Monetary Economics:
Policy and its Theoretical Basis

rd St...

Monetary Economics:
Policy and its Theoretical Basis

Keith Bain

Principal Lecturer, East London Business School
University of East London

Peter Howells

Professor of Economics, East London Business School
University of East London

First published 2003 by
PALGRAVE MACMILLAN
Houndmills, Basingstoke, Hampshire, RG21 6XS and
175 Fifth Avenue, New York, N.Y. 10010
Companies and representatives throughout the world

PALGRAVE MACMILLAN is the global academic imprint of the Palgrave Macmillan division of St. Martin's Press, LLC and of Palgrave Macmillan Ltd. Macmillan® is a registered trademark in the United States, United Kingdom and other countries. Palgrave is a registered trademark in the European Union and other countries.

ISBN 0–333–79255–6 paperpack

This book is printed on paper suitable for recycling and made from fully managed and sustained forest sources.

A catalogue record for this book is available from the British Library.

Copy-edited and typeset by Sarum Editorial Services,
Salisbury, England

Printed and bound in Great Britain by
Creative Print & Design (Wales), Ebbw Vale

Coventry University

Contents

List of boxes, tables and figures ix

Preface xi

1   The Meaning of Money
1.1 Introduction 1
1.2 The various meanings of 'money' 3
1.3 Money in the aggregate 10
1.4 The development of money within economies 15
1.5 Summary 23

2   Definitions of Money in Economics
2.1 Introduction 27
2.2 World views and definitions of money 27
2.3 Economists' definitions of money 33
2.4 Official measures of money 39
2.5 Summary 46

3   The Money Supply Process
3.1 Introduction 49
3.2 Bank balance sheets 52
3.3 The base-multiplier approach to money supply determination 55
3.4 The flow of funds approach 64
3.5 The two approaches compared 66
3.6 Summary 70

4   Money Supply and Control in the UK
4.1 Introduction 73
4.2 Short-term interest rates as the policy instrument 74
4.3 The rejection of monetary base control 82
4.4 Endogenous money 89
4.5 Summary 92

5 The Theory of the Demand for Money

5.1 Introduction 95
5.2 The Quantity Theory of Money 96
5.3 The Cambridge cash balance approach 101
5.4 *The General Theory* and the demand for money 103
5.5 Interest rates and the transactions demand for money 113
5.6 Introducing uncertainty into transactions — models of 116
    the precautionary motive
5.7 Tobin's portfolio model of the demand for money 117
5.8 Monetarism and the demand for money 121
5.9 Microeconomic transactions models of the demand 126
    for money
5.10 The theory of the demand for money: a conclusion 127
5.11 Summary 128

6 Testing the Demand for Money Function

6.1 Introduction 131
6.2 Problems in testing the demand for money 132
6.3 Early demand for money studies 143
6.4 Problems since the 1970s 148
6.5 Sceptical views of a stable demand for money function 162
6.6 Summary 167

7 The Transmission Mechanism of Monetary Policy I — Monetary Policy and Aggregate Demand

7.1 Introduction 171
7.2 The impact of a change in official interest rates on other interest rates 173
7.3 The impact of interest rate changes on consumption and investment as the policy instrument 173
7.4 The transmission mechanism with the money supply as the policy instrument 180
7.5 The money supply with an interest rate control mechanism 195
7.6 Money supply changes in an open economy 197
7.7 Credit availability and expenditure 202
7.8 Summary 203

8 The Transmission Mechanism of Monetary Policy II - Aggregate Demand, Inflation and Output

8.1 Introduction   207
8.2 The simple Philips curve   209
8.3 The new classical model and policy irrelevance   216
8.4 Problems of the new classical model   219
8.5 Credibility and time inconsistency   225
8.6 The independence of central banks   231
8.7 Summary   239

9 The Theory of Monetary Policy

9.1 Introduction   243
9.2 Policy goals and instruments   244
9.3 Rules versus discretion   249
9.4 The choice of monetary instruments   255
9.5 Intermediate versus final targets   259
9.6 The selection of final targets   260
9.7 Central bank policy rules   268
9.8 Summary   271

10 The Open Economy and Monetary Policy

10.1 Introduction   275
10.2 Monetary policy with fixed exchange rates   276
10.3 Brakes on the transmission of monetary influences   279
10.4 Leadership of fixed exchange rate systems   285
10.5 Monetary policy with floating exchange rates   288
10.6 Monetary policy coordination   297
10.7 Capital mobility and the Tobin Tax   306
10.8 Summary   307

11 The Evolution of Monetary Policy in the UK

11.1 Introduction   311
11.2 UK monetary policy before 1985   312
11.3 Financial innovation and monetary policy   328
11.4 Monetary policy after monetary targets   340
11.5 Summary   348

12 The Monetary Authorities and Financial Markets

12.1 Introduction 353
12.2 Central bank leverage 354
12.3 Market constraints 357
12.4 Markets as a source of information 363
12.5 Markets as a test of credibility 369
12.6 Summary 372

13 Monetary Policy in the European Union

13.1 Introduction 375
13.2 The membership of monetary unions 376
13.3 The UK and membership of the euro area 381
13.4 Monetary policy institutions in the euro area 388
13.5 The form of monetary policy in the euro area 396
13.6 ECB monetary policy since 1999 and the value of the euro 401
13.7 Possible reforms of the ECB strategy and procedure 411
13.8 Summary 412

14 Monetary Policy in the USA

14.1 Introduction 417
14.2 The story of central banking in the USA 417
14.3 The aims and form of monetary policy in the USA 424
14.4 The Federal Reserve - independence and accountability 431
14.5 The Federal Reserve - recent monetary policy 434
14.6 Summary 440

Appendices

I The *IS/LM* model 445
II The term structure of interest rates 459

Endnotes 464

References 474

Index 503

List of boxes, tables and figures

Box 1.1	Dictionary definitions of money	4
Table 1.1	Money transmission effects	13
Table 2.1	UK official definitions of money	42-3
Box 3.1	Official measures of money	50
Box 3.2	Commercial and central bank balance sheets	53
Table 3.1	An open-market sale of government bonds	54
Table 3.2	Commercial banks increase their lending	55
Table 3.3	Total transactions volumes in the UK by medium	60
Figure 3.1	The money supply curve	64
Figure 4.1	The supply of bank reserves	75
Box 4.1	Using gilt repo to raise interest rates	77
Box 4.2	The difficulties of monetary base control	84
Figure 4.2	The horizontal 'money supply curve'	91
Box 5.1	Velocity in the Quantity Theory of Money	99
Figure 5.1	The demand for active balances	105
Figure 5.2	The demand for idle balances	108
Box 5.2	Criticisms of Keynes's speculative demand for money	109
Box 5.3	The principal variations on the inventory-theoretic model of the demand for money	117
Figure 5.3	Possible combinations of portfolios	119
Figure 5.4	The effect of a fall in interest rates	120
Box 6.1	Problems in th testing of the demand for money	133
Figure 6.1	Equilibrium in the money market	135
Figure 6.2	The identification problem with endogenous money	136
Box 6.2	Explaining the instability of demand for money functions	148
Box 6.3	Financial innovation and the demand for money	156
Box 7.1	Interest rate control and the transmission mechanism	172
Figure 7.1	The transmission mechanism of monetary policy	178
Figure 7.2	Return to money market equilibrium	181
Figure 7.3	An increase in money supply	184
Figure 7.4	Unstable money demand	185
Figure 7.5	Money supply and wealth effects	187
Figure 7.6	Government spending and money supply	188
Figure 7.7	Expansionary monetary policy with flexible exchange rates	197

Figure 7.8 Expansionary monetary policy with fixed exchange rates 199

Figure 8.1 The simple Phillips curve 210

Figure 8.2 The expectations-augmented Phillips curve 213

Figure 8.3 The Barro-Gordon model 229

Figure 9.1 Choice of instrument with instability in the goods market 256

Figure 9.2 Choice of instrument with instability in the money market 257

Figure 10.1 Monetary policy with fixed exchange rate and capital mobility 276

Figure 10.2 The transmission mechanism of monetary policy with fixed exchange rate 277

Figure 10.3 Short-run freedom for monetary policy after devaluation 280

Figure 10.4 Monetary policy in a fixed exchange rate system 284

Box 10.1 Reducing inflationary pressure in a fixed exchange rate system 286

Figure 10.5 Exchange rate overshooting 292

Figure 10.6 A money supply increase in the Dornbusch model 293

Box 10.2 Monetary policy with floating exchange rates 296

Box 11.1 Capital adequacy ratios as a tax 335

Box 11.2 Monetary control techniques 336

Table 11.1 Broad money targets and outturns, 1980-87 339

Table 11.2 Bank of England repo rate and RPIX, 1997-2001 348

Table 12.1 UK money market rates 355

Table 12.2 Sterling money market volumes, 2001 356

Box 13.1 Characteristics of an area in which the costs of adopting a single currency are likely to be low 378

Box 13.2 Benefits from membership of a single currency area 380

Box 13.3 Monetary developments in the euro area, 1998-2002 389

Box 13.4 Features determining the independence of central banks 391

Table 13.1 Coupon rates and bid yields on benchmark government bonds of euro area members 393

Table 13.2 Exchange rates of the euro against the US$, yen and sterling 402

Table 13.3 Inflation and unemployment rates, money growth and interest rates for the euro area, 1999-2002 407

Table 13.4 Inflation forecasts for the euro area, 2002 411

Box 13.5 Accountability differences: the ECB and Bank of England MPC 413

Box 14.1 The Federal Reserve and the depression of the 1930s 422

Box 14.2 The functions of the 12 district Federal Reserve Banks 424

Box 14.3 Federal Reserve Board of New York's open market operations 428

Table 14.1 Intended Federal Funds Rate, January 1991-December 2001 438

Preface

We have taught monetary economics at the University of East London for many years and have now written a book for our students and, we hope, many other students elsewhere. We have also written a book that seeks to redress the imbalance that has existed, it seems forever, in textbooks on the subject. We can only presume that this imbalance has been present, too, in many of the monetary economics courses taught. Our particular concern in this regard relates to the dominant assumption almost everywhere that the money supply is exogenous, when clearly it is not — and everyone knows that it is not, although not everyone seems yet prepared to admit it, much less to admit the consequences that follow.

This is not a small thing, since the assumption of endogenous money changes many aspects of the subject. It changes entirely one's attitude to the nature of monetary policy and elevates the importance of the supply of money far above that of the demand for money, a reversal of an imbalance indeed. As we note in a footnote in Chapter 6, in 1999, a three-volume set edited by David Laidler was published under the title *The Foundations of Monetary Economics*, which contains 17 papers on the demand for money and none on the supply of money! When you look at the contents of our book you might well, of course, say that we lack the courage of our convictions since there are two rather long chapters on the demand for money. Further, much of the two chapters on the transmission mechanism of monetary policy assume an exogenous money supply. Our response to this is to say that we appreciate the need for students to understand the attitudes of the past as well as the need to change them.

In most universities, monetary economics has not been a mass subject. Many students have found it esoteric and difficult to understand. We, however, believe that it is now an extremely important subject and should be studied by most, if not all, students of economics. After all, the regular decisions of central banks on interest rates are now major news items and will continue so to be. Our view of the importance of the subject has influenced the book in two major ways. Firstly, it accounts for the emphasis on policy. Theoretical aspects of policy and the practice of policy take up five full chapters as well as entering significantly into several others. This is what we believe students should know about and are likely to find interesting. Secondly, it has governed our attitude to mathematics and econometrics. There are equations in this book and we have certainly not avoided difficult material. We give students with quantitative flair much to think about. On the other hand, we do not believe that large numbers of students of economics should feel excluded by an over-concentration on quantitative material.

We have tried throughout to represent fairly all the ideas we discuss. We shall have failed if we have not done this. None the less, we do hold strong views about many aspects of the subject and we should equally have failed if we have not made this clear.

Alas, we do not have secretaries to thank for sterling efforts on our behalf. Perhaps, after many years of working together, we should principally be grateful for each other's forbearance.

KB
PGAH

1 The Meaning of Money

'It is not any scarcity of gold and silver, but the difficulty which such people find in borrowing, and which their creditors find in getting payment, that occasions the general complaint of scarcity of money.'
Adam Smith, *Wealth of Nations* (1776) IV. I

What you will learn in this chapter:

- The nature of monetary economics
- The meaning of 'money' in economics
- The importance of money in exchange
- The changing nature of money and its link with social change
- The relationship between money and credit
- The importance of credit
- The meaning of the 'transmission mechanism' of monetary policy

1.1   Introduction

Monetary economics is a branch of economics centred on money and monetary relationships in the economy. It concentrates on the links between money and prices, output, and employment and so is a development of macroeconomics. Monetary economists have been particularly concerned with the relationship between the rate of growth of the money supply and the rate of inflation, although monetary economics is a much wider area of study than this implies.

Monetary relationships have been studied for several centuries and so the subject contains a great deal of theory. However, we should always recall that the goal of monetary economics lies in a better understanding of monetary policy: what, if anything, governments and/or central banks can do to improve the way in which economies perform through the use of the instruments of monetary policy or, at least, to avoid damaging the performance of the real economy.

Plainly, monetary policy is now regarded as central to the welfare of households and the profitability of firms. The regular decisions of central banks on interest rates are major news items. Changes in exchange rates are part of every day journalism. The question of whether the UK should give up its present currency to join a monetary union is one of the principal political decisions of our day. Monetary policy has become so sensitive that over the past dozen years many countries have made major constitutional decisions regarding the operation of monetary policy.

Despite this, the study of monetary economics is generally regarded as esoteric — a specialist area tackled by a relatively small proportion of undergraduate economics students. An important reason for this can be found in the controversial nature of the material. The subject is full of disagreements and conflict. The standard throw away line, that on any subject two economists will have three opinions, seems to apply to monetary economics *par excellence*. There are few topics within monetary economics in which a set of ideas can be learnt as 'true'. Thus, students find it difficult to understand, and seek to avoid it.

The reason for this controversy and difficulty can be found in the nature of 'money' itself. Money has been a source of fascination in many fields of learning and has been written about by anthropologists, philosophers, and social historians as well as economists. Economists themselves have considered various aspects of money such as the reasons for its existence, changes in its form, and its role in economic growth and development. However, people writing about 'money' are not always dealing with the same thing. Further, the word 'money' is used in everyday speech in a number of ways, generally in different senses from its meaning within monetary economics. The *Oxford Dictionary of Quotations* contains 48 quotations using the word 'money', ranging from the biblical to the music hall - from 'the love of money is the root of all evil' (*Epistle of St Paul to the Ephesians*, vi. 10) to 'I'll bet my money on de bob-tail nag' (Stephen Foster's *Camptown Races*). In many of these quotations, 'money' means 'income' or 'wealth'. This is not new. Adam Smith noted in 1776 that 'wealth and money ... are, in common language, considered as in every respect synonymous' (Smith, 1776, IV, I).

Nonetheless, this is not at all what modern monetary economists mean by 'money'. In modern economics, as in Adam Smith, 'wealth' is produced in the real economy through the production and exchange of goods and services. Money has two clear and separate roles here - in facilitating the act of exchange and in expressing in a common unit the value of the many different goods and services produced. This latter use accounts for the distinction made in economics between 'real' values and 'money' or 'nominal' values. Thus, wealth can be expressed in money terms but 'money' and 'wealth' are certainly not synonymous. However, if 'money' is not the same thing as wealth, what precisely is it?

As we shall see in Chapter 2, even within economics 'money' can be viewed in a variety of ways and different definitions of money often stem from differing ideas concerning the way in which economies function. One of the great historical debates within monetary economics has been over the question of the 'neutrality' of money — whether changes in the quantity of money in an economy have an impact on the 'real' values of output and employment or whether they influence only the general level of prices. There can be little doubt that definitions of 'money' are not neutral in relation to economic analysis. Under these circumstances, we must begin by examining carefully the meaning of 'money'.

1.2   The various meanings of 'money'

The *Chambers 20th Century Dictionary* (1983 p. 814) provides the following definition of 'money':

> *coin: pieces of stamped metal used in commerce: any currency used in the same way: wealth*

From this, we can make two points. Firstly, as we have suggested above, 'money' in monetary economics is not identified with total 'wealth' as in the final element of the definition here. Rather, when we talk of 'money', we are discussing one (quite small) part of wealth. An economist's definition concentrates on the earlier elements of the dictionary definition — 'money' is defined by its use in commerce or exchange. This gives us the common notion of money as a 'medium of exchange' or 'means of payment'. In other words, 'money' is the most liquid part of wealth — that part which can be most readily exchanged for goods and services.

Secondly, 'money' was once identified with 'coin'. We have this, of course, in 'the king was in his counting-house counting out his money (*Sing a Song of Sixpence* in *Tommy Thumb's Pretty Song Book* (c. 1744)'. As shown in Box 1.1, this remains the first definition of 'money' given by the *Oxford English Dictionary*: 'current coin; metal stamped in pieces of portable form as a medium of exchange and measure of value'. This bypasses the common notion that 'money', in primitive societies, took the form of 'commodity money': a commodity that had an intrinsic value but came to be used in the process of exchange because it had a number of characteristics that made it acceptable in that process.[1] These characteristics were found most readily in precious metals and it was convenient to turn these into coins of a pre-determined weight.

Since the conversion of metal into coins probably dates back at least as far as the 8th century BC (Galbraith, 1975), it is reasonable to ignore 'commodity money' in a modern definition. However, we shall return to the concept of 'commodity money' in Section 1.4 below since it is important to a consideration of the way in which economists think about money. The identification of 'money' with 'coin' reinforces the idea of the physical presence of money whereas the idea of 'commodity money' implies that 'money' is essentially abstract and that any asset might potentially serve as money. The abstract nature of money is preserved in the role of money as a 'unit of account'. That is, the use of money allows the value of different goods and services to be expressed in a common unit, or *numéraire*, whether or not exchange takes place.

Box 1.1: Dictionary definitions of money

The *Oxford English Dictionary* provides the following definitions of 'money':

1a Current coin; metal stamped in pieces of portable form as a medium of exchange and measure of value. *Piece of money.*

 b Applied occasionally by extension to any objects, or any material, serving the same purposes as coin.

 c In modern use commonly applied indifferently to coin and to such promissory documents representing coin (esp. government and bank notes) as are currently accepted as a medium of exchange.

2 (With *pl.*) A particular coin or coinage. Also, a denomination of value representing a fraction or a multiple of the value of some coin; in full, money of account.

3a Coin considered in reference to its value or purchasing power, hence, property or possessions of any kind viewed as convertible into money or having value expressible in terms of money.

 b with demonstrative or possessive adj., designating a sum applied to a particular purpose or in the possession of a particular person.

 c considered as a commodity in the market (for loan, etc.)

 d Wages, salary; one's pay.

4 *pl.* Property = 'sums of money', but often indistinguishable from the sing. (sense 3). Now chiefly in legal and quasi-legal parlance, or as an archaism.

5 With defining word, forming specific phrases, as big money; chief money; dirty money; even money; present, real money; single, small money.

The dictionary definition does move on from coin and allows the possibility that money consists of 'any currency'. Currency is, in turn, defined as anything that circulates from person to person in the process of exchange and so we have the possibility that money might take a variety of forms. Nonetheless, for most people the word 'currency' indicates notes and coin or cash or what might be called 'ready money' in everyday use. And yet, the underlying idea remains that 'money' is anything that is acceptable in payment for goods and services, and payment can occur without the transfer of a physical asset. The most obvious example of this is the use of cheques or debit cards to transfer funds from one bank account to another. This leads to the notion that neither the cheque nor the debit card is money but that the bank deposits people can call upon in order to make purchases are money since the exchange is validated by the circulation of the bank deposits to which cheques and debit cards refer

We begin to see the difficulty. 'Money', in monetary economics, does not mean income or wealth. Rather, 'money' is any asset acceptable in exchange for goods and services. We shall see that monetary economists have spent a great deal of time discussing and testing the 'demand for money'. If we define 'money' as a set of assets generally acceptable in exchange for goods and services, the demand for money is only an indirect demand. What people demand are goods and services but they may need money in order to carry out the act of exchange.

The first problem we face, then, arises because a variety of types of asset may allow exchange to take place. This is especially so at an individual level. Consider a person who has decided to give up stamp collecting but who has a philatelist friend. The ex-stamp collector agrees to exchange his stamp albums for a number of CDs. Plainly, the stamp collection has a monetary value — it could be sold to a stamp dealer and the money thus obtained could be used to buy other goods and services. However, the stamp collection is not itself 'money' since for an asset to be considered as such it must be generally or widely acceptable directly in exchange for goods and services, not merely be acceptable in an occasional private transaction. That is, to be classed as 'money', an asset must be exchangeable for goods and services in general.

Thus, 'money' is a sub-set of all those assets that might be acceptable in exchange. Once we acknowledge this, we introduce an element of uncertainty. To decide which assets are 'money' and which are not, we need to say what precisely we mean by 'generally acceptable'. Further, the assets that are generally acceptable in exchange might vary from one country to another or from one period to another within the same country. As Goodhart (1989a) notes, money is a social phenomenon that exists in all societies but that is everywhere different.

Our second problem is more important. We need to say something about the meaning of '*exchange*'. The physical exchange of products is frequently based not on the transfer of money but on the promise to pay later. That is, the purchaser goes into debt, usually being granted credit by the seller, a bank, or some other financial intermediary. One way of coping with this is by introducing the idea that 'exchange' only actually occurs when the debt incurred by the purchase is settled and for this to happen there has to be a transfer of money.

The consequent definition of 'money' as anything that is acceptable in final settlement of debt is a common one but this is radically different from the idea that money allows exchange to occur. Suppose you buy a motor car on credit. You drive the car for two years before you settle the debt. In these circumstances, it is plausible to say that the act of exchange occurred when you obtained the right to drive the car and began to make use of it and that you 'paid' for this right with *credit*. The later settlement of the debt is a consequence of the exchange taking place but is not needed to allow it to happen.

After all, consider the economic consequences of the exchange. Suppose we are talking about a new Ford. Once you have signed the contract to buy the car, the dealer regards the car as sold. It leaves his show room and is replaced by another. Ford regard the car as sold and take this into account when they decide how many cars they are going to produce in the next period, whether they are going to offer their workers overtime or put them on 'short-time' working. These decisions influence Ford's orders for raw materials and the income and hence the expenditure of their workers. All of these and other events follow from the physical act of exchange — the handing over of the car. In addition, it is at this point that the car is registered in your name with the government and you become legally responsible for it. It is true that if large numbers of people do not repay the debt they have taken on there will be an economic impact. It is also true that some people will fail to pay the debt they have entered into and so technically a small number of contracts will never be completed. Companies such as Ford allow in their calculations for bad debts of this kind. It remains that the ability to obtain credit permits a high proportion of the exchange in a modern economy. Further, the physical act of exchange determines legal ownership and produces much of the subsequent economic impact.

The issue becomes clearer when we consider the purchase of goods with a credit card. Over a period of three months, say, a man buys thirty different products using a credit card. He pays a small proportion of the debt he has entered into each month but is still in debt a year later. The seller of each of the products has been paid by the transfer of a deposit from the bank issuing the credit card. The purchaser has legal ownership of all of the products, although they (or other goods) could be later repossessed if he does not pay the bank. It is clear that exchange occurs when the credit card is accepted. In this case, the bank determines the ability to enter into exchange by the limit that it allows on the credit card. However, this credit card limit is not conventionally regarded as 'money' because the purchaser has gone into debt to buy the goods. 'Money' is, thus, a much narrower concept than 'credit'.

The credit card case is more complex than that of the purchase of a car from Ford because the purchaser's debt no longer corresponds directly to any particular good he has purchased. Indeed, it is possible for the bank to which he is in debt to sell that debt on to another firm so that it becomes almost totally detached from the act of exchange. Further, the purchaser could repay his credit card debt by borrowing from another bank or finance company or through re-mortgaging his house. Yet again, debt might be passed on to subsequent generations or be extinguished by bankruptcy or death. The *medium of exchange* is, surely, the credit allowed by the bank rather than the money the purchaser might eventually hand over. There is a logical distinction between money and credit based on the notion that an exchange remains 'incomplete' until the debt has been settled and that this, by definition, requires money. However, from the point of view of the impact of the exchange on others and on the economy as a whole, the distinction between money and credit is of little significance.

We can say that 'money' is likely to be sufficient to enter into an act of exchange (although some companies prefer to be paid by credit card than by personal cheque) but it is certainly not necessary for this. It is true that there is still a range of transactions in which a purchaser must hand over to the seller bank notes and coin or a cheque or debit card that will bring about a transfer of bank deposits. Although one can not yet, for example, pay urban bus fares by credit card, the range of transactions for which this is so has become much narrower in recent years. There may still be some temporary embarrassment or inconvenience from not having immediate access to sufficient money. However, the inconvenience will be very short-term as long as one has wealth or reputation against which one can borrow. For some, the cost of borrowing will be very high, but the ultimate constraint remains the ability to borrow. Exchange is, in general, constrained by the lack of wealth and/or the ability to borrow rather than by the lack of that part of wealth that economists refer to as 'money'.

This understates the importance of money in exchange since it concentrates on the act of exchange itself and gives no weight to the role of money as a unit of account. It is, however, clear that people do not, in anything but the very short term, have to restrict their demand for commodities because of a lack of 'money' as distinct from a lack of wealth or the ability to borrow.

It follows that the notion of an excess demand for money (the demand for money being greater than its supply) can only make sense at an aggregate level. It is true that the great majority of us would like to acquire more goods and services that we are in practice able to do — but this arises not because of a lack of 'money' in the sense in which the term is used by monetary economists but by a lack of wealth. At an aggregate level things may be different. One of the issues we need to investigate is whether the supply of money can be lower or higher than the total amount demanded by persons and firms to enable them to undertake the exchanges they would otherwise be able to make and, if so, what the consequences are.

Pause for thought 1.1:

We have suggested:

(a) that current account deposits are 'money' because they can be used to settle debt through the writing of cheques or the use of debit cars; but

(b) that credit is not 'money' because its use creates an outstanding debt.

What, then, should one make of agreed overdraft limits on current accounts? They can be used to settle other debts but their use creates a debt to the bank. Are they 'money'?

We shall see in Chapter 6, that part of the problem we face in relation to the demand for money function arises from this discord between the macroeconomic and microeconomic significance of money. This shows up particularly as a discord between theory and evidence. Much of the theory of the demand for money is microeconomic in approach but empirical work is concerned with the aggregate demand for money.

Let us recap. At a microeconomic level, we have said, people only have a demand for 'money' in the very short term. This contrasts with the usual story that they have a demand for money in order to carry out planned transactions. However, a person who makes a high proportion of purchases by credit card might require significant amounts of money for only quite small periods of time at the end of each month in order to make the necessary credit card repayments. Thus, it is more accurate to say that people have a demand for what we might call 'spending resources'. A person's 'spending resources' consist of his existing wealth and the amount he is able to borrow, allowing for any existing indebtedness.

This requires us to say something briefly about the meaning of 'wealth'. The simplest approach is to think of wealth as the total of the real and financial assets owned by people. Clearly, wealth is a major determinant of the ability to borrow. However, it is not the only determinant. For example, banks are often quite willing to lend to impoverished students - not on the basis of their existing wealth but because they assume that the students are likely to receive good incomes in the future and that this will enable them to repay their debts. We can allow for this by accepting Milton Friedman's (1957) very broad definition of wealth, which adds 'human wealth' to the total of real and financial assets (non-human wealth). Human wealth consists of abilities and skills that enable people to borrow against likely future income. The willingness of a financial institution to lend may arise from the existing skills or abilities of the borrower or current enrolment on a course of study that will probably develop the necessary skills. Thus, this broad definition of wealth provides a better indication of the ability to borrow and hence a measure of 'spending resources'. Of course, even this is not complete since banks might lend also because the borrowers' parents are well off or because he has a satisfactory business plan, is associated with someone with a reasonable track record in business or much else.

Much is made in many books of the importance of 'liquidity'— generally defined as the ability to convert assets quickly and with little or no risk into money. Assets are often classified in terms of degrees of liquidity, with money itself being the perfectly liquid asset since it is, by definition, directly exchangeable for goods and services. Thus, a house is not a liquid asset because it is difficult to sell quickly and equities are less liquid than money because although they can be sold quickly their prices fluctuate from day to day and one can never be sure of the amount of money one will receive for them when they are eventually sold. However, all assets are effectively made liquid to the extent that one can borrow against them.

As we have suggested above, there are occasions when the possession of 'spending resources', while necessary, is insufficient for undertaking transactions because the resources are not in a form acceptable in exchange (that is, they are illiquid). However, this is usually important to individuals only at the level of convenience, not having, for example, enough cash to buy another beer and with the nearest bank cash machine either five miles away or not functioning.[2] This lack of liquidity can be overcome by an inconvenient trip to a more distant bank machine or by a loan — from the pub owner or a friend or, perhaps with a short delay, from a financial institution.

The only reason why this might not be possible stems from the lack of spending resources as we have defined them above. After all, a person borrowing from a bank takes it for granted that the loan will come in a form that allows him or her to spend. Thus, the lack of 'money' does not except for very short periods constrain individual demand for goods and services and the microeconomic demand for money has little economic significance.

1.3　Money in the aggregate

Of course, it might be argued that if I borrow money from someone else, this is part of the total stock of money currently available in the economy as a whole. Then, *as long as we assume that the total supply of money is temporarily fixed,* we could conceive of a situation in which the supply does not match the current demand for money. But this introduces the important question of what determines the aggregate supply of money — is it fixed or, at least controllable by the monetary authorities, or might 'money' in the aggregate be created by the actions of people in the economy seeking to borrow and to spend? We look at this issue in detail in Chapters 3, 4 and 11.

For the moment, let us assume that the aggregate supply of money is temporarily fixed or that it is growing at a predetermined rate. Then, an unanticipated increase in the demand for goods and services, and the consequent increase in the demand for money to allow the additional desired exchanges to take place, might produce a shortage of money in the aggregate. What does this mean at an individual level? Clearly, those who hold cash or bank deposits will not be immediately affected. Again, there is no physical shortage of notes and coin since these are supplied by the central bank and the mint on demand in exchange for deposits. The shortage, thus, takes the form of bank deposits not growing sufficiently rapidly. Since, as we shall see in Section 3.2, bank deposits are created when banks make loans, the shortage arises through banks being unwilling or unable to meet fully the increased borrowing requirements of consumers at existing interest rates. In this situation, two broad outcomes are possible.

Firstly, the price of borrowing (the interest rate) might rise. This would overcome the shortage if, and only if, the increase in interest rates persuaded people to borrow less and hence to spend less. That is, we are introducing an additional constraint on aggregate expenditure within the ability to borrow: the willingness to borrow. This willingness is tempered by the cost of borrowing. It would also be possible for the authorities to seek to restrict borrowing (credit) in other ways, such as imposing minimum repayment amounts. This is clear enough, but the situation is complicated by the story being told in two, apparently conflicting ways. The first sees the monetary authorities as being completely in control of the money supply (the money supply is exogenous). Then, if they choose to keep the supply of money unchanged in the face of an increased demand for it, market forces cause interest rates to rise. The alternative is to see the monetary authorities as having little or no direct control over the money supply (the money supply is endogenous) but as having control over interest rates. In this case, the monetary authorities respond to what they see as inflationary pressure caused by the initial increase in demand for goods and services by increasing the rate of interest. If this does persuade people to borrow and spend less, the supply of money (or its rate of growth) will fall but, in this case, the influence of the authorities on the stock of money is only, at best, indirect, taking place through the rate of interest and then through the demand for credit.

Expressed in this way, the difference between these channels of influence of the authorities does not seem very important. It remains that the debate over which helps us better understand how the system works has been long and heated and we shall need to consider the issue.

Secondly, as demand for goods and services and the desire to borrow increases, banks might respond by not granting additional loans but by tightening the conditions on which they are willing to lend. Then, some people who previously could borrow would be unable to do so and others would be able to borrow less than previously. That is, people's ability to borrow and hence their spending resources would be restricted — they would be credit-constrained. Again, the money supply would not grow but this would occur without an increase in interest rate being necessary. This might happen because, in an uncertain situation and with *asymmetric information* (discussed in Section 3.5), banks might choose to act in this way. Alternatively, banks might tighten their lending criteria because they are put under pressure to do so by the monetary authorities. That is, the monetary authorities might attempt to influence the ability of people to borrow not by increasing interest rates but by trying to control directly the quantity and/or types of loans made by banks. Examples of this in the UK in the 1950s and 1970s are discussed in Section 11.2.

The question arises here of why banks might not meet an increased demand for loans since these are the source of their profits. The view that the authorities have direct control over the supply of money sees this as occurring through control over the size of the monetary base (high-powered money),[3] on the assumption that there is a reliable and predictable relationship between the size of the monetary base and the quantity of deposits banks can create. If this were the case, banks would not meet the increased demand for loans because they were unable to do so — as they tried to increase their lending they would become short of monetary base. If, however, the authorities could not control the monetary base and/or the relationship between the monetary base and the quantity of bank deposits was unreliable, banks might go on meeting the increased demand for credit as people sought to borrow more in order to increase their spending. The stock of bank deposits, and hence of money, would increase. In other words, the supply of money might simply increase to meet the increased demand for it and the shortage in the aggregate supply of money that we assumed at the beginning of this section might never arise. It is clear, then, that a major issue in monetary economics concerns the way in which money is created and the extent to which the monetary authorities can influence this process.

We assumed above an increase in the demand for goods and services. We could also assume a fall in the demand for goods and services, producing a fall in the demand for credit. This might lead to a reduction in the stock of money, a fall in interest rates and/or an easing of the conditions established by financial institutions for the granting of credit.

We could also begin our story with the monetary authorities. We could assume that the money supply were exogenous and that the authorities wished to change their existing policy, seeking to persuade people to increase or decrease their demand for goods and services. That is, we assume that the demand for goods and services has not changed but that the monetary authorities for some reason seek to change the money supply (or, more accurately, the rate of growth of the money supply) in order to change current spending behaviour. We might imagine, for instance, that an economy has operated at much the same rate of inflation for some time but that now the government seeks to lower that rate. They believe that they can do so by reducing the money supply and forcing up the rate of interest as people seek to maintain their existing demand for goods and services. The increase in the rate of interest is then again assumed to deter people from borrowing in order to spend. For the monetary authorities to seek to follow such a policy, they would need to believe that the relationship between the supply of money and the level of spending in the economy was close and stable. To put it another way, they would need to believe that the demand for money was stable. This, in turn, would imply a stable technical relationship between the amount of money in the economy at any particular time and the total amount of spending able to be undertaken: the velocity of money would need to be stable.

Whatever our starting point, it is clear that the central policy question we are asking is whether the monetary authorities can hope to control spending in the economy by restricting the ability of banks to lend or the willingness of people to borrow or to turn existing wealth into forms that are acceptable in exchange.

Pause for thought 1.2:

Can you explain why a stable demand for money implies a stable velocity of money?

The various possibilities considered above are summarized in Table 1.1. These links between monetary policy and the level of aggregate demand are examined in detail in Chapter 6 under the heading of the *transmission mechanism of monetary policy*. The transmission mechanism, however, has another element. We can see this by continuing to assume an increased demand for goods and services in the economy, leading to an increased demand for money to carry out the desired additional exchanges. But now

Table 1.1: Money transmission effects

Source of change	Money supply	Authorities' response	Interest rate change	Outcome
A: Increase in aggregate demand				
1. Money supply increases	Endogenous	—	—	Aggregate demand rises
2. Money supply unchanged	Exogenous	(i) Restrict money supply	Increases	Aggregate demand unchanged
	Endogenous	(ii) Raise interest rates directly	Increases	Aggregated demand unchanged
3. Money supply unchanged	Endogenous	Restrict credit directly	Unchanged	Aggregate demand unchanged
B: Aggregate demand unchanged but authorities seek to reduce it				
1. Money supply reduced	Exogenous	Reduce money supply directly	Increases	Aggregate demand falls
2. Money supply reduced	Endogenous	Increase interest rates directly	Increases	Aggregate demand falls
3. Money supply reduced	Endogenous	Restrict credit directly	Unchanged	Aggregate demand falls

assume that this increase in demand is met by an increased supply of money. Why might the monetary authorities wish to take some action?

If people are able to borrow freely and interest rates do not rise, the demand for goods and services will increase in line with the plans of consumers (the increased demand will become effective). This increased demand for goods and services might be associated with an increase in prices, depending on the extent to which the supply of goods and services could rise to meet the increased demand (either through production or imports). Plainly, it is the fear of inflation that leads the monetary authorities to act. The important monetary policy issues are the effectiveness of monetary policy in restraining inflationary pressures within the economy and the extent to which actions to control inflation have an impact on the real economy.

We shall see that in dealing with these questions, it is customary to distinguish between the short-run and long run effects of monetary policy. Students are frequently confused, however, over the meaning of the terms 'short run' and 'long run'. This is because much economic analysis is conducted within an equilibrium framework. The system is assumed to be in equilibrium but this is disturbed by a shock, but nothing else is assumed to change. Economic agents respond to the shock in such a way that the system returns to equilibrium. The impact of the shock can then be analysed, *ceteris paribus*. Within money markets, equilibrium implies that the demand for money is equal to the supply of money (or that the rate of growth of the demand for money is equal to the rate of growth of the supply of money).

Within this framework, the term 'long run' relates to the length of time needed for the system to return to equilibrium. That is, in the short run the system is, by definition, out of equilibrium. There can be no calendar-time equivalent to this because in the real world:

- economies are subject to frequent shocks and are never in equilibrium positions
- shocks are likely to cause other elements within the system to change
- these changes may well interact with the initial shock to produce further changes
- shocks and the subsequent changes generate expectations about future changes.

It is thus reasonable to say that monetary policy always takes place within the short run. However, this conflicts with another usage of the terms. For example, according to the economic model used by the Bank of England Monetary Policy Committee, a change in UK interest rates has its maximum impact on the rate of inflation after approximately two years. We might then talk about the short-run effects of monetary policy as being the impact on the economy over six months or a year and the long-run effects as being the impact over two years or longer. This might sometimes be useful but is rather arbitrary and has no relationship with the idea that the long run implies equilibrium. As we shall see in Chapter 8, within an equilibrium framework, the long run describes an ideal world in which all expectations are fulfilled and economic agents are not subject to money illusion — that is, they do not confuse real and money values.

Pause for thought 1.3:

Keynes is widely quoted as having said: 'In the long run we are all dead'. Is this an accurate quotation? In the light of the above discussion, what do you think he might have meant?

We can sum this section up as follows:

• changes in the relationship between the demand for and supply of liquid resources ('money' and 'credit') at an aggregate level can have a variety of important impacts on the economy depending on the extent to which the authorities are able or choose to respond to those changes;

• at an individual level, people are influenced only indirectly, even if strongly — through changes in the interest rate, the rate of inflation, or the ability to obtain credit.

In this section, we have established the following questions to be taken up in later chapters:

1. What determines the supply of money in the economy and changes in that supply?

2. To what extent, if at all, can the monetary authorities directly control this supply?

3. How does the system respond to an increased demand for credit at existing interest rates?

4. Given any limitations on their ability to act, how should the monetary authorities respond to an increased demand for credit?

1.4 The development of money within economies

We have spent a considerable time discussing the meaning of 'money'. We have also looked at the possible links between money, prices, and output in an economy and set down a number of issues to which we must return later in the book. None of this, however, begins to give a clear idea of the important role played by money in an economy. To do this, we need to pay closer attention to the role of money in exchange.

Pause for thought 1.4:

What forms of uncertainty can one identify in an act of exchange of goods and services involving delivery at a future date? How does the existence of 'money' help to overcome these?

In analysing this role, Goodhart (1989a) describes money as one of the social artefacts (along with the distribution network and organized markets) that have evolved to economize on the use of time, which is seen as the ultimate scarce resource. This follows the view that the value of money in exchange arises because of the existence of incomplete information in markets. The collection of information needed to allow efficient exchange involves a heavy use of time, which could otherwise be used in the production of additional goods and services. In other words, in the absence of money, market exchange involves high transactions costs. These costs arise particularly from the uncertainty that results from inadequate information. The use of money, then, reduces uncertainty for market participants and allows a more efficient use of resources (see, for example, Brunner and Meltzer, 1989).

A common approach to the story of money within monetary economics describes an evolution from primitive economies to modern monetary economies in a number of stages. The process begins with primitive economies in which all families were economically self-sufficient and no trade occurred. We then pass through:

• the beginning of the process of exchange but solely through barter;

• the development of the use of commodity money;

• the change in the nature of money from commodity money to coins, bank notes, and bank deposits and the increasing use of electronic transfer of deposits.

This approach to the study of money asks what distinguishes monetary exchange from that which takes place through non-monetary means (barter). The advantages of a monetary economy are then looked at in terms of the costs involved in the process of exchange and the extent to which a movement from barter to the use of money in exchange reduces those costs. We shall look at this approach below, but it is worth noting here that it implies far too simple a view of the way in which economies function.

Firstly, the barter/money distinction indicates a static view of economies — all are classed as one of two simple possibilities. However, exchange is a social process and money a social invention. As such, the role of money in exchange differs from one economy to another and changes over time. In any modern economy, monetary exchange and barter both occur and the extent to which each is practised changes constantly. Indeed, both may occur in a single transaction as in part-payment for a car by trading in an old model. The tendency to think in terms of stereotyped economies can lead to a failure to consider the way in which economic change and the nature of exchange interact. Visions arise of static societies confronted on occasions by exogenous shocks. An equilibrium model of an economy can be a useful analytical device but it is important not to try to impose these models on the much more complex real world. An important recent example was the apparent discovery by monetary economists of 'financial innovation' to explain why their models of the demand for money appeared not to be working. In fact, financial innovation has always been with us and part of the study of monetary economics must be to analyse the interactions among real economies, market processes, and institutions within the economy.

Secondly, the barter/monetary exchange distinction is ahistorical and implies that money came into existence to facilitate exchange. This, in turn, leads to the view that it is possible to analyse a barter economy in which money does not exist and then simply add money. This remains a powerful idea in modern economics and is at the heart of views that 'money is a veil' over the real economy (Pigou, 1949, p.24) and that money is neutral — that it has no impact on the functioning of the real economy. In reality, there is no evidence that barter preceded money anywhere other than in pre-economic societies in which exchange was only ceremonial. Indeed, Wray (1990) argues that money evolved before markets developed and that its use grew much more quickly than the growth of markets.[4] This is not a matter of pedantry since Wray goes on to show that the different views of the origin of money lead to different definitions of money and, in turn, to different analyses of the monetary economy.

The idea of money as an addition to a pre-existing barter economy is sometimes acknowledged to be historically inaccurate, only for the story to be justified, in Samuelson's words (Samuelson, 1973), as a 'reconstruction of history along hypothetical, logical lines'. This raises the question of why economists have sought to reconstruct history in this way. We shall tell this story briefly and seek reasons for its attractiveness along the way.

We begin with self-sufficiency. Modern economics often characterizes such an economy as that of Robinson Crusoe — an isolated individual producing only for himself. This is curious because it ignores the social context of economic action. Since it ignores the role of Man Friday, the servant/slave in Defoe's novel, it also immediately abstracts economic analysis from power relationships. Despite this, we establish production as the central measure of progress. Progress from self-sufficiency then requires the division of labour and specialization. Within a family in a traditional society, a certain degree of specialization is possible — one member of the family catches fish, a second tends the family's animals, a third weaves cloth and so on. Nonetheless, a more thorough exploitation of specialization requires exchange and this implies the establishment of markets. Markets are seen as a logical construct shorn of institutional and social detail and all exchange is thought of as proceeding through markets.

The only available basis for judging welfare in this abstract world is through consumption and the dominant economic question becomes the maximization of individual utility through the most efficient use of scarce resources. Given this starting point, it is only sensible to judge the performance of the economic system in 'real terms'. In practice, people often make judgements in money terms. Indeed, the rich occasionally gain utility by showing the extent of their wealth to others. They may do this by extravagant consumption, but the purpose is often to indicate to others how successful they have been. Nonetheless, orthodox economists reject the notion that anything can be judged in money terms. As we noted above, decisions based on money values are disparaged as examples of money illusion and it is argued that any confusion of money and real values is only inadvertent and temporary. Once people understand the source of the confusion they return, it is assumed, to making judgements in real terms. This is clearly a very psychologically limited view of human behaviour and human society but the aim, remember, is to abstract from such complications.

It is a logical development of this approach to believe that economies can be analysed entirely in real terms. This must follow if we argue that:

• economic behaviour can be separated from social relationships, psychological influences and the institutional context in which economic decisions are made;

• everyone is concerned with the maximization of individual utility; and

• the source of utility is the consumption of goods and services.

Thus, the notion that 'money' is neutral and has no influence on the real economy is not a conclusion derived from the analysis of economic behaviour but an initial assumption of that analysis. It leads to the position that we must be able to analyse economic exchange in a society without money, hence the assumption that exchange through markets preceded money. This leads us to the analysis of exchange by barter. If, however, exchange can occur without money and we assume (incorrectly) that there were societies in a pre-money world in which all exchange took place by barter, we need logical reasons for the invention of money. Wray (1990) argues that 'money naturally develops in a capitalist economy in which property is privately owned and in which production for the market is made possible by proper- ty less workers' (p. xiv). However, in the orthodox story, all economic activity including exchange could develop without money. It seems natural then to explain the presence of money in economies simply in terms of the increased efficiency of exchange allowed by money.

Pause for thought 1.5:

To what extent do you make economic judgements in real terms? Can you think of occasions when you have been subject to 'money illusion'?

This first requires an explanation of why barter is inefficient. This is done through the notion of the double coincidence of wants — that a person who catches fish and wishes to exchange them for pots needs to find a maker of pots who happens to want fish at precisely the same time before an exchange can take place. This implies very large search and information costs. In other words, people spend a lot of time in the process of exchange that could be used in a more efficient system for producing more goods and services. The opportunity cost of a system of exchange by barter is high. This, of course, is an over-simple vision of exchange even by the usual standards of economics and so it became necessary to acknowledge that much more efficient systems of barter existed.

Hence, we have the notion that barter passed through stages of increas- ing efficiency. In particular, the literature discusses fairground barter and trading post barter. Fairground barter occurs when a fair is held for the sale of a particular good in the same place at regular intervals. Then, everyone who has that good for sale, or wishes to buy it, knows that exchange would be much easier if they went to the fair. A common example around Europe was the horse fair. Trading post barter occurs when someone sets up a trad- ing post at which a specified set of goods are bought and sold and advertis- es the location and opening hours. People know that if they were to go to the trading post during its opening hours, they would have a good chance of meeting other people who wished to buy the good they wished to sell or *vice versa*. Thus, both fairs and trading posts considerably reduced search costs involved in the process of exchange. Both of these methods of reducing search costs exist today — in the form, for example, of car boot sales and trade fairs. This shows that they are methods of organization that have no necessary relation with barter since they allow equally for monetary exchange.

Nonetheless, our fable of the way in which exchange developed succeeds in establishing the inefficiency of barter. A second way in which this is done is by concentrating on the role of relative prices in the process of exchange. In a barter system, we are talking about price ratios: how many fish exchange for one pot; how much maize or fish for one cow, and so on. If there are only two goods to be exchanged (fish and pots), there is only one price ratio. With three goods (fish, pots, and maize), however, there are three price ratios (fish/pots; fish/maize; pots/maize). As Visser (1974, pp. 2 and 3) shows, the number of price ratios can be calculated as the number of combinations of two elements from a set of n elements. The formula for this calculation is:

$$\tfrac{1}{2}n(n-1) \qquad\qquad ...1.1$$

where n is the number of goods and services. Thus, in an economy with 4 goods, there will be 6 price ratios; with 100 goods there will be 4,950 price ratios; and with 1,000 goods 499,500 price ratios. Clearly, barter is a very inefficient system for this reason. It is, of course, extremely unlikely that any society proceeded for any length of time without attempting to reduce the number of price ratios with which people had to cope. All that was needed was the adoption of one of the goods as a unit of account in which the price of all other goods could be expressed. This then explains the existence of money. The great reduction in information costs resulting from the use of a unit of account (money) allows people to spend a greater proportion of their time producing goods and services, thus improving their standard of living. The notion of 'information costs' can be considered in more detail. For example, Clower (1971) speaks of two types of cost associated with barter. These are transactions costs and waiting costs (storage costs, the interest foregone on the postponed purchase of an asset and the subjective costs in doing without a good or service).

We may have an explanation of money as a unit of account but this is not sufficient to explain why money actually needs to change hands. That is, why did money develop as a means of payment? Goodhart (1989a) accounts for this by stressing another informational problem associated with market exchange. This is lack of information about the trustworthiness and/or creditworthiness of the counter-party to the exchange. This, he says, truly makes money essential. If everyone in a market could be fully trusted, all exchange could be based on credit and with multilateral credit and a complete set of markets, money would not be needed. An unwillingness of traders to extend credit or to accept other goods as a means of payment means that money is required if some goods are to be purchased. This has become known as a liquidity or cash in advance constraint.

Visser (1974, p.3) points out that the word 'pecuniary' derives from the Latin word pecus which means cattle and that the word 'rupee' comes from the Sanskrit roupya, which 'also has something to do with cattle'. This takes us to the notion that early moneys took many forms as in the colourful list in endnote 1, and gives us the idea of money as commodity money, which we mentioned briefly above. In answer to the question as to why some commodities were used as money rather than others ooffne can point to a number of characteristics a commodity should possess before being used as money. These are that the commodity should be:

• durable
• easily transportable
• easily divisible into small parts
• able to be used in units of a standard value.

In addition, the conditions of supply of the commodity should be stable. If the commodity were subject to sudden increases in supply, people would be worried that the value of a unit of the money would fall sharply and they would not be willing to accept it as a means of payment. Finally, the costs of using the commodity as a means of payment must be small.

We can easily understand from this list why commodity money very quickly took the form of coins of predetermined weight struck from precious metals. The problem with coinage was that people saw very quickly the possibility of reducing the amount of precious metal in coins, for example by shaving off a small amount of metal and keeping the shavings for their own use. This was known as 'sweating the coinage'. The intention was to allow the same amount of precious metal to exchange for more goods than before. The value of the coins in terms of the value of goods they exchanged for thus became greater than the value of the metal in the coins. In other words, the face value of the coins became greater than the cost of producing the coins. This difference was often put to use by princes and kings, among other things to finance the fighting of foreign wars. Thus, it was called 'seigniorage' from the French word *seigneur*, which means a feudal lord of lord of the manor. The word is still much used today in monetary economics and is defined as *the excess of the face value over the cost of production of the currency*. This excess accrues to the issuer of the currency. Thus, the Bank of England produces notes with a face value of £20, which exchange for £20 worth of goods but might cost, say, two pence to produce. The extra £19.98 represents a once-and-for-all gain for the monetary authorities of the country.[5]

The sweating of the coinage was relatively easily accomplished because, before the state took over responsibility for the coinage, there were many competing mints in existence. For example, Galbraith (1975, pp.24-5) notes that:

> A manual for moneychangers issued by the Dutch parliament in 1606 listed 341 silver and 505 gold coins. Within the Dutch Republic no fewer than fourteen mints were then busy turning out money; there was, as ever, a marked advantage in substituting plausibility for quality. For each merchant to weigh the coins he received was a bother; the scales were also deeply and justifiably suspect.

In addition, people saving (or 'hoarding') coins for their future use would hoard those coins containing the highest weight of metal and would seek to use in exchange the coins that had been interfered with such that the amount of metal in the coins was lower than the stated weight. Thus, these would be the coins most likely to stay in circulation.[6] The 'sweating' of the coinage allowed a given amount of issued coinage to purchase more goods and services (to increase the velocity of money). The possibility of making a profit from reducing the amount of metal in coins led to an important development in banking. As Galbraith (1975, pp. 25-6) explains, public banks were set up in the seventeenth century, initially in the Netherlands, to guarantee the value of coins by weighing them and assessing the true value of metal in the coins. At the same time, as nation states became more important, governments began to take over the responsibility for the minting of coins, reducing considerably the variety of coins in circulation.

Financial intermediaries initially issued notes as receipts for coin and gold deposited with them. Thus, initially issued notes were backed by an equivalent amount of gold in reserves. However, as banks realized that their notes were willingly held and accepted in exchange for goods and services, they were able safely to lend on the gold they held on deposit and the modern fractional reserve banking system developed. The issue of notes, too, ultimately became the preserve of the central bank, which held the official reserves of gold. The principal nineteenth century monetary policy debate then concerned the extent to which the central bank note issue should be backed by gold. The Currency School of economists, worried about the possibility of inflation, were in favour of 100 per cent gold backing for the note issue above an initial amount. On the other hand, Banking School economists, worried by the possibility of aggregate demand being restricted by an insufficient issue of notes argued that banks should extend credit to finance real activity according to their own judgement, using liquid assets as backing in addition to gold and maintaining a prudent balance between earning assets and gold reserves.

The terms of this debate have changed as the monetary system has changed, with paper money becoming irredeemable against gold and bank deposits becoming the principal element in money. Nonetheless, the spirit of the debate has not changed. The modern equivalent of Currency School economists remain concerned about the rate of inflation, the rate of growth of the money supply and the relationship between them while continuing to distrust governments whom they see as the source of inflation. The modern equivalent of Banking School economists, on the other hand, place much more emphasis on the role of credit in the economy, stress the role of profit-seeking commercial banks and are more likely to worry about interest rates being too high, restricting real economic activity, than about inflation.

This story takes us through commodity money to fiat money. In an economy with only commodity money, gold coins and bank notes fully backed by gold, it could be argued that if the supply of commodity money and gold were stable, the money supply would be exogenous, since an increase in the demand for goods and services could not call more commodity money into existence. However, we have seen that money is a social artefact and, as such, it develops and alters to meet social needs. If the demand for goods and services is constrained by the inability to obtain 'money' in order to carry out desired transactions, new forms of money develop and/or a higher proportion of transactions are carried out on credit. Thus, it is difficult to see that in any longer term sense, the supply of money was ever truly exogenous. As we shall see, it is extremely difficult to argue that the money supply in a modern economy is exogenous in any sense.

1.5 Summary

Monetary economics is very important in modern economies since monetary policy decisions have a major impact on everyone. However, it is dogged by widespread disagreements. These partly derive from the difficulty of finding a universally accepted definition of 'money'. This is complicated by the variety of meanings the word has in everyday usage. In particular, 'money' is commonly used to mean 'wealth' whereas for monetary economists 'money' refers to only one part of wealth — that part generally acceptable in exchange for goods and services. This does not get us very far towards a precise definition of money since a range of assets is acceptable in the process of exchange. Further, what acts as 'money' is socially determined, is different from one place to another and changes over time.

There is also a problem with the definition of 'exchange'. At an individual level, exchange is constrained by the lack of wealth and/or the ability to borrow rather than by the lack of money. Nonetheless, the quantity of money in the economy may be important at the aggregate level. It is not clear, however, that the monetary authorities are able and/or willing to control the supply of money. Even at an aggregate level, the quantity of money in the economy might be no more than an indicator of the level of economic activity.

The story usually told of the development of money in economies sees it as arising and changing in order to economize on the information costs and time needed in the process of exchange. This is historically inaccurate and biases the debate in favour of the view that money is separate from real economic activity in the economy — that is, in favour of the view that money is neutral.

Key concepts used in this chapter

money	wealth
real values	liquidity
money (nominal) values	exogenous money
the neutrality of money	endogenous money
medium of exchange	transmission mechanism of
credit	monetary policy

Questions and exercises

1. The text refers to the 'regular' interest rate announcements of central banks. How often and when are interest rate announcements made by:
- the Bank of England Monetary Policy Committee?
- the European Central Bank?
- the Federal Reserve Board of the United States?

2. What comprises the wealth of: (a) households? (b) firms?

3. For a short time, in the early years of the British settlement of Australia (the 1790s), rum was used as a currency. What advantages and disadvantages does rum have as a commodity money?

4. What is the significance of the word 'ready' in the term 'ready money'?

5. What limits currently exist on the amount of credit that can be obtained by households? Is there any attempt by the monetary authorities to control the amount of credit available?

6. The words 'exogenous' and 'endogenous' are used widely in economics — not just referring to money. What precisely do they mean? Provide other examples of their use.

7. Provide examples of transactions in our modern monetary economy that take place through barter.

8. How would you explain the phrase 'time is money'? In recent years, 'time banks' have been developed to try to help poor people and communities to overcome some of the problems they face within the market economy. Which constraints on people are time banks trying to ease? Try to find some UK examples of time banks.

9. The text refers to the treatment of the market in economics as a theoretical concept devoid of social and institutional features. Clearly there are many differences among different types of market. But are these important for economists? For example, the business of financial markets used to be conducted face-to-face on the floors of organized exchanges but is now conducted very largely by telephone and the internet. Is this change likely to have had any economic significance? If so, why?

Further reading

Discussions of the meaning of 'money' in economics are often limited to definitions or standard roles of money. For more discursive treatment, you are likely to need to consult older books such as Visser (1974) — but these are not now easy to find. By far the most entertaining book on what money is and how it developed is Galbraith (1975). The early story of money is also told in Glyn Davies (1994). L Randall Wray (1990) provides useful criticism of the simplistic approach to the history of money often taken by economists in the first chapter.

2 Definitions of Money in Economics

'Only 3l. in each 100l. were cash — that is, coin and bank notes, true money', Bon. Price in *Fraser's Magazine*, May 1880, p. 675.

'In international commerce the form of money most used is a bill of exchange, and a good bill is good money', *Westminster Gazette*, 18 June 1903, 2/1.

What you will learn in this chapter:

- How views of the nature of money are influenced by assumptions about the working of economies
- In particular, the impact on definitions of money of assumptions about the level of information in an economy
- Problems in the expression of the Quantity Theory of Money
- Different approaches to the theoretical definition of money in economics
- Official measures of money and how these have changed over time

---

2.1   Introduction

In Chapter 1, we discussed the possible meanings of money and distinguished its meaning in monetary economics from its meanings in everyday usage. In this chapter, we look at the various approaches to the formal definition of 'money' employed by economists. Before this, we look at the way in which the preferred definition of money might depend on the assumptions made about the nature of the economic system and the role of money within that system. We then go on to consider both theoretical and official definitions of money.

2.2   World views and definitions of money

So far, we have said that the only reason for needing a definition of money is to allow us to measure the money supply and that we might want to do this if we believed that we could influence aggregate demand through influencing the supply of money. This leaves open the nature of the link between aggregate demand and inflation, which we shall deal with in Chapters 7 and 8 when we look at the transmission mechanism between money supply and income and prices. We have also suggested that there are difficulties in defining the supply of money. One particular problem is that economists tend to think of 'money' in different ways depending on the general view they hold of how the economy works. To show this, we shall look at two _p...ned views of the functioning of the economy and see what they imply about the nature of money and hence its definition.

Money in a world with high levels of information

We begin by assuming an economic system in which all participants are well informed. Markets tend towards equilibrium. When an existing equilibrium is disturbed, the return to equilibrium is sufficiently rapid that behaviour may be analysed as if the markets were always in equilibrium. That is, we are not saying that the economic system is always in equilibrium — merely that an assumption of equilibrium provides the best way to analyse the system. Thus, we assume that current real income is always at its equilibrium level and that this level is known. Savings decisions, then, reflect the long-term choice between the present and future consumption (of goods and services). This is a real not a monetary decision and is therefore a function of the real rate of interest. All savings are invested and the level of investment determines the rate of growth of capital stock, which in turn ensures the desired future level of output. The real rate of interest is determined by the actions of savers and investors. The plans of economic agents are always fulfilled. There is no uncertainty and no scope for purely financial transactions.

The money supply is exogenous — the monetary authorities determine its size and rate of growth. We define money as all those assets, and only those assets, that are acceptable in exchange. The price of money is the inverse of an index of prices, which we can think of initially as an index of the prices of all goods and services in the economy ($1/P_t$). The technical relationship between money and economic activity is then expressed by the equation of exchange:

$$MV_t \equiv P_t T \qquad \qquad ...2.1$$

where M is the stock of money, $P_t T$ is the value of all transactions undertaken with money (including exchanges of second-hand goods and financial assets as well as of newly-produced goods). V_t, the transactions velocity of money, is the expression of the technical relationship between the stock of money and the flow of transactions and is only likely to change slowly as the financial system changes. Since it is only likely to change slowly, we might even think of it as being constant, although this is not essential. Crucially, V_t should be independent of M, P_t, and T. Shocks to V_t would influence $P_t T$, but, in the absence of such shocks, externally engineered changes in M (exogenous money) would produce predictable changes in P_tT (this is the basis of the Quantity Theory of Money which we meet again in Section 4.2).

We can think of the task of the monetary authorities in measuring and attempting to control the money supply in one of three ways:

- they could attempt to distinguish between those deposits that are held only to allow exchange to take place and deposits held for savings purposes;

- they could attempt to identify a set of assets, changes in the quantity of which would, in the absence of shocks to V_t, induce predictable changes in P_tT.

- they could attempt to identify a set of assets, the size of which is unrelated to V_t.

A common approach to distinguishing between deposits held to allow exchange to occur and savings deposits was to limit the definition of 'money' to non-interest-bearing deposits, on the grounds that people would only willingly forgo interest on those deposits that they required to carry out their planned transactions.

We need to acknowledge at this point a potential problem with the use of T (total transactions). When Irving Fisher published his well-known statement of the Quantity Theory of Money (Fisher, 1911), he distinguished between those transactions related to national income (Y) and those related to financial transactions (F). Thus:

$$MV = P_yY + P_fF \qquad \qquad ...2.2$$

where Y and F are income and financial transactions respectively. Yet, when economists today refer to velocity, they are almost always referring to income velocity, that is to say GDP/M, or PY/M rather than PT/M. Furthermore, income velocity is reported in official statistics. Although a number of other reasons have been put forward, perhaps the principal explanation of this is that a measure of total transactions in the economy is not readily available.

Pause for thought 2.1:

Why is it so difficult to measure the value of all transactions in an economy, including financial transactions and the exchange of second-hand goods? Can you think of ways in which you might try to obtain such a measure?

The substitution of PY for PT produces an awkward point. However we define M, we cannot conceive of a set of assets that are only used in the purchase and sale of newly produced goods and services. Clearly, any asset available as a means of payment for this purpose may also be used for transactions involving second-hand goods and financial assets. We might thus write our equation of exchange as:

$$M_Y V_Y + M_F V_F + M_{SV} \equiv P_y Y + P_f F \qquad \ldots 2.3$$

where M_Y is money held to allow purchases of newly produced goods and services, M_F money held to allow other purchases (of second-hand goods and financial assets) and M_{SV} money held as savings. Thus, to transform $MV \equiv PT$ into $MV \equiv PY$, we are implying that:

(i) M_{SV} is zero and

(ii) $P_f F / M_F V_F$ is constant.

We have assumed (i) above. With well-informed market agents, F and Y will also be closely related since financial transactions will only take place in the pursuit of real ends. That is, as we have noted above, there would be no purely financial transactions. Equally, the prices of second-hand goods would be closely related to those of newly produced goods and services. We can therefore feel comfortable with the transformation of V_t into the income velocity of money (V_y). The price index we need has also changed. We now need an index of the prices of newly produced goods and services (P_y) rather than of all transactions (P_t). This is another big advantage in conducting empirical work since the standard published price indices relate to Y rather than T.

We would, of course, have great trouble in measuring MY but we could still hope to approach the definition of money empirically by:

• attempting to identify a set of assets, changes in the quantity of which would, in the absence of shocks to V_y, induce predictable changes in $P_y Y$; or

•attempting to identify a set of assets, the size of which is unrelated to V_y.

In this case, we would not be attempting to define money directly or descriptively but defining it as anything that produces the results we think should be produced by an accurate definition of money.

Pause for thought 2.2:

Can you explain the reasoning behind wishing to identify a set of assets unrelated to the size of income velocity?

In the absence of shocks, we would be looking for a measure of M that would be associated with a stable or predictable income velocity and, given the assumptions made above, we could do so with some confidence.

In an economy such as this, any conversion of non-money assets into money by individual agents would only produce a redistribution of the existing money balances among people and firms in the economy. It would not increase the total.

Starting from a position of just enough money in the economy to allow the purchase of the equilibrium level of Y at the existing price level, an increase in the quantity of money disturbs the equilibrium: people use excess money balances to attempt to buy more goods and services but, since Y is fixed, the only effect is on P. As P rises, the real value of the money stock falls to its original level. Since the only reason for holding money is to allow the purchase of goods and services, PY goes on rising until the nominal demand for money rises to the new, higher, supply of it. Money is neutral (having no effect on real variables).

Money in an uncertain world

Let us now assume instead that markets do not function well and that disequilibrium is the norm. The future levels of employment and output are unknown. People, being in no position to make rational choices between current and future levels of consumption, can only make consumption and saving plans on the basis of current nominal incomes. Equally, firms do not know the future level of sales and can only base investment plans on the supply cost of capital equipment and the estimated rate of return from various levels of investment. Thus, saving and investment plans are being made by different groups of people on different bases and are very unlikely to match. The economy is dominated by uncertainty. Some people plan to save a high proportion of their income; others to dissave through either using up past savings or borrowing. The ability to convert savings into means of payment will be influenced by both their size and their liquidity (the ease, remember, with which an asset can be converted into a means of payment).

Holders of illiquid financial assets may convert them into means of payment but there is a cost in doing so since other savers must be persuaded to hold them and attitudes towards the risk involved in doing so may change. In the aggregate, such changing perceptions may influence the rate of interest in the economy and hence the level of expenditure.

Money thus has value in itself since (in periods without inflation) there is no risk of loss from holding it. Consequently, savers may choose to hold part of their savings in the form of money and increases in the quantity of money may be held idle as an asset rather than used in the purchase of goods and services. We therefore have a case for widening the definition of money to include assets that are not means of payment but that can be converted into means of payment with little or no risk of loss. The difficulty is that once we move away from the notion of a 'means of payment', it is hard to develop a clear-cut distinction between 'money' and assets that are 'near money'.

Planning to dissave through borrowing introduces another possible limitation on spending plans: the availability of credit. If firms believe that a final payment will ultimately be made, they may extend credit, make exchanges, and produce on that basis. Attitudes to credit may change independently of changes in the quantity of assets available as a means of final payment. Financial intermediaries act to weaken further the link between the means of final payment and production and employment decisions of firms by, in effect, taking over the debt from buyers or sellers.

Consider the implications of this approach to the equations based on the equation of exchange that we considered above:

$$MV_t \equiv P_t T \qquad \qquad ...2.1$$

Firstly, we are no longer at all sure exactly what M is. Secondly, we are likely to have problems in distinguishing between deposits held for exchange purposes and those held as savings. That is, we can no longer assume M_{SV} to be zero. Thirdly, V_t may change in response to changes in M. Hence, even if we continue to assume that the authorities are able to control the level of M, any attempt to restrict $P_t T$ by reducing the quantity of M may be resisted by the easing of restrictions on credit. Thus, any reduction in M might be met in part by an increase in V_t, diluting the impact on $P_t T$. Equally, an increase in M might be associated with a fall in V_t. Of course, if the authorities were able to limit the total amount of final payments for long enough, and, as a result, debts entered into were not paid, credit would no longer be offered, or, at least, the terms on which it was granted would be made tougher. Nonetheless, it is clear that, from the point of view of what determines $P_t T$, we should be interested in the volume of credit in the economy, rather than the money stock.

Fourthly, in the sort of world above, the authorities could not hope to control M with any degree of reliability. Even if they retained the technical ability to do so, the uncertainty surrounding the relationship between M and P_tT would be so great that it would be very inadvisable for the authorities to attempt to manipulate M. External shocks to P_tT would produce changes in M and money would be endogenous. Our task would be to analyse the causes of the external shocks to P_tT.

Finally, there would not be a close link between financial and real transactions or between the markets for second-hand and newly produced goods. In a world with low levels of information, market agents would often make mistakes. Indeed, in the absence of clear and reliable information about the future values of real variables, it may be wisest for people to base decisions on current nominal values. Money illusion (the confusion between real and nominal values), which economists often refer to disparagingly, may be a reflection of rational behaviour in an uncertain world. This would call into doubt the notion that P_tT and P_yY are closely related. This, in turn, would undermine the argument for a stable technical relationship between M and P_yY, even if there were such a relationship between M and P_tT. It would seem highly unlikely that we could find a definition of money that would reliably and consistently be associated with a stable income velocity of money.

From this approach to the economy, we might conclude that we do not need a definition of money at all. If we did, out of a general interest, seek to measure the supply of money as distinct from credit, we would opt for a broad definition that included a range of highly liquid financial assets.

2.3   Economists' definitions of money

We began our discussion in Chapter 1 with a dictionary definition of money and noted that money takes a variety of forms — it is anything that circulates from person to person in the process of exchange and which provides a common unit for expressing the price of goods and services exchanged. It is obviously important for individuals to know what is acceptable in exchange but this is a matter of national, and sometimes local, practice and might change over time. We also need to know how to convert illiquid assets into money and how to seek to obtain liquid resources through borrowing, but, as individuals, we do not need any formal definition of 'money'. Nor do we need any appreciation of how much 'money' exists in the economy. Ultimately, if people have sufficient spending resources they can always obtain money. We have talked above about illiquid assets but all such assets can be converted into money quickly enough if the price is sufficiently low. Even the very poor can borrow from pawnbrokers or 'loan sharks' and, when they do so, what they receive is money. In these cases, it is not 'money' that is scarce. People talk of not having enough 'money' but what they lack is 'spending resources' as we have defined them above: real and financial assets together with the ability to borrow.

Pause for thought 2.3:

What does the word 'money' mean in the following quotation from Shakespeare's *The Merchant of Venice*, Act I Scene III?

'Hath a dog money? Is it possible a cur can lend three thousand ducats?'

Things may be different, however, at an aggregate level. Much depends on whether we accept the notion that the authorities could and should operate on the interest rate by attempting to control the stock of money. In this case, we would need a clear idea of what constitutes the money supply and some ability to measure it. If, however, the authorities attempt to control spending directly by adjusting the interest rate, we do not need to define or to measure 'money' even at an aggregate level. We might still choose to attempt to do so but only perhaps as one of a number of indicators of the desirability of adjusting the interest rate. The fact that we might only have a very limited and specific need for a definition of 'money' in economics may well influence the definition we use, although we should bear in mind that the interest of economists in money is not limited to the macroeconomic relationship between the aggregate money supply and aggregate demand. Let us look, next, at the various approaches to the definition of money in economics.

Descriptive definitions of money

A standard approach is to begin with the three roles attributed to money in the economy. We have mentioned two of these: money as a medium of exchange and money as a unit of account. The third is as a store of value in that the use of money allows for the separation of supply and demand in time. Goods and services can be produced and sold in one time period and the proceeds held in the form of money until a later period when they can be used to purchase goods and services. Exchanges in a monetary economy are accepted as non-synchronized. This is accepted as a benefit because it removes 'the double coincidence of wants' associated with barter — the need to find a buyer for your goods who also happens to sell the goods you desire. In this way, the use of money saves greatly on search and information costs in an economy (see Section 1.4).

The dominant role of these three is usually taken to be money as a medium of exchange. This fits in with the common view of money exemplified by the dictionary definition given in Section 1.2. Further, any asset that performs the role of a medium of exchange is generally held to be able also to act as a store of value and a unit of account. Hicks (1967) denied this, arguing that money could be a medium of exchange without being a store of value as long as, over the course of a day's trading, no individuals have sold more than they have bought and vice versa. However, this would be a very special case and the usual view is that all forms of money are stores of value, whereas the reverse is not true (see Harris, 1985). Thus, acting as a medium of exchange is the only role that clearly sets money apart from other assets.

Pause for thought 2.4:

What is a cash-in-advance constraint? (If in doubt, see Section 1.4). Would money be a medium of exchange but not a store of value if there were a cash-in-advance constraint?

Our discussion above, however, alerted us to a problem with the notion of 'money' as a medium of exchange since credit acts as a medium of exchange but is almost always excluded from definitions of 'money'. One way out is to follow Shackle (1971) and distinguish between the medium of exchange (which includes credit) and a means of payment, in the sense of a means of final settlement of debt. It is this latter idea that most writers have in mind. Among the definitions along these lines, we have:

...a temporary abode of purchasing power (Friedman, 1963);

...any asset which gives immediate command over goods and services (Struthers and Speight, 1986);

...any property right that is generally acceptable in exchange (Fisher, 1911).

These are descriptive or *a priori* definitions of money deriving from the notion of money as a means of payment but also admit of the idea of a store of value. However, none of them gives a precise idea of which assets should be included in a measure of the economy's money stock. Everything depends on what is acceptable.

Nonetheless, the concentration on the role of money as a means of payment led to the common acceptance of the 'narrow' view of money as an asset that would be held only temporarily and not as a form of savings. This implies not just that money is the medium of exchange but also that only the medium of exchange is money. This, in turn, led to the distinction between narrow money and other financial assets based on whether or not interest was paid, since it seemed reasonable to argue that people would only hold in a non-interest-bearing form those funds needed to carry out imminent transactions. Until the middle 1980s, this gave a neat set of assets consisting of cash or fiat money (bank notes and coin) plus non-interest bearing deposits with banks ('sight' or chequable deposits). Fiat money is also known as outside money because it is issued outside the private sector by the monetary authorities, or as 'high-powered' money because it is seen as the monetary base on which the rest of the money supply is constructed. Sight deposits with banks are part of 'inside money' because they are both created by and held within the private sector.

There are two obvious problems with the narrow definition of money. Firstly, its justification is that all other assets must be converted into notes and coin or sight deposits in order to carry out exchange. However, other types of bank deposits and deposits with non-bank financial institutions can be converted so quickly (and at virtually no cost) into narrow money that the distinction is hardly worth maintaining. This has been true for many years but is all the more true when funds can be moved from one account to another through the internet or by telephone at any time of the day or night. Indeed, banks now offer 'sweep' facilities that transfer funds automatically between low interest current accounts and other higher-interest accounts. Equally, other assets do not need to be sold to obtain narrow money but can be used as collateral for a loan that takes the form of narrow money. Under these circumstances, many types of asset are as good as narrow money for the purpose of exchange. Certainly, if our interest lies in the notion of a lack of money acting as a constraint on expenditure or as influencing expenditure plans, the distinction between narrow money and other highly liquid assets is not worth maintaining.

This justifies the widening of the standard definition to include bank deposits other than sight deposits. However, once one moves away from the strict interpretation of means of final settlement of debt and includes liquidity as a criterion it becomes impossible to draw a line between assets that are money and those that are nearly money but not quite. The issue was slightly complicated by the move to the payment of interest on sight deposits in the 1980s since that raised the question of whether some sight deposits might be savings rather than being held because of the function of sight deposits as means of payment. In fact, this merely emphasized a problem that had always existed in the distinction between deposits held for transactions purposes (money) and those held as savings. One only has to acknowledge that people do not know with certainty either the total future value of their wealth or the precise value of the transactions they will be undertaking to realize that the distinction is dubious. Some assets provide convenience because they are acceptable as means of payment or can be easily converted into means of payment. Financial institutions offer a lower rate of interest on these assets because banks are more limited in their ability to make profits from funds deposited with them in this form. Depositors are prepared to accept a lower rate of interest on these assets because of their convenience. What is important is the interest rate differential between assets of differing degrees of liquidity. The attribution in the past of some special significance to the fact that sight deposits paid no interest simply gave a false security to the distinction between them and other kinds of bank deposits.

The second obvious problem with the narrow definition of money is that it ignores the significance of the idea that to be a means of payment, an asset must be generally acceptable. Since acceptability depends on custom and the nature of financial institutions, what is and is not 'money' differs from economy to economy and changes over time.

This leaves us in the position that the narrow definition of money is too precise and does not reflect the complexity of influences on decisions regarding the form in which to hold wealth. However, broader definitions of money are insufficiently precise because there are no clear criteria for deciding what should be included and what left out. Milton Friedman is widely quoted as saying 'money is what money does', implying that anything can be counted as 'money' that performs the role of money. This does not take us very far. There have been attempts to resolve this issue by making use of the 'revealed preferences' of money-holders. This is a microeconomic approach that works on the principle that the best way to find out which assets are 'money' is to discover which assets people treat as money. We start with a narrow definition including only assets that everyone would agree form part of the money stock (notes and coins) and then seek to discover by studying household economic behaviour which other assets are treated as sufficiently close substitutes for the original set that they are, to all intents and purposes, equivalent to money. This leaves open what is meant by a 'sufficiently close substitute' and so remains subjective.

Prescriptive definitions of money

An entirely different approach is to decide on the theoretical nature of the relationship of money with other important variables in the economy and then to define money so as to show that this relationship exists in practice. In other words, one starts with a model of the economy in which 'money' plays a clear role, with the nature of that role depending on the assumptions underlying the model. Here we provide two examples of how particular views of money can be derived from simplified models of the economy in Section 2.2. Once we have the model, we seek a definition of money that validates the model.

Let us assume that we believe money to be neutral. That is, 'money' is a set of assets changes in the value of which have no impact on real variables such as output and employment. We then hope to define money in such a way that empirical tests show this neutrality. Alternatively, we might begin with the view that inflation is caused by a too rapid growth of the money supply. A corollary of this is that the demand for money is stably related to real income. Thus, a demand for money function is constructed, using what seems to be the most likely definition of money for the purpose. However, if the function turns out not to be stable, the definition of money may be changed until a definition of money is found for which demand does appear to be stable. This extremely pragmatic approach is strongly supported by Milton Friedman and reflects the statement quoted above that 'money is what money does'. The underlying belief is that there must be something, the rate of growth of which is closely linked to the rate of inflation, and we may call this something 'money'. The only problem is the practical one of finding an empirical counterpart to the theoretical idea. Money is thus defined in the way that yields the most accurate predictions. This is an example of a general approach to economics that sees the predictive power of models as all-important. It should not worry us unduly if the assumptions made in the construction of models that predict accurately appear to be unrealistic.

It remains that this approach to defining money can lead to frequent *ad hoc* adjustments to the definition in an attempt to produce the correct answer. Given the problems associated with definitions of other variables in the functions, the dubious quality of many of the statistics being employed and the complexity of the time lags involved, there is a danger of exercises of this kind becoming more interesting for the range of econometric techniques used than for any light shed on important economic relationships. It follows naturally that economists who do not start by believing in the theory that inflation is caused by excess growth of an exogenous money supply regard all such empirical exercises with the deepest scepticism.

In any case, there is a potential practical difficulty. No simple combination of assets might produce the desired results. Alternatively, a particular definition may seem to give favourable results when applied to the data for one period but the apparent relationships may break down in later periods. One reason for difficulties of this kind might be that the different assets included in a definition of money may have different relationships with income. For example, notes and coins, sight bank deposits and other bank deposits may each have a stable relationship with nominal income but the relationship may be different in each case. Then, if our definition of money includes all three of these assets and the proportion each forms of the money supply changes over time, the relationship between money as a whole and nominal income will change. Thus, a development of the empirical approach has been to weight the various types of deposit to try to take account of different velocities of circulation. Alternatively, as in the case of Divisia indexes, different degrees of liquidity are measured by rates of interest (the lower the interest rate payable on an asset, the more liquid it is assumed to be). These are discussed in Section 2.4 below.

2.4 Official measures of money

In the last section we have suggested that the way in which one chooses, or would like, to define money is influenced by the way in which one thinks that money works: theoretical perceptions predispose us towards particular definitions. In practice, when it comes to defining monetary aggregates for policy purposes, the authorities have no such luxury. Debates surrounding inside and outside money may require, for example, a measure of non-interest bearing money, but if banks make no distinction between interest bearing and non-interest bearing sight deposits, there will be no such data. Official measures of money have to reflect the behaviour and practices of deposit-taking institutions. This leads us to two rather obvious consequences and an important conclusion. Firstly, pragmatism plays a significant role in the compilation of official monetary aggregates with the authorities having to accept what they can get from the banking system, albeit sometimes with pressure applied. Secondly, the aggregates will change because of changes in banking practice and banking products, as a result, in other words, of innovation. Both of these characteristics are strongly present in the history of UK aggregates, as we shall see in a moment. Before that though we might just pause to note that this is our first encounter in this book with a fundamentally important principle for monetary policy (as opposed to theory), namely that the creators of money are private sector institutions whose responsibilities to their shareholders, and even to their clients, come before their responsibilities as agents of monetary policy. In most economies, the official definitions of money as well as the development of appropriate instruments of monetary control are the outcome of a continuous dialectic between the monetary authorities and the banking system.

Table 2.1 gives a complete listing of all the official monetary aggregates for which data have been recorded in the UK in recent years. It also gives their composition and their status at various times. The latter point needs careful interpretation. The Bank of England has published data for each series at some time. The column headed 'first published' gives the date of first appearance in the *Bank of England Quarterly Bulletin*. Quite often, however, a short back-run of data was also compiled, so date of first publication may not coincide with the beginning of the data series. 'Discontinued' means publication ceased at that date. 'Targeted' is a rather elastic term. It may mean targeted explicitly or implicitly and it may also mean targeted by the authorities even though no series was published, as in the early days with DCE, or targeted according to published ranges — in the heyday of monetary targeting. We have also indicated in the final column those series that have been subject to 'monitoring' rather than 'targeting'. 'Monitoring' means that they were closely observed for the information they might contain about future developments in the economy and thus as an aid to setting the level of interest rates.

The table is laid out so that aggregates are listed in increasingly 'broad' order, although M4 and M5 are replacements for PSL1 and PSL2 rather than further extensions of them. DCE, 'domestic credit expansion', and the Divisia indexes are rather different categories and we discuss them separately below.

Leaving aside the changes in definitions for a moment, what the table shows for the UK is similar to what we would find in any other system, namely that the authorities record data (published or not) for several series. At the narrowest end, all central banks are interested in the magnitude of the monetary base or 'high-powered money'. The reason that is usually given is that base is an essential input into the money-creation process since banks must hold a minimum quantity of base in relation to deposits in order to ensure convertibility of their deposits into cash. This ratio lies at the centre of the deposit-multiplier models of money supply determination. The components of the base are all liabilities of the central bank and it is therefore suggested that officially determined changes in the quantity of the base could create multiple expansions/contractions of the money supply, a technique known as 'monetary base control'. NIBM1, M1, and M2 are progressively wider definitions of what is generally termed 'narrow money'. The first two are narrow in the sense that they focus upon notes and coin plus 'sight' or 'demand' deposits — the media that one would expect to be used primarily for transactions purposes. The appearance of M2 in 1982 illustrates the point we made earlier about institutional changes. If one were interested in money for transactions purposes, it seemed illogical to leave out many building society deposits since, although they were not at that time generally chequable, cash for transactions could be drawn on demand and there was evidence that many such deposits were used by the less wealthy who did not have bank accounts. The same argument applied to National Savings (a government department) accounts. On the other hand, some large building society deposits were clearly savings (as indeed might have been some bank interest-bearing sight deposits) and so M2 was an attempt to cut across both bank and building society deposits to provide another measure of transactions money.

M3 is a measure of 'broad' money in the sense that it includes sight and time deposits, including certificates of deposit (CDs). The components of M3 come closest to providing a universal definition of money — important if one wishes to do comparative empirical work — as the authorities in most countries publish a series very similar to this (in Germany and the USA the series are actually denoted M3 as well).

PSL1 and PSL2 are even broader definitions. The terms stand for 'private sector liquidity — definitions 1 and 2' and indicate a tendency at the time to think of some components as reaching beyond the limits of 'money'. Bank time deposits with long maturities, treasury bills, and certificates of tax deposit could none of them be used for transactions. On the other hand they could be turned, quickly, into sight deposits. It is worth noting that as late as 1979, building society deposits were not only thought of as non-money assets; they were included only in PSL2. This explains why when, in the heyday of monetary targeting, only three years later, it was PSL2 that was chosen rather than PSL1.

The 1986 Building Society Act permitted societies for the first time to make unsecured loans up to a small maximum proportion of their total assets. This was enough, however, to allow them to issue their own cheque books and guarantee cards. This made their deposits virtually indistinguishable from bank deposits as a means of payment. The exclusion of building society deposits from mainstream monetary aggregates (symbol-

Table 2.1: UK official definitions of money

Name	Components	First Published	Discontinued	Targeted
DCE (Domestic credit expansion)	Change in £ bank lending to the non-bank public and private sectors	Dec. 1972	March 1986	1967-9 1976-9
M0 (Wide monetary base)	Notes and coin outside the Bank of England + banks' operational deposits at the Bank of England	June 1981		1984-present[1]
NIBM1 (Non-interest bearing M1)	Notes and coin in circulation + NBPS[2] holdings of non-interest bearing £ sight deposits	June 1975	Feb. 1991	
M1	NIBM1 + NBPS holdings of interest-bearing £ sight deposits	Dec. 1970	July 1989	1982-4
M2	NIBM1 + NBPS holdings of interest bearing retail £ deposits with banks and building societies + National Savings ordinary accounts	Sept. 1982[3]		
M3 (£M3 until May 1987)	M1 + NBPS holdings of £ bank time deposits and certificates of deposits (CDs)	March 1977[4]	July 1989	1976-86
M3c (M3 until May 1987)	M3 + NBPS holdings of foreign currency bank deposits	Dec. 1970[4]	July 1989	

PSL1	M3 - NBPS £ bank time deposits with original maturity >2 years + NBPS holdings of bank bills, treasury bills, local authority deposits and certificates of tax deposit	Sept. 1979	May 1987	
PSL2	PSL1 + NBPS building society £ deposits (excl. term shares) + short-term National Savings instruments	Sept. 1979	May 1987	1982-4
M4	M3 + M4PS5 holdings of building society £ shares, deposits and CDs	May 1987	May 1987	
M4c	M4 + M4PS holdings of bank and building society foreign currency deposits	May 1987	May 1991	
M3H[6]	M4c + public corporations' holdings of £ and foreign currency bank and building society deposits	August 1992		
M5	M4 + M4PS holdings of bank bills, treasury bills, local authority deposits and certificates of tax deposit + short term National Savings instruments	May 1987	May 1991	
'Liquid assets outside M4'	M5 + M4PS holdings of bank and building society foreign currency deposits + further £ liquid assets of M4PS and £ assets of the overseas sector	May 1991		
Divisia	Liquidity-weighted components of M4 (see text)			

Notes: 1 'monitored'; 2 'non-bank private sector'; 3 not to be confused with an earlier version of M2 (Dec. 1970 - Dec. 1971) which was roughly midway between M1 and M3; 4 £M3 and M3 included public sector; 5 'M4 private sector' or non-bank, non-building society private sector; 6 a harmonised measure of broad money, consistent across the EU.

ized by the M3/PSL2 distinction) became unsustainable and so M4 developed alongside M3 as a rival broad money aggregate. The same Act enabled building societies to convert to plc status, in other words to become banks. When the Abbey National Building Society did so in June 1989, this produced a sharp upward break in all those series (excluding NIBM1), which contained only bank deposits. From July 1989, therefore, M3 was discontinued and building society deposits became officially, as many holders had regarded them for years unofficially, 'money'. NIBM1 survived until 1991 because it was unaffected, the Abbey National Building Society having virtually no non-interest-bearing deposits.

1991 also saw major changes in the recording and classification of liquid (non-money) assets. Part of the revision involved discontinuing the publication of M4c and transferring the foreign currency component to M5. But the assets in M5 itself were dramatically supplemented to include, amongst other items, UK-owned off-shore sterling deposits; the overseas sector's holdings of sterling deposits (in the UK and offshore); UK-owned commercial paper, short-dated gilts and, reminiscent of a suggestion first made over sixty years ago by J M Keynes, unused sterling credit facilities such as agreed (but unused) overdraft agreements.

The traditional approach to defining money, as Table 2.1 shows, involves identifying an appropriate subset of financial assets. Measuring the quantity of money then involves the simple aggregation of all those assets in the subset at their nominal value. While this may be an obvious (and straightforward) approach it suffers from both a theoretical and an empirical weakness. At the theoretical level, simple aggregation implies that we are dealing with homogeneous assets. We seem to be saying, for example, that from a monetary point of view, £1bn of CDs is the same as £1bn of notes and coin. The mere fact that CDs pay interest while notes and coin do not, however, indicates some degree of differentiation since otherwise no one would hold notes and coin. At the empirical level, as we saw in Section 1.3, economists are usually interested in the closeness of the relationship between a monetary aggregate and income. This is likely to increase with the extent to which the aggregate is dominated by assets used for transactions. As we also saw in 1.3, however, it is difficult to know exactly where to draw the line between whole classes of assets for this purpose. Notes and coin and sight deposits are all perfectly liquid and are obvious transactions media but we know that time deposits can be switched to sight deposits quickly and cheaply and that other, apparently less liquid, assets have sufficient liquidity that they could still be relevant to transactions, albeit to a lesser degree.

The Divisia approach involves weighting each of the component assets according to the extent to which they provide transactions services. If this could be done accurately, then the resulting index should measure the quantity of money available in the economy for transactions purposes and should be more closely linked to expenditure and income.

The weights given to each asset are often said to represent the 'user cost' of the asset. To measure the user cost, we must first choose a benchmark asset which provides no transactions services. For example, the Bank of England has published a Divisia index going back to 1977 based upon the components of M4 and using the rate on three-month local authority deposits (the 3mLA rate) as the benchmark. In order to construct the index, we subtract the rate of interest on the component asset from the rate on the benchmark asset. Notes and coin are given a weight of one representing the difference between the 3mLA rate and zero. Each other asset, a_i, is then given a lesser weight, w_i, equal to the difference between the benchmark rate and its own rate, i_i, as a fraction of the benchmark-notes and coin differential. In symbols:

$$w_i = (3\text{mLA rate} - i_i)/(3\text{mLA rate} - 0) \qquad\qquad ...2.4$$

The index, D, is then the sum of the nominal value of each asset adjusted for its appropriate weight:

$$D = \Sigma a_i w_i$$

If it is the transactions services of money in which we are primarily interested, then Divisia clearly possesses numerous attractions. There are some problems though. Firstly, it is still not clear that such an index is measuring transactions services alone since bank accounts give access to other banking services for their holders. Secondly, in using interest rate differentials to measure user cost we are assuming that interest rates are equilibrium rates in a perfectly competitive system. A characteristic of the UK monetary sector in the 1980s, however, was a marked increase in competition especially between banks and building societies. For earlier periods, therefore, it seems unlikely that this condition holds. Thirdly, unless we assume that portfolio adjustments are instantaneous, and this is not suggested by evidence, then the weighted components are unlikely to have equilibrium values. For example, if the rate on an asset increases, the differential with the benchmark asset (and thus the weight) diminishes. But until holdings of that asset have adjusted to its new own rate, the re-calculated weight will be attached to an asset quantity which is too small. Since we are dealing with an index derived from numerous assets and interest rates and since the latter are frequently changing, this is more than just a theoretical objection. Lastly, though more a complication than an objection, there is the question of which index to construct and what interest rates to use in its construction. We noted above that the bank of England has an index based upon the components of M4, but such an index could be computed for any of the simple-sum aggregates (excepting M0) and indeed for any other set of assets that we might think relevant. The choice of interest rate for each asset is unlikely to be ambiguous but the choice of the benchmark rate is often more difficult and will depend upon institutional features of the monetary system. The benchmark asset has to be capital certain (to be comparable with other assets in the index) and yet offer no transactions services (if it did, it should be in the index). In most cases, the problem will be one of finding any such asset (there must not be a secondary market, for example). Where there is more than one, and if differentials between the benchmark assets change over time, the logical resolution is to select always the highest benchmark rate.

2.5 Summary

A particular problem in defining money is that economists tend to think of 'money' in different ways depending on the general view they hold of how the economy works. An economist who essentially thinks of the economy as an equilibrium system is likely to stress the importance of the aggregate supply of money and to define it narrowly, concentrating on the medium of exchange role of money. On the other hand, an economist who emphasizes disequilibrium and uncertainty is likely to regard credit as a more important concept than the money supply.

In seeking to produce a precise definition of 'money' amongst all these difficulties, economists have attempted to do so both descriptively, usually starting from the medium of exchange role, and prescriptively, being willing to adjust the definition of money to produce the desired stability in the demand for money function. There have been many official definitions of money and these have changed frequently over the years.

Key concepts used in this chapter

Quantity Theory of Money	narrow money
store of value	broad money
medium of exchange	divisia indexes
means of payment	benchmark asset
inside money	benchmark rate
outside money	

Questions and exercises

1. What is meant by a 'stable equilibrium'? Draw simple diagrams showing (a) a stable equilibrium; (b) an unstable equilibrium. Is the length of time a system takes to return to an equilibrium position important? If so, why?

2. Would it be sensible always to act as if the weather forecast for the following day were always correct if, on average, weather forecasts were correct:

10 per cent of the time?
50 per cent of the time?
90 per cent of the time?

Does this question provide a reasonable analogy with the notion of analysing an economy as if it were always in equilibrium or as if there were perfect competition? If not, why not?

3. List the advantages and disadvantages of holding savings in the form of money.

4. What do you think is meant in the text by a 'purely financial transaction'? Can you provide some examples? Are purely financial transactions necessarily speculative?

5. There is a distinction made in the economics literature between 'consumption' and 'consumption expenditure'. This distinction implies differ-

ent definitions of 'saving'. What are these different definitions and how do they relate to the discussion in the text about information and uncertainty?

6. Distinguish between:
     (a) means of payment and medium of exchange;
     (b) inside money and outside money;
     (c) broad money and narrow money.

7. What is the distinction being made in the text between 'descriptive' and 'prescriptive' definitions of money?

8. Distinguish between 'monitoring' and 'targeting' in the context of money supply measures.

9. List the problems faced by the monetary authorities in preparing money supply statistics.

Further reading

Monetary economics books generally do not discuss money in the way that we have done here in Section 2.2. Many older monetary economics books spent time on definitions of money but these are not now likely to be available in many libraries. Examples included J Struthers and H Speight (1986) and D Fisher (1989).

Equally, official measures of money are less dealt with now than during the brief period in which the money supply was set as an intermediate target. However, Handa (2000) provides a brief discussion of the history of definitions of money as well as the definitions of the principal official measures of money in use at the time the book was written.

3 The Money Supply Process

'Central banks almost everywhere usually implement their policies through tight control of money market interest rates. Academic monetary economists almost everywhere discuss monetary policy in terms of the monetary stock. These facts say something about either central bankers or academic monetary economists, or both.'
W Poole (1991).

What you will learn in this chapter:

- How changes in the quantity of money involve changes in banks' balance sheets
- How the quantity of broad money can be expressed as a multiple of the monetary base
- How the size of this multiple depends upon underlying portfolio preferences
- How the flow of new money can be analysed as the outcome of bank lending
- How these two approaches can be formally reconciled
- But why each is more appropriate to the analysis of a particular type of monetary regime.

3.1   Introduction

In the last chapter we saw that we encounter many problems when trying to define money, especially if we are looking for a definition which actually specifies the assets that should be included rather than simply specifying money's functions. However, we also saw that if the authorities wish to conduct any sort of monetary policy they have to decide which assets they are going to monitor, even if this involves a degree of arbitrariness and requires the frequent redrawing of boundaries.

In practice, most monetary authorities work with three measures of money. These are the *monetary base*, and some measure of *narrow* and *broad* money. For convenience, these are usually identified by numbers. Starting from the narrowest measure, M0 is used to denote the monetary base and consists only of notes and coin outside the central bank plus banks' deposits held with the central bank. Narrow money, M1, consists of notes and coin in circulation outside the banking system together with the non-bank public's holdings of bank sight deposits. M0 and M1 have pretty much the same meaning in all monetary systems. The same cannot be said of the measure of broad money. In the majority of countries this is denoted M3, while in the UK it is denoted M4 and, while we can say that the difference between broad and narrow money is that the former includes time

Box 3.1: Official measures of money - end 2001

Name	Components USA	Size $bn	Components UK	Size £bn	Components Eurozone	Size €bn
M0	Currency outside Federal Reserve banks + bank deposits at FR banks	634.5	Currency outside the Bank of England + banks' operational deposits with the Bank of England	37.3	Currency outside national central banks + banks' deposits with NCBs	426.2
M1	Currency in circulation + sight deposits + travellers cheques + NOW deposits	1178.8	N/A		Currency in circulation + sight deposits	2138.9
M3	M1 + time deposits + money market funds + bank repo liabilities + eurodollar deposits with o/seas US banks	8036.8	N/A		M1 + time deposits + money market funds + bills and bonds with less than 2 years residual maturity	5383.8
M4	N/A		Currency in circulation + sterling sight and time deposits of the non-bank private sector at banks and building societies	942.6	N/A	

Sources: www.Bankofengland.co.uk/mfsd; www.federalreserve.gov/releases; ECB, *Monthly Bulletin*, Feb. 2002 deposits and maybe other assets, exactly which assets are included will vary from one system to another. This merely reflects what we said in Chapter 1, namely that different monetary systems have different institutional structures and these structures change over time. What is accepted as money in one system is not necessarily treated in the same way in another. To illustrate the point, we show the components of broad and narrow monies in the UK, the eurozone and the USA in Box 3.1. The box also gives an indication of the relative magnitudes of the three measures.

In this chapter, we are going to explore how changes in the quantity of money occur. For this purpose, 'money' consists of notes and coin in circulation outside the banking system plus a comprehensive range of bank deposits. It corresponds roughly, therefore, to the national measures of broad money in Box 3.1 and is dominated by bank deposits. The magnitude of bank deposits is important for two reasons. Firstly, it should alert us to the fact that changes in the quantity of money are the outcomes of an interaction between the preferences of banks, their customers and the monetary authorities: the quantity of deposits will not expand (for example) unless banks can find a profitable return from marginal additions to loans and deposits and clients wish to add to loan and deposit portfolios on current terms. Secondly, it should alert us to the likely difficulties that monetary authorities will face when they try to constrain the growth of money and credit. It is not a simple question of modifying their own actions but of modifying the actions of other agents who have no particular interest in co-operating to further the authorities' objectives: indeed, these agents may well feel that the authorities' actions are designed to frustrate their own self-interest.

Before we begin, it is worth noting that what we are describing here is a particular set of institutional arrangements which, while their familiarity may give them a sense of permanence, have not always prevailed. Money has not always consisted of bank deposits and its quantity has not always involved the interaction between the income-expenditure decisions and portfolio preferences of non-bank agents, and the profit-seeking behaviour of banks. Over the years, the importance of a correct understanding of monetary institutions as an essential prerequisite for the understanding of how money 'works' has been stressed by a number of writers (Hicks 1967, Dow 1988, 1996, Niggle 1990, 1991, Goodhart, 2002). The best results from consistently applying this principle are revealed in the work of Victoria Chick (for example, Chick 1986, 1993, 1996).

There are broadly speaking two approaches to the analysis of money supply changes and both involve the manipulation of a series of (related) identities. The reason for manipulating these identities is that they can provide insights, or useful ways of looking at things, which may not be apparent at the outset. The fact that two parallel approaches exist, therefore, suggests that there are rival insights: there are differences of opinion about which insights are worth having. And this brings us to another important issue which is that is that there are different views about how the quantity of money changes, different views, we might say, about the underlying reality. The insights generated by one approach are useful if one thinks the underlying system has one set of characteristics, while the insights of the other are useful if the system behaves in a different way. This will become clearer as we proceed, but it should be stressed at the outset that either approach could be used to analyse changes in the quantity of money in any regime. The fact that each is identified with a particular state of affairs is simply that the insights it gives are more appropriate to those circumstances.

Since 'money' consists overwhelmingly of bank deposits, in order to make any progress at all, we need to be familiar with the balance sheet of commercial banks and of the central bank and we also need to understand how flows of funds between commercial banks themselves, and between commercial banks and the central bank, cause changes in the quantity of deposits and in the liquidity of the banking system. Thus, in section 3.2 we shall look at stylised versions of commercial banks' and a central bank's balance sheets, look at the effect of flows of funds and introduce some notation which will be used throughout the remainder of this book. In section 3.3 we shall analyse money supply changes through the 'base-multiplier approach', giving a simple summary first and then looking at it more formally. In section 3.4 we shall do the same using the 'flow of funds' identity. In section 3.5 we shall show how the two can be formally reconciled and try to explain why the latter approach has generally been favoured in the UK. Section 3.6 summarises. Throughout the discussion we shall point out the nature of the underlying monetary regime which the insights seem to suggest.

3.2 Bank balance sheets

Box 3.2 shows the stylised balance sheets of commercial banks and a central bank. Notice that the assets of commercial banks are arranged in descending order of liquidity. Cb and Db, which we shall later call 'reserves' (R), are generally non-interest bearing but are essential nonetheless because confidence in the banking system depends upon the instant convertibility of deposits into notes and coin, and because payments between clients of different banking companies will require corresponding transfers between commercial banks' deposits at the central bank. The immediate determinant of the size of these reserves will be the volume and composition of customer deposits, time deposits requiring a smaller reserve ratio than sight deposits. Since these reserves are non-interest bearing we can be reasonably sure that banks will hold minimum quantities, either as specified by the monetary authorities (a 'mandatory' reserve ratio) or as dictated by their own experience of what provides a safe level of liquidity (a 'prudential' reserve ratio). This reserve ratio we can denote as R/Dp. These reserves will be supplemented by 'money market loans', that is to say lending in the interbank market and holdings of money market instruments, much of which can be liquidated on demand or at very short notice. There is also a ready market for securities (mainly short-dated government bonds). The most illiquid assets are of course loans and advances (to the public and private sectors). These are generally non-marketable and, in the latter case, can only be called for repayment at the risk of bankrupting the borrowers.

Box 3.2: Commercial and central bank balance sheets

Commercial bank

Assets		Liabilities	
Cb	banks' holdings of notes and coin	Fs	capital and shareholders' funds
Db	banks' deposits with the central bank	Dp	customer deposits
MLb	banks' holdings of loans to the money market		
Gb	banks' holdings of securities		
Lp	loans (advances) to the general public		
Lg	loans to the government or public sector		

Central bank

Assets		Liabilities	
BLcb	central bank loans to the banking system	Db	commercial banks' deposits with central bank
GLcb	central bank loans to government	Cb	notes and coin with commercial banks
Fx	central bank holdings of foreign exchange		
Gcb	central bank holdings of government debt	Cp	notes and coin with the non-bank public
		Dg	government deposits

Notice that the 'reserve' component of bank *assets* appear as *liabilities* of the central bank. This has the effect of interlocking the two sets of balance sheets. Using the symbols introduced in Box 3.2, Tables 3.1 and 3.2 show how two different disturbances in commercial bank balance sheets (i) communicate themselves to the central bank and (ii) affect the money supply and (iii) the liquidity of the banking system.

In the first case, we assume a sale of government bonds to the non-bank public (an example of what is often called 'open-market operations').

Table 3.1: An open market sale of government bonds

Commercial bank				Central bank			
Assets		Liabilities		Assets		Liabilities	
Cb		Fs		BLcb		Cb	
Db	(–)	Dp	(–)	GLcb		Cp	
MLb				Fx		Db	(–)
Gb				Gcb		Dg	(+)
Lp							
Lg							

The non-bank public pays for the sale of government bonds by drawing on its deposits at commercial banks (shown by (–)). At the central bank, commercial bank deposits are transferred (shown (–)) to the government's account (shown (+)). Notice that balance sheets must always balance. For commercial banks there is a matching change (–) on opposite sides of the balance sheet; for the central bank there are compensating changes (–,+) on the *same* side.

What of the money supply and bank liquidity? Since we define the money stock to include bank deposits of the non-bank private sector, the money stock is reduced (by Db (–)). The effect on liquidity is not perhaps so obvious until we remember that 'reserves' ($Cb + Db$) are a small fraction of assets while deposits dominate liabilities. (The reserve ratio, R/Dp, is very small in other words). Since the reduction on both sides of the balance sheet is equal in absolute size, the effect on R is much more pronounced than the effect upon Dp and the reserve ratio falls. The reverse can be easily demonstrated for the case of an open market purchase of government bonds.

For the second example, it helps if we remember that a monetary system is usually a multi-bank system and that what is commercially attractive to one bank is likely to be attractive to many. In this case we shall assume that banks wish to increase their lending and to make the illustration more realistic we must introduce a second commercial bank in order to simulate a multi-bank system.

We begin with commercial bank A which decides that it will increase its lending to its clients. This is shown as Lp (+). Strictly speaking, the addi-

Table 3.2: Commercial banks increase their lending

Commercial bank A		Central bank		Commercial bank B	
Assets	Liabilities	Assets	Liabilities	Assets	Liabilities
Cb	Fs	BLcb	Cb	Cb	Fs
Db (−) [+]	Dp [+]	GLcb	Cp	Db (+) [−]	Dp (+)
MLb		Fx	Db	MLb	
Gb		Gcb	Dg	Gb	
Lp (+)				Lp [+]	
Lg				Lg	

tional loans come into existence only when the clients of *A* make payments. Let us suppose that they make payments exclusively to clients of bank *B*. Customer deposits in bank *B* increase by the same amount (shown as *Dp* (+))as the increase in lending in bank *A*. These payments are matched by a transfer between the accounts of banks *A* and *B* at the central bank. Thus in *A* we have *Db* (−) and in *B* we have *Db* (+). What is attractive to bank *A*, however, is also attractive to other banks in the system, including bank *B*. Thus, bank *B* makes additional loans to its customers who (we assume) make payments exclusively to bank *A*. The process repeats itself, in reverse. We show the changes this time in square brackets. Loans to customers in bank *B* increase, *Lp* [+]. Customers in bank *A* receive the payments as additional deposits, *Dp* [+]. At the central bank, deposits are transferred from bank *B*, *Db* [−] to bank *A*, *Dp* [+]. Notice that at the end of the sequence changes in the two banks' deposits at the central bank cancel (i.e. they remain unchanged) while in each bank loans have increased matched by a corresponding increase in deposits.

What can we say about the money supply and bank liquidity in this second case? Remember that we define money as notes and coin (*Cp*) plus bank deposits (*Dp*). In both banks, *A* and *B*, *Dp* have increased and there is thus a corresponding increase in the money stock. As for bank liquidity, measured by the reserve ratio R/Dp, it is clear that with *Dp* increased and *R* (= *Cb* + *Db*) unchanged, liquidity is *reduced*.

Equipped with this basic knowledge of bank balance sheets and how flows of loans and deposits affect the money supply, we can now turn to the two main approaches to aggregate money supply determination.

3.3 The base-multilier approach to money supply determination

The first characteristic of the base-multiplier (B-M) approach is that it focuses upon stocks. The stocks in question are the stock of monetary base (M0) and the stock of money (e.g. M4). It points out that the latter is a multiple of the former and that this multiple is likely to be stable because of two underlying behavioural relationships. Since the components of the monetary base are liabilities of the central bank, the quantity can be varied at the bank's discretion and, given the stable relationship between M0 and M4, central bank action on M0 will produce a corresponding (multiple) reaction in M4.

Exercise 3.1: Bank loans, deposits and money

Imagine a monetary system with just two commercial banks. Their simplified balance sheets are shown below.

Bank A		Bank B	
Assets	Liabilities	Assets	Liabilities
Cb = 50	Dp = 2000	Cb = 150	Dp = 5000
Db = 30		Db = 50	
Lp = 1920		Lp = 4800	

In addition, the non-bank public holds notes and coin (Cp) of 400.

1. What is the current stock of broad money?
2. What is the reserve ratio for each individual bank and for the system as a whole?

Suppose now that bank A makes additional loans of 50 to a subset of its customers and that some of these customers use 20 to make payments to other depositors of the same bank and 30 to make payments to clients of bank B.

3. Draw up new balance sheets for each bank.
4. What is the total money stock now?
5. What is the reserve ratio for each individual bank and for the system as a whole?

Suppose now that bank B makes additional loans of 100 to a subset of its customers and that some of these customers use 50 to make payments to other depositors of the same bank and 50 to make payments to clients of bank A.

6. Draw up new balance sheets for each bank.
7. What is the total money stock now?
8. What is the reserve ratio for each individual bank and for the system as a whole?

Suppose that the non-bank public now decides to hold 50 of additional notes and coin.

9. What effect does this have upon the total money stock?
10. What effect has it had upon the aggregate reserve ratio?

The latter is certainly a powerful insight. After all it says that the stock of money is given by the size of the base and *in the absence of any deliberate decision on the part of the central bank, the money stock remains constant.* It encourages the impression that the monetary authorities are central and all-powerful in the determination of the money stock because *banks' ability to acquire non-reserve assets (e.g. loans and advances) are reserve constrained.*

But we can also see from this simple summary that this insight depends upon some crucial assumptions about the underlying system. Firstly it assumes the stability of two behavioural relationships: indeed, in its simplest version the B-M approach is sometimes presented as though these relationships are fixed. But this is an empirical question which needs to be examined. (Remember what we said in 3.2 about agents' having *preferences*). Secondly, while it is true that the monetary base consists of central bank liabilities, it does not automatically follow that the central bank either can or even desires to control these liabilities. Finally, there is a question about whether concentrating on stock equilibrium is very useful when the underlying variables are subject to continuous change. Put briefly, a monetary system in which the money supply changes only as the result of the central bank's deliberate adjustment of the monetary base, is a system in which the money supply is *exogenous* — exogenous at least with respect to the preferences of other agents in the economic system. We turn now to a more formal examination of the base multiplier approach.

We begin by defining the two stocks:

$$M \equiv Cp + Dp \qquad \qquad ...3.1$$

and

$$B \equiv Cp + Cb + Db \qquad \qquad ...3.2$$

M is (broad) money and consists of notes and coin in circulation with the non-bank public (Cp) plus their holdings of bank deposits (Dp). In practice, M corresponds to one of the broad money measures in Box 3.1. B, the monetary base, consists of those same notes and coin plus also now notes and coin held by banks (Cb) and banks' own deposits at the central bank (Db). In practice, B corresponds to M0 in Box 3.1. If we now refer to $Cb + Db$ as bank reserves and denote them R, then 3.2 can be rewritten as:

$$B \equiv Cp + R \qquad \qquad ...3.3$$

At any particular time, there will be a monetary base of given value and similarly a given quantity of broad money and it is a simple task to create a ratio of money to base:

$$\frac{M}{B} \equiv \frac{Cp + Dp}{Cp + R} \qquad \text{...3.4}$$

The first insight comes when we divide through by the non-bank public's holdings of deposits.

$$\frac{M}{B} \equiv \frac{\dfrac{C_p}{D_p} + \dfrac{D_p}{D_p}}{\dfrac{C_p}{D_p} + \dfrac{R}{D_p}} \qquad \text{...3.5}$$

For convenience, let $Cp/Dp = \alpha$, and let $R/Dp = \beta$, then we can rewrite 3.5 as:

$$\frac{M}{B} \equiv \frac{\alpha + 1}{\alpha + \beta} \qquad \text{...3.6}$$

The insight is that the volume of broad money, in relation to the base, depends upon the two ratios α, which is the public's cash ratio, and β which is the banks' reserve ratio. Let us suppose for a moment that these ratios are stable (not necessarily fixed) then we can *predict* that:

$$M = B.\frac{\alpha + 1}{\alpha + \beta} \qquad \text{...3.7}$$

and

$$\Delta M = \Delta B.\frac{\alpha + 1}{\alpha + \beta} \qquad \text{...3.8}$$

Notice that in a fractional reserve system, β will have a value less than one and the term $(\alpha + 1)/(\alpha + \beta)$, let us call it m, will be a multiplier. Recall that the base consists of liabilities of the central bank then, if we assume that the central bank is both willing and able to manipulate these liabilities at its discretion, then we get a second, more dramatic, insight, namely that the size of the money stock is determined by the central bank's willingness to supply assets comprising the monetary base. These assumptions amount to a description of a monetary system where the money supply is exogenously determined and we can immediately see why the B-M model tends to be favoured as a way of describing and analysing changes in the money stock in an exogenous regime: by rearranging two simple definitions we are quickly led to this conclusion.

In an unrealistically simple world, α and β might be treated as fixed. But they are both portfolio decisions about which the public and banks respectively are likely to have preferences depending upon relative prices and other constraints. We cannot throw away the standard economic axioms of maximising behaviour just because we are dealing with money. That said, we do not promise an exhaustive account of how maximisation might be achieved, but we can offer some illustration of relevant factors which will bear upon preferences. If we take α, the public's cash ratio, we can say firstly that the decision to divide money holdings between notes and coin ('cash') and bank deposits must surely depend upon any rate of interest paid on deposits, money's 'own rate', which we might denote i_m. The higher the rate paid on deposits (and the wider the range of deposits on which it is paid), the less willing, *ceteris paribus*, people will be to hold cash.

Furthermore, one of the reasons for holding deposits is to have access to the payments mechanism. Just how attractive deposits are as a means of payment depends upon current usage — many fewer transactions involved bank deposits a hundred years ago than they do now — and this depends to some extent upon technological considerations. The widespread use of deposits as means of payment requires the development of an efficient cheque clearing system. Since the mid-1960s the big developments in the payments system have involved electronic payments — automating them first of all so that customers could set up standing order or direct debit instructions and then making electronic transfers possible, most recently in the form of debit cards. As the services offered by deposits increase and improve, so they become more attractive relative to cash.

Technology has almost certainly affected the cash/deposit split through other routes. For a given level of money's own rate and a given level of 'services' from deposits, the decision about how much cash to hold must depend to some extent upon the difficulties of switching between cash and deposits, the so-called 'shoe leather costs' based on the idea that replenishing cash balances involved walking to the bank and standing in a queue. But one of the many achievements of banking technology has been the development of the cash machine or automated teller machine ('ATM') to give it its proper name. These machines now allow a wide range of routine banking transactions to be carried out at remote sites like supermarkets, filling stations, shopping malls and even educational institutions. Given that these facilities make cash replenishment easier, they encourage people to hold smaller cash balances. The effect is likely to be more marked in periods of rapid inflation and high nominal interest rates when the protection of purchasing power offered by interest-bearing deposits will be greatest.

The two examples of technological change we have given, both tend to reduce the public's cash ratio: α gets smaller. This need not be the case *a priori*. It is conceivable that future technological changes will push in the opposite direction. This means that we cannot give a definite sign to the partial derivative of technology (as we could with money's own rate, for example). In practice, however, it is very likely that technological changes have acted over the years towards a reduction in the public's need to hold cash.

Table 3.3: Total transaction volumes in the UK by medium

Millions	1992	1994	1996	1998	1999	Annual rate of change 1992-99
Paper payments	4,190	3,844	3,621	3,394	3,262	-4%
Automated payments	1,962	2,196	2,613	3,056	3,255	+7%
Plastic cards	2,515	3,095	4,069	5,011	5,562	+12%
Cash (>£1)	15,100	14,200	14,200	14,000	14,000	-1%
Other	1,128	1,117	1,114	1,017	962	-2%
Total	24,900	24,500	25,600	26,500	27,000	+1%

Source: *Yearbook of Payment Statistics, 2000* (London: APACS)

Recent changes in payment preferences are shown in Table 3.3. The figures are consistent with our remarks about technology in so far as they show a dramatic increase in automated payments (66 per cent in seven years) and an even more rapid growth in the use of plastic cards (roughly doubled in the same period). On the other side of the picture, the clearing of paper-based payments has declined by 22 per cent and the use of cash by about 8 per cent.

As regards influences upon the public's cash ratio, therefore, we can surmise that α will depend to some extent upon at least two factors, money's own rate and technological conditions.

$$\alpha \equiv \frac{Cp}{Dp} = f(\underset{-}{i_m}, \underset{?}{T}) \qquad \qquad ...3.9$$

Pause for thought 3.1:

In 1999 UK banks caused a stir by suggesting that they would introduce charges for the use of their cash machines which would increase the cost for many customers. In the light of our discussion above, what would have been the likely effect upon the public's cash ratio?

When it comes to banks' decisions about their reserve ratios, therefore, there are numerous influences at work. Remember that banks are profit-seeking firms, that the cash element of reserves yields no interest and that, in most systems deposits at the central bank are also non-interest bearing. This means that holding reserves acts like a tax on banking, an issue we return to in the next chapter.

Banks' decisions to hold reserves will depend firstly upon their cost. Where reserves pay no interest then the cost can be proxied by the return on alternative liquid assets, which might be proxied by the bond rate, i_b. Where reserves do pay interest, then the cost will be the return on reserves, i_r *relative to* the bond rate. The quantity of reserves held will depend also on the cost of being short, that is upon the rediscount rate charged for lender of last resort facilities, i_d. This is the rate of interest announced periodically, usually monthly, by the central bank. In the UK and the eurozone it is a rate of interest charged by the central bank on short-dated repurchase deals with banks, using government bonds as the underlying security. Reserve holdings will also depend upon any mandatory reserve requirement, RR, and, lastly, upon the variability of inward and outward flows to which banks are subject, σ. This last factor is relevant because the primary purpose of reserves is to enable individual banks to meet demands for cash or, more importantly, for transfers of deposits as customers make payments to customers of other banks or to the government. The majority of payments are offsetting (payments from bank A to bank B will roughly cancel); reserves are necessary to meet the balance. Provided this balance is predictable, the need for reserves will be limited to the predicted net flow. If it is unpredictable, then additional funds have to be held. The greater the variance (or standard deviation) of the flows, the greater the margin that will be necessary.

In summary, then:

$$\beta \equiv \frac{R}{Dp} = f(\underset{+}{i_r}, \underset{-}{i_b}, \underset{+}{i_d}, \underset{+}{RR}, \underset{+}{\sigma}) \qquad \qquad ...3.10$$

Given that we now have some idea of the sorts of influences, and the direction of their effect, upon the ratios α and β, the next obvious question is what effect will changes in α and β have upon the size of the multiplier expression in 3.7 and 3.8. From there, we can see their effect on the money supply.

The answer to the first question lies in the value '1'. Because the values of α and β are fractions (in practice, very small fractions) it is the '1' which gives the expression a multiplier value: the numerator is bound to be larger than the denominator. Consider now what happens if we change α and β.

If we increase (for example) α, we increase the numerator and denominator simultaneously and the outcome may therefore appear indeterminate at first glance. But with the numerator already larger than the denominator by virtue of the '1', any change in a must have a bigger effect proportionate effect upon the denominator. If we are looking at an increase, therefore, a given change in α must have a bigger effect upon the denominator than the numerator and the value of the multiplier will fall.

With β, the effect is obvious since it appears only in the denominator. Any change in β must lead to an inverse change in the value of the multiplier.

Exercise 3.2:

1. Suppose that α = 0.05 while β = 0.01, calculate a value for the multiplier.

2. Suppose that the public's cash preferences change such that α falls to 0.04. Recalculate the multiplier value.

3. Calculate a new value for the multiplier if banks increase their reserve ratio to 0.012 (α remaining at 0.04).

Since the money supply depends upon both the base and the multiplier we can write:

$$M = f(B, \alpha, \beta) \qquad \qquad ...3.11$$

and since we know (from 3.9 and 3.10) how α and β are likely to respond to a number of influences, we can substitute into (3.11), to yield a money supply determined as follows:

$$M = f(B, i_m, T, i_r, i_b, i_d, RR, \sigma) \qquad \qquad ...3.12$$

A change in B is a change in the multiplicand; changes in all other variables cause a change in the size of the multiplier itself.

Pause for thought 3.2:

Making explicit use of the B-M analysis, explain how you would expect the money supply to be affected by a rise in interest rates announced by the central bank.

We turn now to how this account of money supply determination can be presented diagrammatically. The account of money supply determination which we have just given is more familiar than it may seem since it is what is assumed, but rarely spelt out, in money market diagrams where a vertical money supply curve intersects a downward sloping money demand curve.

This is what we have drawn in Figure 3.1, though we have given the money supply curve a positive slope for reasons we return to at the end of this section. Before we do that, let us be clear how changes in the variables listed in 3.12 will be reflected in the diagram.

The horizontal axis depicts the quantity of money as a stock. In this space, a money supply curve intersects the horizontal (money) axis at a point where $M = m.B$ (where m is the multiplier). A change in B changes the point of intersection (the supply curve shifts). The same results from a change in any of RR, i_d, i_r, i_m, σ, T since these cause a change in the value of the multiplier.

Notice that we have omitted the bond rate, i_b, from this list. This is because the bond rate must appear on the vertical axis. This is because the purpose of drawing the money supply curve in interest-money space at all is ultimately to discuss money market equilibria, the interaction of supply and demand. With a downward sloping demand curve in the diagram, the rate on the vertical axis must be the opportunity cost of holding money. Strictly, in a modern monetary system, one might argue that this rate ought to be a spread term, representing the difference between the bond rate (appearing as a proxy for the return on 'non-money financial assets' which agents could hold as an alternative) and money's own rate (effectively the weighted average rate on cash and deposits). This is true but does not change the point we are about to make. If we put a spread term on the vertical axis it remains the case that a rise in bond rate increases the opportunity cost of holding money. As the size of the spread increases the quantity of money demanded declines. The crucial point is that it is the bond rate which *must* appear on the vertical axis, either on its own (if money is non-interest bearing) or as part of a spread term.

Now we can see why the money supply curve is drawn with a positive slope. In our discussion of β, we saw that banks would economise on reserves if returns on other assets increased; this would reduce the value of their reserve ratio (3.10) and this in turn (3.12) increases the money supply. In short, the money supply shows some degree of elasticity with regard to the bond rate and *since the bond rate appears in the diagram* on the vertical axis, the effect of changes in the bond rate must be captured by giving a positive slope to the money supply curve.

If as seems reasonable, banks' behaviour towards reserves is dependent upon non-reserve interest rates, the 'vertical' money supply curve must have some positive slope and one might argue that the money supply has acquired some degree of endogeneity, contrary to what we said at the beginning of this section about the B-M approach being associated with exogenous money regimes. Davidson (1988 p.156) does indeed refer to this aspect of the money supply as 'interest-endogeneity'. This form of endogeneity is, however, extremely limited. In a fully-endogenous monetary

Figure 3.1: The money supply curve

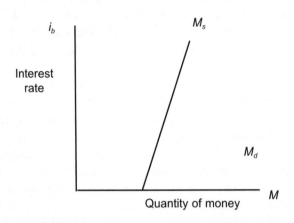

regime, it is generally accepted that continuous expansion of the money stock, with little, if any, effect upon interest rates is the norm. Clearly that is not compatible with what we see in Figure 3.1 where a continuous expansion of the money supply is possible, *ceteris paribus* only if the level of interest rates i_b rises without limit. But the more normal case of course is that the authorities have some range within which they wish to see i_b remain. In circumstances of full-endogeneity continuous expansion requires the authorities to change one of the other variables in 3.12 and we shall see in the next chapter that this is the monetary base, B.

Pause for thought 3.3:

How would you expect the money supply curve in Figure 3.1 to be affected by an increase in the coefficient on the bond rate?

3.4 The Flow of Funds approach

Where the base-multiplier approach focused upon stocks, the flow of funds (FoF) approach concentrates upon changes in stocks, i.e. on *flows*. There is a connection with the B-M approach in that one of the flows is the change in money stock; but the other flow which dominates the FoF approach is the flow of bank *lending* to the non-bank public. This is strictly speaking the net change in the stock of bank loans — the difference over time in the stock of loans taking account of both new loans made and loans repaid. The flow of money is shown as ΔM, the flow of new loans is shown as ΔLp (for new lending to the *non-bank private sector*) and ΔLg (for new lending to the *public sector*).[1] Because it focuses upon flows of new lending and their ability to create deposits, the FoF approach is sometimes known as the 'credit-counterparts' approach.

As with the B-M approach, we begin with the money supply identity:

$$M \equiv Cp + Dp \qquad \qquad ...3.13/3.1$$

and then rewrite it in flows:

$$\Delta M \equiv \Delta Cp + \Delta Dp \qquad \qquad ...3.14$$

We next concentrate on the deposit element and use the bank balance sheet identity to remind ourselves that since deposits (liabilities) must be matched by loans (assets) then the same must be true about changes.[2] On the asset side, loans can be decomposed into loans to the private and to the public sector.

$$\Delta Dp \equiv \Delta Lp + \Delta Lg \qquad \qquad ...3.15$$

Concentrate now on bank loans to the public sector. These are just one way of financing the public sector and, because of its monetary implications and short-term nature, it tends to be a residual source of financing — something to be resorted to after all other forms of finance. So it follows that we can locate the *flow* of new bank lending to the public sector (PSBR) within the public sector's total borrowing requirement:

$$\Delta Lg \equiv PSBR - \Delta Gp - \Delta Cp \pm \Delta ext \qquad \qquad ...3.16$$

where ΔGp represents net sales of government bonds to the general public. Notice that Δext can take a positive or negative value. Δext refers to the monetary implications of external flows. For example, if the public sector buys foreign currency assets with sterling (as it might if it were trying to hold a fixed exchange rate) this adds to the public sector's borrowing requirement. Selling foreign currency assets for sterling reduces the need for sterling borrowing.

We can then substitute 3.16 into 3.15 to show all the sources of change in deposits:

$$\Delta Dp \equiv \Delta Lp + PSBR - \Delta Gp - \Delta Cp \pm \Delta ext \qquad \qquad ...3.17$$

and then substitute 3.17 into 3.14 to show all sources of monetary change. In making the substitution we have tidied up (notice that ΔCp cancels because it enters twice, with opposite signs) and reordered the terms to give 3.18, which is often referred to as the 'flow of funds identity'.

$$\Delta M \equiv PSBR - \Delta Gp \pm \Delta ext + \Delta Lp \qquad \ldots 3.18$$

What insights do we gain from the FoF approach? The explicit message is that changes in the money stock are inextricably linked to lending/borrowing behaviour. But behind this are three implications. The first of these is that changes themselves are what matters — one would not use the FoF approach to analyse a system where stocks dominate everyone's interest. It is an implication of the FoF approach that our interest in money supply is an interest in monetary growth. The second implication is that the monetary base is of little interest. We shall see in the next section that we can rewrite the flow of funds identity so as to include changes in the monetary base, but the fact that the FoF identity is not normally written in that way is significant. One does not adopt a method of analysis which deliberately omits variables which one thinks are important. It points to flows as the important variables and by omitting references to the monetary base it hints that the authorities might need to find some non-base-orientated way of influencing these flows. Equally, one does not normally adopt a mode of analysis which gives a key position to variables of little interest. The third implication of the FoF analysis, therefore, is that if/when the authorities become interested in the magnitude of flows, they should pay attention to lending/borrowing. While the B-M approach creates the impression that bank lending is reserve (*supply*) constrained, the FoF creates the impression that it is (*demand*) constrained by the non-bank private sector's desire for additional credit.

Pause for thought 3.4:

According to the FoF approach, what is the relevance to monetary growth of government debt sales to the non-bank private sector?

3.5 The two approaches compared

While the B-M and FoF approaches are different ways of analysing the quantity of monetary assets, both consist of rearranging identities at least one of which — the money stock and its components — is common to both.

In fact, even though each approach offers a different range of insights and highlights different features of the monetary system as being significant, it is possible to reconcile the two approaches. Indeed it is perfectly possible to analyse money supply changes or flows by using an identity which features the monetary base while one could, if one were so inclined, analyse the existing stock of money in terms of the amount of lending. Each approach is, strictly speaking, agnostic as regards the underlying behavioural characteristics of the monetary system, but each furnishes insights which are more relevant to a certain type of regime and has thus become associated with it. We shall see more of this in a moment, but let us firstly see that the two approaches are formally equivalent.

Pause for thought 3.5:

Using the FoF approach, explain the likely effect on the rate of monetary expansion of a central bank's decision to raise interest rates. (Compare your answer with your reaction to PfT 3.2).

The B-M approach consists of a statement about the monetary base and two behavioural relations (see 3.6). We can write the FoF approach in exactly the same terms if we remember that the monetary base consists of cash held by the non-bank public (Cp) together with bank lending to the public sector in the form of reserve assets ($Db + Cb$). (See endnote 2 for this treatment of bank reserves). Bank lending to the public sector in the form of reserve assets must be equal to total bank lending to the public sector *minus* bank holdings of non-reserve assets (e.g. bank holdings of government bonds, Gb). So (in changes):

$$\Delta B \equiv \Delta Cp + (\Delta Lg - \Delta Gb) \qquad \qquad ...3.19$$

and, substituting 3.16 and rearranging:

$$\Delta B \equiv \Delta Cp - \Delta Gb + (PSBR - \Delta Gp \pm \Delta ext - \Delta Cp\,) \qquad ...3.20$$

From 3.18 and 3.20 we can obtain:

$$\Delta M \equiv \Delta B + \Delta Gb + \Delta BLp \qquad \qquad ...3.21$$

What 3.21 shows is that we can make control of changes in the money stock appear to depend upon control of the base together with two behavioural relationships, in this case the banks' demand for government debt (ΔGb) and lending to the non-bank private sector (ΔLp), almost as easily as making it depend upon flows of new lending.

In the UK, monetary analysis has tended to follow the FoF rather than the B-M approach. Some of the reasons for this are historic. These encouraged the FoF approach years ago and thus ensured a lasting role if only through inertia. But the FoF also has one overwhelming contemporary advantage that we come to in a moment, but which really forms the theme of the next chapter. We look at four older reasons first.

In the UK, analysis for policy purposes has often focused on the broad money aggregates — M3 until 1989 and M4 thereafter. This does not require but it does permit the FoF approach which puts the whole of bank lending on the right hand side. Such an approach cannot be applied to a monetary aggregate containing only a subset of deposits (e.g. M1) since the balance sheet identity requires only that *total* lending is matched by *total* deposits, and there is no way in which a subset of loans can be linked to any subset of deposits. In other policy regimes, in the US for example, the policy emphasis has often been upon these narrower aggregates and the FoF approach does not work.

We noted earlier that the B-M approach emphasises the availability of reserves as a constraint on bank lending while the FoF approach focuses upon the general public's desire for bank credit. The tradition in the UK is for much short-term bank lending to be based upon the overdraft system whereby a maximum credit limit is agreed in advance and the borrower then uses (and is charged for) only that fraction of the loan that is required on a day-to-day basis. Clearly in these circumstances, a proportion of bank lending is done at the discretion of the borrower. Furthermore, it cannot be reserve-constrained. A bank that enters into overdraft contracts must guarantee to meet 100 per cent of the commitment if called upon.

Thirdly, the FoF approach allows all the credit counterparts to monetary growth to be identified separately. This was particularly important in the days when UK governments frequently ran large budget deficits some of which had to be financed by monetary means. With the independence of the Bank of England and the separation of monetary from fiscal policy (since 1997) and a policy of fully-funding budget deficits, this is a less compelling argument than it once was.

Another compelling reason for the popularity of the FoF in the UK involves 'credit rationing'. The literature began with Stiglitz and Weiss in 1981 who advanced a number of reasons why it might be rational for banks to ration the volume of their lending in order to screen out some unsafe borrowers who would be willing and able to pay the going price. The rationality of apparently foregoing profitable opportunities derives from the presence of asymmetric information. It is argued that borrowers have a much better idea about the risks attached to the projects for which they take out loans than do the providers of the loans. It is very difficult for banks to assess the creditworthiness of borrowers and their projects, this gives rise to moral hazard and adverse selection problems. The borrower characteristics that banks might use in the screening are discussed in Leland and Pyle (1977) and Diamond (1984) but the important point from the FoF perspective is that variations in the flow of lending are partly the outcome of banks' lending decisions (Stiglitz and Weiss, 1981) and while this is the case there is little point in focusing upon changes in the availability of reserves.

The final and by far the most powerful reason for the widespread adoption of the FoF framework is that it is easier to apply to the way in which the UK authorities have, in practice, tried to influence monetary conditions. The FoF approach gives a central role to flows of new bank lending and it is the flow of bank credit that the UK authorities have focused on, albeit in differing ways, since 1945. Up until 1971, this control consisted of an evolving collection of direct interventions — 'moral suasion' imposed on banks to discriminate by type of borrower, then by specifying minimum deposits and maximum payback periods for consumer loans. The first of these was a supply-side constraint but the latter were intended to work on the demand for loans as potential borrowers ruled themselves in or out depending upon the severity of the conditions.

In 1971 the *Competition and Credit Control* arrangements swept away all direct controls and stated the intention of relying upon variations in the price of credit, the short term rate of interest, to regulate the demand for credit. In the inflationary years of the 1970s, the authorities had occasional failures of nerve when it was clear that interest rates needed to be held in double figures, and there were occasional outbursts of direct control in the form of supplementary special deposits (a reversion to supply-side control). But in 1981, market methods were restored and the last twenty years have seen a steady convergence in central bank operating procedures towards adjustment of short-term interest rates (Borio, 1997). The short-term rate over which central banks have direct control is the lender of last resort or rediscount rate which we have already met as i_d in 3.10. But in the B-M approach the purpose of raising (for example) i_d would be explained as an attempt to increase the reserve ratio and reduce the size of the multiplier. In practice, raising i_d is assumed to cause banks to raise their lending and borrowing rates and thus to reduce the *demand* for net new bank lending and thus to slow the creation of new deposits. The quantity of reserves and the resulting size of reserve ratios has nothing to do with it. In spite of the occasional appearance of 'ratios' in UK monetary regulations, none of them have been ratios of deposits to reserve assets under the control of the central bank. Monetary regulation has always targeted bank lending and never the quantity of reserves.

Furthermore, it is the *rate* of money (or credit) expansion that has exercised monetary authorities the world over. Nowhere is the stock of any particular interest. A rise in interest rates (today) or a tightening of credit terms (in the past) was never intended to produce an absolute reduction in the *stock* of monetary assets or their credit counterparts. This is quite difficult to deal with in a B-M framework. Recall that we began by saying that the major 'insight' of the approach was that if the authorities did nothing (by way of changing the quantity of reserve assets) then the money stock would be unchanged. But in practice, the money stock expands continuously at the going rate of interest. If the authorities do nothing (to change the level of interest rates), in the real world the money stock *expands* at its current rate. Thus, the real reason why the FoF approach to money supply determination has been so attractive in the UK over the years is that the Bank of England has targeted the flow of new lending and sought to control it through the demand side by changing interest rates. As we shall see in the next chapter, years of experience have proved that there is no realistic alternative and the Bank of England has readily acknowledged the fact.

3.6 Summary

In this chapter we have seen that there are two ways of analysing changes in the quantity of money. One focuses upon *stocks* and looks at the multiple relationship between the monetary base and broad measures of money; the other focuses on *flows* of new loans and new deposits. Although either can be used to analyse changes in money in any monetary system and under any policy regime, each approach carries with it unstated assumptions about the nature of the regime it is analysing and each is easier to use and provides more relevant insights when applied to the type of regime which it is assuming. Thus the B-M approach, through its emphasis upon the stock of monetary base is most helpful in analysing monetary change in a system where the central bank can and does control the quantity of base directly and where the cash/deposit preferences of banks and their clients are stable. The flow of funds or credit-counterparts approach is more helpful in looking at a system where the monetary authorities are more concerned with the rate of monetary expansion and try to influence it through the flow of new bank loans.

Key concepts used in this chapter

monetary base	prudential reserve ratio
narrow money	mandatory reserve ratio
broad money	open market sales and purchases
reserve ratio	credit counterparts
cash ratio	credit rationing

Questions and exercises

1. In the B-M approach, *explain* the effects of the following and show them diagrammatically:

a) an introduction of a mandatory reserve ratio in excess of the prudential ratio currently in force;

b) the development of new deposit liabilities with zero reserve requirements;

c) a dramatic increase in the number and distribution of cash machines.

2. Using figure 3.1, show the difference in impact on money market equilibrium of a given reduction in reserve assets when (a) the money supply curve shows some positive elasticity with respect to the bond rate and (b) when the money supply curve is completely inelastic with respect to the bond rate.

3. How is the LM curve affected by the introduction of some interest elasticity in the money supply curve?

4. In the flow of funds analysis, explain the effect of an increase in the government's budget deficit, *ceteris paribus.*

5. What steps might the authorities take to offset the monetary effects of events in question 4?

6. Why, according to the flow of funds approach, does the choice of exchange rate regime make monetary control more, or less, difficult for the authorities?

Further reading

The base-multiplier account of money supply determination can be found in most intermediate macroeconomic textbooks. To see it presented as the definitive account of the money supply process in specialist textbooks we need to go to the USA. Mishkin (1995), especially chapters 19 and 20, is a good and typical example. Though now rather old, Cuthbertson (1985a) provides one of the clearest expositions of the approach, together with the flow of funds approach and a comparison of the two. Howells and Bain (2002) ch.12 also compares both approaches.

The Bank of England Quarterly Bulletin (1997b) explains that monetary policy in the UK consists of setting interest rates and letting quantities adjust to demand while the *BEQB* (1999) contains a box explaining how interest rates are set. Borio (1997) does the same for a whole range of countries.

4 Money Supply and Control in the UK

'Virtually every monetary economist believes that the CB can control the monetary base and...the broader monetary aggregates as well. Almost all of those who have worked in a CB believe that this view is totally mistaken...' Goodhart (1994) p.1424.

What you will learn in this chapter:

- Why central banks are in a position to exert considerable influence over short-term interest rates
- Why they have chosen to target short-term interest rates rather than the money stock
- Why this choice effectively makes the money stock endogenous
- How the endogeneity of money affects our understanding of a range of issues in monetary economics

4.1 Introduction

In Chapter 11 we look at the evolution of UK monetary policy over the last 50 years or so. What that survey shows is:

(i) that monetary policy has passed through a number of distinct phases, including an initial phase when its influence upon the rest of the economy was regarded as slight;

(ii) that the immediate target of policy instruments has always been the flow of credit and never (not even between 1980 and 1985) the stock of money; and

(iii) that once the Bank of England moved away from direct controls on credit creation (during the 1970s) its chosen monetary policy instrument was the short-term interest rate at which it was prepared to provide liquidity to the banking system.

In the terms of the discussion in our last chapter, therefore, the Bank's main focus of attention has always been on the credit counterparts of the money stock and for most of the time its policy instrument has been the rate of interest and not the monetary base. Thus, as we said in the closing paragraphs, it is hardly surprising that most analysis of the money and credit supply in the UK has been done using the FoF approach.

In this chapter we look firstly at how a central bank is in a position to impose changes in short-term interest rates upon the rest of the financial system (and at some of the constraints there might be). Our illustrations draw upon the behaviour of the Bank of England but, as Borio (1997) shows, operating procedures are now very similar across most central banks. In Section 4.3 we look at *why* central banks have chosen to set interest rates ('prices') rather than the monetary base ('quantities'). In Section 4.4 we explain that this behaviour (widespread as it is) effectively makes the money supply endogenous throughout developed monetary systems and we look at the implications of this for the study of monetary economics. That the circumstances which we analyse are so widely recognised and accepted in central banking and policy circles (see Goodhart, 2002 pp.20-21) raises the interesting question of why the pedagogy of monetary economics (especially in the USA) remains so attached to the misleading insights of the B-M model. Unfortunately, constraints of time and of space prevent us from offering any reasons for the scale and persistence of what amounts, in Charles Goodhart's words to misinstruction (Goodhart, 1984, p.188).[1]

4.2 Short-term interest rates as the policy instrument

As we explain in Chapter 11, the UK monetary authorities have made use of a number of policy instruments over the last 50 years, gradually reducing the range until they were left only with the central bank's official dealing rate. Before 1971, they relied upon lending ceilings, qualitative guidance (to direct funds to particular uses), hire purchase and other credit terms and interest rates. In 1971, all the direct controls were to be jettisoned but in practice interest rates had frequently to be supplemented by the supplementary special deposit scheme. Since 1981, monetary policy has relied entirely upon interest rate changes. We look now at how the central bank can impose a decision about the general level of interest rates, what limits there might be to this power and what the consequences may be for the determination of the money supply.

Our starting point is that banks must be able to guarantee the convertibility into cash of customer deposits.[2] For this purpose they hold 'reserves' of notes and coin and deposits at the central bank. (A glance back at Box 3.2 and the surrounding text may be useful here). In the UK these reserves are very small (less than one per cent of deposits) and are supplemented by loans to the money market which are not quite so liquid but have the benefit that they pay interest. Other things being equal, the demand for loans (and the demand for deposits) expands since both are related to nominal income and this increases as a result of both increases in real income and in the price level. (This is why, when the UK authorities have been concerned about the size of the monetary aggregates — after 1973 and most obviously between 1980 and 1985 — it has been the *growth rate* and not the absolute size which they have targeted). It is thus a fairly simple task for the central bank to ensure that the quantity of monetary base (of which reserves are a part — see equation 3.2) grows slowly enough that at the end of each day the banks involved in the settlement process are short of funds (Bank, 1997a). In addition to this, a large fraction of banks' liquidity consists of previous short-term borrowing from central banks. When these loans mature ('unwinding of official assistance' in the jargon) they need to be refinanced. Provided that the shortage is system-wide, interbank lending and borrowing cannot resolve the shortage and the central bank is then in the position to exploit its monopoly position in the supply of reserves.

Like any monopolist, the central bank can set either the price or the quantity of reserves which it supplies. Two contrasting possibilities, and one intermediate one, are described in Figure 4.1.

Figure 4.1: The supply of bank reserves

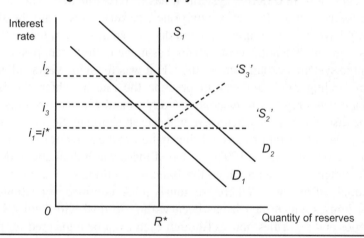

We begin with the situation where the authorities have a fixed target for reserves, R^*. In the event that demand increases from D_1 to D_2, and there is a shortage shown by the distance *AB,* the central bank can hold to its quantity target, in which case bidding by banks for the available reserves will push the rate of interest up from i_1 to i_2. Recall what we said above, namely that if the shortage is system-wide then interbank bidding cannot change the quantity which remains at R^*. The rise in interest rates must bear all of the adjustment.

Alternatively, the central bank may choose to target the rate of interest, i^*. In this case, the bank must supply whatever quantity of additional reserves are required at that rate. The supply curve shifts to the right by the distance AB and the intersection of the rightward shifting supply and demand curves traces out a horizontal locus. The result *looks like* a horizontal supply curve shown by the dashed line which is usually labled S_2. Calling it 'S_2' is a reminder that it is strictly a locus of intersections.

Yet another alternative is that the central bank provides only partial accommodation. The supply curve shifts by just enough to intersect D_2 at a position between A and B, call it C. This has the effect of raising the rate of interest to i_3 and if the adjustment is repeated in response to further increases in demand the locus will produce an upward-sloping 'supply' curve, shown by 'S_3'.

What precisely is the rate of interest shown on the vertical axis and how does it affect any of the money supply components that we saw in Chapter 3? The first point to stress is that it is the interest rate at which the central bank provides reserves to the banking system. In effect, it is the 'lender of last resort rate'. Analytically, it is, i_d or what we called the rediscount rate in Section 3.3. In different systems it has different names. The ECB literature refers to it as the 'refinancing rate', because as we said the shortage that we have been imagining can and does often arise from the maturing of loans of reserves that the central bank has made in the recent past as well as from the system's expansion. In the UK it was for some years called 'minimum lending rate' and was in practice the rate at which the Bank of England was prepared to discount 14-day ('band 1') treasury bills offered by the discount houses when there was a cash shortage. Several changes in money market operations arrived shortly before the Bank of England's independence in 1997 (Bank 1997b). One of these was a dramatic widening of the 'counterparties' with which the Bank was willing to deal in smoothing the supply of reserves. Where previously it had confined its dealings to discount houses, since then it has been willing to deal with banks, building societies and securities houses (though each must be registered for the purpose). Furthermore, instead of providing assistance by the outright purchase of treasury and sometimes commercial bills, since 1997 assistance has been provided by the use of repurchase agreements ('repos'), in a manner very similar to that of the ECB. As Box 4.1 explains, repos are agreements to sell an asset for cash and then to buy it back at a higher price at a specified time in the future. The difference in the two prices is the 'interest' paid from the borrower to lender. Repos are in effect collateralised loans and in money market operations the collateral is government bonds. Thus the rate of interest set by the Bank of England is often referred to as 'repo rate'.

Box 4.1: Using gilt-repos to raise interest rates

A repurchase agreement (repo) is an agreement to buy a number of specified securities from a seller on the understanding that they will be repurchased at some specified price and time. In the UK, there is an established market for repos in government bonds ('gilts'). Since the repos are usually for very short periods, three months at most, repos are classified as money market instruments (even though the maturity of the underlying gilts may be quite long). The difference between the selling and buying price represents interest paid to the repo buyer by the seller. The formula for finding the interest rate is:

$$i = \frac{(R-P)}{P.n} \qquad \qquad ...4.1$$

where R is the redemption or repurchase price, P is the price at sale and n is the length of the repo deal in fractions of a year.

Suppose that the Bank enters into a repo for £1m of government bonds for repurchase at £1,001,900 in fourteen days. From Equation 4.1 we can calculate that it will be setting a price for borrowed reserves of:

$$\frac{(1.0019 - 1.0)}{1.0\,(0.038)} = \frac{0.0019}{0.038} = 0.05 \text{ or } 5\%$$

Suppose now that the Bank wishes to raise interest rates by 25 basis points. Rearranging Equation 4.1 we can find the new repurchase price for future deals in the same securities.

$$R = (i.P.n) + P = (0.0525 \times 1m \times 0.038) + 1m = £1,001,995$$

Raising the repurchase price of £1m-worth of bonds for fourteen days by £95 is equivalent to raising the rate of interest by 25 basis points.

When the central bank changes its official dealing rate, it normally affectsother short-term market rates immediately — pushing them in the same direction and by similar amounts. It does not follow that all changes will be identical, however (i.e. that existing differentials will be preserved). Depending on the competitive nature of the system, banks may find it possible to change deposit rates by more than loan rates or *vice versa*. The transmission of these effects occurs mainly by convention but arbitrage would bring it about very quickly anyway. Banks price many of their products by mark-ups on or discounts to their 'base rates' and these base rates are often linked by formula to the Bank of England's official rate. Money markets are dominated by large institutions who make their profits from lending and borrowing very large sums for short periods at very small interest differentials (hence the need for the 'basis point', a division of one hundredth of one percentage point, in reckoning money market interest rates).

Exercise 4.1: Cutting interest rates

At the moment, the central bank is quoting a repurchase price of £20,050,000 for 14 day repos based on £20m of UK gilts.

Find:

a) the rate of interest that the central bank is setting

b) the price that it needs to quote if it wishes to change interest rates to 6%

Given that it is market rates (not the official rate itself) which affect agents' behaviour, it is not surprising that the transmission of interest rate changes through the money markets and beyond has received quite a lot of empirical attention over the years. In the UK, for example, Spencer Dale examined the link between the Bank of England's 'band 1 stop rate' (the treasury bill rate which was for many years the rate which the Bank set) and market interest rates at maturities of 1, 3, 6, and 12-months and 5, 10 and 20-years, for 30 changes in that stop rate between January 1987 and July 1991 (Dale 1993). His findings were that:

- The response of market rates was generally positive but often 'overshot' the change in official rate (i.e. changed in the same direction by more than 100 per cent of the official change);

- The effect decayed with term to maturity;

- The effect was greatest at turning points of the interest cycle.

- The examination consisted of estimating the equation:

$$\Delta MR(i)_n = \beta(i)\Delta stop_n + \varepsilon_{in} \qquad \qquad ...4.2$$

where:

$\Delta MR(i)_n$ is the change in the market rate of maturity i on the day of the nth change

$\Delta stop_n$ is the nth change in the Bank's band 1 stop rate

$i = 1, 3, 6$ months...20 years

$n = 1,2,3...30$

ε_{in} is an error term.

The first two results were what one would expect. Furthermore, assuming that short-rates are generally below long-rates, the second result tells us something about long-short spreads: they narrow when official rates rise and increase when official rates fall.

Dale and Haldane (1993) also looked at the effect of a change in official rates on market rates. The independent variable was UK banks' base rate (set by reference to the Bank's official rate) changes between March 1987 and October 1992. Market rates were differentiated by type of asset/liability rather than term, as in Dale 1993. The method used was the event-day study, familiar in studies of financial markets' response to news but used also in this context by Cook and Hahn (1989). The findings this time were:

• The mean response of all the market rates to a base rate change is positive but significantly less than 100 per cent.

• The responsiveness of market rates is lower, the lower is the degree of substitutability for the non-bank private sector. Thus, the response to an official rate change is about 30 per cent for personal loans and credit card debt, 38 per cent for corporate loans, above 50 per cent for mortgage and deposit rates.

It is worth noting their conclusion that:

As market rates are sticky, the marginal impact may be less and potentially much less, than suggested by a given base rate change. Moreover, this stickiness suggests that such spreads may contain useful information about the effective stance of monetary policy and hence future movements in activity following a monetary policy shock. (Dale and Haldane, 1993 p.21).

The stickiness of market rates has also been extensively investigated by Shelagh Heffernan (1993, 1997). Following anecdotal evidence of bank and building society failure to pass on interest rate cuts to loan customers Heffernan (1993) showed that the retail banking market was one of complex imperfect competition with sluggish loan and deposit rate adjustment, with LIBOR, the London Interbank Offer Rate, proxying the official rate.

More recently (Heffernan, 1997) used an error correction approach to explore the short- and long-run responses of rates on a number of banking products to changes in official rates. The model was initially estimated for seven different retail bank products using data from four large clearing banks, a number of smaller banks and five large building societies, covering the period (at longest) May 1986-January 1991.

On average, adjustments of chequing accounts and mortgages were 37 per cent complete within a month, but much slower for personal loans. The imperfect competition, noted in the 1993 paper was one reason for the slow response, reinforced by administrative costs. Interestingly, Heffernan makes a comparison with the pre-1971, pre-*Competition and Credit Control*, era when banks operated an interest rate cartel. In these circumstances, she notes, prices adjusted much more quickly because banks linked their product costs/returns directly to official rates by a conventional mark-up. Changes were mechanical and instantaneous.

Other factors might also influence the speed at which changes in the official rate are translated into changes in longer-term interest rates. For example, the administrative costs to the banks in making interest rate changes might cause them not to respond immediately to relatively small changes in the official rate, although much again depends on whether they expect a further change in the official rate in the near future and on what they expect their competitors to do. Banks are in competition with each other for both assets (for example, in the house mortgage market) and for liabilities (in the market for bank deposits). To maintain their spread between borrowing and lending rates (the source of their profits from lending), banks that cut lending rates must also cut deposit rates. An intensification of the competition for bank deposits might, for example, make banks unwilling to lower the rates of interest they were offering on deposits. They might be prepared temporarily to reduce their spread between borrowing and lending rates but even so, they might not follow fully a cut in official rates under these circumstances.

This implies that banks have some choice in deciding whether or not to respond to the prompting of the central bank. In addition to varying the spread between borrowing and lending rates, banks are able to change the conditions under which they are prepared to lend (for example, in the collateral they require for loans). Banks engage as a matter of course in the rationing of credit — not everyone is able to borrow the amount they wish (or at all) at existing bank interest rates. As we saw in Section 3.5, credit rationing may be justified by the existence in the market for loans of *asymmetric information* (we return to this issue in Section 7.7). Thus, to some extent at least banks may choose to respond to tighter monetary conditions by restricting their lending in the hope of reducing the risk associated with their loans.

It should be more difficult for banks to resist attempts by the central bank to push interest rates up since, as we have seen earlier in this section, the central bank has the power to induce a genuine shortage of liquidity in the economy. If banks hold their assets in a more liquid form than is needed, all they are doing is forgoing potential profits. If they hold their assets in a less liquid form than is needed, they ultimately face the possibility of a loss of confidence by the depositors and hence of collapse. Even here, however, there are some limits to the power of the central bank since it would be a very risky policy for central banks to squeeze liquidity to such an extent that the banks genuinely feared collapse. Indeed, for such a policy to be effective, the authorities would have to accept reasonably frequent bank collapses. This, in turn, would reduce the confidence of depositors in the banking system — a result that modern governments do not desire.

For all of these possible reasons for stickiness in medium- and long-term rates, it remains that they are likely to move in response to changes in the central bank's intervention rate at least in the same direction, though by smaller amounts than short rates.

Pause for thought 4.1:

Why might market interest rates not change instantly and exactly in line with changes in official rates?

So far as *monetary growth* is concerned, what matters most is the responsiveness of bank loan rates. If an increase, for example, in official rates is quickly communicated to bank loans, then we move up a downward sloping demand curve for (the flow of) new loans. Consequently, loans and, through the flow of funds identity, deposits grow more slowly. *If* it is also the case that the rise in official rates can cause changes in spreads such that there is a relative cheapening of non-bank sources of credit then better still. This cheapening of the cost of a substitute causes the bank loan demand curve to move inward. In these favourable circumstances, changes in the official rate have the effect of the proverbial 'double whammy'. A change in rates moves us along a curve which simultaneously shifts in a reinforcing direction. This mechanism is quite complicated and we return to it in Section 11.3 where we suggest that various financial innovations in recent years have dismantled these favourable circumstances, so much so that changes in official rates are probably very blunt instruments for controlling monetary growth, supposing that the authorities ever wished to do such a thing.

In spite of all the complications, central banks clearly possess considerable power to influence short-term interest rates in their role as lenders of last resort. However, this does not mean that they can set even short-term rates at whatever level they may wish for domestic policy purposes. One constraint is what is happening to official rates in other major financial centres. This constraint is usually imposed by foreign exchange markets which will quickly make it clear if they think that a central bank is pursuing an interest rate policy which is inconsistent with the current exchange rate. A classic example for the UK is provided by the occasion of the pound's exit from the European Exchange Rate mechanism in September 1992. No one doubted the Bank of England's ability to raise interest rates (which it did, to 15 per cent), but the forex markets judged that the political will would fail to raise them sufficiently unless other central banks (notably the Bundesbank) cut their rates to help sterling. Massive sales of sterling occurred until the exchange rate parity was abandoned. We look at market constraints on central bank policy in more detail in Section 12.3.

In years gone by, a further constraint was imposed by conflicts of policy objectives. From 1945 until the mid-1970s, governments, for whom central banks acted in effect as monetary policy agents, were inclined to list their policy objectives as stable prices, full employment and economic growth — often with a stable exchange rate and balance of payments equilibrium thrown in. The problem, of course, is that four goals are not simultaneously consistent with one instrument (in the imperfections of a real world, at least). Hence interest rates might be raised to protect the exchange rate (as was often the case in the UK) but would be reduced at the earliest opportunity when growth stagnated and unemployment rose. This experience of conflicting objectives underlies some of the arguments for giving central banks independence to set interest rates according to their best judgement *but with only one objective to maximise* — price stability (see Section 8.5).

Given that the short-term interest rate has become the sole instrument of policy for most central banks, attention has turned in recent years to the question of how central banks can be helped to make the 'best' decision regarding the setting of the official rate. This has raised, once again, the 'rules versus discretion' debate, though this time over the setting of interest rates rather than the stock of money (broad or base). This debate, which has a long history is discussed in Section 9.3. One of the best known of the 'rules' suggested for the setting of interest rates was first proposed by John Taylor (1993). The basis of this rule, and its several derivatives, is dealt with in Section 9.7. What matters here is, as Taylor says, that 'Using an interest rate rule...simply makes money endogenous' (Taylor 1999c, p.661). Central banks do, and have for years, set interest rates and not monetary aggregates. Given the fundamental nature of this decision, and its divergence from so much of what economists write about monetary policy, it is time to see why it was taken and why it continues to be reaffirmed.

4.3 The rejection of monetary base control

We have just seen that, given the monopolist's choice between price and quantity, central banks have chosen the rate of interest and not the quantity of reserves as their preferred instrument of monetary policy (Goodhart,

1994). The survey by Borio (1997) shows how central bank practice across the world has converged on the level of short-term rates and indeed upon repo agreements (as opposed to outright sales and purchases) as the way of making changes in the rates. The alternative, control of the monetary base is, in practice, much more difficult than it sounds when presented as the implication of the B-M analysis that we saw in Section 3.3.

The problems, as Goodhart explained in 1994, all stem from the fact that banks must be able to provide *unchallengeable* convertibility between currency and deposits at par, combined with the fact that reserves pay zero (in most cases) interest or at least interest rates which are below money market rates and with fluctuations in flows of funds between the public and private sectors which cause sharp fluctuations in banks' operational deposits. From the first it follows that the demand for reserves is extremely inelastic; from the second it follows that reserve-holding acts as a tax on banking intermediation and so banks will hold minimum reserves. Putting the two together means that money market interest rates must be extremely volatile given net flows in and out of the banking system. Since any interest is better than none, an end of day excess of bank reserves will be dumped in the money market until rates are driven down virtually to zero while a shortage will drive rates up to the penal rate at which the central bank does step in or the banks are prepared to face the penalty for reserve deficiencies.

Pause for thought 4.2:

Explain why non-interest bearing reserves act as a tax on banking intermediaries.

Tinkering with the details can introduce some smoothing. Specifiying the reserve target as an *average* over a period will eliminate day to day fluctuations but will leave rates volatile at the end of the maintenance period. Paying interest on reserves will reduce the distortionary tax efect of reserve holding and lead to larger holdings on average. But a new element is introduced into the demand for reserves as money market rates fluctuate relative to the rate on reserves.

Why banks are not reserve constrained in practice is a question that has received a number of answers over the years, but they all stem from this fundamental dilemma that targeting the quantity of reserves would produce disruptive interest rate fluctuations. We look briefly at the development of these arguments and provide a summary in Box 4.2.

Box 4.2: The difficulties of monetary base control

One implication of the B-M analysis of money supply determination is that the central bank can control the size of the monetary base and that this will produce a predictable and multiple change in the broad money stock. In each major review of the operation of UK monetary policy (1958, 1971, 1980) however, the authorities have rejected such an approach and, indeed, it is difficult to find examples of its use in any developed country. Although policy makers have sometimes stressed the importance of monetary aggregates and the need to control their growth, the chosen instrument has almost always been the short term rate of interest. The reasons for this universal rejection of MBC are many. We give just a brief list below.

If the authorities were able to fix the base, any shock (to the demand for reserves) would have to be accommodated by changes in very short-term interest rates. Because of the convertibility requirement, the demand for reserves is extremely inelastic and these interest rate fluctuations would be very violent.

- While it is true that the authorities know the size of the base *ex post* it is very difficult to control it *ex ante* because it is very difficult to predict the market flows that cause changes. In its daily money market operations, the Bank of England has frequently to intervene more than once because its morning forecasts turn out to be wrong.

- Even if it could forecast accurately, it does not follow that the central bank could undertake the operations necessary to hit the target. If it were necessary to offset a predicted expansion, for example, a sale of bonds or other government debt to the non-bank private sector would be necessary and this cannot be carried out at short notice without major changes to the debt markets. Continuous auctions would be required and once again interest rates (on bonds this time) would become very unstable.

- MBC would probably be inconsistent with other institutional arrangements. For example, it is difficult to see how banks could make overdraft-type commitments to clients if they might suddenly find it impossible to obtain the reserves to cover the additional lending.

- Banks' response to the risk that there might be shortages of reserves would be to hold 'excess' reserves. Since these are non-interest bearing this imposes a tax on all institutions subject to reserve requirements. Such a tax would raise the price and reduce the quantity of bank intermediation.

- Experience shows us that any direct control of quantities will stimulate innovation designed to evade the constraint. Lending via offshore subsidiaries seems one obvious possibility in a world with free capital movements.

The earliest claim that central banks have little choice but to supply reserves on demand rests upon the conflict of policy objectives that would follow from the behaviour of interest rates under reserve targeting. One version appears explicitly in Weintraub (1978) and is linked ultimately to his wage theorem. The growth of nominal income (due to a rise in unit labour costs, or in the mark-up on those costs) results in a rise in the demand for active balances. If the level of real output is to be maintained, the supply of money must increase. If it does not, or does not do so sufficiently, interest rates will rise and this will reduce the level of output and employment. In Weintraub's view, political considerations make this intolerable. Ultimately, the political authorities will instruct the central bank to accommodate the extra demand for money. Similar views, that central banks *could*, if they chose, restrict reserves but choose not to do so for reasons of policy conflicts, appear in Myrdal (1939) and Lavoie (1985). The accommodating behaviour of central banks, seen from this angle, is essentially political in origin and the interpretation has a distinctly 'Keynesian' flavour. In the UK, however, the level of interest rates has always been an issue of political sensitivity. In the early-1970s, for example, when broad money growth touched 30 per cent p.a. the government of Edward Heath pressed the Bank of England to introduce the supplementary special deposits scheme and return to direct controls rather than raise interest rates to the necessary level (see Section 11.2). Goodhart also relates how Margaret Thatcher in the UK, leading a government in the early 1980s which rejected any responsibility for output, growth and employment, and stressed the importance of controlling the monetary aggregates, nonetheless baulked at the prospect of raising interest rates to the levels suggested by the Bank (Goodhart, 2002, p.17).

Given the manifest readiness of governments from the 1970s onwards to sacrifice full employment for low inflation, the accommodating behaviour of central banks needed another explanation. According to Moore (1988a chs. 5-8) and Kaldor (1982, 1985) such pressures can be found in the structure of modern banking systems. The starting point is that central banks, in addition to their role as managers of monetary policy, bear a heavy responsibility for ensuring the stability of their domestic financial systems. This role is commonly referred to as their 'lender of last resort' (LOLR) function and reminds us again of a central bank's monopoly position. Since financial intermediation always involves an element of maturity transformation, intermediaries are always subject to the risk that they may have calls on their liabilities which they cannot meet from their relatively illiquid assets. In the case of an individual institution in difficulties, borrowing within the system is a realistic solution but in the event of a system-wide shortage of liquidity the general sale of assets will be self-defeating as regards the raising of liquidity but it could easily cause a collapse of asset prices with the threat of insolvency and a general debt deflation. The only safeguard against disaster is the central bank's willingness *always* to provide liquidity (Moore, 1988a pp.57-65; Kaldor, 1985 pp.20-25). It needs to be emphasised: this is not a discretionary function. If confidence in the financial system is to be maintained, the public needs to be convinced that this assistance will always be forthcoming. Such reassurance requires an unquestioning response, not a response which is hedged around with conditions (Goodhart, 1984, p.212).

A second structural feature of modern systems explains why such assistance might often be required. Most textbook discussion of the lender of last resort tends to focus upon the shortage of liquidity caused by net withdrawals of cash ('runs on the bank'). However, the same shortage of liquidity, a fall in the R/Dp ratio, will occur when banks increase their lending and in many banking systems banks are contractually committed to make additional loans on demand. This arises from the 'overdraft' facility where banks agree to meet all demand for loans up to a ceiling. Customers then use that proportion of the facility that they require on a day to day basis. Typically, the proportion of the facility that is in use at any one time is about 60 per cent of total commitments. Thus it follows that if the state of trade requires an increase in working capital to bridge the time gap between firms' additional outlays and the receipts from increased sales, requests for loans will always be met. '...if bank loans are largely demand-determined, so that the quantity of bank credit demanded is a non-discretionary variable from the viewpoint of individual banks, this then implies that the money supply is credit driven.' (Moore, 1988b, p.373). If the state of trade[3] means customers demand more advances, banks have no choice (unless they are to break contractual agreements) but to expand their lending. Advances (and deposits) will rise relative to reserves, interest rates will rise and security prices fall, reducing the value of bank assets. Faced with a general shortage of liquidity, the central bank *must*, as we said above, provide assistance. Essentially the same argument is put by Wray (1990, pp.85-90).

There are two further structural features which make it impossible for central banks to resist the demand for reserves. The first is the structure of banks' assets which are overwhelmingly non-marketable loans (rather than marketable securities). Moore highlights the problem by posing a reduction in the monetary base brought about by open market operations of the textbook type. Bank reserves are reduced but banks cannot reduce their balance sheets because calling in loans will bankrupt their customers. This illustration is easily modified to reflect a more realistic state of affairs. Recall that expansion of bank balance sheets is the norm. We must imagine banks making new loans, in response to demand, expecting the additional reserves to be forthcoming, only to find that they are not because of a change in central bank stance. From this point, Moore's argument follows as before. Banks cannot unwind this position without causing chaos.[4]

Lastly, it is worth noting that most monetary regimes which pay any attention to the base/deposits relationship require banks to report on their holding of base at time t, and their holdings of deposits at some earlier period, $t-1$, the system of lagged reserve accounting. The current level of required reserves is thus *predetermined* by the past level of deposits (Moore, 1988a; Goodhart, 1984 p.212). In these circumstances, there is plainly nothing that banks can do to accommodate deposits to reserves. Any desired ratio can only be met by the central bank supplying the reserves.

For all of these reasons, some a matter of choice, others decidedly non-discretionary, central banks accommodate the demand for reserves and confine their policy gestures to setting the price.

Given the ability of banking systems to innovate products and practices in response to regulation (see Section 11.3 for some examples) it is worth considering what might be the outcome if central banks *did* take a less accommodating position.

Suppose, for example, that central banks, under pressure from financial markets perhaps, were forced to impose quantity constraints on reserve availability. Some have argued that this might still matter little since the structure of modern financial systems enables banks to engage in a number of activities which enable them to avoid the consequences of reserve shortages. In this view it is sometimes said that banks can 'manufacture' reserves though this is a little misleading since most of the practices are aimed at reducing the quantity of reserves that are required. If reserves are defined appropriately as the liabilities solely of the central bank then banks can do nothing to avoid a system-wide shortage. What, perhaps, they can do is to economise on reserves so as to avoid the effects of the shortage.

Central to this argument is banks' management of their liabilities. For example, in a period where the central bank is consciously seeking to restrain the growth of reserves, and presumably also the money supply, banks will attract funds out of sight deposits which have a high reserve requirement, into time deposits, CDs and other instruments which have lower requirements. The result is that a given volume of reserves will support a higher volume of lending (and a higher volume of total deposits). It also follows that periods of reserve shortage and consequent liability management will be periods of rising interest rates. Such periods will also be conducive to financial innovation as banks try to find cheaper ways of adjusting to the shortage. An obvious example of this is the development of certificates of deposit where the superior (liquidity) characteristics of the product enables banks to raise funds for a fixed term more cheaply than they could through traditional time deposits.[5]

To date, the only attempt to establish empirically which of the two descriptions (complete accommodation or reserve-economising) is the more accurate was carried out by Pollin, looking at the Federal Reserve. The criteria used were threefold. Firstly, Pollin argued, if 'accommodation' were the rule, then we would expect stationarity in the ratio of loans (L) to reserves (R); secondly, if the Federal Reserve were to provide reserves 'willingly' then borrowed (from the Fed) and non-borrowed reserves would be very close substitutes and there would be no need to develop circumventory products and practices; thirdly, market interest rates would not move independently of official rates (official rates would 'cause' market rates). Formal tests of stationarity in the L/R ratio, of elasticities in the demand for borrowed and non-borrowed reserves and of causality between official and market rates, were all claimed to lend support to the structural view (Pollin, 1991).

The controversy remains, however, since some of the results are open to alternative interpretation (Palley, 1991). For example, the discovery that the L/R ratio is subject to an upward secular trend is advanced by Pollin as evidence that reserves are constrained. On the other hand, as Palley points out, the need to hold reserves against deposits has been recognized for years in the standard banking literature as acting as a tax upon banking intermediation — limiting the amount of each deposit that can be lent out. The fact that the L/R ratio rises over time could merely be evidence that banks are profit seekers wishing to reduce the burden of reserve requirements even when reserves are readily available. Rather similarly, the discovery that there appears to be two-way Sims (1972) causality between Federal and market interest rates (where the logic of complete accommodation would require uni-directional causality from Fed to market rates) could be accounted for by market rates embodying expectations about future Fed rates.

The truth may lie somewhere between the two views, and be heavily dependent on time horizon. It is difficult to see how innovatory behaviour could act quickly enough to alleviate a sudden shortage of reserves but, if only because of their tax-like effects, banks have a long-run incentive to minimise reserve requirements. Wherever the truth may lie, whether central banks passively accommodate the whole demand for reserves or whether they do sometimes impose constraints whose effects must be minimised by banking innovation, the Bank of England's view could not be clearer:

In the United Kingdom, money is endogenous - *the Bank supplies base money on demand* at its prevailing interest rate, and broad money is created by the banking system (King, 1994 p.264. Our emphasis).[6]

4.4 Endogenous money

Having set the official interest rate, central banks must meet such demand for reserves as is forthcoming. This in turn will depend upon banks' deposit liabilities and changes in these will be driven by the demand for loans at the current level and structure and interest rates. Given the importance of loan demand in credit and money creation, therefore, it seems mildly curious that empirical work on the demand for bank loans is so sparse while studies of the demand for money abound (as the next two chapters show!). Of course, one can argue that credit demands cannot create money unless the resulting deposits are willingly held and thus the demand for money is the ultimate constraint on its creation. But this is an equilibrium argument.[7] Buffer stock models of money demand (see Section 6.4) were developed precisely to cope with the possibility that the quantity of money could, at least in the short-run, differ from what agents ultimately wish to hold.[8]

From a present day perspective, where the personal sector's share of bank credit outstanding exceeds that of industrial and commercial companies (ICCs) and other financial institutions (OFIs) combined,[9] it is also curious that such empirical work that exists tends to concentrate upon the demand for loans by firms. Cuthbertson (1985b), Cuthbertson and Foster (1982), Moore and Threadgold (1980, 1985; Cuthbertson and Slow, 1990) all focused attention upon the demand for loans by ICCs. In this literature it is nominal income, sometimes supplemented by wage costs, import costs and taxes, that determine the demand for loans and thus support the view, often quoted in post-Keynesian circles that, given the level of interest rates, the demand for loans (and thus the expansion of deposits) depends upon the 'state of trade'. Bearing in mind both the dominant position of households in the total demand for bank credit and the more rapid rise in spending upon assets relative to GDP in recent years, it is not surprising to find dissenting views on credit demand (Howells and Hussein, 1999). Nonetheless, what follows from all of this work is that once the rate of interest has been set as a policy instrument, the proximate 'cause' of loans and deposits is a demand which originates with the requirements of the economic system.[10] The demand for loans and the supply of credit money are both endogenous.

Notice the contrast with the quantity theory approach in Section 2.2. The Quantity Theory, we said, was the theoretical basis for being concerned about monetary aggregates and maybe even for conducting a monetary policy which targeted the growth rate of money. In the Quantity Theory, causality runs from left to right, from money to nominal income. But no central bank now operates as though it seriously believes this. A fig leaf for the exogeneity of money could be created if it were shown that central bank rate were being set so as to produce a given quantity (or rather growth rate) of the money stock. The Bundesbank certainly published monetary growth rates and 'reference values' for many years and the practice survives in current ECB arrangements. But in both cases, money and credit growth are being used as *information variables*. They are amongst the many inputs into the decision about when and by how much to change interest rates. They feature also for this purpose in the deliberations of the Bank of England's Monetary Policy Committee (Bank, 1999; Treasury 2002 ch.3). But whatever may be said in public, central bank operating procedures ensure that causality (in Quantity Theory terms) runs from right to left. Any reduction in the growth of money and credit aggregates comes from the ability of interest rates to induce a *prior* reduction in the growth of income and output.[11]

The money supply is endogenous and, more importantly for this section, it is endogenous in the 'base-endogeneity' sense, rather than the more limited 'interest-endogeneity' sense that we saw at the end of Section 3.3. To understand this distinction, let us suppose that the money supply *is* determined according to the presuppositions of the B-M model, and that we represent it as in Figure 4.2 below. The money stock changes with changes in the base. This shifts the curve. It also shifts with changes in the size of the multiplier, with one exception. This is the case where the multiplier changes as a result of changes in the bond rate. It was this elasticity with respect to the bond rate (recall) that gave the *Ms* curve a positive slope and thus we said it was possible for an exogenously determined money supply to show signs of 'interest endogeneity'. However, where the central bank sets short-term interest rates, we have just seen that reserves must be free to respond to banks' need for them. The strict analogue of Figure 3.1 in these circumstances is one in which the *Ms* curve is *shifts* as banks find it commercially attractive to increase lending (and thus create deposits). If it so happens that the rate of monetary expansion induced by bank lending happens just to match the growth in the demand for money, then the bond rate (or any other representation of the opportunity cost of money) will remain unchanged and the two continually shifting curves will trace out a horizontal locus as in Figure 4.2 (and the *LM* curve will become horizontal, see Appendix 1).

It should be stressed, however, that there is no reason *a priori* why this should be the case. The question of how the FoF analysis of the money sup-

Figure 4.2: The horizontal 'money supply curve'

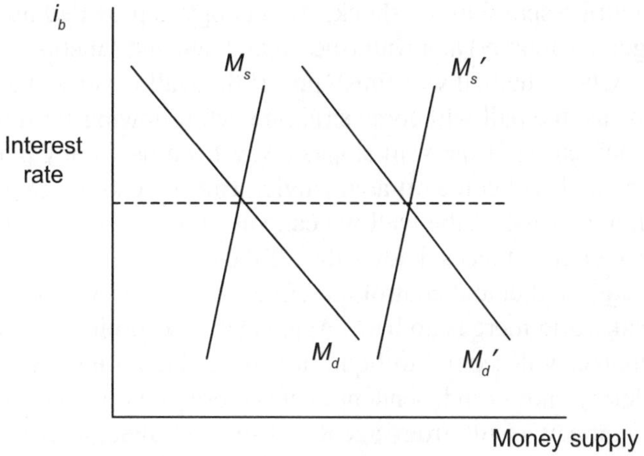

ply relates to the demand for money is a complex one, involving a number of relative interest rates (see the closing paragraphs of Section 4.2 above and the discussion in Section 11.3). Nonetheless, the regime that we have just described is often said to produce a horizontal money supply curve, presumably because the money supply is free to adjust at a *given rate of interest* set by the central bank. But this is erroneous. Anything that may appear horizontal in Figure 4.2 is not a money supply curve in the conventional sense. Neither is it the central bank's official rate that appears on the vertical axis. Thus phrases that describe endogenous money as giving rise to a 'supply curve which is horizontal at the going rate of interest' may have the merit of brevity but are not helpful.

What does matter is that in the real world, inhabited by central banks and policy makers, the precise analogue of the familiar money supply curve drawn in interest-money space is a money supply curve that is continually shifting to the right, whose rate of shift can be influenced, to some degree, by the effect of interest rates on the demand for new loans. In the next few chapters we shall go on to review a lot of work in monetary economics that continues to assume, in the face of the evidence, that this curve shifts only at the discretion of the monetary authorities. Thus, in Chapters 5 and 6, we look at theories and empirical tests of the demand for money. However, with the money supply determined as implied by the FoF approach and as described in this chapter, it is not clear that the demand for money has much policy relevance. In a world where the quantity of money can change independently of other variables the economy can be subject to a genuine 'monetary shock'. Money is a 'cause' and it is essential for policy makers to know how other variables (interest rates, consumption, investment, prices, output etc.) will respond to the shock. An analogy is provided by throwing a ball (exogenous money) at a wall (the money demand function) and wishing to know where the ball will finish up. If the wall is vertical and directly in front of us, the ball will come straight back (allowing for diminishing energy, friction etc.). If the wall slopes away from us, in any plane, however, then the ball will come off at an angle. But if we know enough about the position and shape of the wall we can still predict the trajectory of the ball. In these circumstances, knowledge of the demand for money is essential if we are to predict and control the effects of monetary shocks.

In the real world there is no ball. Agents have portfolio preferences and these preferences will extend to liquid assets, including money. But there are no monetary shocks independent of these preferences. Changes in the quantity of money result from agents' decisions about borrowing from banks, decisions which themselves are made in the light of existing money holdings and the interest rate spread between bank loans and deposits.[12] Issues such as real balance effects and the neutrality of money simply have no practical relevance. Neither do discussions about anticipated versus 'surprise' changes in the money stock. Recognising this fundamental irrelevance to the real world does not empty such debates of intellectual merit.

> There is much of economic theory which is pursued for no better reason than its intellectual attraction; it is a good game. We have no reason to be ashamed of that, since the same would hold for many branches of mathematics. (Hicks, 1979).

The ability to make valid deductions from false premises is highly regarded in some quarters. But it does suggest that some contributions to our understanding of money would fit better in a philosophy than an economics curriculum.

4.5 Summary

No central bank in the developed world targets the money stock or the monetary base. In practice, central banks conduct monetary policy by setting the short-term rate of interest at which they are prepared to make reserves available. Their ability to set the price of reserves stems from their monopolistic position as lenders of last resort in a system-wide shortage of liquidity. The decision to target the price, rather than the quantity, of reserves stems from a number of practical considerations but fundamentally from a rejection of the volatility of interest rates that would result from targeting quantities. Furthermore, the aim of setting interest rates is to achieve a level of aggregate demand consistent with some inflation objective. It is not done in order to achieve a particular outcome for the path of monetary aggregates. What happens to monetary aggregates may be relevant to interest rate setting but only in so far as their growth rates may provide advance information about the likely future path of inflation.

In these circumstances, the money supply is fully endogenous, resulting from the demand for bank credit. Though widely recognised by economists actively engaged with the conduct of monetary policy, and of course by central bankers, there has been a reluctance to recognise the implications in some areas of monetary economics in which assumptions are made and conclusions drawn which amount to misinstruction when presented to students.

Key concepts used in this chapter

lending ceilings	convertibility
qualitative guidance	monetary base control
direct controls	endogenous money
repurchaseagreements	buffer stocks
refinancing rate	interest-endogeneity
counterparties	base-endogeneity
basis point	

Questions and exercises

1. Distinguish between 'interest-endogeneity' and 'base-endogeneity'.

2. Why, in practice, are commercial banks unconstrained in their access to reserves?

3. Explain briefly the disadvantages of attempting to regulate monetary growth by non-price methods.

4. Why is the demand for reserves by commercial banks highly interest-inelastic?

5. Explain what is meant by a repurchase agreement and work an example to show how, by changing the terms of a repo deal, the central bank can raise *and* lower short-term interest rates.

6. Go to the statistical section of the Bank of England's website (www.bankofengland.co.uk/mfsd/) and make a note of (a) the rate of money growth in each of the last four quarters for which figures are available and (b) any changes in the Bank's repo rate over that same period.

Further reading

The use by central banks of short-term interest rates as the sole monetary policy instrument is documented by all the sources below. The reasons for choice of this instrument (as opposed, for example, to the monetary base) and the central bank's ability to impose its choice are explained in Goodhart (1994). The procedures by which rates are set are explained in a box in *Bank of England Quarterly Bulletin* (1999) 'The Transmission Mechanism of Monetary Policy' (May), 161-70, which also explains how the Bank thinks a change in interest rates affects other variables. Borio (1997) confirms the widespread similarity of these procedures across countries. The fact that these operating procedures have the effect of making the money supply endogenous is documented in Goodhart (*op cit*) and in Howells's essay in P Arestis and M C Sawyer (eds) (2001). This also surveys a number of issues arising from the endogeneity of money. H M Treasury (2002) provides the background to the conduct of monetary policy in the UK in recent years. Chs. 3-6 explain the monetary policy framework, the choice of an inflation target and the conduct of an independent Bank of England.

5 The Theory of the Demand for Money

'The force of the guinea you have in your pocket depends wholly on the default of a guinea in your neighbour's pocket. If he did not want it, it would be of no use to you', John Ruskin, *Unto This Last*, (1862).

What you will learn in this chapter

- The implications for economic policy of the Quantity Theory of Money
* The movement from the Quantity Theory to the first theories of the demand for money
- A consideration of Keynes's motives approach to the demand for money and the criticisms of it
- The monetary policy implications of Keynes's theory
- The way in which interest rates were incorporated into the theory of the transactions demand for money
- The development of theories of the precautionary demand for money
- Tobin's development of the portfolio model of the demand for money
- Friedman's approach to the demand for money, its relationship to the Quantity Theory and its implications for monetary policy

5.1   Introduction

Although we have so far talked principally about the money supply, the demand for money has made several appearances. For example, in Section 1.2, we pointed out that if we accept the standard definition of money as a set of assets generally acceptable in exchange for goods and services, money is only demanded indirectly — to allow acts of exchange. We also discussed some of the implications of the existence of an excess demand for money and spoke of a discord between the microeconomic and macroeconomic approaches to the demand for money. In addition, we pointed out at the end of Chapter 1 that the view that the monetary authorities could hope to control the level of aggregate demand in the economy through adjusting the supply of money assumed that the demand for money function was stable. That is, the demand for money was assumed to be a stable function of real income, the price level and interest rates. We returned to this proposition when discussing prescriptive definitions of money in Section 2.3.

We thus provided some basis for understanding why monetary economists have thought the demand for money important, only to suggest in

Section 4.4 that with an endogenous money supply, the demand for money may be of no great practical significance. We shall also see that the rise to prominence of the testing of the demand for money has been accompanied by a reduction of interest in theories of the demand for money.

There is another problem. The teaching of demand for money theory is still dominated by Keynes's motives for demanding money, which is largely rejected by neoclassical economists because it is said to lack 'microfoundations'. That is, it does not conform to the choice behaviour of individual, utility-maximizing market agents. However, mainstream neoclassical theorizing about the demand for money concludes with the proposition that the precise form of the demand for money function should be determined by empirical testing. Since we need to test the aggregate demand for money, several points that arise from the theory quickly disappear from view. The microfoundations of an aggregate demand for money that appears to do well in empirical testing do not seem to matter. Double standards appear to be in operation here.

We attempt to tackle these problems in Chapters 5 and 6. In Chapter 5, we look at the major contributions to the historical development of the theory of the demand for money. We return, in Section 5.2 to the Quantity Theory of Money. Section 5.3 looks at the Cambridge cash balance approach and its relationship to the Quantity Theory. In 5.4, we consider the demand for money in Keynes's *General Theory*. Sections 5.5 to 5.7 treat theories arising from Keynes's work — later views of the transactions demand for money (5.5) and of the precautionary demand (5.6) and, then, Tobin's alternative to the speculative demand (5.7). The monetarist approach to the demand for money is the subject of 5.8, while Section 5.9 provides a brief introduction only to microeconomic theories of the demand for money derived from general equilibrium theory. The chapter concludes with an attempt to tie together a number of the points raised in the chapter.

5.2   The Quantity Theory of Money

Surveys of theories of the demand for money conventionally start with the Quantity Theory of Money. This may seem odd since the Quantity Theory was not a theory of the demand for money at all but dealt with the use of money in transactions rather than with the decision to hold money. Yet, there are three compelling reasons for doing so.

- The Quantity Theory stresses the connection between changes in the economy's money stock and changes in the general price level — the issue at the heart of the monetary debate.

• Many writers on the subject thereafter have seen themselves as opponents or inheritors of the Quantity Theory tradition.

• The varying views on the demand for money can be easily compared using the Quantity Theory equation.

The Quantity Theory of money can be traced back at least as far as the eighteenth century and can be seen as a reaction to the mercantilist identification of money with wealth.[1] In its early days the theory was expounded with varying degrees of rigour but it was generally held that an increase in the quantity of money would:

— (a) lead to a proportional increase in the price level and

— (b) not have a permanent impact on real income.

Some versions of the theory did not require exact proportionality and admitted the possibility of a time lag between the increase in the money stock and the change in the price level.[2]

The Quantity Theory is most familiar to modern readers through Fisher's (1911) version, which we looked at in Section 2.2, when we were constructing a theory of the relationship between money and income in a world in which all participants were well informed. There, we started with the equation of exchange:

$$MV_T \equiv P_T T \qquad \qquad ...5.1$$

where M is the stock of money, $P_T T$ is the value of all transactions undertaken with money and V_T, is the transactions velocity of money. We next assume that V_T, T and M are all exogenous and can be taken as constant. We also assume that the monetary authorities can change the size of M at will. Then, causality runs from the supply of money to prices. We now have:

$$M\bar{V}_T \equiv P_T\bar{T} \qquad \qquad ...5.2$$

This expresses the proposition that an exogenous increase in the quantity of money leads to a proportional increase in the price level and has no impact on real income (money is neutral). It is common to say that T is constant because the economy is making full use of all available resources (including labour). But we should note that this is not just a simple assumption that we can easily relax. The model accepts the classical view of a clear division between the monetary and real sectors of the economy. T is determined in the real sector and cannot be influenced by changes in M. In other words, money neutrality does not follow from the analysis of the role that money plays in an economy. Rather, the monetary sector is merely added on to an already-existing real sector and does not modify it in any way.

We noted in 2.2, however, that Irving Fisher's approach was more complex than this suggests since he distinguished between transactions related to national income and those related to financial transactions:

$$MV = P_Y Y + P_F F \qquad \qquad ...5.3$$

where Y and F are income and financial transactions respectively. If we accept this, and still require T to be exogenous and entirely unrelated to M, we must assume, as we did in the first of our simple models in Section 2.2, that financial transactions only take place in the pursuit of real ends. That is, there are no purely financial transactions — a difficult assumption to maintain even in the 18th century and clearly impossible amidst the speculative behaviour in modern financial markets. This distinction has largely been ignored since Fisher's time. Indeed, most textbook versions of Fisher's statement have replaced T with y, excluding the financial sector from consideration.

A further complexity arises if we pay attention to the precise meaning of M. M was initially limited to currency (in modern terms, the monetary base or high-powered money) but was later extended to include bank deposits:

$$M_C \bar{V}_C + M_D \bar{V}_D = P\bar{T} \qquad \qquad ...5.4$$

where the subscripts C and D indicate currency and bank deposits respectively. M_C is the monetary base. V_C and V_D are assumed to have different values and so variations in M_C/M_D lead to changes in P. As long as M_C/M is constant (people hold a constant proportion of their money holdings in the form of currency), the extension to bank deposits does not change the result. Although this formulation allows us to consider the possibility of a change in M undesired by the authorities, even if they were totally in control of M_C, the Quantity Theory has not been used as a vehicle for the examination of the relationship between the monetary base and the money stock. According to Fisher, an increase in M_C caused prices to rise and hence the real interest rates to fall. This led to an increase in demand for bank loans and an increase in M_D. Nominal interest rates were pushed up until the real rate of interest returned to its initial level.

Although V is usually written as a constant, it is affected by changes in the financial system, in particular by changes in the form in which income is received and payments are made. Thus, V changes over time (and is different from one economy to another) but if we accept that the financial system changes only gradually, we should expect changes in V to happen only slowly. We should also be able to predict quite accurately the direction in which V is likely to move. A standard list of the factors likely to influence velocity in the Quantity Theory approach is provided in Box 5.1. As we stress there the most important assumption is that the nature of the financial system is not influenced by changes in M.

Pause for thought 5.1:

Does it matter, within the Quantity Theory, how rapidly V and T change?

Since T is determined in the real sector, it is influenced by changes in the availability of resources, technology and the skills of the labour force, and grows steadily over time.

The Quantity Theory is, in essence, a long-run theory. We can accept that changes in M might cause short-run changes in V and T during the transition to a new equilibrium without disturbing the central message of the approach. All this requires is that V and T are independent of M in the long run and that M is fully controlled by the monetary authorities. There is no need within the theory to analyse the demand for money since it is clear that the only reason for holding money balances is to undertake transactions. There is also no role for interest rates except during the period of transition to the new equilibrium. The interest rate, like T, is determined in the real sector of the economy. What can we say about the meaning of M in the theory? Plainly, it assumes the existence of a clearly defined set of assets (currency and bank deposits), which can be used to undertake transactions but has no other role in the economy. But we know nothing else except that it is fully controlled by the monetary authorities.

Box 5.1 Velocity in the Quantity Theory of Money (QTM)

We are concerned in the QTM with the transactions velocity of money — the relationship between the flow of goods and services exchanged in a period and the stock of money.

We can write this as: $V = \dfrac{P\bar{T}}{M}$

We have said that V changes slowly over time as the financial system changes. But what types of changes in the financial system are relevant to the size of V? A standard list of such changes reads:

continued...

Box 5.1 continued....

(a) the frequency with which income is received;
(b) expenditure patterns and the timing of payments;
(c) the degree of vertical integration of industry; and
(d) the extent to which credit is used.

We wish to know how much money people need to hold on average over a period in order to finance the exchange of a given quantity of goods and services. The more money they need to hold, the lower velocity will be. How does each of the points listed above fit in with this?

(a) We assume people receive income in the form of money — either cash or direct payments into a sight deposit at a bank. Much depends on what alternatives are available for the holding of wealth in relatively liquid but income-earning form. Can people easily and cheaply move part of their income from money balances into income-earning assets and be able to convert those assets into money when they wish to enter into exchange? The frequency with which income is received is only a small part of what is involved here. Still, other things being equal, we might expect that people are more likely to hold lower average balances of money if they receive their incomes in larger amounts less frequently. Issues of this kind are discussed in Section 5.5. Of course, much depends on the definition we use of M (see Section 2.4 on official definitions of money).

(b) Given the possibility of moving from money to income-earning assets and back, the amount of money people need to hold on average is influenced by the frequency with which they undertake transactions or have to pay for them — *ceteris paribus*, the less often they spend, the less money they need to hold on average.

(c) Some transactions occur for which money is not needed because they take place within a firm — the firm is vertically integrated. The exchange is recorded in the separate books of the various parts of the firm but settlement in money might never occur or occur only infrequently as a net figure.

(d) This follows on from the second part of (b) — the frequency of payment. The greater availability of credit allows exchange to occur but payment to be postponed.

Now answer the following questions. What is likely to happen to the size of V if:

(a) people start to make much greater use of credit cards?

(b) there is a wave of mergers among firms leading to greater vertical integration of industry?

(c) many people who used to pay gas, electricity and telephone bills each quarter, now do so by monthly direct debit payments?

(d) instead of buying fresh food daily from their local markets, people buy frozen food in major shopping expeditions once a month?

(e) people, who used to receive their salaries once a week in cash are now paid monthly directly into their bank accounts?

The replacement of T by y in the Quantity Theory equation implied that real income was a constant proportion of transactions and, as we mentioned above, excluded financial transactions from consideration. This undermined much of the logic of the original Quantity Theory[3] and brought the theory into line with the Cambridge approach and the later portfolio models of the demand for money. In these, the central question is why people wish to hold part of their real resources (real income, wealth) in the form of money, a question which we have seen did not arise in Fisher's version of the Quantity Theory.

Endogenous money and the Quantity Theory

From one point of view, it makes little sense to talk of endogenous money in conjunction with the Quantity Theory since exogenous money was one of its central assumptions. However, it is worth recalling here the point we made in Section 4.4 that if M is not controlled by the authorities, the causal direction of the relationship is reversed. Changes occur in the economy that lead to a change in the demand for bank loans. This, in turn, changes the level of bank deposits and, hence, M. Endogenous money is one, but as we shall see below not the only, way of undermining the conventional conclusions of the Quantity Theory.

The Quantity Theory and rates of change

We have told the story here in the traditional way in terms of the money stock and price levels. As has been clear in earlier chapters, however, in a growing economy, it makes more sense to talk of rates of change. None of the argument is altered thereby. The central message of the Quantity Theory is then that changes in the rate of growth of the money supply determine the rate of inflation.

5.3   The Cambridge Cash Balance Approach

The Cambridge cash balance approach, which first appeared in the UK towards the end of the 19th century, attempted to cast the Quantity Theory into the form of demand and supply analysis, which was becoming prominent in other areas of economics. An assumption of a change in an exogenous money supply clearly prompted a question about the demand for money. An increase in the money supply, *ceteris paribus*, disturbs the equilibrium in the money market and the consequent change must continue until the demand for money increases to the new level of the money supply. It then becomes natural to ask why people choose to hold money. One might still answer this question in terms of the role played by money in exchange, but demand is essentially a subjective concept and the analysis of demand allows psychological factors as well as institutional arrangements to be considered.

In all of the several versions of the Cambridge approach, people wish to hold a part of their real resources in the form of money (thus the concern is with the real value of money demanded):

$$Md/P = kw \qquad \qquad ...5.5$$

where Md is the demand for money; w = real resources (wealth); and k (the *Cambridge k*) expresses the relationship between them. That is, it is a relationship between two stocks (of money and of resources) rather than a relationship between a stock and a flow as in the Fisher version of the Quantity Theory.

The definition of real resources varied but was always a long run concept, retaining an important element of the Classical model. In long-run equilibrium, savings, rather than being held as money, are invested leading to an increase in the economy's resources. The individual's demand for money depends on:

(a) the convenience and feeling of security obtained from holding money;

(b) the expectations and total resources of the individual; and

(c) the opportunity costs of holding money.

The nature of the financial system, which determines V in the Quantity Theory appears here only as an element in (a) and (c).

Since the convenience obtained from holding money derives from its functions as a medium of exchange and store of value, it was still possible to think of k as a constant and to draw the same policy message as that coming from the Fisher version of the Quantity Theory. This can be seen by formally comparing the two. We begin with the Cambridge equation:

$$Md = kPw \qquad \qquad ...5.6$$

Firstly, we need to convert the stock of resources into a flow of output. Since output is produced from the economy's stock of resources and since both theories related to long-term equilibrium, we can assume w/T constant.

Thus, let

$$w = c\overline{T} \qquad \qquad ...5.7$$

giving us:

$$Md = kPc\overline{T} \qquad \qquad ...5.8$$

and:

$$Md1/ck = P\overline{T} \qquad \qquad ...5.9$$

With c and k both constant, we can define Fisher's V as the inverse of ck and write:

$$Md.\overline{V} = P\overline{T} \qquad \qquad ...5.10$$

Finally, we assume the money market to be in equilibrium with $Md = Ms$. Thus,

$$M\overline{V} = P\overline{T} \qquad \qquad ...5.11$$

The two versions of the Quantity Theory appear very similar. In both, as long as money is exogenous, increases in the price level result from an excess supply of money. The demand for money function in the Cambridge version is stably related to w and, hence, to T.

Nonetheless, there are important differences between the Quantity Theory and the Cambridge approach.[4] Firstly, the Cambridge approach makes use of marginal analysis and extends the general neo-classical model to the money market. It is, thus, a forerunner of the later portfolio models of Milton Friedman and James Tobin dealt with below.

Secondly, the factors influencing V in the Fisher version are only a subset of those influencing k in the Cambridge version. The inclusion of the opportunity cost in the Cambridge version makes k potentially more subject to short-term change than is V. The possibility at least exists that people might choose to hold money for purposes other than engaging in the exchange of goods and services. Crucially, it gave a potential role to the rate of interest. Keynes, as early as 1923 in *A Tract on Monetary Reform* (JMK Vol IV), showed how the incorporation of inflationary expectations could produce changes in the price level, in the absence of changes in the money stock. In *The Treatise on Money* (1930 and JMK Vols V and VI), he argued that changing expectations regarding security prices might cause changes in nominal interest rates. In *The Treatise*, his price equation did not include the money stock at all. The opportunity cost of holding money was assuming greater importance.

5.4   *The General Theory* and the demand for money

Keynes's (1936) theory of the demand for money as treated in *IS/LM* analysis is widely known. It is a part of his general model, which deals with the determination of short-run income, output, and employment. In terms of the Fisher equation, T is replaced by y, but y is subject to change since it is endogenous — the real and monetary sectors of the economy are interdependent. The assumption that money is neutral is removed.

The analysis of the monetary sector dealt only with financial assets and was limited to two such assets: money and non-maturing, fixed-interest-rate bonds (consols). This limited choice of assets arises because, in a simple Keynesian model, savers (households) and investors (firms) are separate: households do not own firms and do not invest. Saving is defined as the difference between current disposable income and consumption expenditure. The purchase of real assets by households is part of consumption expenditure rather than a form of saving. Savings are held in the form of money or other financial assets. The plans of investors, on the other hand, are typically long-term. They seek to raise funds for investment by selling fixed-interest long-term bonds to households. The bond market acts as a vital link between the money market and the goods market.

Pause for thought 5.2:

Why might Keynes have assumed only two types of financial asset when we all know that there are many others? Does this form of simplification seriously damage a model in the analysis of events in real world economies?

Three motives are distinguished for holding money: the transactions, precautionary and speculative motives. The first two are related to current consumption expenditure and, following on from Keynes's theory of the consumption function, their principal determinant is current income.

There is a precautionary demand for money because people do not know exactly what their consumption expenditure in the current period will be. The transactions demand for money depends on their consumption expenditure plans, but, in an uncertain world, their plans may not be fulfilled. *Ex-post*, consumption and saving may differ from their *ex-ante* (planned) values, requiring the quantity of money needed for transactions *ex-post* to differ from the planned level. When planned saving is less than planned investment, income rises, causing actual saving and consumption to be higher than planned. The quantity of money needed to undertake consumption is higher than if people's plans had been fulfilled. Equally, when planned investment is lower than planned saving, actual consumption is less than planned consumption and money held for transactions purposes will lie idle. However, the costs of holding too little money are likely to be greater than those of holding too much money, causing people to hold precautionary balances.

Pause for thought 5.3:

What are the likely costs of holding lower money balances than those needed for transactions purposes?

There are, thus, two effects of lack of certainty about the level of consumption on the income velocity of money: (a) more money will be held on average to finance a given value of transactions, causing V to be lower on average than it would otherwise be; and (b) in a recession, V will be lower still. The precautionary demand for money alone allows us to predict that the income velocity of money will move pro-cyclically, rising during booms and falling as income falls in recessions.

Figure 5.1: Demand for active money balances

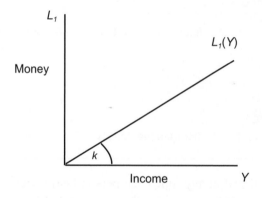

Despite its importance, the precautionary demand for money is usually elided with the transactions demand for money as:

$$L_1 = kY \qquad \qquad \text{...5.12}$$

where L_1 stands for the demand for money for transactions and precautionary motives (active money balances), Y is nominal income, while k expresses the relationship between active money balances and nominal income and is assumed constant. Figure 5.1 shows the demand curve for active balances.

There is no particular role for the rate of interest here. It could be one of many parameters underlying the demand for active money balances and, thus, changes in the interest rate might cause shifts in the curve.

In *The General Theory*, the principal relationship between the demand for money and interest rates derived from the third motive — the speculative demand for money (the demand for idle balances) This provides an argument for an inverse and unstable relationship between interest rate and the demand for money and hence an inverse and *unstable* relationship between the money stock and the income velocity of money.

To understand this relationship, we must consider the choice households face in allocating their savings between money and bonds. Money pays no interest but is free of risk; the reverse is true for bonds. In deciding whether to hold bonds, market agents must compare the interest rate payable on bonds with the risk of capital loss in holding them. This requires a decision regarding the likely future bond price. In the case of bonds that never mature, this depends entirely on the relationship between the rate of interest payable on bonds currently held and the expected interest rate on bonds to be issued in the future.

Pause for thought 5.4

How important is the expected future interest rate in the explanation of the price of bonds that mature:
(a) in 2025?
(b) in 2015?
(c) in 2005?
(d) at the end of 2003?
How does your answer to (a) differ from that to (d)?

Keynes assumed that at any time each person held a view of the likely interest rate in the economy; that is, of the interest rate he regarded as 'normal'. Thus, when a person thought the current interest rate to be below the normal rate, he would anticipate a rise in interest rates and a fall in bond prices and would switch from bonds to money.⁵ The reverse would apply when the current rate was thought to be above the normal rate. For each individual, then, the normal rate was the rate at which he was happy with his present holdings of bonds and money and had no incentive to switch from one to the other.

 regressive expectations endnotes

Pause for thought 5.5

What attitude to risk is being assumed in the theory of the speculative motive for holding money? Is this consistent with the attitude to risk assumed in the precautionary motive?

At any time, the current rate would be below the normal rate of some people and above the normal rate of others. Thus, some people would be switching from bonds to money, some would be moving in the opposite direction, while others would be content with their existing position. For the market as a whole, the average view of the normal rate was important since if the current rate were below this average view, more people would wish to switch from bonds to money than the reverse. The bond price would fall and the interest rate rise until equilibrium was restored.

It would also be true that, given an existing set of individually-held views of the normal rate, a fall in the current rate of interest would lead to an increase in the proportion of people believing the current interest rate to be too low and would increase the number of people wishing to switch into money. That is, falls in interest rate, *ceteris paribus*, cause an increase in the demand for money.

We can now complete the picture. Starting from a position of equilibrium in the money and bonds markets, an unanticipated increase in the supply of money causes interest rates to fall and this increases the demand for money to increase. That is, part of the increased supply of money is held in the form of increased speculative money balances. Let us consider this in terms of a modified form of the Fisher equation:

$$\bar{M}V_Y = Py \qquad \qquad ...5.13$$

where V_Y is the income velocity of money. M is under the control of the monetary authorities as before. An increase in the money supply pushes down the rate of interest and causes an increase in speculative money balances. Since this is unrelated to current income, V_y falls. This weakens the impact of the increase in M on the left-hand side of the equation. How much does V_y fall? This is difficult to say since we do not have any information about the views held by people of the normal rate of interest. However, when interest rates were low, V_y might fall considerably — the interest elasticity of the demand for money would be high — since few people would think it likely that they would fall further. Many people would, indeed, anticipate a rise in interest rates and a fall in bond prices. The demand for speculative or idle balances (L_2) can be written as:

$$L_2 = f(i) \qquad \qquad ...5.14$$

where i is the rate of interest. This negative relationship between the interest rate and the demand for money is shown in Figure 5.2.

Figure 5.2: The demand for idle balances

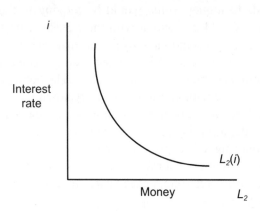

Of even greater importance than the existence of a perhaps powerful negative relationship between the interest rate and the demand for money is the question of the *stability* of the curve. Although each person holds his own view of the normal rate of interest, this must be heavily influenced by his estimate of the views held by other people in the market. Although he might see no objective reason for interest rates to rise, he will know that if sufficient people believe it is going to rise, bond sales will increase and bond prices fall. The most important information to have about a market is what other market participants think and are likely to do. Views of the normal rate of interest are, thus, highly subjective and open to change.

Consider the impact of a change in the average view of the normal rate. We start with the current rate of interest equal to the average view of the normal rate and assume that the average view changes in favour of a higher normal rate. This would cause many people to believe that the current rate was likely to rise and to seek to switch out of bonds into money. Since the current rate has not changed, we can only represent this in Figure 5.2 by shifting the curve to the right. With an unchanged money supply, the demand for idle balances would increase and V_Y would fall, causing a fall in Py. If views regarding the normal rate were at all volatile, the speculative demand for money curve would be unstable.

Even without this possible instability, the theory of the speculative demand suggests that the supply of money and the demand for money are not independent of each other. An increase in the supply of money pushes interest rates down and this encourages an increase in the quantity of money demanded because of the movement of the current rate away from the normal rate.

Keynes's motives approach was for many years the standard theory of the demand for money, although there were important differences from the version given here. In the standard version, the demand curve for speculative balances was linear, which does not allow for the possibility that the demand for money might be much more interest elastic at low rates of interest. In addition, the normal rate of interest was assumed constant, removing the possibility of unpredictable shifts in the demand for idle balances. Thirdly, the role of the bond market in providing investment funds for firms was ignored. Falls in interest rates were assumed to increase investment but the question of how this investment was to be financed was not tackled.

This accounts for a fourth motive for demanding money (the *finance motive*), which Keynes did not include in *The General Theory* but proposed later. The finance motive applies to any large, non-routine expenditure but the need to finance investment projects is crucial. The demand for money to meet such expenditure is only temporary and may be met by the sale of liquid assets or by borrowing from banks. It is of some importance because it provides an additional argument for instability in the demand for money since Keynes argued that investment plans were volatile, being much influenced by the level of confidence of firms.[6]

In summary, Keynes's writings suggest that the demand for money varies inversely with the rate of interest (or, if interest is paid on money balances, with the difference between the interest payable on financial assets and that payable on money balances). In addition, the demand for money curve might shift with changes in expectations about future interest rates and with the need to meet unpredictable expenditure including the financing of investment projects.

Box 5.2 Common criticisms of Keynes's speculative demand for money

1. The theory of portfolio choice is incorrect - the speculative demand implies that people hold all money or all bonds, depending on what they believe is likely to happen to the rate of interest in future. They do not do this in practice.

2. The assumption of regressive expectations is unrealistic. Pg 106 –endnotes.

3. The normal rate of interest is exogenous and no explanation is given of what determines it.

4. The restriction to only two assets — money and consols — is too limiting.

5. The liquidity trap is a logical impossibility since not everyone can switch from bonds to money — someone must hold the existing stock of bonds.

6. Savings deposits should not be included in the money stock.

Keynes's approach to the demand for money was, then, radically different from anything that preceded it, however much its origins can be traced in the works of earlier writers or in his own earlier ideas. Firstly, we are concerned with nominal money balances. Secondly, we have an analysis of short-term *disequilibrium*. Because of this, the demand for money may be highly interest elastic (especially in periods of falling interest rates) and the demand for money function might be unstable.

It is hardly surprising that the theory was much criticized. The most common criticisms are summarized in Box 5.2.

The first criticism concentrates on portfolio choice. In Keynes's theory, any expectation that the interest rate is about to change causes people to hold either all money or all bonds. A belief that the interest rate is about to rise (and bond prices to fall) causes a switch entirely out of bonds into money. The reverse case, an expectation of an interest rate fall, causes people to switch entirely into bonds in order to make the expected capital gain. But rational behaviour dictates portfolio diversification and the holding of a mixture of bonds and money. It is clearly unrealistic, at a microeconomic level, for a fear of a fall in bond prices to cause a switch entirely from bonds to money (and *vice versa*).

This is particularly objectionable to economists who wish to construct macroeconomic models on microeconomic foundations, a view that implies that the behaviour of the economy as a whole can be analysed only as the sum of individual activity. However, treating the economy as the sum of a set of microeconomic decisions might cause us to misunderstand important aspects of the macro economy. It is certainly possible to construct a macroeconomic model that has unrealistic microeconomic assumptions but still produces an accurate analysis of the behaviour of households as a group. In this case, since people hold different views of the normal rate of interest, at any time some people will be moving to holding all bonds, others to holding all money. Yet, as we have seen, a fall in the rate of interest causes a net increase in the demand for money. As long as this increased preference for money over bonds as interest rates fall happens in practice, Keynes's model produces the correct macroeconomic outcome, even if it fails to describe accurately what individual agents do. In any case, the criticism can be handled by increasing the number of financial assets in the model, a point we consider below.

Pause for thought 5.6

Why does rational portfolio behaviour lead to the holding of a mixture of bonds and money rather than all bonds or all money?

2nd
Criticism   The second criticism concerns the assumption of regressive expectations and the lack of explanation of how each agent forms his view of the normal rate of interest. In practice, many examples can be found in markets of extrapolative expectations — where a change in price causes people to believe that the price will continue to move in the same direction. Thus, the assumption of regressive expectations may seem unreasonable. More importantly, since there is no explanation of how people decide on the normal rate, there is no way of analysing the factors that might cause it to change. Again, since people hold different views of the normal rate, we cannot distinguish a clear set of market expectations other than to say, as we have above, that the lower the current interest rate is, the more people are likely to think that the next move will be up. This provides an explanation of the negative relationship between interest rates and the demand for money but gives no indication of the steepness of that slope or of whether the money demand curve is likely to be stable.

However, the assumption of exogenous expectations is important since it explains why market participants can only guess at what other market participants might do in response to a change in interest rates. This unpredictability of the market lies at the heart of the argument for an unstable demand for money. If we knew how market participants formed their views of the normal rate of interest, we would be able to predict accurately how the market was going to behave and the speculative element in the demand for money would disappear.

3rd
Criticism   Thus, the criticism of the normal rate of interest ignores the world to which Keynes's theory applies — one of disequilibrium in which uncertainty is endemic, with knowledge of the future being 'fluctuating, vague and uncertain'. It is not a world in which meaningful probabilities can be assigned to all possible outcomes. Since expectations are subject to sudden change from panic fears and rumours, they cannot be modelled formally as an endogenous variable. Thus, changes in expectations regarding interest rates cause changes in the demand for money (and the demand for bonds), and produce shifts in the demand for money curve.

Further, in the complex world of market psychology, in which much depends on how people think other people will act, many possibilities arise. For example, the majority feeling in the market following an interest rate fall may temporarily be that the interest rate will continue to fall (extrapolative expectations). Nonetheless, everyone will be aware that at some point people will begin to sell bonds in order to realize their capital gains. This is more likely the lower the rate of interest currently is. Everyone will wish to sell out before the market turns, although the attempt to do this will cause bond prices to stop rising and the interest rate to stop falling. Indeed, the fact that the interest rate is changing may, in itself, cause expectations regarding the future rate to change. The idea of regressive expectations based on a normal rate of interest provides a shorthand way of expressing the macroeconomic outcome of a complex set of market interactions. To criticize it as an inadequate theory of microeconomic behaviour is to misjudge its purpose.

Pause for thought 5.7

In football programmes on television, viewers are sometimes asked to choose the best three goals of the month in order. In fact, to win, a viewer must guess correctly what the judges think were the best three goals. Does this provide a reasonable analogy with market behaviour — that what people in markets do is to try to guess what other people think, rather than to attempt to understand underlying real forces?

4th
criticism   Another common criticism relates to the limitation of choice to two types of asset leaving us with only one rate of interest. Gowland (1991) points to the existence of a large number of capital-certain assets, such as building society deposits, whose value does not vary with interest rates. He argues that people not wishing to hold bonds may hold these assets instead of money and that Keynes's theory is a theory of the demand for short-term capital-certain assets in general rather than a theory specifically of the demand for money.

However, Keynes's choice of two assets at the extremes of the spectrum of degrees of liquidity of financial assets was not intended as a realistic description of financial markets but as a means of clarifying important issues. In particular, we have seen that the two-asset model derives in part from the separation of households from firms. In relation to these issues, the inclusion of a variety of financial assets lying between money and bonds on the liquidity spectrum does not change the analysis.

UK firms no longer raise a significant proportion of investment funds through the long-term bond market. Allowing for this merely transfers some of the uncertainty associated with changing interest rates from households to firms. Assume, for instance, that firms borrow investment funds short-term from banks at variable interest rates. Now, any fear of future interest rate rises increases firms' estimates of the likely costs of investment funds and reduces their demand for them. As the government increases the monetary base of the economy, banks may be more willing to lend, but firms become less willing to borrow. Firms accumulating profits for future investment are influenced in their decisions regarding the deployment of their savings in the same way as are households. Fear of a rising interest rate leads them to prefer greater liquidity and they are more likely to hold funds in the form of money or short-term securities than to invest in plant and equipment.

5th
Criticism The final criticism is aimed not at the theory as a whole but at the *liquidity trap* — the extreme state in which any increase in the money stock is held as speculative (idle) balances. In a liquidity trap, therefore, any increase in the money supply has no impact on the interest rate and hence no impact on aggregate demand. A liquidity trap, then, implies the existence of a minimum rate of interest for the economy — a rate that is so low that everyone thinks the next interest rate move must be up. Therefore, everyone believes that bond prices will fall and no one wishes to hold bonds. Everyone switches from bonds to money; but this must involve a fallacy of composition because it is not possible for everyone to hold money rather than bonds. Someone must hold the existing stock of bonds. Gowland (1991) argues further that the bond market will always be in equilibrium (because of low transactions costs and zero storage costs) and that, in the aggregate, it will not be possible for investors to exchange bonds for money. A general expectation that interest rates will fall causes an increased demand for bonds, a rise in bond prices and a fall in interest rates but, at the end of the process, the same quantity of bonds is held as before. Thus, the theory of the speculative demand for money explains who holds money not the quantity of money held. However, this problem also disappears if we assume an uncertain world in which disequilibrium is the normal state of affairs. Then, we could imagine a situation in which all bondholders were *attempting* to sell but could not find buyers. In any case, the liquidity trap represents the extreme theoretical position of the model rather than being a position likely to be reached by any economy.

5.5   Interest rates and the transactions demand for money

The criticisms of Keynes's theory led economists to find other ways of justifying some of Keynes's message, in particular the inverse relationship between interest rates and the demand for money. One approach was to return to the transactions demand for money and to show the way in which this could be influenced by changes in interest rates. The best-known model of this kind is the Baumol/Tobin *inventory-theoretic model* (Baumol, 1952; Tobin, 1956).

In this model, balances set aside for transactions purposes are held temporarily in the form of securities, which may be converted into money when needed to purchase goods and services. The demand for money is then influenced negatively by changes in the interest rate payable on short-term securities and positively by changes in the transactions costs (brokerage fees, transport costs, inconvenience) in the conversion of money into bonds and back again. All information regarding interest rates and transactions costs is known with certainty.

The model seeks to determine how often it is worthwhile switching between money and income-earning assets within a single payments period. From this, we can calculate the optimum stock of money to be held on average over the period. The model assumes that income is received at a steady rate and is all spent during the period.

Let the transactions costs of buying a financial asset be called a. Switching from money into bonds and back into money costs $2a$. Let i_b be the annual yield on the bond. Let income $Y = £1000$ per month, n is the total number of transactions undertaken. Income is spent evenly through the month at £250 per week. Assume firstly that the transactions costs are zero.

In week 1, £250 (Y/n) is held as money and the remaining £750 is used to acquire interest-bearing assets. Then, in each of weeks 2, 3 and 4, £250 worth of the securities is cashed to finance expenditure. Thus, four transactions are involved ($n = 4$). The formula for the initial holding of the asset is:

$$\left(\frac{n-1}{n}\right).Y = \left(\frac{4-1}{4}\right).£1000 = £750 \qquad ...5.15$$

To find the return from holding bonds over the month we need to find the average holding of bonds over the period. Given our assumption of equal expenditure in each week, this is always half of the initial bond holding $\{[(n-1)/2n].Y\}$. In our simple example here, the holding of bonds is £750 in week 1, £500 in week 2, £250 in week 3 and zero in week 4, an average of £375. The profit (π) from holding bonds over the period can be expressed as:

$$\pi = \left(\frac{n-1}{2n}\right).Yi_b \qquad ...5.16$$

Now, allow for transactions costs. If a is a fixed cost, the total costs of n transactions $= na$ and the net profit from holding assets becomes:

$$\pi = \left(\frac{n-1}{2n}\right).Yi_b - na \qquad ...5.17$$

$$= \left(\frac{Yi_b}{2}\right) - \left(\frac{Yi_b}{2n}\right) - na \qquad ...5.18$$

$$\left(\frac{Yi_b}{2}\right) - \left(\frac{Yi_b\,n^{-1}}{2}\right) - na \qquad \qquad ...5.19$$

The next problem is to find the number of transactions (n^*) that maximizes the net return. To do this, we differentiate (5.16) with respect to n and set the resultant derivative equal to zero:

$$\frac{\partial \pi}{\partial n} = \frac{(n^{-2}.Yi_b)}{2} - a = 0 \qquad \qquad ...5.20$$

$$Yi_b/2n^2 - a = 0 \qquad \qquad ...5.21$$

and

$$Yi_b/2n^2 = a \qquad \qquad ...5.22$$

$$n^2 = Yi_b/2a \qquad \qquad ...5.23$$

Therefore

$$n^* = \sqrt{(Yi_b/2a)} \qquad \qquad ...5.24$$

This gives the formula for the optimum holding of cash balances (M_T). On the assumption that expenditure occurs smoothly over each week, the average holding of money is half that held at the beginning of each week ($Yi_b/2n$) and:

$$M_T = \frac{Y}{2n^*} = \frac{Y}{2}\cdot\sqrt{\frac{Yi_b}{2a}} = \sqrt{\frac{Ya}{2i_b}} \qquad \qquad ...5.25$$

Thus, the transactions demand for money is inversely related to the interest rate. Further, the demand for money increases less than proportionately with increases in Y. That is, there are economies of scale in holding money, and to return the economy to equilibrium following an increase in the money stock (assuming that there is only a transactions demand for money), income must increase more than in proportion to the increase in money supply. It follows that monetary policy has a greater impact on economic activity than would otherwise be the case.

However, the extent of economies of scale depends on the nature of the costs involved. If we assume costs to consist of a fixed and a variable element *(a + bE)* where E is the amount withdrawn each time, the formula becomes:

$$\sqrt{\left(\frac{Ya}{2i_b}\right).\left(1+\frac{2b}{i_b}\right)+2Y.\left(\frac{b}{i_b}\right)^2} \qquad \dots 5.26$$

This considerably reduces the economies of scale involved. With fully proportional costs, they disappear altogether.

In general, the model predicts:

(a) a (real) income elasticity of demand for money between 0.5 (fixed transactions costs) and 1.0 (proportional costs);

(b) an interest rate elasticity between −0.5 (fixed costs) and −2.0 (proportional costs); and

(c) nominal money balances increasing proportionately with prices.

The principal ways in which the basic model has been qualified are listed in Box 5.3.[7]

Pause for thought 5.8

If the transactions demand for money is interest elastic, how does an increase in interest rate affect the demand curve for active balances in Figure 5.1?

The empirical relevance of the model has often been questioned. The earliest attacks were in relation to the demand for money of firms.[8] It has also been argued that the possible gains for an individual are so small relative to the costs (especially if the value of time is taken into account) that the rational individual would not bother switching into bonds and back again.[9] In general, there seems little doubt that the relationship between money, interest rates, and transactions is more complex than in the Baumol/Tobin model. Nonetheless, it retains theoretical significance because of its generation of an inverse relationship between interest rate and the demand for money despite the assumption of perfect certainty.

5.6   Introducing uncertainty into transactions - models of the precautionary motive

Inventory models have been modified to allow for uncertainty in the form of a known probability distribution of receipts and payments. These models introduce the possibility of net payments exceeding money holdings (illiquidity). Results vary a good deal depending on how likely this is assumed to be but, as in transactions models, mean holdings of money are inversely related to interest rates and directly related to the brokerage fee.

Miller and Orr's version (1966, 1968), contains thresholds, with people only changing from money to bonds or vice versa at upper or lower thresholds of money balances. Milbourne (1986) took the Miller-Orr framework and considered within it the impact of financial innovation on monetary aggregates.

Box 5.3; The principal variations on the inventory-theoretic model of the transactions demand for money

(i) With fixed or partly fixed transactions costs, a person does not hold securities at all unless the interest income is greater than the transactions costs of converting money into and out of bonds. Then, a change in interest rate may not cause any change in the demand for money. The inverse relationship between interest rate and the demand for money that the model seeks to demonstrate disappears at low rates of interest.

(ii) The frequency of pay periods and the timing of payments may be influenced by institutional and technical changes (for example, the use of credit cards) and by economic factors such as high and variable interest rates.

(iii) Only the interest rate on bonds is included in the model; but if a firm can use an overdraft facility to obtain money, the relevant rate is the difference between the rate charged on borrowings on overdraft and the rate paid on bonds. Again, the demand for money depends on the relative interest rate if the model is extended to include an interest rate or an implicit interest rate (in the form of bank services provided below cost) on holdings of money.

(iv) The transactions demand for money may be modelled such that money holdings are only deliberately adjusted when they reach upper or lower thresholds.

(v) Individuals can be allowed to save part of their income, acquiring interest-bearing assets for holding long-term as well as for short-term reasons.

(vi) Once it is accepted that some people but not others make money/bonds/money conversions with transactions balances, aggregation problems arise. It can then be shown that almost any elasticity is possible depending on the propensity to save and the proportion of income earned by those who do not make any conversions.

The formal inclusion of interest rates into the precautionary demand for money adds further to the case for an inverse relationship between interest rate and the demand for money, without suggesting that the demand for money function might be unstable.

5.7 Tobin's portfolio model of the demand for money

Tobin's model (1958, 1969) can be seen as a response to the common criticisms of the speculative demand model. It introduces a wider range of assets including equities and real assets. Where, in his 1958 article, Tobin limits himself to the same choice as in Keynes, that between money and bonds, he seeks to remove the apparent dependence on the assumption of regressive expectations and to have each individual holding a mixture of money and bonds. Thus, the model is very much concerned with micro-economic choice behaviour. It is generally regarded as a Keynesian model because the model preserves the possibility of an inverse relationship between the rate of interest and the demand for money and because the transmission link between money and nominal income is indirect — money only influences nominal income through changes in interest rate, rather than directly. However, it also produces a demand for money function that is very likely to be stable and so removes the third of the characteristics of the speculative demand model listed above. For this reason, it can be seem as a misrepresentation of Keynes's ideas (Chick, 1977; Dow and Earl, 1982).

To consider the nature of the demand for money in Tobin's model, we need to concentrate on the choice between money and bonds. This depends on a trade-off between the net income receivable on bonds and the degree of risk associated with the total portfolio of bonds and money (which is assumed to be perfectly liquid and non-interest-bearing). The trade-off aris-es because Tobin assumes people in general to be risk-averse, although it is possible to investigate the effect of an assumption that people are risk-lovers. However, because the general uncertainty prevalent in Keynes's model has disappeared, interest rates are thought to be equally likely to rise or fall, irrespective of both the current level of interest rates and what has happened to them in the recent past: expectations regarding future interest rates are neutral.

In these circumstances, the risk associated with bond holding is much more manageable than in Keynes. Now, for any given level of wealth, we can calculate mathematically the impact of a change in interest rate on both the interest income and the capital gain or loss associated with the holding of different quantities of bonds and money. The capital gain/loss becomes a random variable that is normally distributed around the mean, μ. The total return from bond holding (interest payments + capital gain/loss) is also nor-mally distributed around μ. The standard deviation is used as the measure of risk. The various assumptions are reflected in Figure 5.3.

In the upper part of the diagram, the vertical axis shows the expected return on portfolios while the degree of risk associated with the portfolio is on the horizontal axis. The ray from the origin shows the relationship between risk and return for a given level of interest rate on portfolios com-posed of different proportions of bonds and money. Thus, a portfolio con-sisting entirely of money is located at the origin, with a zero return and no risk. As the proportion of bonds in the portfolio increases, so do both the degree of risk and the expected return from the portfolio.

Figure 5.3: Possible composition of portfolios

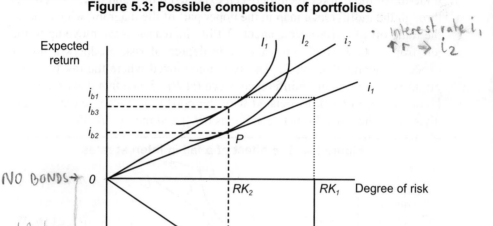

The possible compositions of the portfolio are shown in the lower part of the diagram where $0W$ is the total (fixed) value of the portfolio. The proportion of bonds held in the portfolio is measured down from the origin along the vertical axis. Thus, at the origin, the portfolio contains no bonds, at W no money. The ray from the origin indicates the amount of risk associated with each possible composition of the portfolio, with the extreme positions of all money and all bonds placing us at 0 and RK_1 respectively along the horizontal axis. We can then see from the upper part of the diagram that, at an interest rate of i_1, an all bonds portfolio produces an expected return of i_{b1} along the vertical axis. A mixed portfolio of, say, $0B_1$ bonds and B_1W money involves risk as shown by RK_2 along the horizontal axis and an expected return of i_{b2}. We can see that an increase in the interest rate to i_2 leaves the risk associated with this portfolio unchanged but raises the expected return to i_{b3}.

[margin notes: optimal portfolio ↓; 2 Shaw trade-off between bonds & Money ↓; via indifference map]

To investigate the choice of the optimal portfolio and the way in which this will be affected by changes in the rate of interest, we need to show the trade-off of the market agent between expected return and risk. We do this through the indifference map in the upper part of the diagram, which shows the trade-off of a risk-averse agent. Utility increases as we move up to the left from I_2 to I_1 since on I_2 the same degree of risk produces a higher expected income than on I_1. Utility is maximized where the ray from the origin is tangent to an indifference curve (at P). Since this determines the chosen degree of risk associated with the portfolio, it also determines the division of the portfolio between bonds ($0B_1$) and money (B_1W).

Figure 5.4: The effect of a fall in interest rates

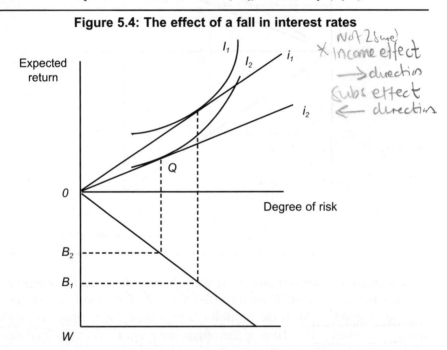

[handwritten on figure: Not 2Sure); ✗ Income effect —→ direction; Subs effect ← direction]

Now we are in a position to consider the impact of an exogenous increase in the money stock. People use excess money balances to buy bonds, causing bond prices to rise and the interest rate to fall: the expected income from any given quantity of bonds falls. The ray in the upper part of the diagram shifts down to the right and (as shown in Figure 5.4) the portfolio-holder maximizes utility at Q on the lower indifference curve I_2. The outcome depends on the relative strengths of the income and substitution effects of the fall in interest rate. Income falls for each degree of risk of the portfolio. To preserve the previous income level, more bonds must be held

[margin note: Income & Subs effects]

(increasing the degree of risk of the portfolio).

The substitution effect operates in the opposite direction since an acceptance of a given amount of extra risk now produces a smaller increase in expected income, making it less worthwhile to choose a higher degree of risk. In Figure 5.4, we make the usual assumption that the substitution effect outweighs the income effect so that a fall in interest rate produces a fall in the holding of bonds and an increase in the demand for money. Thus, part of any increase in the money stock is held in the form of idle money balances, reducing the possible impact on nominal income and causing monetary policy to be weaker than it would be otherwise.

Since the outcome for each individual depends on the relative strengths

---

Pause for thought 5.9

When interest rate rises, is it the income or the substitution effect that causes the demand for money to fall? Why?

---

of income and substitution effects and since there may be some risk-lovers in the economy, there is no reason to believe that the demand for money will be highly interest-elastic; nor that the aggregate demand for money curve will be unstable. The curve will only move if there is a widespread change in people's attitude towards the risk associated with holding bonds. However, since there is no general uncertainty in the economy and since risk is defined as the standard deviation of a normal distribution, this is unlikely. Certainly, there is no possibility of the demand for money curve shifting in response to an increase in the stock of money.[10] ✳

5.8   Monetarism and the demand for money

The term 'monetarism' was first used by Brunner (1968) and has since been defined in a variety of ways. Mayer (1978) identifies twelve propositions associated with monetarism, but for our purposes here, we can be content with what he identified as the narrow meaning — the view that changes in the money stock are the principal cause of changes in nominal income. In line with this, we continue to assume an exogenous money supply and concentrate on Milton Friedman's demand for money.

Money is demanded by two groups:

(a) ultimate wealth holders (for whom money is simply one way in which they may hold wealth); and

(b) business enterprises (for whom money is a productive resource).

The theory concentrates on ultimate wealth holders. Their demand for money can be analysed in the same way as the demand for any asset. We can consider the demand for money as a whole rather than needing to consider separate 'motives' for holding money. Thus, the demand for money function contains:

(i) a budget constraint (either permanent income or wealth);

(ii) the prices of the commodity itself (money) and its substitutes and complements (Friedman sees the counterparts of these as being the rates of return on money and other assets);

(iii) other variables determining the utility attached to the services rendered by money relative to those provided by other assets (these may include the degree of economic stability, the variability of inflation, and the volume of trading in existing capital assets);

(iv) tastes and preferences.

When Friedman refers to 'wealth' as the budget constraint, he intends total wealth — the sum of *human* and *non-human* wealth. Since this is impossible to measure, Friedman suggests the use of permanent income (the expected future stream of income generated by the stock of human and non-human wealth) as a constraint. There is also a theoretical complication with the use of total wealth as a budget constraint since there are institutional restrictions on the conversion of human into non-human wealth and so human wealth is less liquid than non-human wealth. Friedman explains this by saying that it is only possible to buy or sell the services of human wealth, not the wealth itself. Another way of thinking about it is to compare the relative ease of obtaining a bank loan using as collateral: (a) non-human wealth (a portfolio of government bonds, say); and (b) human wealth (an expected degree, which will allow the holder to earn a higher salary in the future). This difference in liquidity between the two forms of wealth means that the composition of wealth influences the demand for money. An increase in human wealth relative to non-human wealth reduces the overall liquidity of wealth and will cause people to hold the non-human proportion

Pause for thought 5.10:

Why is it possible only to buy or sell the services of human wealth, not human wealth itself?

of their wealth in a more liquid form than previously. In other words, the demand for money will increase.

Friedman's demand for money function

Putting all this together, we arrive at Friedman's 1970 version of his revised quantity theory:[11]

$$Md/P = f\,[Yp,\ w;\ i_m,\ i_b,\ i_e,\ (1/P).dPe/dt,\ u] \qquad ...5.27$$

where:

• P is the price level. It is included because the demand for money is a demand for real balances and a change in P changes the real value of money holdings. Thus, P is *positively* related to *Md*.

• *Yp* is permanent income, introduced as a proxy for wealth because of the difficulties involved in measuring wealth. As in Friedman's consumption theory, permanent income was taken as an exponentially weighted average of past and current levels of income. *Yp* is *positively* related to the demand for money.

• w is non-human wealth/wealth and is *negatively* related to the demand for money.

• i_m is the rate of return on money itself and is *positively* related to the demand for money.

• i_b is the rate of return on bonds, abstracting from the possibility of capital gains and losses. It is *negatively* related to the demand for money.

• i_e is the rate of return on equities, abstracting from the effects on equity prices of changes in interest rates and the rate of inflation. It is *negatively* related to the demand for money.

• $(1/P).dPe/dt$ is the expected rate of inflation, included as the rate of return on real assets. It is also *negatively* related to the demand for money. Note that the demand for money is positively related to the price level, but negatively related to the expected rate of inflation.

• u is a portmanteau symbol standing for other variables affecting the utility attached to the services of money and also includes tastes and preferences. It may be either negatively or positively related to the demand for money.

The rates of return in the above equation are expected variables. Although we have indicated the likely signs to be attached to the variables in the above equation, in Friedman's view the signs should be determined principally by the data.

Although this is a theory of the demand for money and we have seen that the original Quantity Theory (as distinct from the Cambridge version) was not a theory of the demand for money, Friedman regarded his theory as a 'restatement' of the Quantity Theory.[12] We can show why with some assumptions and a little manipulation. Let us first multiply both sides of (5.27) by $1/Yp$. This gives us:

$$Md/(PYp) = g[i_b, i_e, i_m, (1/P).dPe/dt, w, u] \qquad ...5.28$$

Next, assume that the demand for real balances is stably related to the small number of variables we have on the right hand side and replace the whole expression by k. Then we re-arrange to produce:

$$Md = kPYp \qquad ...5.29$$

As we did with the Cambridge version of the Quantity Theory, we can define k as the inverse of velocity and arrive at:

$$MdV = PYp \qquad ...5.30$$

With the money market in equilibrium, we have:

$$MV = PYp \qquad ...5.31$$

This looks very similar to the Fisher version of the Quantity Theory. Of course, $1/k$ in this model is quite different from Fisher's V. The factors determining Fisher's V appear only as one element in u in Friedman's model. Friedman's theory can be defended as a restatement of the Quantity Theory if the money supply is exogenous, causality runs from left to right, the demand for money is a stable function of the small number of variables summed up in k, and Yp, as a long-run measure of real income grows steadily over time. Then, the price level is explained by changes in the stock of money. We could easily, as we did with the Quantity Theory itself, express this in terms of rates of change and say that Friedman's theory supports the view that the cause of inflation is a too-rapid growth in the money supply.

Friedman made use of permanent income in the above equation to explain apparently conflicting long run and cyclical tendencies. His historical studies of money in the US economy suggested that in the long-run as income rose, V fell but that over the business cycle, there was a tendency for V to rise in booms and fall in recessions. The argument rested on the proposition that if the demand for money were a function of permanent income, it would fluctuate less *ceteris paribus* than if it were a function of current income. As income rises in the boom of a business cycle, people continue to base their demand for money on their permanent income, which is now lower than current income because part of current income is positive transitory income. The demand for money falls in relation to current income and V rises. In the trough of the business cycle, transitory income is negative, the demand for money rises in relation to current income, and V falls.

We have not said anything about the demand for money of business enterprises. Friedman himself says little except to point out some differences from that of ultimate wealth holders. Thus, he notes that:

(i) The constraint is different; it is not permanent income or wealth since firms can influence the total amount of capital in the form of productive assets by borrowing through capital markets. Not much work has been done on the best scale variable for firms. Friedman suggests three possibilities: total transactions, net value added, and net worth.

(ii) The distinction between human and non-human wealth is not relevant for firms.

(iii) The rates of return relevant to firms are different from those for ultimate wealth holders, for instance, bank loan rates may be more important for firms than for households.

Despite these differences, Friedman treats the equation for ultimate wealth holders as the aggregate demand for money function for the economy, while observing that the inclusion of firms makes problems of aggregation more difficult. The problem of aggregation, however, causes little real difficulty. This is because of Friedman's methodological approach. Having indicated a number of variables likely to be of importance in an aggregate demand function, he argues that the ultimate test of theories is their ability to predict accurately. Since he believes the demand for money to be a stable function of a small number of variables, the variables to be included in the equation, the form that they take and the relationship between them may be changed in order to produce the desired result. Testing, in effect, takes over from theory, although the aim of the testing is to demonstrate that the basic theory is correct.

Before the middle of the 1950s, there had only been a small amount of empirical work on the demand for money. Since Friedman's formulation of his demand for money function, however, relatively little attention has been paid to the theory of the demand for money.

5.9   Microeconomic transactions models of the demand for money

Since Friedman's Revised Quantity Theory, theoretical work on the demand for money has been far outweighed by the huge number of empirical studies. We have already considered the post-Keynesian advocacy of endogenous money and mentioned the buffer stock approach to the demand for money in Chapter 4. Since the buffer stock approach is best seen as an attempt to find a theoretical justification for empirical results, we return to it in Chapter 6. Apart from these, the only developments have been microeconomic transactions models that have grown from attempts to justify the holding of money for transactions purposes within general equilibrium models. The most prominent models of this kind (McCallum, 1989; McCallum and Goodfriend, 1992; Dowd, 1990) analyse the demand for money in terms of the *shopping time* saved in carrying out transactions through the use of money (as distinct from barter). Shopping time saved has value since it can be used to earn income or to obtain utility from other uses.

In McCallum and Goodfriend's (1992) version, an agent maximizes present and future utility from the consumption of goods and leisure. He currently holds a stock of bonds and money (the purchasing power of which is eroded by expected inflation); and the economy provides a stream of opportunities for the earning of further income by selling labour services and for re-arranging consumption over time through a capital market in which bonds may be bought and sold. Consumption goods can be obtained in exchange for income only by shopping for them.

The amount of time required for shopping increases with the quantity of consumption goods bought, but is negatively related to the size of real money balances carried on shopping trips. It follows that a decision to hold more money now, *ceteris paribus*, reduces shopping time, leaving more time for current leisure and/or increased labour supply and future real income. Equations can be derived from the model for current and future demands for consumption, leisure, bond holding, money holding, and the supply of labour.

These are highly theoretical models that were principally intended to overcome criticisms that general equilibrium theory did not provide a role in the economy for money. The demand for money function that can be derived from them can be compared with Friedman's. In McCallum and Goodfriend, the demand for money is related to inherited assets; expected unearned income (non-human wealth); current and expected future wage rates (human wealth); interest rates and inflation rates. Since decisions about current money holding are part of a utility-maximizing strategy governing future plans as well as current behaviour, the demand for money depends on expected future values of interest rates and inflation as well as current values. The model also implies that the current volume of market transactions is chosen simultaneously with the demand for money — real income does not determine the demand for money: both are simultaneously influenced by deeper underlying forces.

5.10 The theory of the demand for money: a conclusion

The central issue dealt with in this chapter has been the question of the stability of the demand for money function. This has long been seen as crucial in relation to economic policy because it determines whether the authorities can hope to influence the rate of growth of nominal income by controlling the rate of growth of the money supply. All of the writers we have dealt with here, with the exception of Keynes, have proposed theories that support the idea of stability. Although there are important differences between the views of, say, Tobin and those of Friedman, strictly from the point of view of the relevance of demand for money theory to economic policy, the important distinction is between Keynes and the others; and a large proportion of that debate rests on the dispute over the speculative demand for money.

We have seen that the major criticisms of Keynes's theory arise from its claimed lack of microfoundations. The problem with theories based upon microeconomic reasoning is that they provide us with individual demand for money functions and leave aside the problem of aggregation, even if difficulties involved in it are mentioned from time to time. This becomes a genuine difficulty when we arrive, as we have done with Friedman, at the proposition that theories can be best judged by their ability to predict. Clearly, if we are to say anything at all meaningful about policy, it is the aggregate demand for money that we need to predict. We shall see in Chapter 6, that this leads to the opening up of a gulf between the theories discussed here and the empirical work, and casts doubt on both.

There is, of course, an even more serious problem. All of the reasoning about the importance of the demand for money is based upon the importance of knowing what factors in the economy will change in order to cause the demand for money to return to equality with an exogenously determined money stock. We have seen in Chapter 4 that this is at odds with reality. We shall see in Chapter 7 that this can cause serious differences to arise in the approach taken to the transmission mechanism of monetary policy.

5.11 Summary

The Quantity Theory of Money is not a theory of the demand for money but has been very influential and can be related to later theories of the demand for money. The theory contained a number of variations and was far from the inflexible idea that is studied today. However, the simplified model based upon the equation of exchange and assuming a constant transactions velocity of income provides the important policy messages that lie at the heart of one of the major approaches to monetary economics — that changes in an exogenous money supply produce proportional changes in the general level of prices and that money is neutral in relation to real income. The replacement in the expression of the Quantity Theory of transactions by income undermined the logic of the original theory but brought it more closely into line with the first major theory of the demand for money, the Cambridge cash balances approach, which was being developed at the same time. The Cambridge approach introduced important changes because the demand for money was treated at a microeconomic level and was, like other demand functions in economics, subjective. However, most proponents of the Cambridge approach accepted the policy conclusions of the Quantity Theory. This was not true of Keynes who, in 1936, proposed a radically different theory of the demand for money based upon the motives for holding money. This gave interest rates a much more important role in the theory and raised the possibility that the demand for money function might be unstable. This led to the view that monetary policy might be relatively weak, especially when the economy was in a depression. It also raised the question of whether the authorities could hope to control the rate of inflation through changes in the rate of growth of the money supply. In doing this, it elevated the role of fiscal policy in the management of the economy.

Keynes's theory was heavily criticized, particularly because it was said to be overly concerned with the short run and lacked microfoundations. There followed a series of attempts to explain the demand for money so as to retain some of Keynes's message (notably that the demand for money was interest-elastic) but to do so in a less controversial way. These included the incorporation of interest rates into transactions and precautionary models of the demand for money and the reformulation of the speculative demand for money as an asset demand. Even the notion of interest-elasticity was reduced greatly in importance in Friedman's demand for money theory. Friedman saw his theory as a return to the spirit of the Quantity Theory in the sense that he sought to re-establish the importance of controlling the money supply as the means of controlling inflation. This required a return to the acceptance of a stable demand for money function. Although Friedman's initial approach was theoretical, he suggested that the form of the demand for money function could only be determined by empirical testing. Thereafter, apart from some developments that grew out of general equilibrium theory, the focus of academic work on the demand for money shifted away from theory to econometric testing.

Key concepts in this chapter

Quantity Theory of Money	normal rate of interest
equation of exchange	active money balances
transactions velocity of money	idle money balances
income velocity of money	disequilibrium
stability of the demand for money function	liquidity trap
	inventory-theoretic model
motives for demanding money:	portfolio models of the demand for money
transactions motive	
precautionary motive	human wealth
speculative motive	non-human wealth
finance motive	
The Cambridge k	shopping time

Questions and exercises

1. Economics generally tells us that one must analyse the factors influencing both the demand for and supply of important variables. Why, then, might the demand for money not be of great importance from the point of view of economic policy?

2. Why is the Quantity Theory of Money not a theory of the demand for money? What is it a theory of?

3. Given the various points mentioned in Box 5.1 as influencing the velocity-of money, would you expect the long-term velocity of money to have increased or decreased over the past fifty years?

4. How is the interpretation of the Quantity Theory equation affected by the assumption of endogenous money?

5. Why is the Cambridge k more likely to change than is V in the Quantity Theory?

6. Both the precautionary and the speculative motives for holding money arise from the existence of uncertainty — uncertainty about what in each case?

7. Why is the speculative demand for money a demand for idle balances? What happens to the velocity of money when idle balances increase?

8. Why was the speculative demand for money so controversial?

9. Both the inventory-theoretic model of the transactions demand for money and Tobin's portfolio model are commonly called Neo-Keynesian models. Why?

10. Why did the testing of the demand for money grow rapidly at the expense of theorizing about the demand for money after Friedman published his theory?

11. What are the particular characteristics of monetarist models of the demand for money?

12. In Chapter 1, we mentioned the view that the value of money in exchange arises because of the existence of incomplete information in markets. How does this relate to shopping time models of the demand for money?

Further reading

A great deal has been written about the theory of the demand for money. For a quite different approach to the historical approach taken here, see Howells and Bain (2002). Other good textbook treatments can be found in Laidler (1993) and Gowland (1991). For more detailed treatments than is found here see Lewis and Mizen (2000) or Handa (2000). For an essay on the demand for money that manages to dismiss Keynes in a few lines as a victim of money illusion see McCallum and Goodfriend (1992). Post-Keynesian explanations of Keynes's finance motive for holding money are in Rousseas (1986) and Wray (1990).

6 Testing the Demand for Money

'Money is a Merchandize, whereof there may be a glut, as well as scarcity', Sir D North, *Discourses upon Trade* (1691).

What you will learn in this chapter:

- The weakness of the link between the theory of the demand for money and the testing of it
- The difficulties in carrying out any demand for money test
- The form and results of early demand for money tests
- The problems that arose with the stability of demand functions in the 1970s and 1980s
- The possible link between financial innovation and tests of the demand for money
- Econometric explanations of the instability shown in testing in the 1970s and 1980s
- The buffer stock approach to the demand for money
- Sceptical views regarding the stability of the demand for money function

6.1   Introduction

As we saw at the end of Chapter 5, the focus of academic work on the demand for money since the late 1950s has been empirical. There are a number of problems associated with testing the demand for money. To begin with, the theory we are meant to be testing is based upon theories of household demand (or, much less often) of the demand for money by enterprises. However, we wish to draw messages for monetary policy about the aggregate demand for money. In Section 6.2, we consider the lessons we might draw from theory about the form of the aggregate demand function. Unfortunately, we discover that theory is not very helpful in this regard. We go on to consider the many difficulties involved in testing demand for money functions. In section 6.3, we look at results. Testing seeks to establish whether the demand for money function is a stable function of a small number of variables, as Friedman has claimed (see Section 5.8). Early tests suggested that this was indeed the case. We look at this work, but then confront the problem that a number of studies carried out in the mid-1970s in the USA and the UK seemed to raise doubts about the *stability* of the function. These tests provide the focus of attention of Section 6.4. Since that time, much of the effort put into demand for money studies has gone into explaining the apparent instability. Most researchers have attempted to show in one way or another that the problems were, indeed, only apparent and did not seriously undermine the conventional theory of the demand for money. The principal areas of endeavour have been in improving the econometric techniques used and in studying financial innovation and its effects on the demand for money. As well, the buffer stock theory of the demand for money was developed to show how some of the empirical findings could be explained within the framework of neoclassical theory. In section 6.5, we look at views sceptical about the notion of a stable demand for money.

6.2 Problems in testing the demand for money

We suggest in Section 4.4 that if money is endogenous, the demand for money might not be very important. However, since much of past monetary economics has assumed an exogenous money supply, the demand for money has seemed central to many of the debates on the value of monetary policy.[1] Consequently, we sufficiently felt the need to conform to past views to spend Chapter 5 looking in some detail at the theory of the demand for money, only to find that it raised a number of questions but did not provide answers. In particular, the theories differed over two issues that would be crucial if the supply of money were exogenous:

1. The extent to which the demand for money is sensitive to changes in the rate of interest; and

2. whether the demand for money function is likely to be stable.

The only possible way of resolving these issues appeared to be through testing. A logical starting point for this is to derive from that theory the independent variables we wish to include in the equation to be tested. Based on our discussion in Chapter 5, this might give us a list something like the following:

- The interest rate on representative non-money assets, possibly including the rate of inflation

- The interest rate on money

- The transfer costs of switching between money and non-money assets

- The level of current income or wealth/permanent income

- The variance of income

- The expected change in the rate of interest

- An index of prices.

Unfortunately, we can immediately see several practical difficulties associated with testing any equation derived from this list. These are summarized in Box 6.1. We consider each of them below. However, we must first mention a more general problem. Where we are required to make choices regarding the form of the variables to be included in the testing equation (for example, among different definitions of money), we shall see that theory provides little or no help. This usually results in the choice being made on pragmatic grounds — which form of the variable 'tests better'. But what does this mean? It means that we do not ask whether the demand for money is stable. Rather we ask how we can construct a demand for money function that appears to be stable over a particular period. The presumption of almost all of the thousands of tests that have been conducted over the past half-century has been that the demand for money is stable. Equations that don't produce the right result are discarded. The proposition can never be disproved because there are always changes that can be made to the equation being tested or new tests to be conducted. It is a rigged game. Still, let us do as we promised and look at each of the difficulties separately.

Box 6.1: Problems in the testing of the demand for money

(a) There is no agreed definition of money for testing purposes;

(b) The demand for money is not directly observable;

(c) The assumption of an endogenous money supply creates an identification problem;

(d) There are problems in the choice between income and wealth as the scale variable and difficulties in the measurement of wealth;

(e) There are problems with the selection of the interest rates;

(f) Variables, all of which should be included as independent variables may be correlated with each other, making it difficult to isolate the specific relationship between each variable and the demand for money;

(g) Some of the variables in our list may not be easily measured or measurable at all;

(h) There are problems in the choice of time period for the testing.

(a) There is no agreed definition of money for testing purposes

Theories are of little help here. The transactions motive for holding money suggests a narrow definition (currency + sight deposits), but there are problems with theories based on the speculative demand or the proposition that money yields a flow of services. In the latter case, the definition of money must be an empirical matter. Some Keynesians stress the difficulty of distinguishing money from 'near-money' and are, thus, likely to prefer broad definitions to include assets that are close substitutes for narrow money in terms of liquidity.

When we have settled on a preferred definition of money, we must match it as closely as we can to an official definition used in the collection of money stock statistics. We have seen in Section 2.4, the extent to which official definitions change over time, and in Box 3.1, the variety of definitions of money in use in different countries. This has always made the choice difficult, but the use of official definitions has been complicated by financial innovations that have changed both the roles of financial institutions (and thus the extent to which their liabilities may act as money) and attitudes towards the various types of financial assets. Consequently, most empirical work settles for the most readily available and consistent definitions and ignores questions of theoretical justification. Most use currency + the sight deposits of banks or add banks' time deposits.

Pause for thought 6.1:

Why might there be a difference between:

(i) the relationship between interest rates and demand deposits; and

(ii) that between interest rates and time deposits?

Attempts to use broader definitions run into additional complications. Then, explicit interest rates may be payable on some elements of the chosen measure but not on others. Some elements may be positively related to interest rate changes, others negatively. Further, the demand for non-interest-bearing components of the stock is likely to be more closely related to income than that for interest-bearing components since the latter are more likely to be held as part of savings balances. One way of trying to deal with these problems is to replace the conventional aggregates with Divisia indexes, which we discussed in Section 2.4. In these, weights are attached to the various types of deposit to take account of different degrees of liquidity as measured by rates of interest. Some success has been achieved with the use of these in demand for money functions in the sense indicated above — Divisia indexes tend to give a better statistical fit than unweighted aggregates and demand for money functions incorporating them appear more stable (Chrystal and MacDonald, 1994; Belongia, 1996). This may well be because they are better able to deal with financial innovation than are the conventional aggregates (Mullineux, 1996). None the less, many problems remain including that of the implicit interest rate on sight deposits (Barnett *et al*, 1984; Lindsey and Spindt, 1986).

(b) The demand for money is not observable

We can observe the quantity of money currently being held but not whether it is being *willingly* held. If the money market is in disequilibrium, with people, on average, attempting to increase or decrease their money holdings, measuring the quantity of money does not measure the demand for money.

  If we assume the money market is always in equilibrium and the money supply exogenous, we can make progress. Consider Figure 6.1. Let the money supply be MS_0, the interest rate i_0 and the money supply equal to the demand for money $(Md) = 0A$. Let the money supply increase to Ms_1. The interest rate falls to i_1, as we move instantaneously to a new equilibrium at Y with $Ms = Md = 0B$. With a further increase in the money supply and a further fall in interest rate to i_2, we move to Z with $Ms = Md = 0C$. Then, we might assume that the demand for money curve is being traced out as the exogenous money supply schedule shifts along an unchanging demand for money curve.

Figure 6.1: Equilibrium in the money market

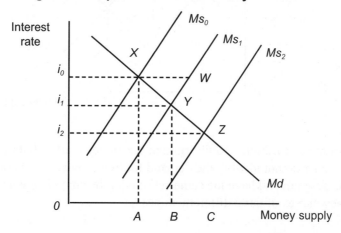

However, Figure 6.1 applies only if we are confident that we are not inadvertently measuring the supply function or the combined effects of both demand and supply. Before we can relate observations of the money supply to the level of income and the rate of interest and call the result a demand for money function, we must be sure of two things:

(i) that the supply function of money shifts independently of the demand function (that is, that the money supply is exogenous, as assumed in Figure 6.1); and

(ii) that such observations lie on the same demand for money function.

(c) Endogenous money supply creates an identification problem

It would be perverse of us to continue to assume (i), given our support for the notion of endogenous money in earlier chapters. Consequently, let us assume the money supply is endogenous, with the same set of variables influencing both the supply of and the demand for money. Then, the demand and supply curves move together. One possibility is shown in Figure 6.2.

Figure 6.2: The identification problem with endogenous money

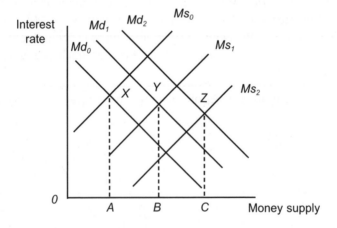

We continue to assume equilibrium in the money market, but now the points X, Y and Z do not identify the demand for money curve. We could draw the same diagram and have the same set of equilibrium points with demand for money curves of quite different slopes.

Pause for thought 6.2:

If we assume an endogenous money supply, can we identify a money supply curve from information about changes in the money stock as interest rates change?

Investigators attempt to overcome this problem by employing techniques that enable supply and demand functions to be fitted simultaneously, but there is clearly a serious problem. If we drop the equilibrium assumption, another problem emerges, even if we assume an exogenous money supply. In Figure 6.1, following an increase in the money supply from Ms_0 to Ms_1, the initial movement may be to W rather than directly to Y. We would, then, need to consider the speed of the movement to Y and the path taken.

(d) Problems in the choice between income and wealth as the scale variable

We suggest above that choosing a narrow definition of money implies a concentration on the role of money as a medium of exchange. This, in turn, seems to lead to the use of *GDP* or Total Final Expenditure (*TFE*) as the scale variable. Unfortunately, the demand for money is a stock variable while *GDP* and *TFE* are flow variables.[2] This can cause difficulties. In addition, in demand for money theories in which the demand for money is an asset demand rather than a transactions demand, wealth, a stock variable, is the constraint on the holding of money. Early empirical work on demand for money functions was dominated by this controversy over the choice between measured income and wealth as the scale variable.

The first difficulty in trying to resolve this issue is that the desire to include wealth always introduces measurement problems. Khusro (1952) and Grice and Bennett (1984) constructed a series on financial wealth for the UK and used it in their studies. However, this is a much narrower wealth concept than is suggested by the theory. Data permitting the construction of long time series for various broad measures of the aggregate level of private sector nonhuman wealth, real as well as financial, exist only for the USA. Even there, broad measures have seldom been constructed because of aggregation problems, especially the problem of double counting in the aggregation of the wealth of households and firms combined.

Because of the absence of reliable statistics for wealth, it was often represented in studies by data on permanent income. This has the added benefit of incorporating income from human as well as non-human wealth, as required by Friedman's theory (see Section 5.8). On the other hand, permanent income is not observable. It has most often been measured as an exponentially weighted average of current and past values of income, on the assumption of adaptive expectations. Later, rational expectations were used. This might still lead to the modelling of expectations formation as some sort of averaging process of current and past values of income, but this would depend not on exponentially declining weights but on the way in which income moves over time.

In general, wealth seemed to perform better (that is, produce more stability) than income (Meltzer, 1963; Chow, 1966; and Laidler, 1971). The support for wealth was, however, not conclusive. These studies used permanent income as the wealth variable. When promising results were obtained in studies using a lagged dependent variable in formulations with measured income (Feige, 1967; Laidler and Parkin, 1970; Goldfeld, 1973), it was suggested that the apparent superiority of permanent income might have arisen because it captured important adjustment lags rather than demonstrating the benefit of including a long-term measure. However, later studies (Hall, Henry and Wilcox, 1989; Adam, 1991) appeared to confirm that models of broad money in the UK performed better with the inclusion of an explicit wealth term.

Pause for thought 6.3:

Why is there a problem in including in an equation for testing a variable (such as human wealth), the measurement of which depends on a separate theory of the way in which expectations are formed?

A variety of alternatives has been tried. Consumption has been used as a proxy for wealth because it moves more closely with permanent than with measured income (Mankiw and Summers, 1986; Faig, 1989). Another possibility explored was the inclusion of both wealth and income terms. Expenditure has been used as a broader alternative to income (Goldfeld and Sichel, 1990; Mankiw and Summers, 1986; Hall, Henry and Wilcox, 1990). This takes us back to the idea of transactions as the constraint and closer to the spirit of the Quantity Theory. Some studies have, indeed, attempted to employ the value of transactions, but this also produces many measurement problems. We return to the use of transactions in Section 6.5.

e) Problems with the selection of the interest rate

There would be little point in including the interest rate on more than one non-money financial asset since interest rates on financial assets tend to move together. This leaves us with the question of which interest rate to choose. Theoretically, the answer should be the rate available on the closest substitute for money since this should best represent the opportunity cost of holding money. However, the closeness of substitutes varies with the definition of money, which itself varies as innovations in very liquid assets take place. Even with a constant definition of money, the choice of the closest substitutes for money changes through time.

Still, short-run commercial debts seem closer substitutes for money than long rates and, therefore, more relevant. On the other hand, long rates are more representative of the average rate of return on capital in the economy and incorporate expectations of future inflation rates. On both grounds, they may be thought a better guide to the general opportunity cost of holding money than the yield on short-run commercial debts. In any case, while theoretical considerations may be of some help, the choice, in practice, of the most appropriate interest rate requires knowledge of institutional detail. For example, the rate on long-dated gilts might seem correct in a financial system in which secondary trading was thin and costly and securities were generally held to maturity. The growth and development of the secondary gilts market, however, and the changes, especially after 1986 in the UK,[3] made all gilts extremely liquid. Long gilts like shorts can be sold cheaply and easily for cash in 24 hours.

Whether or not absolute changes in the rate(s) on non-money assets represent changes in the opportunity cost of money depends on what is happening to money's 'own rate'. In a world where bank deposits do not pay interest, money's explicit own rate is zero and absolute changes in rates on non-money assets necessarily indicate changes in opportunity cost. An intermediate situation applies where deposits pay interest but at rates that are probably low but, above all, are sticky. This was the position in the UK until the changes of *Competition and Credit Control* introduced in 1971. Once deposits began to pay market-related rates, changes in money's own rate meant that changes in the 'spread' or differential between the rate on money and the rate on other assets indicated a change in the opportunity cost of holding money. Furthermore, where some deposits (and notes and coin) still pay no interest and where banks offer premium rates for differing terms and conditions, theory suggests that money's own rate should be indicated by a weighted average of deposit rates.

In theory at least, the spread between money's own rate and the rate charged on bank lending should also influence the demand for money since spending in excess of income can be financed either by running down liquid assets or by borrowing. Sprenkle and Miller (1980) pointed out that when the rate on overdrafts and the rate on deposits are equal, the demand for overdrafts will become infinite. The significance of this observation is widely recognized in studies of the demand for bank lending. It is less frequently recognized that there is also an implication for the demand for money since the attraction of overdrafts, when this spread approaches zero, arises from a reluctance to run down liquid assets. Clearly, the growth of interest bearing deposits and the resulting changes in money's own rate are involved here as well. Furthermore, financial innovation may be implicated in changes in the other part of the spread, the cost of bank lending. Competition between banks and building societies to lend for house purchase in the 1980s, and again 2000-02, led households in the UK to build up their holdings of floating rate debt.

This also altered dramatically the composition of their bank debt as the share made up of personal loans and overdrafts diminished while the share of mortgage debt rose. Before 1990, mortgage lending was charged at rates close to base rates with the result that at any given level of interest rates the average cost of bank debt, weighted by its components, was falling. The attractiveness of borrowing from banks while building up liquid assets was possibly further reinforced by the increasing ease with which bank credit became obtainable — a decline in the non-pecuniary costs of borrowing.

Pause for thought 6.4:

What are the non-pecuniary costs of borrowing?

In practice, the choice of interest rate may be limited to a small number of series by the availability of data over a long period. For this reason, studies in the USA were constrained for a long time to use either the yield on 20-year corporate bonds or the yield on 4 to 6 month prime commercial paper.

Much work has been done on the term structure of interest rates. Laidler suggests that the most satisfactory theory says that (with suitable adjustment for risk) expected holding period yields on assets of various maturities tend to be equalised by the market. If the planned holding period of money and bonds is a short one, then the yield on 4- to 6-month commercial paper is more likely to be a good measure of the opportunity cost of holding money than the yield to maturity on 20-year bonds. However, it has been argued that these two series moved very closely together and thus that, for the purposes of testing for the importance of interest rate on the demand for money function, one was probably as good as the other.

(f) Independent variables may be correlated with each other

When this occurs, the easiest thing to do is to omit one of the variables. However, this might then become a source of problems. Consider a simple testing equation. By assuming linear relationships, we may write the demand for money function as:

$$\frac{Md}{P} = \beta_0 + \beta_1 y - \beta_2 i + v \qquad \qquad ...6.1$$

with P being an index of prices, y a measure of real income, i a representative interest rate and v a random variable. This is just a straightforward statement of the demand for money as a function of income and interest rates. For testing purposes, we could convert this into:

$$m_t = \beta_0 + \beta_1 y_t + \beta_2 i_t + v \qquad \qquad ...6.2$$

where m_t equals $(M/P)_t$, a measure of the real value of the money supply, while t indicates the current period. This is usually linearized by taking logs, which smoothes out the data and converts parameter estimates into elasticities, making them easier to interpret. The equation becomes:

$$ln\ mt = ln\beta_0 + \beta_1.lnY_t + \beta_2.lni_t + v_t \qquad \qquad ...6.3$$

A common required addition is the lagged dependent variable (the real value of the supply of money in the previous time period): $\beta_3\ lnm_{t-1}$. This simply accepts that there are bound to be time lags in adjustment and thus it is a reflection of the idea that a movement to a new equilibrium following a change in one of the independent variables will not be instantaneous. However, in the early days of testing it was assumed that these time lags would be quite short and thus that the role of the lagged dependent variable would not be very great. It was hoped to establish this by testing. The other principal hopes in testing were that:

(i) the signs would be as indicated by the theory (most obviously a negative relationship between i_t and m_t;

(ii) that the constants would indeed turn out to be constant;

(iii) that the independent variables (Y_t and i_t) would between them predict a high proportion of the demand for money); and

(iv) that v would prove to be random, indicating that it did not incorporate a missing variable with a systematic relationship with the demand for money.

Suppose, however, that testing shows that v is not random and, thus, that the income and interest rate terms explain only a proportion of variations in m_t. Part of the variations is explained by v. This might be caused by the omission from the equation of an explanatory independent variable. The variable may, in turn, have been omitted because it was correlated with either y or i.

An obvious example relates to nominal interest rates and the expected rate of inflation. An equation containing both of these terms is difficult to estimate because of the high degree of correlation between the two. The correlation makes it difficult to isolate the specific relationship between each variable and money. For this reason, although Friedman included both terms in his theoretical demand for money equation, the usual practice for testing purposes has been to include only the nominal rate of interest. With expected inflation omitted, however, the equation is likely to perform particularly badly in inflationary periods. Other variables often omitted on similar grounds are a wealth term and the own rate of interest.

(g) Some variables in the list may not be easily measured or measurable at all

Transfer costs are difficult to measure since they vary from one individual to another and from one company to another depending on the circumstances. Since it is usually assumed that transfer costs are likely to change slowly over time, they are usually left out of aggregate demand for money equations.

There are no objective *ex-post* measures of the expected variables included in the list. The best we can do is to estimate expected future values of variables based on forecasts using currently available information (making a judgement in doing so as to the best available forecasting model). These estimates can then be entered into the demand for money equation on the assumption of rational expectations — that agents do, indeed, make use of the best available forecasting models. A more usual approach is to replace the expectational variable with an available proxy or to represent it econometrically in some other way (for example by a dummy variable or a trend term).

(h) There are problems in the choice of time period for the testing

Supporters of the notion of a stable demand for money only claim stability in the long run. However, if the demand for money is unstable in the short run, we need to be able to explain why, and do it in such a way that this instability is compatible with long run stability. Further, long run studies (which typically use annual observations or temporally averaged data) face problems because the definitions of many of the variables change over time. Some elements omitted from the equation because they are assumed constant, such as payment systems, do change over time. In any case, the distinction between long run and short-run studies is arbitrary. There is no theoretical definition of the long run in macroeconomics other than the period necessary for the economy to return to equilibrium — a definition that is useless for empirical work.

What can we learn from testing?

One result of these problems is that the standard regression equation used in demand for money testing makes relatively little use of theory beyond taking as a starting point the need to include both an income term and an interest rate term. It is hard, therefore, to argue that it is the theory being tested. Rather, we start with a view of the world that leads to a belief in a stable relationship between the demand for money and real income and we seek to confirm this. Failure to do so does not produce a re-evaluation of the theory or a change of world view but a determination to change the equation and try again. A chapter on the testing of the demand for money in a recent book (Handa, 2000) contains the sub-heading, 'The desperate search for a stable money demand function'. This is an accurate description of much that has gone on. None the less, let us look at the results of all this endeavour.

6.3   Early demand for money studies

Before Keynes's *General Theory*, estimates were made of the velocity of circulation over long periods, with the aim of relating changes in long-run velocity to institutional changes (fitting in with the classical quantity theory of money). After the publication of *The General Theory*, attempts were made to show a positive relationship between interest rates and velocity (and thus an inverse relationship between interest rates and the demand for money). The aim was to demonstrate that an increase in the money stock would produce a fall in velocity, reducing the impact on nominal income. Other studies (Tobin, 1947; Bronfenbrenner and Mayer, 1960) sought to distinguish between idle and active balances and then to relate idle balances to interest rates, on the assumption that interest rates only influenced idle balances and had no role to play in the transactions or precautionary demands for money. Tobin's study covered the period 1922-45, with idle balances taken to be zero in 1929. The study found a relatively close negative relationship between interest rates and idle balances. Bronfenbrenner and Mayer also found a clear negative relationship between the demand for idle balances and the rate of interest. The main problem with both studies lay in arbitrary definition of idle balances. This led to the growth of general demand for money studies in which no distinction was made between the two types of balances. These became by far the most common form of study from the early 1950s on.

The form of general demand for money studies

We suggested above that general demand for money studies involve the testing of equations of the type:

$$m_t = \beta_0 + \beta_1 y_t + \beta_2 i_t + v \qquad \qquad ...6.2$$

This is a reduced form equation that regresses the demand for a measure of money on measures of income and interest rate. No attempt is made to derive the parameter estimates of an underlying structural model. This has been taken by some writers as a 'monetarist' approach,[4] although Friedman argued that the dispute over the use of large models was almost entirely independent of the Keynesian-monetarist controversy. Mayer (1978) points out that small reduced-form models go well with the view that changes in the money stock have effects through a large number of channels, since a large structural model would not be able to pick all these up and a reduced-form approach might be more reliable. He also suggests that the approach suits monetarists because they are concerned only with the supply of and demand for money, not with allocative detail. If one takes the stability of the private sector as given, there is no need for large models to examine erratic factors in various sectors.

Pause for thought 6.5:

What is implied if, in equation 6.2, v is not a random variable?

The vast majority of reduced-form studies have used highly aggregated time-series data. These studies set out to find:

(a) which variables should be included in the function, for example, income or wealth, long or short interest rates;

(b) whether the demand for money is correctly specified in real terms (that is, whether the price elasticity of the demand for nominal money balances is equal to unity);

(c) the interest elasticity of the demand for money; and

(d) whether the function is stable, with
    (i) significant and stable co-efficients; and
    (ii) most of the variation in the demand for money accounted for by variations in interest rate and income.

Equations of this type were estimated, using different sample periods and different forms of both the dependent variable and the explanatory variables. Functions were estimated for both the long-run (using annual data over periods ranging from around 30 to over 100 years) and the short-run (mainly with quarterly data, mostly over time periods between 5 and 20 years).

Most short-run studies incorporated time lags, with equilibrium assumed to occur only in the long run. In these models, long-run equilibrium was disturbed by a change in income or interest rates but, because of adjustment costs, agents were assumed to adjust only slowly towards the new equilibrium level of desired money balances. Thus, a two-stage decision process was assumed: in the first stage, the long-run optimal amounts of assets to be held were determined; in the second stage the optimal speed of adjustment to long-run equilibrium was decided. The adjustment path was assumed to have no impact on the optimal long-run demand for the asset.

The second stage decision was modelled according to the partial adjustment hypothesis: that the change in the demand for money in the current time period is a fraction, θ, of the gap between the desired (long-run or equilibrium) demand and the actual demand in the previous period. Thus, $0 < \theta < 1$, and the smaller θ is, the slower is the adjustment to the new equilibrium. We have:

$$m_t - m_{t-1} = \theta(m_t{}^* - m_{t-1}) \qquad \qquad ...6.4$$

where $m_t{}^*$ is the long-run equilibrium level of real money balances.
    Adding m_{t-1} to both sides gives:

$$m_t = \theta m_t{}^* + (1 - \theta)m_{t-1} \qquad \qquad ...6.5$$

This shows that the observed demand for money at time t is a weighted average of the desired money demand at that time and the demand for money in the previous period with θ and $(1-\theta)$ being the weights. Equation 6.2 could then be taken as a simple long-run relationship for the demand for money, with 6.5 being substituted into it:

$$m_t = \theta\beta_0 + \theta\beta_1 y_t + \theta\beta_2 i_t + \theta v + (1 - \theta)m_{t-1} \qquad ...6.6$$

Dynamics were later introduced into the equation by replacing current income with expected income. This was usually modelled with adaptive expectations but, later, rational expectations were incorporated. Other models sought to incorporate the learning process of agents (Cuthbertson and Taylor (1987a, 1989). Partial adjustment equations were formulated in both real and nominal terms. The approaches were different but the results similar.

The interdependent asset adjustment model (Brainard and Tobin, 1968) provided a variation on simple partial adjustment models. In these, the speed of adjustment in money holdings depended on disequilibrium in other asset markets as well as in the money market. Less formal interpretations were based on the idea that economic agents altered their behaviour according to 'signals' that they were out of equilibrium (simple feedback models).

Pause for thought 6.6:

Explain the role of the lagged dependent variable in testing equations of the demand for money.

The results of early general demand for money studies

Early long-run studies included those of Latané (1954), Meltzer (1963), Laidler (1966, 1971) and Chow (1966) all for the USA, and Kavanagh and Walters (1966) and Laidler (1971), for the UK. Short-run studies of note included Heller (1965) and Goldfeld (1973) for the USA, and Laidler and Parkin (1970) and Goodhart and Crockett (1970) for the UK.

Despite considerable variations in detailed results, there was considerable agreement up until the early 1970s in both the USA and the UK. It was broadly accepted that:

(i) the demand for money was interest elastic but elasticities were relatively low. There was a general tendency for UK figures to be higher. Despite the existence of a small number of extremely high figures in short-term studies, long-term elasticities were, on balance, greater than short-term ones, indicating the existence of a time lag. No evidence was found for an infinite elasticity of the demand for money, seemingly denying the existence at any time of a liquidity trap. The elasticity found was generally lower when short interest rates were used.

(ii) No clear preference had at that stage been established between income and wealth. Current income, permanent income and wealth had all proved statistically significant. Widely different income elasticities were estimated but most studies produced similar results, although again results differed between the USA and the UK. Most US studies produced estimates close to unity, as against figures comfortably below one in the majority of UK long-run studies. UK results thus appeared to provide some support for the existence of economies of scale in the demand for money.

(iii) The demand for money appeared to be correctly specified in real terms but with an adjustment lag.

(iv) Time lags between interest rate and income changes and the demand for money seemed from long-run studies to be relatively short with three-quarters of the adjustment occurring in the first year and 90 per cent within two years. However, this was called into doubt in short-run studies in both the US and the UK, which suggested much longer lags.

(v) The importance of expected inflation in normal times remained open to doubt, especially in US studies.

(vi) Demand for money functions appeared to be reasonably stable.

(vii) No clear preference was established between narrow and broad definitions of money. In general, the interest elasticity of the demand for money was found to be lower, the broader the definition of money used. There was some suggestion that if a narrow definition of money were used, a long interest rate produced better results, whereas a short interest rate was preferable with broad money.

Thus, the conclusions of the various tests were relatively favourable to the monetarist position. The inverse relationship between money and interest rates seemed clearly to have been established but this posed no problems so long as the long-run elasticity was small and the function was stable.

The stability of the demand for money appeared to be confirmed by Friedman and Schwartz (1963) in a study of velocity. They found that measured income velocity in the USA had fallen on average by one per cent per year over the previous century, from 4.6 to 1.7 but that short-run variations in velocity were relatively small compared with changes in the money stock. This suggested that the demand for money had been reasonably stably related to nominal income around a long-run upward trend. Further, they claimed that the short-run variations that had occurred had reinforced rather than offset movements in the size of the money stock (in contrast to the notion embodied in Keynes's speculative demand for money).

6.4 Problems and responses since the 1970s

In the 1970s, problems appeared in both the UK and the USA — where Goldfeld named the problem 'the case of the missing money' (Goldfeld, 1976). In the USA between 1973 and 1975, real money balances steadily declined, whereas demand for money equations estimated with data for the 1950s and 1960s had predicted a mild decline in 1974 followed by a recovery in 1975. Thus, existing demand for money equations were seriously *over-predicting* the demand for money.[5]

In the UK, too, the demand for money function began to show signs of instability. There, however, equations from the 1950s and 1960s *underestimated* the demand for money (Artis and Lewis 1974, 1976; Hacche, 1974). Equations also broke down in several other OECD countries (Atkinson and Chouraqui, 1987).

Box 6.2: Explaining the apparent instability of demand for money functions

1. The problem was econometric in nature — demand for money equations had been misspecified or the dynamics of short-run models were inadequate. All that was needed was to improve the econometrics.

2. There had been changes affecting the arguments of the function, resulting in unpredictable shifts in the demand for money function and/or in the slope of the function. To retain belief in the long-run stability of the function, one then had to argue that such changes were limited to particular periods of time and that once the system had adjusted, long-run relationships would re-emerge. Financial innovations were thought to have been mainly responsible for upsetting earlier predictions.

3. Blame was placed upon the assumption of equilibrium and new approaches to disequilibrium were developed, notably the buffer stock approach to the demand for money — a formalization of the importance of the liquidity of money. A distinction is drawn between 'demanding' money as a means of payment and being willing to 'accept' it temporarily because the costs of adjusting stocks of money are less than those associated with adjusting stocks of less liquid assets.

We should add, however, that some Keynesians and post-Keynesians have argued that the demand for money function should be expected to be unstable and that the findings of the 1960s were an aberration; while others have been highly sceptical about the value of any form of econometric testing as an aid to understanding the complex interaction between people and markets.

The problem showed up in ways other than the failure of equations to predict accurately. For example, extending the data used for estimating equations to include the 1970s produced changes in the coefficient on the lagged dependent variable (for both narrow and broad money), indicating changes in the length of time lags. The coefficient also tended to be very low, suggesting unreasonably long time lags.

Things began to go wrong again in both the United States and the United Kingdom in the early 1980s when income velocity began to fall sharply and demand for money functions estimated on pre-1982 data seriously underestimated the demand for narrow money in the mid-1980s (Stone and Thornton, 1987).

Several explanations of these problems have been put forward, most of which have sought to preserve belief in the view that the demand for money is, in the long run at least, stably related to real income and interest rates. These explanations are summarized in Box 6.2 and considered individually below.

Improvements in econometric techniques

Many criticisms were made of the early econometric tests. For example, Baba *et al* (1992) criticized the standard demand for money equation on a number of grounds, including the omission of the inflation rate and the inadequate inclusion of the own rate on money, as well as incorrect dynamic specification. Concern about the dynamic specification of equations led to the recognition of the inclusion in equations of non-stationary variables (trended variables — such as the money stock and national income — that increase over time and so have no constant mean). Least squares regressions with non-stationary series can produce spurious regressions, biased coefficients and invalid statistical inferences. Non-stationary variables can be made stationary (detrended) by taking differences but using differenced data does not provide estimates of the long-run relationship between dependent and independent variables in the estimating equation. Tests were developed to determine whether variables are stationary or non-stationary (unit root tests) but the problem remains with those money demand functions containing non-stationary variables.

Pause for thought 6.7:

Can you think of non-stationary variables other than money and national income?

However, it was discovered that one might be able to combine data series of non-stationary variables in a linear way to produce a stationary series.

Such combinations are said to be cointegrating and the vectors of the coefficients of these combinations are called the cointegrating vectors. The existence of a cointegrating vector among a set of variables implies an equilibrium (long-term) relationship among them. Variables might drift away from the equilibrium relationship in the short run but the technique of cointegration can provide evidence of the long-run relationship.

Unfortunately, several cointegrating vectors might exist among a set of variables. Among n variables, there are potentially $n-1$ cointegrating vectors. If two or more cointegrating vectors are found, it is not clear from the econometric estimation which vector relates to which economic relationship. To identify a cointegrating vector with a particular economic relationship, such as the demand for money function, judgements must be made based on the expected signs and sizes of the coefficients. Sometimes none of the available vectors possess both the signs and sizes of coefficients expected from economic theory. This could be caused by the sorts of problems that apply to all testing, which we have outlined above. There are ways of trying to get around the difficulties but it remains that, in relation to the demand for money function, even if there appears to be a long-term equilibrium relationship amongst, say, income, the demand for money and interest rates, it may be difficult to obtain reliable estimates of the interest-rate and income elasticities. In any case, the existence of such a long-term relationship does not, in itself, tell us anything about causality and so does not resolve the endogenous versus exogenous money debate.

Further, discovering the existence amongst the data of a long-term equilibrium relationship still leaves the problem of the short-run dynamics. These were tackled by the development of error correction models (ECM). These began to be used in the late 1970s to replace partial adjustment in short-term demand for money models. ECMs combine short-run and long-run elements without imposing restrictions on the lag structure or tying short-run and long-run effects to a single parameter. They were the outcome of the general to specific modelling strategy (Hendry *et al*, 1984) in which a very general equation was used as the beginning point of the search for the best specification of the model. The ECM technique is often combined with the cointegrating procedure to try to explain short-run deviations from the underlying long-run relationship.

In one particular application of cointegration, researchers tried to verify the existence of a cointegrating relationship between the current aggregate price level and the long-run equilibrium price level, labelled *P*-Star. Based on the income version of the Quantity Theory of Money, *P*-Star models assume a long-run equilibrium velocity (that may be either constant or have a deterministic trend) and define *P*-Star as money per unit of real potential output. In other words, the Quantity Theory equation becomes:

$$P^* = (M/y^*)V^* \qquad \qquad ...6.7$$

with y^* and V^* representing long-run equilibrium levels of output and velocity. The models are then used to indicate the existence of inflationary pressures in the economy by comparing current levels of income and velocity with their long-run equilibrium levels. If current income is above long-run equilibrium income, $(y > y^*)$, then, *ceteris paribus*, current income must fall in the long-run, with the existing monetary pressures in the economy being transferred to the price level. Equally, if current velocity is below its long-run level, it must rise in the long-run generating increased expansionary pressure that must fall on y or P. Plainly, if $y = Y^*$, all additional monetary pressure will fall upon P. Thus, short-run movements in the price level are modelled as the product of an output gap, $(Y - Y^*)$, and a velocity gap, $(V - V^*)$. However, the *P*-Star approach suffers from the same problems as other cointegrating studies in that, to obtain definite answers, one must impose on the models assumptions drawn from economic theory, notably here the assumption of a long-run equilibrium velocity of money. We are also left to explain the short-term deviations of V from V^*.

In general, while cointegration studies have been judged useful, they have not yet been able to establish a stable demand for money function with a specific form and invariant coefficients for out-of-sample data. We need, therefore, to consider the principal explanations of the continuing problems with the function.

Shocks to the demand for money function

Economists have proposed a number of possible causes of sudden shifts in the demand for money function in the 1970s and 1980s. These have included:

(i) financial innovations associated with institutional change in the financial sector;

(ii) uncertainty about the rate of inflation as a result of the large swings in inflation rates in the 1970s and 1980s;

(iii) currency substitution, especially following the movement away from fixed exchange rates in the early 1970s.

Although we shall say a little about the second and third of these, we concentrate here on the impact of financial innovations since this has produced by far the greatest amount of lucubration.

(i) Financial innovations and the demand for money

Institutional change is not new. For example, one of the earliest and most fundamental innovations, whose consequences foreshadowed those that would follow from many later ones (Niggle, 1990; Chick, 1986), was the switch from fiat to credit money as banks discovered that they needed to cover only a small proportion of their liabilities with cash. This led the money supply to become the product of private sector institutions whose principal loyalty was to shareholders.

Many institutional changes affect the trend of velocity. They do not always do so in the same direction, but each change has a predictable impact. With financial innovation, for example, transactions costs diminish and, following the Baumol-Tobin inventory model of the transactions demand for money, the quantity of narrow money demanded is, *ceteris paribus*, likely to fall; the income velocity of money should slowly increase over time. On the other hand, the increasing monetization of the economy should have produced a downward trend in velocity. The development of near-money substitutes often associated with financial innovation should produce a fall in the demand for money relative to *GDP* and, hence, an increase in velocity. However, if the increasingly close money substitutes bear interest, a rise in money's own rate of interest relative to other rates may follow, increasing its attraction as a liquid asset and tending to reduce velocity. The net result of all such developments is reflected in the income-elasticity of the demand for money (> 1 with falling velocity; < 1 with rising velocity).[6]

Pause for thought 6.8:

What meaning can you attach to the idea that money might be a luxury good?

But what specific innovations were thought to relate to the question of the apparent instability of the demand for money function in the 1970s and 1980s? The deregulation of financial markets, the introduction by banks of interest-bearing demand deposits, the impact of technological change on financial services, the liberalization of international capital flows and the imposition or removal of controls on bank lending all came into the debate. Policy measures specific to particular economies also played an important role in the discussion, notably, for the UK, the relaxation of lending controls over the period 1971-73.

Technological innovation in the banking and payment systems reduced brokerage charges (including the cost of changing deposits into cash or non-money assets into deposits). Where extensive (and expensive) specialist labour and premises had been previously required, cash deposit and withdrawal facilities began to be offered by retail stores whose computer networks already allowed for payment by credit and debit cards. Electronic communication and ATMs also lowered the cost of entry into some areas of banking activity. Increased competition led to a narrowing of spreads.

These changes had three consequences. Firstly, it gave an opportunity to economize on non-interest bearing cash and an increased desire to hold deposits, giving banks command over a greater proportion of monetary base. Secondly, the virtual automatic access to credit lines provided by plastic cards made it more attractive to hold both debit and credit positions simultaneously, as well as raising the question of whether the unused credit should not be included in a 'truer' measure of money. Thirdly, ATMs offering current balance statements and on-screen home banking services reduced considerably the need for significant holdings of precautionary balances by making it easier for people to manage their money balances with precision.

It has been argued that there is little to worry about in relation to the demand for money function since there is no long run problem. Perhaps the strongest statement of these views came from economists writing in the *Federal Reserve Bank of St Louis Review*. For example, they concluded on one occasion that the US demand for money function had shifted down in 1974 without affecting the income- or interest-elasticities. Hafer and Hein (1979) argued that simply including long-term interest rates in the function and redefining money would overcome the apparent difficulties of the 1970s. In a similar vein, it was proposed that problems arising from the growth of interest-bearing cheque accounts could be countered and the instability of the income velocity of money reduced by excluding interest-bearing cheque deposits from the definition of money. Further, Hafer (1985) claimed that errors resulting from institutional change and financial innovation would, in any case, tend to cancel out in the long-run. However, when demand for money functions estimated on pre-1982 data seriously underestimated the demand for narrow money in the mid-1980s, the notion of simple shifts in the function with nothing else changing had begun to disappear. This later failure was put down to a combination of the effects of: (a) financial innovations; (b) the sharp increase in the volume of the interest-bearing components of the money supply; (c) cyclical movements in GNP; and (d) possibly an increased interest-elasticity of the demand for money.

Suggesting that financial innovation causes occasional shifts in an essentially stable relationship does not explain why the innovations occur when they do. Institutional change is, in effect, assumed exogenous. In practice, it is much more likely that anything that shifts the function will change the elasticities (the slope of the demand curve will change as well as the curve shifting). Consider, for example, the impact of monetary policy. A period of high interest rates may encourage the development of financial innovations, allowing money balances held for transactions purposes to be reduced. This introduces the possibility of a ratchet effect — when interest rates are high, it pays to spend time and effort on the development of financial innovations. In the 1970s and 1980s, for instance, we saw the introduction of concentration accounts (in which funds deposited in other accounts are automatically transferred at the end of each working day), zero balance accounts (that allow firms to do without transactions balances at banks, yet give them the opportunity to write cheques) and automated teller machines. Having been introduced, such innovations are not reversed when interest rates fall again because the costs involved are mainly set-up costs such as computing hardware and software. In this case, it was, therefore, likely that financial innovation increased the interest-elasticity of the demand for narrow money (as movements between demand deposits and high interest-bearing deposits became much easier) as well as causing a downward shift in the function. Thus, monetary policy measures may affect the demand for money indirectly through inducing financial innovations.

Pause for thought 6.9

Do you think the introduction of internet banking has been an important financial innovation? What effect, if any, do you think it will have on the velocity of money?

Since the principal aim of explanations of the apparent demand for money instability has been to retain belief in a stable long run function, it is not surprising that most explicit attempts to include the effects of institutional change on the demand for money, has focused on long-run changes. While Friedman and Schwartz (1982) employed dummy variables to allow for selected institutional changes, the major studies to include institutionally-related variables have been by Bordo and Jonung (1981, 1987, 1990), Siklos (1993), Klovland (1983) and Akhtar (1983). The variables have included bank offices per head of population, the proportion of the labour force employed outside of agriculture, and the ratio of currency to total money stock and of non-bank to bank financial assets. Other efforts have involved the inclusion of past peak levels of interest rates on the grounds that the incentive to innovation comes from changes in costs of which interest rates are an important part (Judd and Scadding, 1982; Goldfeld, 1992).

Again, we have the argument here that an innovation, once adopted, is not usually reversed even when interest rates fall.

Attempts to incorporate the effects of financial innovation by varying the definition or measurement of the independent variables have been concerned largely with the use of Divisia indexes as measures of the money supply (discussed above) and interest rates. In particular, the significance of money's own rate in the demand for broad money has been recognized. The own rate can be entered implicitly as an element in the differential between money's own rate and the rate on other assets (Lee, 1967) or explicitly with the rate on other assets appearing independently (Klein, 1974). Taylor (1987), for example, used quarterly data (1964-85) and general to specific modelling techniques to estimate an equation for changes in UK real M3 balances, which contained a spread term. This was the difference between three-month treasury bill rate, representing the rate on non-money short term assets and the maximum of the seven day deposit rate and high interest cheque account rate, representing money's own rate. The same spread was also significant in the long-run steady state solution. Taylor also reported results obtained by excluding money's own rate and concluded that money's own rate was a key explanatory variable.

Adam (1991) estimated long and short-run equations from quarterly data for UK real M3 1975-86 using a weighted average own rate on money, with the weights and interest rates reflecting each of the components of M3. Other, opportunity cost, interest rates were the yield on bonds (including capital gains) and on eurodollar deposits (adjusted for expected depreciation of sterling), recognising thus the 'innovations' of euromarkets and the abolition of exchange controls. Both money's own rate and the rate on foreign assets were significant in the long-run equation.

We have noted above that empirical work on the demand for money has employed a variety of scale variables in an attempt to capture the effect of, variously, income, wealth, or transactions. This variety is driven more from the controversies that still surround the motives for holding money than by a recognition that financial innovation had changed the appropriate variable. However, it can be argued that the boom in financial activity in the 1980s and 1990s caused non-income transactions to rise as a proportion of total transactions. This raises the possibility of using transactions rather than income as the scale variable. In a comparison of the demand for broad money in the UK and Germany, Arestis, *et al.* (1995) found the coefficient on real GNP for Germany was close to unity, while for the UK it was nearly 1.7. The latter is what one would expect if the demand for money were following a transactions series that was growing more rapidly than GNP.

Many attempts to adjust equations to reflect institutional change did not produce satisfactory results. This may have been largely because of the difficulty of capturing in equations the many ways in which institutional change may influence agents' actions. A particular problem is that, to the extent that they are induced rather than autonomous, the factors causing financial innovations may be taken into account elsewhere in the equation. Yet, however difficult it may be to measure the effects empirically, the scope for financial innovations to modify the demand for money, in various contradictory ways, is considerable. A summary is provided in Box 6.3.

Box 6.3: Possible effects of financial innovation on the demand for money

• liability management affects money's own rate and thus the opportunity cost of holding money

• a change in financial transactions relative to GNP transactions may make GNP an inappropriate scale variable

• a reduction in transactions costs may reduce the demand for precautionary balances but may also lead to more borrowing and larger debit and credit positions

• by creating ever closer money substitutes, innovation may lead to an increase in velocity

• cheaper access to cash may reduce the demand for cash and thus reduce the public's cash ratio, with implications also for money supply

• better access to balance sheet information may reduce the demand for precautionary balances

• better access to financial innovation generally may make agents more sensitive to interest rate differentials leading to more frequent switching between components of broad money.

(ii) uncertainty about the rate of inflation

Most work under this heading has related to uncertainty about the rate of inflation caused by the large swings in inflation rates in the 1970s and 1980s and the changes in exchange rate expectations following the move to floating exchange rates in the early 1970s. Associated with this have been fears arising from the loss of the link between the dollar and gold in the Bretton Woods exchange rate system and the erratic policies which this allowed (Friedman, 1986, 1988). The suggestion is that high rates of inflation in the 1970s reduced the willingness of agents to hold money, producing an increase in income velocity; while the process of disinflation in the 1980s helped to explain the sharp falls.

(iii) currency substitution

It has been argued that instability in domestic demand for money functions may be explained by currency substitution since foreign currency may act as a substitute for domestic currency in economic agents' portfolios either directly or indirectly. Direct currency substitution occurs when economic agents shift into foreign currency when they expect depreciation of the home currency. This may occur because they anticipate expansionary monetary action by the authorities. Occasionally, agents may lose faith completely in the domestic currency and seek to hoard foreign currency.

Indirect substitution takes place through the capital market: assume economic agents revise upwards the expected return on foreign bonds. Selling domestic bonds and buying foreign bonds puts upward pressure on domestic interest rates and perhaps downward pressure on foreign interest rates. With a given demand for money function and, in a floating exchange rate system, a given money supply, interest rates cannot move. Thus, the increased demand for foreign bonds causes the exchange rate to rise (that is, the home currency depreciates) to a level where the expected future fall compensates for the relative fall in the attractiveness in foreign bonds. This fall in the value of the domestic currency promotes inflation. To the extent that the domestic authorities validate the inflationary expectations, total domestic money supply does not fall (the decline in reserves is matched by the increase in the domestic component of the money supply). Meanwhile, in the country to which capital is flowing, reserves are rising, increasing the money stock. The net result is an increase in the world money stock.

With fixed exchange rates, the problem does not arise. Capital exports occur, the domestic money supply falls and the foreign money supply increases until foreign and domestic interest rates differ by an amount expressing the relative attractiveness of foreign and domestic bonds to investors.

This argument was most strongly put forward by McKinnon (1982, 1984a, 1984b) who rejects floating exchange rates on these grounds. It follows from this analysis that the breakdown of the Bretton Woods fixed exchange rate system in the early 1970s was a likely cause of instability in the demand for money function. Some influence of changes in exchange rate expectations have been found. For example, funds were repatriated to France and placed in interest-bearing accounts after France's 1969 devaluation. Nonetheless, over the period 1960-77, neither the collapse of the Bretton Woods system nor severe exchange rate crises in the UK, nor switches between pegging and floating in Canada seem to have had any significant effect on the demand for money.

Pause for thought 6.10:

If currency substitution was important before the beginning of 1999, what effect should the introduction of the euro have had on the stability of the demand for money function in the EU?

The buffer stock response to demand for money problems

We mentioned earlier that demand for money studies allowed for some slowness in adjustment to long run equilibrium positions and sought to model this through partial adjustment. This slowness was justified principally by the existence of time lags but questions were raised about the basis for the inclusion of such lags in financial markets, especially since transaction costs in these markets are usually assumed low.

This concern increased in the 1970s when the evidence appeared to suggest that time lags were lengthening. Indeed, it was argued that following the sharp increase in UK money supply in the mid-1970s, it had remained in excess of the demand for money for several years. It was suggested that, if the supply of money were exogenous but the system out of equilibrium, the 'independent' variables in the function could not be independent at all but must be determined by the interaction of demand and supply. This led some to reject single equation estimations and to claim that the demand for money could only be estimated as part of a complete model of the economy. Since this poses many problems, various simplified approaches were tried. For example, the interest rate was treated as the variable that bears the main burden of adjustment when the demand for money and the supply of money are in disequilibrium. This was modelled by either:

(i) regressing the rate of interest (the dependent variable) on the money supply, now treated as the independent variable, inverting the demand for money function (Artis and Lewis, 1976; Laidler, 1980, 1982; Goodhart, 1984; Wren Lewis, 1984); or

(ii) relating the inverse of velocity to real income, interest rate, lagged velocity and a variable designed to capture exogenous changes in the money stock (for instance, changes in currency holdings, bank reserves, and domestic borrowing requirements).

Both of these methods produced improved results and evidence of stability. However, the value of the inversion of short-run demand for money functions was called into doubt in relation to narrow money by both Hendry

(1985) for the UK and MacKinnon and Milbourne (1988) for the USA.

Some writers accepted that, in practice, monetary authorities act to supply the amount of cash people demand. In other words, narrow money (M1) is assumed to be demand-determined, although equations that have the money supply as the dependent variable conflict with traditional monetarist analysis. That is, short-run demand determines supply, but takes time to adjust to its long-run equilibrium level. Artis and Lewis (1990) query the partial adjustment of the supply of money to the quantity demanded at an aggregate level. They argue that although individuals can adjust to long-run equilibrium by building up money stocks through asset sales, this is only possible at an aggregate level under certain circumstances, for instance when the central bank chooses to stabilize interest rates rather than to control the money stock or when the country is a member of a fixed exchange rate system.

The best known attempt to explain why adjustment may be subject to long and variable lags was provided by Laidler (1984) in the form of the buffer stock approach to the demand for money. Credit is also given, amongst others, to Darby (1972) who first used the term. Other writings on money as a buffer stock include those by Goodhart (1989c), Cuthbertson (1985a) and Cuthbertson and Taylor (1987b).

The buffer stock idea derives from the notion that, given risk and uncertainty, not all events are correctly anticipated and so, following a shock, at least one variable won't be equal to its planned value. However, one can arrange one's affairs so that the shock will fall on a predetermined variable — the buffer. In the buffer stock approach to the demand for money, people accept deviations in money holdings around their equilibrium levels. Assume, as an example, that a long-run equilibrium is disturbed by an expansion of the money supply, causing money holdings to be temporarily greater than the demand for money. To return portfolios to equilibrium, agents would seek to move out of money into other financial or real assets. However, in the short-run, they might choose instead to absorb the shock by holding excess money balances. There are two clear reasons for behaving in this way:

(a) It requires both time and information to monitor money balances continuously (money, this becomes a substitute for information, and

(b) because the adjustment of portfolios is not costless, agents wait until they are convinced that the change is not merely transitory.

It is only when money holdings deviate too much from the equilibrium level (they hit a 'ceiling' or a 'floor'), that funds are transferred out of or into money balances to take them back to the long-run equilibrium level.

Money is assumed to act as a buffer in this process because it is liquid and the costs of adjusting money balances are likely to be less than the cost of adjusting holdings of other assets. If it is relatively easy to borrow, credit might also act as a buffer; but if borrowing is inflexible, money will be the ony buffer and money balances can be expected to fluctuate more.

As we have seen above, it can be objected that transaction and information costs in the financial sector are relatively low, and thus that adjustment should be quick. However, adjustment may be slowed due to stickiness in both interest rates and goods prices and may be spread over a number of months or even quarters. Buffer stocks are then willingly held during this gradual process of adjustment. Economic agents hold money precisely because it acts as a buffer rather than having to strive for an exact value of their money holdings as presupposed in the deterministic demand for money models such as the Baumol/Tobin inventory-theoretic model. Instead they wish to keep their money holdings within a band, monitoring them only at intervals.

Pause for thought 6.11:

Provide some other examples of the use of the idea of buffer stocks.

It follows from the buffer stock argument that observed changes in the real stock of money may reflect either:

(i) a change in one or more of the determinants of the long-term or 'target' demand for money, or

(ii) a shock to the nominal stock of money not accompanied by changes in the conventional money demand variables sufficient to keep the economy on its long-term money demand schedule.

The approach also suggests that instability in the demand for money found in econometric research need not reflect unstable demand for money but rather time-consuming adjustment processes. There is a particular problem with models that assume equilibrium, which are said to be 'backward-looking'. The demand for money function in a 'backward-looking' model may be unstable if:

(a) any of the costs of adjustment change, or

(b) there is a change in government behaviour leading to a change in income.

These problems account for the development of 'forward-looking' models that employ rational expectations. In Cuthbertson and Taylor's (1978b) forward-looking buffer stock model, in which a change in the money supply may lead to a revision of expected income and price levels, a cost function measuring the cost both of being away from equilibrium and of changing money holdings is added to a conventional money demad function. In order to minimise this cost function, agents form expectations of future values of real income, the interest rate and the price level. The model distinguishes between expected and unexpected changes. Whereas an expected future increase in price level or real income or an expected fall in interest rate will produce an immediate increase in money holdings, unexpected changes of this type will not initially do so unless they represent news about a change in the process generating the variable in question. Again, an exogenous increase in the money stock will be communicated only slowly through the money demand function to the price level, real income and the interest rate.

Laidler (1982) claimed that, in the presence of monetary shocks, only the buffer-stock argument offered a convincing theoretical rationale for the presence of a lagged, dependent variable in relatively successful short-run money demand equations. Cottrell (1986) argued that non-demand-related changes in the money stock are common, occurring especially under interest-rate targeting and other supposedly accommodative monetary regimes. Cuthbertson and Taylor (1987b) also suggest that the buffer-stock hypothesis helps to account for both temporal instability in conventional money demand functions and the presence of a long and variable lag in monetary policy. The hypothesis has also been used to explain the finding that the short-term income elasticity of money is low (c.0.2 for the USA) whilst long-term income elasticities are much nearer to unity.

It is clear, then that if buffer-stock money is quantitatively important, conventional specifications of the short-run money demand function are appropriate and, indeed, that any single-equation estimates of the determinants of the demand for money are likely to suffer from serious simultaneity problems. Although the quantitative significance of buffer-stock money has been difficult to establish, Lastarpes and Selgin (1994) suggest that this might have been due to inadequacies in past tests of the hypothesis. Using more recently developed econometric techniques to measure the dynamics of real and nominal money in the USA, they conclude that, especially for M1, exogenous nominal supply shocks play an important role in determining real money balances in the short-run.

6.5 Sceptical views of the stability of the demand for money function

Although heavily outnumbered by believers in the stability of the demand for money, sceptics can be found. They fall broadly into three groups.

a) Believers in endogenous money.

b) Economists who accept the importance of the demand for money function and the testing of it but found the problems of the 1970s and 1980s unsurprising. For them, the instability apparent in tests demonstrated that the function was indeed unstable and that it was the seeming stability of the 1950s and 1960s that was more apparent than real. They put forward a variety of possible reasons for instability.

c) Economists who deny the usefulness of econometrics in attempting to understand economic relationships.

(a) Endogenous money

We have dealt with this at some length in Section 4.4. There we point out that the extreme form of the endogenous money hypothesis holds that there is no demand for money function independent of the supply of money. People are willing to hold whatever money is created through the banking system. We have made it clear in 4.4 that we do not accept this view because we make a clear distinction between the demand for bank loans and the demand for money. It is the demand for bank loans that drives the process and creates money and there remains a question as to why people are willing to hold the quantity of money created. However, this is clearly a secondary question entirely lacking the importance it has when money is assumed exogenous. We discuss a role for the demand for money within an endogenous money model in Section 7.5.

(b) Unstable demand for money functions

There are several arguments supporting the belief that the demand for money function should be unstable even with an exogenous money supply. We outline the principal candidates below.

(b1) Institutional changes (financial innovation)

As we suggested earlier in the chapter, financial markets are subject to waves of institutional changes. The conventional view is to recognize that such changes may cause discrete jumps in demand for money functions but to see these as short-term movements that do not undermine the view that the long run demand for money function is stable. This is because the long-run stability is assumed to depend solely on the rationality of agents and to assume most institutional changes are exogenous, although we have mentioned above the possibility of a link between policy changes and institutional changes. The only problem according to this view is with the modification of short-term demand for money equations.

An alternative approach (Foster, 1992) sees institutional changes affecting the supply of money as the driving force in the market. This may be coupled with the endogenous money approach to the demand for money to construct an explanation of changes in the money stock over time.

(b2) Keynes's speculative demand for money

We have explained Keynes's theory at some length in Section 5.4. The argument for instability rests on (i) the speculative demand for money; and/or the finance motive for holding money. We also note that neoclassical writers reject the speculative motive on several grounds largely related to the liquidity trap, the assumption of a normal rate of interest, and the all-or-nothing choice between bonds and money in the model.

We note in 6.3 that some early work attempted to show a positive relationship between interest rates and velocity while other studies sought to relate idle balances to interest rates. The latter studies found a relatively close negative relationship but this could be explained by an asset demand for money and did not demonstrate instability. Also, there were problems with the arbitrary definition of idle balances and this approach was abandoned.

Pause for thought 6.12

Vocabulary test: Is there a difference in meaning between 'to refute' and 'to deny'? If so, what is it?

Later studies contented themselves with looking for a liquidity trap. A Keynesian speculative demand curve indicates that the interest elasticity of the demand for money should increase as interest rate falls (the curve flattens out at low interest rates), culminating in a liquidity trap when the curve becomes horizontal. This is explained in the theory by the proposition that at lower rates of interest more people would believe that the current rate was below the normal rate and, therefore, that the next rate move would be up, producing a fall in bond prices. Thus, it was argued that evidence that the interest rate elasticity of the demand for money was not higher at lower rates of interest would cast serious doubt on the existence of a liquidity trap. This appears to be the case. Studies of the demand for money in the 1930s, when interest rates were low, do not show a higher interest elasticity of the demand for money than in other periods. In addition, regressions incorporating data from the 1930s predicted the velocity of money in later decades accurately. The absence of a liquidity trap, however, does not refute the possibility of instability — the possibility that the speculative demand curve moves unpredictably.

Nonetheless, most economists who see themselves as true adherents to the Keynesian tradition (Post Keynesian rather than New Keynesian or neo-Keynesian) are likely to follow the endogenous money path (despite Keynes's acceptance of an exogenous money supply) and/or to concentrate on the finance motive for holding money. The finance motive, which did not figure in Keynes's *General Theory*, has been ignored entirely by mainstream economists. We mention it briefly in Section 5.4. It is defined by Wray (1990 p.120) as 'a propensity to hoard cash in preparation for funding an investment project'. Keynes thought investment was highly unstable because investment decisions depended on the price ratio between capital assets and current output together with financial market conditions and were made under conditions of uncertainty. He saw the markets for capital assets and current output as separate and prices in the two markets as influenced by different factors. Shocks in financial markets could produce large and rapid changes in expectations regarding the future. The combination of these elements meant that investment was subject to rapid and unpredictable change. Clearly then, the finance motive could provide a source of instability in the demand for money function. There have been no attempts to test for the existence or nature of the finance motive.

Minsky (1978, 1986) developed a theory of financial fragility, which grew out of Keynes's views regarding investment decisions and theories of endogenous money. According to Minsky, instability derives from waves of credit expansion and deflation. In booms, firms make more use of debt financing; both households and firms reduce their holdings of cash and liquid assets relative to debt. Banks increase their loans. This credit expansion increases the money value of assets and this, in turn, justifies further borrowing. The debt/real assets ratio continues to rise. However, this cannot continue forever. At some point the boom falters. This leads to crisis, credit contraction and collapse. In a world like this, there is no room for a stable demand for money function or exogenous money. Minsky claimed evidence for his hypothesis in the 1987 stock market crashes (Minsky, 1991).

(b3) Transactions *vs* income velocities

The income term in demand for money functions is most commonly represented by GNP but GNP is a poor measure of the work money has to perform as a medium of exchange. So too is gross domestic final demand (GNP - inventory adjustments - net exports). The idea of this is that spending on goods drawn from inventories or on imports calls for transactions balances without affecting GNP directly, but use of it instead of GNP does not make much difference in equations. Gross national expenditure (GNP + Imports − Exports) has also been used and in one study produced a better fit than GNP in 12 out of 16 countries for the two decades ending in 1975 (Bomberger and Makinen 1980). However, such concepts do not represent the total money value of all transactions, even abstracting from the underground economy. Variations in the degree of vertical integration in industries or in financial transactions may also change the volume of money demanded independent of changes in interest rate or GNP. Thus, parameters of the demand for money function may shift.

Total transactions are larger than income transactions by an amount that reflects, *inter alia*, the volume of intermediate transactions involved in the production process (itself a reflection of the degree of integration in production), the volume of financial transactions and the volume of transactions in existing assets or second-hand goods. The latter include a large proportion of total house sales/purchases. In adopting *Py* rather than *PT* the point is often made that total transactions are likely to be stably related to income transactions and that the distinction between the two is, therefore, unlikely to matter. This is certainly convenient, but not very compelling. Clearly, Irving Fisher did not think it probable and Keynes explicitly denied its likelihood in the first volume of *The Treatise* (1930). Various attempts have been made in recent years to develop a *PT* series and to compare its movements with *Py* or GDP. For the UK, Cramer (1986) worked from input-output data to produce a series up to 1980, which showed significant deviations from *Py* for short periods of four to five years but in the long run followed income fairly closely. The study ended, however, before the deregulation of financial markets and the boom in financial (relative to GDP) activity that occurred in the UK in the 1980s. Following Keynes and using cheque and electronic payments data, Bain and Howells (1991) constructed a *PT* series that showed a dramatic upward divergence from GDP, from a multiple of approximately two to three between 1979 and 1989. Interestingly, this study deliberately omitted all transactions through the CHAPS and 'Town Clearing' systems. These are 'same day' payments mechanisms used predominantly by financial firms but also in the settlement of housing transactions. Including CHAPS and Town Clearing data not only makes the *PT/Py* multiple much larger but also increases dramatically the divergence over time. It seems at least worth considering the possibility, therefore, that financial innovation could have a fairly direct effect upon transactions velocity by causing a rise in financial and second-hand transactions relative to those involving newly produced goods and services.

This distinction between income and transactions velocities and the possibility that financial innovation may somehow be implicated, raises another interesting possibility although it is more strictly related to supply and only indirectly to the demand for money. The endogeneity argument is based upon (deposit-creating) advances being demand-determined. The demand for bank lending originates ultimately from the expenditure needs of deficit units. The desire to spend in excess of one's income can reflect a desire for newly produced goods or services or for financial assets or for second-hand goods. There seems no good reason, therefore, why *GDP* rather than *PT* should appear in bank lending equations. Indeed, theory suggests the reverse. Suppose now that the demand for bank lending were shown to be sensitive to *PT* rather than to *GDP*. Bank lending follows total transactions and grows more rapidly than if it were closely linked to *GDP*. Bank lending and the money supply grow more rapidly than income and income velocity must fall. Financial activity thus not only affects transactions velocity but also is causally implicated in the fall in income velocity. The study by Howells and Biefang-Frisancho Mariscal (1992) suggests some support for this line of reasoning. Of course, in equilibrium, the resulting deposits must be held. It would be interesting to see the effect of using a *PT* series as the scale variable in demand for money studies.

When this problem is taken into account, as Visser (1991) notes, parameter instability in conventional demand for money functions is hardly a surprise. It is clearly to be expected over longer periods as the underlying relationships change continuously. Even if they did not, but the true demand for money function was non-linear, linear estimates would show parameter instability. Visser suggests it is possible that the apparent stability in the demand for money function up to 1973 was unique and unlikely to be repeated. We may note here that the inclusion of bank debits as an additional transactions variable alongside GNP helped to improve the performance of money demand equations in the early 1980s (Judd and Scadding, 1982).

(c).The rejection of econometric testing

Some Post Keynesian economists deny the value of econometric testing altogether, although the relationship between Post Keynesian economics and econometrics is a somewhat troubled one (Downward, forthcoming). For example, according to Downward, Davidson argues that, in general,

> the neoclassical research programme invokes the axiom of 'ergodicity'. This implies that the world is predetermined and immutable. In the case of probabilistic inferences, therefore, as the past is a good guide to the future, objective or subjective probabilities will ultimately converge on the true values of the parameters of the probability distribution.

This explains why they believe inferences can be drawn from statistical/econometric analysis. Keynes, on the other hand, saw decision-makers in financial markets as facing uncertainty rather than risk, implying a much more profound ignorance of future events that could not be treated mathematically nor insured against. An uncertain world, in this sense, is not conducive of econometric analysis.

6.6 Summary

Although the demand for money might not be very important, the opposite has always been assumed within monetary economics. The theory of the demand for money raises a number of questions but does not provide definite answers. It seems, therefore, that tests of the theory need to be conducted, particularly to discover the interest elasticity of the demand for money and whether the demand for money function is stable. One way of approaching this is to use the theory to draw up a list of the variables that should be included in an equation to be tested. However, drawing up such a list reveals a number of specific problems as well as the more general problem that when we attempt to choose the form of the variables included, theory provides little guidance. Consequently, equations to be tested are constructed largely on pragmatic grounds. Further, the tests carried out do not in any genuine sense test the theory. Rather, they seek to confirm the view that the demand for money is stable.

The specific problems relate to the definition of money, the subjective nature of the demand for money, the existence of an identification problem when money is endogenous, the choice of a scale variable, the choice of interest rate, the existence of correlations between independent variables, difficulties in measuring some of the variables suggested by theory, and the period over which tests should be conducted. These problems together with the approach taken towards testing raise serious doubts concerning the value of the tests. Nonetheless, we looked at the results that have been produced.

Some early studies were related to Keynes's theory of the speculative demand for money, but since the middle 1950s, the great majority of tests have been of reduced form equations in which the demand for money is regressed on income and interest rate using highly-aggregated data. These tests set out to confirm a number of beliefs derived from conventional theories of the demand for money. Early tests were favourable in the sense that the results appeared to conform to those theories. In particular, the demand for money appeared to be stably related to real income and not to be highly interest elastic.

However, problems emerged in the 1970s. Tests in both the US and the UK indicated instability in the function together with the lengthening of time lags. A variety of attempts were made to explain how these results could be explained without disturbing an underlying belief in the long run stability of the function.

These included major attempts to improve the dynamic specification of the equations being tested and to take account of shocks that might temporarily have disturbed the function, notably from financial innovation. Attempts were also made to explain the problems with time lags. These led to the development of buffer stock models, which see adjustment to shocks occurring through changes in money balances. There have been a number of successes in these different approaches but it has not been possible to restore the confidence in the stability of the demand for money that existed up until the mid-1970s. None the less, most economists still appear to believe that the demand for money function is stable in the long run.

However, sceptics can be found. Notable among these are believers in the endogeneity of money, those who give considerable importance to Keynes's finance motive for holding money and those who doubt the value of statistical/econometric inference in a world of uncertainty.

Key concepts used in this chapter

stability of the demand for money function

interest elasticity of the demand for money

identification problem

scale variable

own rate of interest on money

omitted variable

lagged dependent variable

reduced-form equations

cointegrating vectors

partial adjustment equations

error correction models

dynamic specification

buffer stock models

non-stationary variables

ergodicity

Questions and exercises

1. It is widely accepted in science that it is not possible through empirical testing to prove anything. All one can do is to refute hypotheses. How scientific, then, is the testing of the demand for money?

2. Consider the list of variables that the text suggests might be included in an equation for the demand for money based on theory. Link each variable to a particular theory discussed in Chapter 5.

3. In what way is it favourable to monetarist views if:
(a) the interest elasticity of the demand for money is low?
(b) the demand for money is correctly specified in real terms?

4. Consider the equation:
$$m_t = \theta\beta_0 + \theta\beta_1 y_t + \theta\beta_2 i_t + \theta v + (1 - \theta)m_{t-1}$$
Does the assumption that the time lag on the income term should be the same as that on the interest rate term cause any problems?

5. Explain the following statement from the text and give some examples:
'However, the closeness of substitutes varies with the definition of money, which itself varies as innovations in very liquid assets take place. Even with a constant definition of money, the choice of the closest substitutes for money changes through time.'

6. Why might it be reasonable to replace an expectational variable in an equation with a dummy variable or a trend term? What is being assumed when a trend term is used?

7. Explain each of the effects suggested in Box 6.3.

8. What is implied about the relationship between money and interest rate when money is made the independent variable and interest rate the dependent variable — that is, when the demand for money function is inverted?

9. In the light of Keynes's view about the difference between risk and uncertainty, explain each of the following ideas from Keynes:

(a) it might be rational (rather than simple money illusion) for workers to make labour supply decisions based on relative money wages rather than real wages;

(b) households base their consumption and savings decisions on current income rather than wealth.

Does the second of these lead you to think differently about the choice of scale variable in the demand for money function?

10. '…the main *prima facie* objection to the application of the method of multiple correlation to complex economic problems lies in the apparent lack of any adequate degree of uniformity in the environment.' (Keynes 1939, p567).

Discuss this statement in relation to the question of the value of econometric testing.

Further reading

Readers will find much more econometrics and details of the tests in other textbooks — for example, Lewis and Mizen (2000), Handa (2000) or the older but still useful Artis and Lewis (1991). Notice too that many of the tests mentioned here date from before 1990. This is true of other books also as (possibly finally under pressure from endogenous money), interest in the demand for money function appears to have been waning in recent years. This means that older survey articles are still very helpful. Examples of these include: Artis and Lewis, 'Money Supply and Demand' in Bandyopadhyay and Ghatak (eds) (1990) and Cuthbertson and Barlow, 'Money demand analysis: an outline', in M Taylor (ed) (1991)

Sceptical views are harder to come by but readers could start with Paul Davidson's 'Reality and Economic Theory' (1996).

7 The Transmission Mechanism of Monetary Policy - I

'A man who has more money about him than he requires is tempted to spend it. It is apt to "burn a hole in his pocket".' S. Smiles, *Thrift* (1875) viii p.125

What you will learn in this chapter:

- The ways in which interest rate changes affect consumption expenditure
- The ways in which interest rate changes affect investment expenditure
- The factors affecting the size of these changes
- The importance of degrees of confidence and expectations;
- The different views of the transmission mechanism assuming an exogenous increase in the money supply
- The implications of these views for the demand for money
- The importance of the type of exchange rate system for the monetary transmission mechanism
- The possibility of monetary policy changes being transmitted to expenditure through the availability of credit.

7.1   Introduction

We are concerned in this and the following chapter with what happens in the economy following a change in monetary policy. We are particularly interested in the impact that monetary policy has on the nominal income of the economy and, through this, on the level of output and the rate of inflation. The series of links between the monetary policy change and the changes in output, employment, and inflation are known as the *transmission mechanism of monetary policy*. This can be broken up into two elements — the impact of monetary policy changes on aggregate demand; and the effect of changes in aggregate demand on output, employment, and prices. In this chapter, we consider the first of these. Chapter 8 looks at the second part of the transmission mechanism.

We have seen that a monetary policy change may take one of three forms:

• a change in the short term rate of interest at which the central bank is willing to lend to the banking sector in order to relieve any shortages of liquidity within the monetary system (interest rate control);

• a change in the monetary base in the expectation that this will alter the money supply, or its rate of growth (monetary base control);

• changes in the regulations that apply to banks in an attempt to influence the rate of growth of their lending (direct controls).

We saw in Chapters 3 and 4, however, that the Bank of England and other monetary authorities, now use only the first of these. In Chapters 4 and 11, we explain the practical difficulties associated with the other two methods of control in more detail. Here, because of this predominance of interest rate control in modern monetary policy, we begin by examining the transmission mechanism assuming this form of policy. We do this in Section 7.3, concentrating on the effect of an increase in interest rates. The arguments in this section can be reversed for a reduction in interest rates. This approach to the transmission mechanism is summarized in Box 7.1.

Box 7.1: Interest rate control and the transmission mechanism

The interest rate control (endogenous money) approach to the transmission mechanism in six steps (Goodhart, 2002):

1. The central bank determines the short-term interest rate

2. The private sector determines the volume of borrowing it wishes to undertake from the banking sector at the current set of interest rates.

3. Banks adjust their own relative interest rates, marketable assets, and interbank and wholesale borrowing to meet the credit demands upon them

4. These bank actions determine the money stock and its various sub-components (e.g. demand, time and wholesale deposits). This determines the volume of bank reserves needed, taking into account any required reserve ratios

5. This determines how much the banks need to borrow from, or pay back to, the central bank in order to meet their demand for reserves

6. In order to sustain the level of interest rates set under Step 1, the central bank uses open market operations to satisfy the banks' demand for reserves established under step 5.

However, much of the theoretical literature has assumed, against the evidence, an exogenous money supply, and the operation of monetary policy through changes in the money supply or in the monetary base. Thus, in Section 7.4, we consider the theoretical arguments associated with an assumed exogenous increase in the supply of money. Recently, it has been suggested that the money supply might play a role in the transmission mechanism even within a model constructed on the assumption of interest rate control. This approach involves a distinction between a credit channel of transmission (the impact of the change in interest rates) and a money channel (second and later round effects on nominal income of money supply changes that follow from the initial interest rate change). We look briefly at this argument in Section 7.5. In Section 7.6, we return to the connection between monetary policy and exchange rates, which is identified in 7.3 as providing a possible transmission link. Section 7.7 discusses the possibility of transmission occurring through credit availability.

7.2   The impact of a change in official interest rates on other rates

In changing short-term interest rates - the interest rate on gilt sale and repurchase agreements at the two-week maturity in the case of the Bank of England (repo rate), the official refinancing rate (refi) in the case of the European Central Bank — the monetary authorities expect to bring about changes in the general level of interest rates in the economy. The link between the short-term rate on which the central bank chooses to operate and other interest rates in the economy is discussed in detail in Section 4.2. There, we conclude that the effect of a change in the Bank's intervention rate is an empirical question and may change over time. In general, short rates adjust quite quickly and in the same direction as the official change. The effect on medium and longer-term rates is much less certain. Although there are exceptions (examples of which are given in 4.2), they, too, are likely to move in the same direction but by smaller amounts than short rates. The next step is to consider the effects on the economy of these changes in interest rates brought about by central banks.

7.3   The impact of interest rate changes on consumption and investment

It is widely accepted that this is influenced by changes in the real rate of interest (the nominal rate of interest less the expected rate of inflation). Changes in nominal interest rates brought about by central bank changes in its short-term interest (repo) rate will, given the expected rate of inflation at the time, result in changes in the real rate of interest in the economy. Thus, we need to look at the ways in which real interest rate changes induced by central bank policy affect private sector spending.

The principal components of domestic private sector demand are consumption and investment expenditure.

Pause for thought 7.1:

(a) Why are equity prices likely to fall following an increase in interest rates?

(b) Why might they not fall?

Consumption expenditure derives from current income but consumption decisions depend also on expected future income, the level of wealth and on the ability to borrow against existing wealth. Thus, monetary policy is likely to influence household consumption through several channels. For example, an increase in interest rates:

• makes saving from current income more attractive

• increases repayments on existing floating-rate debt and thus lowers disposable income

• increases the cost of borrowing and thus increases the cost of goods and services obtained on credit

• lowers the price of financial assets and hence influences estimates of private sector wealth

• lowers house prices or, at least, slows the rate at which they are increasing and this, too, influences estimates of household wealth and lowers the value of the collateral against which households seek to borrow.

If households believe that the interest rate changes will lower aggregate demand, they might also become concerned about the impact on output and employment. Increased worries about future employment will cause households to lower their estimates of expected future income from employment and become more cautious about current expenditure. Any fear of an impending recession might, in addition, cause banks to tighten the conditions they apply to loan applications, making it more difficult for people to obtain credit even if they remain willing to borrow credit.

Of these various influences, changes in repayments on floating-rate mortgages are particularly important in the UK since loans secured on houses make up about 80 per cent of personal debt, and most mortgages carry floating interest rates. *All of these operate in the same direction — we expect an increase in interest rates to reduce consumption expenditure.*

Yet, not everyone will reduce consumption expenditure as interest rates rise. The discussion so far has implied that interest rate rises reduce the disposable income of all households, but this will not be true for those consisting of people living off income from savings deposits. Nor is it true for people whose expected future income depends on an annuity to be purchased in the near future. In both of these cases, higher interest rates imply a higher income. Thus, interest rate changes have redistributional effects. When interest rates increase, net borrowers are made worse off and net savers better off. However, the groups made better off (net savers) are highly likely to be dominated by those made worse off (net borrowers) and so we continue to expect increases in interest rates to reduce household consumption expenditure.

The same applies to investment expenditure. An increase in interest rates:

• raises external borrowing costs for firms that raise funds through bank loans or from bills or bonds markets;

• increases the rate at which they discount back expected future returns from investment, making investment projects less attractive;

• increases the return from the savings of firms, retained from past profits, raising the opportunity cost of financing investment internally;
• increases the difficulty and cost of raising investment funds through the issue of new capital on the stock market;

• increases the costs of holding inventories of goods, which are often financed by bank loans;

• lowers asset prices, reducing the net worth of firms and making it more difficult for them to borrow.

Pause for thought 7.2:

Why might firms take actions leading to reductions in employment when the central bank *does not* change the rate of interest?

The way in which firms respond to monetary policy changes also depends on the way in which those changes affect estimates of future aggregate demand since these are a major influence on their forecast future sales and hence on estimated future profits. Thus, if a change in the official interest rate — or, indeed, a failure to change it — reinforces a view that aggregate demand is likely to fall in the future firms may respond by 'restructuring' and cutting back employment by greater amounts than might be expected simply on the basis of the direct effects listed above.

As with households, not all firms will be affected in the same way or to the same extent. Much depends on the nature of the business, the size of the firm and its sources of finance. An increase in interest rates improves the cash flow of firms with funds deposited with banks or placed in the money markets, although this does not imply that they will make use of their improved position to increase investment. It is more likely, indeed, to encourage firms to hold greater quantities of financial assets or to pay higher dividends to shareholders. The cash flow of firms whose short-term assets and liabilities are more or less matched will be little affected by changes in short-term interest rates but are still likely to be influenced by changes in longer-term rates. Further, despite the above list, the impact of changes in the official interest rate on the cost of capital for particular firms is difficult to predict, especially for large and multinational firms with access to international capital markets. Nonetheless, it remains true that for firms taken together increases in interest rates are highly likely to lead to reduced investment expenditure.

Open economy influences also need to be taken into account. Other things being equal, an increase in domestic interest rates should increase the attractiveness of the currency in foreign exchange markets, raising the value of the currency. This damages the international competitiveness of domestic firms since it raises the prices of their goods when expressed in foreign currencies and, in the short run at least, they have little scope for reducing costs of production and lowering domestic currency prices. Thus, they must reduce their profit margins, accept a loss of market share in export markets or both. Problems arise in domestic markets also. Import-competing goods face increased competition from foreign products because their prices are now lower in domestic currency terms. Difficulties are likely to follow also for domestic firms that are not in direct competition with foreign firms because of changes in the composition of household spending that results from changes in the relative prices of domestic and foreign goods. For example, households may respond to a reduction in the domestic currency price of foreign holidays by cutting back on expenditure on books or CDs in order to take a foreign holiday. Of course, it is only those changes in exchange rate that are brought about by monetary policy changes or expected changes in monetary policy that we are concerned with here. Exchange rates may be affected by many other factors.

Again, different sectors will be affected in different ways by monetary policy induced exchange rate changes. The manufacturing sector is the most exposed to foreign competition and thus is likely to suffer most from increases in the value of the domestic currency. Agriculture, financial and business services, and those parts of the service sector heavily reliant on the arrival of foreign tourists are also likely to be strongly affected.

Pause for thought 7.3:

Can you think of situations in which an increase in domestic interest rates will not cause an increase in the value of the domestic currency?

Expectations and confidence about the future clearly play a major role in all of this. It follows that the size of the likely fall in aggregate demand depends crucially on:

(a) whether the present increase in interest rates had been expected; and

(b) whether the present increase leads to expectations of further increases in future or quick reversals of policy;

(c) expectations regarding future inflation rates.

Inflationary expectations are particularly important since much of the influence of interest rate changes on the expenditure of households and firms relates to changes in *real* interest rates (the rate of interest adjusted to take into account the expected rate of inflation). Monetary policy operates directly on nominal interest rates. Much of the above discussion takes inflationary expectations as given, in which case a change in nominal interest rates is equivalent to a change in real interest rates. However, monetary policy may well have an influence on inflationary expectations. Indeed, it is commonly the intention of the monetary authorities that it should do so. Hence, if an increase in interest rates lowers market expectations of the future rate of inflation, the real rate of interest will increase by more than the nominal rate. Those areas of expenditure particularly influenced by real rates of interest (e.g. investment expenditure by firms and housing expenditure and expenditure on consumer durables) will be affected more than would have been the case had inflationary expectations remained unchanged.

Pause for thought 7.4:

Are the effects of a reduction in interest rates likely to be the exact reverse of the effects described above for an increase in interest rates?

We can conclude from this section that:

• monetary policy influences aggregate demand in a variety of ways;

• the relationship between interest rate changes and changes in aggregate demand might be quite powerful;

• the relationship between interest rates and aggregate demand is inverse — increases in interest rates reduce aggregate expenditure; reductions in interest rates cause aggregate expenditure to increase

• nonetheless, the relationship between interest rates and aggregate demand is complex

• interest rate changes affect the distribution of income as well as the level of aggregate demand.

Figure 7.1: The transmission mechanism of monetary policy

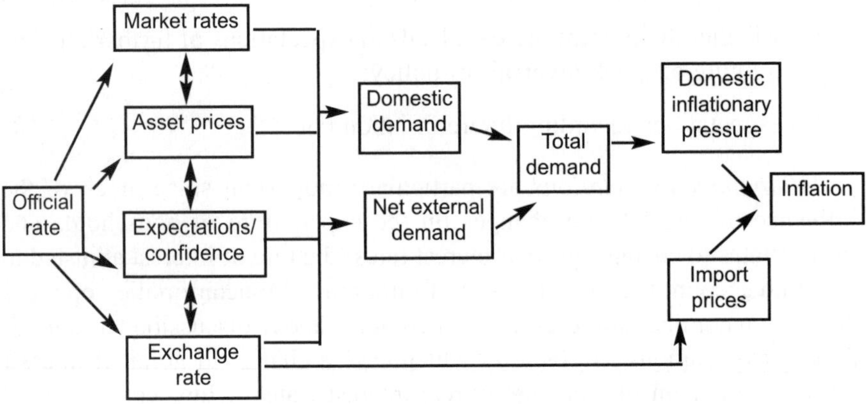

Source: adapted from *Bank of England Quarterly Bulletin*, May 1999

Knowing the direction in which aggregate demand is likely to change when interest rates change is of very limited use. We need to know how powerful a policy instrument monetary policy is, whether the size of the impact of a given change is predictable and how long it will take for the full impact of a change in interest rates to be felt in the economy. Clearly, the size of the impact of a monetary policy change and the length of the time lags involved in the process may well vary from one economy to another. Nonetheless, we can make some general points about time lags.

The approach to the transmission mechanism of monetary policy considered here is summed up in Figure 7.1, which is taken from the Bank of England.

There are several different time lags involved in monetary policy. We can distinguish the following:

- the length of time it takes for the authorities to observe changes in the economy and to decide on a change in the official short-term rate of interest (policy decision lag);

- the length of time it takes for the change in the official rate to feed through to other interest rates in the economy (institutional lag);

- the length of time required for interest rate changes to affect the disposable income of households (income lag);

- the length of time required for changes in short-term and long-term interest rates to affect the expenditure of households and firms (expenditure lag);

- the length of time needed for changes in expenditure to be reflected in changes in the rate of inflation, output, and employment (real response lag).

Pause for thought 7.5:

Why does it take so long for interest rate changes to affect the rate of inflation?

Evidence from industrial economies generally suggests that once the monetary authorities have changed the official rate it takes about twelve months for the full impact of the change to be felt on demand and production. It takes a further twelve months for the full effect on the rate of inflation to be felt. This in itself presents serious problems for the monetary authorities since it means that they must be constantly looking forward trying to assess the likely state of inflationary pressures two years ahead on the assumption of unchanged policies and then trying to estimate the impact of a policy change. Given that the interest rate is only one influence among many on expenditure, this is clearly very difficult. However, things are even worse because the time lags of twelve months and two years mentioned here are only approximate and are only averages. The time lags associated with any particular act of monetary policy may be much shorter or much longer — they are highly variable and will depend, among other things, on the state of business and consumer confidence, how this confidence is influenced by monetary policy changes, events in the world economy, and expectations about future inflation.

7.4   The transmission mechanism with the money supply as the policy instrument

In Section 3.5, and in Chapter 4, we saw that central banks do not in practice attempt to control the quantity of money directly. In other words, the
money supply is not an instrument of policy. Nonetheless, a strong school
of theoretical monetary economics has always argued that the monetary
authorities could, and should, control the money supply through monetary
base control. Sufficient numbers of economists have in the past believed
strongly enough in the stability of the link between the monetary base and
the money supply that the latter has commonly been treated as a policy
instrument. Thus, most textbook analyses of the transmission mechanism
begin with an assumption of a given change in the money supply, as if the
authorities could automatically bring this about. For example, monetary
policy is often treated in this way within the *IS-LM* framework.

Consequently, we shall look at this approach here, not least because it
implies a much more important role for the demand for money and looks at
the problems facing monetary policy in a rather different way from the discussion above.

We begin with an assumption of equilibrium in the money market, with
the demand for money being equal to the supply of money. We then propose an increase in the supply of money. This causes a temporary excess
supply of money (the supply of money is greater than the demand for it).
Market agents seek to return to equilibrium. Their actions produce changes
in the economy that cause the demand for money to increase to the level of
the newly increased supply of money. Thus, we are not asking what effect
a change in monetary policy is likely to have in a particular economy at a
particular time. Rather, we are asking what would have to change in an
economy to return the money market to equilibrium, if an existing equilibrium were disturbed by a monetary policy change. This assumes crucially
that nothing else changes at the same time. This is an example of comparative static equilibrium analysis and is a world away from our approach to
the monetary transmission mechanism above. There, for example, we point
out that a change in interest rates might have a variety of impacts depending on the way in which the change affects expectations and consumer confidence. Here, we assume such things as confidence and expectations to be
unchanging.

It is clear that the nature of the demand for money is crucial in this
approach to the transmission mechanism since we need to know what
changes must occur in the economy to increase the demand for money by

the amount required to return us to equilibrium. The relationship between the demand for money and the interest rate becomes vital. This is illustrated in Figure 7.2.

Figure 7.2: Return to money market equilibrium following an increase in the money supply

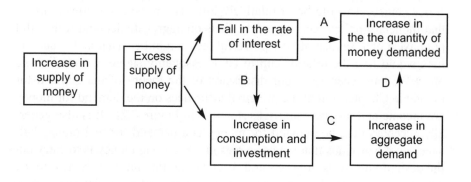

Assume to begin with that the demand for money is highly interest-elastic (implying the existence of assets that are close substitutes for money). Then, link *A* in Figure 7.2 is strong and only a small fall in interest rates might be required to return the money market to equilibrium following an increase in the supply of money. In this case, a significant proportion of the increase in the supply of money is held in the form of money balances and there is relatively little impact on aggregate demand. In the terms of the Quantity Theory equations in Section 2.2, an increase in M produces a fall in V and thus does not have a full impact on Py on the right-hand-side of the equation. The impact on Py would be weaker still if the interest rate effects on consumption and investment expenditure were weak (link *B* in Figure 7.2), although our discussion in Section 7.3 above suggests that this is not generally the case.

Pause for thought 7.6:

Which of the theories of the demand for money considered in Chapter 5 suggests the possibility of a highly interest-elastic demand for money?

With these assumptions of a highly interest-elastic demand for money and interest-inelastic consumption and investment expenditure, monetary policy would be a weak instrument of policy.

However, if we were to reverse these assumptions we would obtain the opposite results. If interest rate changes have relatively little impact on the demand for money, the principal way in which the economy moves back to equilibrium following an increase in the money supply is through increases in aggregate demand that require people to hold more money to finance additional purchases of goods and services. This implies a powerful transmission mechanism linking monetary policy with aggregate demand.

Of course, it would be of relatively little use to the authorities to know that monetary policy had powerful effects on aggregate demand if they did not have a precise idea of how powerful they might be. That is, the authorities would like the relationship to be a reasonably stable and predictable one. We have seen from our discussion of the theory of the demand for money in Chapter 5, that the principal influences on the demand for money are income and interest rate (links A and D in Figure 7.2). It is also generally accepted that the demand for money is a demand for real money balances on the grounds that the basic reason for holding money is to carry out the desired purchases of goods and services and that utility is related to the consumption of goods and services rather than to the amount spent upon them. Thus, it is generally accepted that there is a fairly close and positive relationship between the price level and the demand for money. If this is so, we can write:

$$\frac{Md}{P} = f(y,i) \qquad\qquad ...7.1$$

where Md is the demand for money, P is an index of prices, y is real income, and i is a representative interest rate on non-money assets. Since, in equilibrium, the demand for money is equal to the supply of money, it follows that a stable relationship between the supply of money and aggregate demand (Py) requires a stable relationship between interest rates and the demand for money (link A in Figure 7.2). In Chapter 6, we looked at the attempts to test the demand for money function for stability. In this chapter, we shall see that differences in the theory of the transmission mechanism are closely linked to theoretical views of the demand for money.

We can express the argument about the importance of the stability of the demand for money also in terms of the income velocity of money. If the impact of changes in the supply of money on aggregate demand is predictable, the income velocity of money (Py/M) must also be predictable.

To move towards an answer to these questions, we need to look closely at the way in which an increase in the supply of money affects other variables within the economy. We begin by assuming that economic agents distribute their wealth among the various assets to maximize utility and that the system is in equilibrium with all agents content with their current pattern of asset holdings. Each asset market is also in equilibrium but equilibrium positions are disturbed by any changes in the total stock of wealth, the expected real rates of return on assets, the perceived degree of risk associated with each asset, or the agents' attitude to risk.

The response of agents to a change in the supply of any asset affects relative asset prices and disturbs the equilibrium positions in other asset markets. Portfolio effects are concerned with the way in which disequilibrium spreads from one asset market to another. At the same time, any change in the supply of an asset, *ceteris paribus*, changes the size of the stock of wealth and agents take this, too, into account in moving to a new equilibrium. In an open economy, portfolio effects may be brought about through changes in the exchange rate.

Portfolio effects of an increase in the stock of money

For monetarists, how the money supply changes is of little relevance to this argument — we are merely interested in the effects any change will have. This explains Milton Friedman's famous assumption of money being dropped from a helicopter. No matter how the money supply is changed, there will be *both* portfolio and wealth effects.

For Keynesians, however, it is possible to separate the wealth and portfolio effects of an increase in the supply of money by assuming that the central bank increases the stock of money through open market operations — buying government securities and issuing money in return. We have an increase in the private sector's holdings of money, matched by a reduction in private sector holdings of government debt. We assume for the moment that this leaves total private sector wealth unchanged, although we shall return to this issue later.

There are three distinct views as to how portfolios will be re-arranged, with the differences hinging on the range of assets taken into account and on the extent to which various assets are thought to be good substitutes for each other. However, since the monetarist approach combines both portfolio and wealth effects, we consider it separately and look first at portfolio effects within Keynesian models, starting with the analysis in Keynes's *General Theory* (Keynes, 1936).

Keynes and the speculative demand for money

We spent some time looking at Keynes's theory of the speculative demand for money in Section 5.4. We saw there that this theory led to the view that the supply of money and the demand for money are not independent of each other. An increase in the supply of money pushes interest rates down and this encourages an increase in the demand for money because of fears of a future interest rate rise. Thus, interest rates may not need to fall much to persuade people willingly to hold the now larger supply of money. In other words, the demand for money is likely to be highly interest elastic and the impact of any increase in the money stock on interest rates is bound to be small. The increase in investment is small, producing only a small (multiplied) increase in nominal income. From the firms' point of view, the lower the interest rate becomes relative to its previous level and, thus, the higher is their demand for investment funds, the more difficult it is to raise long-term fixed-interest funds from savers. We can represent the above account in an *IS/LM* diagram. For details of the derivation of *IS* and *LM* curves, see Appendix I.

Figures 7.3: An increase in money supply

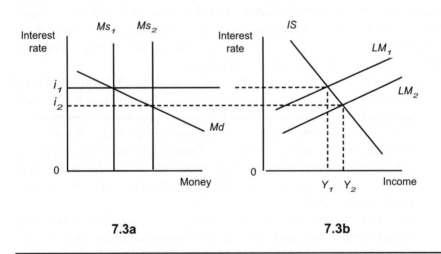

7.3a   7.3b

Figure 7.3a shows a demand for money curve (*Md*) that is drawn with a shallow slope reflecting the assumption that the demand for money is highly interest-elastic. The supply of money curve is here drawn vertical in contrast with the more realistic, positively sloped money supply curve in Figure 3.1. This is simply because here we are continuing to assume, against the evidence, that the authorities have complete control over the money supply. In Figure 7.3a, an exogenous increase in the supply of money (shown by the shift from *Ms₁* to *Ms₂*) produces only a small fall in interest rate, from *i₁* to

i_2. Nonetheless, because the demand for money is highly interest elastic, most of the burden of the return to equilibrium in the money market is borne by this change in interest rate. Investment increases only slightly, income rises slightly producing a small increase in the transactions demand for money. This is shown in Figure 7.3b by the relatively flat *LM* curve moving only slightly down to the right (from LM_1 to LM_2), producing only a small change in *Y*.

The main messages of this model are:

1. The transmission mechanism between increases in the money stock and the level of nominal income is indirect, operating through the rate of interest.

2. Monetary policy is weak because of the high interest elasticity of the demand for money implied by the impact of interest rate changes on bond prices.

3. The demand for money may well be unstable.

Figure 7.4: Unstable money demand

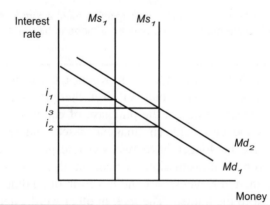

If this last were true, the link between exogenous changes in the money stock and nominal income would be not only weak but also unstable and unpredictable. For example, in figure 7.4 below, the exogenous increase in the money stock, from Ms_1 to Ms_2, may be associated with an outward movement (of uncertain extent) of the demand for money curve from Md_1 to Md_2 resulting in an even smaller fall in the rate of interest. The *LM* curve in Figure 7.3b would, in this case, shift by an even smaller (and uncertain) amount.

Tobin's portfolio model and the transmission mechanism

In Section 5.7, we dealt with that part of Tobin's theory that deals with the choice between money and bonds. However, we pointed out that Tobin also introduced a wider range of assets including equities and real assets. Consider the impact of so doing.

Now, an exogenous increase in the money stock is shuffled along through the assets from more to less liquid. Thus, households use the excess supply of money in the first instance to buy bonds (as in Keynes's model), pushing bond prices up, and interest rates down. As interest rates on bonds fall, equities become relatively more attractive than bonds and households switch to equities, driving up their price and lowering the rate of return on them. Firms wishing to expand have the choice of acquiring additional existing capital stock by taking over other firms or investing in new capital stock. As share prices rise, the market valuation of existing firms increases and takeovers become less attractive than the purchase of new capital stock. Thus, investment increases. The principal determinant of investment, therefore, is the yield on equities.

Pause for thought 7.7:

Would it change the essence of Keynes's transmission mechanism if, instead of introducing equities into the model, we introduced a range of bills and bonds of different maturities?

In one sense, this is the same story as in Keynes, but using a different interest rate. The process remains indirect. Yet, there is a distinction. In Tobin, households are able through the purchase of equities to own firms and this eliminates the gulf between financial assets and real assets in Keynes's model. We no longer have two separate groups acting from diverse motives. Tobin's transmission mechanism also suggests different motives for saving than in Keynes. A bond is a form of lending and pays a fixed rate of interest to the holder. The rate, in other words, does not vary with the way in which the bond is used, and acquiring the bond does not bestow ownership of real assets. Ownership of shares does bestow ownership of real assets and entitles the holder to a share in the future flow of profits from the use of those assets. This brings us much closer to the classical view of saving as a real decision involving a trade-off between current and future consumption. We might also suggest that if households own firms, they control the level of investment and there is no longer any reason for a mis-match of the plans of savers and investors. The uncertainty that permeates Keynes's model has disappeared: we have an equilibrium rather than a disequilibrium model. It is not surprising, therefore, that this leads us in the direction of a stable demand for money function (see Section 5.7)

Wealth effects of an increase in the stock of money

In Keynesian approaches, monetary policy carried out through open market operations does not create wealth effects. Everything that follows does so through the re-arrangement of portfolios and the interest rate is, therefore, central. Governments, supported by the monetary authorities, can also increase the money supply by increasing government expenditure and financing the increase by borrowing from the central bank or the banking sector.[1] This has wealth effects since the increase in the money supply is not matched by a reduction in private sector holding of government debt. In this case, though, we have a mixture of monetary policy (the increase in the money supply) and fiscal policy (the increase in government expenditure) and the wealth effects could be attributed to fiscal policy.

Figure 7.5: Money supply and wealth effects

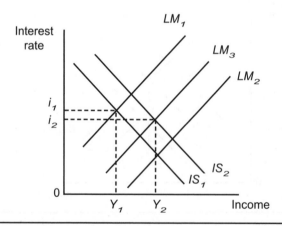

However, it has been argued that even monetary policy carried out through open market operations might produce wealth effects. If this were true, an increase in the money stock would produce an increase in private sector wealth, leading to an increase in the holding of each type of asset, including money itself, financial assets of all kinds, and real assets such as capital equipment and consumer durables.[2] Then, there would be a direct link between changes in the stock of money and expenditure on goods and services. The interest rate channel of transmission would be much less powerful and monetary policy more powerful *even if* the demand for money were highly interest elastic (indeed, even in a liquidity trap).

This is shown using IS/LM diagrams as in figures 7.5 and 7.6.

Figure 7.5 shows the wealth effect only, without considering how this might arise. An increase in the stock of money shifts the *LM* curve down from LM_1 to LM_2 but the increase in the demand for money resulting from the increased wealth moves it back to some extent and it finishes at LM_3. At the same time, the increased wealth causes consumption to increase, shifting the *IS* curve out from IS_1 to IS_2. The strength of the wealth effect resulting from the increase in the supply of money depends on the extent to which the *IS* curve moves in comparison with the counteracting backwards movement of the *LM* curve to LM_3.

Figure 7.6 shows an increase in government expenditure financed by an increase in the supply of money. In this case, we have two movements in the *IS* curve, from IS_1 to IS_2 as a result of the increase in government expenditure and from IS_2 to IS_3 from the wealth effect.

Figure 7.6: Government spending and money supply

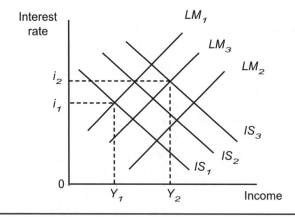

If we ignore the money-financed fiscal policy case and concentrate on pure monetary policy, we are left with two questions:

- does an increase in the supply of money through open market operations produce a wealth effect?

- if it does, how strong is that effect?

Clearly, if there is a strong wealth effect, the argument that monetary policy is weak is severely damaged.

Pause for thought 7.8:

Compare the notion of the net wealth of the private sector with Friedman's version of wealth in Section 5.8. Why does no one include human wealth in the net wealth of the private sector?

In considering whether there is a wealth effect, we must first look at the notion of wealth being used here. It is usual to refer to the *net wealth of the private sector.* We divide the economy into three sectors: the private, the public sector, and the foreign. The net wealth of the private sector is defined to include all private sector assets that are not also liabilities of other members of the sector—that is, it includes private sector assets for which the corresponding liabilities are those of the public sector or the foreign sector. Thus, many financial assets are excluded because they create corresponding liabilities within the private sector. For example, equities are assets to shareholders but are liabilities of firms within the sector. If we rule such assets out, we are left with four categories of asset to investigate:

- real assets;
- assets that are liabilities of the foreign sector;
- inside money; and
- assets that are liabilities of the public sector.

The first two are straightforward. Both real assets held by the private sector and private sector assets that are liabilities of the foreign sector are clearly part of private sector net wealth. However, there are measurement problems. There are severe difficulties in measuring the net value of the stocks of private sector housing and consumer durables. Thus, in most studies, only the capital stock of firms is included as part of private sector net wealth. The value of foreign assets can alter rapidly with changes in exchange rates.

Inside money, remember, consists of bank deposits, which are assets to the holders of the deposits but are liabilities to the banks with which they are held. Since banks are part of the private sector, some attempts have been made to exclude inside money from the definition of private sector net wealth. This, however, ignores the fact that the whole monetary system is based upon the presumption that banks do not have to repay deposits and need only hold small prudential balances to meet the day-to-day calls upon them. If we add central bank willingness to act as lender of last resort to ensure that the system does not fail, it seems reasonable to accept inside money as a part of private sector net wealth.

On the other hand, there are conceptual problems with private sector assets that are liabilities of the public sector. There are two assets of this kind: outside (high powered) money and government securities. It has been argued that the public sector's only source of funds is ultimately from the private sector in the form of taxation and that, therefore, public sector liabilities are liabilities of the private sector. Remember, however, that our interest is in how the private sector perceives public sector liabilities.

Few people deny that outside money is part of private sector net wealth. Technically, fiat money is a liability of the central bank and must be backed by government securities or foreign exchange reserves held by the central bank. Despite this, it is argued variously:

(a) that it is not, in practice, a government debt since it never has to be repaid (Pesek and Saving, 1967)

(b) that it is a debt but that the government is not concerned about the level of it (Gurley and Shaw, 1960), or

(c) that the issue of it certainly leads to a change in economic behaviour and that this is more relevant than the formal accounting position (Goodhart, 1989b).

However, there has been controversy over whether or not the private sector sees its holding of government securities as net wealth. Since interest payments on bonds and the repayment of principal must come from future taxation revenue, one can argue that taxpayers as a group regard public sector debt as a liability. In this case, government borrowing imposes a future burden on taxpayers.

In the extreme (Ricardian equivalence) view (Barro, 1974), the discounted present value of this burden exactly equals the value of the bonds to bondholders. Asset and liability cancel out and government bonds are not part of private sector net wealth. It follows that any increase in the economy's stock of outside money (however the increase is brought about) is an increase in net wealth. Pure monetary policy (open market operations) has wealth effects.

Opponents of this view object that bondholders and taxpayers are not identical groups and hence any assessment of tax liability will not fully match the value of bonds to bondholders, especially as at least part of any tax liability will be met by future generations.[3] Neoclassical economists have responded with highly formal models of overlapping generations that assume perfect knowledge of the future and in which the present and the future are, in effect, unified.

It can also be argued against Ricardian equivalence that the extent of any future liability must be related to future income (and hence future ability to pay) and that, therefore, any bond-financed increase in government expenditure does not create an effective liability for future generations as long as it results in an increase in future real income. This occurs in a Keynesian model if the economy is at less than full employment. The bond-financed increase in government expenditure increases output and employment and this, in turn, induces additional private sector investment adding to the economy's capital stock. In this case, the present generation will see government bonds as assets and will not offset a perceived future liability against them.

On the other hand, as we see in Chapter 8, in a neoclassical model, unemployment is at its natural level and the increase in government expenditure merely displaces (crowds out) an equivalent amount of private sector expenditure. There is no addition to real income to ease the burden on future generations of repaying the increase in government debt.

Seen in this way, the argument about wealth effects of an increase in the money stock resolves itself into an extension of the familiar argument in intermediate macroeconomics concerning the slopes of *IS, LM* and aggregate supply curves. A typical neoclassical model with a steeply sloped (or vertical) *LM* curve and a vertical aggregate supply curve has as a corollary strong wealth effects following an increase in the money stock. Wealth effects provide an additional support for the view that monetary policy is strong. In a Keynesian model, with a shallow *LM* curve and a positively sloped aggregate supply curve, an expansionary monetary policy through open market operations does not generate significant wealth effects. Indeed, in the end the effect may even be negative.

We should also note criticisms of the whole idea that only the size of private sector net wealth is important. Chick (1977) argues that the relationship between wealth and expenditure is influenced by the composition of wealth: specifically, by its liquidity. She argues that as long as inflation rates are low, an exogenous increase in the money stock should have a greater impact on expenditure than an equal increase in other, less liquid, assets. In addition, consumers may increase their liquidity by borrowing. Expenditure plans, in other words, are based on both estimates of the market value of assets and the cost and availability of borrowed funds. Chick goes further, claiming that it is fallacious to net debt out from wealth since, while existing debt does have to be paid off and this discourages consumption, people go into debt in order to consume. Existing debt is a current liability but, at the time spending decisions are made, the burden of debt is only potential.

In addition, other types of wealth effect are possible. Notably, to the extent that an increase in the money stock (however it is brought about) drives down interest rates, there is a capital revaluation effect (windfall gain) in the form of an increase in the market value of capital-uncertain financial assets already held.

Much also depends on government responses to changes in interest payable on government securities. Thus, the bond-coupon effect describes the impact of changes in government interest payments on disposable income: the repurchase of government securities through open market operations (combined with any fall in interest payments) lowers government interest payments and lowers the current income of bondholders, producing a possible negative impact on consumption. Yet again, lower interest rates improve the cash flow of net debtors such as the company sector, possibly encouraging investment. Expenditure decisions may also be influenced by the way in which the economy's stock of wealth is distributed between creditor and debtor units of the different sectors in the economy since each sector may respond differently to changes in its wealth.

Pause for thought 7.9:

Can you now appreciate how much easier life becomes if we assume that the money supply is increased by dropping money from a helicopter? Is this the ultimate form of outside money?

These points lead to the view that a much more disaggregated analysis is needed than is provided by the notion of an exogenous increase in the money stock increasing net wealth and producing movements in *IS/LM* curves.

A monetarist transmission mechanism

In monetarist views of the transmission mechanism between changes in the stock of money and the level of nominal income, money is different from all other assets. Consequently, no asset is a good substitute for money but money substitutes equally for all other assets. That is, the cross-elasticity of the demand for money with respect to the yield on any one particular asset is low. If we assume that all interest rates move together and talk of a single interest rate, as we saw in Chapter 6 happens very largely in the empirical testing of the demand for money, the monetarist stress on the uniqueness of money explains the belief in a very interest-inelastic demand for money. This helps to explain the difference of view between Keynesians and monetarists over the 'price of money'. For Keynesians, the interest rate is the price of money; whereas monetarists think of the price of money as the inverse of the price level.

Pause for thought 7.10:

It is sometimes said that, in Keynesian models, increases in the money supply influence investment but not consumption but in monetarist models, both consumption and investment are affected. What explains the difference?

Monetarists argue that the Keynesian concentration on the interest rate as the channel through which the monetary transmission mechanism works derives from the common assumption of fixed prices, which leads to a lack of interest in relative prices. For monetarists, on the other hand, transmission occurs through a number of channels as the result of changes in relative prices. We begin, as usual, in equilibrium. Demand equals supply for all types of asset and an increase in the stock of money disturbs all of these equilibrium positions. Interest rates fall, the prices of financial assets rise, the demand for existing real assets rises forcing up the prices of existing real assets leading to increased demand for new assets. The range of relevant rates of interest is greater and includes implicit rates of return on real assets (the flow of services from them).

Brunner and Meltzer (1972) developed the best-known monetarist model of the transmission mechanism. This focuses on stock effects as well as on changes in relative prices. According to Mayer (1978), this brings the system towards a classical equilibrium. In the Brunner and Meltzer model, there are three types of capital goods:

(a) those for which there are separate prices for existing stock and new output (for instance, plant and machinery);

(b) those for which the prices of existing and new stock of comparable quality are the same (including housing and cars);

(c) those for which there is no market for existing stock (certain types of consumer durables).

Then an increase in the money stock leads to:

• an increase in equity prices and hence greater demand for new type (a) goods; and

• an increase in prices of type (b) goods, stimulating their production.

The rise in prices of real capital assets and the fall in the rate of return on financial assets act to raise the market value of wealth and hence the desired stock of type (c) goods as well as the consumption of non-durables. With regard to non-durables, as asset yields are lowered, there will be three effects on the savings/dissavings decision:

(a) a substitution effect — a fall in the opportunity cost of consumption (and, thus, dissaving) provides a stimulus to current consumption through an increased incentive to run down accumulated assets and to borrow;

(b) an income effect, working in the opposite direction — a fall in interest rate lowers the flow of income and thus potential future consumption from any given level of saving.

but also:

(c) windfall gains - as asset prices rose, the net wealth of the private sector increases and, since wealth is a determinant of consumption, so does consumption.

There is much less emphasis on interest rates than in Keynesian models. Nominal interest rates do fall following an increase in the stock of money but this is reversed as prices increase and the real value of the money stock returns to its initial level. The monetarist transmission mechanism operates more through a real balance (wealth) effect than through substitution, because of the weak substitutability of money for other assets. Hence, monetarist models are characterized by:

1. A wider range of assets than even in Tobin-style Keynesian models, including implicit rates of return on real assets.

2. Direct impact of changes in the money stock on nominal income.

These increases in nominal income cause the demand for money to rise to return us to equilibrium in the money market. Income needs to rise considerably and monetary policy is powerful. A corollary is that interest rates on financial assets are driven down considerably as part of the excess supply of money is used to purchase financial assets. However, this fall has little or (in the extreme) no effect on the demand for money since people are assumed to know (or to form correct expectations regarding) future rates of interest and thus to have no fear of capital loss from holding illiquid financial securities. This again makes clear the importance of the assumption of uncertainty in Keynesian models.

7.5   The money supply within an interest rate control mechanism

Much of the debate about the nature of the transmission mechanism has been concerned with causality and the direction of causality. The assumption of endogenous money implies that changes in the money supply are a consequence of economic activity and should, therefore, follow them. The money supply does not play a causal role within the economy but is created by the demand for loans. For monetarists, on the other hand, changes in the money supply should precede changes in output and prices. This appears to be something we could test empirically. Alas! It is not so easy.

Monetarists have always interpreted the empirical evidence to suggest that changes in the quantity of money have systematically led changes in output and inflation rather than lagging behind them. However, other interpretations of the evidence are available. For example, Laidler (2002) notes that the cyclical nature of output and inflation might produce misleading appearances. Alternatively, he suggests, forward-looking agents might be adjusting their money holdings in line with expected output and prices before these variables actually change. In both cases, the quantity of money might only seem to be leading.

A problem also arises from the existence of time lags. Remember that in Section 7.3, we suggested that a reduction in interest rates would not have its full effect on output for around twelve months and two years might elapse before the full effect was felt on prices. However, the impact on the money supply occurs as soon as banks meet the increase in demand for loans consequent on the fall in interest rates. Indeed, we shall see in Chapter 9, that one of the arguments for using the money supply as an intermediate target of monetary policy is precisely that the time lag between the instrument change and a change in the money supply is relatively short. Thus, timing evidence can tell us little about causality and certainly does not provide the basis for an attack on the endogenous money version of the transmission mechanism.

However, Laidler and others have proposed an addition to that version. This continues to recognize the importance of the credit channel through the impact of changes in interest rates on borrowing and spending, but suggests that the quantity of money might still have a role to play in transmission. In doing this, the importance of the demand for money function is re-established. The interest rate change is identified as the first round in the transmission mechanism. Consider an interest rate reduction. This causes an increase in borrowing and creates deposits and hence money. However, the demand for loans, which creates the supply of money, is not the same thing as the demand for money. Laidler suggests that the increase in the quantity of money resulting from an increased demand for loans might be greater than agents as a group wish to hold. This might arise because the interest rate change disturbs relationships between indebtedness to the banking system and desired stocks of durable goods.

Consider a simple case with two market agents. Interest rates are lowered by the central bank. A increases his borrowing and buys durable goods. B deposits the funds in a bank and both bank deposits and the money supply rise. This is the first round effect. B temporarily has excess money balances. Everything depends on what he does next. If he uses his excess balances to repay existing loans from banks, the money supply falls until it matches the demand for money. There is no separate 'money channel'. Only the credit channel operates. On the other hand, he might use the newly acquired deposit to buys goods, repay a loan to a non-bank or, indeed, make a loan himself. In all of these cases the portfolio disequilibrium is passed on to someone else, the quantity of money does not fall and the demand for money remains below the increased supply of money.

As output and/or prices change following the first round effects on spending, the demand for money increases and we eventually return to equilibrium in the normal way. Nonetheless, the impact of the initial interest rate change differs depending on the response of agents to the increased quantity of money. It is this, which Laidler regards as the second-round effects of the interest rate change or as the money transmission channel. The strength of this effect clearly depends on the nature of the demand for money.

Pause for thought 7.11

In Section 4.4, we consider the view that the demand for money is a constraint on the demand for credit since credit cannot create money unless the resulting deposits are willingly held. We dismiss this as only an equilibrium argument. How does the role for the demand for money envisaged here by Laidler compare with that argument?

One can regard this approach as adding very little. After all, no one would argue that all interest rate changes have the same effects. We have suggested above that much depends, for example, on expectations. It is, indeed, largely because the same interest rate change might have significantly different effects on output and inflation and might take varying periods to do so that the conduct of monetary policy is extremely difficult. It remains that the interest rate change is the causal agent and that money is endogenous. However, identifying a secondary money channel might be one way of explaining puzzling empirical evidence and might help us to understand better the way in which interest rate changes have their effects.

7.6   Money supply changes in an open economy

We have seen in Section 7.3 that changes in the money stock may also influence the level of nominal income through exchange rate changes. The analysis of the effectiveness of monetary policy in an open economy is based upon the Mundell-Fleming model — an open economy model, which adds a *BP* (Balance of Payments equilibrium) curve to the *IS/LM* model (Fleming, 1962; Mundell, 1963).

Figure 7.7: Expansionary monetary policy with flexible exchange rates

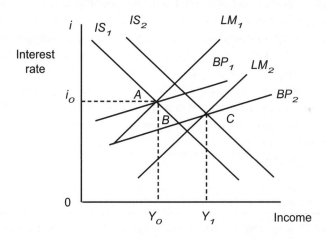

This model was developed in the 1960s when most currencies were linked through the Bretton Woods fixed exchange rate system. Consequently, the BP curve is drawn on the assumption of fixed exchange rates. The *BP* line shows all combinations of income and the rate of interest at which the balance of payments is in balance. Exchange rate devaluations or revaluations cause the *BP* curve to shift. A devaluation of the currency improves the current account of the balance of payments and allows overall balance of payment equilibrium at a lower rate of interest — the *BP* curve shifts down.

As pointed out in Appendix 1, in the normal case for developed countries, the *BP* curve is drawn flatter than the *LM* curve because capital is assumed highly mobile internationally. Thus, only small increases in interest rate are needed to attract a sufficient capital inflow to offset balance of trade deficits resulting from increased income. Figure 7.7 shows this normal case.

Here, we have assumed an increase in the money supply, which shifts the LM curve down from LM_1 to LM_2. Income rises and interest rate falls. The increase in income causes a deterioration in the current account of the balance of payments while the fall in interest rate causes a deterioration in the capital account. The outflow of currency causes a depreciation of the exchange rate shifting the BP curve down. However, the depreciation improves the international competitiveness of domestically produced goods and this is reflected in a rightwards shift of the IS curve. The new equilibrium is established at point C. At this point, the balance of payments is again in balance and both goods and money markets clear but the expansionary monetary policy has produced a higher income and lower interest rate. Monetary policy under these circumstances is more powerful than in the equivalent closed economy case, in which the new equilibrium position would be at point B. Although the improvement in competitiveness resulting from the exchange rate depreciation is likely to be eroded over time by inflation, it remains that any change in the exchange rate brought about by an increase in the supply of money has a significant short-run impact. This creates a more direct link between money and nominal income than in either a closed economy or an open economy with fixed exchange rates.

Pause for thought 7.12

Remembrance of theories past: How is the competitive advantage gained from an exchange rate depreciation eroded over time by inflation?

If we assume a system of fixed exchange rates, the position changes entirely since the BP curve does not move. Thus, an expansionary monetary policy, which shifts the LM curve down and moves the economy to point B, generates a capital outflow as domestic interest rates have fallen below world rates. Since the current account also moves into deficit as income rises, we have a deficit in the balance of payments as a whole. This, together with the developing current account deficit, creates an overall balance of payments deficit. This is shown in Figure 7.8, in which point B lies below the BP curve. Currency flows out of the country and the money supply falls.

We can divide an economy's money stock into two elements: a domestic component (D), assumed exogenous, and the central bank's holding of international reserves (IR):

$$M = D + IR \qquad\qquad ...7.2$$

The initial increase in D shifts the LM curve down and creates the balance of payments deficit. As long as the deficit remains, R is falling, offsetting the initial money supply increase, and pushing the LM curve back towards its original position. Ultimately, we return to A.

Figure 7.8: Expansionary monetary policy with fixed exchange rates

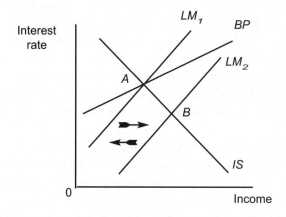

In practice, the balance of payments deficit puts downward pressure on the value of the currency, but the authorities need to intervene, for example by using their international reserves to buy their own currency, in order to preserve the agreed fixed rate of exchange.

If the exchange rate is fully fixed, the length of time the economy takes to return to A depends on the degree of capital mobility since this determines the speed with which capital flows out of the country as the domestic interest rate falls below world levels. With our assumption here of a high level of capital mobility, the return to A occurs rapidly. Increases in income are very temporary. The authorities might try to slow down the movement back to A by attempting to reduce capital mobility through the use of capital controls, but this has become increasingly difficult to do with the growth of offshore financial markets.

Pause for thought 7.13

How would you define 'sterilization', as the word is used here?

Governments might attempt to sterilize the effect on the monetary base of the balance of payments imbalance by undertaking open market operations. Assume the authorities wish to follow an expansionary monetary policy as in Figure 7.8, but the consequent balance of payments deficit frustrates this desire. It therefore accompanies its expansionary monetary policy with an open market purchase of government securities, which has the effect of adding monetary base to the economy, reversing the tendency of the *LM* curve to move back to the left.

However, this can only help to prolong the expansionary phase for a short period. To the extent that sterilization works, it keeps the interest rate below the world level and causes further outflows of capital, again reducing the monetary base. It remains that as long as the balance of payments remains in deficit, international reserves continue to fall and the central bank will soon run out of these. Thus, with fixed exchange rates and mobile capital, the ability of the authorities to operate a more expansionary or more contractionary monetary policy than that of other countries is severely constrained.

Some flexibility exists to the extent that the fixed exchange rate system allows the exchange rate of a currency to move within a band around the fixed central rate. This means that the monetary authorities can allow the value of the currency to drift down (pushing down the *BP* curve) to remove the balance of payments deficit as long as the exchange rate remains within the agreed bands. Normally, however, they must intervene before the lower band is reached in order to avoid damaging speculation against the currency. Nonetheless, the wider the band is, the greater the freedom the authorities have to run a monetary policy different from that of the other members of the fixed exchange rate system.

There are several points to note in this analysis. Firstly, in the floating exchange rate case, the extent of the initial movement of the *LM* curve remains important. Thus, in a Keynesian model, the *LM* curve does not move much, the balance of payments does not deteriorate much and the impact on the exchange rate is only small. Monetary policy under floating exchange rates is more powerful in monetarist models than in Keynesian models.

Secondly, we should not, in practice, expect such rapid adjustment of exchange rates and balance of payments positions as is implied here. The process is slowed down by the presence of a non-tradable goods sector. In any case, the goods market may adjust more slowly to the disturbance than the asset market. Such rigidities in the system might produce exchange rate overshooting, even with rational expectations (Dornbusch, 1976). We consider this in Section 10.5.

Thirdly, the analysis above is simplified to the extent that a change in exchange rate only causes the *BP* curve to shift. In fact, an exchange rate change should also have an impact on the marginal propensity to import and hence on the slope of the *BP* curve. An exchange rate depreciation should improve the international competitiveness of a country's output and hence lower the marginal propensity to import. Thus, a fall in the value of a country's currency should flatten the *BP* curve; an exchange rate appreciation should make it steeper. However, in the normal case, we are assuming that the slope of the *BP* curve is influenced to a much greater extent by the degree of mobility of capital than by the size of the propensity to import. Consequently, allowing for changes in the propensity to import as the exchange rate changes does not make a significant difference to the analysis.

Finally, there are a number of problems with the Mundell-Fleming model. Above all, the international competitiveness of a country's goods and services depends crucially on differences in rates of inflation among countries, but the *IS/LM* analysis assumes constant prices. Once we start talking of inflation, we introduce the distinction between nominal and real interest rates and the difficulty that the interest rate shown on the vertical axis should be the real rate of interest for analysis of the goods market but the nominal rate of interest for analysis of the money market. We discuss this point further in Appendix I.

In addition, the model is concerned only with flows whereas a full equilibrium requires stocks to be in equilibrium, not just flows. The model assumes that a capital outflow continues as long as domestic interest rates are below world interest rates. It is this that causes monetary policy not to work under fixed exchange rates. This implies that differences in interest rates provide the only basis for choosing among domestic and foreign bonds. If, however, we allow for the existence of exchange rate or default risk, in equilibrium people hold a mixture of foreign and domestic bonds. An expansionary monetary policy drives down the domestic interest rate and causes a switch from domestic to foreign bonds, but only until a new stock equilibrium occurs; and, to the extent that foreign bonds are regarded as more risky than domestic bonds, this happens with the domestic rate of interest below the world rate. Once the new stock equilibrium has been reached, the flow of capital ceases.

Yet again, the model considers only the overall equilibrium of the balance of payments, not its full equilibrium, which occurs only when both current and capital accounts are separately in balance. The problem here is that a current account surplus matched by a capital account deficit (or vice versa) is not sustainable since, as we have suggested above, the flow of capital implied by the lack of balance in the capital account continues only until the new stock equilibrium is reached. Once this occurs, there will no longer be a flow of capital to offset the current account imbalance.

Lastly, once we use the model to deal with floating exchange rates, or admit the possibility of exchange rate devaluations or revaluations in a fixed exchange rate system, we need to take into account expectations regarding exchange rate changes. This is not done in the Mundell-Fleming model.

Despite these problems, the model remains useful for considering open economy influences on the transmission mechanism of monetary policy and we return to it in Chapter 10.

7.7 Credit availability and expenditure

Because of the important role played in Keynesian models by the level of credit, Keynesian economists have often argued that monetary policy may operate not only through interest rate changes but also through changes in credit availability. We discussed the importance of credit availability to the FoF approach to the money supply in Section 3.5.

Two types of rationing in credit markets have been distinguished: (a) potential borrowers are not able to obtain a loan irrespective of the interest rate they are willing to pay; (b) a loan of a given amount is offered at a specified interest rate with no possibility of obtaining a higher loan at a higher interest rate. This implies that money markets are in disequilibrium, with the demand for loans being greater than the supply of them by financial institutions. We have here a sticky price model in which interest rates do not (or can not) rise sufficiently to return the market to equilibrium.

Earlier forms of the argument saw either government-imposed controls on interest rates or a failure by financial institutions to follow profit-maximizing behaviour as the cause of credit rationing. Examples include the 'sticky rate effect' and the 'locking-in effect' both stressed by the Radcliffe Committee (1959). The sticky rate effect concerned the slowness of building society interest rates to adjust relative to those of banks. Thus, when interest rates were rising, the building societies lost funds to banks (leading to a rationing of loans). When interest rates were falling, they gained funds from banks. The locking-in effect described the failure of financial institutions, unwilling to realize capital losses on currently held assets, to adjust their portfolios following a sharp fall in asset prices. They were said to feel locked in to their existing portfolios.

More recently, writers have argued that loans are not homogeneous from the lender's point of view, with different loans carrying differing degrees of risk. If we begin in a position of equilibrium and then assume an increase in the demand for loans, lenders may prefer to minimize risk, rationing new loans on a non-price basis (limiting loans to particular categories of borrowers, increasing collateral requirements, or, in the hire-purchase finance market, raising initial deposits or shortening maximum repayment periods).

A recent resurgence in interest in credit availability transmission channels has been based upon imperfect and asymmetric information. For instance, credit rationing by lenders may be an optimal response in a situation in which the potential borrower has greater knowledge than the lender of the uses to which the funds will be applied and of the risks associated with them. The problem for lenders is increased to the extent that borrowers have an incentive to conceal the riskiness of their projects from lenders. These models lead to the proposition that increases in interest rates tend to discourage safe borrowers and to increase the average riskiness of lending. Hence, rather than rationing through higher interest rates, lenders meet an increased demand for loans by rationing credit. Surveys of this material may be found in Blinder (1987) and Miles and Wilcox (1991).

Two types of argument follow from the credit availability doctrine depending on the monetary policy instrument employed by the authorities. The first (assuming an exogenous money supply) is just a changed form of the transmission mechanism that plays down the role of interest rates. A government-induced reduction in the money stock may be met by an increased demand for loans as agents seek to finance their expenditure plans but interest rates do not rise: the transmission is through credit rationing.

Things are more complex for a monetary authority that uses interest rates as its monetary policy instrument. A tight monetary policy based upon increases in the rate of interest may bring about an increase in the average riskiness of lending and in the level of defaults on loans. Thus, the deflationary impact of a tight monetary policy may be very great and may be difficult to control. This formed part of the explanation by Keynesian economists for the depth of the recession in the UK in the early 1990s.

7.8   Summary

This chapter deals with the link between monetary policy and changes in nominal income, leaving the link between nominal income and real income to Chapter 8. Monetary policy may be conducted in one of three ways but in recent times has been conducted very largely through central bank control of short-term interest rates. These have a strong impact on general interest rates in the economy, which in turn influence both consumption and investment expenditure. Although a reduction in interest rates does not cause the consumption of all households and the investment of all firms to increase, the overall relationship between interest rates and expenditure is a negative and potentially powerful one. Much depends on the expectations of households and firms regarding future changes in interest rates and the likely direction the economy will take.

Although monetary authorities do not use the money supply as an instrument of policy, much of the theoretical literature on the monetary transmission mechanism assumes an exogenous money supply, manipulated by the authorities. This literature remains important because it raises questions concerning the likely usefulness and strength of monetary policy. The standard approach, through the *IS-LM* model, concentrates on portfolio effects and sees the transmission of money supply changes as occurring entirely through the interest rate. The Keynesian speculative demand model raises doubts about both the usefulness and strength of monetary policy - the former because it allows the possibility of an unstable demand for money function, the latter because it produces an argument for a highly interest-rate-elastic demand for money. This model has been criticized on several grounds. One of these has been to argue that even pure monetary policy has wealth effects and that there is a direct transmission of monetary policy through wealth effects in addition to any transmission through interest rates. In monetarist versions of the transmission mechanism the direct link between the money supply and expenditure becomes the most important.

The chapter concludes with an outline of the theoretical approach to the link between monetary policy, exchange rates and expenditure and with the possibility of transmission occurring through credit availability rather than through interest rates. Amongst the debate over monetary policy, we can identify a number of positions, which can be summarized as:

Keynes:
Changes in the money supply are not likely to have a powerful effect on aggregate demand particularly when the economy is in recession; the size of any effect will be unpredictable since the demand for money function might be unstable.

Neo-Keynesian (Tobin):
The effect of a change in the money supply on aggregate demand is both more powerful and more predictable than in Keynes.

Monetarist:
The effect of a change in the money supply on expenditure is both direct and powerful. However, monetarist economists recognize long and variable time lags in policy, which lead them to prefer the operation of monetary pol-

icy by following a monetary rule (see Chapter 9) and believe that the long-run impact of money supply changes falls only on prices not on output (see Chapter 8).

Post-Keynesian:
Post-Keynesians accept the propositions listed under Keynes above but add that the money stock is endogenous and thus cannot be controlled by the Central Bank even if it would like to do so.

Key concepts in this chapter

transmission mechanism of
 monetary policy

interest rate control

monetary base control

cost of borrowing

inflationary expectations

real money balances

portfolio effects

wealth effects

speculative demand for money

normal rate of interest

liquidity trap

net wealth of the private sector

Questions and exercises

1. How might the impact of a change in UK interest rates be affected by:
(a) demand conditions in the USA;
(b) the expected future policy of the Federal Reserve Board?

2 Following a stock exchange crash in 1987, there was a temporary fear of a recession because of an anticipated reduction of consumption expenditure.
(a) What was the basis of this fear?
(b) Was the fear justified?
(c) Would things be any different now?

3. What difference would it make to the strength of UK monetary policy if all mortgages were fixed-interest-rate loans:
(a) in the short run; (b) in the long run?

4. How are interest rate changes likely to affect the distribution of income between:
(a) rich and poor; (b) borrowers and lenders; (c) old and young?

5. The text describes consols (non-maturing bonds) as 'relatively illiquid'—relative to money.
(a) Why are they 'relatively illiquid'?
(b) Rank them in terms of liquidity among the following range of assets: money, houses, jewellery, treasury bills, gold bullion, long-term bonds maturing in one year's time, life insurance policies.

6. Provide examples from everyday of life of different forms of expectations — static, regressive, extrapolative.

7. Draw *IS/LM* diagrams with differently sloped *LM* curves and consider the impact in your diagrams of assuming different slopes.

8. If there is a 'normal rate of interest' in money markets, what factors might cause it to change?

9. How far ahead do people typically look in making market decisions? Provide examples of different forms of market behaviour in this regard.

10. Provide examples of the three types of capital goods distinguished by Brunner and Meltzer in formulating their version of the monetarist transmission mechanism.

11. How useful is it in a Mundell-Fleming model to assume perfectly mobile international capital flows? What happens in the diagram with differently sloped BP curves?

Further reading

The best source of material on the transmission mechanism in the UK is the Bank of England (1999) article from which we have borrowed Figure 7.1. This can also be found at www.bankofengland.co.uk

A discussion of the transmission mechanism with an equivalent diagram can also be found in Chapter 3 of the ECB (2001) and at www.ecb.int.

The material on the transmission mechanism with exogenous money is scattered but Gowland (1991) is a reliable source of the principal ideas and covers some aspects in more detail than here, The Mundell-Fleming model can be found in many books on macroeconomics, international economics, and foreign exchange. Two sources are Acocella (1998) and L S Copeland (2000).

8 The Transmission Mechanism of Monetary Policy - II

'But it is pretty to see what money will do.' Samuel Pepys, *Diary*, 21.3.1667

What you will learn in this chapter:

- The empirical basis for the existence of an unemployment/inflation trade-off through the simple Phillips curve
- How the expectations-augmented Phillips curve introduces money illusion into the analysis to deny the existence of a long-run unemployment/inflation trade-off
- The distinction in the Friedman/Phelps model between the short run and the long-run
- Friedman's simple monetary growth rule for monetary policy
- The basis of the New Classical model and of the proposition that aggregate demand policy is completely ineffective
- Criticisms of the New Classical model
- The use of the policy ineffectiveness theorem to develop the ideas of credibility and time consistency
- The case for central bank independence based on the importance of credibility in monetary policy
- More general arguments for and against central bank independence

8.1 Introduction

In Chapter 7, we considered the impact of changes in interest rates and the money stock on nominal income. However, our ultimate concern is with their effect on real variables and on the rate of inflation. To complete the picture, therefore, we need to consider the links between nominal and real income.

Before Keynes's *General Theory*, this was the preserve of the Quantity Theory of Money, which suggested that, in anything other than the short run, any change in the rate of growth of the money supply would simply lead to inflation. Real income (output) was assumed to be determined by the real forces of saving (thrift) and productivity and not by monetary factors. As we have seen, this required a stable demand for money and hence a stable income velocity of money. There was thus, effectively, no transmission mechanism between changes in the money supply and output. Long-run real interest rates could not be influenced by monetary policy. Classical theory argued that they were determined by the behaviour of savers and investors, as set out in the loanable funds theory of the determination of interest rates. Both saving and investment decisions, and hence the real rate of interest, depended on long-term considerations. The monetary authorities could influence nominal interest rates, but these were of no long-run significance for the real economy.

This picture was disturbed by Keynes's *General Theory* and by the interpretations made by Keynesians of this theory. In this view, the nominal interest rate was determined by the demand for and supply of money and provided a vital link between the real and monetary sectors of the economy. Changes in nominal interest rates could bring about changes in real interest rates and have an effect on the real variables of output and employment. Further, the demand for money was held not to be stable and hence control of the money supply would not have a predictable effect on nominal income. The interest rate became the accepted monetary policy instrument but, as we saw in Chapter 7, monetary policy was thought to have only a weak effect on nominal income, especially when the economy was in recession. However, whenever the economy was operating at less than full employment, any impact on nominal income implied also an impact on output since inadequate demand was argued to be a major cause of unemployment.

This approach explained the standard Keynesian models in which the general price level was assumed to be constant and hence no distinction was made between nominal income and output. An increase in demand implied an increase in output and employment. It was always acknowledged that excess demand would cause prices to increase when the economy was at full employment as inflationary gaps (the gap between aggregate demand and aggregate supply at the existing price level) developed. In more detailed models, prices had to rise before the economy was at full employment because an increase in employment required a reduction in real wages and this could only occur through an increase in the general price level. There was thus an inherent notion of a trade-off between reductions in unemployment and increases in the price level. Despite this, there was little enquiry into this trade-off until 1958 when A W Phillips first constructed the Phillips curve (Phillips, 1958). Section 8.2 deals with the original Phillips curve and the subsequent attack on the idea of the existence of a long-run trade-off between wage inflation and unemployment in the Friedman-Phelps expectations-augmented Phillips curve. Section 8.3 then discusses the New

Classical model, which assumes forward-looking (rational) expectations and in which the trade-off disappears altogether, even in the short- run.

Unfortunately for the New Classical model, it is clear from the evidence that there is a short-run trade off between inflation and unemployment. A monetary policy shock does have real effects, at least in the short-run. Further, the impact of such a shock on unemployment precedes the impact on the rate of inflation. Thus, in Section 8.4, we look at the many criticisms of the New Classical model and at recent attempts to explain the inflation/unemployment trade-off.

Despite these criticisms, the New Classical model had a powerful effect on the way in which people looked at economic policy. In particular, it led to the policy irrelevance proposition that the authorities cannot influence real variables by boosting or squeezing aggregate demand. Section 8.5 introduces the notions of credibility and time consistency and spells out the idea that the economy can only reach the optimum (zero) rate of inflation if the monetary policy of the authorities is held to be credible by market agents. Ways of obtaining credibility are listed, including the granting of independence to the central bank. This leads us into Section 8.6, which considers the question of the independence of the central bank.

8.2 The simple Phillips curve

After World War II, the UK government accepted for the first time the obligation to try to run the economy as close to full employment as possible, although the term 'full employment' was never precisely defined. Keynes's *General Theory* had suggested that economies in deep recession could reduce unemployment by expanding aggregate demand and that, in such circumstances, fiscal policy was likely to provide a more powerful instrument than monetary policy. There appeared to be empirical support for these ideas. Unemployment had been high in the 1930s when demand was low; it was non-existent during the war years when demand for everything outstripped supply; and it seemed in the 1950s that expansionary demand management could reverse small increases in unemployment.

Pause for thought 8.1:

What definitions might one use for the term 'full employment'?

After 1958, the idea that governments could effectively choose the level of employment and output up to some critical full employment level, enjoyed what appeared to be overwhelming empirical support from the work of A W

Phillips (1958). The Phillips curve plotted the relationship in the UK between the recorded level of unemployment (U) and the rate of change of money wages ($\dot{W}$) from 1861 to 1957. The rate of change of money wages was used as a proxy for inflation since price inflation data was not available for the early years. Figure 8.1 shows a simple Phillips curve with wage inflation on the vertical axis. However, it was easy to move from wage inflation to price inflation by allowing for increases in labour productivity and the Phillips curve is almost always drawn in price inflation/unemployment space.

Pause for thought 8.2:

How would one modify Figure 8.1 to convert it into a diagram with price inflation on the vertical axis?

The implication seemed clear. The evidence suggested firstly that the economy could be run at various levels of employment and, consequently, output. Secondly, it suggested that the level of unemployment could be reduced without producing inflation until it fell to the level of unemployment at which the curve cut the horizontal axis (5.5 per cent in Phillips's original study). Thirdly, the government appeared able to choose to run the economy at even lower levels of unemployment if they so wished, but at the cost of inflation. They could, for example, choose point B in Figure 8.1. The original study suggested that an unemployment level of 2.5 per cent required acceptance of a 2 per cent rate of inflation. Thus was born the idea of a stable trade-off between unemployment and inflation.

Figure 8.1: The simple Phillips curve

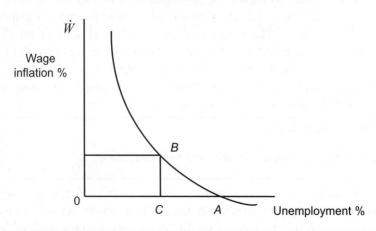

Empirical support for the Phillips curve trade-off was found in many economies in the early 1960s, but Phillips's statistical study needed theoretical support. Much of standard Keynesian macroeconomics assumed constant prices. Where prices were introduced, the analysis was in terms of the price level rather than the rate of inflation. Lipsey (1960) and others provided some theoretical support. However, neoclassical economists remained sceptical because, in conventional microeconomic analysis, employment (and hence unemployment) levels depended on the real wage, not the money wage as implied by the Phillips curve. One way of bringing the statistical evidence into line with microeconomic theory was to assume a zero rate of expected inflation. In other words, workers always took the existing money wage as equivalent to the real wage — a restatement of the existence of money illusion.

When, in the late 1960s, inflation rates began to rise steadily and the points showing the unemployment/money wage inflation combinations began to appear well off to the right of the curve plotted by Phillips in 1958, Friedman and Phelps were separately able to exploit this approach to explaining the trade-off (Friedman, 1968; Phelps, 1967). The result was the Friedman/Phelps expectations augmented Phillips curve. Of the many attempts made to explain the movement away from the original Phillips curve, the Friedman/Phelps model conformed best to the standard theory that rational labour market decisions were based on real wages. In other words, it was an extension of the dominant neoclassical theory of market behaviour. This ensured its survival ahead of other theories that depended on institutional changes and the existence of class conflict to explain the growth of cost inflation.

By incorporating a theory of expectations formation into the model of worker behaviour, the Friedman/Phelps model allowed workers to take expected inflation into account. In so doing, it introduced the possibility of the money wage being different from the real wage. If, then, workers' estimate of the rate of inflation were correct, there would be no money illusion and the labour supply decisions of workers would be based on the true real wage rate. The Friedman/Phelps model assumed the use of adaptive expectations by workers, with workers basing their expectations of inflation on a weighted average of past inflation rates. Their expectations are said to be backward looking. This means that past errors are built in to future forecasts (the errors are serially correlated). When inflation is increasing, workers systematically underestimate the rate of inflation and *vice versa*. Thus, if inflation were to increase steadily over a number of years, workers would expect higher and higher inflation rates and would push money wages up to reflect this. Consequently, the gap between the money wage rate and the equilibrium real wage rate would grow — workers would demand higher and higher money wage rates to supply the same quantity of labour as before. The combinations of unemployment and the rate of inflation experienced by the economy would appear above and to the right of the curve plotted by Phillips. Thus, according to Friedman/Phelps, there was a different short run Phillips curve for every expected rate of inflation.

On each such short run curve, there would be one point at which workers' estimate of the real wage would be correct, and this would be the long-run position. Linking these long-run positions together provided the vertical long-run 'Phillips curve' at the level of unemployment that existed when the labour market was in equilibrium. This was called the 'natural rate of unemployment'. It extended the previously existing notion of 'voluntary' unemployment resulting from workers placing too high a value upon their leisure by allowing also for unemployment caused by structural factors (such as the level of economic development and the characteristics of the labour market). Crucially, however, it did not include unemployment caused by lack of aggregate demand — at the natural rate of unemployment, unemployment is balanced by job vacancies. Thus, government could only hope to reduce the natural rate of unemployment by microeconomic policies that affected the structural characteristics of markets or the incentives faced by economic agents in making their work/leisure choices, not by increasing aggregate demand.

Pause for thought 8.3:

In what sense might an unemployed worker who is seriously looking for work but never receives a job offer be 'voluntarily unemployed'?

The natural rate of unemployment could occur with any rate of inflation and would do so as long as the expected rate of inflation was equal to the actual rate of inflation. The notion of a long run trade-off between unemployment and inflation had been completely removed. The rate of inflation would be explained, as in the Quantity Theory of Money, by the rate of growth of the money supply. The model, thus, supports the simple rule of monetary policy proposed by Milton Friedman — that the rate of growth of the money supply in a stable price environment should be kept equal to the rate of change in real income.

Short-run trade-offs between unemployment and inflation could exist but only because the economy was out of equilibrium. We start at point *A* in Figure 8.2, with the rate of inflation having been at zero for some years and with workers expecting it to remain at zero. We assume, next, that the authorities increase the rate of growth of the money supply in the hope of reducing unemployment. Inflation unexpectedly increases to two per cent. The real wage falls but workers continue to offer labour to the market as if it had not done so. At the lower real wage rate, employers hire more workers and expand production. Output and employment increase and we move along the short-run Phillips curve from A to B. However, workers gradually adapt their expectations to take into account the true rate of inflation and, so long as the rate of inflation remains at 2 per cent, they will eventually forecast it correctly. Money wages are pushed up to restore the initial real wage and the economy returns to equilibrium, again at the natural rate of unemployment but at a higher rate of inflation than previously. That is, the original short-run Phillips curve applied only as long as expected inflation remained at 0 per cent. When expectations were changed, the curve shifted to cut the long-run vertical Phillips curve at the, now expected, actual rate of inflation of 2 per cent.

Figure 8.2: The expectations-augmented Phillips curve

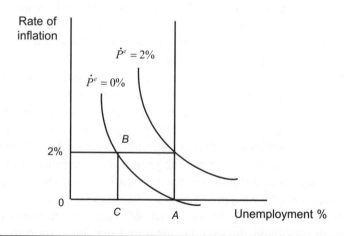

Further attempts by the authorities to reduce unemployment by increasing the rate of growth of the money supply push inflation higher but, in the long run, produce no reduction in unemployment. It follows that any level of unemployment below the natural rate of unemployment is available only temporarily and is associated with accelerating inflation. For this reason, the natural rate of unemployment became widely known as the NAIRU (the non-accelerating-inflation rate of unemployment).[1]

The expectations-augmented Phillips curve was bad news for governments wishing to control unemployment by managing aggregate demand. It implied that increases in aggregate demand could reduce unemployment but only in the short run and only at the expense of accelerating inflation. Each attempt by the government to lower unemployment below the NAIRU would ratchet up the rate of inflation. In fact, the news was even worse since it was also argued that increasing inflation interfered with the operation of the price mechanism and reduced the efficiency of the economy. This would cause the NAIRU to rise. This view assumed that higher rates of inflation meant more volatile inflation and hence an increased chance of incorrect inflationary expectations.

Pause for thought 8.4:

Is it reasonable to assume that inflation is more volatile at higher average rates of inflation? Can the rate of inflation also be volatile if the average rate of inflation is low?

The most prominent explanation of the damage done to the price mechanism by volatile inflation came from Lucas (1972, 1973). He assumed that firms know the current price of their own goods but only learn what happens to prices in other markets with a time lag. When the current price of its output rises, a firm has to decide whether this reflects a real increase in demand for its own product or a general increase in prices resulting from random demand shocks. In the former case, the rational response would be to increase its output; in the latter case, it should not do so. That is, firms have to distinguish between absolute and relative prices. The signal that should be provided to producers by changes in relative prices is being confused by the possibility of inflation, especially by volatile inflation. Firms face a signal extraction problem. The greater the variability of the general price level, the more difficult it is for a producer to extract the correct signal, and the smaller the supply response is likely to be for any given change in prices. Far from there being a trade-off between unemployment and inflation, the accepted theory now suggested that inflation caused unemployment to increase. To reduce unemployment in the long-run, governments were required to keep inflation low and to attempt to lower the NAIRU through supply-side measures.

There was also bad news for those authorities who started with a high rate of inflation and wished to get it down. Reducing the rate of growth of the money supply would push inflation down but workers would continue for some time to expect the previous high rate of inflation and would continue to push money wages up in line with their expectations. Real wages would rise, output would fall, and unemployment would increase beyond the NAIRU. The amount of output lost in order to bring about a fall in inflation was called the sacrifice ratio. Of course, in the long run, workers would adjust their expectations and unemployment would fall back to the NAIRU. However, the short-term costs in terms of lost output and increased unemployment could be high, especially since the theory did not indicate how long it would take workers to adjust their expectations.[2] The 'long run' is a logical construct —- the time that it takes for workers to obtain full information about changing prices. However, in a constantly changing world, this could be a very long time. Indeed, there is no reason to believe that any economy ever reaches the long-run. Thus, within the Friedman/Phelps model, monetary policy might have considerable and continuing real effects.

Pause for thought 8.5:

The argument here implies that workers determine the rate of growth of money wages — they build the expected rate of inflation into money wages, so that if their expectations are correct, the real wage remains unchanged. Is this an accurate picture of wage bargaining?

There are other objections to the theory. Firstly, the evidence that inflation was very costly for economies even at low levels was not strong. The principal loss for an economy identified by Friedman and others (called the shoe leather cost of inflation) was a welfare cost, which depended on people switching from money to other assets because of inflation. However, if one accepts the Keynesian proposition that there are close substitutes for money, this cost might not be very great at low inflation rates. Further, one could argue that low rates of inflation might be desirable since a zero rate of inflation for the economy as a whole would require prices to be falling in some sectors and falling prices have always been associated with low levels of confidence. Of course, as we have noted above, the model suggests that continuing attempts by the authorities to exploit the short-term unemployment/inflation trade-off produce accelerating inflation and so eventually the costs of inflation must increase, whatever one's view about the closeness of substitutes for money. Even so, much time might pass before the costs of inflation become serious for an economy.

Secondly, the view that inflation was caused by the monetary authorities implied a belief in a stable demand for money function and an exogenous money supply, which, as we have seen in earlier chapters, are both open to serious doubt — especially in the case of exogenous money (see Chapter 4).

Thirdly, unemployment might also have long-run impacts. It has been argued that increases in unemployment damage confidence leading to lower investment and economic growth and might lower the skill levels of workers causing reductions in labour productivity. That is, increased unemployment in the short-run could cause higher unemployment in the long run and the long-run costs of unemployment might be greater than the long-run costs of low inflation.

The debate over the expectations-augmented Phillips curve thus led to many attempts to enumerate and compare the various costs of both inflation and unemployment. If the costs of unemployment were high relative to those of low rates of inflation and if economies never reached long-run equilibrium positions, there was still a case for attacking unemployment by expanding aggregate demand. Nonetheless, the Friedman/Phelps model, together with the experience of stagflation in many developed economies in the 1970s, was influential in the increasing acceptance by governments of the limitations of demand management policies. Governments everywhere began to pay much greater attention to the supply side of the economy.

Pause for thought 8.6:

Memory test: Define 'stagflation'?

8.3   The new classical model and policy irrelevance

The opposition to demand management policies was soon strengthened with the development of the new classical model in which the rational expectations hypothesis was applied to a model of continuous market clearing. Rational (forward-looking) expectations are informed predictions of future events and are essentially the same as the predictions of the relevant economic model, which is assumed the correct model for the economy. It follows that the expected rate of inflation is an unbiased predictor of the actual rate of inflation. Mistakes may be made because the available information is incomplete but expectations are correct on average. That is,

$$\dot{P}_t^e = \dot{P}_t + \varepsilon_t \qquad \qquad ...8.1$$

where ε_t is a random error term, which (i) has a mean of zero and (ii) is uncorrelated with the information set available when expectations are formed. Thus, forecasting errors are not serially correlated. The assumption of rational expectations could be seen as a clear advance because they are compatible with all other aspects of the model in a way that adaptive expectations are not. Adaptive expectations require an additional hypothesis — how market agents adapt expectations to take account of previous errors. The assumption of rational expectations, however, means that the expectations of agents are always the values of the variables produced by the model itself.

The rational expectations hypothesis suggests that market agents make the best use of all available and relevant information in their forecasts of inflation—rather than simply taking account of past rates of inflation, as in adaptive expectations. Since the rate of growth of the money supply is relevant information in the monetarist model to which new classical economics applied rational expectations, market agents are assumed to consider government policy in making their forecasts. In other words, government is incorporated into the model. In all previous models, government was exogenous.

The assumption of continuous market clearing implies that prices are free to adjust instantaneously to clear markets. It follows that anyone wishing to work can find employment at the market-clearing equilibrium wage and thus that all unemployment is voluntary. The combination of the rational expectations hypothesis and the assumption of continuous market clearing implies that output and employment fluctuate randomly around their natural levels. Thus, unemployment fluctuates randomly around the NAIRU. All we are left with of the Phillips curve is the vertical line at the NAIRU. Increases in aggregate demand do not produce systematic reductions in unemployment, even in the short-run. All they do is increase inflation. Acceptance of the new classical model denies that there is any advantage to be had from demand management.

Pause for thought 8.7:

Is it reasonable to call a vertical line at the natural rate of unemployment 'a vertical Phillips curve'?

Another way of making the same point is to say that rational market agents fully anticipate the actions of the authorities and incorporate this information in their expectations of the rate of inflation. That is, if the monetary authorities seek to increase the rate of growth of the money supply in the hope of reducing unemployment, market agents realize this and correctly forecast that the rate of inflation will rise. Workers then push wages up in line with the correctly forecast inflation and real wages; employment and output all remain unchanged. The level of unemployment does not fall. Thus, fully anticipated changes in monetary policy are ineffective in influencing the level of output and employment even in the short run. This is known as the policy ineffectiveness or policy irrelevance theorem.

According to this theorem, the only way in which the authorities can influence output and employment through demand policies is to take market agents by surprise. For example, an unexpected increase in the money supply causes workers and firms to see the consequent increase in the general price level as an increase in relative prices. They react by increasing the supply of output and labour and the economy moves to a new short-run aggregate supply curve. Both employment and output temporarily increase. As in the expectations-augmented Phillips curve, once agents realize there has been no change in relative prices, output and employment return to their natural levels at the higher price level. However, there are two important differences from the expectations-augmented Phillips curve.

Firstly, market agents include the rate of money supply growth in the information they use to forecast inflation and quickly realize that inflation is about to rise. They thus adjust their inflation forecasts much more quickly than in the expectations-augmented Phillips curve case, where agents do not realize what is happening until inflation actually rises.

Secondly, the authorities are unable to exploit the possibility of the temporary trade-off between inflation and unemployment. If they try to reduce unemployment through monetary shocks at all frequently, agents learn that this is what the authorities do when unemployment reaches undesirable levels. Workers and firms anticipate the monetary shocks and are no longer taken by surprise. In other words, any short-run trade-off between inflation and unemployment disappears if the authorities try to exploit it.

The more often the authorities try to engineer reductions in unemployment through monetary shocks, the less easily are workers and firms fooled and the more vertical is the short-run Phillips curve. The incorporation of government into the model ensures the policy invariance result. If market agents believe that increases in the rate of growth of the money supply have no real effects but only cause increases in the rate of inflation, government cannot have an impact on output and employment by increasing the rate of growth of the money supply. When governments do this, market agents immediately respond by raising their inflationary expectations, the short-run Phillips curve moves out and the economy remains at the NAIRU. Money is once again neutral.

8.4   Problems of the new classical model

As we mentioned in 8.1, a major problem for the new classical model is that money is not neutral in the short-run. It is widely accepted that a monetary shock does have an impact on output and unemployment and that this impact occurs before the shock begins to influence the rate of inflation. There have, thus, been many attempts to explore the weaknesses of the new classical model and to produce new explanations of the non-neutrality of money. We can divide these attempts into five groups:

- modifications to the model that accept continuous market clearing;
- complete rejections of equilibrium models;
- new Keynesian models that reject market clearing in the short run;
- criticisms of the natural rate hypothesis;
- attacks on the use of rational expectations.

Modifications to the continuous market clearing model

Relatively small changes to the model can restore the power of governments to reduce output fluctuations at the cost of an increase in price fluctuations and, thus, remove the neutrality of money, without attacking the principal assumptions of the new classical model. These include:

(a) Progressive income tax structures push workers into higher tax brackets as inflation rises, affecting employment and output. Tax changes might also affect net-of-tax real rates of interest and, hence, influence borrowing and lending.

(b) Changes in the rate of inflation might influence investment and, thus, the long-run rate of growth. For example, higher inflation makes holding real capital more attractive relative to money, and might stimulate investment.

(c) Higher inflation might have a positive impact on consumption as saving in the form of financial assets becomes less attractive.

(d) Price movements in a model with asset holdings might produce real effects:

(i) through changes in the real value of nominally denominated government assets provided they are considered to be net wealth; and

(ii) through distribution effects that might occur even with assets issued by the private sector, as creditors and debtors react asymmetrically to changes in the real value of debt.

However, these are only likely to have real effects if the price level changes are unexpected and this conflicts with the forward-looking assumptions of the new classical model.

(e) With fixed exchange rates in an open economy, the relative prices of tradable and non-tradable goods change in response even to expected changes in the money supply.

The complete rejection of equilibrium models

At the opposite extreme are criticisms that reject entirely the assumption of continuous market clearing, arguing that real world prices are not perfectly flexible and markets do not continuously return to equilibrium. The neo-classical identification of the long run with equilibrium, which leaves dise-quilibrium as a short-run phenomenon based on imperfect knowledge, is replaced by a view of the world dominated by uncertainty in which dise-quilibrium is the norm. Equilibrium is a special case, unlikely ever to be reached. When markets do clear, it is often not through the process of price adjustment. Lack of information about the future leads to coordination fail-ures among markets.

Pause for thought 8.8:

How can markets clear other than through price changes? Does any other form of market clearing lead to a genuine equilibrium?

This certainly overcomes the policy ineffectiveness problem despite the introduction of rational expectations into the analysis, but there remains the problem of explaining the transmission mechanism from money to prices and output. A number of general disequilibrium models were produced in the 1970s (Benassy, 1975; Barro and Grossman, 1976; Grandmont, 1977; Malinvaud, 1977). These were fix-price models, although absolutely fixed prices were not required for monetary and fiscal policy changes to produce real effects. However, the models lacked plausible explanations of how prices are determined in an economy not at a market clearing equilibrium. Consequently, they had little long-term influence on the debate.

New Keynesian models that reject market clearing in the short-run

A less strong criticism of continuous market clearing accepts the existence of a long-run equilibrium and the tendency for economies to return to equi-librium positions. However, this may take a considerable time, not because of incorrect expectations but because of institutional features of the market.

One set of these theories, sticky price wage models, concentrates on the labour market. The best known of these assume long-term overlapping wage contracts (Taylor, 1979). When trade unions enter into a contract in which wages are fixed for one or two years, even if workers form expectations rationally and are able to forecast the actions of the policy authorities, they are unable to react to new information. Thus, an inflationary monetary shock pushes up aggregate demand and prices rise but, during the life of wage contracts, money wages cannot rise. Real wages fall and employment and output increase. It is only as some wage contracts end that money wages are pushed up and the monetary impulse begins to have a more powerful impact on the rate of inflation. Equally, following a disinflationary monetary shock, in the short term real wages are pushed up and output and employment fall. This means that there is a period during which the authorities might exploit a trade-off between unemployment and inflation. Monetary policy is again useful.

To support this model, we need an explanation of why workers and firms enter into long-term wage contracts. New Keynesian economists see these as the product of rational behaviour given the conditions in real world labour markets. For instance, the theory of implicit contracts assumes incomplete labour markets (workers do not have full access to insurance against risk). There is also asymmetric information and workers and firms have different degrees of risk aversion. The outcome is the standard labour contract in which the wage is held constant and the worker's job is guaranteed over the period of the contract, no matter how well or badly the firm is doing.

Pause for thought 8.9:

What form might asymmetric information take in negotiations between employers and workers over labour contracts? Which side may be better informed about what?

Another possible explanation of the failure of the labour market to clear continuously is provided by the insider-outsider model, in which workers already employed by firms have an advantage over unemployed workers. In neoclassical models, the real wage is kept at the market clearing level through competition between workers for jobs. Workers with jobs cannot push their wages above the equilibrium level because there are other workers willing to take their places at a lower wage rate. However, in real world labour markets, there is often no genuine competition between employed and unemployed. Employers know the abilities and attitudes of the workers they already employ, but must make judgements about unemployed workers based on limited information, such as the length of time the potential worker has been unemployed. Firms often assume that a long period of unemployment implies something personally unsatisfactory about the worker, or that the period of unemployment has reduced his potential productivity, or both. Again, the firm has spent time and money training its existing work force and would face costs in both getting rid of existing workers and hiring new workers. For these reasons, firms are willing to pay higher wages to existing workers than would be accepted by unemployed workers.

Existing workers (insiders) take advantage of their position to push the wage above the market clearing level, causing employers to hire fewer workers than they would in a competitive market. The unemployed workers remain unemployed. In practice, unemployed workers seldom receive job offers and are not in a position to show their willingness to undercut the wage paid to the existing workforce. Equally, employers are seldom in a position to discover the wage at which unemployed workers might be prepared to do the job. Unfortunately, the sticky wage theory also conflicts with reality. If there is no competition from the unemployed, there is no reason for money wages to rise more rapidly in booms than in slumps. Since prices rise more rapidly in booms, we might expect real wages to move contra-cyclically — falling in booms and rising in slumps. This does not happen.

Pause for thought 8.10:

Why might the insider/outsider model apply better to skilled than to unskilled workers?

Consequently, attention has shifted to new Keynesian models of the price-setting behaviour of firms. These assume monopolistic competition in goods markets and incorporate costs of adjusting prices. Firms have market power and, thus, are able to set prices above marginal cost. Consequently, they always wish to sell more at prevailing prices. A monetary shock influences both aggregate demand and the demand for labour and leads firms to adjust output and employment. That is, it has real effects. In a recession, there is excess supply in both the goods and labour markets. This theory of the goods market is often combined with a model of the labour market that produces above-equilibrium real wages. Mankiw (2001) points out that this approach runs into difficulties when economists attempt to develop dynamic models of price setting. The most common approach to this assumes that price adjustment is costly and, hence, infrequent. These models produce a form of Phillips curve, frequently referred to as the new Keynesian Phillips curve.

Mankiw sets out an illustrative model in which the current inflation rate becomes a function of inflation expected to prevail in the next period and the deviation of unemployment from its natural rate. If expected inflation is held constant, higher unemployment leads to lower inflation, much as in the Friedman-Phelps model. Again, however, the model runs into trouble when confronted with evidence. Oddly, according to the model, credible monetary disinflations are likely to produce booms (Ball, 1994) whereas, in practice, monetary disinflations typically lead to recession. Mankiw also argues that the new Keynesian Phillips curve is incapable of producing empirically plausible impulse responses to monetary policy shocks. He assumes a plausible response of inflation to a monetary policy shock and then shows that the new Keynesian Phillips curve implies an implausible result for unemployment — a monetary contraction causes unemployment to fall!

Criticisms of the natural rate hypothesis

We have seen that the new Classical model depends on the concept of the natural rate of unemployment — the rate of unemployment at which the labour market clears and does not exert pressure on the rate of inflation. This implies that the natural rate is independent of the actual rate of unemployment in the economy and raises the question of how easy it is to identify the natural rate. There are problems under both headings. According to Mankiw, the natural rate of unemployment 'is impossible to know with much precision' (Mankiw, 2001, p. C47).

Further, there is evidence in support of hysteresis — the notion that the current level of unemployment has an impact on future unemployment levels. If this is true, there is no single 'natural rate' for an economy and increases in unemployment resulting from disinflationary monetary policy persist into the long term. Money is not neutral even in the long run. Ball (1997) provides support for this. His analysis of the growth of European unemployment in the 1980s shows that countries with larger decreases in inflation and longer disinflationary periods experienced larger increases in their natural rates of unemployment. In a 1999 paper, Ball shows that these larger increases in the natural rate of unemployment could be linked back to a failure to pursue expansionary monetary policy in the early 1980s. That is, monetary policy influenced both actual unemployment and the natural rate of unemployment. Shocks to US real GDP are also typically very persistent, offering support for the existence of hysteresis.

Criticisms of the assumption of rational expectations

There have also been several criticisms of the rational expectations hypothesis. It has been argued, for example, that the form of learning applied in the rational expectations model is unrealistic. Acocella (1998) also suggests that the new classical model is a model of a stationary society and that the 'rationality' of human beings in this system ignores 'creative rationality', which involves the attempt to transform society and the environment rather than just accepting what already exists.

Empirical work on the new classical model

Two statements are made in response to criticisms that the assumptions of the new classical model are unrealistic: that markets act as if the assumptions were true; and that the only way of judging a model is through testing its predictions — if the model predicts well, the underlying theory must be a sufficiently good representation of reality. We, thus, need to say a little more than we have so far done about the empirical work done on the new classical model.

Pause for thought 8.11:

Memory test: Where previously in this book have we come across the proposition that 'the only way of judging a model is through testing its predictions'.

Much of this empirical work involves testing one of the implications of the policy irrelevance hypothesis — that deviations of real variables from trend result from people being surprised by movements in the general price level. In other words, only unanticipated monetary policy has real effects. Anticipated monetary policy should be neutral. On this basis, early work (Barro, 1977, 1978) appeared to support the policy ineffectiveness proposition. Using annual data for the US economy from 1941 to 1976, Barro's study suggested that, while output and employment are significantly affected by unanticipated monetary growth, anticipated monetary growth has no real effects. However, subsequent studies (Mishkin, 1982; Gordon, 1982), found evidence that output and employment are affected by both anticipated and unanticipated monetary policy. By 1989, Goodhart (1989a, ch.13) was able to report 63 tests of the policy irrelevance hypothesis for seven different countries. Of these, 17 appeared to confirm the hypothesis that only unanticipated monetary shocks had real effects. The great majority suggested that monetary policy had real effects, whether it was anticipated or not.[3] More recent testing has not altered that balance.

Quite apart from the formal testing, it seems hard to accept that major booms and recessions can be explained by frequent, large and persistent errors in the inflation expectations of market agents, especially given the quantity and quality of information that is available about current changes and likely future movements of the price level. It seems far more likely that monetary policy's impact on real variables is the result of one or more of the arguments critical of the new classical model. The most likely candidate is the failure of real world markets to clear perfectly and instantaneously.

8.5 Credibility and time consistency

Nonetheless, to develop our next set of propositions, we need to ignore the criticisms of the new classical model. We must return to the policy irrelevance proposition and to the idea that the expectations of market agents regarding the rate of inflation depend on their view of the likely behaviour of the authorities, specifically the expected rate of growth of the money supply. In such a world, the monetary authorities could assist market agents in the formation of expectations by following a clear monetary rule or, at least, announcing targets for the rate of growth of the money supply. There would be no point in attempting to mislead market agents because, to be effective, they would need to do so in a consistent direction. That is, if the authorities wanted to reduce unemployment they would always need to cause the money supply to grow at a faster rate than their announced target. However, market agents would soon realize that the money supply always grew at a faster rate than the authorities' target and would adjust their inflation expectations accordingly. In other words, agents would make a judgement regarding the credibility of the policy announcements of the authorities.

The credibility of a particular policy statement would depend on:

(a) the performance of the policy authorities in the past (their *reputation)*

and

(b) the nature of the policy institutions.

Even if the policy authorities were not to be trusted, institutional arrangements might prevent them from attempting to mislead the public. For example, the authorities might be *pre-committed* to following a particular policy. This might make their policy statements credible in the view of market agents. This is related to the notions of *time consistency* and *inconsistency*. Kydland and Prescott introduced these terms in 1977, although the ideas behind them are not new. A time consistent equilibrium is another version of long-run equilibrium. A time inconsistent equilibrium is one that, for one reason or another, cannot be sustained.

Pause for thought 8.12:

Is there any point in the authorities announcing targets for the rate of growth of the money supply, if they cannot guarantee the achievement of those targets?

In Kydland and Prescott's model, the policy maker is engaged in a strategic dynamic game over a period with sophisticated forward-looking private sector agents (agents who employ rational expectations). They argue that, in such circumstances, '...discretionary policy, namely the selection of that decision which is best, given the current situation, does not result in the social objective function being maximized' (Kydland and Prescott, 1977, p.463). If a government formulates and announces an optimal policy and private agents believe this, in subsequent periods the policy may not remain optimal. This is because, in the new situation, the government has an incentive to renege on the previously announced optimal policy. This change in the optimal policy over time is known as time inconsistency. More formally, the optimal policy computed at time *t* is time-inconsistent if reoptimization at time t+n produces a different optimal policy. The fact that policies may be time-inconsistent significantly weakens the credibility of policy announcements by the authorities since market agents are always aware that the authorities might not carry out the promises made in the first period.

Kydland and Prescott employ the new classical version of the Phillips curve to illustrate this view that discretionary policies are incapable of achieving an optimal equilibrium. Assume that the monetary authorities can control the rate of inflation perfectly, that markets clear continuously and that economic agents have rational expectations. Then:

$$U_t = UN + \psi(\dot{P}_t^e - \dot{P}_t) \qquad \qquad ...8.2$$

where *UN* is the natural rate of unemployment and ψ is a positive constant. Kydland and Prescott assume that there is a social welfare function of the form:

$$S = S(\dot{P}_t, U_t) \qquad \qquad ...8.3$$

where $S'(\dot{P}_t) < 0$ and $S'(U_t) < 0$. That is, both inflation and unemployment are undesirable and so a reduction in either or both increases social welfare. A consistent policy seeks to maximize (8.3) subject to the Phillips Curve constraint in (8.2).

The form of game proposed by Kydland and Prescott is a dynamic non-cooperative Stackelberg game in which the dominant player (the government) acts as leader and the remaining players react to its strategy. Both market agents and the government seek to maximize their own objective functions subject to their perception of the strategies adopted by the other player. Thus, the government, as leader, decides on its optimal monetary policy taking into account the likely reaction of the followers. The response of market agents, in turn, depends on their expectations of the future behaviour of the government.

Pause for thought 8.13:

Why should games between market agents and the government be non-cooperative?

Barro and Gordon (1983) constructed a model to illustrate the ideas of Kydland and Prescott. This represents equations 8.2 and 8.3 by an expectations-augmented Phillips curve and a set of indifference curves showing the willingness of the community to trade off inflation against unemployment. The more concerned the community is about unemployment relative to inflation, the steeper the indifference curves will be. The point of tangency closest to the origin represents the highest welfare point available.

If the economy is at the natural rate of unemployment (on the vertical Phillips curve) with zero inflation, it is always possible for the government to expand the economy along the short-run Phillips curve associated with an expectation of zero inflation. In doing so, it reaches an indifference curve closer to the origin than the one the economy is currently on. Welfare is temporarily increased. The reduction in unemployment is at the expense of higher inflation but the combination is thought preferable to the existing one. If we think of the social welfare function as indicating electoral popularity, democratically elected governments will always opt to expand the economy in this way. Hence, the position with zero inflation and the natural rate of unemployment is time inconsistent in a democracy because a democratically elected government always seeks to expand the economy. The point of tangency between an indifference curve and the short-run Phillips curve associated with an expectation of zero inflation yields the highest level of popularity the government can achieve by deceiving voters.

We know from the expectations-augmented Phillips curve analysis that the economy cannot remain at this point since points to the left of the natural rate of unemployment imply mistaken expectations. The government has brought the economy to this point by causing a higher rate of inflation than that expected by market agents. As soon as market agents realize this, they adjust their inflation expectations. Money wages rise to restore the original real wage and unemployment moves back to the natural rate — we return to a point on the vertical Phillips curve but at a positive rate of inflation.

Although we are now worse off than when we started, there appears once again to be a welfare gain to be had by expanding the economy along the new short-run Phillips curve. The process continues until we reach a point at which the existing short-run Phillips curve is tangent to an indifference curve on the long-run Phillips curve. At that point, there can be no welfare gains from expanding the economy since any move would take us to an indifference curve further away from the origin. Thus, this point is *time consistent*. It is on the vertical Phillips curve, with the expected and actual rates of inflation equal (there is no money illusion). The elected government can obtain no advantage from seeking to move the economy away from this position. However, the position is sub-optimal since the economy could have the same level of unemployment with a zero rate of inflation.

This time consistent rate of inflation varies from country to country depending on the form of the social welfare function and on the level of the natural rate of unemployment. Countries in which governments can increase their popularity markedly through short-term reductions in unemployment have high equilibrium inflation rates. Countries in which people are more concerned about inflation have lower equilibrium inflation rates.

The addition of rational expectations to the analysis removes all intermediate steps. Starting from zero inflation and the natural rate of unemployment, the economy moves up the vertical Phillips curve to the time consistent position at the equilibrium rate of inflation. This occurs because rational market agents understand that the government is always seeking to expand the economy and they immediately build the expected (equilibrium) inflation rate into their price- and wage-setting behaviour. The Barro-Gordon model is shown in Figure 8.3. A government from a high inflation country cannot easily lower the equilibrium inflation rate. Any announcement of a tighter monetary policy than that followed in the past will not be credible to market agents. We begin at E. The monetary authorities announce a target rate of inflation of zero, to be achieved by reducing the rate of growth of the money supply. If this announcement is credible to

market agents, they revise downwards their expected rate of inflation, causing the Phillips curve to shift down from E to U^*. However, market agents
are aware that if this occurred, the authorities would renege on their promise and increase the rate of growth of the money supply in order to move to
S, with the result that the economy would finish at E. Consequently, the
announcement of a zero target rate of inflation is not credible. Market
agents continue to build into their wage-setting behaviour, the old, higher
rate of inflation.

Figure 8.3: The Barro-Gordon model

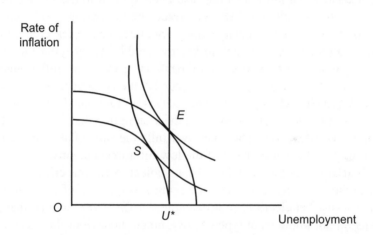

What then happens if the monetary authorities do follow the announced
policy? The rate of inflation falls and now lies below the expected rate of
inflation. Real wages and unemployment rise (we are now to the right of
the vertical Phillips curve with unemployment above the natural rate). The
economy could remain in this position for a prolonged period, at a high cost
in terms of additional unemployment. If, after some time, market agents
begin to believe the government has changed and lower their expectations
regarding the equilibrium inflation rate, we temporarily reach U^*, only for
the process to begin again.

Thus, only unanticipated increases in nominal income have an effect on
real variables. All of the transmission channels from money to nominal
income lead to the same result: no impact on real variables either in the
long- run or the short-run. One escape route from this position is provided
by the government accepting pre-commitment to a tight monetary policy.

However, governments can improve the situation by building up a reputation for keeping the inflation rate low. If they were to act always according to their announcements, the long-term equilibrium could occur at zero inflation and the natural rate of unemployment.

In macroeconomic policy terms, governments might pre-commit by the acceptance of fixed or *a priori* rules. This approach is considered in Chapter 9. An alternative to pre-commitment is the transfer of power over macroeconomic policy from elected governments to non-elected bodies such as independent central banks, which are assumed not to face the temptation to re-optimize because they do not face elections. Another possibility is to disband the central bank and privatize the supply of money.

The Barro-Gordon model has also been applied to the foreign sector in relation to the choice between fixed and floating exchange rates. Governments whose monetary policy announcements lack credibility with their own citizens might seek to borrow credibility by tying the domestic currency to a country whose central bank has greater anti-inflationary credibility. Then, as we shall see in Chapter 10, the issue becomes the credibility of the fixed exchange rate system. This, in turn, can be used to support a move to full monetary union — on the assumption that the central bank of the union is independent and takes over fully the anti-inflationary stance and credibility of the central bank of the low inflation economy.

The Barro-Gordon model has been subject to various criticisms in addition to those arising from the underlying assumptions of rational expectations and market clearing. For example, Driffil (1988) argued that private agents do not know what type of government behaviour they face because they have incomplete information. They analyse the various policy actions and announcements and attempt to determine whether the government is strongly anti-inflation ('hard-nosed') or relatively soft on inflation ('wet'). However, life is made difficult for them because they are aware that 'wet' governments have an incentive to masquerade as 'hard-nosed' and may engage in 'the dissembling actions of an impostor' (Blackburn, 1992). This might mean that hard-nosed governments face a high sacrifice ratio when they follow disinflationary policies because agents mistakenly regard them as wet. The 1997 decision of the newly elected Labour government to hand over monetary policy to an independent Bank of England can be interpreted in these terms (Milesi-Ferrettti, 1995; Bain, 1998).

Pause for thought 8.14:

Why might 'wet' governments have an incentive to masquerade as 'hard-nosed'?

8.6 The independence of central banks

The dynamic time inconsistency theories were widely regarded as providing a strong case for independent central banks as a pre-commitment device. Rogoff (1985c) suggested that the appointment of conservative inflation-adverse central bankers would prevent the excessive use of discretionary stabilization policies and the inflationary bias that they imply.

This provided support to the anti-discretionary policy view that had been developed over many years by public choice theorists and others. Public choice theory applies the methodology of neoclassical economics to the political process and assumes that governments seek to maximize the utility of individual members of the government by retaining power. Politicians act to maximize votes. Since elections occur frequently, governments are principally interested in the short-run impact of their policies. This implies that voters are shortsighted and judge the position of the economy only at the time of elections, forgetting what happens between elections. This leads to a number of different types of argument suggesting that democratically elected politicians are likely to favour policies that are more inflationary than is desirable for the economy in the long run.

For instance, voters can be divided into smaller groups, each of which seeks increased government expenditure in a particular area — health, education, roads, defence etc. Politicians seek to win votes by promising higher expenditure in all these areas. Thus, government expenditure rises inexorably. Governments are then faced with the problem of financing this. Beyond a certain level, it becomes politically unpopular to raise taxes. If taxes are not increased, government borrowing must increase. However, if governments borrow by selling increasing quantities of bonds to the non-bank sector of the economy, interest rates are pushed up. In a modern economy, with large numbers of voters burdened by mortgages, interest rate rises are also unpopular. Thus, vote-seeking politicians increase government expenditure and finance this by borrowing through the banking sector, thus increasing the money supply and causing inflation.

Another approach has been to consider the government as a unit, which seeks to gain advantage for itself at the expense of its citizens. It can do this by creating inflationary surprises because any expansion of the money supply provides seigniorage (see Section 1.4) to the issuer of money.

Pause for thought 8.15:

Memory test: Define 'seigniorage'.

This may take a number of forms. For example, by causing inflation the government reduces the real value of the national debt. In effect, an expansionary monetary policy acts as a tax on the savings of the citizens. Of course, the expectations-augmented Phillips curve suggests that each time the government creates an inflationary surprise, it ratchets up the rate of inflation while achieving no long-run increases in employment or output.

This, in turn, fits in with the view that governments create political business cycles — unnecessary cycles with real costs for the economy, which are generated by the need for governments to face elections. Governments expand the economy in order to win elections, only to be forced to deflate the economy after the election as the inflationary impact of the expansionary policy is fully felt. This makes governments unpopular between elections but puts them again in a position to expand the economy in time to win the next election. This does not, in itself, produce ever-increasing inflation but involves real costs for the economy, as inflation falls following each election only at the expense of high, albeit short-term, unemployment. The economy faces a regular and unnecessary stop-go cycle, which creates uncertainty and interferes with longer-term growth prospects.

These arguments, too, face problems. Attempts to find evidence for the existence of political business cycles have not, on balance, been successful. Studies that find no evidence of electoral cycles outnumber those that do. All theories depend on the shortsightedness or limited vision of the voter in contrast with the rational and well-informed market agent. In any case, all these arguments have a rather dated feeling since elections in the 1980s and 1990s in most countries were won, in the main, by political parties promising low taxation and low inflation rather than high government expenditure and low unemployment as suggested by the anti-discretionary policy theories.

This reflects an over-simple view of the political process in many public choice models, in which all citizens are assumed to have similar preferences. However, since unemployment (especially long-term unemployment) is heavily concentrated among unskilled workers and poorer sections of the economy, the chances of becoming unemployed are much greater for some people than for others. Equally, the losses arising from inflation vary widely depending on household indebtedness and holdings of financial assets. In general, middle income households with mortgages and significant holdings of financial assets, but whose workers have a lower than average risk of becoming unemployed are likely to be more worried by inflation fluctuations than by output fluctuations. The reverse is likely to be true for working class households. In addition, elections are often decided by

changes in the voting behaviour of relatively small groups of floating voters in swing constituencies. In the UK, the great majority of these swing
constituencies have been in the suburbs of cities and in small towns and
have been predominantly middle class. Consequently, in order to be elected, political parties have needed to signal a greater concern with inflation
than with unemployment (Bain, 1998).

Pause for thought 8.16:

Mortgages are a debt. The real value of debts falls with inflation. Yet, the text
suggests that holders of mortgages might be particularly worried by fluctuations in
the rate of inflation. Is this likely to be the case? If so, why?

Because the theoretical arguments in favour of central bank independence are open to criticism, its supporters have sought to add strength to their
argument through empirical studies. These have looked at the degree of
independence of central banks and attempted to find correlations between
this and the rates of inflation in the respective countries. These studies have
largely claimed to find such correlations within developed economies as
well as failing to find correlations between the independence of central
banks and rates of economic growth. The implication is that countries with
politically independent central banks can maintain lower rates of inflation
with no loss in terms of economic growth.

In one of the earlier major studies, Alesina and Summers (1993) examined 17 OECD countries over 35 years. They used a composite index of
central bank independence based on a number of indicators of independence, the chief of which they identified as:[4]

(a) the ability of the central bank to select its policy objectives without
the influence of government and the frequency of contacts between the
government and bank officials

(b) the selection procedure for choosing the governor of the central
bank, including the length of tenure of the governor

(c) the ability to use monetary instruments without restrictions

(d) the requirement of the central bank to finance fiscal deficits.

When they examined the correlation between this index of independence
and some major economic indicators, they found that more independence
was accompanied by lower inflation; but was not associated with lower

unemployment, a more stable economy, higher growth; or less volatile rates of economic growth. They, thus, suggested that 'while central bank independence promotes price stability, it has no measurable impact on real economic performance' (p.151). That is, the study appeared to support the view that central bank independence could reduce inflation without cost.

Australia and the UK both had more stable rates of growth than Japan, the USA, and Germany, all of which had central banks that were more independent. Spain, Australia, and Italy all had higher average annual rates of growth over the period 1955-87 than Germany despite having less independent central banks and higher average inflation rates. The same results held for the sub-period between 1973 and 1987. Of course, this is also undermined to some extent by arguments about the cost to an economy of inflation since there appeared to be no truth in the claim that countries with below average or stable inflation rates had above average rates of economic growth.

However, the study enabled Issing, then the chief economist of the Bundesbank, to argue that '...as regards the relationship between monetary stability and employment, the findings are pretty unambiguous, and, except in the very short-term, the hypothesis of an alleged conflict in the sense of a trade-off between inflation and unemployment may be considered quite refuted' (Issing, 1993, p.14).

There were, however, several difficulties with these studies. Firstly, doubts were raised about the index employed. While there was general agreement on the characteristics associated with independence, they had to be weighted to produce a composite index of independence. Different researchers could use different sets of weights and, hence, rank central banks differently in terms of independence. There were also problems in deciding whether central banks fulfilled the various criteria, especially when there were differences between the constitutions of the banks and their performance. For example, the average length spent by governors in office might, in practice, be rather different from the term of office specified in the constitution. Again, Issing (1993), in distinguishing between functional independence (related to the legal framework) and personal independence asked how the courage, steadfastness, and skill of the members of the decision-making body could be measured. Crawford (1993) suggested that Alesina and Summers had either overlooked differences in customs and traditions among countries or handled them arbitrarily. Overall, although it was accepted that the Bundesbank ranked highly on any index, there was sufficient doubt about other central banks to query the apparent correlations between independence and inflation rates.

Secondly, the existence of a correlation between central bank independence and low inflation does not necessarily indicate a causal relationship from degree of independence to inflation rates. Any correlation could be accidental or a third factor might be responsible for both the independence of a central bank and the low rate of inflation. For example, the low rates of inflation in Germany may have been due principally to a strong anti-inflationary attitude among German people following politically and socially damaging episodes of inflation. This meant that there was, for a long period, little or no disagreement among the major political parties over the need to keep inflation rates low. This made it easy for the government to accept the conduct of monetary policy by an independent central bank. German governments may well have followed much the same monetary policy as that chosen by the Bundesbank. Even Alesina and Summers acknowledge that the excellent anti-inflationary performance of Germany might have had more to do with the public aversion to inflation than the existence of an independent central bank.

Pause for thought 8.17:

Knowledge of history: When did Germany experience politically and socially damaging episodes of inflation?

Further, in the cases of both the USA and Germany, a major reason for establishing an independent central bank was to limit the extent to which regions of the countries were dominated by distant financial and political centres: both the Federal Reserve and the Bundesbank have strong regional representation on their central governing boards. It can be argued that this kept the central banks in touch with the real economies in the regions and led to some tempering of monetary policy. Thus, while control of inflation may have remained the central aim of policy in Germany (reflecting a national consensus), there has been little feeling that the interests of the financial sector of the economy have dominated the central bank. Any reading of the reports of the US and German central banks shows them to have been highly pragmatic institutions. Thus, it seems clear that any relationship between the nature of a central bank and inflation performance within its economy is a highly complex one and that simple correlations between them do not advance the argument far.

Other writers sought explanations for differences in monetary policy in the other functions central banks were required to carry out. For example, Issing (1993) stressed the importance of the German decision to separate the monetary policy role (given to the Bundesbank) from that of responsibility for bank supervision (given to the Federal Banking Supervisory Office).

Again, changes during the period in the degree of independence of central banks and in rates of inflation presented difficulties. Inflation rates had tended to converge, which might have been due to increased central bank independence, but might also have been influenced by other factors such as changing government views of the possibility of exploiting a trade-off between inflation and unemployment or changes in labour market organization. Indeed, Campillo and Miron (1997) argued that the empirical correlation between inflation and central bank independence disappeared once other potentially explanatory variables that might account for cross-sectional variations in average inflation rates were incorporated into the analysis. Such factors included a measure of political instability, the ratio of imports to GDP, the ratio of debt to GDP, and income.

Despite these doubts, the 1990s saw a widespread acceptance among economists and politicians of the desirability of politically independent central banks. This was translated into action in many countries. In Europe, the Maastricht Treaty on European Union (1992) required that the national central banks of all members of the future monetary union should be politically independent while the European Central Bank itself would be independent of all governments and of the European Commission. This was largely responsible for the increased independence granted to the central banks of France, Spain, and Italy. This requirement of economic and monetary union was needed to help to persuade financial markets that monetary policy after monetary union would be as determinedly anti-inflationary as Bundesbank policy had been. Market confidence in the future single currency was needed, in turn, to convince the low inflation countries, notably Germany, to give up their domestic currencies.

This need to persuade financial markets was part of the acceptance, in a world of highly mobile capital, of the dominance of financial markets. It is now taken for granted that a country's long-term interest rates might fall if only, and only if, governments can convince the financial markets of the credibility of their expressed determination to keep inflation low. Handing control of monetary policy over to the central bank was seen as one way of achieving this, since financial markets have more trust in the anti-inflationary credentials of central banks than in those of elected governments.

We, therefore, have a classic example of self-fulfilling beliefs. We have suggested that the theoretical arguments in favour of taking the control of monetary policy out of the hands of elected governments are not strong and that the empirical evidence is rather weak. It remains that, so long as these views are accepted in financial markets, it is in the interests of governments to accept them also. Strength is added to this proposition by the view that governments are not, in practice, giving up a great deal since the increased mobility of international capital has made it increasingly difficult to operate national monetary policies markedly different from those being followed in other countries.

Despite the widespread support for central bank independence, there has been much concern over the question of accountability. 'Accountability' has been defined (ECB 2001 p.126) as 'the principle that an institution with decision-making authority is held responsible for its actions'. Clearly, the bank should ultimately be accountable to the public since it administers monetary policy on behalf of the economy as a whole. The only way this can happen is through accountability to parliament and/or the government in power. However, the political system in operation in developed countries is representative democracy. Thus, for accountability to the public to have any meaning at all, it must be clear to the public what the bank is trying to achieve and what it is doing in order to meet its objectives. If this is not so, members of parliament will not be able to represent the views of their constituents over the behaviour of the bank. This introduces the different but related (and often confused) issue of transparency. The European Central Bank defines 'transparency' narrowly as requiring the provision of information about the internal decision-making process and more broadly as 'explaining how monetary policy is used to achieve the mandate assigned' (ECB, 2001, p.57). We shall return to both issues when we consider individually the Bank of England, the ECB and the Federal Reserve. Here, we are concerned particularly with the issue of accountability.

Concern over accountability has been expressed in a variety of ways. For public choice theorists, members of boards of independent central banks, like everyone else, seek to maximize their own utility and it is not clear that this coincides with the maximization of social welfare. For example, Milton Friedman preferred the idea of a monetary rule to central bank independence partly because he was worried that central bankers might be strongly influenced by particular interest groups, notably by the banking sector. Many on the left of the political spectrum have deplored the loss of democracy involved in allowing important economic decisions to be made by unelected people. Even Rogoff (1985c), who was strongly in favour of monetary policy being put in the hands of an independent conservative[5] central banker , accepted that there might need to be a clause in the central bank constitution allowing policy makers to overrule the central banker when the economy was hit by large shocks.

The analysis of the behaviour of independent central bankers has some-times been cast in the form of a principal/agent problem, with the government (on behalf of the society) as the principal and the central bank as the agent. The difficulty lies in ensuring that the agent acts to achieve the goals of the principal. In terms of the theory earlier in the chapter, any doubt about the behaviour of the agent results in a time consistency problem, even in the case of independent central banks. Thus, much has been written on the question of the constitution of central banks, including attempts to design an optimal incentive contract for the central banker, which would leave him with full flexibility but avoid the time inconsistency problem (Walsh, 1995). Blinder (1997), however, rejects this approach because the principal (the government) may not have an incentive to enforce the contract on the central banker (the agent). That is, even if an optimal contract were designed for the central bank, the time inconsistency problem would still remain but would be shifted from the central bank back to the government.

Lohman (1996) takes a rather different line. She suggests that monetary authorities able to grant independence to a central bank in order to bring about lower inflation should, logically, also be able to operate directly a monetary policy that would ensure lower inflation. All that is needed is for the public (now regarded as the principal) to be able to punish the monetary authorities (now the agent) for failing to deliver the low inflation that we are assuming the public ultimately want. This requires policy decisions to be made visible so that the public can easily monitor what the authorities are doing. Thus, visibility and accountability are the best guarantees for monetary stability in a democracy. There might still be a case for delegating monetary policy to an agent with clear responsibilities at arm's length from the government to increase the possibility of monitoring by the public and parliament by distinguishing one public task from others. However, she sees this as quite different from independence.

We can relate this argument to an earlier point — the idea that central bank independence can only be achieved when there is general public agreement (as shown by election results) on the overriding importance of controlling inflation. In this case, the independence of the bank might not be the cause of low inflation but simply the institutional arrangement chosen to deliver it. It also raises another issue - the distinction between goal independence (freedom to set the goal of monetary policy) and instrument independence (freedom to set the value of instruments in order to achieve the goal). A central bank (such as the Bank of England) that has instrument independence but not goal independence could be judged to fall into

Lohman's second category of a delegation of monetary policy, which is quite different from full central bank independence. Much depends on the sanctions available to the government if the central bank fails to deliver the goal set by the government.

8.7   Summary

The Quantity Theory of Money had suggested that, in the long run at least, increases in the money supply led directly to increases in prices. Keynes's *General Theory* had analysed the way in which monetary policy could influence not only prices but also output and, hence, the level of unemployment. The Phillips curve showed the statistical relationship between rates of (wage) inflation and levels of unemployment, implying that governments could trade off higher inflation against lower unemployment or vice versa. The Phillips curve was criticized because it showed a relationship between money wages and unemployment whereas, according to the neoclassical theory of the labour market, labour demand and supply depended on real rather than money wages. Thus, when the Phillips curve relationship broke down in the late 1960s, it was quickly replaced by the expectations-augmented version of the Phillips curve in which there was a separate short-run Phillips curve for each expected rate of inflation. In the long run, the trade-off disappeared — the long-run Phillips curve was vertical at the natural rate of unemployment. Any attempt by the monetary authorities to reduce unemployment by increasing aggregate demand through monetary policy would have no long run impact on unemployment but would cause accelerating inflation. This, in turn, would interfere with the efficiency of the market economy and cause the natural rate of unemployment to rise.

Attempts to reduce the rate of inflation by unanticipated reductions in the rate of growth of the money supply would cause unemployment to rise above the natural rate, where it would stay until workers' expectations of inflation adjusted to the lower level of inflation in the economy. This idea of the cost (in unemployment) of reducing the rate of inflation was named the sacrifice ratio. A major objection to this model was that the 'long run' had no clear meaning in calendar time, indicating only the period needed for the economy to return to equilibrium. Thus, a monetary policy that expanded aggregate demand might succeed in reducing unemployment for quite a long period and might be seen as worthwhile. This would be particularly the case if there were hysteresis effects in the labour market, with the short-run reductions in unemployment producing longer-run gains in employment.

The opposition to the macroeconomic policy of aggregate demand was, thus, strengthened with the development of the new classical model. It, in effect, removed the short run from the analysis by combining rational expectations with a market-clearing model of the economy. In this model, workers would correctly anticipate expansionary monetary policy and would increase their wages in line with the money supply increases. Real wages and employment would be unchanged. Aggregate demand policy could have no real effects even in the short run. This was a full return to the neutrality of money. There are, however, a number of problems with both aspects of the new classical model (rational expectations and market clearing) and a number of ways in which the model can be modified to re-introduce real effects from a monetary change. Recent empirical work also appears to conflict with the existence of money neutrality.

Nonetheless, the new classical model had a very powerful impact, not least because it led to the development of the ideas of credibility, reputation, and time consistency in economic policy. These played an important role in the growing, and ultimately successful, support for the independence of central banks. According to the theory, politicians could be expected to follow inflationary policies in the attempt to win elections. Removing the control of monetary policy from them and placing it in the hands of independent central banks would lower the expected rate of inflation in the economy and would considerably improve the sacrifice ratio. The rate of inflation should be lower and the rate of economic growth should be higher in countries with independent central banks. It is by no means certain, however, that making the central bank politically independent is in itself sufficient to lower the rate of inflation. The relationship between the independence of central banks and economic growth is even weaker.

Key concepts used in this chapter

Phillips curve	policy ineffectiveness/policy irrelevance
expectations-augmented Phillips curve	credibility
natural rate of unemployment	reputation
non-accelerating-inflation rate of unemployment (NAIRU)	pre-commitment

adaptive (backward-looking) expectations

money illusion

signal extraction problem

sacrifice ratio

time consistency/inconsistency

forward-looking expectations

central bank independence

accountability

Questions and exercises

1. Where would the combination of inflation and unemployment in the UK in 2002 lie on the original Phillips curve diagram?

2. Why is the natural rate of unemployment referred to as 'natural'?

3. Explain the basis of Milton Friedman's simple rule of monetary policy — that the rate of growth of the money supply in a stable price environment should be kept equal to the rate of change in real income.

4. Why was the 'shoe leather cost' of inflation so called? What other costs are there of anticipated inflation?

5. The model to which new classical economists applied rational expectations is described in the text as 'market clearing' and 'monetarist'. How are these descriptions related? What must have been the principal assumptions of the model?

6. Why does 'the combination of the rational expectations hypothesis and the assumption of continuous market clearing' imply that output and employment fluctuate randomly around their natural levels?

7. How useful do you think equilibrium models are in analysing a world that is never in equilibrium?

8. The *Chambers Twentieth Century Dictionary* defined 'hysteresis' as:

the retardation or lagging of an effect behind the cause of the effect: the influence of earlier treatment of a body on its subsequent reaction.

How then can hysteresis occur in labour markets? How can the existence of hysteresis in labour markets be used to argue against the neutrality of money?

9. Why should central bankers be particularly adverse to inflation?

10. Is the argument over the independence of central banks being biased in favour of independence by the assumption of forward-looking market agents but myopic voters?

11. How are the following arguments discussed in this chapter affected, if at all, by an assumption of endogenous money?

(a) the expectations-augmented Phillips curve

(b) policy irrelevance

(c) central bank independence.

Further reading

The expectations-augmented Phillips curve, new classical models, and the policy irrelevance theorem can be found in any recent intermediate macroeconomics text. A good account, together with criticisms, is provided by Acocella (1998). This also discusses public choice views and political business cycles.

Treatment of the issues relating to central bank independence are scattered through countless articles in journals. A good reference, especially in relation to credibility and accountability is H M Treasury (2002) ch.2. The arguments in favour of central bank independence can be found in many places, including Cukierman's (1992) book, and in two publications from the early 1990s by the Institute of Economic Affairs: Otmar Issing (1993) and Wood, Mills and Capie (1993). For more rounded views see Eijffinger and de Haan (1996). For more scepticism, see Forder (1998, 1999) and for an attempt to defend democracy, see Bain and Howells (1996).

9 The Theory of Monetary Policy

'The best thing undeniably that a government can do with the Money Market is to let it take care of itself.' Walter Bagehot, *Lombard Street*, (1873).

What you will learn in this chapter:

• The nature of monetary policy goals and instruments
• The problems in defining and ordering policy goals
• Theil's social welfare approach to macroeconomic policy.
• Tinbergen's fixed targets approach to macroeconomic policy
• The distinction between targets, intermediate targets and indicators of policy
• The arguments against discretionary policy
• Problems associated with monetary policy rules
• Arguments concerning the choice of monetary instruments
• The issues concerning the decision whether to make use of an intermediate target
• The issues concerning the choice of the final target of monetary policy
• The nature and basis of Taylor rules of monetary policy

9.1 Introduction

The central question for any macroeconomic policy concerns the extent and nature of government intervention. A discretionary or activist monetary policy involves frequent government intervention in an attempt to achieve relatively precise goals. An alternative to such a policy is to seek only to provide a stable medium to long-term monetary framework within which private economic agents make their own choices. This may be based on the acceptance of medium- or long-term rules that remove the ability of the monetary authorities to make discretionary changes. Alternatively, as we saw in Chapter 7, monetary policy may be taken out of the hands of the elected government and trusted to an independent central bank. A more extreme action would be to privatize the issue of money itself, replacing monetary policy by a set of institutional arrangements, the sole aim of which is to control inflation in order to preserve the value of the monetary unit.

The idea that the authorities, whether elected or not, should operate a monetary policy, of whatever form, implies the existence of policy goals and of instruments that may be utilized to achieve those goals. This chapter explores the nature of the goals and instruments of monetary policy and the relationships among them. Section 9.2 looks at the theory of the relationship between the goals and instruments of economic policy, without paying particular attention to monetary policy. The choice between a discretionary (active) policy and policy rules is considered in 9.3. Section 9.4 concentrates on the instruments of monetary policy dealing specifically with the choice between short-term interest rates and the money supply, although we make clear that the money supply is in practice an intermediate target of policy rather than an instrument. The second part of the chapter investigates the range of targets available to the monetary authorities. 9.5 examines whether the authorities should seek to achieve their goals through an intermediate target or should aim directly at their final targets.

9.2   Policy goals and instruments

Goals (or target variables) are substantive objectives, the achievement of which increases the material well-being of the population. As we shall see in Chapter 11, the choice made by governments among the goals of macroeconomic policy has varied considerably over the past sixty years, but throughout the 1980s and 1990s, primacy was given almost everywhere to the control of inflation on the assumption that a low rate of inflation was a *sine qua non* for the achievement of low unemployment and high rates of economic growth.

There are two issues here. Firstly, we have the debate over the Phillips Curve that we considered in Chapter 8 — the question of whether lower unemployment can be traded off against higher inflation. Secondly, if we conclude that the authorities can indeed succeed in reducing unemployment through macroeconomic policies,[1] we need to know the economic and social costs of both inflation and unemployment. A particular problem arises over the distinction between the short-run and the long-run. If inflation acts to increase the long-run equilibrium rate of unemployment, but policies aimed at reducing inflation produce an increase in unemployment in the short-run, how do we decide between short-run and long-run costs and benefits? The answer depends on the extent of the short-run and long-run effects as well as on the length of time it will take for the long-run to come to pass. Bear in mind that the people unemployed in the short-run as a result of anti-inflationary policies will be different from those who might obtain jobs in the long-run as a result of these policies. Arguments based on the notion of improving the welfare of the economy as a whole frequently conceal judgements about the distribution of income and other benefits both among various social groups and between present and future generations.

We must also accept that long-run impacts of policy are often difficult to judge because of the possibility of change in many of the factors influencing the economy. Thus, we might accept the proposition that inflation produces inefficiencies within the market economy and, in this way, increases the natural rate of unemployment in the long run, but argue also that anti-inflationary policy has hysteresis effects in labour markets, resulting in long-run costs. For example, the skill levels of workers may be seriously affected by increased spells of unemployment.

Pause for thought 9.1:

What sort of 'inefficiencies' might inflation cause that affect the level of employment in the long-run? How do these inefficiencies vary with the rate of inflation?

The operation of policy naturally requires rather more than a general statement of goals such as 'the control of inflation'. At some point, numbers must be attached to goals, converting them into targets.[2] Even if there is general agreement over the nature of policy goals, there may be discord over the precise targets that are desirable or practicable, in the light of the available instruments and the associated costs. For instance, attitudes towards inflation may change with its level. At modest rates, inflation may seem no more than an irritant and, possibly, a constraint on the achievement of other objectives. Rampant inflation may, on the other hand, seriously undermine both economic and social relationships and become a major source of welfare loss. It follows that, even if we are willing to accept the control of inflation as the dominant macroeconomic objective, we may well require strong justification for propositions that it should take precedence over all other policy goals, irrespective of the existing rate of inflation and level of unemployment.

An instrument of policy is a variable that the policy authorities control directly, being able to determine its value independently of other variables in the system. What constitutes an instrument is partly a technical question. For example, we have seen (in Section 4.2) that the monetary authorities effectively have direct control over short interest rates but directly control neither long interest rates nor the stock of money since these depend also on the actions of private sector financial institutions and the personal sector.

The derivation of precise targets from policy goals can be treated formally. In the 1950s and 60s, it was believed that there were a number of objectives of policy. It was thought that governments could achieve some of these objectives or could move part of the way to several of them but that different policies would have varying degrees of success in relation to different objectives. Thus, it seemed important to know how success in achieving one objective could be compared with success in achieving others.

Theil (1964), sought to answer this question by postulating a social welfare function that expressed the relationships among various goals and the constraints implied by the structure of the economy. Such a function would, for example, indicate how much damage to British exports the government was prepared to accept through increases in the value of sterling in order to bring about particular rates of inflation. If we limited ourselves to two objectives, a social welfare function could be expressed in the form of a community indifference map. The most common textbook example takes as the two objectives the reduction of unemployment and the reduction of inflation. This map is then imposed on a diagram showing the original form of the Phillips curve, which represents the constraints on policy. The government, then, simply selects the point at which the Phillips curve is tangential to a community indifference curve to determine the government's specific targets.

More generally, we can say that the aim was to solve a stochastic optimization problem by maximizing the social welfare function or minimizing a weighted function of deviations of actual values from their socially desired levels.[3] This approach leaves open the question of how the social welfare function is determined, assuming that it is possible to arrive at a social evaluation of objectives through democratic processes.[4]

Other problems associated with this approach are:

(a) it assumes that deviations above or below a target are equally bad;

(b) it might lead to undue caution in terms of what is feasible (there is too much stress on constraints);

(c) policy makers do not behave in this way.

An alternative view sees governments as satisficers, periodically manipulating instruments all together in discontinuous reactions to crises. Such governments have utility functions with acceptable-level goals rather than specific targets. The satisficing levels of targets are reached by the resolution of conflict between different parts of the organization e.g. the Prime Minister versus the Chancellor of the Exchequer or the Bank of England versus the Treasury. Thus, targets are flexible.

The best known formal approach to macroeconomic policy remains Tinbergen's analysis (1952, 1956) of the relationship between numbers of fixed targets and instruments.[5] This takes as given: (a) the structure of the economy; (b) the target variables and their numerical values; and (c) the nature of the instrument variables. Tinbergen then asks what values must be given to the instrument variables if the policy targets are to be achieved. In algebraic terms, we have to solve a set of equations representing the economic system. These contain: target variables (values known); and instrument variables (values unknown). Of crucial importance is the relationship between the number of targets (knowns) and the number of instruments (unknowns).

This analysis gives rise to Tinbergen's Rule: that to achieve any given number of targets, a government must have under its control at least an equal number of independent policy instruments. But there are many difficulties: target variables may be inter-related or inconsistent; instruments may not be independent of each other and some variables may, depending on the policy and the policy environment, be either instruments or targets.

Further, a government may technically have a policy instrument under its control but be prevented by practical and/or political considerations from using its full range of values. The freedom a government has to change interest rates, for example, may depend on the need to defend a fixed exchange rate or on the proximity of the next election.

Pause for thought 9.2:

Why might the pattern of home ownership be a constraint on the rate of interest as a monetary instrument?

The existence of uncertainty produces additional problems. There may be uncertainty over the structure of the economy or over which is the best model of its operation as well as over the effects of instruments. In this regard, it can be demonstrated that performance is improved by using more instruments than targets. Each instrument may be imperfectly used but weaknesses may to some extent be offsetting. If one instrument is given the wrong value, other instruments may also need to be given sub-optimal values in order to produce the best available result.

The relative effectiveness of instruments in achieving particular targets is also of considerable importance. Even if the authorities have instruments sufficient in number and in flexibility to achieve their targets, there remains the question of which policy to apply to which target. One approach to this problem is to direct each policy instrument at that target over which it has the greatest relative influence. Robert Mundell (1962) referred to this as the principle of effective market classification. He chose as targets external balance (balance in the balance of payments) and internal balance (full employment with low inflation) and, as instruments, the interest rate (monetary policy) and the budget balance (fiscal policy). He then showed that in a fixed exchange rate system, using fiscal policy to achieve internal balance and monetary policy to achieve external balance would move the system towards equilibrium, while the reverse would send the economy further and further away from equilibrium.

Another possible approach is to allocate each instrument to a separate authority, giving each authority the responsibility for hitting one well-defined target as nearly as possible (Meade, 1978). For such decentralization of policy to be successful, we require each instrument to have a strong impact on one policy goal and relatively little impact on all other goals. One obvious example of this is to allocate monetary policy to an independent central bank, which is given the responsibility for controlling inflation (considered in Section in 8.5).

A problem of particular relevance to monetary policy stems from the fact that the relationship between instruments and final policy goals is far from direct. Lying between instruments and goals are proximate or intermediate targets: a set of variables that the authorities cannot control directly and that do not have a direct impact on economic welfare but that may be important determinants of final goals and that we may thus wish to target. The most obvious example of a possible intermediate target in monetary policy is the rate of growth of the money supply.

Other variables may act as *indicators* — variables that we do not wish to control but that tell us what is happening or is likely to happen to intermediate targets or final goals. Indicators that give advance warning of what effect policies are having on policy variables are called leading indicators. Indicators should be variables for which statistics are reliably and readily available and that have close and statistically stable relationships with policy instruments. Thus, ideally, policy-induced and exogenous effects on the indicator should be separate and identifiable.

Pause for thought 9.3:

In what ways may the spread between short-term and long-term interest rates be considered as a leading indicator? How is its value as an indicator limited by difficulties in distinguishing policy-induced from exogenous effects? (Hint: see Section 12.3).

The best example of an indicator in the recent history of British monetary policy is M0, a measure of the wide monetary base of the economy. Although a target has been set for its rate of growth since 1984, very few people have defended M0 as an intermediate target since no evidence has been found that it is causally related to GDP. Equally, it is not an instrument since the government cannot control it directly (see Box 4.2). The principal defence for it has been as a coincident indicator of consumption and perhaps therefore a leading indicator of economic activity.

9.3 Rules versus discretion

Discretionary economic policy has been attacked on several grounds over the past thirty years. The strongest assault has come from public choice theorists who argue that granting discretion to politicians and the civil servants who advise them is bound to lead to excessive government spending and the residual financing of budget deficits with consequent high rates of inflation that act to transfer resources from the private to the public sector (the 'crowding out' debate). This is not an attack on particular groups of politicians and bureaucrats but stems from the application of economic principles of maximization and self-interest to the democratic process. All governments are held to be myopic since rational politicians are concerned only with obtaining and retaining power. Thus, they choose policies that may be popular in the short-run, even if they have undesirable long-run consequences for the economy. It follows that governments should be constrained to follow rules that take into account the longer-term needs of the economy.[6]

A rather different case against discretionary monetary policy has been in terms of its feasibility:[7] that an activist policy is too difficult to operate and is bound, in practice, to make things worse rather than better. There are several strands to this argument.

Firstly, a beneficial application of discretionary policy requires that the authorities know with some precision how different policies are likely to affect the economy. There are many problems here. To begin with, there are costs involved in the collection, preparation, presentation and analysis of statistics. Some statistical series are notoriously inaccurate and figures may be changed retrospectively. Definitions may also change over time, as we have seen in Chapter 2 with definitions of the money stock. Hence, it is arguable that governments do not know what is happening currently to many important variables, let alone what is likely to happen to them in the future.

It is plainly vital for the successful practice of discretionary policy that forecasters, at the very least, are able to forecast turning points in economic activity: when, for example, an economy is likely to move out of recession if governments continue with their present policy. Unfortunately, the history of macroeconomic forecasting has not been a happy one. Forecasters failed, for instance, to forecast correctly the size of the 1987 boom in the UK and the timing, size and duration of the subsequent recession. Governments also need to know how the economy is likely to respond to policy changes — but this implies a much greater knowledge of the structure of the economy than currently exists.

These problems are exacerbated by the existence of time lags in the policy process. Even if policy makers were able to recognize when action should be taken and decide quickly and correctly on the nature of that action, there would be administrative limitations on the speed with which it could be taken. Worse, a policy change may not have the desired effect on target variables for a considerable time. Obviously, the longer the time lags are, the more difficult it is to forecast the nature of other changes that will have been happening in the economy independently of the policy action. Everything becomes more difficult if the lags are not only long but also variable.

Pause for thought 9.4:

Make a list of all the lags that may be involved between a development in the real economy (say a fall in GDP growth below trend) and the earliest appearance of any evidence of the effect of a change in instrument(s) designed to correct it.
Note that you are being asked to consider the time between actual *occurrence* (of the event) and *recognition* (of the results of policy).

Once a policy action has been taken, there is a clear need to consider how the outcome relates to the policy targets and whether it is possible to say why things have gone right or wrong. If things have gone wrong, has it been because of inadequate knowledge of the system, wrong choice of instruments, incorrect information regarding the performance of the economy, or exogenous shocks that would have been difficult or impossible to allow for adequately? Again, the achievement of objectives does not necessarily mean that the policy pursued was the best one available. It may have been possible to do better (the objectives set were, under the circumstances, too modest). Again, policy goals may have been achieved for reasons that had nothing much to do with the policy followed (for example, there was considerable disagreement about the true causes of the fall in inflation in the UK in the early 1980s and of the rapid rates of growth in the United States in the same period). Yet again, the objectives may have been achieved at too high a price in terms of the impact of the policy on other variables (such as the distribution of income).

All of these problems raise doubts about the feasibility of discretionary policy and lead us by a different route to the proposition that all governments can do is to set fixed medium-term or long-term policy rules that will provide a stable framework within which the private sector can act.

Such rules are said to reduce both the costs of acquiring information and uncertainty about current and future government policies. This was the basis of the Medium Term Financial Strategy (MTFS) introduced by the UK government in 1981 (discussed in Section 11.2).

This second form of argument against discretionary policy is not, however, absolute. Models have been developed showing that active monetary policy may be stabilizing even in the presence of lags. Empirical estimates of the actual effects of policy in the UK have produced conflicting judgements regarding its success. Defenders of discretionary policy, while acknowledging the difficulties, are able to claim that knowledge of the working of economies has increased over the years and that better forecasts will be made in the future.

Different views of the rules versus discretion debate have also been taken under conditions of uncertainty. The treatment of uncertainty in policy decisions started with Theil (1964), who included additive random shocks. He showed that if the policy-maker knew the structure of the economy, the optimal policy would be the same as the policy under conditions of certainty — that is. it would be 'certainty-equivalent'. Things became more difficult, however. when uncertainty was introduced in a multiplicative fashion and Brainard (1967) argued that this weakened the case for use of monetary policy to stabilize output. Friedman (1960, 1968) argued that a non-activist fixed rule was optimal under uncertainty.

Bertocchi and Spagat (1993) argued against this. They constructed a model in which the authorities learn. The policy-maker, in solving a problem of intertemporal minimization of output variability optimally takes into account the information revealed by policy actions and updates his knowledge of the economy. At each stage of the process there is a potential trade-off between the minimization of output variability and the value of the information that can be obtained through a discretionary policy. It follows that monetary policy should be active in two senses:

(a) it should be responsive to new information;

(b) it should seek to generate information even if it is costly to do so.

Friedman's fixed money supply rule is not optimal since the learning leads to adjustments in the monetary action. They presented cases in which it was optimal to bear some costs in terms of current output performance in order to gain information for the formulation of future monetary policy. Experimentation pays. Even passive learning without experimentation leads to an activist monetary policy (that is, one that responds to new information).

In any case, the argument for a rule leaves open the question of the nature of that rule: evidence is needed that there is a rule that will work better than discretionary policy. Most arguments by supporters of a fixed monetary rule have been for a money supply rule. The simplest form of monetary rule proposed is one that requires the central bank to set the rate of growth of the money supply equal to the rate of growth of real income plus the desired rate of inflation, π. A slightly more complex rule would be:

$$\Delta m = \Delta y^* - \Delta v^* + \pi \qquad \qquad ...9.1$$

where y^* and v^* are long-run equilibrium values of output and velocity (Tödter and Reimers, 1994).

Preference for a money-supply rule has been based largely on the view that a fixed-interest rate rule would be unworkable. For example, Friedman argued that it is the nominal interest rate that is observable whereas concern should be with the real interest rate, which is not observable because of problem of modelling price expectations. Stable nominal rates of interest only indicate a stabilising monetary policy if real rates of interest are constant and inflationary expectations are not changing. Maintaining a stable nominal interest rate in the face of rising inflationary expectations would involve a declining real rate of interest and hence would be expansionary; the reverse would be true if inflationary expectations were falling.

It was further argued that interest rates were very sensitive to exogenous influences and could only be kept within a target range if that range were very wide. Any attempt to keep them within a narrow band against the dictates of the market would be destabilizing. Wicksell (1898) and Sargent and Wallace (1975) argued that if monetary policy attempted to set the interest rate and not the money supply then the price level would be indeterminate, but this proposition has since been qualified (Sargent and Wallace, 1982).

Fixed rules need not be simple but may involve feedback in which rules depend on what is happening to the goals of policy and the specification of circumstances (contingent rules) under which policy actions will change. However, once feedback is included in rules, the distinction between fixed rules and active policy becomes blurred. It is for this reason that supporters of rules generally preclude the inclusion of feedback in the rule.

The choice of a money supply rule presents a problem since, as we have seen above, the money supply is an intermediate target rather than an instrument. That is, it cannot be controlled directly by the authorities. This raises the question of whether or not the government is technically able to conform to a fixed money supply rule. As we shall see in Section 11.2, in relation to the Medium Term Financial Strategy of the British government in the first half of the 1980s, it is one thing to propose a rule, another thing entirely to be able to put it into operation.

The argument in favour of rules against discretion in economic policy has taken an entirely different form over the past twenty years through the application of rational expectations to the question of the effectiveness of government policy. The rational expectations hypothesis sees economic agents as efficiently applying all relevant knowledge to the best available model in order to predict future values of economic variables. Strictly speaking, economic agents need only act as if they know the best model of the economy. That is, it is sufficient if they derive their expectations from someone who does know the best model. However it is achieved, the forecast of a rational agent is the forecast generated by the model itself. It follows that if government policy is relevant, it too will be fully taken into account. If the best model of the economy were the neo-classical market-clearing model, government policy would not be able to move the economy away from those values determined by the operation of markets. Monetary policy would have no effect on real variables in either the short- or the long-run. This is the strong policy invariance proposition examined in Chapter 8. The hypothesis of rational expectations has also been used to criticize forecasting with the aid of large econometric models of the economy (the Lucas critique). The structural parameters in such models are invariant with respect to policy changes, but if policy changes are fully taken into account in private sector decisions, these parameters will change with alterations in the policy regime. Consequently, econometric models produce errors when used to forecast beyond the period over which the data was collected in order to estimate the model. If forecast errors are inevitable, the chances of stabilization policy making things worse (rather than just having no effect) increase considerably. Much depends in practice on how different the new policy is from the old one. A small change in policy may not change the parameters sufficiently to undermine seriously analysis based upon the model.

There are a number of ways of re-introducing the possibility of government being able to affect real values. This will be so, firstly, if the government has an informational advantage over the private sector, although in this case an argument has to be made as to why the government should not make available to the private sector all the information it has. Such an argument may be based on the resource costs involved in collecting and distributing information — it may save resources if the government collects information and then chooses its policies to produce the same results as would have transpired had information been costless and fully available to the private sector.

A second counter-argument depends on the existence of labour contracts of more than one period in length. This prevents workers from adjusting immediately to changes in rational inflation-rate expectations and introduces a fixed-price element into the model. Models may thus be partly rational, for example with full market clearing in asset markets but with 'sticky prices' in goods and labour markets. Much work has been done in recent years in developing models in which price and wage stickiness is derived from rational behaviour.[8] Other modifications may be introduced to the model that allow government to be able to reduce output fluctuations at the expense of higher price fluctuations.

Thirdly, the government may also be able to influence real values in the short-run if it succeeds in taking the private sector by surprise by reneging on its policy promises. As we saw in Section 8.5, Kydland and Prescott (1977) demonstrated that there may be welfare gains for the government from such behaviour. The problem for governments is that agents will quickly adjust once they realize the true nature of government policy and so the welfare gains will be limited to the short-run. Worse, the credibility of future government statements will be damaged.

Assume that the government announces a strong intention to bear down on inflation and a determination to keep the rate of growth of the money stock at a low level; but the markets do not believe that the government is prepared to push interest rates up sufficiently high to achieve its monetary growth targets and thus believe that inflation will be above the government's aim. Workers will make high wage claims to preserve their real wage in the face of the expected high inflation; employers will be prepared to make high wage settlements and will push up prices to allow for the expected increases in both wage and other costs. High inflationary expectations will cause the rate of inflation to remain high, for some time at least, irrespective of what the government actually does.

These arguments lead to the claim that governments should pre-commit themselves to fixed policy rules rather than engaging in discretionary policy.

In addition to the general questioning of the rational expectations hypothesis itself, there have been two main criticisms of this approach to economic policy. Firstly, questions have been raised about the process by which agents arrive at knowledge of the best model of the economy. This is a particular problem following major changes in the economy, for example from fixed to floating exchange rates. The rational expectations hypothesis does not allow for the possibility that agents will take time to learn what the best model is under the new circumstances. Secondly, much of the strength of the criticisms of discretionary policy derive not from the assumption of rational expectations, but from its application to the neo-classical market-clearing model (Laidler, 1990, ch.5). Discretionary policy again becomes feasible when rational expectations are applied to non-market-clearing models.[9]

Pause for thought 9.5:

Why will monetary shocks have real output effects if (only) part of the economy is made up of fix-price markets?

An intermediate notion in the rules versus discretion debate is that there is a continuum of rules and discretion, not a clear-cut distinction between them. The 'extent' of the discretion left in any monetary arrangement is determined by:

- the nature and precision of the targeted variables;

- the immediacy of the link between policy actions and the attainment of the targeted variable;

- the transparency of the policy strategy.

The idea of imposing rules on the policymaker's behaviour is to make policy actions predictable and to hold the authorities accountable for their performance. At one end of the continuum, the authorities' objective function is precisely specified and is directly attainable through policy actions, and the public is fully informed about the policy strategy. The degree of discretion then rises with reductions in each of the three areas above.

9.4 The choice of monetary instruments

We have dealt with the question of monetary policy instruments in Chapter 3 and shall return to it in Chapter 11, where we deal with the choice between interest rate control, monetary base control and direct controls. However, as we have pointed out in Section 9.2, it is frequently assumed that the money supply is an instrument and the choice of instrument is treated as if it were between the rate of interest and the money supply.

As we have seen, this is not an issue in basic *IS/LM* analysis. The model assumes full knowledge of the economy and complete control by the authorities of the money supply. We do not ask how this is achieved: the money supply is an instrument rather than an intermediate target. The only intermediate target is the nominal income level itself. This is clearly unsatisfactory, because of both the assumed certainty about the economy and the treatment of the money supply as an instrument.

Poole's (1970) analysis of the choice between monetary instruments tackles the first of these problems by introducing uncertainty into one or other of the curves in an *IS/LM* model. The curves move, but do not change their slopes (the disturbances are additive rather than multiplicative). In the face of these shifts, the monetary authorities must choose between the interest rate and the money supply as an instrument with the aim of minimizing the instability of income. As is shown in Figure 9.1, with exogenous shifts in the IS curve (between IS_2 and IS_3 with IS_1 being the mean or expected position), the policy of keeping the supply of money constant and allowing the interest rate to carry the burden of the shock causes income to vary only within the range Y_2Y_3; whereas the use of the interest rate as an instrument, allowing the money supply to vary, produces much greater income changes (from Y_4 to Y_5). Thus, it would appear that if the principal source of uncertainty for the economy lies in the goods market, the money supply is the preferred monetary instrument.

Figure 9.1: Choice of instrument with instability in the goods market

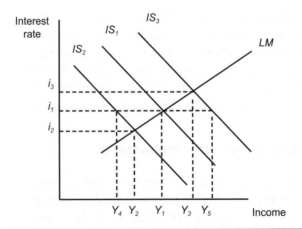

However, the situation is reversed if the source of uncertainty is in the monetary sector, causing unpredicted shifts in the *LM* curve. Since the money supply is assumed to be under the control of the government, these shifts must have their origin within the demand for money function. It follows that a policy of fixing the interest rate (at i_1 in figure 9.2) and allowing the money supply to vary to offset the random shock to the demand for money keeps the income level at Y_1; whereas, with a constant money supply the *LM* curve shifts with the impact of the shock and income varies within the $Y_2 Y_3$ range. Therefore, in the face of instability in the money market, the interest rate is preferred as an instrument over the money supply.

Figure 9.2 Choice of instrument with instability in the money market

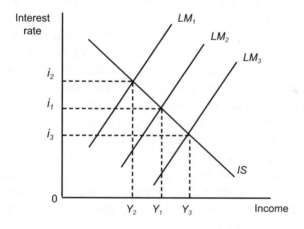

This has particular significance in the debate between Keynesians and monetarists, since Keynesians hold that the principal source of instability lies in the money market as a result of the instability in the demand for money function. On the other hand, monetarists (as we saw in Chapters 5 and 6) believe the demand for money function to be stable but see the expenditure multiplier (and hence the *IS* curve) as unstable. On this limited basis, then, Keynesians would be more likely to opt for control of the interest rate; monetarists for control of the money supply, although they generally argue against short-run discretionary changes in the stock of money, preferring the use of a medium- or long-term rule to govern its rate of growth.

Poole's model was a sufficiently potent piece of analysis to spawn a number of offspring. For example, it has been used in relation to the choice between a monetary target and an exchange rate target, with the answer depending again on the origin of the shocks to the system. Nonetheless, the model has been subject to many criticisms.[10]

Firstly, despite the introduction of instability in either the goods market or the money market, it assumes a great deal of knowledge about the structure of the economy, with the only source of uncertainty being stochastic disturbances. It is this assumption that invalidates discretionary policy as a form of response and requires either a money supply or interest rate rule to be chosen. It has been shown, however, that if the stochastic shocks are serially correlated and the authorities have time to understand what is happening to the economy, Poole's results fall. Again, the conclusions may be invalidated by the introduction of lags into the system or if there is uncertainty about the slope of the *IS* curve rather than its position (B. Friedman, 1975; Goodhart, 1989a).

Secondly, problems arise from the use of the *IS/LM* model in Poole's analysis. *IS/LM* analysis only allows changes in the supply of money to operate indirectly through the interest rate (the Keynes effect) whereas, as we have seen in Chapter 7, monetarists see changes in the money supply as also having a direct impact on consumption and investment. Although the *IS/LM* model assumes constant prices, equivalent results to Poole's have been developed with variable prices and rational expectations, strengthening the case for a money supply target (Blanchard and Fischer, 1989). This is because, with a constant money stock, aggregate demand changes that cause prices to vary will tend to be stabilized through the Keynes and Pigou effects; whereas they will be intensified by changes in the money stock under an interest-rate strategy.

Yet again, the assumption that the money supply may be an instrument causes difficulties. In practice, the relationship between instrument and intermediate target (the money supply) may not be stable. As we saw in Chapter 2, there are many possible measures of the money supply, each with a potentially different relationship to the final goal. We may have a theory that highlights the rate of growth of the money supply but does not specify sufficiently closely the meaning of the term. In such circumstances, monetary policy may be described more generally, for example, as a desire for 'sufficiently tight monetary conditions'. The obvious difficulty, then, is in knowing whether monetary conditions are indeed 'sufficiently tight'.

9.5 Intermediate versus final targets

We have proposed two possible broad approaches to the operation of monetary policy. The first is the idea that there needs to be an intermediate or proximate target for which desirable values should be set. Policy instruments should then be adjusted to achieve those values. The alternative approach is to use the final target only but to identify indicators or information variables that provide information as to what is likely to happen in the future. These should not, however, be treated as targets since this introduces an extra source of error into the system (Waud, 1973).[11]

Intermediate targets should be stably related to both instruments and the final target and should, ideally, be observable. Exogenous influences on the intermediate target should be separate and identifiable. There are many possible intermediate monetary policy targets, including the exchange rate, the level of credit, various budgetary measures, the money supply, domestic credit expansion (DCE)[12] and nominal income. However, most of the argument in favour of the use of an intermediate target has taken the money supply as that target.

We have seen that this was largely based on the belief in a stable emand for money (and hence in the medium-term stability of velocity), whereas volatile expectations about future inflation were thought to make it difficult to use interest rates as a guide the stance of monetary policy. Goodhart (1989b) pointed out that the case for intermediate monetary targets was even accepted by many moderate Keynesians in the 1970s. There are, however, several difficulties associated with the choice of the money supply as an intermediate target.

Firstly, there are a large number of measures of money and thus a problem in choosing which measure to target. This has been largely dismissed as a second-order problem on the grounds that alternative measures tell much the same story except in the very short term.

Secondly, the money supply is particularly prone to exogenous influences, such as the impact from overseas and financial innovations. One of the principal reasons for the rejection of monetary targetry in the UK in the 1980s was the view that financial innovation had so changed the nature of financial assets and the reasons for holding them that a consistent measure of money had become impossible. However, it has been argued that financial innovation has made all assets more liquid and hence all measures of money understate its true growth. In the view of Gowland (1990), the official response should have simply been a slower growth rate of the money supply.

Thirdly, money supply statistics are published less frequently than statistics for some other potential intermediate targets and are published with a time lag. Thus, the money supply is less observable than, for example, are interest rates. Fourthly, there are the doubts over the possible instabilities in short-run relationships between monetary aggregates, economic activity and inflation that we have dealt with in earlier chapters.

Fifthly, since the money stock is not exogenous, there are the problems involved in meeting money supply targets. The attempt to do so might involve high costs in terms of the required degree of interest rate fluctuations. Sixthly, post-Keynesians have argued that money has such powerful effects that the attempt to control it might have dramatic and unpredictable effects. This leads to the view that the authorities should let the money supply adjust to shocks.

9.6 The selection of final targets

Monetary authorities that reject intermediate targets may either target a final variable or choose to follow a central bank operating rule more complex than the simple monetary rules discussed above. The former involves a further choice between inflation targeting, nominal GDP targeting, and the tracking of a weighted index of monetary conditions including the exchange rate. We shall deal with each of these in turn before looking at the most commonly proposed policy rules for central banks.

Inflation targeting

The ideas behind inflation targeting are not new but can be traced at least to Wicksell (1898) while Sweden operated monetary policy with a price level target in the 1930s. That said, the practice of inflation targetry is largely a product of the 1990s. The first country to adopt such a target was New Zealand in 1990 followed by Canada and Israel in 1991, the UK in 1992 and by many more countries since.

An inflation target has the advantage that the central bank has a single objective for monetary policy. Both a nominal income target and a monetary conditions target, in contrast, allow for deviations in more than one economic variable. On the other hand, the existence of an inflation target might lead policy makers to seek to bring about a disinflation in the face of adverse supply shocks, thus causing greater deviations from equilibrium output. However, the most common argument against an inflation target is that it is not transparent because of the long time lag between policy instrument change and result. Estimates of the time taken vary but recent evidence suggests that the optimal forecast horizon for inflation targeting is six to eight quarters. Anything less and there would be a risk that not all of the policy measures would have worked themselves through. Yet, inflation targeting offers much greater accountability than money supply targeting because it is relatively easy to judge whether the independent central bank has been successful in achieving its target and to call it to account for any misses. The problem remains that the central bank should only be called to account after two years to allow for the transmission period. It is this that leads to the other attempts at accountability: inflation reports, press statements, minutes of policy review meetings and cross examination by parliamentary committees (see Section 11.4).

Once a central bank has opted for inflation targeting, there are several issues that must be considered in order to define the target. Artis, Mizen and Kontolemis (1998) list the issues as:

(a) Which inflation rate should be targeted and how should it be measured?

(b) When an inflation target is specified, how far ahead should the target be set? If the target is set consistently with the transmission lag the intermediate variable for monetary policy becomes an inflation forecast target.

(c) Does a central bank need both goal and instrument independence?

(d) Has the quite widespread change to an inflation targeting framework caused a regime change in inflation behaviour.

Which inflation target?

Inflation targeters have, to date, chosen some version of the consumer price index, largely on the grounds that, if the central bank is to be accountable to citizens, the price index chosen should not exclude products that make up a large part of the typical consumer's expenditure. This might interfere with another desirable feature — that the index should not be too volatile since the attempt to maintain a volatile index at a fixed level could require the central bank to adjust interest rates frequently and this could create greater uncertainty in financial markets. Certain items in a consumer price index are particularly volatile. These include items with strong seasonal effects such as food and those that have jumps corresponding to supply shocks such as energy prices. As a general rule, supply shocks produce a once-and-for-all jump in the price level rather than adding to sustained inflationary pressure. Changes in indirect taxes are an obvious example and some countries

— Finland, New Zealand and Canada — target an index which excludes indirect taxes. In the UK, an index, RPIY, which excludes mortgage interest payments and indirect taxes has been published and analysed by the Bank of England for some time. However, excluding the effect of all such shocks could create considerable differences between the rate of inflation as measured by the central bank and that observed by the citizen. This then undermines the arguments for inflation targeting which are based upon the simplicity which it brings to the understanding and monitoring of monetary policy.

The price index should also not respond perversely to changes in the monetary policy instrument. The most obvious example of this occurs when the central bank raises interest rates in order to reduce inflationary pressures in the economy. This causes mortgage interest payments to rise and pushes up inflation as measured by an index including them. Again, removing mortgage interest payments from the index conflicts with the notion that the index used for inflation targeting should conform with the public view of the rate of inflation. Nonetheless, these payments are excluded from the index which is actually used by the Bank of England, called 'RPIX' (the retail price index *ex*cluding mortgage payments).

Artis, Mizen and Kontolemis (1998) consider the possibility of a wholesale price index target for the ECB on the grounds that these consist largely of traded goods for which the law of one price might be expected to hold and thus there should be less variation in the rates of inflation across member countries. However, wholesale price index inflation turns out to be more volatile than consumer price index inflation.

One possibility is to surround the central target by a band of some kind. For example, the ECB's target rate of inflation is given as between 0 and 2 per cent, rather than as a single figure. In the UK, a single figure is given (2.5 per cent) but a band of one per cent up and down exists in practice since it is only when the inflation rate goes below 1.5 per cent or above 3.5 per cent that the Monetary Policy Committee must send an open letter to the Chancellor of the Exchequer explaining their actions and what they intend to do to move the inflation rate back towards the target. Such a band allows some volatility in the recorded rate of inflation and reduces the degree of variation needed in short-term interest rates. It also reduces the scope for inflation 'surprises'. It is very unlikely that any monetary policy could consistently deliver a point target, as the economy is buffeted by various events all of which have some small effect upon inflation. It would therefore be foolish to undermine the credibility of policy makers by debiting every small deviation of outturn from target. However, if the bands were set too wide, the discipline of the target would be lost.

Another suggestion is to use adjusted measures of central tendency such as trimmed means and medians. The aim is to measure 'core' inflation without arbitrary omissions by excluding components that are at the tails of the distribution on the basis of information regarding the distribution of relative price movements. Other possibilities include the weighted median or a measure based on the common trend of the individual price indices. Artis, Mizen and Kontolemis (1998) make a comparison of different measures and decide that, over the period of inflation targeting in the UK up until that point, there had been very little to separate the various possible ways of attempting to measure core inflation.

Given the width of the band, what should its mid-point be, what is an 'optimal inflation target'? If the object of monetary policy is price stability then an obvious target appears to a rate of increase in the RPIX of 0 per cent. However, there is both a theoretical and a statistical case for setting the target above 0 per cent (Yates, 1995).

One theoretical argument is that most economies are subject to a degree of price rigidity (especially, but not exclusively) in labour markets. If resource allocation requires relative price changes, then it is easier to achieve these by differential rates of price increase than it would be if some nominal prices had actually to fall. Another argument is that there may be circumstances (the Japanese recession may be a case in point) where the authorities feel the need to secure negative real interest rates. This is impossible without a positive rate of inflation.

The statistical case for a positive target is based upon upward biases in price indexes. Most indexes are based upon a survey of purchasing patterns taken at intervals. Between the intervals, buying habits are assumed to be fixed, though in practice they will adjust with people switching away from goods and services whose prices are rising more rapidly. However, since this substitution will not be picked up until the next survey, the index has an upward bias. Estimates of this, and other biases, suggest an upper bound of around 0.6 per cent. Partly for these reasons, but partly also in order to set a credible target having regard to recent inflation experience, the first target was expressed in October 1992 as a range of 1–4 per cent; in June 1995 the Chancellor announced that policy would aim at '2½ per cent or less' while retaining the range; in 1997 this was modified to 2½ per cent, +/– 100bp. The arguments for stating an explicit target within a range are (again) that it simplifies the judging of performance and that it prevents the range from becoming a 'range of indifference' where agents come to believe that the authorities are aiming only to come within the upper limit (Haldane 1995a).

Some writers deny the value of a single measure of inflation and argue that the best results would come from a mixture of measures from many models that include 'off-model' information allowing for inflationary risks and potential regime shifts.

Pause for thought 9.6:

If the objective of policy is price stability, why are positive rates of inflation always chosen as targets?

The inflation forecast as target

Svensson (1997) suggests that, because of the long lags in the monetary transmission mechanism, inflation targeting is actually inflation forecast targeting. That is, instead of altering the instrument to ensure that a specific target is hit in m-quarters time, the monetary authorities might form an optimal sequence for the policy instrument derived from a forward-looking policy rule based on a forecast horizon for expected inflation. The forecast horizon (n) need not necessarily coincide with the target horizon (m). Unless the target horizon is chosen carefully, the use of an optimal forecast horizon that is model-specific may result in a missed target at a time $t + m$. If different authorities choose the different horizons, the central bank may be held responsible for missed targets even though it is optimising using an acceptable loss function to derive n. In the UK, the Bank of England is free to specify the policy horizon and thus to equate n and m. This gives the Bank of England a degree of goal independence since it is able to choose the horizon *ex ante* (currently set at around eight quarters) over which it will be judged on its performance *ex post*. However, the choice of the optimal horizon is not easy.

It is also hard to forecast inflation. Over the period 1971-96, average errors in the forecasting of inflation by HM Treasury were 0.71 for four quarters ahead and 3.31 for eight quarters ahead. Over the shorter period from 1993 to 1996 (during which inflation rates were lower), the errors were −0.45 and −1.04 respectively, indicating that forecasts had been too high. Forecasts also understate inflation volatility. Thus, the Bank of England questions the value of setting a target for forecasts in terms of a single measure and stresses the role of judgement. As we shall see in Sections 11.4 and 12.5, they prefer the use of fan charts and probability distributions from the Bank's own model, private sector forecasts and cross-sectional information. This brings into question the transparency of MPC decisions since they are based on a forecast of inflation two years hence, which is influenced by subjective information not in the public domain. There is also the question of whether the Bank's forecast should be subject to outside checking — for example, by comparison with private sector forecasts. However, these are usually unconditional forecasts that incorporate the Central Bank's own reaction function as seen by the Bank forecasters. This can lead to problems of multiple equilibria or even non-existence.

In the USA, the Fed has always outperformed the private sector forecasts. This raises the question of what private sector forecasts tell us. If the private sector believes that the central bank's target is credible, it will publish the target as its forecast and no one will learn anything. This implies that the divergence between the forecast and the target is a measure of the bank's credibility. That, in turn, gives the bank an incentive to produce the target in its own forecast in order to suggest that policy is correctly set. That is, if the central bank regards proximity of inflation forecasts to target as a measure of its own credibility, it may seek to create (self-fulfilling) expectations of falling inflation over the two-year horizon.

Svenson (1997) thus argues for an independent body charged with producing strictly conditional forecasts based on present policies given by constant short rates or market expectations. The central bank would then be required to deposit its own forecast models with the independent body, reducing the opportunity for covering tracks. The independent body could assess which mistakes were avoidable and which were likely to be made by any good forecaster.

Instrument and/or goal independence

Monetary authorities may fall into one of three categories in terms of their degree of independence. Firstly, they may not be independent at all. As we saw in Section 8.5, this now applies to very few monetary authorities because of the strong move towards independence for central banks sine the late 1980s. Secondly, they might have only instrument independence. That is, the inflation target might be set by the government while the monetary authority is able to choose how to use the available monetary instruments to achieve that target. This is the formal case with the Bank of England, although we have followed Svenson (1997) above in suggesting that the ability of the Bank of England to set its own policy horizon gives it some degree of goal independence in practice.

Thirdly, the central bank may be granted both goal and instrument independence. That is, it may be allowed to set its own target as well as having the freedom to manipulate policy instruments in the pursuit of that target. Of course, in such cases the constitution of the central bank will include the broad policy goals that should guide the central bank in the setting of targets. In this sense, the European Central Bank has both goal and instrument independence.

A particular problem arises where the authorities have both goal and instrument independence. This relates to the changing of the inflation target. Changing the goal for good reasons must be part of a good contract. The problem is how to provide this flexibility without giving the impression that the central bank can always escape blame for a poor performance by shifting the goal posts. One possibility is to provide an escape clause, allowing the government to override the central bank. However, this can only operate in extreme circumstances or we shall return the position of the market judging that monetary policy is subject to regular political interference. The ECB has a particular problem of credibility because it polices its own contract. One suggestion has been for the use of a nominal income target to justify changes in the inflation target. This would allow the inflation target to be flexible without the credibility of the target being undermined by political intervention.

Nominal income targets

Nominal income targets also have a number of disadvantages. Firstly, national income data is generally quite long delayed, of uncertain accuracy and subject to minor revisions. This means that policy makers could only react to new information about the target variable on a quarterly basis rather than on the monthly basis possible with price data. Further, nominal GDP figures represent the lagged consequences in the economy of previous policy decisions rather than giving a reasonable indication of where the economy may go in the future if no policy action is taken now.

Secondly, moving to nominal income targets involves giving exactly equal weight to a percentage deviation of real output from its desired level as to a divergence of prices from the price level target. Hall (1986) proposed placing weights on output and price level deviations so as to reflect more closely some social welfare function weighting of unemployment on the one hand and price level instability and uncertainty on the other. This would be a considerable improvement on a simple nominal income target.

Thirdly, there would be a possible conflict between an independent central bank and the government over the nominal income target. Fourthly, other instruments (for example, fiscal policy) that influence nominal income are not under the control of the central bank. Finally, it is difficult to combine a good thing and a bad thing in a single target. For example, one may want to react to a shock to prices by encouraging through policy measures a (partial) offset to output, in pursuit of stability. However, the attainment of a nominal income target might require the authorities to seek to raise prices in order to offset a fall in output due, say, to a bad harvest.

Despite these criticisms, a case may be put for placing more emphasis on nominal income targets in establishing and publicly explaining the longer-term strategy and framework of policy within which intermediate targets and shorter-term operating rules are decided. In addition, supporters of nominal GDP targeting have emphasized its operability (since it depends only on variables known to the policy-makers) and robustness.

Frankel with Chin (1995) makes a theoretical case in favour of a commitment to a nominal GNP target on the part of the monetary authorities, as compared with two other popularly proposed targets, the money supply and the exchange rate. Bean (1984) and West (1986) had shown conditions under which a nominal income rule would stabilize output more effectively than a money rule. However, in their framework, it would not make sense for the monetary authorities to adopt any rule, if the alternative were the ability to use discretion to respond to new disturbances. Frankel with Chin adds an exchange rate rule to the list of candidates and adopts a framework of time consistency for weighing advantages of rules versus discretion.

There has been a good deal of debate in recent years over whether or not nominal GDP targeting leads to instability. It is clear in this debate that much depends on the precise form of the model and the assumptions about how expectations are formed in the Phillips curve. For example, Ball (1999) used a small closed economy model to show that nominal GDP targeting can lead to instability. Ball had inflation expectations simply taken to be last period's inflation rate. Svensson (1997) suggests that Ball's assumption that policy affects output before inflation lies at the heart of the instability result. McCallum (1997) argues that the Ball-Svensson instability result is a special case and not very interesting. He shows that the stability properties of the system come down to how the Phillips curve, or supply-side of the economy. is specified in the model. Using a model with forward-looking rational expectations, he shows that nominal GDP-targeting does not generate instability. Dennis (2001) extends Ball's model to uncover the role inflation expectations play in generating the instability in that model. He allows inflation expectations to be a mixture of backward-looking and forward-looking terms and shows that nominal GDP targeting is unlikely to lead to instability. He argues that if inflation expectations in the

Phillips curve contain even a small element of forward-looking behaviour the system is stable. He further shows that in Ball's model where exact targeting causes instability moving to inexact targeting restores stability.

Targeting an index of monetary conditions

Targeting an index of monetary conditions allows the formal incorporation of a number of variables relevant to the monetary policy decision, rather than leaving various elements to be included subjectively by the policy makers, as in the case of the Bank of England's emphasis on the judgement of the policy makers. Targeting an index is more open and, to the extent that a satisfactory index could be established, would make the monetary authorities more accountable.

Making monetary policy decisions on the basis of a number of important variables rather than just the rate of inflation or nominal income also might have specific advantages. For example, one component of any monetary conditions index would be the exchange rate. Taking the exchange rate into account would ensure that the external consequences of a tight monetary policy were taken into account, avoiding the achievement of a low inflation rate through excessive exchange rate appreciation. The incorporation of the exchange rate in the index would also address the question of who should take care of the exchange rate in a world of delegated responsibility for monetary policy.

However, there would be severe problems with the choice of the components of a monetary conditions index and the establishment of the weights to be attached to each component. It seems unlikely at present that a reliable and broadly acceptable index of monetary conditions could be established.

9.7   Central bank policy rules

The aim of central bank policy rules is to provide a clear and transparent guide to the conduct of monetary policy. They should depend on variables that can be easily measured and for which statistics are available without long time lags. They should be able to be estimated by econometric methods and should explain the past history of the monetary policy instrument. Such rules fall into two categories: simple instrument rules and targeting rules.

The best known of the former type are Taylor rules (Taylor 1993). A Taylor rule is a rule for the setting of short-term interest rates in order to achieve a target rate of inflation. The required short-term interest rate depends on the rate of inflation for the previous period, the extent to which the past inflation rate deviated from the target rate of inflation, the extent of the deviation of output from its natural rate and the equilibrium real rate of interest. The rule may be written:

$$i_t = \pi_{t-1} + \theta_1(\pi-\pi^*)_{t-1} + \theta_2(\frac{(y-y^*)}{y^*})_{t-1} + (i_t - \pi_t)^* \qquad ...9.2$$

where i_t is the required short-term interest rate, π_{t-1} is the inflation rate in the previous period, $(\pi-\pi^*)_{t-1}$ is the deviation of inflation in the previous period from the target rate of inflation, $\left(\frac{(y-y^*)}{y^*}\right)_{t-1}$ represents the deviation of output from its natural rate and $(i_t - \pi_t)^*$ is the target real rate of interest. θ_1 and θ_2 are constants and were set by Taylor at 0.5.

Looking at this equation, one can see a number of potential problems:

• it is difficult to determine a desired real rate of interest;

• both the idea and the measurement of the natural rate of growth of output(the NAIRU) are problematic;

• no account is taken of the exchange rate.

One can extract estimates of the desired real rate of interest from financial instruments such as indexed government bonds but such estimates are subject to error and may bias the equation in one or other direction. Despite a few difficulties, a Taylor rule has the virtue of being simple and relatively easy to compute. It simply involves collecting data on inflation and output (though calculating the output gap may not be straightforward). But given these two inputs and an estimate of the real interest rate, instrument setting is completely mechanical. In particular, there is no room for judgement. As McCallum has suggested, policy decisions could be turned over to 'a clerk armed with a simple formula and a hand calculator' (McCallum, 2000).

The last two decades have seen extensive research carried out on simple instrument rules (see for example, Clarida, Gali and Gertler, 1998; McCallum, 1999 and Taylor, 1999b). One notable finding is that such a rule performs quite well as a description of how interest rates have been set in many economies, even though no central bank has actually adopted an instrument setting rule of the Taylor type. For example, Taylor (1993 and 1999a) showed that his rule could accurately describe US monetary policy decisions in the past. However, it is not altogether surprising that there should be some correspondence between monetary policy, however it was being operated, and a version of the Taylor rule, provided that policy makers were setting interest rates primarily in relation to trends in output and inflation. Targeting the money stock, 'leaning into the wind' and explicit interest rate setting will all produce a positive link between interest rates and inflation and output. The interesting question is the size of the coefficients on the output and inflation gaps and Taylor (1999a) shows that these have risen steadily in the US, through successive phases of monetary policy, until they approximate now the coefficients in his rule.

Gerlach and Schnabel (2000) showed that the setting of interest rates throughout the EMU countries between 1990-98 also followed a path prescribed by an application of the Taylor rule. At first sight, this may seem surprising for the Bundesbank which for much of the period was widely regarded as a 'money targeter'. But Bernanke (1996) was the first to argue that the Bundesbank was really targeting inflation and the claim has since been confirmed by Muscatelli *et al* (2000) and Svensson (1999, p.641).

However, the rule has performed less well when applied to explaining interest rate setting in the UK economy and other small open economies. This may well be due to the omission of such important state variables as the exchange rate, the terms of trade and foreign interest rates (Svensson, 2000). Attempts to take account of these variables in an instrument-setting rule require assumptions about the speed with which such changes affect domestic prices and makes the rule very much more complex than any Taylor-type rule. The fact that the Bank of England does take such additional variables into account (and exercises a good deal of judgement, see Section 11.4) no doubt accounts for the comparative failure of Taylor rules to describe Bank of England interest rate setting.

Over the years, the basic rule has been modified in a number of ways. These include adding a forward-looking element to take account of lags in the monetary transmission mechanism. Such modified versions have approximated monetary policy reasonably well in a range of other countries. Ball (1999) found that Taylor rules are optimal regardless of the preferences of policy makers and that inflation forecast targeting can always be expressed as a Taylor type rule by substituting forecast output and inflation gaps for actual deviations. Thus, his model appears to unite Taylor rules and inflation targeting and shows them to have many desirable properties.

Svensson (2001), by contrast, maintains that *targeting* rules are quite different from *instrument* rules and suggests that we should stop talking about monetary policy rules (with the assumption that these are instrument rules) and concentrate instead on developing a 'prescribed guide for monetary-policy conduct' embracing both targeting and instrument rules. If we cannot do that, then we would do better to describe the conduct of policy in terms of targeting rules, since it is targeting rules that central banks have adopted in practice. He also argues that a specific targeting rule, of the kind adopted by the Bank of England, has a number of advantages. For instance, it relies on more information than a simple instrument rule, allows the use of judgement and is more robust to model variation that an instrument rule. Consequently, it is likely to lead to better monetary policy outcomes than an instrument rule — which may be why real world monetary policy making prefers targeting rules to instrument rules.

9.8   Summary

While economies are subjected to shocks, be they real shocks (to terms of trade, investment, productivity etc) or monetary shocks (exchange rates, demand for money, supply of money etc.) there is a widespread presumption that the authorities should take some responsibility for stabilisation. *How* this is to be done separates commentators into two broad camps: those who argue for an activist or discretionary policy and those who argue for medium-term, rule-based policy.

Within each of these positions there are further controversies. If the authorities are to make short-run responses to shocks, what is the best instrument to use in given circumstances? Assuming that the response is to come from monetary policy, should the authorities use interest rates or the money stock? Furthermore, since the connection between instrument changes and their effect on the objectives of policy is quite long, what intermediate target should be adopted in order to monitor the progress of policy. While this is a subject of frequent debate in the theoretical literature, we know that in practice central banks are committed solely to the use of short-term interest rates. If we opt for a rule-based policy is the best rule a money supply rule, or an interest rate rule?

In recent years, the debate about rules and discretion has been calmed by shifting the conduct of monetary into the hands of independent central banks. These have considerable discretion in their use of the interest rate instrument (and the scale of this discretion was clearly demonstrated during 2001). Being independent of political pressure, however, removes some of the objections to discretionary policy which were frequently levelled at such policy when conducted by government. There has also been a substantial move toward focusing solely on a final target, usually the rate of inflation itself, looking at variables in an intermediate position only as leading indicators of the future likely path of inflation. There remains an argument over rules for the setting of the interest rate instrument. 'Taylor-type' rules appear to give a good description of the way in which interest rates are set in practice, though no central bank is formally committed to their use.

Key concepts used in this chapter

policy goals	indicators
policy instruments	discretionary policy
policy rule	Medium Term Financial Strategy
hysteresis	contingent rules
satisficing	rational expectations
Tinbergen's rule	Lucas critique
Keynes effect	inflation targets
Pigou effect	nominal income targets
intermediate targets	Taylor rule
monetary conditions index (MCI)	

Questions and exercises

1. Distinguish between 'goals', 'targets', 'instruments' and 'indicators'.

2. It is often said that 'in the long-run' inflation reduces output and employment. What costs might be incurred in the short-run and why might these fall upon those who may not benefit from a long-run reduction in inflation?

3. 'Tinbergen's rule' says that a government with x policy objectives must have at its disposal at least x independent instruments. Explain the difficulties that confront the use of this rule in practice.

4. Outline the arguments against discretionary macroeconomic policy.

5. Explain how the rational expectations hypothesis has been used (a) to support the adoption of monetary rules and (b) to criticise the feasibility of forecasting.

6. Explain the problems associated with the choice of the money supply as an intermediate target.

7. What are the arguments for basing an inflation target on (a) RPIX and (b) RPIY?

8. Compare and contrast the merits of inflation and nominal income as monetary policy targets.

9. Why does the ability of the MPC of the Bank of England to set its own policy horizon give it some goal independence?

10. Explain the view that inflation targeting in practice means the targeting of the central bank's inflation forecast rather than the rate of inflation itself.

11. Why do you think central banks have not adopted an instrument setting rule of the Taylor type?

Further reading

The best recent coverage of theories of macroeconomic policy is in Acocella (1998). Amongst older books, M Peston (1982) is very helpful. Acocella also discusses the goals of macroeconomic policy at some length.

A collection of essays which discusses most of the issues raised in inflation targeting is in Haldane (1995b). Amongst them, Bowen explains the thinking behind inflation targets in the UK while Yates discusses issues involved in designing inflation targets. Useful on UK experience also is Haldane (1995a) in the *Bank of England Quarterly Bulletin*.

A more recent discussion of targets and rules for the conduct of policy is Cecchetti *et al* (2000) while Gerlach and Schnabel (2000) show that the setting of interest rates in the EMU has in practice approximated what would have followed from a Taylor rule.

A broader survey of monetary policy rules is provided by Taylor (1999b).

For an elaboration of the idea that inflation targeting amounts in practice to the targeting of central bank inflation forecasts see Svensson (1999).

Two essential articles for any study of the conduct of monetary policy are provided bu Goodhart in the *Economic Journal* (1989b and 1994).

10 The Open Economy and Monetary Policy

'Money speaks sense in a language all nations understand', Aphra Behn, *The Rover* (1681).

'The best money to take to the United States, is either guineas or Spanish milled dollars;Bank of England notes will not do', *Noble's Instructions to. Emigrants,* U.S. 107, 1860.

What you will learn in this chapter:

- The ineffectiveness of monetary policy with perfect capital mobility and fixed exchange rates
- The transmission of the monetary policy of the leader within a fixed exchange rate system
- The factors slowing down the transmission of monetary influences
- The difficulties involved in attempts to sterilize foreign impacts on the domestic money supply
- The factors influencing leadership within fixed exchange rate systems
- The issues relating to the question of the neutrality of money in a system with floating exchange rates
- The arguments for and against monetary policy coordination amongst countries
- The nature of the Tobin Tax and arguments for and against its application

10.1   Introduction

The impact of monetary policy in an open economy depends on the nature of the exchange rate system in operation. In section 7.5, we considered the impact of changes in the money stock on nominal income in a fixed exchange rate system and showed that, with fixed exchange rates and mobile capital, monetary policy has only a temporary impact on the level of income and, in the longer run, is completely ineffective. On the other hand, with freely floating exchange rates and mobile capital, monetary policy is more effective than in the closed economy case. In section 10.2, we consider the case of perfectly mobile capital under fixed exchange rates. In 10.3, we go on to consider ways in which countries might hope to preserve some monetary independence while retaining membership of a fixed exchange rate system. Section 10.4 looks at the question of leadership in fixed exchange rate systems. In 10.5, we turn to floating exchange rates and consider the relationship between monetary policy and the exchange rate.

In 10.6, we introduce the issue of policy coordination and look at both rule-based and discretionary coordination. 10.7 looks briefly at the arguments for and against the introduction of a Tobin Tax on international capital flows in the hope of restoring a degree of independence to each country's monetary authorities. The question of monetary policy in the euro area is considered in Chapter 13.

10.2 Monetary policy with fixed exchange rates

We return to the Mundell-Fleming model introduced in section 7.5. Now we assume fixed exchange rates and perfect capital mobility. Perfect capital mobility requires foreign and domestic bonds to be perfect substitutes. Any small change in interest rates that causes the world interest rate to vary from the domestic rate causes a flow of capital, which reverses the interest rate change. Domestic interest rates, thus, cannot vary from world rates. Domestic monetary policy is completely ineffective. An expansionary monetary policy does not cause even a temporary increase in income. This is illustrated in Figure 10.1, in which the BP curve is drawn as a horizontal line at the world interest rate. An expansionary monetary policy in a closed economy shifts the LM curve from LM_1 to LM_2, but in an open economy with perfect capital mobility, this does not happen. Any tendency for the domestic interest rate to fall below the world rate (i^*) causes a capital outflow and immediately pushes the interest rate back to the world level. Indeed, any expectation of a fall in the domestic rate of interest has this effect. The economy stays at point A with income at Y_1.

Figure 10.1: Monetary policy with fixed exchange rates and capital mobility

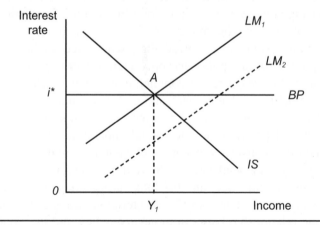

This leaves the question of what determines i^*. It could be determined through the agreement of all member countries of the system or by the most powerful economy within the system. The latter case is known as asymmetric leadership since the leading country is in a different position from all other members. Only it is able to determine its own monetary policy. We discuss the question of the factors influencing leadership in section 10.4 below. For the moment, we assume that there is such a leader and make use of the Mundell-Fleming model to show how the leader's monetary policy is transmitted to the other member countries of the system. We keep the assumption of perfectly mobile capital.

We begin at A in Figure 10.2, with the domestic economy in equilibrium at a full employment income level, Y_1. The strong country tightens its monetary policy, forcing the world interest rate up to i^*_1. Capital immediately flows out of the domestic economy, putting downward pressure on the value of the domestic currency. The domestic monetary authorities act to protect the exchange rate, either directly by restrictive domestic open market operations (selling domestic bonds, forcing down bond prices and forcing domestic interest rates up to i^*_1) or by buying domestic currency on the currency markets, causing international reserves to fall. In both cases, the money stock falls and the domestic interest rate is driven up. The LM curve

Figure 10.2 The transmission of monetary policy with fixed exchange rates

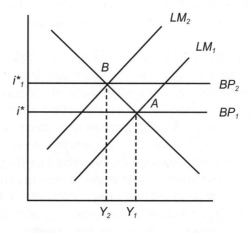

moves back to LM_2. We move to point B, at a lower level of income than previously. Domestic monetary policy is being determined by the strong country within the system. This simple example illustrates a major argument put forward within small countries for joining a fixed exchange rate system. This assumes that the domestic authorities wish to reduce inflation but find it difficult to do so because, in the light of the past performance of the economy, their announced anti-inflationary policy lacks credibility in the eyes of market agents. Inflationary expectations continue to be built into the economy's inflation rate. The fixed exchange rate system provides the possibility of a link with a strong anti-inflationary country, which forces a tight monetary policy on the domestic economy.[1] In effect, the government with the inflation problem borrows a reputation for financial prudence from the strong country in the system.

Pause for thought 10.1:

Why might a country's anti-inflationary statements lack credibility in the eyes of market agents?

Opponents of fixed exchange rates argue, rather, that the monetary policy forced on the domestic economy through the exchange rate link may run counter to the interests of the domestic economy. This happens when the business cycles of the two countries are not synchronized or when the countries have different views of the desirable short-run relationship between inflation and unemployment. Let point A in Figure 10.2 now represent a level of income at which there is high unemployment and low inflation. Meanwhile, the strong economy is experiencing boom conditions and high rates of inflation. It applies a tight monetary policy, forcing up interest rates just at the time when the domestic economy requires an easing of monetary policy.

Clearly, a fixed exchange rate system (or a single currency covering a number of countries) is likely to face fewer problems if the business cycles of the member countries are synchronized and if external shocks to the economies are symmetric — that is, they effect all member economies in broadly the same way. Another issue of importance is the extent to which monetary policy has real effects. If monetary policy does not have real effects in the long run, applying the incorrect monetary policy for a country's position on its business cycle causes short-run pain but does not damage the real economy in the long run. However, if there are hysteresis effects, then the application of a tight monetary policy during a period when the economy is already experiencing high unemployment increases that unemployment in the short run and results in long term damage.

The strong country might take some account of the needs of the other members in choosing its policy. However, if it feels that it would, for political reasons, have to compromise its own policy preferences too much, the strong country would have little incentive to join the system in the first place. In any case, if the strong country does take account of the needs of the weaker countries in determining its policy, it may, by lowering the anti-inflationary credibility of its own monetary policy, damage the anti-inflation credentials of the system as a whole. This, in turn, would reduce the potential gains for the small countries from being a member of the system.

The strong country need not adopt an anti-inflationary stance. Expansionary policy is transmitted through a fixed exchange rate system just as is deflationary policy. Much depends on what gives the strong country its position within the system. The Bretton Woods adjustable peg exchange rate system was criticized because the macroeconomic policy of the USA in the later years of the system's operation was more inflationary than that desired by other major countries and US inflation was being transmitted to other countries through the fixed exchange rates. US inflation made US goods uncompetitive and this, together with the capital outflow resulting from low US interest rates, produced a balance of payments deficit. The principal trading partners of the USA found themselves in balance of payments surplus, their international reserves increased and so did their money stocks.

10.3   Brakes on the transmission of monetary influences

Theoretically, countries wishing to follow a less deflationary or less inflationary policy than the system as a whole, while retaining membership of a fixed exchange rate system may do so by:

- devaluing or revaluing the domestic currency, although this needs to conform to the rules of the system and/or be approved by partner governments; or by

- sterilizing the monetary influences spilling over from the policy followed by the strong country.

Let us consider these two possibilities. Countries devaluing their currencies within a fixed exchange rate system obtain a competitive advantage that produces a current account surplus, although there may be long time lags in this process.

Pause for thought 10.2

Why are there long time lags between exchange rate devaluations and improvements in the balance of trade?

Countries are, thus, able to maintain a balance of payments balance for any given level of income at a lower interest rate. The *BP* curve moves down to BP_2, as shown in Figure 10.3. This enables the authorities to run a more expansionary monetary policy. Interest rates fall (the *LM* curve shifts down to LM_2), capital flows out of the economy and the current account surplus is offset by a capital account deficit.

Figure 10.3 Short-run freedom for monetary policy after devaluation

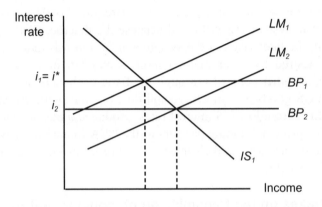

However, the current account gain is likely to be only temporary. Domestic prices are likely to rise, undermining the competitive advantage obtained from the devaluation. As the current account surplus disappears, the balance of payments moves into deficit and interest rates need to rise again to reverse the capital outflow. If the government wishes its monetary policy to continue to be different from that of the system as a whole, further devaluations become necessary. The possibility that one devaluation will be followed by others reduces the credibility of the existing fixed exchange rate and damages any reputation for an anti-inflation stance the government might have been trying to build up. Workers and firms build higher inflationary expectations into wage demands and price-setting formulae and speculators are likely to put pressure on the currency. Nonetheless, the competitive edge granted by the devaluation may last over a sufficiently long period to be judged useful.

A country wishing to follow less expansionary policies than the strong country in the system may be forced to revalue at regular intervals. The initial revaluation removes (again after a lengthy time lag) the current account surplus that had been driving up the country's reserves and inflating its money supply. Yet this, too, is likely to be only temporary; meanwhile expectations of further revaluations are likely to reinforce the tendency for capital to flow in from the inflating economy. The result may be an overall balance of payments balance, this time with a current account deficit being offset by a capital account surplus. The inflationary tendencies emanating from the strong economy are countered temporarily but at the expense of lower output and employment.

Although some policy independence may be granted by occasional exchange rate changes, this cannot occur as a matter of course. Regular changes in exchange rate parities in a fixed exchange rate system undermine the system's basis. Firstly, exchange rate uncertainty remains and risk premiums will be demanded on currencies thought at all likely to devalue. Secondly, it opens up the possibility of countries seeking to gain advantage through devaluations. Thus, fixed exchange rate systems must be constructed on the principle that large changes in exchange rate parities should occur infrequently and should be allowed only if a country can show that its balance of payments is in 'fundamental disequilibrium'.[2] The ability to alter exchange rate parities within a fixed exchange rate system can provide only an escape route for economies in serious difficulties rather than granting monetary policy independence.

A country can also try to avoid inflationary influences from abroad by using domestic monetary policy to sterilize the impact on domestic money stocks of the inflating economy's balance of payments deficit. This operates through the open market sale of government securities, soaking up excess money balances. Domestic bond prices fall and interest rates rise. The increase in reserves is offset by the decline in the domestic component of the money stock. The high domestic interest rate damages investment and, in time, affects both employment and the rate of economic growth. Nonetheless, faced with the threat of imported inflation, governments have often chosen sterilization. It cannot, however, operate effectively in a world with high capital mobility since the high interest rates attract further capital inflows from abroad, merely compounding the initial problem.

International capital was sufficiently mobile by the late 1960s to make sterilization difficult for countries such as Japan, Switzerland, and Germany, which regarded US policy as over-expansionary. To try to make it work, they had to operate draconian capital controls to limit the inflow of capital. Countries wishing to avoid deflationary monetary impulses from abroad without changing their exchange rate parities also require capital controls, this time to prevent the outflow of capital. In the absence of both exchange rate adjustments and capital controls, the weak country is constrained to remain at point *B* in Figure 10.2.

We should not rule out entirely the possibility of operating a fixed exchange rate system with capital controls. They played an important role in the EMS up until 1991 and have been resorted to in emergencies since then. However, they are widely regarded as undesirable and have become increasingly difficult to enforce with the development of offshore financial markets. In the modern world, they can probably only be enforced for short periods, at best. The difficulties caused to monetary authorities by the international mobility of capital has led to a call by some economists for a tax on international capital movements in the hope of slowing them down. We consider this in Section 10.7 and look at related issues in 12.3.

However, even as things are, the chances of some degree of monetary policy independence within a fixed exchange rate system are not quite as slim as we have so far suggested. In the real world, even without capital controls, capital is not perfectly mobile. In addition, fixed exchange rate systems usually allow some freedom for the exchange rate to move around the established exchange rate parities. There are normally, also, some limitations on the free international flow of goods and services. Finally, changes in central parities do not always generate expectations of further changes in the same direction. Let us consider each of these points briefly.

Capital mobility

Capital is not perfectly mobile internationally unless securities issued in different countries are considered perfect substitutes for each other across international borders. This may not occur because of the existence of political or exchange rate risk, different credit ratings of firms and governments or lack of information on the part of market participants. As we showed in Section 7.5, any immobility of capital gives the authorities some opportunity to maintain temporarily an interest rate different from world rates.

Pause for thought 10.3:

Memory test: why is the monetary freedom granted by a small amount of capital immobility only temporary?

(If in doubt, return to section 7.5)

Bands around exchange rate parities

All fixed (but adjustable) exchange rate systems maintain bands around the established central parities within which market-determined exchange rates may move. These bands may be narrow, as with the ± 1 per cent of the Bretton Woods system between 1945 and 1971, or broad, such as the ± 6 per cent for currencies within the broad band of the exchange rate mechanism of the EMS in operation until July 1993. Following the turmoil in the EMS in that month, an extremely wide band of ± 15 per cent was adopted, although this was intended to be only temporary and was not fully used.[3] Its sole purpose was to reduce the scope for profit-making attacks on currencies by speculators.

The rules of the system may prevent the full use of the band. In the EMS system, currencies were required to stay within their bands both against the European Currency Unit (Ecu) — a weighted currency basket consisting of the currencies of all members of the European Union (EU) — and against each other single currency. This meant in practice that the range of variation before July 1993 was limited to 2.25 or 6 per cent against the strongest or weakest currency in the system. Further, governments could not allow their currencies to fall to the bottom of the allowed band since this raised expectations of a possible devaluation and encouraged speculation against the currency.

Nonetheless, the existence of bands around parities can provide governments with a limited amount of monetary policy freedom. This applies if the central exchange rates to which the bands apply are thoroughly credible. Consider Figure 10.4. Here we again assume perfect capital mobility and show an initial equilibrium with the *IS*, *LM* and *BP* curves intersecting at point *A*. We assume this equilibrium to be at the country's central rate of exchange within a fixed exchange rate system. BP_1 and BP_2 show the BP curves that would apply at exchange rates 2.25 per cent above and below the existing central rate. Next we assume that the domestic monetary authorities expand the money stock, pushing the *LM* curve down to LM_2, intersecting the *IS* curve at *B*, which implies an exchange rate still within the allowable band. In the usual way, however, the fall in interest rate causes capital to flow out, the money stock falls and the economy moves back to *A*.

It remains that *B* may be a position of short-run equilibrium if it is fully believed that the exchange rate will move back to its original position. The expected increase in the value of the currency causes agents to be willing to hold the currency even at a rate of interest temporarily below the world level.

If the value of the domestic currency stays below its central rate for any length of time, expectations of a movement back to the central rate begin to be undermined and capital again begins to flow out, leading to expectations of a future devaluation. Thus, the degree of independence of domestic mon-

etary policy granted by the existence of bands around central rates of exchange is strictly limited and conditional, but some short-run freedom is provided and this freedom is greater the wider is the band.
Limitations on free trade

Figure 10.4: Monetary policy in a fixed exchange rate system

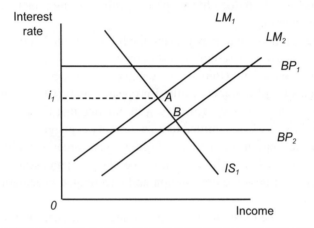

Some freedom may be retained also through the ability of a government to protect the current account of its balance of payments using commercial policy (tariffs, quotas and other non-tariff barriers). Although the capital account is a much more potent source of instability, expectations of devaluation are often triggered by current account weakness. Extra tension was caused in the EMS in the early 1990s because of the move (under the Single European Act of 1986) towards a unified market within the EU, severely limiting the ability of member governments to protect their current accounts through trade restrictions as well as leading to the removal of restrictions on capital movements within the EU.

Expectations of future devaluations following a devaluation

Finally, one devaluation does not always convince the financial markets that others will follow. Consider a case in which a country maintains a fixed parity for an extended period but steadily loses competitiveness over that period. Its rate of inflation may be converging on that of the strong country within the system, but only slowly. Under these circumstances, many come to appreciate that the existing parity cannot be maintained and that devaluation is necessary to restore competitiveness. The secret is either to make small adjustments to the exchange rate when needed, such that each change does not engender significant inflationary expectations and/or to accompany the devaluation with other policies aimed at preserving the credibility of the government's anti-inflationary stance.

To sum up this section, we can refer to the 'inconsistent quartet',[4] which states that governments cannot at the same time maintain all of the following:

(1) free trade

(2) full capital mobility

(3) fixed exchange rates

(4) national autonomy in the conduct of monetary policy.

This does not apply to the strong country of the system, which is able to determine its own monetary policy, as long as it is able to withstand the political pressure emanating from other members in cases where interests conflict.

10.4   Leadership of fixed exchange rate systems

We have so far been assuming that any fixed exchange rate system is characterized by asymmetric leadership — with a single country occupying a dominant position. This was certainly true of the Bretton Woods system and was widely held to be the case in the EMS, which was often referred to as a DM-zone. Yet, the two cases are notably different.

The USA owed its position as leader of the Bretton Woods system to its overwhelming strength at the end of the Second World War, which led the system to be constructed around the US dollar. Confidence in the system was provided by the large US gold holdings and the link established between the US dollar and gold by which the USA agreed to redeem any foreign holdings of dollars at a fixed gold price. This, together with the strong demand for US goods in the period after the war, encouraged other governments to hold dollars in their international reserves, making the dollar the international intervention currency. Later loss of confidence in the US dollar destroyed the basis of the system. The nature of the system gave it an inflationary bias since the USA suffered no penalty from operating expansionary policies in both the economic and political fields. In addition, up until the late 1950s, other members wanted US expansion (in the economic field at any rate) to help post-war reconstruction. Tight US monetary policies in these periods would have been very unpopular. Indeed, the Bretton Woods treaty contained a scarce currency clause to discourage the USA from taking actions that would make its currency difficult to obtain in the amounts required by other members.

Leadership in the EMS developed differently. German leadership came from market confidence in the Deutschemark (DM). The strength of the DM relative to other currencies meant that agents required a risk premium to persuade them to hold other currencies. This confidence in the DM was a reflection of the anti-inflation record of the German government and of confidence in its future anti-inflationary stance. In theory, changing policies and performances of different governments could cause leadership to pass into other hands — what markets had delivered, markets could take away. Leadership based on a credible anti-inflationary stance has two side effects.

Box 10.1: An attempt to reduce deflationary pressure within a fixed exchange rate system - the Basel-Nyborg agreement

The Basle-Nyborg agreement (1987) sought to introduce into the EMS two anti-deflationary devices. Firstly, when a currency fell to the bottom of its band against another currency, both central banks had to intervene, using the strong currency to buy the weak one (before 1987, most intervention in the system had been carried out in dollars). The weak currency country borrowed the strong currency through the Very Short Term Financing Facility of the EMS. Thus, in the short term, the weak currency country's reserves did not fall but the act of buying back its own currency reduced the domestic component of its money supply. The strong currency country issued more of its domestic currency, both to lend to the weak currency country and to buy the weak currency itself in the market. The net result was an increase in the money stock of the strong currency country.

Secondly, the agreement relaxed the terms of the Very Short Term Financing Facility by:

• extending the loan period, lengthening the period over which a more expansionary policy was forced on the strong currency country; and

• widening access to borrowing.

Before 1987, borrowing was only allowed for marginal interventions: those required because a currency had reached a prescribed intervention limit. After 1987, countries could borrow for intra-marginal interventions before a currency came under threat. Thus, theoretically, a government concerned about the tightness of the monetary policy in the system could apply a limited degree of short-term expansionary pressure on the strong currency country. However, the strong currency country could still sterilize the monetary effects of intervention through selling additional securities in open market operations. If it did this, the full burden of any adjustment was forced back onto the weak country and the deflationary bias of the system was preserved.

Firstly, it introduces a potentially deflationary bias to the system. To maintain its position and its apparent independence the leader must continue to operate strongly anti-inflationary policies. Then, as we have seen, these policies are transmitted through the fixed exchange rates to other members. This raises the question of exactly how 'independent' the leader is — it is free to determine its own monetary policy, but only as long as that policy is what the market expects.

Pause for thought 10.4:

What was the monetary policy significance of the German short-run Phillips curve becoming more or less steep?

Secondly, political pressures seem bound to ensure that the country able to deliver the most convincing inflation performance over a run of years, is the one with the best short-run unemployment-inflation trade-off. This means that the pain of convergence on the inflation rate chosen by the leader for the system is not only unequal across the system but also greater for followers than for the leader. This is likely to intensify the deflationary bias.

However, membership of the system itself may have changed the German unemployment-inflation trade-off. Thus,[5] membership may have made the German short-term Phillips Curve less steep since part of the inflationary impact of any German monetary expansion was transmitted abroad through the fixed exchange rate system. Germany could then reduce unemployment at less cost in terms of domestic inflation than previously. If this were so, membership would provide an incentive for the German authorities to follow more expansionary policies than would be the case with floating rates.

On the other hand, it is equally plausible[6] that membership of the fixed exchange rate system made the German Phillips Curve more steep since the exchange rate could no longer adjust to compensate for any loss of competitiveness resulting from domestic inflation. In practice, German policy in the 1990s was influenced much more by the problems it faced in digesting the East German economy than by judgements as to what was happening to the unemployment-inflation trade-off in the West German economy.

Systems can be designed to try to overcome tendencies towards deflation. In Box 10.1, we set out an example of this taken from the operation of the exchange rate mechanism of the EMS. However, as is explained in the box, it is difficult to force strong currency countries to follow more expansionary policies than they wish to do. The only way out appears to be through cooperation among members to establish a monetary policy suitable to all. This requires all countries to make policy concessions and, as we have already noted, there is often little incentive for the strong country to do so. Of course, if the alternative is a floating exchange rate system characterized by conflict, the strong country may accept cooperation, even if it involves some sacrifice on its part in terms of policy choices. However, to the extent that this happens, the anti-inflationary stance of the whole system may be weakened.

For the world economy, the asymmetric leader path is no longer available. Although the US dollar remains the dominant world currency, the balance of economic power is more evenly spread across three economic power blocs than it was in the 1940s and 1950s. The issue of cooperation in monetary policy has thus become increasingly important. We say more about this in Section 10.6.

10.5   Monetary policy with floating exchange rates

Our limited analysis in Section 7.5 concluded that monetary policy was more effective in an open economy with floating exchange rates than in a closed economy for two reasons:

• the exchange rate freedom grants the economy monetary independence and allows the authorities to choose the domestic inflation rate;

• the exchange rate movements have an impact on the real economy by changing the international competitiveness of the country's output.

Thus, an increase in the money supply causes income to rise and the interest rate to fall. The increase in income causes a deterioration in the current account in the balance of payments while the fall in interest rate causes a deterioration in the capital account. There is a net outflow of currency (the supply of domestic currency increases) and the exchange rate depreciates. The depreciation improves the international competitiveness of domestically produced goods and this causes a further increase in income. This analysis implied that the exchange rate changed to restore the goods and money markets and the balance of payments to equilibrium.

Income, then, increases, but the size of any real effects of monetary policy depends on the extent to which this reflects an increase in the price level, rather than output. This, in turn, depends on the extent of the depreciation that follows the monetary expansion. If the value of the currency falls in proportion to the increase in the money supply, the full weight of the expansion falls on the price level. There are no real effects. Money is neutral. To allow us to say more about this, we need to look briefly at theories of the determination of exchange rates in floating exchange rate systems.

The simplest model of exchange rate determination is the flexible price monetary model. This assumes that capital is perfectly mobile (domestic and foreign bonds are perfect substitutes), markets are competitive, transactions costs are negligible, and investors hold exchange rate expectations with certainty. Uncovered interest rate parity (UIRP) holds — that is, the expected rate of depreciation of a currency equals the interest rate differential between domestic and foreign bonds. Thus, if the interest rate on UK bonds were two per cent above the interest rate on US bonds, investors would expect sterling to depreciate by two per cent against the dollar. The key determinants of exchange rates are the supply of and demand for money.

We assume, also, that all prices are perfectly flexible. Purchasing power parity (PPP)[7] holds and money markets clear continuously. The demand for money is stably related to real income and stably and negatively related to the rate of interest.

$$m - p = \eta y - si \qquad \qquad ...10.1$$

where m is the log of the domestic money stock, p is the log of the domestic price level, y is the log of domestic real income, and r is the rate of interest. The same relationship holds abroad and thus:

$$m^* - p^* = \eta y^* - si^* \qquad \qquad ...10.2$$

Since PPP is assumed, we can write:

$$s = p - p^* \qquad \qquad ...10.3$$

where s is the exchange rate. Further, since UIRP holds, we have:

$$Es = i - i^* \qquad \qquad ...10.4$$

(the expected rate of depreciation of the home currency equals the difference between the domestic and foreign interest rates).

Re-arranging and substituting in 10.3 gives:

$$s = (m - m^*) - \eta(y - y^*) + \sigma(i - i^*) \qquad \qquad ...10.5$$

That is, the rate of exchange is determined by the supply of money and the demand for money function at home and abroad.

We can use this model to consider the impact of expansionary and contractionary monetary policy changes. *Ceteris paribus*, an increase in the rate of growth of the domestic money supply causing the domestic money supply to grow more rapidly than the foreign money supply causes domestic prices to rise more rapidly than foreign prices and, to maintain PPP, the domestic currency must depreciate. A ten-percentage point increase in the rate of growth of the domestic money supply causes the domestic currency to depreciate by ten per cent. Money is neutral in this case.

However, the predictions of this model are not supported by evidence, which is not surprising since neither PPP nor UIRP hold in the short run. Consequently, the model has been modified to allow for exchange rate over-shooting in the short run. That is, we continue to assume the existence of long-run equilibrium rates of exchange and to incorporate both UIRP and PPP. We also assume rational expectations and so market participants in the model make the best use of all relevant information and employ the best model for forecasting future exchange rates. Therefore, they know what the long-run equilibrium exchange rate is. Despite this, exchange rates over-shoot their long-run equilibrium positions. That is, if the exchange rate is pushed above its equilibrium it will fall well below the equilibrium rate before once again rising towards equilibrium. Equally, an exchange rate pushed below its equilibrium rate will not move directly back to equilibri-um but will rise well above it before returning to equilibrium. This result is achieved by assuming the existence of sticky prices. The best-known sticky price model was developed by Dornbusch (1976).

In Dornbusch's model, the goods and labour markets are slow to adjust whereas the asset market adjusts immediately. Exchange rates are deter-mined in the asset market and, thus, exchange rate changes are not matched, in the short run, by price changes. That is, we depart from PPP in the short run but return to it in the long run.

The model is described by four equations:

(a) uncovered interest rate parity

$$Es = i - i* \qquad \qquad ...10.6$$

(b) the demand for real money balances

$$m - p = \eta y - \sigma i \qquad \qquad ...10.7$$

(c) purchasing power parity

$$\overline{s} = p - p* \qquad \qquad ...10.8$$

(d) regressive exchange rate expectations in the short-run:

$$E_s = \theta (\overline{s} - s) \qquad \qquad ...10.9$$

where $\overline{s}$ is the equilibrium or long-run exchange rate and $\theta > 0$.

That is, in each period the expected change in the exchange rate is given by a fraction (θ) of the difference between its current value and the long-run equilibrium value.

Thus, the model has four endogenous variables:

· domestic interest rate
· the expected change in the exchange rate and
· the current value of the exchange rate
· the price level.

There are four exogenous variables:

· the foreign interest rate
· the long-run equilibrium exchange rate
· real income and
· the stock of money.

Pause for thought 10.5:

Memory test: where in this book have we commented critically on the assumption of an exogenous money supply?

The diagrammatic solution of the model gives a relationship between the exchange rate and the price level with the asset market always in equilibrium as in Figure 10.5, in which equilibrium is at N, with p^e and s^e. Note that the exchange rate is here expressed in direct terms. That is, as we move along the horizontal axis s increases but this means that the value of the home currency falls (one has to pay more home currency for one unit of foreign currency).

In Figure 10.5, AA represents asset market equilibrium. The negative slope of AA reflects the assumptions of an exogenous money supply and UIRP. This latter assumption tells us that if interest rates on domestic bonds fall, currency will flow out to buy foreign bonds. This flow will continue until people come to expect a sufficient appreciation of the currency to balance the interest rate differential between domestic and foreign bonds.

XX represents equilibrium in the goods market. This slopes up since an increase in the price level leads to a fall in domestic demand because:

(a) the real exchange rate falls (competitiveness declines) and

(b) the real value of the exogenous money supply falls, pushing domestic interest rates up.

To return the goods market to equilibrium, the value of the currency must fall (s must rise). Thus, the price level and the exchange rate are positively related. Below XX, there is excess demand for goods and prices will be rising. Above XX, there is excess supply of goods and prices will be falling. We assume that the asset market is always in equilibrium (that is, we are always on AA). If we are at M_1, there is an excess demand for goods and prices rise slowly. We move along AA towards N. As prices increase, aggregate demand falls and s falls (the domestic currency appreciates), compensating investors for low domestic interest rates caused by the high real money balances.

Figure 10.5: Exchange rate overshooting

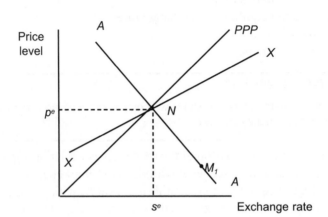

Assume now a once and for all unanticipated increase in the supply of money. The AA curve shifts out to A_1A_1 in Figure 10.6. There is no permanent effect on the current account of the balance of payments and PPP holds at the new equilibrium at N_1 (X_1X_1 shifts up). Investors realize this. The movement to long-run equilibrium takes place in two stages. We start at N. The unexpected increase in the money supply pushes up XX and the market knows that the new equilibrium will be at N_1 with an exchange rate of s^{e1}. That is, the market knows the domestic currency will depreciate.

However, because domestic prices are slow to rise, the initial effect is to increase real money balances and lower domestic interest rates, causing people to sell domestic currency, pushing the exchange rate instantaneously to s_2. At s_2, investors can see the prospect of a sufficient exchange rate appreciation to compensate for the lower interest rate on domestic bonds and the currency depreciation ceases.

There follows a gradual adjustment to the new equilibrium exchange rate, s^{e1}, as prices increase in the goods market. Therefore, we have overshooting of the exchange rate even with rational expectations. If we dropped this assumption and assumed that the market did not know the long-run equilibrium position, they would try to infer the truth from what others were doing and there would be much wilder movements in s.

Figure 10.6: A money supply increase in the Dornbusch model

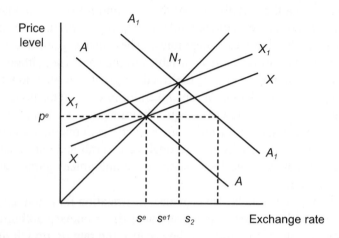

Another well-known model (Frankel, 1979) combines inflationary expectations with the sticky price element of the Dornbusch model. As in Dornbusch, the expected rate of depreciation of the domestic currency is positively related to the difference between the current exchange rate and the equilibrium exchange rate, but here it is also a function of the expected long-run inflation differential between the domestic and foreign economies.

$$E_s = \theta\left(\overline{s} - s\right) + \dot{P}^e - \dot{P}^{e*} \qquad \ldots 10.10$$

The long-run equilibrium exchange rate in this model is determined by the relative supplies of and demands for money in the two countries just as in the flexible monetary model. The gap between the current exchange rate and its long-run equilibrium value is now proportional to the real interest rate differential between the two countries. If the expected real rate of interest on foreign bonds is greater than the expected real rate of interest on domestic bonds, there will be a real depreciation of the domestic currency until the long-run equilibrium exchange rate is reached. When this occurs, real interest rates will be the same in the two countries and any difference in nominal interest rates must be the result of differences in inflation rates. As in the Dornbusch model, an unanticipated monetary expansion in the domestic economy causes the exchange rate to overshoot its long-run equilibrium level.

Other similar models have been developed, distinguishing for example between the speeds of adjustment of the prices of tradable and non-tradable goods or of volumes and prices of exports and imports (known in the balance of payments literature as the J-curve). The central feature of these models is that they retain most of the assumptions of the standard approach to foreign exchange markets while attempting to produce results closer to the reality of volatile exchange rates. They also suggest that the monetary authorities can influence real variables in the short run, although not in the long run. The importance of the freedom granted to the monetary authorities depends on the length of time taken for prices and the nominal exchange rate to move to their long-run equilibrium positions. Expansionary monetary policy could obtain worthwhile reductions in unemployment for significant periods. If a sticky-price model were combined with a labour market model with hysteresis, these short-run employment gains could become long-run gains.

Sticky-price models also provide a justification for a gradual approach to monetary policy. For example, assume the monetary authorities wish to reduce the rate of inflation. If they reduce the rate of growth of the money supply sharply and interest rates rise, but prices do not change in the short run, the nominal and real exchange rates fall sharply (overshooting the long-run equilibrium level), causing problems for exporters and import-competing industries. Unemployment results. If prices were slow to change, these real problems would persist for a considerable time. The position would be worse if the short-run overvaluation of the currency caused bankruptcies of domestic firms and serious loss of market share in important industries. The short-run cost of reducing inflation could be high. This leads to the view that monetary policy should be applied gradually to allow the economy to adjust slowly.

Pause for thought 10.6:

Why does a *fall* in the exchange rate of a country's currency cause problems for exporters?

There remain two problems with sticky price models from the point of view of monetary policy. Firstly, although PPP does better in long run than in short run tests, the evidence that it holds in the long run is not convincing. This increases the strength of the argument that monetary policy in an open economy has a long run impact on real variables. Secondly, all monetary models do not allow a distinction to be made between open market and foreign exchange operations.

Suppose the monetary authorities seek to improve the country's competitiveness by lowering the value of the currency. They buy foreign bonds with domestic currency, increasing the supply of the domestic currency on the market. The exchange rate of the domestic currency rises (its value falls) and the current account of the balance of payments improves. However, the country's holding of foreign exchange reserves increases and the money supply rises, creating inflationary pressure. The inflation then removes the competitive advantage obtained from the higher exchange rate of the domestic currency. The monetary authorities aim to counter this by selling domestic bonds to reduce the domestic component of the money stock. Consider this in terms of equation 7.2 in Section 7.5:

$$M = D + R \qquad\qquad ...7.2/10.11$$

The authorities attempt to increase R and reduce D so that the money supply does not change, but the exchange rate does, but this type of operation is not possible within the framework of a monetary model of exchange rate determination because domestic and foreign bonds are perfect substitutes. Changes in D and R have equivalent effects on the exchange rate. This is another way of saying that in a monetary model, the monetary authorities cannot influence the real exchange rate (except in the short-run, in sticky price models).

Portfolio models of the exchange rate overcome this by dropping the assumption that foreign and domestic bonds are perfect substitutes. Uncovered interest rate parity does not apply. We assume that residents of the domestic economy think foreign bonds are more risky than equivalent domestic bonds and hence require a higher rate of interest on foreign bonds to be persuaded to hold them. This inclusion of differential risk in the analysis allows open market operations and foreign exchange operations to have different effects on interest rates and exchange rates, and introduces the possibility of monetary authorities making use of sterilized foreign exchange operations. Monetary authorities now have a wider choice of policy actions. These are considered in Box 10.2.

We have so far seen that with mobile capital the following applies:

(a) in fixed exchange rate systems, the target of monetary policy is the exchange rate — domestic inflation rates are determined by the monetary policy of the whole system;

(b) in floating rate systems, the monetary authorities can target the domestic rate of inflation.

In practice, however, exchange rates in floating exchange rate systems do not float freely. Central banks intervene to varying degrees to influence exchange rates. Sometimes the intervention is light, with the intention only of smoothing out fluctuations in exchange rates. On other occasions, central banks join together to intervene strongly in the foreign exchange market in the hope of influencing the direction in which exchange rates are moving or to try to keep rates within unspecified target ranges. In this case, monetary policy may be aimed either at internal or at external objectives. Problems under these conditions are discussed in Section 12.3.

Box 10.2 Monetary policy with floating exchange rates

If domestic and foreign bonds are not perfect substitutes, the monetary authorities may choose among:

(a) an exchange rate operation
(b) an open market operation and
(c) a sterilized exchange rate operation.

(a) They might seek to expand the economy by buying foreign bonds from the private sector, using newly created monetary base. The private sector's holding of money increases while its holding of foreign bonds falls. The exchange rate rises and the domestic interest rate falls to maintain equilibrium in the money market.

(b) They might purchase domestic bonds from the private sector, again causing the exchange rate to rise and the domestic interest rate to fall; or

(c) They might combine an expansionary exchange rate operation with a deflationary open market operation, leaving the money supply unchanged. The exchange rate rises but now the domestic rate of interest also rises. The higher interest rate compensates the private sector for their increased holding of domestic bonds relative to foreign bonds while the depreciation of the currency raises the domestic currency value of its now smaller holding of foreign bonds.

Although the exchange rate and the interest rate move in the same directions in (a) and (b), the two policies may have different effects. The exchange rate operation has a greater effect on the exchange rate while the open market operation has a greater effect on the interest rate. Which policy has the greater impact on output and employment depends on the impact of an interest rate change on investment relative to the impact of an exchange rate change on the balance of trade.

10.6 Monetary policy coordination

One of the standard arguments for floating exchange rates is that they isolate an economy from external shocks, allowing the authorities to pursue their own independent monetary policy. However, it has become clear that all economies are interdependent and are subject to spillovers from the domestic monetary policies of other economies. Further, the degree of interdependence among countries has been growing. This happened particularly in the early 1970s because of:

(i) increased capital flows after the collapse of the Bretton Woods fixed exchange rate system

(ii) alterations in terms of trade following large changes in world oil prices

(iii) a greater degree of openness to foreign trade and

(iv) the development of offshore financial markets.

Our particular interest here is in what has been called 'sensitivity independence', defined by Cooper (1985) as the amount of adjustment a country has to make to foreign events under conditions of normal economic activity. This is determined by factors such as the marginal propensities to spend on foreign products or assets, the elasticity of substitution between foreign and domestic products or assets, the elasticity of substitution in production and the relative size of the economies in question. The theoretical approach to macroeconomic policy coordination calls upon a number of areas of macroeconomic theory, as well as making use of games theory to incorporate in models the notions of credibility and reputation, and the sustainability and time consistency of policy.

Pause for thought 10.7:

What does 'uncovered' mean in the phrase 'uncovered interest rate parity'?

The first stage in the analysis of macroeconomic interdependence among economies was the investigation of the channels along which influence flows from one economy to another. The beginnings of a case for some form of policy coordination can be derived from the simple open economy multiplier. For a small economy, it is clear that increased linkages with the rest of the world weaken the impact on domestic targets of domestic fiscal policy. Models can, however, be greatly complicated by dropping the small country limitation, by making different assumptions about the nature of the exchange rate regime, by introducing various forms of price or wage stickiness, or by considering the timing and nature of tax policy changes needed to pay for government expenditure increases.

The analysis of monetary linkages builds on the Mundell-Fleming model, making varying assumptions about the exchange rate regime, the degree of international capital mobility, and country size. Depending on the assumptions made, spillovers from domestic macroeconomic policy may be positive or negative. The importance of spillovers became clearer, however, with the recognition of price spillovers operating through the terms of trade linkage (Hamada, 1976). This plainly meant the end of arguments that a country could fully insulate itself from events and policies in the rest of the world. Even with perfectly flexible exchange rates, the terms of trade transmission works.

Pause for thought 10.8:

What do the terms of trade describe?

Cooper (1969) examined the impact of spillovers on domestic policy using a simple model with fixed exchange rates and constant prices. He argued that the greater is the degree of interdependence (and the stronger are spillovers), the less will be the effectiveness of policies in non-cooperating economies. Greater interdependence, in other words, leads to either worse results from domestic policies and longer periods away from equilibrium, or greater costs to restore targets to their desired values.

In Canzoneri and Gray's (1985) model, the governments of two identical countries both attempt to achieve full employment output without increasing inflation. Both countries are subject to supply shocks. The paper is concerned with the monetary transmission mechanism, specifically with the impact of an expansion of the money supply in each country. Canzoneri and Gray consider three possibilities:

(a) beggar-thy-neighbour in which monetary expansion in one economy has a negative effect on output in the other economy

(b) locomotive in which the spillover effects are positive and

(c) asymmetric in which monetary spillovers have different signs, the result depending on the size of the exchange rate and interest rate changes following the domestic monetary expansion as well as the import content of the foreign price index. The outcome is an empirical question, depending on the structure of the economies involved.

It has been shown that it is possible both for an instrument's spillovers to change signs over time and for an instrument to have impacts of different signs depending on the target at which it is aimed.

Specific conclusions of theoretical models must, however, be treated with caution since many depend on the sign or relative size of particular coefficients while the models assume that the economy's behavioural parameters are unchanged under different conditions. They thus founder on the Lucas critique. In addition, there have not been enough empirical studies to produce clear ideas about the likely direction and size of spillovers in practice. We are only left, following Hughes-Hallett (1989), with a set of not very surprising theoretical conclusions:

1. Spillovers vary with the policies pursued in other countries

2. There are multiple transmission mechanisms that operate simultaneously

3. Net spillover effects depend on the particular circumstances of the economies concerned

4. The impacts of spillovers crucially depend on the size of the economy, the degree of asset substitutability, relative price and wage flexibility and exchange rate flexibility.

Games theory has been used to analyze the desirability of policy coordination. This commenced with the development of models incorporating two simple forms of policy decisions by national governments in an international context — Nash non-cooperative games in which either governments act independently taking the decisions of other governments as given or one country acts as leader;[8] and cooperative games in which countries attempt to pursue some common interest, attempting to maximize the sum or product of the utilities of the national governments. The problem is to elucidate and, if possible, to quantify the gains from co-operative decisions.

Non-cooperative models suffer from a variety of defects. For example, they consider only static decisions and thus allowance cannot be made for predictable future effects of current decisions. Further, the restrictions on the assumptions regarding the behaviour of the other country's policy makers presupposes that policy makers already know the form of the equilibrium decision rule: but this can only be so in special circumstances. Despite these difficulties, the sub-optimality of non-cooperative decisions is accepted.

The presence of significant policy spillovers forms the basis of a well-known model (Hamada 1976, 1985) illustrating the case for international policy coordination between countries. It is a two-country model, with each country targeting its inflation rate and balance of payments position in a fixed exchange rate regime. Each country controls a single policy instrument — the level of domestic credit creation. Neither country can attain both objectives by acting alone except by coincidence. In one version of this model with demand-constrained output and price inertia, Nash non-cooperative behaviour gives the system a deflationary bias. Coordination is clearly preferable. This fits in with the general conclusion that non-cooperative decisions are socially inefficient except under special conditions.

However, it is one thing to argue for the inefficiency of non-cooperation, but quite another to accept the need for coordination. To begin with, one can produce cases where Nash non-cooperative behaviour is superior to cooperation. Perhaps the best-known example of this is Rogoff's international inflation game in which governments gain from unexpected inflation (Rogoff, 1985b). In Rogoff's model, governments fix exchange rates and then agree to raise their domestic money supplies. By cooperating, they are able to exploit the gains to be had from inflation surprises. Their citizens lose out. This assumes that the private sector can be taken by surprise. Most models rule this possibility out by assuming forward-looking expectations. Without surprises, the costs to the private sector of anticipated inflation remain, but an understanding of the nature of government policy by the private sector leads to a rapid reduction in their willingness to hold government debt except at interest rates that fully take government policy into account.

Pause for thought 10.9:

Why might governments wish to cause inflation at the expense of their citizens?

One can also show that the degree of sub-optimality of non-cooperative decisions can be affected by the strength of preferences of national policy makers, by the economy's policy responses, and by capacity constraints. We can only conclude that the size of net gains (or losses) from cooperation can only be determined by empirical analysis.

In attempting to bridge the gap, however, between theory and reality, economic theory has paid most attention to a different set of difficulties — if governments succeed in reaching an agreement to coordinate macroeconomic policies, how can we be sure that such policies will be sustained in each country? There are two separate issues here.

The first deals with the relationship between the state and the private sector. As we have seen in Section 8.3, if rational expectations are assumed and thus the private sector cannot be taken by surprise by the government, the effectiveness of macroeconomic policy depends on that policy being credible to the private sector. If this is not the case, macroeconomic policy is ineffective. One way out for governments is to pre-commit themselves to their stated policy. An obvious example is the pre-commitment of monetary policy through membership of a fixed exchange rate regime as long as the exchange rate parity is itself credible.

The second issue relates to the temptation felt by governments to renege on their agreements with other governments. The issue hardly arises in the Hamada two-country model since an attempt by one country to improve its position by reneging on the agreement will be met by a withdrawal of the other country from the agreement — both countries move back to the original sub-optimal non-cooperative equilibrium and are worse off. The threat of such action prevents either country from reneging. However, with more than two participants, the question of the credibility of threats becomes relevant. Where the incentive to renege on agreements cannot be removed by credible threats to retaliate, policy coordination cannot be sustained.

There are two ways out of this dilemma. The first is to concentrate on the notion of reputation. Governments may adopt a longer term view of coordination than is implied by the one-off bargains that dominate the world of policy models. Consequently, they may be willing to forgo potential short-term gains available from reneging on agreements in order to make future bargains possible. Yet again, the loss of reputation in the field of macroeconomic policy coordination might be thought likely to affect a country's standing in other international negotiations. This is an example of the problems involved in analysing macroeconomic policy in isolation. It is clear that the outcomes of G7 economic summits have been influenced by much more than narrow macroeconomic considerations.

The second way out is to develop arguments in favour of rule-based rather than discretionary policy coordination. The acceptance of rules means that all governments are pre-committed to agreed polices, removing the dangers apparent in cases where some parties are effectively pre-committed but others are not.

A considerable number of empirical studies have been undertaken. These have produced mixed results regarding the benefits from macroeconomic policy coordination. On balance, where studies have shown gains from coordination, they have tended to be rather small, although the gains appear to increase with the persistence of disturbances that lead to coordination. They also appear to increase over time. In the long run, gains from cooperation in the face of permanent supply or demand shocks may be very considerable. Such studies are of some interest in themselves but the ability of researchers to vary the results by making relatively small changes in their models means that they can, at best, provide only luke-warm support for policy coordination.

The obvious question that remains is why more has not come from the interest, at all levels, in increased policy coordination. There have been many meetings on economic issues of the heads of government of G7, supported by considerable academic lucubration. Yet very little of substance has resulted and what has resulted has been subject to much criticism. Perhaps the most substantial outcome has been the development of two major proposals for international macroeconomic cooperation: Williamson and Miller's target zone proposal[9] and McKinnon's currency substitution proposal . These have led to a good deal of argument and this has, in itself, underlined the difficulties involved in making serious progress towards macroeconomic policy coordination at a world level. A brief outline of the two proposals helps to make the point.

Williamson and Miller proposed that interest rate differentials between countries should be varied to keep real exchange rates within a given, wide band around the agreed equilibrium level for the real exchange rate (chosen so as to give medium — to longer-run current account equilibrium). The target zone would have 'soft buffers' so that authorities would cease defending it in the face of large unexpected shocks. The zone would also be regularly adjusted in line with actual changes in exchange rates. Domestic fiscal policy should be used to achieve domestic targets for nominal demand growth. Although these targets should take account of the need to reduce inflation to zero, countries would be able to give greater or lesser weight to the inflation objective relative to capacity utilization.

Pause for thought 10.10:

What is a soft buffer?

McKinnon, on the other hand, proposed fixing the exchange rates of the currencies of G3 (USA, Japan and the EU) approximately at purchasing power parity. G3 would then agree on a constant expansion rate for the combined money supply of the three members. If portfolio holders increased their demand for one of the currencies at the expense of another, the authorities would simply accommodate this at the existing exchange rates. The money stock of the country whose currency was in demand would expand more rapidly; the rate of growth of the other country's money supply would decline. Much academic work followed on target zones for exchange rates.[10]

Although it is worth noting that both Keynesians and monetarists may support some form of international coordination, the difference between the two proposals outlined above is pronounced. It is clear that there has been little, if any, convergence in the views of economists. If we add to these disagreements among economists, the many other issues likely to divide governments of the major industrial countries, as well as such problems as sustainability and time consistency, we cannot be very hopeful about the prospects for a rapid movement even to a simple rule-based regime. Certainly, there has been no progress in recent years towards a more fixed exchange rate system at international level. The prospect of full discretionary coordination of macroeconomic policies is remote.

Policy coordination in practice

The first significant attempt at discretionary policy coordination was the setting up of the annual economic summit of the G7 countries in 1975, seen as an important new forum for policy coordination following the breakdown of the Bretton Woods system (an example of rule-based coordination). Later meetings of some importance in terms of macroeconomic policy included the Bonn Summit of 1978, the Plaza Accord of 1985, and the Louvre Accord of 1987. Two problems arise in attempting to deal with these: that of attempting to judge their success or failure; and that of trying to account for that success or failure. The crucial question is whether failure is an indication that any such exercise is bound to fail; or whether there are particular lessons to be learnt that might allow more successful policy coordination to be undertaken in the future.

In 1974, the finance ministers of the industrial countries agreed not to have competitive devaluations. However, after 1975, the USA chose a policy of loose fiscal policy and tight monetary policy; while Europe and Japan used contractionary policies (largely, government expenditure cuts and tight monetary policy). The Bonn Economic Summit in 1978 endorsed the view that coordination at this time might have considerable benefits; the USA called for joint action to expand the major economies as a locomotive for the world economy. However, when Germany tried to carry out its part of the programme alone, it quickly ran into trouble. From 1980 to 1982, there were further calls for joint expansion but by then the USA were opposed to joint action. It has been argued that had the OECD countries other than the USA accepted fiscal expansion in return for reduced US budget deficits, US inflation would have been lower, while export demand would have increased via a fall in the value of the dollar. The other OECD countries would have grown faster and had less unemployment. Developing countries would have increased export earnings and reduced their indebtedness. There was a start on this kind of programme with the Plaza Agreement (late 1985) between G3: it was agreed that monetary policies should be coordinated to manage worldwide reductions in interest rates. 1986 saw the fiscal counterpart to the Plaza Agreement: budgetary changes were to be coordinated to lower the value of the dollar together with fiscal expansions in Japan and Germany to compensate for any contractionary tendencies in US policy. Yet in practice, little happened although interest rates and the dollar did start to fall. In 1987, in the Louvre Accord, finance ministers decided to try to maintain exchange rates within agreed target zones, but the arrangement was abandoned after the 1987 stock market crash.

At one end of the spectrum of opinions on recent attempts at policy coordination, are those who do not see the economic summits as attempts at policy coordination at all. In Kindleberger's presidential address to the 98th annual meeting of the American Economic Association in 1985, he asserted that '...the commitment to consultative macroeconomic policies in annual summit meetings of seven heads of state has become a shadow play, a dog-and-pony show, a series of photo opportunities ....with ceremony substituted for substance'.[11] Portes argues somewhat differently, questioning not their effectiveness but the motives behind them, seeing the global macroeconomic policy attitudes of 1979-85 as '...the very antithesis of policy co-ordination'.[12] In his view, the spirit behind policy coordination should be a desire to produce more efficient outcomes, but he saw the G7 summits as attempts to alter the balance of power within the existing economic system by bringing about changes in fellow-members policies in one's own interests.

Pause for thought 10.11:

What do you think a 'dog-and-pony show' might be? To what aspects of such a show might Kindleberger be referring in the quote above?

At the other end of the spectrum lie the views of those who do, indeed, see G7 and G3 meetings as coordination but who believe that all such attempts are likely to do more harm than good. Such views are based on a central belief in the efficiency of markets, a Public Choice school interpretation of the aims and ambitions of bureaucrats who attempt to manage markets, and a feeling that economists are '...abysmally ignorant about the macro-economic processes and the dynamics of forces that determine the fate of national economies'.[13]

Horne and Masson (1988) provide a good example of the 'lessons to be learnt' approach to the summits. They distinguish between 'procedural' and 'substantive' achievements. At a procedural level, they suggest that the summits were a success, establishing '...an increased awareness of policy interactions, a recognition of the role of exchange rate factors in macroeconomic policy formulation, and the need for mutually consistent medium-term strategies'.[14] However, they argue that the record has been much less convincing at a substantive level. The 1978 Bonn economic summit, which endorsed the view that coordination at this time might have considerable benefits but which led to an apparent over-expansion of the West German economy, is selected particularly as an example of the pitfalls of international fine-tuning. Currie (1990) suggested, on the other hand, that criticism of the macroeconomic aspects of the Bonn summit may have been unfair and contrasts the '...detailed analysis and negotiation that took place prior to the Bonn summit with the sketchy and hasty preparations for the Plaza and Louvre Accords'.[15] He reserved his ire principally for the shortcomings of the Louvre Accord, which he saw as an example of stupid coordination since its targets for exchange rates were not supported by a willingness to adjust the underlying macroeconomic policies.

The failure of the Louvre Accord set back the development of international policy coordination. Very little has happened at the level of the world economy since 1987. The notion of international macroeconomic policy coordination seems, temporarily at least, close to expiry. We are left with attempts by governments to exert pressure on other governments. For example, in 2001, as the US economy headed into recession and as the Federal Reserve cut interest rates sharply, American economic policy advisers on several occasions expressed their unhappiness at the failure of the European Central Bank to follow suit. However, there was no suggestion that there should be an organized exercise in policy coordination to reduce the possibility of world recession.

Exercises in international policy coordination since the collapse of Bretton Woods were not limited to the economic summits. Of equal importance was the operation of macroeconomic policy within EU member countries. The EMS was an example of rule-based policy coordination. The widening membership of the exchange rate mechanism of the EMS, with most members moving into the narrow band, together with the increasing freedom of capital movements within the EC, ensured a high degree of coordination of monetary policy. This later developed into the movement to the monetary union of 12 members of the EU. This is dealt with in Chapter 13.

10.7 Capital mobility and the Tobin Tax

We have seen that internationally mobile capital reduces the freedom of policy makers to act independently. In a fixed exchange rate system, monetary policy is, at best, effective for only a short period. In a floating exchange rate system, rapid flows of capital cause fluctuations in exchange rates, which add to uncertainty and cause problems for policy makers. These problems are discussed further in Section 12.3. Here, however, we wish to consider the application of a small tax to international capital flows. This was first proposed by the American Nobel Prize-winning economist, James Tobin (1978) and has become universally known as the Tobin Tax. The original plan was for a uniform tax on capital flows, levied by all countries, to make 'hot money' round trips unprofitable and to remove the dominance of capital account movements over exchange rates. The tax rate most commonly suggested is 0.1 per cent, although figures up to 0.5 per cent have been put forward by various writers.

There have been many criticisms of the proposal and, until recently, it languished in occasional journal articles. Following the Asian financial crisis of 1998, however, the proposal was taken up particularly by groups campaigning against the impact of globalization on developing countries. It has now attracted support from some governments. It was supported by the Canadian parliament in 1999.

Some criticisms of the Tobin Tax have been practical. For example, it has been argued that capital flows for long-term investment are desirable and certainly should not be taxed. The aim should be to reduce, or at least slow down, speculative capital flows, but it would not be possible to discriminate accurately between the two types of flows. It has also been claimed that the proportion of international capital flows that are genuinely speculative in nature has been exaggerated. Another practical difficulty is that many international assets are not controlled by a single authority or group of authorities and this makes it difficult to keep track of all capital flows. Many already go unrecorded. The application of the Tobin tax would provide another incentive for investors to evade official attention and would lead to a large increase in unrecorded flows. In addition, there is the problem that the tax would need to be imposed by all financial centres but would provide an incentive for some centres not to charge the tax as a way of attracting new business.

Quite apart from the practical objections, neo-classical economists argue that the Tobin Tax is undesirable because it is not a first-best policy and would have undesirable side effects. It would favour inertia and local asset bias in portfolios and would infringe Pareto-efficiency conditions. From this viewpoint, the underlying problem should be identified and policy should be aimed directly at that problem. For example, if the problem were the slow adjustment of goods market prices (as in the Dornbusch over-shooting model), the first-best policy would be one aimed at the rigidities in goods markets. Of course, if such policies were themselves impracticable, one could argue for the Tobin Tax as a second-best policy.

The tax has also been criticized by post-Keynesians. Davidson (1997) accepts that speculative flows create problems. He stresses the relevance of Keynes's beauty contest analogy to foreign exchange markets. This is the view that market behaviour largely consists of people trying to guess what other people in markets are likely to do. This can easily lead to wild speculation and panics. However, he argues that the usual magnitude proposed for a Tobin tax would be a negligible deterrent to short-term speculation and would probably be a greater deterrent to real trade flows and arbitrage activities. He makes an alternative proposal for preventing currency speculation, based on Keynes's 1940s writings. He suggests a need for rules and structures to prevent crises, pointing out that when Keynes analysed this problem, he saw that a system of outright prohibition of international hot money flows would be required.

In recent years, the tax has been supported as a source of funds for sustainable development. It is argued that if the tax were applied and were to fail in its primary purpose of slowing down flows of hot money, it would provide large funds that could be used for the assistance of poorer countries. This assumes that countries could arrive at a decision as to how the funds would be best used.

10.8 Summary

The impact of monetary policy in an open economy depends on the nature of the exchange rate system. When a fixed exchange rate system is in force and capital is mobile, monetary policy is weak. If capital were perfectly mobile, monetary policy would be completely ineffective. In this case, a small country within the system could not determine its own monetary policy. The monetary policy of the system could be that of an asymmetric leader or it might be determined by the group of countries acting together. In either case, there could be problems for a small country whose business cycle was not synchronized with those of the other members of the system. This would be particularly the case if there were hysteresis effects, which caused an incorrect monetary policy to have a damaging long-run impact on the economy.

Countries may retain some freedom in monetary policy if the system has relatively wide bands around the fixed exchange rate parities or if governments are able to devalue or revalue their currencies within the system without damaging either the system or the anti-inflationary reputation of the government. The authorities also on occasions attempt to preserve monetary independence by engaging in open market operations to sterilize the impact of monetary influences from abroad. However, this cannot be effective for long in a world of highly mobile capital. This also applies to the attempt to preserve monetary independence with capital controls. The leadership of a fixed exchange rate system may be determined by the nature of the system or by the attitudes of governments and financial markets. In the latter case, the country most trusted to keep inflation low and to preserve the international value of its currency is likely to become the leader. Then, there is a possibility of the leading country following a tight monetary policy that could have a deflationary impact on other members.

Monetary policy is effective if exchange rates are allowed to float. The precise nature of the impact depends, however, on what determines exchange rate movements. In simple monetary models of the exchange rate an increase in the rate of growth of the money supply leads to a proportional change in the exchange rate, preserving purchasing power parity in both the short and the long run. That is, monetary policy is neutral. However, purchasing power parity certainly does not hold in the short run. Exchange rates are much more volatile than domestic prices. The overshooting exchange rate model attempts to explain the volatility of exchange rates. The best-known version of this approach makes use of the idea of sticky prices in goods markets. In this case, monetary policy has real effects in the short run, although it again becomes neutral in the long run. Monetary models suffer from the disadvantage that they preserve the assumption of perfect capital mobility and do not allow a distinction to be made between open market operations and foreign exchange operations. This is overcome in portfolio models of the exchange rate.

Floating exchange rate systems are sometimes defended because they allow countries to preserve independent monetary policies. However, even with floating exchange rates, the monetary policy of a country can have an impact on other countries. This possibility has increased as countries have become more and more interdependent economically. This raises the question of the desirability of international monetary policy coordination. Although a good deal of time has been spent developing policy coordination models, the size of any net benefits from policy coordination remains unclear. In practice, little progress has been made in discretionary monetary policy coordination among the major economies.

THE OPEN ECONOMY AND MONETARY POLICY 309

Key concepts used in this chapter

target ranges

spillovers

perfect capital mobility

synchronized business cycles

devaluations/revaluations of the exchange rate

sterilization of monetary influences

capital controls

exchange rate parities

exchange rate bands

intervention currency

uncovered interest rate parity

purchasing power parity

overshooting exchange rates

macroeconomic policy coordination

rule-based coordination

Questions and exercises

1. How is the deflationary policy of a strong country transmitted through a fixed exchange rate system?

2. Why might a revaluation of a currency only temporarily reduce a Balance of Trade surplus?

3. Why does a wide band around fixed exchange rate parities (as with the 15 per cent band in use in the EMS between 1993 and the end of 1998) make life more difficult for currency speculators?

4. What factors are likely to determine leadership within a fixed exchange rate system?

5. What meaning or meanings might be attached to the notion of the equilibrium exchange rate?

6. Show on a Mundell-Fleming diagram the impact of:
   (a) a country revaluing its currency within a fixed exchange rate system;
   (b) a decision to widen the exchange rate bands within a fixed exchange rate system.

7. Memory test: What are hysteresis effects? Where are they mentioned in this chapter? What point is made in relation to them?

8. Is the assumption in the Dornbusch model of sticky goods market prices realistic? What about the other assumptions of the model?

9. What is the relationship between purchasing power parity and the neutrality of money?

10. Memory test: what is the Lucas critique? Where is it referred to in this chapter?

11.In what senses is:

   (a) the Williamson-Miller target zone model Keynesian?
   (b) the McKinnon fixed exchange rate model monetarist?

Further reading

The Mundell-Fleming model is dealt with at length in most second level macroeconomics texts. It is particularly well used and discussed in Acocella (1998). Textbooks that cover exchange rate economics well include the third edition of Copeland (2000) and the second edition of Pilbeam (1998). Most of the material on policy coordination dates from the late 1980s and early 1990s, when it was rather more popular as a topic than it has been recently. Recommended are the essays by Currie in Llewellyn and Milner (1990) and by Hughes-Hallet in Greenaway (1989).

11 The Evolution of Monetary Policy in the UK

'In the United Kingdom, money is endogenous - the Bank supplies base money on demand at its prevailing interest rate, and broad money is created by the banking system' Mervyn King (1994) p.264.

What you will learn in this chapter:

- The small part played by the explicit targeting of money and credit aggregates in the history of UK, monetary policy
- How financial innovation undermined the experiment in monetary targeting in the 1980s
- Why the short-term rate of interest has emerged as the main instrument of monetary policy
- How the Bank of England sets interest rates through its operations in gilt repo.

11.1 Introduction

In Box 2.1, we saw that for policy purposes, money is defined and measured in similar ways in most economies. Furthermore, we saw that money consists overwhelmingly of bank deposits and that these are the liabilities of private sector profit making firms and that the monetary authorities can therefore have only indirect control over the creation and destruction of money. In this chapter, we are going to look at how monetary policy has evolved over the years, at what factors have caused policy to change and thus at what lessons have been learned. In Chapter 4 we saw how changes in the quantity of money occur. Here we shall start, in the next section, by looking at the conduct of monetary policy in circumstances where the authorities think that changes in the quantity of money matter. We should stress at the outset that the UK authorities have always been rather half-hearted in their commitment to this view. For most of the period from 1950 to 1985 monetary policy was conducted with at least some vague idea that the quantity of money probably did matter, but that other things — the level of interest rates, the exchange rate, the availability of credit, overall 'liquidity' — were also important. It was only from 1967 to 1985 that specific targets for monetary growth were set (but not always publicly) and only between 1980 and 1985 that the pursuit of these targets took clear precedence above all else. Section 11.2 ends in the mid-1980s with the final abandoning of monetary targeting.

The reasons for its end are various but many of them had to do with changes in the monetary and financial system which made the behaviour of monetary aggregates less important and also less controllable. We shall see that there is a certain irony here, since many of the innovations which undermined monetary targeting sprang from a policy of financial deregulation introduced by the same government which was at the same time insisting on the importance of hitting its monetary targets. In Section 11.3 we look at the process of financial innovation and how it undermined both the rationale and the feasibility of monetary targets during the 1980s.

In Section 11.4 we look at how monetary policy has evolved since the demise of monetary targeting. This takes us through a period in which the authorities targeted the exchange rate (against the Deutschemark) and then targeted the rate of inflation itself. In these circumstances, and in contrast with those outlined in 11.2, money and credit growth rates are demoted, firstly to being a subsidiary target and then to at most one of many possible indicators of the future trend in inflation. In these circumstances, the central bank sets interest rates with an eye on the likely rate of inflation some eighteen to twenty-four months ahead. Given the level of interest rates, banks are free to meet all creditworthy demand for loans that are forthcoming and the central bank ensures that sufficient reserves are available. These 'loans create deposits' and the money supply has become endogenous. We close Section 11.4 by looking at how the central bank sets interest rates and at why, in the present conduct of monetary policy, the money supply is endogenous.

Section 11.5 summarises.

11.2 UK monetary policy before 1985

As we shall see in a moment, UK monetary policy passed through a number of very different phases between the end of World War II and the mid-1980s. Dividing the historical record into precise sub-periods is always controversial, but we can probably say that there were three identifiable phases — 1945 to 1971, 1971 to 1979 and 1979 to 1985. It was only in the last of these periods that monetary policy tried to focus explicitly and single-mindedly upon the growth of the money stock, though shifts in this direction can be seen during the second period, roughly the 1970s.

Adopting a monetary policy in which control of the monetary aggregates is the main objective must obviously be based upon some theoretical notion of how monetary variables affect the rest of the economy and specifically upon the idea that the aggregates themselves are capable of having an independent, causal effect. The thinking is broadly that which we saw in Section

5.2. Beginning with the equation of exchange and converting it to growth rates (since this is what usually interests us) we have:

$$\dot{M} + \dot{V} \equiv \dot{P} + \dot{y} \qquad \ldots 11.1$$

As in 5.2, this identity is turned into a theory by placing some restrictions on the following variables:

y : that it grows at a 'natural rate' determined by population and productivity growth;
V: that it reflects custom and usage of money in the payments system and evolves very slowly;
M: that it is determined independently of other variables in the system.

In its pragmatic version, these restrictions are held to apply only in the long-run; short-run deviations are allowed. Notice three important conclusions that follow from these restrictions:

• Causality runs from left to right as a result of money's independence

• The monetary arrangements implied by the B-M approach (see section 3.3) would do very nicely as an explanation of this independence

• $\dot{P}$, the rate of change in the general price level, is the residual variable which will adjust to accommodate any tendency for the rate of growth of money to vary from the rate of growth of output.

The message, of course, is that the rate of monetary expansion determines the rate of growth of nominal spending ($\dot{M} + \dot{V}$) and if, in the long-run, this differs from $\dot{y}$, the rate of growth of real output, the difference will be reflected in the rate of inflation.

Pause for thought 11.1

In 2001, the Bank of England was content to observe the M4 money stock growing at an annual rate of about 7 per cent, while being confident that inflation would be close to target at 2.5 per cent. If real output was expected to grow at 2 per cent, what was the Bank assuming about the likely behaviour of velocity?

As we shall see now, such ideas played little part in the first phase of post-war monetary policy. In fact, it took quite a long time for such ideas to gain what was a rather fleeting hold over policy.

Monetary policy from 1945 to 1971

For these twenty-six years, British monetary policy was effectively determined by a theoretical approach, an institutional imperative, and membership of the Bretton Woods fixed exchange rate system. The theoretical approach was Keynesianism, an interpretation of the ideas of Keynes in which his strong views about the ineffectiveness of monetary policy in a depression were generalized to cover all phases of the business cycle. In terms of the *IS/LM* model, which was a popular if not always accurate exegetical device for Keynes's ideas in this period, the *LM* curve was believed to be flat and the *IS* curve steep. Thus, monetary policy was believed to be weak and fiscal policy strong.

Although Keynesian theory of the day did not reject monetary policy out of hand, it was certainly not thought possible to conduct it through controlling the stock of money. While accepting that planned expenditure was the key to behaviour of nominal income, the ability to carry out these plans was held to depend on the 'liquidity' of the economy, rather than on the narrower concept of the stock of money. For example, the ease with which people borrow from *any* source (not just banks) would affect their ability to spend. We discussed this at some length in Section 1.2. Secondly, the existence of many close substitutes for money meant that it was difficult to define the supply of money let alone to measure it. The existence of close substitutes (including non-bank borrowing) meant that spending could vary independently of changes in the money stock which was just another way of saying, in Quantity Theory terms, that velocity was highly variable. All of this was powerfully expressed by the *Report* of the Radcliffe Committee which deliberated for two years over the working of the UK monetary system.

> It is possible…to demonstrate statistically that during the last few years the volume of spending has greatly increased while the supply of money has hardly changed: the velocity of circulation has increased. We have not made use of this concept because we cannot find any reason for supposing, or any experience in monetary history indicating, *that there is any limit to the velocity of circulation.* (Radcliffe, 1959, para 391 our emphasis). [1]

This left monetary policy preoccupied with the general level of liquidity. Interestingly, Radcliffe opted for changes in the cost of borrowing (the rate of interest) rather than direct controls (lending ceilings) as the best way to influence liquidity. In practice, however, the level of interest rates was largely determined by the general tenor of macroeconomic policy. The principal objective of policy throughout the period was full employment, constrained by the need to achieve a balanced balance of payments within a fixed exchange rate system. The full employment target, combined initially with the need to reconstruct the economy following the war, led to a policy of low interest rates, punctuated by an occasional rise to protect the value of the pound sterling.

The institutional imperative derived from the dual role of the Bank of England as a central bank with responsibility for monetary policy and the country's international reserves, and as banker to the government with the responsibility for marketing government debt issues. The domination of fiscal over monetary policy was reflected in the priority given to the debt marketing responsibilities among the Bank of England's tasks. The generally accepted view of the UK market for government debt at the time was that it was dominated by *capital* risk aversion. This led naturally enough to the view that the size of the market could be maximised by keeping bond prices steady and this in turn meant a combination of stable interest and a policy of 'leaning into the wind' by the Bank, buying and selling debt as the market weakened or strengthened. However one looks at money supply determination, the Bank's position in these circumstances is severely compromised. In the flow of funds identity for example (see equation 3.18) it has to take any fiscal deficit as given. Its ability to sell debt to the non-bank private sector is inhibited by views about the debt market with the result that residual financing (ΔL_g) broadly follows the deficit. Equation 3.20 puts it in B-M terms. Ignoring the external position, the monetary base expands to the extent that sales of government debt do not fund the PSBR. Worse even that this, interest rates were already serving two masters — the needs of the government debt market and the exchange rate. In these circumstances, giving primary attention to the rate of money and credit expansion would have been a practical impossibility.

Pause for thought 11.2:

Why does the presence of capital risk aversion in the bond market discourage frequent changes of interest rates?

This lack of access to both the monetary base and interest rates as instruments of monetary control meant that when, occasionally, the rate of money and credit expansion did reach the policy agenda as in the 'credit squeezes' of 1956 and 1964-5, control could only be conducted through the use of direct controls over bank behaviour . This fitted neatly with the needs and spirit of the immediate post-war period which reflected the very weak position of the economy following the war as well as a general Keynesian suspicion of unregulated markets. National indebtedness and fears regarding the scarcity of US dollars meant that controls over capital flows were inevitable.[2] In an economy in which rationing of consumer goods also existed for many years and in which a number of industries had been nationalized,[3] controls over the behaviour of banks hardly seemed alien.

Controls over banks, however, remained well after they had begun to be dismantled in other areas of the economy. They continued to be used throughout the 1960s, even though this was against the advice of the Radcliffe Committee. Borrowers, with the clearing banks unable to meet their requirements, sought other sources of funds. This contributed to the rapid growth of non-bank financial intermediaries, greatly weakening the effectiveness of direct controls. The first response of the authorities was to widen their application, with lending ceilings being extended in the late 1960s to secondary banks and hire purchase finance companies.

Apart from major devaluations of sterling in 1948 and 1967, balance of payments balance was sustained through macroeconomic policy. This was largely achieved through stop-go fiscal policies although interest rates had to be raised from time to time to protect sterling from speculative pressures. This was particularly true in the period before 1967 during which the government battled to avoid devaluation.

By the end of the 1960s, all of the elements which had contributed to the formation of monetary policy in the previous 25 years were being called into question. Inflation rates had risen and the term 'stagflation' had been invented to refer to the periods of 'stop' which combined low rates of economic growth and rising unemployment with stubborn rates of inflation. Keynesian confidence that the macroeconomy could be managed at or near full employment had begun to wilt. Furthermore, conditions attached to an IMF loan in 1967 included requirements that the government restrict lending to the private sector and reduce the budget deficit in order to reduce domestic credit expansion (DCE).[4] Although it was expressed in terms of credit rather than money stock, this was the first statement that the aggregates must themselves be directly targeted, though the method was unspecified.

In brief, monetarism began to elbow Keynesianism aside and this was associated with a strengthening of belief in the efficiency of markets. From the point of view of the operation of monetary policy, this was doubly significant. Firstly it stressed the importance of targeting the monetary aggregates and it also hinted at methods. As we saw a moment ago, direct controls had always suffered from the ability of market participants to find their way around them and something of a game of cat and mouse had emerged between the authorities who made a rule, ingenious financial institutions which found a way round it, and the authorities who revised the rule to block the loophole and so on. However the monetary aggregates were to be restrained, direct, or non-market, controls should play no part.

To reinforce the theoretical shift, there was also a partial change in the institutional constraints. As we saw in Equation 3.18, the money supply will change when the central bank uses exchanges between domestic currency and foreign assets as it is obliged to in a fixed exchange rate regime. This can severely hamper any attempt to target the domestic money supply and is one widely recognised source of money supply endogeneity. By 1970, however, the Bretton Woods fixed exchange rate system had begun to unravel and powerful claims were being made for floating exchange rates. In future, monetary authorities would have more freedom to target the domestic money stock.

1971-79: 'Competition and Credit Control'

By the end of the 1960s the authorities were becoming increasingly concerned at the effect of the accumulation of controls on the structure and in particular the competitiveness of the banking system. The objections to the battery of 'requests', 'guidelines', 'ceilings' and other forms of direct control were set out by the Governor of the Bank of England in 1971 (Bank 1971a). The objections were those which routinely apply to all non-price methods of rationing: they encourage inefficiency, inequity and evasion.

Inefficiency arose, it was alleged, by diverting funds (priced below the market clearing level) into projects (typically in exports and manufacturing) which were favoured by government policy but whose return was less than that on other projects (often connected with property development or consumer goods). Inequities arose at many points. For example, the regulations discriminated against those institutions to which they applied, in favour of those to which they did not. Typically the burden of control fell most heavily upon the clearing banks to the benefit of existing non-bank financial intermediaries and of newly created secondary banks whose characteristics were designed to keep them just outside the reach of the controls.

The growth of new markets and institutions exempt from the controls yields a wealth of examples of regulation-induced innovation.[5] More importantly here it was a demonstration of the classic black market effect of non-price regulation. As soon as controls frustrate both sides of the market (banks and their clients) they create a market incentive for evasion. This in turn requires new regulation, and expenditure upon the resources required for enforcement. Furthermore, it also distorts the meaning of existing indicators and deprives the authorities of valuable information. It was this experience of seeing controls imposed at one point countered by circumventory innovations elsewhere ('squeezing the balloon' as it became known in Bankspeak) that eventually led to an extensive review of operating procedures in 1970.

At the same time, controlling the volume of bank credit was starting to emerge as a potential intermediate target of monetary policy partly, as we have seen, under pressure from the IMF, but also as the state of monetary economics itself came to link monetary aggregates with nominal income more directly through a stable demand for money function. In the terms that we adopted at the beginning of this section, the discovery of a stable demand for money function was tantamount to confirming that, contrary to the Radcliffe Committee's contention, velocity was subject to very little change. The quantity of money that people wished to hold (M) was a stable fraction of total spending (Py). Velocity changed only slowly and thus the effect of changes in P would be predictable changes in Py. (Notice that stability in V only creates a predictable *association* between M and Py. It says nothing about causality, but this was assumed, with little debate, to run from M). What emerged from a period of extensive discussion and consultation was a set of proposals known ever after as *Competition and Credit Control (CCC)*. These proposals were introduced in September 1971 and the title is significant since the package was trying to achieve two objectives which did not necessarily fit easily together. On the one hand, the 'competition' part of the proposals was designed to reduce the discrimination between institutions — banks, secondary banks and finance houses — and to foster competition between banking firms. The principal targets here were an interest rate cartel operated by the banks which kept deposit rates down and made them 'sticky' or unresponsive to changes in other short-term rates, and bank charges, which were higher than in other countries with developed banking systems. On the other hand, the *CCC* proposals were intended to provide a more satisfactory method of controlling the expansion of money and credit than the market-distorting interventions of the past. The details of *CCC* are reported in many places,[6] but briefly:

• all quantitative restrictions on lending by banks and finance houses were to end

• all agreements and conventions on interest rates were to end

• the Bank would no longer support the gilts market by buying bonds with more than one year to maturity

• 8 per cent cash ratio reduced to 1.5 per cent and extended to all banks

• 28 per cent liquid assets ratio replaced with a reserve asset ratio of 12.5 per cent for banks and 10 per cent for finance houses with assets over £5m

• the Bank to be able to call for 'special deposits', with interest payable at treasury bill rate, from all banks.

The removal of directives and requests naturally raised the question of what form control of credit or monetary aggregates should take in future. Given the disillusion with direct controls, it is not perhaps surprising that the emphasis was to be on 'market methods', that is to say on price. Changing the market price of credit, it was argued, would be indiscriminate between institutions and would remove the incentives to collusion between borrowers and lenders that inevitably arose when interest rates were held at non-market-clearing levels. The intention was, therefore, to vary short-term interest rates which, it was hoped would cause changes in the demand for loans and the demand for the deposits which the loans created. The details of *CCC* have thus to be seen as a way of giving the authorities the ability to make those changes quickly and predictably, and to make them in a non-discriminatory way. The history of the initial failure and the subsequent patching up of *CCC* reflects the progressive discovery that these demands were not particularly responsive to interest changes, especially in periods of rapid inflation.

Pause for thought 11.3:

Why might the demand for bank loans be interest-inelastic?

Given the prevalence of official ratios in the history of UK banking, and the prevalence of bank deposit multipliers in textbook accounts of money supply determination (see Section 3.3), it is important to emphasise that the reserve asset ratio (like all ratios before and since) and the calls for special deposits were never intended to operate as part of a monetary base control system where the Bank would seek to change the quantity of deposits by changing the supply of reserve assets. The objective was stated by the Governor in an often quoted passage:

> It is not to be expected that the mechanism of minimum reserve asset ratio and Special Deposits can be used to achieve some precise multiple contraction or expansion of bank assets. Rather the intention is to use our control over liquidity, which these instruments will reinforce, to influence the structure of interest rates. The resulting *change in relative rates of return* will then induce shifts in the current portfolios of both the public and the banks (Bank, 1971b, p.10, our emphasis).

The key phrase is 'our control over liquidity'. This refers to the Bank's position as a monopoly supplier of funds in times of a general shortage (lender of last resort). In times of shortage the Bank can make funds available at a rate of its own choosing and this rate then sets the floor for other lending rates. In these circumstances the role of the reserve asset ratio (and a call for special deposits for that matter) is solely to speed up the process of interest rate adjustment. Essentially, the reserve asset ratio was intended to force banks with a reserve shortage to meet the problem by withdrawing call money from the discount market where the Bank could immediately put pressure on short-term rates by its response to the discount houses' requests for help. By classifying a wide range of bank liquid assets as reserves the authorities hoped to deter banks from meeting the shortage by disposing of these assets. Of course, a significant disposal — of gilts, for example — would eventually cause interest rates to rise with similar implications for the cost of bank advances and the flow of lending. But the interest rates affected, and the length of time required for the effect, would be more diffuse and less certain.

Clearly, and it is worth repeating, the reserve asset ratio was not intended and could not be used as the centrepiece of a fractional reserve-multiplier system and was there only to help in the manipulation of interest rates. It is the Bank's lender of last resort function and its willingness to vary interest rates which is crucial. Reflecting on the conduct of monetary policy as it was envisaged under *CCC*, the Bank later said:

> Importance was now attached to the monetary aggregates; their rate of growth was to be controlled by the market instrument of interest rates. (Bank, 1978).

It is easy to see the FoF approach at work here.

As regards debt management the authorities can adopt one of two attitudes. They can emphasise a support function giving priority to maintaining stable debt prices, buying and selling debt so as to smooth market fluctuations, and accepting whatever monetary consequences, via residual financing, may follow from that. The alternative is to emphasize the control (of money supply) function — selling whatever volume of debt is necessary to limit residual financing to whatever is consistent with monetary targets, and accepting whatever price/yield fluctuations follow from that. Each approach carries a number of detailed implications for the way in which the authorities operate in the market.

As we saw in the last section, in the pre-*CCC* period the authorities saw the support function as more important than control. This was consistent with the Keynes-Radcliffe scepticism about monetary aggregates and the consequent emphasis on interest rates. It also reflected some of the Bank's (often unsupported) views about the nature of the government debt market in the 1950s and 1960s as we saw in the last section, namely, that the market was dominated by capital risk aversion and that frequent changes in price might diminish the market for debt as a whole by driving large numbers of potential investors away.

The announcement, slightly predating *CCC*, that the Bank would no longer be willing to buy stock with more than one year to maturity obviously signalled a major shift in the direction of the control function. This was consistent with a desire to give more attention to the growth of money and credit arguments, though it is worth emphasizing again that this priority itself emerged only from 1973 onwards. The arguments in the preparation of *CCC* reflected a wider range of growing doubts about the policy of 'leaning into the wind'. The first questioned the ability of the tactic to deliver its fundamental objective. While stabilising debt prices may maximize present demand it does not follow that long-term demand is similarly affected. It may be that a policy which gave more variable yields and more monetary control now, would do more for demand in the long term if the greater degree of monetary control produced lower and more predictable inflation rates. Furthermore, the ability of the tactic to maximize present demand could be called into question since there was no real evidence that the market was dominated by sceptics. Thirdly, the policy was contradictory. 'Leaning into the wind' involved selling debt and then buying it (or some other debt) back if the market weakened. The argument that supporting the market must conflict with the need to vary interest rates for monetary control purposes was therefore only one of several objections.

Allowing prices/yields to fluctuate more gave the authorities more potential control over residual financing of the government deficit, but left them with the problem of how to sell debt on a falling market. In the early years of *CCC* when, as we shall see, monetary and fiscal policy were both expansionary, this was not a problem. Indeed, in 1972 and 1973 the Bank provided support for the market for short periods. The situation became pressing in 1975, however, when large public sector deficits combined with a desire to control monetary growth required large sales of gilts. The response was twofold. The most dramatic part of the strategy was to raise short-term interest rates sharply in order to bring them down later and encourage investors to join the market to benefit from capital gains. This amounted to treating the demand for gilts as a function not just of the *level* of interest rates but as a (negative) function of *changes*, a fall in rates from their peak causing the demand curve to shift outward. The first use of the device, subsequently christened the 'Duke of York tactic' for obvious reasons, was in October 1975. Between then and March 1976 over £3bn of central government debt was sold to the non-bank private sector. The tactic was used on a further nine occasions before 1979. [7]

The other element in the authorities' attempt to increase the marketability of debt was to experiment with new types of stock and new methods of issue. In March 1977, the Bank invited the first subscriptions for part-paid stock and followed this with two issues of stocks with variable interest rate payments linked to treasury bill rate, offering holders some compensation for declining capital values when interest rates were rising. Although the possibility of moving away from the fixed price/tap system of issue was widely discussed in 1975 and 1976, the first experiment — with a partial-tender issue — had to wait until 1979.

Finally, amongst the changes often associated with *CCC* was the change from Bank Rate to Minimum Lending Rate (MLR). The switch was not part of the provisions but may be argued to have followed necessarily from the change in debt management which allowed greater fluctuations in interest rates. Bank Rate had functioned both as the 'last resort' rate and as the basis on which many other rates were set by conventional mark-ups. Its level for the coming week was announced each Thursday though, during years of interest rate smoothing, the announcement consisted most frequently of 'no change'. With many rates linked to it by convention, changes in Bank Rate became increasingly momentous events which acquired a corresponding amount of inertia. When interest rates, including the treasury bill rates at which the Bank was effectively supplying liquidity, were allowed to fluctuate more freely, it became inevitable that market rates sooner or later would move out of line with a sticky Bank Rate. Like most things, this was easily predictable with hindsight but it took experience to learn. In October 1972, Bank Rate was replaced by what later became known as Minimum Lending Rate (since that is what it was). MLR was determined as treasury bill rate plus 0.5 per cent rounded up to the nearest 0.25.

As we said earlier, the dominant theme of monetary policy until 1973 was expansion. A succession of tax-cutting budgets and, as it turned out, easy credit led to a rapid rise in the PSBR, a dramatic deterioration in the balance of payments and unprecedented increases in money supply. In the four quarters of 1972 M3 grew by 4¾ per cent, 7½ per cent, 4¼ per cent and 5 per cent; equivalent to 27 per cent at a year-on-year rate. In the 1972 Budget Statement Chancellor Barber had indicated that not even the sterling exchange rate would hinder recovery. Predictably, the existing exchange rate immediately became difficult to maintain and sterling was floated on 23rd June. Until 1973, therefore, there was still a recognisable Keynesian flavour to monetary policy: unemployment still topped the list of potential economic problems and it was still believed that a combination of monetary and fiscal measures could deliver (sustained) changes in the level of output and employment.

Nonetheless, in the background, views about the influence of monetary aggregates were beginning to change.[8] By the spring of 1973 unemployment had fallen by over 200,000 on the figures of a year earlier. Furthermore, from a small but rapidly declining surplus in 1972, the current account of the balance of payments was sent into deficit in the first quarter of 1973 and by summer was clearly headed for a very large deficit for the year. Inflation was 9 per cent and rising and unfilled vacancies were at a record level. The first tentative steps towards restraint came in July with a 1.5 point rise in MLR and a call for Special Deposits equal to 1 per cent of eligible liabilities to be made in August. In November, MLR was raised again (to 13 per cent) and a further 2 per cent call for SDs was made. Between the two calls, further lending guidelines were issued and the general drift away from *CCC* gathered pace with an *official* interest ceiling on deposits (for the first time in the UK), the reintroduction of hire purchase term controls in December and the appearance of a completely new device, the Supplementary Special Deposit scheme (or 'corset'), for imposing quantitative limits on the growth of deposits.

Under the SSD scheme, the Bank of England would issue target rates of growth of interest bearing liabilities (IBELs) for banks. Growth rates in excess of these targets were taxed in a steeply progressive manner by requiring banks to make non-interest bearing SSDs with the Bank of England. The scheme operated on five occasions between December 1973 and June 1980 with variations in the target rates and in the scale of penalties.

Once begun, the most interesting feature of the retreat from *CCC* was its speed and extent. As we have just seen, within the second half of 1973 monetary policy came once again to be firmly based on direct controls in spite of *CCC*'s high hopes. There are various possible interpretations: the interest rate mechanism was ineffective or too slow. Alternatively, the mechanism was sound but the authorities declined to use it. 'Willing the end but fearing the means?' is Gowland's interpretation[9] and this is supported by an inside view from the Treasury. Browning (1986, p.284) admits that it was Government pressure that forced the Bank to find some alternative to further interest rate increases in the second half of 1973, because of the special circumstances of the energy and industrial crises. For the Bank, this is confirmed by Goodhart[10] though he stresses also the unexpected technical problems which confronted interest rate methods as a result of liability management and the consequent difficulty of.creating the appropriate relative interest rate changes. It is very significant for Goodhart's case that the two most dramatic innovations in the second half of 1973, interest rate ceilings on deposits and the corset, were both intended to limit the rise in deposit rates when other interest rates were increased, thus restoring some of the authorities' ability to influence the key relativities.[11] In 1972 and 1973 annual growth rates of M3 had reached 25 and 27 per cent respectively. The effect of the corset was to bring this down quite sharply during 1974 to 6 per cent in 1975. But by then, the annual rate of inflation, assisted by the first oil crisis, had reached 24 per cent.

The symbolic end of Keynesian monetary policy came in 1976 when Prime Minister Callaghan, addressing the Labour Party Annual Conference against a background of a collapsing pound and rumours of forthcoming cuts in public spending, announced that it was impossible for governments to spend their way out of recession, efforts to do so having only a temporary effect before being replaced by higher prices. Within three months the rejection of fiscal policy was accompanied by the first publication of monetary targets.

In 1976 inflation had begun to moderate but by then the major focus of attention was the PSBR, at £10bn equivalent to almost 10 per cent of GDP. Repeated speculation about the need for large cuts in public spending and splits in the governing Labour Party, helped by the misinterpretation of government policy toward the exchange rate, led to a thirty per cent depreciation between February 1975 and September 1976. The year ended with the government negotiating a loan from the IMF of $4bn over two years to support sterling. In exchange, the government agreed to major cuts in public spending and increases in revenue through to 1978 and agreed also to limit domestic credit expansion (DCE), the counterpart of sterling M3 (£M3), to a target range of 9-13 per cent. Money supply targets were at last out in the open.

The experiment with monetarism

The 1980 Budget speech announced the Medium Term Financial Strategy (MTFS) which projected declining target rates of growth for £M3 and for a PSBR forming a declining proportion of GDP. With inflation at 21 per cent it was always going to be difficult to hold monetary growth to its target (7-11 per cent) and interest rates were raised to 17 per cent in November. Even at this level, *real* rates were negative but this did not prevent an outcry from the personal and corporate sectors. Scepticism about both the ability of interest rates to constrain monetary growth and about the connection between monetary growth and nominal incomes had already been expressed. The arguments in favour of such a hostage to political fortune were essentially to do with information. Published targets, especially if the accompanying rhetoric made them sound credible, would give the private sector a framework of financial stability within which it could plan more effectively; publicized targets were an indication that negotiators who tried to thwart their implications by raising prices or wages excessively would know they would encounter heavy costs

— in bankruptcies and unemployment — and would modify their behaviour more quickly and without the need for a costly learning process. It was also argued that target growth rates, published for some years ahead, would impose a discipline on governments which might otherwise be tempted to depart from the counter-inflationary objective for reasons of short-run political expediency .

The level of interest rates and the UK's new role as a major oil producer pushed the (nominal and real) exchange rate to very high levels and it was this which exerted the major deflationary pressure and caused the dramatic rise in unemployment (from 1.3m to 2.2m) during 1980.

By the turn of the year there was some evidence that inflationary pressures were easing (helped to some degree by external events) and interest rates were reduced to 14 per cent. The 1981 Budget was sharply deflationary, however, and inflation continued to fall in spite of rapid monetary growth (14.5 per cent) distorted by a Civil Servants' strike. Exchange rate worries reversed the interest rate trend in the autumn but rates declined again through 1982.

The overwhelming commitment to monetary targets in this period, combined with a desire to remove the direct controls on credit which had crept back into use after the failure of *CCC*, provoked an extensive review of monetary control techniques. The result was a rejection of the arguments for monetary base control. Instead, the authorities opted for a return to the spirit of *CCC* but with a number of institutional changes which, they hoped, would make interest rates more effective than they had been ten years earlier.

The starting point was the identification of institutions to whom the arrangements should apply. These were described as the 'monetary sector' (a term later substituted by 'banking sector' after the Banking Act, 1987) and comprised all banks 'recognized' under the Banking Act, 1979. By including also 'licensed deposit takers' it abolished the two-tier structure of recognition established in *CCC*. It also included the Trustee Savings Banks, the National Girobank, the Banking Department of the Bank of England, and such banks in the Isle of Man and the Channel Islands as chose to join.

Members of the monetary sector were required to maintain ½ of one per cent of their eligible liabilities as *non-operational* deposits at the Bank of England in order to provide resources and income for the Bank. In addition, banks were required to hold such *operational* balances as they thought prudent. Notice, this was not mandatory but a matter of judgement for banks, though banks were required to notify the Bank of England of any significant change which they proposed to make to this prudential ratio.

The most significant provisions concerned banks' relations with the discount market where the Bank wished to strengthen its leverage over short-term interest rates. The new arrangements extended the range of banks whose bills were eligible for discount at the Bank of England. Eligibility required an agreement to maintain at least four and an average of six per cent of eligible liabilities as secured call money with discount houses, money brokers and gilt-edged jobbers. This was intended to achieve two things. Firstly, it ensured an adequate supply of bills in which the Bank could conduct the open market operations by which it intended to provide liquidity and indicate its interest rate preferences; secondly it would ensure that banks would have significant assets subject to the change in interest rates which the Bank could engineer.

All other ratios were abolished along with the continuous posting of minimum lending rate although the possibility of announcing a rate in special circumstances was retained. The Bank instead committed itself to maintaining interest rates within an unpublished band. The possibility of calling for special deposits, however, was retained.

The disinclination to publish an official dealing rate was part of the desire, observed with *CCC*, to depoliticize interest rate changes — to make them seem more market determined. Without a pre-announced dealing rate, discount houses would have to offer bills to the Bank at a price of their own choosing. This could, at least in theory, be held to reflect the scale of the shortage 'in the market'. Nonetheless the Bank retained the right to reject the offers if it was unhappy with the corresponding discount rate. The impression that interest rates were market determined was to be further promoted by the Bank's preference for dealing only in 'band 1' bills (those maturing within 14 days), seemingly leaving longer-term rates to be determined by the market.

Faced with the desire to slow the rate of monetary expansion, the mechanism envisaged the Bank pushing up band 1 rates by buying bills at a larger discount than had hitherto been the case, if necessary rejecting offers of bills from discount houses until the shortage of liquidity produced the appropriate rate of discount at the houses' initiative. Convention, though ultimately market forces if necessary, would ensure that all short-term rates would rise in response to reports of the Bank's action (see Section 12.2): amongst these would be bank base rates and thus the rate on advances. Assuming some negative interest-elasticity, a movement up the curve would slow the flow of new bank lending and therefore the rate of increase of the money stock. If the rise in the level of absolute rates meant also a widening of the bank lending-money and non-money-asset - money differentials, then the slowdown would be reinforced by an inward shift of the curve. We look at this process in more detail when looking at liability management later in this chapter.

By 1982, evidence that £M3 velocity was declining had become irresistible. For this reason, and with their confidence in monetary targets beginning to waver, the authorities extended the range of indicators they were prepared to consider (while maintaining publicly announced targets for broad money). From 1982-85 additional evidence on the deflationary stance of policy came from employment, output, various measures of inflation, asset prices and also, by 1983, two additional monetary aggregates — M1, a narrow definition and PSL2, a very broad definition (see Table 2.1).

Bank lending, however, continued to grow very rapidly (at around 20 per cent p.a.) suggesting, without some drastic action, a similar growth in bank deposits. Some of the growth came from the banks' aggressive entry into the mortgage market. There was plenty of evidence from earlier periods that the demand for bank lending was interest inelastic but the demand for 'home loans' appeared particularly insensitive to high interest rates. Houses had proved the one successful hedge against inflation in the 1970s and prices were rising very rapidly again in the early 1980s. Capital gains on dwellings in the UK are generally tax-exempt and there were at the time quite widespread tax subsidies on mortgage interest payments.

By the end of 1982, base rates were just above 10 per cent and, with a general election not far away, the authorities were not willing to use interest rates to tackle this explosion in lending. Instead, they resorted to 'overfunding' the PSBR, introducing a number of novelties in the form of government stock that they issued but also putting some upward pressure on long-term interest rates. As a means of reconciling the rapid growth of private sector borrowing with much lower monetary targets, this device was entirely successful but had the inevitable effect that the UK banking system was regularly short of liquidity. This was remedied initially by the Bank buying treasury bills from the banking system and, when the stock of these ran out, buying large quantities of commercial bills. In effect, the Bank was lending short to the corporate sector, selling gilts in order to do so: a practice which was always open to the criticism that the corporate sector should have been able to borrow in the bond market on its own behalf. The practice ceased in 1985 when worries about distortions (to relative yields) combined with increasing scepticism about the value of money stock targets.

By the mid-1980s, therefore, it was clear both that the authorities' ability to target the broad money stock with any degree of accuracy by using interest rates, had been severely undermined, and that the rationale for monetary targets had itself broken down in the face of sharply falling velocity.[12] Both were recognized by the Bank of England when the Governor announced the end of formal targets from 1986.

11.3 Financial innovation and monetary policy

We have just seen that the policy of using interest rates to target the rate of growth of the money stock has a history going back to 1971, reaching its most explicit form after 1980 before ending suddenly in 1985. Its demise was brought about by a coincidence of circumstance. Firstly, interest rates became ineffective in controlling the aggregates while falling velocity removed most of the point of targeting the aggregates. Ironically, there was a certain amount of good luck here: the instrument failed just when the policy became point-less. The explanation often given for this state of affairs commonly makes reference to 'financial innovation' and 'liability management', and we need to look in more detail at just how it is that changes in financial products and processes can have such a major impact on the conduct of monetary policy.

Since financial innovation is a continuous process, it is unlikely that events of the period 1980-85 are unique in having some impact on the monetary system. This means that we should be prepared to look rather more broadly at the topic and recognise a number of developments which have caused major monetary changes with at least potential relevance to policy. We want obviously to look at the falling velocity episode but we will look at three others as well. The first is 'regulation Q' and the growth of eurocurrency markets; the second is the 'bill-leak' and the Supplementary Special Deposit scheme; the third is off-balance sheet activity. We will then look at liability management and the 1980s. We take them in chronological order.

Regulation Q and the eurocurrency markets

Under the Bretton Woods system the US$ functioned as an intervention currency, an international means of payment and store of value. The worldwide demand for dollars to which these roles gave rise was met by a combination of US balance of payments deficits and dollar borrowings from US banks, the resulting deposits being held until the early 1960s, mainly with US banks. In the mid-1960s, however, the US authorities began to impose controls on currency outflows which limited access to these deposits for overseas holders. This combined with two further, long-running, disadvantages. The first was 'regulation Q' which limited interest payments on deposits. The second problem, mainly relevant to Eastern bloc countries, was that cold-war tensions created the risk that dollar deposits might be impounded for political reasons. The result was the growth of dollar deposits placed with European banks and, later, with European subsidiaries of US banks.

Since reserve, deposit insurance, capital and other regulatory requirements are usually imposed with respect to banks' holdings of deposits in the domestic currency and act as a tax on deposit business, a further contributory factor to the long-term growth of eurocurrency business was the ability of Eurobanks to offer their services at more competitive rates than domestic institutions.[13]

At the end of 1990, estimates of the growth of the eurocurrency market, put it at over $5,000bn, having increased three-and-a-half-fold during the 1980s. 'Eurobanks' (and 'eurocurrencies') are misnomers. Most such banks are departments or subsidiaries of major banks with a clear national identity. Most major countries are involved, although the largest shares lie with banks whose headquarters are in Japan or the USA. Equally 'eurocurrency' may refer to currencies with no european connection whatsoever. In this context, the prefix 'euro-' simply means a deposit held in a bank outside the country in whose currency the deposit is denominated. Hence dollar deposits in a Tokyo bank are eurodollars. The use of the term 'euro-' is a reminder that the practice of holding deposits outside their country of denomination began with the holding of US$ in 'european' banks.

From an economic point of view, there is nothing fundamentally different between a bank which specializes in eurocurrency business and a bank which concentrates on domestic deposits and lending. Both engage in maturity transformation, and in so far as they create assets and liabilities which are more attractive to end users than would be the case if the latter dealt directly with each other, then they help to mobilize funds which might otherwise have lain idle. However, there are two possible consequences of eurobanking activity which have attracted considerable attention.

The first is the effect upon world money supply and liquidity. If, as we said above, eurobanks are able to mobilize funds which would otherwise lie idle (through the usual processes of maturity and risk transformation) then private sector liquidity is increased. Furthermore, if we introduce into the banking system a further layer of institutions whose liabilities are money, as is plainly the case with any eurocurrency, then we introduce the possibility of further multiple deposit creation against a limited quantity of reserves. Most eurobanks hold reserves with major US banks or with major banks operating in the domestic monetary system. Imagine, for example, that a US resident moves dollars from a domestic US bank to a eurodollar bank which holds reserves with the domestic bank. In the domestic bank, there is no loss of deposits but there is a rearrangement of ownership of deposits (from a non-bank to the eurobank). In the eurobank, there is an increase in customer deposits matched, of course, by an increase in reserves. However, the bank's liquidity has increased on the assumption that its reserve:deposit ratio is less than one. (The effect is the opposite of the sale of government bonds in Table

3.1). If its response is then to increase its advances and if those advances are redeposited, then a further expansion of the eurobank's balance sheet is possible. Numerically at least, the significance clearly depends upon two ratios, the reserve ratio and the redeposit ratio. Estimates of the size of the eurodollar multiplier are very uncertain and have a wide range, mainly because it is difficult to identify dollars in a US bank which are being held as reserves against eurodollars in a eurobank which is a branch of the domestic US bank.

A second consequence, or group of consequences, arises from the increasing difficulty of operating an independent domestic monetary policy in the absence of exchange control (i.e. post-1979 for the UK). Clearly, any attempt to control domestic monetary expansion can be partially thwarted at least by frustrated UK borrowers taking out eurodollar (for example) loans and exchanging the proceeds for sterling in the spot market. Such would be a predictable response whatever form the domestic monetary restrictions took. Furthermore, high UK interest rates, which would be part of a restrictive monetary policy, may attract an inflow of eurocurrencies which could then be exchanged for sterling at a guaranteed price (under fixed exchange rates), increasing both the money supply and UK banks' cash reserves. In principle such an inflow can be sterilized by sales of securities but there is the obvious danger that security sales themselves widen the gap between domestic and Eurocurrency interest rates, leading to an increased inflow. With floating exchange rates the impact falls upon the exchange rate itself rather than on the money supply.

The 'bill-leak'

We saw in section 11.2 that the *CCC* arrangements envisaged the use of interest rates to limit monetary growth but that this commitment faltered in the period of rapid growth after 1973 when it became clear that interest rates would have to rise to levels that were considered politically unacceptable. The emergency measure was the Supplementary Special Deposit scheme which allowed the Bank of England to specify growth targets for interest-bearing eligible liabilities (roughly speaking interest-bearing deposits) and then to impose steeply progressive penalties on banks whose IBEL growth exceeded the target. The object was to discourage banks from raising deposit rates when the Bank of England raised minimum lending rate. This enabled the Bank to open up a differential between deposit and other market rates and the thinking behind this was twofold. Firstly, making deposits relatively less attractive than other assets reduced the tendency for borrowers to hold the proceeds of loans as bank deposits (preferring government securities, for example). Since balance sheets must balance, the inability to attract deposits itself made it difficult for banks to lend. Secondly, the change in relative interest rates made borrowing less attractive. By widening the loan-deposit spread, using existing liquid assets (i.e. deposits) to finance a deficit, becomes marginally more attractive than taking out new loans. (Other relativities are also involved in what is quite a complicated story. We return to it under 'liability management' below).

The point about all this is that during the periods when the corset was in force, banks were deterred from increasing their lending. Nonetheless, firms still needed credit and banks were fretting at the loss of the interest income from loans unmade. One partial solution which quickly surfaced was the guaranteeing of commercial bills of exchange. Given the most highly developed discount market in the world, it had long been possible for firms to raise short-term funds in London by the sale of bills at a given discount for a specified period. Indeed, for large corporations this had been a standard method of short-term finance since the early nineteenth century. The disadvantage for smaller firms, or at least for firms with no established reputation in the discount market, was the rate of interest (discount) they would have to offer on the bill. This was bound to be greater than the cost of a bank loan, since the firm would have an established relationship and a credit record with the bank, while in the discount market it was asking buyers to hold the bills of an unknown debtor. The cost of bill finance was bound to contain a significant risk premium.

Pause for thought 11.4:

Give some examples of the *relative* interest rates that may influence (a) the demand for deposits and (b) the demand for bank loans.

For firms in this position, one solution was to 'buy' reputation from their bank by getting the bank to guarantee the bill. With the bank's guarantee the bill would trade at the finest rates of interest since the risk of default was virtually eliminated. The bank, of course, would charge for this service, but provided that the guarantee fee was less than the interest saving, then the firm would gain from a reduction in the cost of bill finance while the bank would earn fee-income which would provide some compensation for the interest foregone on loans that it was unable to make. By the end of the 1970s the 'bill-leak' was very large indeed.

In effect, the corset introduced a form of non-price rationing. Non-price rationing almost always has two consequences. The first is that it encourages evasion. Such evasion often takes place in what is often called a 'black market' in which both sides, buyers and sellers, try to find a form of behaviour which allows them to achieve the results the authorities wish to prevent while appearing not to do so. The bill-leak was typical of behaviour of this kind. Firms could borrow and spend pretty much as they originally planned; buyers of the bills acquired assets which had almost the same liquidity as bank deposits; and banks received income from arranging loans. The second, less obvious consequence of non-price rationing but one which follows directly from evasion, is that the authorities lose information. In the present case, they no longer knew what the size of the loan market was or what volume of liquid assets agents were holding. The statistics which they regularly collect are those for bank loans and deposits. When the corset was in force, these statistics suggested that spending should be under control, but the reality was very different.

For UK banks, the bill-leak was their first experience of a larger category of activity known as 'off-balance sheet operations'. They learned quite quickly.

Off-balance sheet operations

It is a curious characteristic of traditional banking business, that the size of the business is directly reflected in the balance sheet. As more loans and deposits are 'produced' the balance sheet expands. Compared with the balance sheets of other types of enterprise, a bank's balance sheet is much more informative about the business. Hence, when the authorities wish to monitor banking activity it is hardly surprising that they focus upon the structure of bank balance sheets and when they wish to impose controls, these controls are specified in terms of balance sheet components (notice the growth rates for IBELS referred to in the last section). Avoiding these constraints, or at least minimising their impact often, therefore, involves engaging in income-earning activity which has no direct, corresponding, balance sheet entry.

'Off-balance sheet' operations are activities which generate income for banks without creating assets or liabilities which normal accounting procedures would place in their balance sheets. As with most other innovations, the interest in off-balance sheet operations lies not in their novelty but in their recent rapid expansion and increasing variety. Lewis (1988) listed some 60 off-balance sheet activities. These were divided roughly equally between 'financial services' and those giving rise to 'contingent claims'. The former included activities such as tax and financial planning, investment advice, portfolio management, insurance broking, credit/debit card services and (most recently) estate agency. The latter included the issuing of guarantees of many kinds, securities underwriting, market-making in securities and arranging swap and hedging transactions. One of the themes running through the growth of off-balance sheet operations, and much discussed in the financial innovation literature, is 'securitization'. This refers both to the increasing use by ultimate lenders and borrowers of capital markets, in preference to bank intermediation, and to the practice by banks themselves, more especially in the US, of selling off loans from their asset portfolio, turning them into marketable securities — shifting them off the balance sheet.

Clearly, at an institutional level, one can view this growth of off-balance sheet activities as representing a significant change in banking operations. On a more theoretical level, however, one should take seriously the argument that off-balance sheet activities are essentially the same as the '...traditional on-balance sheet lending and borrowing operations of banks [which] can be seen to be packages of information and risk-sharing (or insurance) services' (Lewis, 1988, p.396). By taking a customer's deposit a bank (traditionally) creates a very secure, very liquid asset, repayable at par and turns it into a long-term liability for a borrower. The bank protects both from risk by its superior information and by its size. The interest rate 'spread' is the price that lenders and borrowers pay for this service. Nothing is fundamentally different when a bank accepts a bill or issues a standby letter of credit. The holder of the bill (or letter) enjoys a transfer of risk to the bank for which s/he pays by accepting a lower interest rate on the loan than would have been the case without the bank's guarantee; the borrower pays a fee to the bank for the benefit of the lower interest charge required by the market. Furthermore the bank is willing to accept the risk in the guarantee because it has information which enables it to make a reasonable assessment of the individual default risk and to price it bearing in mind the average default rate on the total pool of guarantees.

When it comes to identifying the consequences, actual and potential of the expansion of off-balance sheet activity, one can say as with the growth of Euromarkets, that by supplying services which customers want, banks are helping to mobilize funds which might otherwise have lain idle and are generally adding to the liquidity of the financial system. However, the consequences which are of more concern to the authorities are rather different. The first is the one that we saw in connection with the bill-leak. It opens up a range of opportunities which may well be used in response to regulations which are specified in terms of balance sheet size or composition.

The corset was a specifically UK regulation and one which the authorities applied intermittently during the 1970s to deal with a specific problem. Of more widespread and durable significance have been the regulations governing the capital adequacy of banks, laid down, amended and refined since 1988 by the Basle Committee and known as the 'Basle Accords'. The basic principle involves the use of 'risk-asset ratios'. Bank assets are divided into five categories, each of which is given a risk-weighting. For example, 'cash' has a weight of 0 while, at the other extreme, commercial loans have a full weight of 1. The approach is, broadly, to take the market value of assets in each category and multiply by the risk-weighting, to give a risk-adjusted value for each. These are then aggregated to give an overall value for the bank's risk-adjusted assets. This is then compared to the bank's capital base, which itself is carefully defined and subject to rules of composition. The Basle Committee set a lower limit of eight per cent for the ratio of capital to risk-adjusted assets, though national bank supervisors have discretion to set higher limits.

The effect of such ratios for a bank operating near the limit is to make the further expansion of its loan portfolio very costly and may indeed make it unprofitable. Box 11.1 illustrates this and makes the point again that regulation has the effect of acting like a tax. In the circumstances, some banks have responded by the practice of securitization. This involves setting up a separately capitalised 'special vehicle' whose job it is to buy bundles of loans from the bank. It does this by issuing bonds whose interest payments are guaranteed by the income from the loans (after deductions by the originating bank and the special vehicle). The result is that the sale of the loans frees up an equivalent amount of capital (assuming that the loans' risk-weighting was 1), lowering the risk-asset ratio, while leaving the bank with some income from the loans — the fees for setting up the loan and a small fraction of the interest.

Liability management

The last of these illustrations bring us to the circumstances which were widely regarded as being responsible for the demise of monetary targets in the UK, in the mid-1980s.

Given a decision to make monetary targets the centre of monetary policy, there exists, in principle, a wide range of techniques which can be used in an attempt to control the aggregates. Box 11.2, which draws on Gowland (1984 pp.9-10) lists 14.[14] Bewildering as the range may look, however, the chosen technique (or techniques) must either restrict banks' ability to lend, restrict clients desire to borrow or reduce the community's willingness to hold the resulting deposits. In each case the restriction may come in the form of quantity ('direct') control or price ('market') incentive. Control of the monetary base, as implied by the B-M analysis is an example of a quantity restraint on

Box 11.1: Capital adequacy ratios as a tax

Imagine a bank which has the following, simplified, balance sheet.

Assets £bn

		Risk weights	Risk adjusted value	Liabilities £bn	
Loans	80	1	80	Time deposits	100
Bonds	30	0.4	12	Sight deposits	36
Bills	32	0.25	8	Capital	8
Cash	2	0	0		
Total	144		100		144

Suppose that the prime loan rate = 6%, while deposit rate = 4% and the cost of capital (the required return on the bank's equity) = 15%

Notice that the bank is operating at the limit of its capital adequacy ratio (= 8%). In these circumstances, additional lending (e.g. of £1bn) requires a matching increase in capital of £0.08bn if the ratio is to be maintained, accompanied by £0.92bn of additional deposits. The net income effect of this expansion can be calculated as:

	Expenditure	Income
£1bn of additional loans at 6% =		£60.0m
£0.08bn of additional capital at 15% =	£12.0m	
£0.92bn of additional deposits at 4% =	£36.8m	
		-£48.8m
Profit		£11.2m (=1.12%)

Without the capital adequacy constraint, the bank would have been able to finance the additional loan solely by additional deposits, which are much cheaper than new capital. The effect of this can easily be compared with the situation above.

	Expenditure	Income
£1bn of additional loans at 6%		£60.0m
£1bn of additional deposits at 4%	£40.0m	-£40.0m
Profit		£20.0m (= 2%)

The effect of the capital adequacy requirement is to reduce the return on additional lending from 2 per cent to 1.12 per cent. The bank may feel that such a return is inadequate. In these circumstances, it has a number of choices. It can abandon its expansion plan. Alternatively, it can charge more for the loans and/or pay less for deposits. The result will depend upon the elasticities of deposit supply and loan demand but it is likely that the expansion will be smaller than the £1bn envisaged. Or, it can securitise the loans, avoiding the capital adequacy requirement but having to meet the costs of the securitization deal. In all of these cases the outcome will be some combination of a lower volume of additional lending and a higher price — exactly as if a tax had been placed on bank lending.

a bank's ability to lend. As we have already seen, quantity controls (at any of the three pressure points) had been widely rejected by the time monetary targets became a serious feature of monetary policy and the plan was to use price (interest rates) to deter borrowing and deposit holding. Unfortunately, just when the techniques were applied in their purest form, institutional changes undermined the strategy in a fatal manner.

We recall that one aspect of the *CCC* arrangements was the ending of the bank's interest rate cartel and the beginning of competitive bidding for deposits to fund the rapidly growing demand for bank loans after lending ceilings were removed. At this stage the competition involved banks competing between themselves for wholesale deposits, that is to say large time deposits held mainly by the corporate sector. The effect, however, was to raise the level of interest paid on wholesale deposits relative to other rates and also to make it more sensitive to market movements. Taking the Bank of England's treasury bill rate as a benchmark, 7-day deposit rates were approximately half that rate at end-1971; ten years' later the proportion was 0.87.[15]

The 1980s saw the extension of this competition to retail deposits. Once again, deregulation played its part. The starting point was the entry of banks into the mortgage market in 1981. From this stemmed the break up of the building societies' interest rate cartel in 1983, the rise in building society deposit and advances rates to market clearing levels and the consequent demise of mortgage rationing. As building societies moved onto the offensive, they entered into money transmission services by issuing chequebooks.

Box 11.2: Monetary control techniques

Variable	By price	By quantity
Deposits of the M4PS	Y	Y
Bank lending to public and private sectors	Y	Y
Non-bank lending to the public sector	Y	Y
Variations in the PSBR	N/A	N/A
Variation in the size of the base	N	Y
Variation in the size of the reserve ratio	Y	Y
Tax on banking	Y	N
Licensing	N/A	N/A

But these were of limited attraction without the benefit of cheque guarantee cards and these in turn were impossible to issue under the Building Societies Act, 1962, which prevented societies from granting unsecured loans. To remove this and other restrictions the societies set about lobbying the government for a change in the legislation.

Pushing on an open door where deregulation was concerned, the societies were quickly rewarded with the Building Societies Act, 1986, which broadened both the sources and destinations of societies' funds. In particular, large societies were permitted a limited amount of unsecured personal lending. This apparently minor change had momentous results. Since societies could now legally permit customers to be overdrawn, they could, for the first time, issue cheque guarantee cards. This made building society cheque accounts indistinguishable from those of banks except for the considerable advantages that societies paid interest on all positive balances, stayed open longer and were generally seen as more user-friendly by the public. The change in building society regulation, therefore, ensured that banks which had, since 1983, grudgingly paid interest on selected cheque accounts with restricted use, would have to follow. The first announcement came from Lloyds Bank in December 1988. The increasing tendency to pay interest on sight deposits has a number of possible consequences. Firstly it raises money's 'own rate' by increasing the weighted average return on deposits. This in turn narrows the spread between lending and deposit rates, and is one way by which the cost of bank intermediation may fall. Borrowing to finance spending becomes cheaper relative to using existing liquid assets; at the same time, money's own rate increases relative to other assets. In short, money and bank credit both become more attractive at all levels of income and at any level of *absolute* rates. Looking at it in terms of a conventional money demand diagram, the demand curve shifts out as money's (interest) services increase.

Nowhere was the effect more obvious than in a comparison between the targets and outturns for monetary growth and the rate of inflation. Under the Medium Term Financial Strategy (MTFS) starting in 1980, targets for £M3 were set, for usually the next three years, as a series of declining ranges. Table 11.1 shows the large, frequent overshoots in broad money growth rates and the steady decline in inflation, the overshoots notwithstanding.

The consequence of increasing the range of deposits on which interest is paid (as well as bidding up the rate itself) raises the weighted average return on money relative to all other assets and liabilities. Broad money becomes more attractive as a savings medium. Velocity falls and the link with spending is broken.

The rise in money's own rate led to a decline in velocity and undermined the main rationale for monetary targets. But this was not all. The tendency for deposit rates to become more market-sensitive and to follow changes in official rates quite closely made it simultaneously more difficult to hit the target. The reason for this lies in the way in which a change in official interest rates affects the flow of new loans and new deposits. Briefly, the flow of new loans and deposits depends to some degree upon *relative* interest rates and these are increasingly difficult to influence when all rates move in sympathy with changes in official rates.

Exercise 11.1

Imagine a family with a monthly income of £2000 and annual expenditure of £24,000. It spends the whole of its income each month at a constant rate. In addition it holds a minimum precautionary balance of £800. Deposits do not pay interest.

1) Calculate the household's average money holding over the year;

2) Recall that 'velocity' is the relationship between money holdings and total expenditure, calculate an annual velocity figure for this household;

3) Suppose now that banks begin to pay interest on positive balances of £1,000+ and our household increases its precautionary balance to £1000, all else remaining the same

Recalculate the velocity figure.

Three rates (and thus three relativities) are involved: money's own rate, the rate charged on bank loans and the rate on short-dated non-money assets (NMAs). To understand how this works, it is simplest to assume firstly that money's own rate is fixed and that the central bank raises its official dealing rates. This increase is followed, through a mixture of convention and arbitrage, by an increase in all other rates — closely in the case of short rates, more flexibly in the case of medium and long rates — with the notable exception of the rate on money. At this point, therefore, bank lending rates and rates on short-dated non-money assets have risen relative to money's own rate and by the same amount. This rise in the opportunity cost of holding money predictably induces some switch from money to NMAs with the result that the price of the latter is bid up and yields fall back from the level to which they initially adjusted in response to the rise in official rates. (This process is being described as taking time and proceeding in steps but this is a logical sequence, necessary only for exposition. In practice, adjustment is very rapid). We now have a change in *two* relativities. NMA rates have risen relative to money, while bank lending rates have risen even further (and therefore relative to

Table 11.1: Broad money targets and outturns, and inflation, 1980-87 (%p.a.)

£M3 targets announced	outturns						
	1980/1	1981/2	1982/3	1983/4	1984/5	1985/6	1986/7
March 1980	7-11	(6-10)	(5-9)	(4-8)			
March 1981		6-10	(5-9)	(4-8)			
March 1982			8-12	(7-11)	(6-10)		
March 1983				7-11	(6-10)	(5-9)	(4-8)
March 1984					6-10	(5-9)	(4-8)
March 1985						5-9	(4-8)
March 1986							11-15
Outturn	18.5	13	11.5	10	12	15	20
Inflation rate	16.5	11.5	7.1	4.7	5	5.9	3.2

Source: Artis and Lewis (1991) p.136; www.statistics.gov.uk

NMAs as well as relative to money). We can now see that the rise in official rates affects the demand for bank loans through two channels. Firstly, the absolute rise in loan rates pushes us up a downward sloping (flow) demand curve for bank loans. But just as important, in raising the cost of bank loans relative to the return from NMAs, the change has, in effect, cheapened the cost of a (partial) substitute for bank credit. Issuing short-dated bonds and even shorter money market instruments is an alternative to borrowing from banks for firms at least (recall the episode of the bill-leak). In our virtual diagram, not only do we move up the curve, but the curve simultaneously shifts inward. In these circumstances, change in official rates have considerable influence over the demand for loans, and this influence is to some degree independent of the elasticity of demand for bank loans with respect to loan rates themselves.

Pause for thought 11.5:

The possibility of 'liquidity trap' is usually associated with very low interest rates. If, however, the demand for money depends upon *relative* interest rates, do we need to revise this view?

While explaining what happens in an ideal world is necessarily complex, it is a relatively simple task to see what happens when circumstances move against the authorities as they did in the 1980s. Suppose now that money's own rate adjusts instantaneously to a change in official rates. All short-rates now move together. This means that there is no increase in the opportunity cost of holding money, no switch to NMAs and no change in the money-NMA-bank loan relativities. In the diagram again, an increase in rates (for example), pushes us up the loan demand curve, but the position of the demand curve is unchanged. The elasticity of the bank loan demand curve becomes critical to control of the monetary aggregates.

The importance of being able to influence relative interest rates in order to achieve control of the monetary aggregates has been stressed by a number of commentators (Gowland, 1978, 1984 pp.8 and 67; Goodhart 1984). It was also part of the rationale behind the corset episodes of the 1970s as we saw towards the end of the last section. By giving banks a disincentive to accumulate interest bearing deposits, it was hoped to drive a wedge between deposit and other short-term rates. Regulation Q had a similar effect. With deposit rates sensitive to market rates, it is very doubtful that the growth of monetary aggregates could again be targeted successfully by the use of interest rates. With direct controls ruled out because of their distortionary effects and control of the monetary base ruled out for reasons we come to in the next section, it is doubtful that monetary targeting will ever be attempted again.

It is time now to look at UK monetary policy after the demise of monetary targets.

11.4 Monetary policy after monetary targets

Ceasing to pursue impossible targets which were anyway becoming irrelevant, was clearly a sensible decision. However, the authorities remained convinced that the main objective of monetary policy was to minimise inflation and achieve an approximately stable price level, the danger in abandoning money supply targets was that agents would be left without any means of identifying the stance of monetary policy and thus of any way of anticipating future movements in the price level. Since one of the major objections to inflation is that it makes price signals harder to interpret and increases the chance of agents making allocation errors, 'uncertainty' was clearly unacceptable.

The initial solution to the problem was to focus attention on the exchange rate. The argument here was that a 'lax' monetary policy — defined as one which was likely to produce a future inflation rate above that of the UK's major competitors — would lead to a declining value of the pound against other currencies. Conversely, a rising exchange rate indicates a 'tight' monetary policy and a lower (than competitors') rate of inflation. The argument was not wholly convincing, partly because it placed a great deal of confidence in financial markets' ability to interpret events correctly. This required that they operated with the 'correct' model of how *current* official interest rates were linked to *future* inflation, a level of modelling sophistication which the authorities themselves had failed to achieve in years gone by, and then that this prediction of future inflation would be fully and instantly incorporated in exchange rate movements. This amounted to saying that forex markets were both rational (in the choice of model) and efficient (in the use of the resulting information). These are characteristics of financial markets which many commentators would be reluctant to credit, but it ushered in a period, continuing to the present, in which feedback from financial markets became quite influential in monetary policy making.

In the circumstances, the obvious step might have been for the pound to join a fixed exchange rate regime which would have *compelled* the authorities to adjust the policy stance whenever the pound deviated from its specified value. But the only show in town, for this purpose, was the European Monetary System and Mrs Thatcher's opposition to Britain's joining the EMS (and the more general euro-scepticism of a large section of her party) made it impossible. This left the UK's Chancellor (Lawson) to operate a monetary policy in which the pound was linked covertly to the Deutschemark. From the autumn of 1985, UK short-term interest rates came to be determined almost entirely by movements in the £:DM exchange rate. The choice of the DM as the basis of an exchange rate target made some sense in terms of trade flows but the most compelling reason was that the DM had historically been a strong currency, German inflation had been low (since the reform of the monetary system in 1948) and much of the credit for this, rightly or wrongly, was attributed to the Bundesbank. In effect, the UK authorities were 'buying' credibility for their monetary policy from an institution which had it to spare.

At the same time, and presumably to mitigate the *volte-face* involved in dropping monetary targets entirely, the UK authorities began publishing 'guidelines' for the growth of M0. It was emphasized at the time that this was not a precursor to a shift to monetary base control but was rather because its relationship with nominal GDP had been subject to less disturbance than that of other aggregates and because it would function as a *leading indicator* of future changes in nominal GDP. From the spring of 1987, the exchange rate target became more overt, though still unannounced.

The pound was held in a very narrow range against the DM, its upper limit was clearly 3.00DM though its lower limit was uncertain. The strength of the pound throughout 1987 allowed scope always for a cut in interest rates (as indeed occurred after the stockmarket crash in October) but not for a rise. By

1988 this was becoming a problem since further surges in bank and non-bank credit, a rapidly deteriorating trade balance and rising house prices suggested a return of inflationary pressures and the need for a rate rise, even though the pound remained strong. So long as markets believed the 3.00 DM exchange rate was secure, the German-UK interest differential caused capital inflows which then required intervention by the authorities which itself caused increases in broad money. The dilemma was resolved by a rise in interest rates in the second quarter of 1988. By the autumn, foreign exchange markets caught up with the deterioration in the UK's position and short-term interest rates rose steadily (to 13 per cent by December) while the pound became weaker. Base rates reached a peak of 15 per cent in October 1989 and remained there for the following year.

In the hope that formal membership of the European exchange rate mechanism would persuade forex markets of the authorities' long-run commitment to reduce inflation and secure the pound sufficiently to allow some easing of interest rates, the UK joined the ERM in October 1990 with 2.95DM as the central rate of the wider, 6 per cent, band. Interest rates were cut by one percentage point. At the time of joining, doubts were raised both as to the wisdom of the move in principle (by Sir Alan Walters, a long-run opponent of ERM membership) and of the chosen rate (by opposition political parties). In the event, the sceptics received some support as the authorities struggled to hold the pound above its lower limit (effectively set at DM2.87 by the strength of the Spanish peseta). Further evidence of the deepening recession and a decline in the headline rate of inflation, and a reduction in Spanish interest rates in February 1991, allowed the UK authorities' the tentative step of a half-point cut.

The main reason for the UK's entry to the ERM was to increase the credibility of its anti-inflationary policy by 'buying' some of Germany's reputation for financial prudence. To begin with, the policy showed some signs of success in so far as interest rates were reduced steadily by a series of half-point cuts through 1991, reaching 10.5 per cent by September, while sterling slipped only slightly from its DM2.95 target to end the year at DM2.89. Helped by the progressive cuts in interest rates, the lagged response of inflation to stagnation in the real economy was very sharp when it came. From 10.9 per cent in September 1990, the headline rate fell to 4 per cent by September 1991. Ironically, this contributed as much as anything else to sterling's difficulties in the ERM in 1992.

By the spring of 1992, credibility was once again the problem. With inflation running between 3 and 4 per cent and base rates around 10 per cent, *ex post* real rates fluctuated between 6 and 7 per cent. Even at these levels the

DM:£ exchange rate slumped repeatedly to 2.85 while the real economy showed increasing signs of being in very serious recession. By the summer of 1992, non-oil output had fallen for six consecutive quarters — to nearly 5 per cent below its peak in 1990(2). Amongst the novelties of this particular slowdown was the sharp fall in output from services as well as manufacturing. The rise in unemployment (from 5.6 per cent in spring 1990 to 10.1 by autumn 1992) was thus spread geographically more evenly so that London and the South East were badly affected. It was in this region that the highest levels of personal sector floating-rate indebtedness had developed during the property boom of the mid-1980s and it was here, therefore, that the more dramatic cases of personal sector gearing and indebtedness were to be found. By the middle of the year the concern with falling house prices had crystallized in the problem of 'negative equity', preventing people from moving house and threatening banks and building societies with insolvency if they repossessed property from defaulting borrowers.

By the summer, opinion was widespread that, faced with a choice of even higher interest rates or abandoning the exchange rate, the government would have to choose the latter. The UK was not alone with this problem. The lira, the Irish punt, the peseta and escudo were all subject to speculative pressure as their weak economies suggested the need for interest rate reductions. The only way of avoiding widespread realignments within or defections from the ERM seemed to lie with a cut in German interest rates. The Bundesbank, however, was concerned about rapid monetary growth, domestic inflationary pressures and the costs of reunification and used the occasion to enhance even further its own credibility, by demonstrating its total independence of the general clamour. The crisis came in September 1992 when doubts about the willingness of some countries to ratify the Maastricht treaty called into question the durability of the ERM itself. Sterling, which had been very weak throughout August, came under heavy selling pressure in the middle of the month. The Bank used its powers to announce an MLR of 12 per cent (in effect raising base rates from 10 per cent) on the 16th September, accompanying it with a statement of intent to raise it to 15 per cent from the following day. This, plus large-scale intervention buying, failed to stop the pressure and sterling was withdrawn from the ERM on the evening of the 16th September. On the 18th, interest rates were reduced to 10 per cent, beginning a steady decline that continued through the first half of 1993.

Leaving the ERM in 1992 left UK monetary policy with the same problem that it had in 1985: how to find a target which would enable agents to judge the policy stance. The new monetary policy framework announced in October 1992 contained two features. The first was the adoption of an explicit inflation target. Instead of adopting an intermediate target in the hope that it had some reliable connection with the ultimate objective of policy, the ultimate objective itself would be directly targeted. Interest rates were now set with a view to their effects upon inflation some eighteen months ahead. One way of interpreting inflation targeting is to see it as an encompassing case of monetary targeting or exchange rate targeting. In the latter cases, the authorities are setting interest rates with a view to achieving a low inflation rate, using just one source of information (monetary growth, exchange rate etc.) disregarding all else.[16] In an inflation targeting regime, interest rates are still set with the same objective but the decision draws upon all relevant variables. These include money and credit growth, the exchange rate, wage trends, asset prices, employment figures, the 'output-gap', surveys of 'confidence' etc. and may change over time.[16]

The second feature was a much greater degree of openness and transparency in policy making. By the time the Bank of England gained its instrument independence in 1997, this contained five elements. Firstly, a quarterly *Inflation Report* would be published showing the information on which the Bank was making its interest rate decisions. Secondly, the minutes of the meetings between the Governor of the Bank of England and the Chancellor of the Exchequer at which interest rates were set were also published. After 1997, when the Bank of England was given independence in the setting of interest rates, the latter was replaced by the minutes of the monetary policy committee (MPC) which again gave commentators some insight into how decisions were arrived at and also revealed the pattern of voting. Thirdly, representatives of the Bank and the MPC could be called to give evidence on their conduct to the Treasury Select Committee. Fourthly, if inflation were to deviate by more than one per cent from target, then the MPC would be required to write an 'open letter' to the Chancellor of the Exchequer in order to explain the horizon over which it intended to bring it back into the target range (in effect, making explicit the policy reaction function). Finally, the Bank of England's *Annual Report* would be subject to parliamentary scrutiny and debate. The argument behind this openness was that, over time, private sector agents would 'learn' how the MPC decided on the appropriate interest rate and would eventually be able to anticipate the Bank's next decision. Eventually, changes in interest rates would cease to be 'news' since, by the time they were announced, they would already be incorporated in private sector decisions. The economic advantage of this, rather like the advantage of low and stable inflation rates, is that another source of 'shocks' to the economy would be eliminated and fewer incorrect decisions would be made by private sector agents. It is worth noting that the lack of comparable openness has been a source of recurrent criticism of ECB operating procedures (see Section 13.7). Evidence from financial markets suggests that both the introduction of inflation targeting (and most of these arrangements) in 1992 and again the switch to central bank instrument independence in 1997 had positive effects on credibility and openness (see Section 12.5).

The rate of inflation, which had been running at over nine per cent in 1990, fell to two per cent in 1993 and remained in the two-three per cent range until 1997 when the Bank of England was given formal independence. The observation that countries with an independent central bank tended to have better inflation records than those without had been made for some years. We examined the arguments behind this alleged superiority in Section 8.5. But we might note here that one of the reasons advanced was the increase in 'credibility' that we met earlier when UK monetary policy was linked to the £:DM exchange rate. In this case, an unelected and independent central bank is less likely to be subject to political pressure if and when it has to make unpopular interest rate decisions. It should be remembered also that by 1997 it was clear that some form of European monetary union would be inevitable in the near future and plans were already underway for the creation of a European Central Bank modelled on the Bundesbank. *If* the UK were to join at some point in the future, then the Bank of England would need to have the independence from government that other national central banks in the European System of Central Banks would have. Changes were also made to the way in which the Bank of England imposed interest rate changes through its money market operations to bring them into line with European practice. This involved the greater use of gilt repurchase agreements (strictly *reverse* repos) and less reliance on the outright purchase of treasury and other eligible bills. (See Sections 4.2 and 12.2).

At the same time, it was decided to relieve the Bank of England of two functions which it had carried out for centuries, the management of government debt and supervision of the banking system. In both cases, the intention was to increase the Bank's sense of independence and to increase its freedom to set interest rates as required by the inflation trend with as few distractions as possible. The responsibility for debt management passed to a newly created 'debt management office' or DMO, an agency of the Treasury, in 1998. This was a recognition of the occasions, referred to above, where the Bank had sometimes felt it necessary either to resist changes in interest rates in order to stabilise bond prices or to adjust them to counter trends in bond prices (the episodes of 'leaning into the wind'). From now on, the state of the gilts market would be ultimately a Treasury responsibility. Similar thinking played a small part in the decision to transfer banking supervision to the Financial

Services Authority. A decision had already been taken to centralise the regulation of all types of financial activity in the FSA, but the advantage from a monetary policy point of view was that the Bank would no longer be in possession of detailed information about the state of individual bank balance sheets. It would not know, therefore, which, if any, banks might be threatened by poorly performing loans and consequently it would not be deterred from raising interest rates by the knowledge that such an act might cause a bank failure.

With the coming of independence, the responsibility for setting interest rates passed to the Monetary Policy Committee. This consists of nine members. Five of these are Bank staff (the Governor, the two Deputy Governors and two Executive Directors — with responsibility for monetary policy analysis and for monetary policy operations). Four are appointees of the Chancellor of the Exchequer. Voting is by simple majority and the Governor has a casting vote in the event of a tie. The Treasury also sends a representative, in order to brief on fiscal policy and other issues which the Treasury thinks the MPC may like to consider. This provides for some degree of policy coordination but the representative plays no part in the discussion (except to answer factual questions) and does not vote. The Committee meets according to a regular monthly schedule, though the facility exists for additional meetings and one was in fact held on 18 September 2001. Meetings are usually scheduled for the first Wednesday/Thursday after the first Monday of the month, with the policy decision being announced at 12.00 noon on the Thursday. The making of policy thus follows a monthly cycle and contains three elements:

- Briefings in advance of the policy decision meeting

- A two-day meeting at which decisions are made and implemented immediately

- Production and publication of the minutes.

We can begin the cycle with the circulation of briefing material to committee members. This is mainly material relating to data releases and market developments, prepared by bank staff. On the Friday prior to the decision meeting, there is a half-day meeting at which senior Bank staff present reports on major features of the economy under a set of standard headings such as 'demand and output', 'the labour market', 'monetary and financial conditions' etc. Members of the committee may ask for further information or analysis and this is done by the Bank staff on the Monday and Tuesday following. The policy meeting begins on Wednesday afternoon when members identify the key issues (broadly, the same headings as used in the Friday meeting) and their likely implications for inflation. Following discussion on each issue, led by the Deputy Governor, members are left to reflect overnight. On the Thursday morning the Governor summarises the discussion of the previous day and asks members to confirm or amend his summary. Each member is then asked to state his or her view of the present situation and the appropriate stance of policy. The Governor then puts a motion which he hopes will command a majority. In all cases, members who are in a minority are asked to confirm their preferred level of interest rates. These will be published in the minutes so that the weight of opinion and sentiment in the MPC can be clearly observed by the public. A press statement is prepared for release at 12.00 noon and where a change in interest rates is decided upon the statement will normally give a brief indication of why the MPC made the change.

The final part of the cycle involves the preparation of the minutes of the meeting. A first draft is circulated for comment in the week after the meeting and a final version is agreed on the following Monday for publication on the Wednesday two weeks after the meeting. Although the minutes show the voting decisions of individual members, their comments and arguments are unattributed. The purpose of this is to encourage the freest discussion in the meetings.

Alongside its routine of monthly decision meetings the MPC is also engaged in a detailed inflation forecasting exercise. This follows a quarterly cycle and culminates in the publication of the Bank's *Inflation Report*, normally in the week following a policy meeting of the MPC. The work normally takes about eight weeks (thus beginning about seven weeks before a policy meeting). The cycle begins with a review of any research commissioned by members at the end of the previous forecast cycle. It then moves to an examination of the latest trends as projected by Bank staff. These are based upon the Bank's suite of econometric models, on information extracted from current financial market prices and yields (see Section 12.4) and on inputs from independent forecasting bodies like the National Institute of Economic and Social Research (see Bean, 2001). Over the following weeks there is a series of meetings in which particular issues are the subject of discussion between MPC members and Bank staff. A week before publication the forecasts are put together, data and trends updated by Bank staff and a final view of risk and plausibility of the forecast is taken and added to the *Report*. The full text of the *Report* is published in hardcopy and is also available on the Bank's website at: www.bankofengland.co.uk/inflationrep/index.html

Table 11.2 shows the changes in repo rate made by the MPC since 1997 and the annualised rate of inflation measured by RPIX at the time.

Table 11.2: Bank of England repo rate and RPIX 1997-2001

Date		Repo %	RPIX % p.a.
1997	6 May	6.25	2.5
	6 Jun	6.50	2.7
	10 Jul	6.75	2.7
	7 Aug	7.00	2.8
	6 Nov	7.25	2.9
1998	4 Jun	7.50	2.8
	8 Oct	7.25	2.5
	5 Nov	6.75	2.5
	10 Dec	6.25	2.6
1999	7 Jan	6.00	2.5
	4 Feb	5.50	2.5
	8 Apr	5.25	2.7
	10 Jun	5.00	2.2
	8 Sep	5.25	2.1
	4 Nov	5.50	2.1
2000	13 Jan	5.75	2.1
	10 Feb	6.00	2.2
2001	8 Feb	5.75	1.9
	5 Apr	5.50	2
	10 May	5.25	2.1
	2 Aug	5.00	2.6
	18 Sep	4.75	2.3
	4 Oct	4.50	2.2
	8 Nov	4.00	2.2

Sources: www.bankofengland.co.uk/mfsd and *Inflation Reports* (various)

11.5 Summary

In this chapter we have seen that monetary policy in the UK since 1945 has passed through a number of phases. Until 1971, policy followed a broadly Keynesian line. The objective was to minimise unemployment subject to a balance of payments constraint which occasionally caused a weakness in the (fixed) exchange rate. The instruments of policy consisted of direct controls on the growth of money and credit, in so far as this was thought important, and short-term interest rates when sterling weakened. From 1967, the concern with inflation began to replace unemployment and, after 1971, the authorities tried at least to switch instruments as well by relying entirely upon short-term interest rates. In practice, these had to be supplemented by direct controls in the form of supplementary special deposits. With the end of fixed exchange rates in 1972, the value of sterling was less of a problem. From 1979 to 1985, minimising the rate of inflation was the sole objective of monetary policy and for this brief period there was a firm conviction that the growth of the monetary aggregates should be the sole intermediate target of policy. Short-term interest rates were reinstated as the instrument of policy, this time with no help from direct controls. By 1985, strict control of the monetary aggregates looked both unfeasible and unnecessary. Since the mid-1980s, therefore, monetary policy has become more pragmatic. Minimising inflation is still the dominant objective and interest rates are still the instrument but the intermediate target, which began as the sterling:Deutschemark exchange rate was abandoned altogether in 1992 when the rate of inflation became both the target and objective. The pragmatism of policy can be seen most clearly in the eclectic (and flexible) range of indicators which are used in forming judgements of the likely future trend in inflation and thus of the required level of interest rates.

Viewing the experience of UK monetary policy through the analytical frameworks of Chapter 3, reveals three things. Firstly, the quantity of money has been a matter of relatively little concern. The need to limit the growth of DCE was forced upon the authorities in 1967 and the authorities tried to restrain money and credit growth within unpublished limits between 1973 and 1979. But it was only from 1980 to 1985 that monetary aggregates were explicitly targeted. Secondly, when the aggregates were important, it was their rate of growth that was targeted. Stocks were of no relevance. Thirdly, while it is true that the quantity of money can always be expressed as a multiple of the monetary base and true that banks must hold a minimum fraction of the base in order to ensure convertibility, the UK authorities have never tried to control the base directly. Even during the period of explicit monetary targets, the policy instrument was short-term interest rates whose function was to restrain the growth of demand for money and credit; the base required to support this growth was available on demand.

Key concepts usd in this chapter

liquidity

equation of exchange

Quantity Theory of Money

velocity of circulation

capital risk aversion

domestic credit expansion

leaning into the wind

Duke of York tactic

special deposits

Supplementary Special Deposits

Medium Term Financial Strategy (MTFS)

overfunding

off-balance-sheet operations

risk-asset ratios

securitization

monetary base control

inflation targeting

credibility

openness

Further questions and exercises

1. Explain why policy makers have generally come to the conclusion that the only effective instrument of monetary policy is the short-term rate of interest.

2. Outline the disadvantages of trying to limit the growth of money and credit by 'direct' controls.

3. 'It is not that the demand for lending has become less sensitive to changes in relative interest rates. If anything, it has become more so. The problem lies in the increasing inability of the authorities to cause changes in relative rates by changing the level of absolute rates.' (Goodhart, 1984). Explain how this situation has come about.

4. Explain how central banks are able to set the level of short-term interest rates.

5. Explain briefly why 'credibility' and 'openness' are desirable properties in the conduct of monetary policy.

6. What features of the UK's monetary policy framework contribute to credibility and openness?

7. Why might responsibility for the government debt market inhibit a central bank's conduct of monetary policy?

8. Why might giving the central bank responsibility for banking supervision make it more difficult for the bank to pursue an independent monetary policy with price stability as the primary target?

9. Explain how capital adequacy requirements impose a tax on banking.

10. Why might the presence of capital risk aversion in the bond market make the conduct of monetary policy more difficult?

11. Why does a rise in money's own interest rate, *ceteris paribus*, tend to increase the rate of monetary growth?

Further reading

The history of monetary policy in the UK since about 1971 is dealt with in Artis and Lewis (1991) and in Hall (1983). Goodhart (1989b) brings the story more nearly up to date. The latest developments can be followed in H M Treasury (2002) and in the regular 'markets and operations' section of the *Bank of England Quarterly Bulletin*. A critical view of policy in earlier years is in Dow and Savile (1988).

Bank of England (1999) 'Monetary Policy in the United Kingdom' *Bank of England Fact Sheet*, (available at www.Bankofengland.co.uk) gives a succinct explanation of the way in which monetary policy is formulated and carried out. A detailed explanation of the way in which the MPC works is in Bean (1998 and 2001) and the thinking behind the setting up of the MPC and the movement towards independence at the Bank of England is in Bean (1998).

A classic work on financial innovation and its relevance to monetary policy is Podolski (1985) though this focuses mainly on the implications for money supply. Goodhart (1986) gives a broader account. More recent work includes Lewis and Mizen (2000) ch.12, though their linking of financial innovation solely to the demand for money must be read in the light of our remarks about the potential irrelevance of the demand for money in chapters 4 and 5. Chapter 24 in Howells and Bain (2002) takes a broad look at the implications of financial innovation.

Statistical data on money and interest rates can be found at www.bankofengland.co.uk/mfsd

12 The Monetary Authorities and Financial Markets

'It's official. There is a Greenspan put option'. *Financial Times*, January 4, 2001.

What you will learn in this chapter:

- Why central bank action on official short-term rates has so much leverage over market rates
- How the behaviour of financial markets may place constraints upon central bank policy-making
- How information can be derived from financial markets that can help in making economic forecasts.

12.1 Introduction

In two other sections (4.2 and 9.4) where we refer to central bank instruments of monetary policy we drew attention to the recently emerged consensus that the only satisfactory instrument is the short-term rate of interest. We have also shown (in Section 4.2 especially) how central banks can use repo and similar money market deals to set the price at which reserves are made available to the banking system and we looked at how changes in official rates are reflected in other, market, short-term rates. In this chapter we are concerned with a broader question but one to which the interest rate setting process nonetheless has some connection. The big question is the relationship between central bank decision-making and financial markets and one way of caricaturing the relationship is one of a struggle for power. The central bank wishes to set domestic interest rates at some target level for the achievement of its policy objectives but is reluctant to do so for fear that markets (typically the forex or bond markets) will react badly, pushing the exchange rate or long-term interest rates to undesirable levels. A variation on this theme, often expressed by critics of 'globalisation', is that the size and instability of international capital flows makes it virtually impossible for any but the very largest monetary authorities to operate an independent monetary policy (Cornford and Kregel, 1996; Mosley, 1997). If there is any truth in such a picture, however, one must wonder how it is that individual central banks, by changing the return on fairly small-scale flows through domestic money markets can rattle the whole interest rate edifice. Furthermore, in the general consensus that market solutions are best and the subsequent privatisation of monetary policy, policy makers have become increasingly willing to use financial markets as sources of information and prescience, superior to their own. Finally, the reaction of financial markets to monetary policy actions may offer a way of testing the credibility and transparency of the policy makers. Given that both are seen as desirable characteristics, financial market responses may be giving us an important report on progress. To say the least, the relationship between policy makers and financial markets is interesting and complex.

In the next section (12.2) we look at why it is the case that central bank money market transactions, which are usually quite small in relation to total money market flows, can have such a powerful effect on domestic interest rates. In section 12.3 we look at the contrary evidence, namely that markets can sometimes impose formidable constraints upon policy. In section 12.4 we examine the slightly different, but very interesting issue: the extent to which markets can provide information which is useful in the forecasting of likely future developments in the economy. In section 12.5 we review the arguments that evidence from market reactions suggests that inflation targeting (and subsequently instrument independence) have increased the credibility and openness of the Bank of England's monetary policy making.

12.2 Central bank leverage

In Section 4.2, we saw how the Bank of England sets interest rates through its operations in UK money markets, mainly through deals in gilt repos, and that the approach of other central banks was essentially similar.

The term 'money markets' refers to a range of markets for short-term loans. 'Short-term' in this context means an original maturity of less than one year, though in practice most money market instruments have an even shorter initial maturity while the average *residual* maturity is much less, between two and three months. The term 'money market' is usually used in the plural to denote the existence of a number of different instruments and markets. These range from what is sometimes called the 'traditional' or 'discount' market wherein bills are issued at a discount to their maturity value and have their yields quoted as a rate of discount rather than a conventional interest yield, to the interbank market which is a 'market' in which banks lend and borrow between themselves, the resulting deposits being non-negotiable. Other money markets include the CD market (in which time deposits can be made negotiable by trading the certificates of ownership) and the gilt repo market. The latter is a market for what are in effect collateralised loans, the collateral being government bonds. Note that government bonds are normally thought of as capital market instruments, having much longer initial (and in most cases residual) maturities than money market instruments. The fact that repos are classified as money market instruments reflects the fact that the repo is for a short period, while the residual maturity of the underlying bonds can be anything, provided only that it exceeds the maturity of the repo deal. The pricing of repos, with an illustration of how a change in price causes a simultaneous change in yield is given in Box 4.1.

The participants in money markets are banks, other financial institutions, large corporations and the central bank. Money markets are, in other words, wholesale markets dominated by professional institutional traders. The minimum denomination of the instruments is large and the personal sector has little if any direct access. Some banks offer money market accounts, offering money market interest rates but restricted as to the number of withdrawals/transfers of deposits per period of time and subject also to a high minimum threshold for each transaction. Some mutual fund managers also offer unitised investment facilities for individuals wanting to get access to money market instruments indirectly. Given that the markets are dominated by professional, well-informed traders and that the instruments are very close substitutes for each other (short-term, minimal risk), it is not surprising that spreads across the market are small and that rates move closely together. Changes in yields and in spreads are often reckoned in 'basis points' (1bp = 0.01 per cent) because they are so small. Table 12.1 shows the yields on a range of UK money market instruments in September 2002.

Table 12.1: UK money market rates

	Overnight	7-days	1-month	3-months
Interbank sterling	3.86 - 3.38	3.75 - 3.5	3.97 - 3.84	4 - 3.88
Sterling CDs			3.91 - 3.88	3.94 - 3.91
Bank bills			3.88 - 3.84	3.88 - 3.81
Discount market deposits	3.75 - 3.5	3.94 - 3.69		

Source: Adapted from the *Financial Times*, 21/22 September 2002, p.18

Exercise 12.1:

How would you explain the interest differentials shown in table 12.1?

Money markets are also large. Table 12.2 shows the total amount out-standing for a range of UK money market instruments at the end of June 2001 and the average daily turnover in these instruments during the previous three months. Set against these magnitudes central bank operations are usually very small. Table 12.2 shows the average daily money market shortage with respect to which the Bank of England had to take a position in the same period. The table shows the shortage averaged about two per cent of the total daily turnover and less than half of one per cent of the amount outstanding.

Table 12.2: Sterling money market volumes, £bn 2001(Q2)

	Amounts outstanding	Daily turnover (ave.)
Gilt repo	128	17.9
Interbank (overnight)	177	11.1
CDs, bank bills		
and eligible bills	143	12.4
Other	95	66.0
Total	543	107.4
Money market shortage (daily ave.) = 2.3		
Money market shortage as %	0.4	2.1

Source: *Bank of England Quarterly Bulletin*, Winter 2001, tables F, G and I

As we saw in Chapter 4, changes in central bank rates certainly do communicate themselves instantly to the money markets and we even know something about how the official changes are reflected in market rates, albeit with lags and spread impacts in some cases. But the big question is not 'how?', it is 'why?'. Why should decisions by central banks to change their official lending rate have so much leverage in these markets that many of the market adjustments are instantaneous, when the volume of funds in which they deal directly is a minute fraction of the total funds flowing through these markets? To the extent that there is an analogy between central bank intervention to set interest rates and central bank intervention to deliver a desired rate of exchange rate the analogy is not encouraging.

Central banks, and the Bank of England more than most, have frequently failed to defend a particular rate of exchange.

The beginnings of an answer can be found in Section 4.2. In a system wide shortage of liquidity, the central bank is the monopoly supplier while the demand for central bank money is extremely inelastic (Goodhart, 1994 p.1424). The next step involves recognising that while the central bank may act only on a small fraction of money market flows, relying a great deal on convention to do the rest of the work, it could if it wished *impose* its will by the sheer scale of its operation if it so chose — and markets know this. Potentially, central banks are much bigger players in domestic money markets than they could ever be in foreign exchange. The creation of central bank money is virtually costless and the central bank can create as much as it needs to buy whatever quantity of securities (repo deals) is necessary to force or keep down market rates. Conversely, when it comes to imposing a rise, its power is limited only by the quantity of securities it is prepared to sell. Provided that markets know this, there is no need for an everyday demonstration.

An alternative (but not exclusive) explanation was offered by Dow and Saville (1988). This is that without central bank stabilisation, it would be very difficult for money market participants to know what the 'correct' day to day risk-free rate should be. In many monetary systems, government banks with the central bank and thus transactions between government and private sector could have big daily effects upon money market rates and they would be very hard to predict (since their timing — critical if the banking system requires end of day settlement — arises as much from administrative decision as from any economic 'fundamentals'). In these circumstances, where relevant information is very scarce, market participants are easily swayed by official statements. Provided that there is *some* action to back up the official announcement, the announcement itself is the key. Viewed like this, the setting of short-term interest rates relies less on open market operations and more on what has become known as 'open mouth operations'.

12.3 Market constraints

There are, we have just seen, several ways in which we may try to explain the influence that central banks have over domestic, short-term, interest rates. Recall now, some of the things that we saw in Section 8.6, when we discussed the trend towards central bank independence. The precise nature of this independence varies across regimes but minimally it includes free-

dom from political interference in the setting of interest rates and a requirement that the chief objective in the setting of such rates is price stability.
This obligation actually adds to central bank powers. This is because it
removes any dilemma that might arise from trying to pursue several incompatible objectives at once. Such 'conflict of objectives' was commonplace
for policy makers (governments and/or central banks) for 30 years after
1945 as they tried simultaneously to achieve 'full employment', 'high'
growth, a balance of payments equilibrium and low inflation. In the UK, the
oscillation between these objectives was christened 'stop-go' policy. It also
spawned the 'Theil-Tinbergen' literature on matching the number of instruments to targets that we discussed in Section 9.2.

Given that central bank interest decisions have a major effect on market
interest rates, given that they are free to set interest rates without political
interference and given that they have a single objective, one could draw the
conclusion that central banks have unlimited powers to set interest rates at
whatever level they choose. This would be a major exaggeration and in this
section we consider some of the constraints under which central banks
work. One such constraint arises where monetary policy involves *intermediate* targets. Even with a single (inflation) *objective* conflicts can be rein-
troduced if policy is guided by more than one intermediate target. Such targets might be some combination of exchange rate, money growth, credit
expansion and so forth. Finding an interest rate which enables a central bank
to hit simultaneous intermediate targets could be as difficult as finding one
which achieves multiple final objectives. But we are more interested here in
constraints which arise from financial market behaviour. Many of these can
be seen to be related to the credibility of central bank behaviour: they appear
as the result of partial or incomplete credibility (Treasury, 2002, ch.2). One
simple, but recent, example is provided by market reactions to the succession of cuts in repo rates that the Bank of England instigated during 2001.
The main purpose, in a low inflation environment, was to limit the effect on
the UK economy of what looked like a developing world recession.
However, as we stressed in Section 4.2, the central bank only has direct control over a current and very short-term nominal interest rate while it may be
other rates which matter to spending decisions. These may be longer-term
rates, and/or *real* rates or even expectations of future short-rates. These rates
were much less influenced by the Bank's relaxation of monetary policy. In
February 2002, the price of short-term interbank interest rate futures (see
Section 12.4 below) suggested a strong belief on the part of market participants that short-term rates were about to rise again and such expectations
naturally worked against the efforts of the Bank to loosen monetary policy.

Pause for thought 12.1:

Why do you think that the interest rates futures market would react 'fast and furiously' to comments by the Governor of the Bank? Might the reaction have been different ten years ago? If so, why?

On February 19th, the Governor felt forced to make an announcement that this was not likely and markets 'reacted fast and furiously' to price in lower interest rate expectations (*Financial Times*, 20.2.02). This was another triumph, at least temporarily, for 'open mouth operations', and it is arguable that it would not have had the effect that it did in the early 1990s when Bank of England policy statements lacked the credibility that they have now (see Section 12.5 below). Even so, it still shows how the effects of central bank policy can be modified by market reactions.

We are used to defining an open economy as one in which exports plus imports exceed a certain fraction of its GDP. For open economies thus defined, developments in the real economies of its trading partners will always be important. Typically, these developments involve divergent productivity trends which eventually have their effect upon competitiveness and show up in balance of trade trends and maybe eventually the exchange rate. This familiar concept of openness and its implications we might call 'real economy openness'.

Since the 1970s, under pressure from the World Trade Organisation and national governments (especially in developed economies) this openness has been promoted as policy. Alongside it, however, has been the growth of 'financial openness' with the progressive liberalising of capital markets. The result, predictably, has been a rapid growth in international capital flows, in relation to real GDP, and in relation to international trade flows. Much of this capital, therefore, is mobile in pursuit of the best returns and will respond to quite small differences in perceived risk/return combinations. In the absence of a fixed exchange rate regime, such flows inevitably cause fluctuations in exchange rates and since the monetary authorities usually have an exchange rate 'preference' (even if there is no explicit target) they can hardly be indifferent to these flows.

Frequently, therefore, it is foreign exchange flows and the reaction of forex markets that central banks must anticipate. The most dramatic example, applying to the UK in recent years, is provided by the end of the UK's membership of the ERM in 1992. The details are set out in Section 10.4. The Bank of England was endeavouring to maintain an exchange rate of DM2.95:£1 at a time of rapidly rising unemployment and against background information that the UK was seriously uncompetitive with other ERM members at that exchange rate. In that particular case, the forex market took the view not so much that interest rates were 'wrong' but that the appropriate interest rates were simply unattainable. The situation was made worse by existing interest differentials between sterling and the DM and the reluctance of the Bundesbank to reduce its rates despite pressure from other EU partners. With unemployment climbing into double figures, the market gambled that the authorities (remember that the Bank of England was not then independent) would not tolerate the level of interest rates necessary to maintain DM2.95. Bearing in mind that forex dealers themselves had a great deal of influence over what level of interest rate would be necessary to achieve this, it was perhaps a reasonably safe bet. A simpler way of looking at the episode is to say that markets simply did not see DM2.95 as a credible rate of exchange, given the state of the real economy. It also shows how the choice of appropriate interest rate can be heavily influenced by the level of rates being set in other major centres. On any interpretation, it was the reaction of forex markets which brought the policy to an end.

As a recent paper by Cornford and Kregel (1996, p.2) shows, the breakdown of fixed exchange rates in the 1970s and the increase in international capital flows has been accompanied by a step increase in volatility, particularly of exchange rates. The standard deviation of percentage monthly changes has rose from 0.4 in the 1960s to about 1.7 since the 1980s. Their explanation for this is that the bulk of such flows now are asset flows, largely unrelated to trade and represent the application of standard capital asset pricing model principles to an ever increasing portfolio of risky assets. Under the CAPM, rational investors are assumed to diversify across the whole market of risky assets. As barriers to capital flows are reduced, additional currencies and assets become part of the whole market portfolio. Portfolio managers are then required to hold these additional currencies and assets with effects on their price which is analogous to the effect on the price of a stock which becomes a member of the FTSE-100, for example. The job of fund managers (to continue the analogy) is to earn the best returns by exploiting return differentials. Many of the newcomers to the whole market portfolio, 'emerging' markets for example, have very high yields. This may reflect a higher level of risk but if the fund manager is ill-informed about the level of risk then funds will flow to these markets, pushing up their exchange rates. Exchange rates (and asset prices and returns generally, for that matter) are no longer determined by fundamentals. Not only do these circumstances make it more difficult for central banks to pursue the single price stability objective (because of effects on import prices), they are simultaneously bound to consider the exchange rate effects of interest changes. Such difficulties have spawned a substantial literature on possible means for limiting international financial flows (see Section 10.7).

More specific examples of markets constraining central bank behaviour are provided by the short history of European monetary union. In Section 13.6, we refer to the difficulties for the ECB in setting an appropriate rate of interest caused by forex markets steadily marking down the value of the euro against the US dollar (from about US$1.18 in January 1999 to US$0.86 when notes and coin went into circulation in January 2002). A more interesting example, since it involves market sentiment in the design even of the institutions of policy, occurred in the spring of 2002 when the French government commissioned a report on the functioning of the ECB with a view to possible reforms. One such reform was the suggestion that the inflation target should be changed from 'between 0 to 2 per cent' to 'between 1 and 3 per cent' to remove the alleged deflationary bias which arises from setting zero as the lower limit and thus risking falling prices. Another proposal was for the ECB to publish more information about how its decisions are arrived at and to be open to examination about the decisions. In deciding upon the wisdom of these proposals, much discussion centred on the reaction of financial markets. It was argued against raising the inflation target that this would alarm financial markets and lead to further weakness in the euro while, on the other hand, markets would respond positively to suggestions to make ECB policy-making more transparent.

On 19 October 1987, the UK stock market declined very sharply, losing about 30 per cent of its value over two days. The collapse followed a large fall on Wall Street at the end of the previous week. In both cases the central banks, the Bank of England and Federal Reserve responded by cutting interest rates and indicating their readiness to create liquidity to meet the borrowing needs of financial institutions whose stability might be threatened by the fall in asset values. In the UK case at least, it was widely argued (e.g. Goodhart, 1989b) (after the event) that the Bank's willingness to ease monetary conditions was excessive, lasted for too long and helped to fuel what became known as the Lawson boom. As we saw in section 11.4, the UK was subject to strong inflationary pressures from the beginning of 1988. The cut in interest rates began to be reversed in June and eventually reached a peak (of 15 per cent) in October 1989. This incident was the first of several in which central banks acted to support financial markets. Another was the liquidity crunch associated with the dramatic falls in South East Asian stock markets and exchange rates in 1998. Here again, central banks, led by the Federal Reserve cut interest rates and made clear their readiness to provide liquidity. And, whether as a result or not, the S E Asia 'crisis' was limited in its effects to less than commentators feared. This apparent new role for central banks eventually gave rise to the remark by the *Financial Times* which we quote at the beginning of this chapter. We are familiar with the role of central banks as lenders of last resort to financial institutions. If central banks have become lenders of last resort to markets as well then the effect is rather like giving investors access to a free, market wide, put option. The 1987 and 1998 incidents suggested that stock markets had acquired limited downside risk. Unsurprisingly, prices eventually reflected this. Though US shares fell sharply in the stock market crash of 1987, they then appreciated at a record-breaking pace into the new millennium. The broad-based S&P 500 index of top US companies, for example, increased 360 per cent from its pre-crash peak of about 330 in August 1987 to its recent peak of just over 1,500 in August 2000, an average annual growth rate of about 12 per cent. This asset price boom implied that, relative to the past, estimated dividend growth rates had risen, the risk premium had fallen, or there was a bubble. (Miller *et al*, 2002 p.C172)

Shiller (2000) explains the behaviour of stock prices in the 1990s as an example of a 'bubble' — driven ultimately by psychological factors which encouraged the view that rising prices would go on rising. Cecchetti *et al* (2000) first drew attention to the possibility that the price trend may have something to do with reduced risk by carrying out a small survey of major fund managers and chief economists in London and New York in early 2000. 'The results are quite clear. All respondents believe that the Fed reacts more to a fall than a rise, and all except two believe that this type of reaction is in part responsible for the high valuations on the US market.' (Cecchetti *et al.*, 2000, p.75). To see by what order of magnitude perceptions of stock market risk would have to change in order to justify the price levels of the late 1990s, they computed a long-run equity risk premium for the period 1926-97 of 4.3 per cent p.a. They then took the actual level of dividend yield on the S&P500 in early 2000 and added a dividend growth rate for three different assumed rates of growth ('low', 'medium' and 'high'). Comparing these three different equity returns against the long run real rate of interest suggested actual equity risk premia for early 2000 ranging from -0.1 (assume slow dividend growth) to 1.8 (the fast scenario) (Cecchetti *et al.*, 2000, table 3.1). As Miller *et al.* subsequently pointed out (2002, p.C173), the dividend yields required to restore the risk premium to 'normal' levels needed to be some 2-3 times higher than they actually were. Another way of expressing this is to say that, given the actual dividend yields, stocks were overvalued by the order of 50-67 per cent.

Could it be then that the long price boom was largely due to a reduction in the equity risk premium brought about by central banks acting as lenders of last resort to securities markets? This is the issue tackled by Miller *et al.*(2002). The paper shows how the belief that the Fed can prevent market prices from falling by more than 25 per cent from a previous peak reduces the equity risk premium from its long-run normal level of 4.3 per cent to about 2.6 per cent. This still does not justify the stock price levels of 2000, and the effect is weakened still further if agents perceive the insurance as only partial credible. But Miller *et al.* do not claim this is the only source of market overvaluation. Shiller's argument that the late 1990s represent a classic price bubble is almost certainly true for technology stocks; there may well be genuine reasons for a lower risk premium to do with better risk management and/or distribution. What they show is that beliefs in the stabilising effect of central bank behaviour may have played a substantial part in the stock market boom.

The problem for policy-makers, and central bankers especially, is how these beliefs about free stockmarket insurance can be unwound without causing a major market collapse. A dramatic collapse, through its effects on wealth and the cost of capital, would have a major deflationary effect. This is especially true in the United States where the direct ownership of stocks is much more widespread. While these beliefs persist, and until a controlled way of eliminating them can be found, central banks have to tread very carefully, especially when it comes to raising interest rates.

12.4   Markets as a source of information

Until the mid-1980s the setting of policy instruments was based to a large degree on the forecasts of future economic developments derived from large-scale, structural, models of the macroeconomy. However, the lack of forecasting success of these models, together with the Lucas critique which appeared to explain why they were bound to fail, forced a reappraisal of this approach during the 1980s (Fisher and Whitley, 2000). The result, in the UK at least, was a shift towards a 'suite' of small-scale models of limited but critical relationships. This was a period of growing optimism in the abilities of markets, illustrated by widespread privatisation of public assets, deregulation of financial markets and the growing conviction that even central banks might benefit from independence from government. Thus it is perhaps not surprising that markets came to be seen as potential sources of wisdom and prescience from which information might be derived which would be a useful supplement to traditional forecasting methods (see Bean,

2001 p.438). In the history of forecasting, this has something in common with the 'leading indicators' approach, initiated by Burns and Mitchell (1946).

Pause for thought 12.2:

What sort of central bank behaviour might give rise to speculation that it was operating a market wide *call* option? Why might a central bank want to give such an impression?

The starting point in the argument that financial markets might be particularly useful sources of information is that the return on virtually all financial assets lies in the future. From this it follows that in their *current* pricing of financial assets, agents must be taking a view about future states of the world. Then it is argued that if these views are well-founded, or at least contain no systematic bias, *and* if the views can be derived from the current prices (or yields) then markets may be able to tell us something useful, on average, about the future. The unstated implication of the argument is that the disaggregated pursuit of self-interest by large numbers of agents, combined with their ability to learn quickly from mistakes, is likely on balance to produce a better forecast of the future than the painstaking construction of mathematical models embodying relationships estimated from past data.

Pause for thought 12.3:

Why should markets know anything about the future?

One example of the use of financial markets for this purpose is discussed in Appendix 2 and involves the term structure of interest rates in the government bond market. Ignoring, for the moment, any term-varying risk premium that might be involved in the return on bonds of longer maturities, the term structure of interest rates should be such that current long rates reflect current expectations of *future* spot rates. Restricting the discussion to a 'two-period' yield curve and assuming all yields are equilibrium yields, then:

$$(1+i_2)^2 = (1+i_1) \times (1+E\,^2i_1) \qquad \ldots 12.1$$

which says that agents must be indifferent between investing for two periods at the current two period (i.e. 'long') rate, i_2, and investing for one period at the current one period (i.e. 'short') rate, i_1, and reinvesting in a year's time in the one year rate *expected* in the second period, E^2i_1. From this we can solve for the expected future one year rate, E^2i_1, as follows:

$$E^2i_1 = \frac{(1+i_2)^2}{(1+i_1)} - 1 \qquad \qquad ...12.2$$

Since the future one year rate, $^2i_1$ is only *expected*, it is likely in practice that:

$$^2i_1 = E^2i_1 + \varepsilon \qquad \qquad ...12.3$$

but provided that ε is a normally behaved error term, then E^2i_1 will be an optimum forecast of $^2i_1$ and the *current* relationship between short and long rates tells us something useful (i.e. correct on average) about future short rates.

Exercise 12.2:

One year spot rates are 5 per cent while 2 year spot rates are 6 per cent. If the term premium on two year rates is 25 basis points, what does this relationship tell us about one year rates expected in a year's time?

Further more, if we now introduce the so-called Fisher hypothesis which says that the nominal rate of interest, i, is composed of a stable real rate, r, and an inflation premium, π, then:

$$E^2i_1 + \varepsilon = r + {}^2\pi \qquad \qquad ...12.4$$

Again, provided that ε is well-behaved (and provided that we know the stable real rate), then E^2i_1 contains an optimum forecast of inflation.

In practice, the picture is further complicated by the need to estimate a term premium which has to be extracted from our expectations of future rates, and as we say in Appendix 2, more fundamentally compromised by the empirical evidence that the current difference between long and short rates does not forecast the path of future short rates particularly well. Nonetheless, while we may be sceptical of the ability of the term structure to forecast the absolute level of future short rates (and future rates of inflation) it might still be the case that *changes* in the shape of the yield curve (a steepening, for example) tells us something about the future *direction* of changes in short-term interest rates and inflation (upwards, in this case).

Methods for estimating the term structure and the useful information that the Bank of England draws from such estimates is discussed in Anderson and Sleath (1999).

One reason why the Bank wishes to know the markets' expectations of future interest rates is that it wishes to know whether or not a given change in its repo rate is likely to surprise markets or not (we discuss the importance of this issue in the next section). In this case, the Bank wishes to know market expectations of two week repo rates for dates in the near future. With the exception of very short-dated gilts, bond yields are less than ideal since bonds are much longer term instruments than 14-day repos. But guidance may be possible from money market yields. The Bank of England currently makes judgements about market expectations of official repo rate movements from a range of market ('general collateralised' or 'GC') repo deals, interbank loans, short sterling futures contracts, forward rate agreements and swap contracts involving six month LIBOR and the sterling overnight interbank average rate (Brooke, Cooper and Scholtes, 2000). The approach is very similar to the one that we described for estimating future interest and inflation rates from the gilt yield curve and the difficulties and limited results illustrate well some of the points we made above.

Firstly, yields have to be collected from instruments which are strictly homogeneous in all respects but term. The advantage of the gilts market is that it contains a large population of bonds with varying terms to maturity but with absolutely identical risk. Money market instruments all carry a degree of risk which is greater than gilt repos with the central bank (GC repo probably comes closest). Hence estimates of future central bank repo rates derived from, for example, interbank rates, are found to have a systematic upward bias when their predictions of official rates are compared with the actual outturn. Unsurprisingly the bias increases with the length of forecast horizon, rising to about 100bp at two years. Brooke *et al* estimate that interbank rates probably contain a credit risk premium of around 25bp. But this leaves the conclusion that the remainder of the bias is due to some unknown term premium or systematic expectational errors. Similar considerations (albeit with different values) apply to the whole range of money market instruments. 'No particular money market instrument is likely to provide a "best" indication of Bank repo rate expectations at all maturities' (Brooke *et al*, 2000 p.398). In practice the Bank estimates two forward curves, one based on CG repo and the other on a combination of instruments based on LIBOR (London interbank offer rate) but subjects both to a degree of *ad hoc* adjustment.

With the development in recent years of markets for financial derivatives designed explicitly to allow agents to take positions regarding future events, the range of potential market information has expanded dramatically. In 1995 and 1997, for example, Malz showed how information in options prices might be used to indicate the probability of exchange rate realignments in the ERM (Malz, 1995, 1997). Options are contracts which give agents the right to buy or sell an asset at a given future date for a given price (the 'exercise' or 'strike' price). 'Call' options are options to buy and will be exercised if the market (or spot) price is above the strike. Thus the price of a call option is telling us something about the market's perception of the probability that the spot price *will* be above the strike price. Since the lower the strike price, the greater the probability that it will be exceeded at a given future time, the price of the call varies inversely with the strike price. Clews, Panigirtzoglou and Proudman (2000) show how an implied risk-neutral probability density function (pdf) can be extracted from a short sterling call option. A series of pdfs (from a series of calls) then tells us the probability (as seen by the market) that the sterling three month interest rate will fall within a particular range on a future date. These estimates then form the basis of the famous fan charts in the Bank's quarterly *Inflation Report*.

Given that the flow of benefits from virtually all financial assets lies in the future and thus that current price must incorporate something of agents' views of the future, scarcely any class of assets is immune from the search for potentially useful information. So far, we have considered the possibility of uncovering markets' expectations of future interest rates (of different kinds) and possibly of inflation. More ambitiously, it has been suggested in recent years that financial markets might be made to yield information about future developments in the real economy.

As with many fundamental insights into the working of financial markets, Irving Fisher (1907) was amongst the first to point out that changes in the spreads between the returns on different fixed income securities might foreshadow changes in the macroeconomy. The idea was further explored by Merton (1974), since when the growth in confidence in market wisdom has led to a near-explosion of empirical studies. The basic idea draws on the inverse relationship between risk and return. Thus, in any given economy, government paper will have the lowest rate of return, followed by 'AAA' bonds issued by the corporate sector and so on up to the returns available on 'junk' or sub-investment grade bonds. The spreads represent compensation for different degrees of risk and, provided the risk is correctly priced, must function simultaneously as an index of the risk contained in each security. It is a short step from here to assuming that changes in the spread are indicating changes in the degree of risk. The principle is familiar, indeed crucial, to investors making a choice *between* fixed interest securities on the basis of relative prices and yields. Hence we saw the collapse in Marconi's bond price and quadrupling of its yield after the disastrous profits warnings in 2001. What Fisher was pointing out, however, was the possibility that *aggregate* movements in corporate bond yields and thus in the corporate-gilt spread might tell us something not about changes in the riskiness of individual firms but about the degree of risk facing the corporate sector as a whole. If it did this, then it might be telling us something about the proximity of recession (the spread widens) or boom (the spread narrows).

Why should there be a connection between the economic cycle and the corporate-gilt spread? There are essentially two arguments which are mutually reinforcing. Firstly, the perception of the future possibility of recession causes investors to revise downward their estimates of firms' future cash-flows out of which bond interest (and eventually the principal) have to be paid. The risk of default increases and so prices fall and yields rise. Secondly, the rise in yields represents an increase in the cost of capital for firms. Faced with a test that they cover this higher cost, fewer investment projects will pass. Firms will reduce the quantity of real capital demanded and this reinforces the recession. Notice that, since we are interested in *spreads,* nothing here contradicts the wisdom that faced with the prospect of a recession there is a 'flight to quality' or certainty by investors — from equity towards bonds. This undoubtedly happens and means that bond yields in the aggregate fall relative to the return on equity. But *within* the range of bond yields corporate yields will widen relative to government yields because there will be a 'flight' from both equity and corporate bonds toward government paper.

As we noted above, studies of bond spreads and their forecasting ability are many. Surveys include Stock and Watson (1989), Bernard and Gerlach (1996) and Dotsey (1998). Specific applications to the UK include Davis (1992) and Davis and Henry (1993) who found that including financial spreads in VAR models of output and prices improve our ability to anticipate turning points. The theory, and its application to monetary policy making at the Bank of England is explained by Cooper, Hillman and Lynch (2001). One interesting feature of the recent work carried out at the Bank is that it suggests recent developments in these spreads are harder to link to the economic cycle than earlier episodes, say in the early 1990s. This is because the widening of spreads during 2000 was much more concentrated and was dramatic in particular sectors of the economy (notably in telecom and technology firms). This widens the *average* corporate-gilt spread but may be more indicative of sector- or firm-specific difficulties than a general downturn. On the other hand, the widening of these specific spreads will not be irrelevant to the broader picture if the firms concerned had previously been responsible for a large fraction of aggregate investment which they are forced to abandon by the sharp increase in the cost of capital.

Exercise 12.3:

Suppose that the differential between 'AAA' corporate bond yields and yields on government bonds have normally averaged about 75bp. In the last two quarters you have observed this spread fall to about 40bp. About 20 per cent of the corporate bond market (by value) consists of bonds issued by firms in the media and communications industries and shares in these firms have increased sharply in value over the last year. What useful information, if any, might you be able to draw from the change in bond spreads? Explain any difficulties you may have in drawing conclusions.

The most recent efforts to extract information about macroeconomic trends from financial market data involves profit warnings. In the UK London Stock Exchange and the Financial Services Authority require firms to disclose to the Company Announcements Office without delay any change in the company's condition which might lead to substantial movement in the price of its listed securities. Recent work at the Bank has examined the response of returns on a company's securities to trading statements in general and to negative trading statements ('profits warnings') in particular. Two notable results, though not especially relevant to policy, are that returns begin their response to the warnings up to two days before they are made and the adjustment is complete on the day of the announcement (lending support to the semi-strong version of the efficient market hypothesis) and that the response to negative statements is much stronger than the response to positive statements. More relevant to the question of whether company news can provide useful leading information about the state of the macroeconomy is the correlation between the number of profit warnings per month and *subsequent* GDP growth. Preliminary results suggests that it may be (Clare, 2001).

12.5   Markets as a test of credibility

In Section 8.4, we explored the Kydland and Prescott argument that elected governments would always be faced with the problem of time inconsistency in their formulation of appropriate monetary policy. Knowing this, private sector agents are unlikely to believe governments whose stated aims are to reduce high rates or maintain low rates of inflation. This lack of credibility then means that if governments do try to carry out such policies, inflation expectations lag behind the declining (actual) rate of inflation with the result that the economy lies to the right of the vertical Phillips curve with high unemployment and low output — a situation that may have to persist for some time. Various ways of gaining credibility were noted, including linking the exchange rate to that of a low inflation country and/or removing monetary policy from the hands of government altogether and handing it over to an independent central bank. Credibility matters to the monetary authorities then because it means that agents will incorporate policy statements more quickly into their own plans and any necessary adjustment in market behaviour will be carried out at lower cost.

An optimum monetary policy does not just require that the monetary authorities are *believed*, however. It also requires that their actions can be seen and understood. Thus in addition to *credibility*, policy also requires what has come to be called *transparency* . This is an unfortunate term since what is required is that policy actions and the reasons behind them can be clearly *seen*. Henceforth we use the term 'accountability' since having to account for one's actions involves to explain and justify. The argument for accountability is that private sector agents can learn and then *anticipate* what the authorities' reactions will be in any given set of macroeconomic conditions. We shall see in Section 13.7 that the ECB's lack of accountability has had the effect of making its thinking obscure and that this has confused financial markets. By contrast, with a high degree of accountability, policy actions themselves contain little 'news' since markets would already know what the authorities were going to do. Since the ideal monetary policy is one in which prices can be stabilised without increasing instability elsewhere (in growth, output, unemployment etc), the best the monetary authorities can achieve is a predictable monetary policy. In principle, this could be achieved by having a simple rule, for example one which linked interest rates to the money growth rate. The rule could then be built into a policy reaction function so that agents could observe *actual* money growth trends and anticipate monetary policy changes. Experience has told us, however, that money growth rates do not contain sufficient information about the likely course of future inflation. It is the failure of any single indicator to provide adequate information about future inflation rates that has led to the direct targeting of inflation itself, with forecasts being based upon a wide range of variables. Once the forecast is known it could then be fed, along with a measure of the output gap into a well-publicised version of the Taylor rule and agents could read off the next change in interest rates. Beyond accepting the general principle that its interest rate decisions involve paying some attention to trends in both inflation and real output the Bank of England uses a more judgmental approach. This means that if private sector agents are to learn about the setting of interest rates, they have to learn alongside the Bank, or more specifically the Monetary Policy Committee, and this requires a great deal of openness on the part of the Bank. As we saw in Section 11.4 the Bank of England first adopted an inflation target in 1992. Since then it has worked to create transparency by scheduling and announcing the dates of the monthly monetary policy meetings, issuing press releases immediately following each meeting, publishing minutes of the meeting together with a record of the votes (since 1997) and, most importantly perhaps, publishing the quarterly *Inflation Report* which contains the information on which the decisions are based. It may be hard work, but this should make it possible for analysts to learn over time how interest rates are likely to move in the face of given macroeconomic trends.

Given the importance of credibility and accountability, therefore, it is not surprising that central banks should look for evidence on their performance and financial markets are an obvious place to look. For example, if policy is 'transparent' then changes in short-term interest rates should generally be anticipated and the prices and yields of short-dated assets should show little response on the day of the announcement. If policy is credible, and if the central bank is promising lower inflation (for example) in the future, then the yield curve should slope downward , after allowing for any term premium. Attempts to use information from financial markets in this way in recent years are many and varied. In the case of the UK where there have been two major changes in the monetary policy framework in the last ten years - the adoption of inflation targeting in 1992 and the independence of the Bank of England in 1997 — several of the studies have been of the 'before and after' variety.

In 1998, for example, Mervyn King (Deputy Governor of the Bank) published a study showing the *changed* shape of the yield curve after the announcement of Bank of England's independence. Long-term yields fell by about 40bp in response to the announcement, suggesting that the bond market took the promises of a low inflation environment in years ahead more seriously from an independent Bank of England than they did from its predecessor (King, 1998). Independence, even when limited to instruments, did indeed seem to add to credibility.

Haldane (1999) looked at changes in the shape of the yield curve in response to changes in official rates for the period 1984 to 1997 and for the two sub-periods 1984-1992 and 1992-1997 by calculating the average change in yields at various maturities in response to a one per cent change in official rates. The results suggested (a) that yield-curve 'jumps' in response to an official change were significantly different from zero over the whole period; (b) that the 'jump' was largest at short-maturities (up to two years) where it seemed that about one-third of the official change was not fully-anticipated and (c) that the jumps were very much smaller for the later period than for the earlier one, suggesting that the switch to inflation targeting and the information that went with it had reduced the news content of monetary policy announcements.

Exercise 12.4:

Two central banks increase their refinancing rates by 50bp. The consequence in country A is that the whole yield curve shifts upward by c.50bp. In country B, the yield curve is unchanged at the short end and *falls* at the long end by 30bp. What conclusion do you draw about the credibility and openness of the two banks?

More recently, Clare and Courtenay (2000) have updated these findings by looking for evidence of the news content in monetary policy announcements before and after the movement to independence, studying the minute -by-minute change in price in a variety of interest and exchange rate contracts. Their findings seemed to suggest that the *immediate* impact of the announcement was generally greater after May 1997, though the total impact when cumulated over the day was less. The latter is some evidence that the news content of announcements has fallen since independence. The former, they suggested, may be due to 'pre-positioning'. Traders now know exactly when the announcement will come and are waiting for it.

12.6 Summary

The relationship between monetary policy making and financial markets is complex. On the one hand, central banks appear to have considerable influence over short-term interest rates, an influence which looks surprising when the scale of their intervention is set against total money market flows. However, markets can still set formidable constraints on central bank operations. This is especially true for small, open, economies for example whose central banks find that they can only set interest rates within what financial markets regard as a 'credible' range, a range which is often set by reference to interest rates being set in other, major, financial centres. The behaviour of asset prices can also complicate the setting of interest rates, especially if markets come to believe that central banks are unwilling to see a major fall in prices. On the other hand, because of their forward looking nature financial markets may be capable of yielding useful information about future economic and financial developments (or at least about markets' perceptions of such developments). Furthermore, the information in such markets can be used to give feedback on the degree of credibility and transparency in the conduct of policy.

Key concepts used in this chapter

money markets

basis points

conflict of objectives

volatility

capital asset pricing model

fundamentals

call options

put options

stockmarket insurance

leading indicators

term structure of interest rates

yield curve

LIBOR

probability density function

policy credibility

Questions and exercises

1. Why do money market rates move so closely together?

2. Why do central bank repo deals have such a large impact on money market interest rates?

3. What are 'open mouth operations'? On what does their influence depend?

4. Why do international capital flows make the conduct of monetary policy more difficult?

5. Why might central banks be concerned about major price fluctuations in asset markets?

6. Why might the yield on corporate bonds fluctuate relative to the yield on government bonds? What assumptions would you have to make in order to draw information about the economic cycle from these yields?

7. You observe a yield curve which slopes upward for maturities up to two years and then slopes gently downward levelling off at 10 years and beyond. What might this tell you about market expectations of future interest rate developments. Make explicit any assumptions you have to make.

8. What useful forecasting information might there be in (a) company profit announcements and (b) corporate-government bond spreads. Explain how you might go about trying to extract that information.

Further reading

A comprehensive survey of the problems caused for monetary policy makers by inrenational capital flows is provided by Cornford A and Kregel J (1996). For more detail of specific incidents involving sterling's exit from the ERM and the crises in Mexcio and Thailand, see H M Treasury (2002).

On the economic information which may be contained in current financial market prices and yields see Bernard and Gerlach (1996) or Clare (2001) or Cooper, Hillman and Lynch (2001).

Useful sources on central bank support for financial markets are Cecchetti, Genberg, Lipsky and Wadhwani (2000) Miller, Weller and Zhang (2002).

Haldane (1999) shows how changes in the yield curve may indicate something about the credibility of central bank policy.

13 Monetary Policy in the European Union

'The Mony of this kingdom is of a good Alloy', Morland, *Geog. Rect., Asiat. Tartaria* (1685) p.396

What you will learn in this chapter:

• The difficulties involved in determining the desirable membership of a single currency area
• The application of the general arguments about membership of a single currency area to the question of UK membership of the euro area
• The nature of the monetary policy institutions in the euro area
• The form of monetary policy in the euro area
• An approach to the analysis of ECB monetary policy since 1999 and of the impact of that policy on the value of the euro
• A comparison between the monetary policy institutions of the euro area and the UK.

13.1 Introduction

In the lead up to the establishment of monetary union in Europe and since the establishment of the euro as a single currency in January 1999, the issue of monetary union has been much debated. A number of economists continue to argue that the European single currency project will produce many problems and eventually fail. There has also been much argument over future membership of the euro area both for present members of the EU — the UK, Denmark, and Sweden — and for prospective members of the EU. The issue of the desirable membership of a single currency area is considered in Section 13.2. Section 13.3 deals with the particular case of UK membership of the euro area. In 13.4, we move on to look at the existing monetary policy institutions of the euro area, while 13.5 examines the form of monetary policy and the way in which it has been influenced by the movement towards monetary union. Section 13.6 considers monetary policy as practised by the European Central Bank since January 1999 and looks particularly at the relationship between monetary policy and the value of the single currency. The chapter concludes with a comparison between the practice of monetary policy in the UK since June 1997 and that of the ECB and asks whether reforms of the ECB institutions or approach to policy are desirable.

13.2 The membership of monetary unions

In principle, there is no difference between the operation of monetary policy in a single nation state such as the UK and in a monetary union consisting of a number of nation states. In each case, a central bank operates a single monetary policy for the whole country or group of countries. In these times of independent central banks and the dominance of price stability as a policy goal, the constitutions and practices of the central banks are likely to have much in common. In no case are monetary policy decisions of the central bank likely to suit all regions or all economic sectors. Much of the debate over the European single currency has been of the 'one interest rate does not suit all' variety — that a policy decided by the ECB in Frankfurt might be helpful for some member states but not for others. Yet it is also true that an increase in interest rates by the Bank of England that suits the south east of England might not please manufacturing industry in Scotland or Northern Ireland. A difference between the two cases only arises if it is more likely that a central bank decision will be wrong for some parts of the euro area or that it will do more damage to some parts of the area than is the case for the UK. We are talking about questions of degree rather than principle. We could, thus, express the issues at the heart of the debate through the following questions:

- How likely is it that the interest rate set by the central bank of a monetary union will be unsuitable for some member countries?
- How much damage is the wrong interest rate likely to do to those economies that it does not suit?
- Are there other types of flexibility in the economy of the monetary union that will help the disadvantaged economies to cope with the wrong interest rate decisions?
- Are the likely costs of wrong interest rate decisions for some parts of the area likely to outweigh the benefits expected from the single currency?

The usual theoretical approach to these questions is known as optimum currency area theory. This seeks to determine the optimum size and composition of a single currency area. The logic is clear. Start with a very small single currency area. Then, as the area is enlarged, the costs increase and the net benefits (benefits–costs) of having a single currency decline. At some point, the benefits and the costs become equal and we have reached the optimum size. Beyond this, it would be advantageous to retain more than one currency. However, the question is more complex than this for two reasons.

Firstly, the composition of the area is important. In practice, we are not concerned with the idea that an existing single currency area (such as the UK or France) should introduce additional currencies, even if this seemed justified by a strict application of optimum currency area theory.[1] Rather, we are interested in which existing nation states should give up their currencies and join a single currency area. Thus, we ask which countries should be members and this introduces considerations other than the geographical area of the union.

Secondly, the size of both the costs and benefits of a group of countries moving to a single currency and a single monetary policy is uncertain and strongly disputed. This is true of the economic costs and benefits considered alone and is true, *a fortiori*, when one acknowledges that the movement to a single currency is inevitably a political as well as an economic project. This is especially true in the case of Europe where integration has always been expected to deliver dividends in terms of lasting international peace and harmony. Here, we shall largely endeavour to keep to economic arguments, but the political issues cannot be forgotten.

Pause for thought 13.1:

Do not peace and harmony, in turn, deliver economic benefits? Is it ultimately possible to distinguish clearly between economic and political factors?

We cannot, then, be precise about the size of an optimum currency area. All we can do, at most, is to ask whether the benefits of a single currency appear to outweigh the costs for a specified set of countries — for example, the current 12 of the euro area, the EU 15, or the enlarged EU we are likely to have in the near future. To do this, we start by enquiring about the characteristics of groups of countries for which the costs of adopting a single currency are likely to be low. These are based on the idea that the principal costs are:

(a) the loss of the ability to adapt to changing economic circumstances by altering the exchange rates between the currency of the domestic economy and those of the other member countries and

(b) the loss of an independent monetary policy.

Box 13.1 sets out the most important of these characteristics.

The conditions listed in point 1 in Box 13.1 are seldom, if ever, fully met amongst groups of countries. Adopting a single currency across a number of countries introduces an element of rigidity into macroeconomic policy and there are costs associated with doing so. However, the extent to which countries fail to meet these conditions varies. Further, flexibility in other areas of the economy might keep the costs associated with the adoption of a single currency relatively low. We need to estimate how large these costs are in particular cases. Unfortunately, this is extremely difficult to do and is complicated by the possibility that increased integration of the European economy might either increase or decrease the likelihood of future shocks affecting member countries symmetrically.

Box 13.1: Characteristics of an area in which the costs of adopting a single currency are likely to be low

1. The economies should be sufficiently similar that:

    (a) shocks affect them symmetrically and do not create balance of payments imbalances among member countries;
    (b) business cycles are synchronized so that all member countries want interest rates to be moving in the same direction;
    (c) monetary policy changes affect them in similar ways.

2. Where balance of payments imbalances arise among the countries, there should be sufficient labour market flexibility and capital mobility to keep the costs of adjustment relatively low.

3. There are fiscal mechanisms that automatically transfer resources within the single currency area from rich regions with low unemployment to depressed regions with high unemployment.

On the one hand, to the extent that the growth of the market allows greater specialization through economies of scale, member countries might diverge and shocks become less symmetrical. On the other hand, to the extent that production is driven increasingly by consumer preference for variety and trade is increasingly intra-industry in nature, production patterns are likely to converge and shocks to become more symmetrical.

It is also difficult to be certain about the impact of wage flexibility and capital mobility. Wage flexibility requires money wages to fall to allow countries to recover from slumps in the economy. Where the slump is caused by an external demand shock and the immediate problem is a lack of demand, wage flexibility hardly provides an efficient adjustment mechanism.

Pause for thought 13.2:

Does it follow that, because of the operation of economies of scale, there will be greater specialization among member countries? Alternatively, might geographical areas in which industries specialize overlap national boundaries?

Labour market flexibility requires labour to be able to move easily between jobs and between member countries of the single currency area. It is unlikely that this is always beneficial since one possible outcome is that young and skilled workers move leaving depressed regions to become more depressed.

In any case, even if we were to accept wage and labour flexibility as unmitigated advantages, we might have to admit that neither exists in practice. For example, wages and labour markets are certainly not flexible across the euro area. The numbers of people moving from employment to unemployment and vice versa are much greater in the USA than in the euro area. The risk of employees becoming unemployed is smaller in the euro area, but those who become unemployed in the euro area have much less chance of getting back into work than have their American equivalents. In the 1990s, about half of the unemployed in Europe had been out of work for more than a year. In the USA, this was true of only about an eighth of the unemployed. In addition, the adoption of the single currency might reduce wage flexibility by increasing wage transparency, encouraging trade unions to push for greater equality of nominal wages across the single currency area.

A good deal depends on the level of economic and financial integration. Clearly, where there is a high level of economic integration, the conditions in point 1 of Box 13.1 are more likely to be met and the benefits of a single currency would be higher. Further, the provision of fast, cheap and reliable financial services across an internal market should allow that market to function more effectively, increasing the level of economic integration. Again, the higher is the level of financial integration the more mobile capital becomes. Only small interest rate differentials are required to produce large capital movements and, as we saw in Section 10.2, independent monetary policies become impossible to sustain in the absence of frequent and, perhaps, large movements in exchange rates. This would mean that a country wishing to be part of an economically and financially integrated area but to retain its own currency might have to accept a high risk premium in its domestic interest rates to offset potential fluctuations in the value of the currency in the minds of international investors. This leaves open the question of whether increased capital mobility might itself cause convergence or divergence among member economies. There are arguments in support of both sides of this issue, but the evidence in Europe so far suggests that it is more likely to favour convergence.

When the costs of the single currency have been estimated, they need to be compared with the benefits from its adoption. The most important benefits are listed in Box 13.2.

Box 13.2: Benefits from membership of a single currency area

1. Transactions costs associated with the exchange of currencies and of keeping records in multiple currencies are reduced.

2. There is greater price transparency across the single market, which might increase competition and raise the level of efficiency across the market.

3. Welfare gains result from the reduction of uncertainty:

   (a) the variation of profits around the mean is likely to be smaller;

   (b) real exchange rate uncertainty is likely to fall, reducing uncertainty about the future prices of goods and services and allowing better investment and consumption decisions to be made; and

   (c) real interest rates should be lower because the risk premium built into interest rates falls with the removal of exchange rate risk.

4. There are possible benefits from having a major international currency:

   (a) countries whose currency is used by other countries obtain seigniorage in the form of additional revenue to the central bank (in Europe's case, the ECB) as the issuer of the money;

   (b) the international use of the euro might also help domestic financial markets.

These, too, are difficult to judge and, indeed, might not all be positive. There is no doubt that there are some savings on transactions costs. However, there are differences of opinion over the size of these savings in particular cases. By any measure, the gains under this heading for the euro area are absolutely large but only small in relation to GDP. There is also plenty of evidence that price discrimination occurs across national markets in Europe. However, we do not yet know how much of this discrimination will be removed as a result of the greater price transparency produced by a single currency. After all, there are other barriers to the free movement of goods and price discrimination remains in national markets such as that of the UK.

There is little evidence that the use of multiple currencies greatly impeded trade and the efficient allocation of resources in Europe. Trade grew rapidly across the EU in relation to GDP throughout the period 1957-1999, before the introduction of the single currency. The evidence about the impact of reduced uncertainty on profits and investment is also mixed.

Overall, it is extremely difficult to come to clear conclusions about whether the loss of the exchange rate instrument in the euro area might result in net benefits or net costs in the long run. This is likely to be the case in any ambitious single currency project.

Pause for thought 13.3:

Why might a reduction in uncertainty lead to better investment decisions and an increase in the efficiency of the market? How do market agents normally protect themselves against uncertainty?

13.3   The UK and membership of the euro area

The above arguments have been highlighted by the debate over UK membership of the euro area. The single currency was established in January 1999 with 11 members. Greece had applied but was excluded at that point because it did not meet the requirements of convergence established in the Maastricht Treaty of 1992. However, Greece became the twelfth member of the area on 1 January 2001. This left three EU members outside of the single currency area.

Denmark had met the convergence conditions in 1999 but had chosen not to join following the rejection of membership in a national referendum. The decision was confirmed in a second referendum conducted on 28 September 2000. At the second referendum, the margin was the quite large one of 53.1 to 46.9 per cent against membership. The size of the 'no' majority made it unlikely that the question would again be asked of the Danish people in the near future, although at the beginning of 2002, opinion polls in Denmark suggested that there was then a willingness to join. Sweden, which joined the EU in 1995, had not become a member of the European Monetary System and was in no hurry to join the euro area. The UK had obtained an opt out from membership of the euro area in the Maastricht Treaty and was also not technically eligible in 1999 because it had not been a member of the exchange rate mechanism of the EMS when the decision on single currency membership was made in 1998. In practice, sterling would almost certainly have been granted membership from January 1999, but the government chose to exercise its option to remain outside.

The question was then whether the UK would join in the future and, if so, when. In 1998, the government indicated its willingness to join in principle but said that it would not recommend UK membership until the economic case for doing so was 'clear and unambiguous'. The factors to be taken into account in making that decision were expressed in the 'five economic tests' set out by the Chancellor of the Exchequer, Gordon Brown, in July 1997. The government also committed itself to seeking the people's permission to join through a referendum.

The five economic tests were:

(1) Are business cycles and economic structures compatible so that we and others could live comfortably with euro interest rates on a permanent basis?

This relates to point 1 in Box 13.1. We have identified three separate issues there, although 1(a) and 1(b) are closely related. 1(a) asks whether external shocks are likely to affect the UK economy in the same way as they do the other 12 member countries of the EU. 1(b) concerns the issue of timing. We have the general argument that the UK economy might require interest rate cuts when the German economy, say, requires interest rate increases or vice versa. In both cases, the debate centres on the level of convergence of the UK economy with the rest of the euro area.

Opponents of UK membership of the single currency often hark back to UK experience as a member of the EMS between 1990 and 1992. In 1992, the UK economy was heading into recession and there was a strong argument for interest rate cuts. However, the Bundesbank increased German interest rates and this required the UK government to keep interest rates up in order to defend the exchange rate of sterling against the DM. Of course, in 1992, the UK government could have devalued but that would not be an option within the single currency and so is not relevant to the present debate. This 1992 example is commonly taken to be evidence of incompatible business cycles, but is better thought of as an example of an asymmetric shock.

The Bundesbank decision to push German interest rates up stemmed from its fear of rising inflation in Germany as the German government attempted to assimilate the East Germany economy following German reunification without raising tax rates. That is, the Bundesbank chose to keep monetary policy tight because it was worried that fiscal policy was becoming too loose. Thus, this was to a significant extent a special case. Shocks of the size of the reunification of Germany do not occur often. In any case, even if we take this as evidence of incompatible business cycles, we are now a decade on and it is possible that business cycles are no longer incompatible. What more recent evidence do we have?

In October 1997, H M Treasury published an assessment of the tests,[2] which stressed the crucial nature of business cycle convergence and argued that, at that time, the timing of the UK business cycle remained significantly different from that of the rest of the EU. In support of this proposition, it mentioned that official UK interest rates at the time were 7 per cent in comparison with rates of just over 3 per cent in Germany and France. Further, it argued that forward-looking measures indicated that significant differences would remain into 1999 and beyond. The particular worry was that had the UK joined the euro area at the beginning of 1999, euro interest rates would have been too low for the UK, resulting in an inflationary boom in the UK.

Pause for thought 13.4:

Does a consideration of the difference between nominal interest rates provide a conclusive test of business cycle incompatibility? What factors other than different positions on the business cycle might have caused UK interest rates to be above those of Germany and France in 1997?

This brings us to the question of how well the UK economy is currently integrated with the rest of the euro area in 2002-3, when H M Treasury was again charged with making an assessment of the degree of UK convergence with the euro area.[3] Clearly, the degree of integration has increased greatly over the past 30 years as the proportion of the UK's trade that is with euro area members has increased. Since this is a continuing process, if the UK is judged to be insufficiently integrated at the moment, there might be some date in the future when this will no longer be so. However, one cannot be precise about this. It is a matter of judgement and different people judge the matter in different ways. It is also possible that membership of the single currency would speed up the process of integration, although, as we have suggested above, some economists also argue that the single currency will increase divergence even among the existing euro area members.

Point 1(c) in Box 13.1 relates to other arguments associated with the 'one interest rate does not fit all' argument. That is, it is argued that the UK economy is different from the European economy in other ways than in possibly having incompatible business cycles. There may be differences between the UK and other members in production, tax, financial and wage setting systems and other differences in institutional sturctures, which would cause a change in a common European monetary policy to have a significantly different impact on the UK economy from that experienced by other members. For example, in financial markets, floating interest rate mortgages have been much more common in the UK than in other euro area economies. This raises the possibility that interest rate changes have a more powerful impact on household income and consumption in the UK than in the other economies.

This also can be viewed as an extension of what happens in any single economy. British interest rate decisions are often criticized for not taking into account the needs of some sectors of the economy, for example manufacturing industry in the Midlands and the North. It is possible that the problem with a single monetary policy for Europe is as much a regional problem as a national one — that is, that if the UK were a member of the single currency area, a particular interest rate decision might suit, say, the regions centred on Paris, Hamburg, Madrid and London but cause unhappiness in the south of Germany, north-east France, the Basque country of Spain and France and Scotland. In the debate about UK compatibility with the rest of the euro area, there is probably a tendency to overstate the extent to which all parts of the UK economy are similar. Nonetheless, it is also possible that interest rate changes do have significantly different impacts on national economies.

(2) If problems emerge is there sufficient flexibility to deal with them?

This concerns the flexibility of the labour market and of fiscal policy (points 2 and 3 in Box 13.1 — that is, with possible escape routes if the UK economy were affected differently from other euro area countries by economic shocks or monetary policy decisions and its exchange rate with these countries could no longer change.

There are two fiscal policy issues. The first relates to the lack of automatic fiscal stabilizers across the euro area because tax and government spending decisions remain largely in the hands of national governments. Thus, regions that are badly affected by shocks to the euro area economy or by monetary policy decisions are not automatically supported by transfers from well-off regions through the budget. All that is left are discretionary disbursements from the structural and cohesion funds of the EU. These are very small relative to the euro area GDP and must deal with the large, existing regional disparities.

The second fiscal policy issue concerns the attempt by the European Commission to constrain the fiscal policy freedom of euro area member countries by the application of the Stability and Growth Pact. Article 103 of the Treaty on European Union specifies that where the European Council finds economic policies of a member state that endanger the proper functioning of economic and monetary union, it may make policy recommendations to that member's government and may publish them. In all areas other than that of fiscal deficits, members need not accept these recommendations. Article 104c forbids member states from having excessive budget deficits and charges the European Commission with the task of monitoring the budgetary situation and the stock of government debt of member states. The Commission may report to the Council that an excessive deficit exists. The Council may then make policy recommendations that the member state in question is obliged to follow. Failure to do so may ultimately lead to the imposition of financial sanctions in the form of a non-interest-bearing deposit or a fine.

Detail was added to this clause by the agreement of the Stability and Growth Pact of 1997, which set out rules for government borrowing of euro area members after January 1999. These rules converted the three per cent of GDP limit on budget deficits in the Maastricht convergence conditions into a permanent ceiling that might only be breached under exceptional circumstances. These were defined as a natural disaster or a fall in GDP of at least two per cent over a year. This would only occur in a severe recession. In cases where GDP has fallen between 0.75 per cent and two per cent in a single year, EU finance ministers have discretion over whether to impose penalties. Members who break the three per cent barrier in other circumstances are required to make heavy non-interest bearing deposits with the European Central Bank. These deposits would be converted into fines should the member's budget deficit remain above the three per cent limit.

Pause for thought: 13.5

Is there a general problem with the enforcement of supranational rules within the EU? What powers of enforcement does the European Commission have short of expelling or suspending members?

Since there is discretion in the application of fines, we do not yet know to what extent the Stability and Growth Pact will be enforced. In one sense, the firm application of the Pact would make little sense since the fines would make it even more difficult for governments to get their borrowing back below three per cent of GDP. The restriction of fiscal policy in this way would also remove another element of flexibility in the management of national economies and would increase the costs associated with the loss of freedom to change exchange rates. The first major test of the Pact appeared imminent in February 2002 when the European Commission was poised to warn Germany and Portugal over the size of their budget deficits. However, in the event, ECOFIN accepted the assurances of the two governments that they would bring their budget deficits under control.

The role of labour market flexibility is also controversial. Again, we have two concerns here. The first is with the ability of the euro area as a whole to recover from negative economic shocks because of labour market inflexibility arising from government regulations regarding wages, working hours, employer rights to fire workers, and, in general, the 'freedom of management to manage'. The EU's concern with social policy and workers' rights is often pointed to as a basic reason for slow EU growth in comparison with growth rates in the USA.

Pause for thought 13.6

Should the EU be prepared to weaken social policy and reduce the rights of workers if that is what seems to be needed to have faster rates of economic growth?

The second issue is the lack of labour market mobility across the euro area. It is normally argued that the much greater degree of labour mobility in national economies such as the USA provides a safety valve for regional pressures as labour moves from high to low unemployment areas, helping to balance the unequal impact of asymmetric shocks or policies. Labour mobility might be hampered again by labour market regulation as well as by other aspects of social policy and regulations governing the housing market and pensions.

It is not clear that the weakening of employment and social policy would have much effect on euro area labour mobility, given the continuing language and cultural differences and lack of information regarding employment opportunities and living conditions across national boundaries. It is also not clear, as we have suggested above in 13.2, whether greater labour market mobility always has a positive impact.

(3) Would joining EMU create better conditions for firms making long-term decisions to invest in Britain?

It is difficult to say much about this in advance. There has not (since 1999) been a large-scale loss of foreign investment to the UK, but it is difficult to read much into this since the investment decisions of firms are influenced by many factors and we cannot know what would have happened to incoming investment had sterling joined the euro area in 1999. For example, during the period 1999-2002, the UK economy performed well in relation to most of the euro area economies and this must have helped to persuade firms to stay in or come to the UK. A period of weakness in the UK economy or a period of sharp growth in, say, France and Germany could easily produce a loss of foreign investment to the UK irrespective of whether the UK joins the euro area. Further, were the UK to join, the question would remain counterfactual since we should not know what would have happened had the UK not joined. We have a certain amount of anecdotal evidence. Several large firms have made it clear that they would prefer the UK to be in the euro area and might possibly relocate from the UK into the euro area were the UK to remain outside the single currency for much longer. There have also been some investment decisions in favour of the euro area against the UK that have been said to relate largely to the UK's being outside the euro area. However, it is hard to judge these statements and actions. Some of the unhappiness on the part of foreign firms with the UK's failure to join the single currency in 1999 has related to the strength of sterling against the euro. Attitudes might change considerably were sterling to weaken significantly against the euro.

(4) What impact would entry into EMU have on the competitive position of the UK's financial services industry, particularly the City's wholesale markets?

As with (3), it is hard to know in advance and would be difficult to judge in retrospect. There is no obvious reason why the City of London should benefit from the UK remaining outside the single currency. Thus, the question appears to be whether continued failure to join might cause the City to lose business to Paris or Frankfurt. There is no evidence that this has occurred since January 1999, but this does not preclude it from happening in the future. The majority City of London preference is for the UK to join but one cannot quantify the potential gains here in order to weigh them against other possible losses.

(5) In summary, will joining EMU promote higher growth, stability and a lasting increase in jobs?

This is even more difficult than the earlier questions. Indeed, ultimately, it cannot be answered. The UK's failure to join at the beginning of the EEC in 1957 may well have contributed to the relatively poor performance of the economy in the subsequent years, although we cannot know for certain that this was so. Equally, some past monetary unions have failed. However, arguments of this kind do not provide much guidance for the future. This really is a catchall condition and answering it would involve an attempt to weigh up all of the possible economic advantages and disadvantages, none of which can be quantified with any degree of precision, if at all. This is hardly surprising since little economic analysis of future events produces 'clear and unambiguous' support for anything. Indeed, if we were to accept those words at face value, the five economic tests would seem to provide an argument for the UK's never joining the single currency.

The problem, then, with the five economic tests is that they are sufficiently open to interpretation that the decision when to hold a referendum on membership remains much more likely to be decided by political factors. For example, there is a feeling that the government would be unwilling to hold the referendum and recommend a 'yes' vote until they were confident they could win the vote. There is nothing, of course, inherently wrong with this since there can be little doubt that the single currency is to a significant extent a political project and political advantages of greater European integration should not be left out of the equation. In addition, there is little doubt that economic problems following the joining of the euro area would be attributed (whether justly or not) to single currency membership but these would be less likely to lead to social and political upheaval if membership had been supported by a clear majority of the people in a referendum.

Pause for thought 13.7

Should UK membership of the euro area be decided solely on economic grounds?

13.4 Monetary policy institutions in the euro area

The euro area was formally established on 1 January 1999 and trading in the euro commenced on 4 January. Box 13.3 sets out euro area developments from immediately before the establishment of the single currency area until February 2002.

Monetary policy in the single currency area is conducted by the European System of Central Banks (ESCB), which consists of the European Central Bank (ECB) and the national central banks of the member states. The ESCB is under the control of the Governing Council and the Executive Board of the ECB. To ensure independence of the ESCB from the European Commission and the governments of member states, the national central banks, although continuing to be owned by their governments, were made to become independent of the political process in their own countries.

Box 13.3 Monetary developments in the euro area 1998-2002

Jun 1 1998	Establishment of ECB and ESCB
Sep 26 1998	Denmark and Greece agree to participate in ERMII with fluctua tion bands around parity of 2.25% and 15% respectively
Oct 13 1998	ECB announces a target inflation rate for the euro area of less than 2%
Dec 1 1998	ECB announces a reference value for monetary growth (M3) of 4.5%
Dec 22 1998	ECB sets its main refinancing interest rate at 3%
Dec 31 1998	Conversion rates of the 11 participating currencies into the euro established from Jan 1 1999
Jan 4 1999	Trading begins in euro and ERMII commences operation
Apr 9 1999	ECB cuts refinancing interest rate from 3% to 2.5%
Nov 5 1999	ECB raises refinancing interest rate 50 basis points to 3%
Dec 3 1999	Euro falls below parity with the US dollar for the first time
Feb 4 2000	ECB raises refinancing interest rate by 25 basis points to 3.25%
Mar 17 2000	ECB raises refinancing rate 25 basis points to 3.5%
Apr 28 2000	ECB raises refinancing rate 25 basis points to 3.75%
Jun 9 2000	ECB raises refinancing rate 50 basis points to 4.25%
Jun 19 2000	Greece granted membership of the single currency from Jan 1 2001
Jun 28 2000	ECB changes refinancing operations from fixed to variable interest rate system
Sep 1 2000	ECB raises minimum refinancing rate from 4.25 to 4.5%
Sep 22 2000	ECB is joined by the US, UK and Japanese central banks in inter-vention in the currency markets to support the weakening euro
Sep 28 2000	Danish referendum decides against membership of the euro area
Oct 6 2000	ECB raises minimum refinancing rate 25 basis points to 4.75%
Oct 25 2000	The euro falls to US$0.8250 - the lowest level of the euro against the dollar
Jan 3 2001	The euro rises above US$0.95 for the first time for over 5 months
May 11 2001	ECB cuts minimum refinancing rate 25 basis points to 4.5%
May 31 2001	The euro again slumps below US$0.85
Aug 14 2001	The euro creeps above US$0.90
Aug 31 2001	ECB cuts minimum refinancing rate 25 basis points to 4.25%
Sep 18 2001	ECB cuts minimum refinancing rate 50 points to 3.75%
Sep 19 2001	In the wake of the September 11 attack, the euro reaches US$0.93178 before starting to slip back again
Nov 9 2001	ECB cuts main refinancing rate 50 points to 3.25%
Jan 1 2002	Euro notes and coin become legal tender in the 12 euro area countries
Jan 2 2002	The euro gets a temporary boost on the back of the issue of the currency and again perks up above US$0.90 - this effect lasts only two days

Article 105(2) of in the Treaty on European Union set the ESCB four basic tasks:

(a) to define and implement the monetary policy of the Community;[4]
(b) to conduct foreign exchange operations;
(c) to hold and manage the official foreign exchange reserves of the member states; and
(d) to promote the smooth operation of payments systems.

Article 105(1) of the Treaty established the primary objective of the ESCB as the maintenance of price stability. The ESCB was also required, without prejudice to the goal of price stability, to support the EU's general economic policies and to act in accordance with the principle of an open market economy with free competition, favouring an efficient allocation of resources.

The general economic policies of the EC are stated in Article 2 of the Treaty as being to promote throughout the Community:

• a harmonious and balanced development of economic activities
• sustainable and non-inflationary growth respecting the environment
• a high degree of convergence of economic performance
• a high level of employment and social protection
• the raising of the standard of living and quality of life and
• economic and social cohesion and solidarity among Member States

Article 3a further requires that in attempting to achieve all of this, member states and the Community should comply with the guiding principles of stable prices, sound public finances and monetary conditions, and a sustainable balance of payments. This gave it a set of objectives similar to those of the Bundesbank, which had been obliged by law to safeguard the currency while supporting the general economic policy of the German federal government.

Although pursuit of general economic policy objectives is not meant to prejudice the achievement of price stability, there is clearly scope for interpretation under circumstances in which an apparent conflict exists between tightening monetary policy and one or more of the general objectives. 'Price stability', after all, does not necessarily mean the lowest possible level of inflation. Indeed, with a central bank composed of people from a number of countries with different economic conditions and problems, one might expect a range of interpretations of it. Nonetheless, control of inflation was intended to be central. Further, the objective of low inflation is statutorily protected since the ESCB's objectives can only be changed by the unanimous decision of the Council of Ministers.   The European Parliament has no influence on the objectives of monetary policy.

Pause for thought 13.8:

What do you think 'price stability' means?

The possibility of the system's objectives being interpreted in different ways makes the composition of the ECB extremely important and raises the question of how the political independence of the decision-makers within the system can be ensured. Box 13.4 lists factors widely accepted as relevant to the degree of political independence of a central bank.

Box 13.4: Features important in determining the independence of a central bank

1. The existence of statutory guarantees of independence
2. The nature of the statutory objectives set for the central bank
3. Methods of appointment and removal of senior officers, the board of directors and the President
4. The length of the President's term of office
5. The presence or absence of government officials on the bank's board
6. The extent to which the bank is bound by instructions from the government and the range of instruments at the bank's disposal
7. The limits on central financing of the government
8. The ease with which any of the above features can be altered by government.

The ECB does well under the headings listed in Box 13.4.   The Executive Board of the ECB, which runs the bank, comprises a president, vice-president and four other members appointed by the Heads of State on a recommendation from the European Council after consultation with the European Parliament and the Governing Council of the ECB. All six members are required to be of recognized standing and professional experience in monetary or banking matters. In other words, they should be representatives from the world of finance, making it likely that their interpretation of 'price stability' will be conservative.

The term of office for Executive Board members is eight years and is non-renewable. Members of the Executive Board may be compulsorily retired but only for misconduct, which is defined to include the taking of instructions from a member government. To compulsorily retire an Executive Board member, the Governing Council or the Executive Board must apply to the European Court of Justice. Governors of national central banks must be appointed for at least five years and may end their terms prematurely only for serious cause, notified either by themselves or the ECB council. That is, they cannot be removed by their own national governments. The long and non-renewable term is meant to reduce the possibility of Board members following the wishes of governments in the hope of being reappointed to their positions.

Pause for thought 13.9:

Why might representatives of the world of finance be expected to have a conservative view of 'price stability'? What is a conservative view of price stability?

The Governing Council consists of the Executive Board plus the governors of the national central banks. Thus, the membership rose to 18 with the entry of Greece to the monetary union at the beginning of 2001. Voting, on all issues except those related to the bank's capital, is on a one-person one-vote basis, with decision by simple majority. This makes it possible for the representatives of the national central banks to outvote the Executive Board members and for smaller members of monetary union to outvote large members such as Germany on all issues other than those related to the ECB's capital. This provided an extra reason for the insistence that the national central banks be politically independent.

Where the bank's capital is involved, voting power is proportional to the member states' subscribed capital and the Executive Board has no votes. The subscribed capital, in turn, is determined by equal weighting of (i) the member states' shares of the population and (ii) GDP at market prices, averaged over the previous five years. Subscriptions are revised every five years.

The ECB is responsible for the note issue, open market operations, the setting of minimum reserve requirements and other aspects of monetary control and supplies liquidity to the banking system. It can make use of the national central banks to carry out open market operations. However, the ESCB is not permitted to lend to governments except through the acquisition of their paper in the secondary market. Article 104 of the Treaty explicitly prohibits the provision of overdraft or other credit facilities by the ECB or national central banks to any EU member state public body.

As we saw in 13.3, to strengthen the control of high-spending member governments, the Maastricht treaty forbad excessive government deficits and the 'bailing out' of indebted member governments by EU governments or institutions. Thus, in theory, member governments continue to face different degrees of default risk with the consequence that bond issues of different governments should continue to carry different rates of interest to reflect the market's assessment of the default risk associated with each government's debt issue. It was being suggested in bond markets in early 1997 that the formation of monetary union could see the dramatic downgrading of the debt of countries such as Belgium and Italy because of their high levels of public debt as a proportion of GDP. However, as can be seen from Table 13.1, this has not happened. Table 13.1 shows the bid yield on selected benchmark government bonds of monetary union members on February 9 2002. There are three possible reasons for the similarity of the bid yields in this table for bonds with approximately the same maturity dates.

Table 13.1 Coupon rates and bid yields on benchmark government bonds of euro area members

Country	Redemption date	Coupon (%)	Bid yield (%)
Austria	31/7/2003	4.3	3.73
	31/1/2011	5.25	5.07
Belgium	30/4/2004	7.25	3.99
	30/9/2011	5.0	5.12
Finland	30/11/2003	3.75	3.84
	28/2/2011	5.75	5.09
France	31/1/2004	4.0	3.86
	31/10/2011	5.0	5.00
Germany	30/9/2003	3.75	3.76
	31/7/2011	5.0	4.90
Greece	31/1/2004	6.6	3.97
	31/5/2011	5.35	5.28
Ireland	31/10/2002	2.75	3.46
	30/4/2010	4.0	5.11
Italy	28/2/2004	5.0	3.94
	28/2/2012	5.0	5.14
Netherlands	31/1/2004	5.75	3.90
	31/7/2011	5.0	5.04
Portugal	31/8/2004	3.625	4.13
	30/6/2011	5.15	5.16
Spain	31/7/2004	4.5	4.06
	31/10/2011	5.35	5.11

Source: *Financial Times*, 9/10 February 2002 p.17

The first is that the financial markets believe that the other governments would rescue a member country in danger of defaulting on its loans, despite the 'no bail out' rule. The second is that the worry about countries running large deficits in monetary union has been excessive. Indeed, it can be argued that the fiscal discipline on a member of a monetary union is greater than that on nation states outside monetary union because members of monetary union cannot finance their budget deficits through increases in the money supply. The third is that the markets believe that the threat of fines under the Stability and Growth pact, together with the power granted in the Maastricht Treaty to the European Council to monitor economic developments in each of the member states, will be effective in persuading potentially high spending countries to keep a tight control of their budgets. For one or more of these reasons, the market does not price the bonds to include a significant default risk.

The Maastricht Treaty separated the operation of monetary policy from the prudential supervision of credit institutions and the stability of the financial system. The latter remains the responsibility of the member states, although the ESCB is expected to ensure the smooth conduct of policies relating to prudential supervision and the ECB may, with the unanimous approval of the European Council and the approval of the European Parliament, be given specific tasks in this area (Article 105.6). This conforms to the German model in which prudential supervision was not carried out by the Bundesbank but by the separate Aufsichtsamt (the Federal Banking Supervisory Office).

Any attempt to place significant power in the hands of an unelected body such as the ECB raises the question of the accountability of that body to governments and, ultimately, to the citizens of the member states. Accountability under the Maastricht Treaty is weak. This is not surprising since:

- the aim of making central banks independent is to prevent as far as is possible the contamination of monetary policy decisions by the attitudes and actions of the democratic political system and

- there is a general problem of accountability within the European Union.

What accountability there is, takes the following forms:

1. The ECB is subject to audit and is under the jurisdiction of the Court of Justice;

2. The President of the European Council and a member of the European Commission are allowed to attend meetings of the Governing Council of the ECB but are not allowed to vote;

3. The ECB is required to report annually on its activities to the Council and the European Parliament, and the President and other members of the Executive Board are heard by the relevant committees of the parliament at either side's request.

None of this gives any power to anyone to genuinely call the ECB to account. Disapproval can, of course, be expressed but there is no provision beyond this. There is another difficulty, which we shall come across below. Accountability requires transparency, in the sense that people should be able to know what the ECB is doing in order to fulfil its mandate. This, in turn, requires full knowledge of what that mandate is. Of course, we do know this in a general sense — the achievement of price stability. But this requires interpretation.

The aim of all of these regulations was to create a strongly independent central bank. Indeed, it is, in a sense, more politically independent than the Bundesbank itself. When the Bundesbank and the German government held different views regarding economic policy, the Bundesbank had a single and united opponent that was able to point to its electoral support. Within the monetary union, the counterpart of the German government is a group of governments that may be of different political persuasions and whose countries may be experiencing different economic problems. Consequently, it is less likely that the Executive Board of the ECB will confront a united political view than was the case with the Bundesbank.

And yet, despite all of the attempts to preserve the political independence of the ECB, to enforce strict convergence conditions for membership and forbid loose budgetary policies, the view of both the financial markets and leading economists before the establishment of the single currency was that the euro, in the long-term, would be a weaker currency than the DM had been. One reason for this view stemmed from the high proportion of intra-EU trade of monetary union members. This makes the EU a relatively closed economic area with its external trade making up only a small percentage of GDP. This, it was held, would cause the ECB[5] to be less concerned about the external value of the euro than the Bundesbank was about the DM and to behave like the US Federal Reserve — pursuing internal price stability but being largely indifferent to the impact of the exchange rate on foreign trade. This would make it more open to pressures for weaker monetary policy to stimulate economic growth, particularly given the slow growth and high rates of unemployment in much of the EU in the late 1990s. A supporting argument was that the euro would be a broader-based reserve currency than the DM and, thus, would be less likely to be driven artificially high on occasions.

13.5   The form of monetary policy in the euro area

Several issues relating to the operation of policy needed to be settled in advance of 1999. There were three principal issues:

- The determination of a target rate of inflation;
- Whether to target the inflation rate directly or to target an intermediate variable such as the rate of growth of the money supply;
- The choice of the policy instrument.

The target rate of inflation

The ECB, unlike the Bank of England, chooses its own target rate of infla-tion. However, this is referred to as a 'quantitative definition of price sta-bility' rather than as a target because the Bank denies that it is engaged in inflation targeting (ECB 2001). However, we are also told that the quanti-tative definition 'provides a yardstick against which the public can hold the ECB accountable' (ECB, 2001, p.38) and that 'The ECB is required to pro-vide an explanation for sustained deviations from this definition and to clar-ify how price stability will be re-established within an acceptable period of time' (ECB, 2001, p.38).

This makes it sound close enough to a target for us to use the word. Initially, the ECB announced a price stability definition of an annual increase of less than two per cent in the newly developed Harmonised Index of Consumer Prices (HICP). This was quickly changed to a range of 0 - 2 per cent to indicate that falling prices were not acceptable. This still left some concern that the policy might be too strict, particularly given the prob-lems surrounding the use of price indexes in general and the HICP in par-ticular. According to Eurostat, the statistics bureau of the EU, the HICP takes account of the latest economic research. However, national price indexes are probably more likely to overestimate inflation than the reverse; the same is likely to be true of the HICP.

It has been difficult to know how the ECB has been interpreting its own target range. A range of 0 - 2 per cent appeared to imply that the ECB would be equally happy with an inflation rate of 0 per cent as with one of two per cent and that one might expect a successful monetary policy in the ECB's terms to produce a long-term average rate of inflation of around 1 per cent. This implies a very tight policy especially given the probability that the HICP overstates the true rate of inflation. Further, since we are dealing with 12 economies, an average inflation rate across the euro area of 1 per cent could well involve falling prices in some national economies. It, therefore, seemed unlikely that this would be the genuine aim of policy. Matters were complicated when calculations regarding money growth and velocity trends suggested that the ECB was aiming at a point target of 1.5 per cent (Svensson, 2000).

A second problem derives from the fact that the HICP is a measure of headline inflation. That is, the measure is influenced by all factors including external shocks, even if these have only short-term effects, and policy changes, although they might be intended to reduce longer-term inflationary pressure. This contrasts with many other central banks, which frame the inflation target in terms of core or underlying inflation, such as the RPIX in the UK (see Section 9.6). This seeks to measure sustained domestic inflationary pressure. The use of a headline rate leaves an element of uncertainty as to how the central bank is likely to react to an external shock. The ECB has argued that it retains a degree of flexibility because its concern is with medium-term inflationary trends — but this leaves open the question of the length of the medium term. The ECB defends the choice of a quantitative definition of price stability as a means of providing both transparency and accountability. However, this is not achieved if the meaning of the definition is unclear. In other words, the form of the target reduces the transparency of ECB decision-making and leaves the financial markets uncertain about the basis of ECB decisions.

Inflation or monetary targeting?

The ECB had to decide whether simply to target the ultimate objective - the achievement of a low inflation rate — or to choose an intermediate target through which it would hope to control the rate of inflation. The likely intermediate target was some measure of the money supply. We have seen in Chapter 9, that the use of a money supply target has the advantage that the time lag between adjusting short-term interest rates and changes in the objective are shorter than if the intermediate target is nominal income or if no intermediate target is used. Further, there are fewer exogenous influences upon it than is the case with a GNP or inflation target. However, the use of an intermediate money supply target only makes sense if there is a stable short-run demand function for money. For this reason, where the short-run money demand function had been manifestly unstable over the past twenty years, as in the UK, the use of a single money supply target had been abandoned. Germany, on the other hand, continued to use a target for broad money. Although, in practice, the Bundesbank had appeared to pay as much attention to the rate of inflation as to the broad money target, it had continued to recommend the use of a broad money target for the ECB. This was despite the existence of evidence that in the second half of the 1990s, the German demand for money function was starting to become unstable because of financial liberalization and increased financial innovation in Germany. As well as causing short-term instability in the demand for money function, financial liberalization had made it harder for central banks to control the money supply because it had become harder to influence relative interest rates between money and other financial assets.

This meant that there were sufficient uncertainties to make it inadvisable to depend on a single measure of the money supply as an intermediate target. A money supply target could have been based on past relationships between the money supply and inflation or on a model of the economy of the monetary union but there was a serious possibility that it would be of little use in making monetary policy decisions. In addition, a failure to achieve the single money supply target would have added to the uncertainty regarding the strength of the ECB's monetary policy.

Thus, instead of a money supply target, the ECB set a monetary growth reference value for a broad measure of the money supply, M3 (see Box 3.1 for the composition of M3). The monetary growth reference value was established as the first pillar of the ECB's monetary stability strategy. The second pillar of the strategy is a broadly based assessment of the outlook for price developments and the risks to price stability, using other available indicators. These other indicators include the output gap, forecasts of economic growth, and a forecast of the rate of inflation itself. Factors taken into account are considered in more detail in 13.6 below.

Pause for thought 13.10:

Why did the ECB forecast an annual fall in the velocity of money?

The monetary growth reference value was set at 4.5 per cent per annum and has been left unchanged during the first three years of the ECB's operations. This figure was based on what the ECB referred to as the plausible assumptions of a medium term rate of growth of 2 to 2.5 per cent per annum and an annual decline in the velocity of money of 0.5 to 1 per cent, together with the target rate of inflation of less than 2 per cent.[6] The ECB made it quite clear from the beginning that the figure of 4.5 per cent for monetary growth was not a target and that figures above 4.5 per cent would certainly not automatically trigger interest rate rises. The reference value is also described as a medium-term concept. In the view of the ECB, temporary deviations from it are not unusual and do not necessarily have implications for future price developments.

The choice of instrument

The ECB had first to decide upon its system for providing liquidity to the banking system. This is done principally through the main refinancing operations, weekly open market operations that provide liquidity to the banking system through repurchase agreements (repos)[7] with a maturity of two weeks. Initially, this operated through a system of fixed rate tenders, with the fixed rate known as the main refinancing rate — 'refi' for short. This rate became the focus of attention at the regular announcement of the interest rate decision of the ECB's Governing Council.[8]

In a fixed-rate tender, when the total amount for which banks bid is greater than the amount the central bank is prepared to lend, each bank receives the same proportion of the amount for which they bid. This encourages banks to bid for more than they really want since they know they are unlikely to receive all that they bid for and they know the interest rate they will have to pay on the funds they receive. This gives an advantage to large banks, which have the collateral to be able to support large bids for funds. It also makes it difficult for the central bank to judge the true demand for money in the system.

Thus, it quickly became clear that the ECB would prefer a variable rate tender in which banks indicate how much they are willing to borrow from the central bank at various rates. A cut-off rate of interest is then declared. Bids above this cut-off rate are fully filled while bids at the cut-off rate are filled proportionately. This gives the central bank a better idea of the state of demand in the market and of market expectations about future interest rates. The official refinancing rate is then simply a minimum rate of interest — no funds are provided by the central bank below this rate but it is possible for funds to be lent to the banks above this rate. For this reason, the ECB was wary about changing to the variable rate system. This was particularly the case because the large euro area economies were in recession during the first year of the ECB's operation. This had led the bank to cut the refinancing rate from 3 per cent to 2.5 per cent on 9 April 1999 and it had a clear desire at this point to keep interest rates low. During this period only about five per cent of total bank bids for funds were being met by the ECB and there was little doubt that the interest rate at which funds were actually provided under a variable rate system would be higher than the minimum rate.

The change to a variable rate tender was made on the 28 June 2000. By then, the main refinancing rate was on its way up as the ECB became more concerned about inflation. The ECB wished to keep interest rates as steady as possible under the new system and so moved to variable rate tenders just after it had increased the refinancing rate by a half percentage point — a larger increase than many in the market had expected. Changing the system at that time made it less likely that the rates at which funds would actually be provided to the banks would be much above the official refinancing rate, which from that point became the minimum rate.

The main refinancing operations of the ECB are supported by two other types of open market operations: longer-term refinancing operations and fine-tuning operations.[9] Longer-term financing operations are conducted monthly through repurchase agreements with a three-month maturity. The purpose of these is to prevent all liquidity in the money market from having to be rolled over every two weeks and to provide access to longer-term refinancing. As their name suggests, fine-tuning operations are conducted irregularly with the aim of smoothing the impact on interest rates of unexpected liquidity fluctuations in the money market.

When the refinancing rate is announced by the ECB's Governing Council, two other rates are also declared. These are the ECB's rates on its marginal lending facility and on its deposit facility. The marginal lending facility provides the possibility of emergency overnight borrowing to meet liquidity needs. The rate of interest for such borrowings is always set above the refinancing rate.[10] On 22 January 1999, after a brief adjustment period, the marginal lending interest rate was set 150 basis points (1.5 per cent) above the main refinancing rate. From 9 April 1999, this difference was reduced to 100 basis points (1 per cent) and the gap between the two rates has remained unchanged from that date. The deposit rate applies to overnight deposits and is always set below the refinancing rate. The gap between these two rates has stayed steady at 100 basis points (1 per cent) since 9 April 1999. The main refinancing rate (refi) is by far the most important of the ECB's rates.

Another question was whether to support the control of short-term interest rates with the requirement that banks hold mandatory minimum reserve ratios. Before monetary union, this was practised in the majority of EU member countries in the belief that it allowed the central bank more easily to manage short-term interest rates by creating a predictable demand for reserves at the central bank under circumstances in which bank balance sheets were growing rapidly in response to increased demand for credit. However, because reserves at the central bank usually do not receive interest, the ratios act as a tax on banks and, as required reserves grow, banks push up loan rates to make up for the lost interest and to restore overall rates of profit. This in turn puts downward pressure on the demand for credit.

The Bank of England argued that minimum reserve ratios were not required in deep and liquid financial markets since the central bank could achieve its objectives in such markets solely through open market operations. It was also suggested that the use of minimum reserve ratios conflicted with the Maastricht Treaty requirement that policy should be conducted in accordance with the principle of an open market economy with free competition, favouring an efficient allocation of resources.

Despite these objections, the ECB settled for a minimum reserves system with banks required to hold with the national central bank members of the ESCB a reserve ratio of 2 per cent of the liability base. This was defined to include: overnight deposits; deposits with agreed maturity up to two years; deposits redeemable at notice up to two years; debt securities issued with agreed maturity up to two years; and money market paper. A lump-sum allowance of €100,000 may be deducted from an institution's reserve requirement. The Governing Council argued that without the use of a minimum reserve system, the ESCB would be faced with a relatively high volatility of money market interest rates and would need to engage frequently in open market operations. This could undermine the operational efficiency of monetary policy as markets have difficulty in distinguishing policy signals made by the ECB from technical adjustments necessary to reduce the volatility of interest rates. It argued, too, that a reserve ratio system would safeguard the role of national central banks as providers of liquidity to the banking system. However, the Council acknowledged the burden that such a system places on banks if reserves at the central bank do not earn interest. It thus decided to pay interest on the required minimum reserves holdings at the main refinancing interest rate.

13.6 ECB monetary policy since 1999 and the value of the euro

It is difficult to judge the effectiveness of ECB monetary policy. Firstly, we must allow for the time lags in monetary policy and accept that the performance of the euro area economy in 1999 and perhaps a good proportion of 2000 had more to do with the monetary policies of the central banks of the member countries before 1999 and with the attempt by various governments to meet the Maastricht convergence criteria. Secondly, despite the setting of an inflation target and a monetary growth reference value, it has not been easy to know precisely what the ECB has been attempting to do.

Table 13.2: Exchange rates of the euro against the dollar, the yen and sterling 1999-2002

Date	$/€	Y/€	£/€
4 Jan 99	1.18738	133.159	0.71556
1 Feb 99	1.13027	130.046	0.68874
1 Apr 99	1.07802	129.536	0.67097
1 Jun 99	1.04463	125.483	0.64863
3 Aug 99	1.06798	122.966	0.66023
1 Oct 99	1.07172	112.627	0.64761
1 Dec 99	1.00678	103.069	0.63077
27 Jan 00	0.98947	103.804	0.60455
1 Mar 00	0.97029	100.166	0.61208
1 May 00	0.91240	99.322	0.58664
4 Jul 00	0.95107	101.024	0.62789
1 Sep 00	0.89942	95.140	0.61559
25 Oct 00	0.82737	89.366	0.57468
26 Oct 00	0.82733	89.672	0.57764
1 Dec 00	0.87678	97.478	0.60996
11 Jan 01	0.95246	111.922	0.63610
1 Mar 01	0.92923	108.983	0.63865
16 Mar 01	0.89273	109.718	0.62571
18 May 01	0.87690	108.495	0.61340
1 Jun 01	0.84650	100.643	0.59820
3 Jul 01	0.84786	105.54	0.60307
1 Aug 01	0.87928	109.79	0.61346
4 Sep 01	0.88691	105.94	0.61383
10 Sep 01	0.89907	108.85	0.61636
11 Sep 01	0.91277	108.70	0.62070
19 Sep 01	0.93178	109.34	0.63323
1 Oct 01	0.91608	110.17	0.61958
1 Nov 01	0.90446	110.20	0.61834
1 Dec 01	0.88984	110.26	0.62594
2 Jan 02	0.90343	119.28	0.62512
4 Jan 02	0.89502	117.25	0.61926
31 Jan 02	0.85926	115.10	0.60844
15 Feb 02	0.87312	116.14	0.60972

Source: Pacific Exchange Rate Service - http://pacific.commerce.ubc.ca/xr/

In practice, the interest rate decisions appear to suggest that a medium-term average rate of inflation of 2 per cent would be perfectly acceptable and that monthly figures between 2 and 3 per cent do not, in themselves, suggest a failure of policy. Thus, the Governing Council appears to become concerned when the monthly rate moves above 2 per cent only if there is evidence of growing inflationary pressure that would continue in the medium-term, pushing the rate higher. However, as we have pointed out in 13.5, it is difficult to know how long the medium term is in the minds of the members of the Governing Council. It has also been difficult to determine the attitude of ECB members towards the desired value of the euro.

Pause for thought 13.11:

Whose monetary policy was most important in determining the rate of increase of the HICP during 1999? If your answer is not the ECB's, why not?

We have mentioned the doubts that surrounded the likely policy of the ECB and hence the likely strength of the euro following its launch in January 1999. The constitution had been designed partly to convince the markets that the euro area would be a low inflation area with a strong currency. However, the ECB was a new institution and new institutions ultimately only establish a reputation through their behaviour over a number of years. In January 1999, no one knew precisely how the ECB would behave.

Despite these doubts, no one forecast the dramatic fall that took place in the value of the euro, particularly against the US dollar and the Japanese yen, in its first two years of life. The extent of this fall is shown in Table 13.2. The euro, having begun trading on 4 January 1999 at a rate of €1 = $1.1743 rose on the first day to close in New York at $1.18738. However, from then until the close on 25 or 26 October 2000 (the days when the euro seemed to have finally reached its low), the euro fell 30.3 per cent against the dollar, 32.9 per cent against the yen, and 19.7 per cent against the pound sterling. It then recovered, reaching $0.95246 on 11 January 2001 but failed to sustain this improvement, falling back below $0.90 in March 2001.

There were many reasons for the fall in the value of the euro. Its fall against the US dollar was partly a reflection of the strength of the US dollar as the USA economy continued to grow rapidly and European firms invested heavily in the USA.

In addition, because the markets had no clear no notion of how low the ECB were prepared to see the euro fall before they took action, market agents frequently 'tested the market' — they sold euro to see if falls would produce some indication of likely future action by the ECB. This doubt about the policy likely to be followed by the central bank was increased by the tendency of members of the Executive Board to make conflicting statements about the euro. The markets did not like this apparent lack of leadership. Nor were they convinced that the ECB would, despite its constitution, be truly immune from political pressure. This concern was strengthened by the confusion over the length of the term of office of the first President of the ECB, Wim Duisenberg of the Netherlands.

Duisenberg was appointed in 1998 to serve an eight-year term. However, there had been conflict over his appointment because of the fear of some member states, notably France, that Duisenberg's approach to policy would be too conservative and that monetary policy might be deflationary. It was generally understood that there had been a behind-the-scenes agreement that Duisenberg would not serve his full term of office and would be replaced by a French nominee, although the exact terms of the agreement were unclear. There was a widespread view that Duisenberg would serve only four years, although he consistently denied this. In the event, in February 2002, he announced that he would be retiring from the job on his 68th birthday, on 9 July 2003. By then, he will have served just over five years of his term of office.

Pause for thought 13.12:

If there had been a fear on the part of some member countries that Wim Duisenberg would be a too conservative President of the ECB, why did the value of the euro rise slightly, when, in February 2002, he announced his retirement?

In addition to the worry about leadership, because the euro was a new currency, there was no firm view as to the long run exchange rate indicated by economic fundamentals. The starting exchange rate of the euro was simply a weighted average of the values of the 11 participating currencies at the end of December 1998. There was no reason to believe that the new currency would behave in the same way as this weighted average had done before 1999. Indeed, it was probably the case that recessions in the major economies would have a more depressing impact on expectations about the future of the European economy than was suggested by the weights applied in the old ERM.

Under these circumstances, other factors that might normally not have had much impact on the currency provided additional excuses for selling the euro. These included the resignation of the president and members of the European Commission and the NATO bombing of Serbia and Kosovo. The feeling was that only genuine news about improved fundamentals of the currency would push the value of the euro up, whereas it would fall merely because of rumour and political uncertainty. Thus, the fall resulted from a mixture of genuine economic news, the existence of uncertainty about the attitudes of the authorities and a variety of short-term political factors. The doubts about when the euro would 'bottom out' encouraged speculators to continue to sell the euro.

For most of 1999, the ECB was able to take a relaxed view of the value of the euro. At this time, the major European economies were in deep recession with high levels of unemployment and low rates of growth. There was little inflationary pressure in these economies and the HICP showed inflation rates well within the ECB's target range of 0 – 2 per cent. This is shown clearly in Table 13.3, which sets out changes in the ECB's main refinancing rate since January 1999, together with inflation, unemployment, and money growth rate figures over the period for the euro area. We need to note that at the beginning of 2001, Greece became a member of the euro area, requiring some small adjustment of the statistics. We should also note that the base of 100 for the HICP represents average 1996 prices. At the beginning of the operations of the ECB in January 1999, the HICP stood at 102.8.

In the first half of 1999, there was little desire to invest within Europe and the ECB was able to keep interest rates low to help the recovery of the European economy. The HICP remained almost stationary for much of the year. The ECB's initial interest rate of 3 per cent was lowered in early April to 2.5 per cent and was then left unchanged for seven months. By November, however, although the inflation rate was still well within the target range, it had begun to rise. The monetary growth rate had climbed to 6.2 per cent, the euro was plunging towards parity with the dollar and unemployment, while still high, was beginning to fall. The ECB responded to what they saw as developing inflationary pressure by pushing the main refinancing rate back to 3 per cent.

The euro continued to fall, breaching parity with the dollar for the first time on 27 January 2000. Despite a temporary fall in January 2000, the monetary growth rate remained well above the reference value and unemployment continued slowly to decline. The ECB responded with a series of quarter point interest rises in February, March and April and a half point rise in June. Under this pressure, monetary growth fell back towards the reference value and the euro picked up to some extent. This was misleading since it began to fall again sharply in August and September. Meanwhile the inflation rate continued to rise, reaching 2.8 per cent in September. The

ECB appeared now to be genuinely concerned about the possible inflation-ary effects of the weakening currency. Interest rates were again increased in September and on 22 September 2000, the ECB joined with the central banks of the USA, Japan and the UK to purchase euro in the attempt to prop up the currency. This, together with a further interest rate rise in October, had no immediate effect and the euro reached a low of $0.825 during the day's trading on 26 October.

None the less, the euro area economy appeared soon after to be respond-ing to the ECB's rate rises. By January 2001, the inflation rate had fallen towards the target range; the monetary growth rate had reached the refer-ence value for what was to turn out to be the only month of the first 36 months of the operation of the ECB; and the fall in unemployment had vir-tually come to a halt. The ECB felt able to relax. Following the October 2000 increase, the main refinancing rate was left unchanged for seven months. During this period, however, the US economy had started to head toward recession and fears of a global recession had begun to emerge. The Federal Reserve had begun to slash US interest rates and the financial mar-kets were expecting the ECB to follow suit. The problem for the ECB was that monetary growth was again heading for 5 per cent and the inflation rate was under pressure from rising world oil prices as well as the weak euro. The impact on the HICP of the temporarily high world oil price provides a good example of the problem mentioned in 13.5 of using a headline rate of inflation as the target of monetary policy. It is at least possible that the ECB was unduly slow to cut interest rates because of the high rate of inflation as shown by the HICP, which reached a peak of 3.4 per cent in May 2001.

Following the May cut, the ECB resisted pressure for further cuts until the end of August. In the period between May and August, the inflation rate began to decline but remained well outside the target range. Monetary growth continued to rise. The 11 September attack on the World Trade Centre in New York and the Pentagon in Washington DC led to increased worries about world recession and the ECB responded with a half-point cut in rates on 18 September and a further quarter-point cut in November. By this time inflation had fallen to 2.1 per cent, just outside the target range.

The monetary growth rate continued to climb but this was dismissed by the ECB. It argued that the relatively high growth of M3 was the result of people shifting into the liquid and relatively safe short-term assets that make up M3 because of the uncertainty following the September 11 attacks in the USA. Support for this view was drawn from the fact that the growth of pri-vate sector credit had been continuously falling over recent months. None the less, the ECB then felt that the main refinancing rate, which stood after

Table 13.3 Inflation and unemployment rates, money growth rate and official interest rate for the euro area January 1999-February 2002

Date		Inflation rate [1]	Money growth rate[2]	Unemployment rate[4]	Interest rate[3]
1999	Jan	0.8	5.8	10.4	3.0
	Feb	0.8	5.3	10.3	3.0
	Mar	1.0	5.4	10.2	3.0
	Apr	1.1	5.3	10.2	2.5 (9 April)
	May	1.0	5.5	10.1	2.5
	Jun	0.9	5.5	10.1	2.5
	Jul	1.1	5.9	10.0	2.5
	Aug	1.2	5.7	10.0	2.5
	Sep	1.2	6.0	9.9	2.5
	Oct	1.4	5.7	9.8	2.5
	Nov	1.5	6.2	9.7	3.0 (5 Nov)
	Dec	1.7	6.1	9.6	3.0
2000	Jan	1.9	5.3	9.5	3.0
	Feb	2.0	6.2	9.4	3.25 (4 Feb)
	Mar	2.1	6.6	9.3	3.5 (17 Mar)
	Apr	1.9	6.7	9.2	3.75 (28 Apr)
	May	1.9	5.9	9.1	3.75
	Jun	2.4	5.3	9.0	4.25 (9 Jun)
	Jul	2.4	5.1	8.9	4.25
	Aug	2.3	5.4	8.9	4.25
	Sep	2.8	5.0	8.8	4.5 (1 Sep)
	Oct	2.7	4.9	8.7	4.75 (6 Oct)
	Nov	2.9	4.7	8.7	4.75
	Dec	2.5	4.9	8.7	4.75
GREECE	JOINS		EURO	AREA	
2001	Jan	2.4	4.5	8.5	4.75
	Feb	2.6	4.8	8.5	4.75
	Mar	2.6	4.7	8.5	4.75
	Apr	2.9	4.7	8.4	4.75
	May	3.4	5.3	8.4	4.5 (11 May)
	Jun	3.0	5.5	8.5	4.5
	Jul	2.8	5.7	8.4	4.5
	Aug	2.7	6.0	8.4	4.25 (31 Aug)
	Sep	2.5	6.9	8.5	3.75 (18 Sep)
	Oct	2.4	7.4	8.5	3.75
	Nov	2.1	7.8	8.5	3.25 (9 Nov)
	Dec	2.1	7.7	8.5	3.25
2002	Jan	2.5			3.25

Notes: 1 annual rate of growth of Harmonized Index of Consumer Prices. 2 annual rate of growth of M3   3 ECB's main refinancing (refi) rate at the end of month (date of interest rate change in brackets)   4 Unemployment as a percentage of the labour force
Source: *ECB Monthly Report*, various months, Tables 2.4, 4.1 and 5.4

the November cut at 3.25 per cent, had been reduced sufficiently. On 6 December 2001, the Governing Council left the rate unchanged. It is worth concluding this brief account of the ECB's decisions by listing the factors that were considered in making this decision. As listed in the ECB's *Monthly Report* of December 2001, they were:

- quarter-on-quarter real GDP growth was close to zero in the third quarter of 2001and economic activity seems to have remained subdued in the fourth quarter;

- surveys in November continued to indicate low business and consumer confidence;

- conditions existed for economic growth to improve during 2002;

- the fall in oil prices and the expected continued decline in consumer price inflation would lead to higher growth in real disposable income;

- participants in financial markets were being more optimistic about growth prospects in the euro area and in the world economy;

- forecasts by the international institutions and by ECB staff were for a strengthening of growth in the euro area.

Thus, we can interpret the decision of the 6 December as follows. The inflation rate was above the target range but had been falling for the previous six months and was highly likely to continue to fall. This view was supported by the weak GDP figures and the low level of confidence in the economy. The money supply was growing at a rate well above the reference value — but this seemed to be the result of temporary factors and had no implication for future inflation. Therefore, there was certainly no need to increase interest rates.

The current weakness of the economy and the low levels of confidence might suggest, rather, the need for further interest rate cuts. However, the ECB believed that, on current policies, the growth rate in the euro area would increase in 2002 and 2003. In support of this, it quoted the forecasts of other organizations and a revival of confidence in financial markets (following the conventional wisdom discussed in Chapter 12 that financial markets are constantly looking ahead). It argued in the report that structural reforms had taken place in the euro area but that further reforms would be needed if higher rates of growth than the 2 – 2.5 per cent per annum built into its calculation of the monetary growth reference point were not to be inflationary. Thus, it decided that a further cut in interest rates in December

2001 might cause inflationary pressures to develop in late 2002 and 2003 that would cause the inflation rate to become unacceptably high. The Governing Council of the ECB, therefore, chose to leave interest rates unchanged.

In the light of the performance of the euro and the targets established for itself by the ECB, what can we say about European monetary policy since 1999? First of all, we should note that, in the 37 months during which the ECB has been responsible for monetary policy, the inflation rate has been within the target range on only 16 occasions. All of these were in the early months of operation of the ECB when, as we have suggested above, the inflation rate was being influenced more by the separate monetary policies in existence before 1999 than by anything done by the ECB. Indeed, inflation was outside of its target range for 20 consecutive months from June 2000 to January 2002. Despite this, we are not in a position to suggest that ECB policy has failed since, as we have indicated above, its approach to policy is sufficiently opaque to leave us uncertain regarding the precise intentions. Inflation has certainly not run out of control and shows no sign of doing so. Indeed, the forecast for 2002 shown in Table 13.4 suggests that the average annual inflation rate for the euro area in 2002 will be only 1.5 per cent, well within the target range.

Part of the problem stems from the dubious role of the monetary growth reference value. In December 2001, the ECB reaffirmed the monetary growth reference value as 4.5 per cent, but we have noted a tendency to attribute growth rates above this level to temporary and irrelevant factors. It should be clear from other sections of the book that we have no problem with the downgrading of a monetary target. However, it seems odd that monetary growth continues to be acknowledged as the 'first pillar' of policy when all that occurs is that 'developments of M3 are continuously and thoroughly analysed by the ECB in the broader context of other monetary indicators and information from the second pillar to assess their implications for the risks to price stability over the medium term.'[11]

To conclude, we need to mention two other possible concerns regarding monetary policy in the euro area. The first concerns the unevenness of inflationary pressures across the area. The Organization for Economic Cooperation and Development (OECD) figures for the annual increase in consumer prices (per cent, p.a.) in the euro area for the year 2001 were:

Austria	1.9	Germany	1.7	Netherlands	4.4
Belgium	2.9	Ireland	4.2	Portugal	3.7
Belgium	2.9	Italy	2.4	Spain	2.7
France	1.4	Luxembourg	1.7		

Thus, some euro area countries have inflation rates well above the ECB's target range. These figures show a difference of 3 percentage points between the lowest and highest inflation rates. Whether this is a problem depends on the extent to which above- or below-average inflation rates for individual countries are temporary or long-lasting. There are a number of factors including different patterns of consumption and weather conditions and variations in the timing and magnitude of government policies that can account for temporary deviations in inflation rates from the average. It is also possible that, in the early years of monetary union, the process of 'catching up' causes differences in inflation rates. That is, some countries experience faster rates of economic growth and consequent higher inflation rates.

A problem only arises if the inflation rate in a country remains stuck well above or below the average for a significant period or if there is a clear lack of synchronization of business cycles. If a country's inflation rate remained well above the euro area average for, say, two to three years and showed no sign of moving back towards the average, it would seem that the ECB's monetary stance was too weak to tackle the underlying inflationary pressures in the country. The higher rate of inflation would begin to undermine the country's competitiveness — and this can no longer be tackled by a devaluation of the national currency. Equally, a particularly low rate of inflation might indicate that the centrally determined monetary policy was being too restrictive for the country in question.

In recent years, particular concern has been expressed about the position of Ireland because the inflation rate had reached 5.9 per cent in the year 2000 and had shown little sign of falling in the early months of 2001. However, as the figures show, the Irish inflation rate fell back towards the average in the later part of 2001 and the forecast inflation rates for the euro area for 2002 shown in Table 13.4 suggest that the Irish inflation rate will fall more or less in line with the euro area average. According to this forecast, the difference between highest and lowest inflation rates will fall back to 2.6 percentage points in 2002.

Therefore, it is not yet clear that there is a problem of divergent inflation rates in the euro area as it is currently constituted. We shall need to wait longer to see how the situation develops. If a problem is revealed by the forecast figures for 2002, it is that monetary policy may have been too tight from the point of view of the German and French economies.

The ECB's view regarding divergent inflation rates is that it needs to determine its monetary policy on the basis of average economic performance across the euro area and leave individual countries to deal with any excessive inflationary pressures that remain with fiscal policy. This, however, does not tackle the reverse problem of a country suffering the deflationary effects of an over-tight inflation rate since attempts to use fiscal policy to correct for this may run into difficulties with the Stability and Growth Pact.

Table 13.4 Inflation forecasts for the euro area 2002

Country	Inflation forecast for 2002
Germany	0.9
France	0.9
Italy	1.8
Spain	2.5
Netherlands	2.6
Belgium	1.7
Austria	2.0
Finland	1.8
Greece	3.1
Portugal	2.3
Ireland	3.5
Luxemburg	1.4
Euro zone	1.5

Source: ABN-AMRO

The last possible concern stems from the political desire for the euro to challenge the US dollar as the major world currency. Some have argued that the early weakness of the euro would undermine the attractiveness of the currency for financial markets and prevent it from challenging the US dollar. However, the euro has done reasonably well in international securities markets, although the US dollar clearly remains the currency of preference for the issue of securities. This is hardly surprising and any slowness in the growth in use of the euro is almost certainly attributable more to the diversity of traditions, practices, regulations and tax regimes across the euro area that prevent the full integration of the euro area capital market.

13.7 Possible reforms of the ECB strategy and procedure

The ECB has faced criticism because of both its perceived lack of accountability and its monetary policy strategy. Svensson (2000) suggests that claims by the ECB that it is open and credible carry little weight when it is clear that it is less accountable than the central banks of New Zealand, Sweden and the UK. We have seen that there has been a particular problem with the ECB, that it has been difficult to understand the Governing Council's interpretation of its mandate and, hence, difficult to judge its success. The problem of accountability is highlighted by the comparison with the Monetary Policy Committee of the Bank of England, set out in Box 13.5. Suggested reforms of the ECB have included the publication of an inflation forecast and greater openness regarding the voting record and decision-making process of the Governing Council.

The monetary strategy criticisms have concentrated on the inflation targets set and the role of the monetary growth reference value in the policy deliberations. Proposals have included the move to the use of a core rate of inflation in place of the headline rate provided by the HICP and a raising of the target rate to a range of 1 – 3 per cent. There has been no suggestion, however, that the euro area should move to the UK system of having the inflation target set by the political system.

13.8 Summary

In principle, the practice of monetary policy is the same in a monetary union as in a single country. However, the success of any monetary policy is strongly influenced by the size and composition of the area that it covers. Thus, when a single currency area is established across a number of nation states, we must ask whether this makes economic sense and must look at the costs and benefits associated with a country's giving up the possibility of changing its exchange rate. To do this, we must look at the characteristics of the countries involved. In particular, we must look at the extent to which the separate economies are coordinated and at the extent to which other elements in the economies are sufficiently flexible to cope with the loss of a traditional instrument of policy. In particular, we must look at the labour market and fiscal policy. In carrying out this exercise, we must realize that there are no precise answers and we must not forget that important political issues are also involved.

To help it to decide whether or not to join the euro area, the UK government has set out 'five economic tests' based on a mixture of general principles about the membership of monetary union and specific issues of importance to the UK, notably the impact of the decision on the City of London and on inward foreign investment. The Chancellor of the Exchequer has suggested that the UK will not join unless the answers to the questions

Box 13.5: Accountability Differences between the ECB and the MPC of the Bank of England

1. The ECB sets its own inflation target (currently 0-2%); the UK inflation target is set by the Chancellor of the Exchequer (currently 2.5%). Thus, the Bank of England has instrument independence but not goal independence. The ECB has both.

2. The Bank of England practices inflation targeting, setting its interest rate with the aim of meeting the inflation target set by the government. The ECB has two pillars of policy: (i) the monetary growth reference point (currently 4.5 %); (ii) a broadly based assessment of the outlook for price developments and the risks to price stability, using other available indicators. The ECB has an inflation rate target but its intentions in relation to that target are not always clear.

3. The Bank of England issues minutes of the meetings of its Monetary Policy Committee and voting records so that it is known whether the decision was closely contested and how individual members voted. The ECB publishes neither minutes nor voting records. Indeed, it is forbidden from publishing voting records. All that is issued after the meeting is a not-very-detailed press release.

4. The Bank of England publishes a three-monthly inflation report that sets out the Monetary Policy Committee's inflation forecast together with an assessment of the factors likely to influence the rate of inflation over the following two years. The ECB does not publish an inflation forecast. It does publish a weekly financial statement, monthly and quarterly reports and an annual report, the last of which comments on its monetary policy over the last two years.

5. The MPC of the Bank of England is subject to biannual interrogation by the Treasury Select Committee of the House of Commons. The President of the ECB appears quarterly before the European Parliament's Committee on Economic Affairs and answers questions. Transcripts of these hearings are published on the ECB website.

6. If it misses its target by one per cent or more in either direction, the MPC is required to write an open letter to the Chancellor of the Exchequer setting out the reasons for its failure and explaining what steps it will take to remedy the situation.

7. The Annual Report of the Bank of England goes to parliament; the ECB's annual report goes to the European Parliament, Commission and Council.

8. The Court of the Bank of England commissioned a review of monetary policy-making, which was published in 2000.

posed in the five economic tests are clearly and unambiguously in favour of membership. However, there are very few clear and unambiguous answers to major economic questions.

Monetary policy in the euro area is conducted by the European System of Central Banks, which consists of the European Central Bank and the national central banks of the member states. The constitution of the ECB was modelled as closely as possible on that of the Bundesbank. All constituent elements are required to be politically independent and the principal task of the Bank is to achieve low and stable inflation. The European parliament has no influence on the objectives of monetary policy. Because of the determination to convince markets that the ECB would be fiercely politically independent, it is now only weakly accountable to the governments and citizens of the euro area. This has sometimes resulted in the reasoning behind its decisions being opaque and has led to some uncertainty in financial markets about its likely future course of action. This has been particularly true in relation to its attitude towards the value of the euro. This was one factor behind the large slide in the value of the euro against the US dollar in the first two years of the euro's life.

The ECB, in its explanation of its policy, refers to two pillars of its inflation strategy — a monetary growth reference value, and an assessment of the outlook for the future using a range of other indicators. In practice, however, it is probably closer to being engaged in inflation targeting than anything else, although it has not always been clear how it has been interpreting its own inflation target range of 0 - 2 per cent.

Key concepts used in this chapter

optimum currency area	European System of Central Banks
symmetric and asymmetric shocks	European Central Bank
synchronized business cycles	Governing Council of the ECB
labour market flexibility	Executive Board of the ECB
convergence/divergence of economies	political independence of central banks
Stability and Growth Pact	accountability of central banks
the main refinancing rate (refi) of the ECB	Harmonized Index Of Consumer Prices (HICP)

monetary growth reference value

target inflation rate

fixed rate tender

variable rate tender

minimum reserve ratio

Questions and exercises

1. How useful is the exchange rate as an instrument of policy:
    (a) in a closed economy?
    (b) in a very open economy?

Why is the answer different in the two cases?

2. In 13.2, we suggest that wage flexibility does not always provide an efficient means of adjusting to external shocks. What is the basis of that argument?

3. Why might the business cycles of the UK not be synchronized with those of the 12 current members of the euro area?

4. Do you think that the business cycles of Ireland are likely to be better synchronized with the rest of the euro area than are those of the UK? If so, given Ireland's long-standing economic links with the UK, why might this be so?

5. What does the Executive Board of the ECB do? What does it not do?

6. In Table 13.1, compare and comment on the following sets of interest rates:
    (a) the bid yields for French, Netherlands and Greek bonds with a redemption date of 31 January 2004;

    (b) the bid yields for German and Netherlands bonds with a redemption date of 31 July 2011;

    (c) the bid yields for French and Spanish bonds with a redemption date of 31 October 2011.

7. Why is the accountability of the central bank an important issue?

8. In the text, we say:

'A supporting argument was that the euro, as a broader-based reserve currency than the DM would be less likely to be driven artificially high on occasions.'

Explain this statement. How did it relate to the question of the likely future strength of the euro?

9. When the ECB began operation at the beginning of 1999, how did it ensure that all members of the Executive Board would not end their terms of office at the same time? What would be wrong with the terms of all six members of the Board ending on the same date?

10. Outline the arguments for and against fixed and variable rate tenders as the instrument for the provision by the central bank of liquidity to the banking system.

11. Look at the latest interest rate decision made by the ECB and explain it in terms of the first and second pillars of the ECB's monetary strategy.

Further reading

For a good text book account of the economics of monetary integration, see: P De Grauwe (2000). Among a wide range of other text books with useful material on European monetary policy, we would also recommend Eijffinger and de Haan (2000).

The European Central Bank has published a detailed account of all aspects of its monetary policy as European Central Bank (2001). This is fully downloadable as a pdf file from the ECB's website: www.ecb.int

An extraordinary amount of material of all types and levels, from newspaper reports to difficult academic articles is available on the website of Giancarlo Corsetti of Yale and Bologna Universities at: www.econ.yale.edu/~corsetti/euro/

14 Monetary Policy in the USA

'The almighty dollar is the only object of worship.' Anon.
Philadelphia Public Ledger, 2.12.1836

What you will learn in this chapter:

• The story of the development of central banking in the USA
• The structure of the Federal Reserve System
• The approach to monetary policy of the Federal Open Market Committee of
  the Fed
• The way in which monetary policy is implemented by the Fed
• The extent to which and ways in which the Fed is independent and accountable
• The nature of the monetary policy practised by the Fed in recent years.

14.1 Introduction

The United States central bank, the Federal Reserve System, is widely
regarded as the most powerful economic policy institution in the world and
its present Chairman, Alan Greenspan, as the single person having the most
influence. This is a testament to the size and strength of the US economy,
the return to importance of monetary policy in the minds of economists,
industrialists, and politicians and, perhaps above all, the dominance of
financial markets in the modern imagination. We have indicated at several
points in this book that the real power of the monetary authorities is rather
less than this might suggest, but the Fed certainly has sufficient impact to
mean that no account of current monetary policy could omit consideration
of it. Thus, in Section 14.2, we provide some necessary background historical information and look at the structure of the Federal Reserve System.
We also look at the position within the system of the Federal Open Market
Committee, the body responsible for US monetary policy. In 14.3, we consider the form of US monetary policy. In 14.4, we consider the independence and accountability of the Federal Reserve, while 14.5 looks at recent
US monetary policy.

14.2 The story of central banking in the USA

The current US central bank, the Federal Reserve System (the Fed), was not
established until the early years of the 20th century. Unlike the Bank of

England, the Fed was set up as a central bank rather than evolving into one from a privately owned bank of discount, deposits and note issue. Two early attempts were made to set up a corporate central bank, chartered by the state, but owned by private investors.

The First Bank of the United States commenced business in 1791 and survived until 1811. The Second Bank of the United States also survived for twenty years (1816-36).[1] Both met with strong opposition. This came partly from banks given operating charters by state governments (state-chartered banks). The state-chartered banks wanted a share of the national government's banking business and did not like the attempts by the central banks to exercise control over them. For example, in 1791, the First Bank of the United States had attempted to control the number of bank notes issued by state banks.

However, not all the criticism was self-interested. There was a strong feeling that the central banks were too large and privileged and that this conflicted with the democratic ideals of the USA. This attitude is well illustrated by a statement made in 1836 by the US president, Andrew Jackson, that the Second Bank of the United States was a 'concentration of power in the hands of a few men irresponsible to the people'.[2] One problem was the private ownership of the bank, which included some foreign investors. A second was the geographical concentration of the bank.

From the beginning, the development of US banking was influenced by two major fears — of centralized authority and of domination by moneyed interests. These fears reflect the origins of the US nation state. Settlement from Europe had been by separate, relatively small groups often fleeing from religious or political domination — the first united action by settlers was the struggle against the distant authority of Britain. The two fears combined to produce a determination to prevent the financial system being controlled either by large institutions in the financial centre of New York or by political forces concentrated in Washington. The result was an idiosyncratic banking system that consisted of large numbers of small independent banks, restricted from opening branches across state boundaries.[3] In the 18th and 19th centuries, any attempt to control the operation of banks from the centre met with deep suspicion. The failure of the early central banks was one reflection of this.

In the absence of a central bank, for much of the 19th century the federal government had to act as its own banker. In doing so, Treasury officials gradually realized that funds might be added to or withdrawn from the private sector on a discretionary basis to prevent financial panics and as an element of macroeconomic policy. That is, the Treasury began to develop a central monetary policy. This also met with opposition since the Secretary of the Treasury was a political appointee, feeding the fear of the political control of money and finance and, hence, the economy. We find here, too, an early example of the view at the heart of much of the modern argument for independent central banks that the Treasury, because it was controlled by politicians, would have a long-run bias towards easy money and inflation. Perhaps more importantly, it was thought that the Treasury might favour particular financial, geographic, and economic interests.

Pause for thought 14.1:

What was the point of stopping banks from opening branches in other states?

However, the extreme decentralization of the banking system caused problems. In recessions, small banks regularly ran into problems and this frequently led to runs on banks, multi-bank panics, and the collapse of many banks. This was not helped by the absence of a central bank. There were nine multi-bank panics between the closure of the Second Bank of the United States and the end of the first decade of the 20th century. Consequently, following the panic of 1907, a commission of enquiry was set up and the *Federal Reserve Act*, which established the Federal Reserve System, was passed in 1913.

The form of the system was strongly influenced by the continuing fear of excessive control from the centre. Instead of setting up a single bank, the 1913 Act brought into being twelve regional Federal Reserve banks over-seen by the Federal Reserve Board in Washington D.C. The system was designed to provide a broad view of economic activity in all parts of the country. By the time the Fed was set up, US commercial banks consisted of both nationally chartered and state-chartered banks.[4] All nationally chartered banks were required to become members of their regional reserve bank. State-chartered banks could choose to become members, as long as they met standards set by the Fed. The regional reserve banks do not receive funds from the central government. They were individually chartered and required to raise their own capital, which is contributed by the member commercial banks in each district. They are profit making and twice a year pay their member banks a dividend on the subscribed capital at a fixed rate of six per cent. Earnings above those needed for operations and the payment of the dividends are paid to the US Treasury at the end of each year. The income of the district banks comes from fees paid for the services provided to commercial banks and from interest on their holdings of US

Treasury securities and loans to the commercial banks.

Each district reserve bank has its own president and board of directors. Board membership should reflect the interests of the various sectors of the economy including business and industry, agriculture, labour, the financial sector and consumers. To this end, reserve bank boards consist of nine members: six representatives of nonbanking enterprises and the public and three of the banking industry. Reserve bank presidents serve five-year terms while the members of the boards of directors serve for three years. Where there are branches of a federal reserve bank, each branch also has its own board of directors to try to ensure that local interests are always taken into account.

When the banks were set up in 1913, the regional reserve banks retained considerable power. They had a monopoly of the nation's note issue, acted as fiscal agents of the government, banks of rediscount and reserve for member banks, and lenders of last resort in their districts. They were involved in the regulation and supervision of the banking system although, because of the late establishment of the Fed, this had to be shared with already established state banking authorities and federal agencies. The intention of the decentralized structure was to ensure a sufficient supply of credit in each region. This was to be achieved principally by each reserve bank re-discounting commercial paper at rates set according to each regional its view of the needs of its region. Further, each bank was able to determine for itself which bills were eligible for rediscounting.

Member banks held legally prescribed reserves as deposits in their reserve banks and in return were entitled to rediscount their eligible commercial paper at the banks when in need of temporary liquidity. They were also able to use the Fed clearing facilities including electronic funds transfers and the currency and information services of the banks. It was anticipated that the availability of these services to members would encourage state-chartered banks to join the system.

Pause for thought 14.2:

Why might state-chartered banks have chosen not to join the Federal Reserve System?

The original Federal Reserve Board comprised five members[5] appointed to staggered ten-year terms by the US president with the Secretary of the Treasury and the Comptroller of the Currency as *ex-officio* members. The Board was required to oversee and supervise the operations of the reserve banks, co-ordinate their activities, and handle the System's relations with the federal government. At the beginning, the Federal Reserve Board had little authority to initiate policies and no power to coordinate monetary policy across the country. Indeed, the Board probably had less power than the unofficial Governors' Conference set up by the regional reserve banks under the chairmanship of the Governor of the Federal Reserve Bank of New York.

The possession of the chairmanship of this unofficial body was merely one indication of the growing power of the New York bank. This arose largely because New York had by far the largest money and capital markets in the USA and the Federal Reserve Bank of New York soon started to act as agent for the other reserve banks in the purchase of securities. Following the entry of the USA into the First World War in 1917, government borrowing increased greatly and had to be financed. Government paper began to dominate commercial bills in the portfolios of the banking system. The principal objective of the Fed became, in effect, to finance the centralized needs of the Treasury. Since government securities were largely placed on the New York capital market, their prices were strongly influenced by the policies of the New York Reserve Bank.

Regional policy diversity began to decline. When, in 1921, the New York bank raised its interest rate to 7 per cent, the other reserve banks soon followed. In 1922, the New York Governor set up a committee of five governors to coordinate open market operations and between that year and 1928, the Fed began increasingly to act as a unified central bank.

However, in the late 1920s and again during the Great Depression, serious disagreements over policy resurfaced, both among the regional banks and between them and the Board. During the depression, the Federal Reserve Bank of New York favoured expansionary policies to stimulate the economy. Following the appointment by President Roosevelt in 1933 of a new Governor, the Board also favoured expansion, but this was opposed by several of the other district Banks and did not happen. This led to a campaign to increase the power of the Board. The behaviour of the Fed immediately before and during the depression is the subject of Box 14.1.

In the early 1930s, multi-bank panics and collapses continued.[6] As a consequence of these problems, two major pieces of bank legislation were enacted — the Banking Acts of 1933 (the Glass-Steagall Act) and 1935. The Glass Steagall Act introduced the federal insurance of bank deposits and restrictions on the activities of insured banks, in an attempt to reduce the riskiness of the system. Among other things, the Act prohibited interest payments to owners of federally insured sight deposits and authorized the setting of limits on rates paid on federally insured savings deposits of vari-

Box 14.1: The Federal Reserve and the depression of the 1930s

There are differences of opinion regarding the performance of the Fed in the lead up to the stock market crash of October 1929, although it is widely held that it did not perform well. There are two issues:

1. To what extent did Fed policy in 1927 fuel the speculative boom in equity prices of 1928 and 1929?
2. Was the Fed responsible for the financial crash and the conversion of that crisis into a general, deep, and long-lasting economic slump?

In the spring of 1927, the Fed cut its rediscount rate from 4 to 3½ per cent and sold government securities, adding liquidity to the banking system. Did the provision of liquidity cause the speculative fever that followed? Or was the Fed at this point acting as a passive supplier of liquidity? The Fed raised interest rates in August 1929. In nominal terms, the money supply steadied and then fell. It did not grow during 1928, fell by 2.6 per cent from August 1929 to October 1930 and continued to fall until March 1933. Was this the cause of the stock market crash in October 1929?

Friedman and Schwarz blame the Fed on both counts, particularly for the collapse. As believers in exogenous money, they argue that the restrictions on liquidity brought about the crisis. Other economists reject both propositions. Galbraith (1954, p. 15) rejects the view that the Fed's actions encouraged speculation in the early stages of the boom as 'formidable nonsense' as, in his view, the interest rate was relatively high. Temin (1976) rejects the Friedman and Schwarz argument about the causes of the crash on a number of grounds, one of which was that interest rates fell rather than rose. If the fall in money supply had been the cause of the crash, that part of the transmission process that worked through the interest rate should have been:

$$\downarrow \text{ money supply} \rightarrow \uparrow \text{ interest rate} \rightarrow \downarrow \text{ investment and consumption} \rightarrow \downarrow \text{ income}$$

A standard monetarist argument, of course, requires that the exogenous reduction in the money supply does not have real effects in the long run. To explain these, Friedman and Schwarz depend on the banking collapses that followed the Wall Street crash. 8,812 banks collapsed between 1930 and 1933 and total bank deposits fell by 42 per cent between 1929 and 1933. These clearly had a large impact on the real economy. Thus, money is not neutral in this case because of institutional failures brought about by the Fed's actions. Temin, however, argues that the problem had begun with consumption. A fall in consumption would have caused a fall in the transactions demand for money, causing interest rates to fall. The falls in the money supply would have occurred as a result of the decline in demand for bank loans. In fact, most interest rates declined sharply after the 1929 crash.

Kindleberger (1996) worries, however, that this still leaves the fall in consumption to be explained and finds none of the several explanations of this convincing. He also worries that neither the monetarist nor the Keynesian view explains the fact that industrial production had started to fall in advance of the financial crash. It fell in September 1929 and then continued to fall sharply so that an index of industrial production that had stood at 127 in June 1929 had fallen to 99 by December. Kindleberger relies on the instability of the credit system to explain the facts. He quotes the view of Simons (1948) that changes in business confidence had led through an unstable credit system to changes in liquidity and effects on the money supply — which is again seen as endogenous here.

Whether the Fed was responsible or not, however, no one has a good word for them in this period. Galbraith, indeed, describes them as 'a body of startling incompetence' (1954 p.33).

ous maturities. The regulation issued by the Federal Reserve in exercising its authority over deposit rates was known as Regulation Q.[7]

The 1935 Act replaced the Federal Reserve Board with the Board of Governors of the Federal Reserve System. The new Board comprised seven members, each appointed by the President with the advice and consent of the Senate. Membership of the Board should provide 'a fair representation of financial, agricultural, industrial and geographic divisions'[8] again indicating concern about the concentration of power in the centre and the possible neglect of the needs of industry. The new Board was given additional powers, including the authority to adjust member-bank reserve requirements, order the Federal Reserve Banks to change their discount rates, restrict discount window loans to member banks deemed to be making excessive loans for speculative purposes, and limit the volume of loans made by member banks. The term of Board members was lengthened to fourteen years.

The Federal Open Market Committee (FOMC) was set up to conduct monetary policy. The FOMC comprises the seven members of the Board of Governors, the president of the Federal Reserve Board of New York and four other reserve bank presidents, serving one-year rotating terms. The district banks are grouped for this purpose to ensure that all areas of the country are always represented on the FOMC. For example, the presidents of the Cleveland and Chicago Federal Reserve Banks alternate since they come broadly from the same part of the country. The presence of the seven Board members gives the Board a permanent majority on the FOMC.

The form of the Federal Reserve System established by the 1935 Act remains in place today. As the Bank of England did until its reform in 1997, the US central bank carries out all possible functions of a central bank, being:

- the bank to the banking system
- the bank to the US government
- the body responsible for monetary policy
- the operator of the payments system
- a major part of the system of supervision and regulation of depository institutions

It also has a responsibility for the protection of consumers' rights in dealing with banks and for promoting community development and reinvestment. The modern role of the 12 district Federal Reserve Banks is set out in Box 14.2.

Box 14.2: The functions of the 12 district Federal Reserve Banks

Although monetary policy has, since 1935, been centralized and rests with the Board of Governors of the Federal Reserve System, the 12 district Federal Reserve Banks continue to play a number of important roles.

• They provide 5 of the 12 members of the FOMC and have the specific task of helping the Committee stay in touch with the economic conditions in all parts of the country

• They supervise banks and bank and financial holding companies, helping to maintain the stability of the financial system

• They provide financial services to depository institutions

• They market and redeem government securities and savings bonds and conduct nationwide auctions of Treasury securities as well as maintaining the Treasury's funds account

• They provide payments services — the safe and efficient transfer of funds and securities throughout the financial system

• They distribute coins and currency

• They are heavily involved in research and have an educational role

• The Federal Reserve Bank of New York carries out open market operations and intervenes in foreign exchange markets on behalf of the Board of Governors.

14.3 The aims and form of monetary policy in the USA

Policy objectives

The monetary policy goals of the Federal Reserve System were initially broad. They included the provision of an 'elastic currency' — ensuring sufficient liquidity in the banking system to guard against bank panics. Price stability was important, but so were the other standard goals of macroeconomic policy. In the 1970s, the Fed listed its broad objectives as 'to help counteract inflationary and deflationary movements, and to share in creating conditions favourable to sustained high employment, stable values, growth of the country, and a rising level of consumption'.[9]

As with other central banks, however, the goal of price stability has dominated since the beginning of the 1980s. The Fed now sums up its objectives as 'price stability and sustainable growth'. However, in practice, the two goals almost appear to become one. For example, in his testimony to the US Congress in July 2001, the Chairman of the Board of Governors,

Alan Greenspan, said, 'Certainly, should conditions warrant, we may need to ease further, but we must not lose sight of the prerequisite of longer-run price stability for realizing the economy's full growth potential over time.'[10]

In other words, price stability is now seen as the *sine qua non* for the achievement of sustainable growth, an issue discussed Section 9.2.

Pause for thought 14.3:

What is an 'elastic currency?'

None the less, the representative structure of the Fed appears to lead to greater attention being paid to the real economy and to economic perform-ance across the country than is the case with many other central banks. Unlike the ECB and the Bank of England, the Fed does not specify the goal of price stability in the form of a target rate of inflation. The minutes of its meetings show that the FOMC heeds a wide variety of real and monetary indicators in arriving at its decisions and appears to pay considerable atten-tion to anecdotal evidence of business conditions in diverse industries and regions.

At its January/February meeting each year, the FOMC establishes annu-al monetary growth ranges.[11] These are specified, on a fourth-quarter-to-fourth-quarter basis, for the broader monetary aggregates, M2 and M3. The aim is to identify monetary growth ranges that are consistent with the Committee's policy goals for inflation and economic growth. However, the FOMC is aware of the potential instability of money velocities and accepts that monetary growth rates have not recently been reliable guides for mon-etary policy. They are now just one indicator among many. The Committee also sets an annual monitoring range for the growth of aggregate debt of all nonfinancial sectors — allowing credit growth to be given at least an equal role in policy deliberations as that given to monetary growth.

Instruments and intermediate targets

Similarly to the Bank of England and the European Central Bank, the Fed seeks to achieve its monetary policy targets by changes in short-term inter-est rates. In the case of the Fed, the interest rate that is central is the Federal funds rate (Fed funds rate). This is the rate that depository institutions pay when they borrow reserves overnight from each other in order to meet reserve requirements set by the Federal Reserve, and to ensure adequate bal-ances in their accounts at the Fed to cover cheque and electronic payments clearances. The Federal funds rate often has a strong impact on other short-term rates.

Since the *Monetary Control Act* (MCA) of 1980, the Fed has set reserve requirements for all depository institutions, whether or not they are members of the Federal Reserve System. The MCA authorized the Fed's Board of Governors to impose a reserve requirement of from 8 to 14 per cent of sight deposits and of up to nine percent of nonpersonal time deposits, but not to impose reserve requirements on personal time deposits except in extraordinary circumstances. The reserve requirement on sight deposits is currently 10 per cent, although concessions apply for the first part of the total[12] while no reserves are required for time deposits. The lack of reserve requirements on time deposits means that important components of the broader money measures M2 and M3 can expand without any concern about reserve levels. In practice, reserve requirements now play only a very limited role in monetary policy and the Fed's reserve requirements are changed only infrequently.

Pause for thought 14.4

The Fed has long wanted to pay banks interest on the reserves that must be held with them, but the US Congress has refused to allow this. Why do you think the Fed would like to pay interest? Why does the Congress say no?

Reserves may be held as vault cash or as deposits at the Fed. Banks that fail to meet their reserve requirements can be subject to financial penalties. Required reserves are calculated on net sight deposits, using 'contemporaneous reserve accounting'. That is, they are based on deposits more or less concurrently held. This is not fully contemporaneous but is calculated as a daily average[13] over a two-week period: a bank's average reserves over the period ending every other Wednesday must equal the required percentage of its average deposits in the two-week period ending Monday, two days earlier. Thus, banks can work out how much they must hold in the last two days to raise their average reserves over the period to the required average.

Banks short of reserves can borrow in the Federal funds market or from the discount window of the Fed. Reserves borrowed from the discount window are referred to as borrowed reserves. Nonborrowed reserves constitute the bulk of total reserves. They are supplied principally through Fed open market purchases of Treasury Bills in the secondary market.

A discount window is operated by each of the 12 regional reserve banks and each decides its own discount rate (the rate that applies to borrowings at the discount window), although approval for changes to the discount rate must be obtained from the FOMC. The discount window is usually held below the Federal funds rate. This means that, in theory, it provides the cheapest way of acquiring reserves. Indeed, if the gap between the Fed funds rate and the discount rate grew sufficiently large, there would be an opportunity for round tripping — with banks borrowing from the discount window and lending at the Fed funds rate. However, the Fed's aim is to keep the discount window for lender-of-last resort borrowing, after banks have exhausted other borrowing possibilities. Thus, the Fed discourages the use of the discount window, certainly for profit but also as a normal way of making up shortfalls in reserves.

To do this, the Fed operates rules governing the extent and frequency of borrowing and ultimately may turn away frequent borrowers through the discount window. This means that banks realize that if they borrow too often from the discount window, they may be unable to do so when they have a genuine need. In addition, too frequent borrowing by banks through the discount window creates a bad impression in the financial markets. Thus, there are non-pecuniary costs (commonly known as 'frown costs') in borrowing from the discount window that more than balances the difference between the Fed funds rate and the discount rate. Banks, then, are only likely to borrow from the discount window for reserves purposes in emergencies. Rather, they seek to borrow reserves that they require initially in the Federal funds market, despite the greater financial cost of doing so.

Under current arrangements, the FOMC, which normally meets eight times a year, sets a target for the Fed funds rate and the Federal Reserve Bank of New York conducts open market operations on the Fed's behalf to try to ensure that the rate remains close to the target. To do this, the New York Reserve bank must forecast each morning the total reserves (the reserves required together with any additional reserves the banks might wish to hold minus those reserves that will be borrowed through the discount window). If it decides that the quantity of reserves available is too low or too high, it seeks to adjust this by direct intervention in the government securities market, making use of repos,[14] matched transactions[15] and outright purchases/sales of securities. Outright purchases of Treasury Bills are made when the Fed projects that commercial bank needs for reserves will last for a period of several weeks; repos and matched transactions when it projects only a temporary shortage or surplus of reserves. When the FOMC wishes to influence the Fed funds rate, it does so by directing the New York Fed to vary the supply of reserves through its open market operations. A purchase by the Fed reduces available reserves relative to demand

and tends to push the Fed funds rate up. A sale puts downward pressure on the rate. In this way, the New York Fed seeks to keep the Fed funds rate close to the FOMC's target rate. Some details of the process of open market operations are provided in Box 14.3.

Box 14.3: Federal Reserve Bank of New York open market operations

At the end of its regular meetings, the FOMC issues a directive to the New York Federal Reserve, which indicates the approach to monetary policy considered appropriate in the period until its next meeting. This guides the day-to-day decisions regarding the purchase and sale of securities by the manager of the System Open Market Account at the New York Fed. Each working day, information is gathered about the market's activities from a number of sources.

• Discussions are held with the primary dealers in government securities

• Discussions are also held with banks in the large money centres about their reserve needs and plans for meeting them

• Data is received on bank reserves for the previous day

• Projections of factors that could affect reserves for future days are received from reserve forecasters

• Information is received from the Treasury about its balance at the Federal Reserve.

Forecasts of reserves are then made and a plan of action for the day is developed and reviewed with a reserve bank president currently serving as a voting member of the FOMC. A summary of this discussion is sent to members of the FOMC later in the day to allow the FOMC to monitor closely the implementation of its directive. Conditions in financial markets, including domestic securities and money markets and foreign exchange markets are also reviewed each morning. The Trading Desk of the New York Fed then enters the government securities market to execute any temporary open market operations (repos or matched sale-purchase transactions) by sending an electronic message to the primary dealers, asking them to enter bids (if the Fed is selling) or offers (if the Fed is buying) within 10 to 15 minutes. The terms of the operation are stated but not its size — this is announced after the operation is completed. The dealers' bids/offers are evaluated on a competitive best-price basis and the dealers are notified whether their bids/offers have been accepted or rejected. This usually happens about five minutes after the bids/offers were due. Outright sales and purchases are arranged at various times during the day, following a similar procedure.

This system clearly makes the money supply endogenous. Once the target interest rate has been set by the FOMC, non-borrowed reserves are supplied by the Fed through open market operations on demand from the banking system. As we have said above, no use is made of reserve ratios to control the rate of expansion of the banks' balance sheets. We have a straightforward attempt to control the public's demand for loans through interest rate control as practised by both the Bank of England and the ECB. The Fed has, however, attempted to introduce some control over the rate of growth of the money supply from time to time over the past 30 years.

Pause for thought 14.5:

If reserve ratios are not used to control the rate of expansion of bank balance sheets, why are they set?

From 1970 to 1979, the FOMC tried to achieve this by specifying at each meeting both a target rate for Fed funds and a target range for the rate for the period up to the next meeting. Then, if the money supply was judged to be rising too rapidly, the New York Reserve adjusted the supply of reserves to allow the Fed funds rate to drift up towards the top of the target range. Nevertheless, once the top of the target interest rate range was reached, additional demands for reserves would be met and the stock of money would be allowed to rise. That is, the money supply again became endogenous. Although it was true that extra pressure could be applied by raising the top of the target range at the next FOMC meeting or, indeed, between meetings,[17] the Fed was not controlling the money supply effectively during this period.

A more wholehearted effort was made from October 1979, when the Fed sought to engage in what Fazzari and Minsky (1984) referred to as 'practical' monetarism — the use of the quantity and rate of change of a monetary aggregate as the intermediate target of monetary policy. Interest rate targets were replaced by targets for non-borrowed reserves. Increases in Fed funds rates brought about by increases in the demand for reserves would, then, not be limited by the target range for interest rates. In theory, this was a move in the direction of monetary base control. Yet, the Fed still failed to control reserve growth.

One reason given in the early 1980s for this continued lack of control was that from 1968 a system of lagged reserve accounting had operated for calculating the reserves required by banks. As we point out in Section 4.3, the current level of required reserves was thus predetermined by the past level of deposits and there was nothing banks could do to accommodate deposits to reserves. The required reserve ratios could only be met by the Fed supplying the reserves.

Yet, when the change was made to contemporaneous reserve accounting in 1984, the Fed's ability to control reserves did not improve. This was because banks were able to respond to reductions in open market purchases of securities by the Fed (aimed at squeezing bank reserves) by seeking to economize on reserves and by increasing competition for other sources of them — the Fed funds market, international sources and idle cash balances of firms.[16] When these sources failed, banks could still borrow from the discount window. Thus, interest rates were pushed up and the Fed was again seeking to control bank behaviour through prices rather than quantities.

Goodhart (2002, p.16) argues that this episode of 'experimental monetarism' was not a genuine attempt at monetarism at all, but simply a ruse to get Congress and the US public to accept higher interest rates than would otherwise have been politically possible, by persuading them that aggregates mattered and that the level of interest rates was an unfortunate side effect. If this is a correct reading of the situation, it shows again the political pressures to which interest targeting is subject (see Sections 4.3 and 11.2).

In 1982, the Fed introduced another variant by targeting borrowed reserves, only to find that it was again, in effect, supplying reserves on demand. An increase in the demand for reserves would cause the Fed funds rate to be bid up and, as it rose further above the discount rate, banks would increasingly turn to the discount window as a source of reserves. This would push the quantity of borrowed reserves above target. To avoid this, the Fed would have to engage in open market purchases to increase bank reserves because only in this way could they sufficiently discourage banks from using the discount window to enable the target for borrowed reserves to be met. We were back to interest rate targets. Nonetheless, Lewis and Mizen (2000) argue that the post-1982 system was more flexible than that in use before October 1979 because the Committee was more easily able to choose, depending on the source of the increase in the demand for reserves, between providing additional reserves through open market operations and allowing interest rates to be pushed up. The result was that the Federal funds rate fluctuated much more from day-to-day. In other words, policy became more discretionary in nature — hardly likely to be approved by monetarists. During the 1980s, the focus of policy gradually shifted back toward targeting a specified level of the Federal funds rate, a process that was largely complete by the end of the decade, taking the system back to simple interest rate control. From the beginning of 1995, the FOMC has announced its target level for the Federal funds rate after each meeting.

Overall, despite the changes in practice from time to time, there can be little doubt that the US money supply has been endogenous throughout the period discussed.

14.4   The Federal Reserve - independence and accountability

Independence

When it was established in 1913, the Fed was intended to be independent of:

(i)   private financial business interests;

(ii) duly constituted government authorities (executive and legislature); and

(iii) partisan political interests.

By the usual standards applied (see Box 13.4), the Fed is highly independent politically and has been since its inception apart from a period during the Second World War and up to 1949. Although the seven members of the Board of Governors are political appointments, their long and staggered terms (even if the majority of Governors do not serve the full fourteen years) ensures that any one government cannot stack the Board with its own appointees in order to ensure the results it wants. The duties and powers of the Fed are not enshrined in the US constitution but are statutorily protected and difficult to change. The Fed has full control of its policy instruments and has the freedom to interpret the mandate given to it. The government has no direct representative with voting power on the FOMC.

This leaves us with the interesting question of independence from 'private financial business interests'. This is interesting firstly, because it is mentioned at all. The usual assumption in the modern literature is that 'independence' in connection with central banks means independence from politicians and governments. We have seen, however, why independence from financial and business interests was included as a requirement for the Fed — again the general concern over possible domination by 'moneyed interests' especially in New York. We have seen also that at every point in the constitution of the Fed, attempts are made to ensure representation of all industries and geographical areas. The representation of consumers of banking services is also considered in the membership of the Boards of the regional Reserve Banks. Yet, there remains a potent distrust of the Fed in parts of American society. This can be found on both the right and left of US politics. On the right, it is part of the rejection of all big government and centralized institutions.

On the left, it is often seen as over-concerned with the world of finance. For example, Greider (1987) sees the Fed as a non-elected body with an anti-inflationary bias that restrains economic growth in order to preserve the value of financial assets, most of which are owned by wealthy people. It may be that the Fed appears to pay considerable attention to the real economy in the regular deliberations of the FOMC. It remains that any politically independent policy-making body is bound to be strongly influenced, if not controlled, by experts from the field. For independent central banks, this means control by bankers and experts from other areas of finance, who may well share values that do not chime with those of the majority of the people, especially of workers and the poor. Further, the very nature of the task that the FOMC performs brings its members into touch daily with the representatives of high finance. In this time of the partial eclipse of older democratic ideals, in which in all countries and all areas of life public decisions are being made increasingly by committees of unelected experts, the independence of the Fed from private financial interests is not an issue. However, it will continue to surface from time to time in the future.

Pause for thought 14.6:

Do you think it would be possible to have a politically independent central bank that was also independent of the financial sector of the economy?

Accountability

The Fed's mandate has been changed by Acts of Congress over the years but, at any time, is clearly stated and known. The Fed's interpretation of its own mandate also changes as conventional economic wisdom changes. Thus, the objectives of price stability and economic growth, which were once thought to be conflicting, have now effectively become the single goal of price stability. Again, however, the Fed's general interpretation of its mandate is always clear. We have seen, however, that the Fed does not set an inflation target. Nor does it publish an inflation forecast or report such as that of the MPC of the Bank of England. This reduces transparency since we lack knowledge of precisely what the Fed regards as 'price stability'. And, indeed, this can be interpreted differently at different times. On the other hand, this is hardly worse than the case of the ECB, which has a quantitative target but still succeeds in leaving us unclear what its intentions are.

Furthermore, the Fed is a more open institution than is the ECB. The principal form of Fed accountability is through its twice-yearly reports to Congress — in February and July each year. The report is presented by the Chairman of the FOMC (who is also the Chairman of the Board of Governors). The Chairman is then subject to questions by Committees of

Congress. The February report provides a comprehensive review of the economic and financial situation in the country and reviews a wide range of indicators relevant to monetary policy. It also includes specific annual growth ranges for money and debt aggregates, consistent with expectations for inflation and growth of employment and output. In July, the Chairman reports any revisions to the plans for the current year, along with preliminary plans for the following year. Questioning by Congress committees can be detailed and tough. The reports are published by the Fed.

The meetings of the FOMC are also quite open. Although there are only twelve voting members, attendance at the meetings is much wider. The seven presidents of the regional reserve banks who are not currently voting members of the FOMC attend and are allowed to speak. At the October 2001 meeting, another 35 people were present, including the Manager of the New York Fed's Open Market System, and economists and associate economists of the various divisions of the Office of the Board of Governors, several of whom provided reports to the Committee on the present state of the economy and the financial markets. The decisions of the FOMC meetings are published immediately after the meeting.

At its December 1998 meeting, the FOMC decided also to announce immediately major shifts in its view about prospective developments relevant to the likelihood of a future increase or decrease in the targeted Federal funds rate. The aim was to communicate to the public more quickly the FOMC's assessment of the balance of risks and its policy leanings. The Fed became worried, however, about the impact that these statements were having on the markets and now releases a statement after each meeting, whether or not it feels that there have been changes affecting future developments. These statements choose among a set of standard phrases to express the Committee's view. Thus, throughout 2001, all post-meeting statements concluded with the phrase that, in the view of the Committee, 'the risks are weighted mainly toward conditions that may generate economic weakness in the foreseeable future'. Minutes of FOMC meetings are published a few days after the following FOMC meeting and full transcripts become available five years later. Minutes include voting records, although these are often not very useful. This is because the FOMC attempts to reach consensus before motions are put to the vote and so, when the vote is taken, there is frequently no dissenting voice. No votes were recorded against decisions through the whole of 2001.

It follows from this, that the Fed's monetary policy is fairly transparent and its reasoning well understood. The views of the people, on whose behalf the FOMC is meant to be acting, can be expressed through elected members of Congress twice a year. However, there is no political representation at FOMC meetings and a question we raised in relation to the ECB appears here also concerning the political remedy available if the people are unhappy with the Fed's actions.

This brings us back to the question of independence from the financial sector since financial markets can be seen to be the only part of the economy capable of damaging the Fed in response to the Fed's policies. Through their actions, the financial markets can make it much more difficult for the central bank to fulfil its mandate and can damage the reputations of central bankers. We have seen, in Chapter 13, a good example of this in relation to the value of the euro. The result of this is that the central bank might well feel itself more accountable to financial markets than to the political system. It is of interest in this regard that, as we report above, the Fed recently changed the way in which it expresses its views about the future prospects of the economy because of concern over the way in which its comments were being interpreted in the financial markets. This, of course, provides another reason why the desire expressed in the constitution of the Fed when it was set up in 1913, that it should be independent of both private financial business interests and duly constituted government authorities might not, in practice, be possible.

14.5 The Federal Reserve — recent monetary policy

The year 2001 saw the Fed principally concerned with the weakness of the US economy. As the US economy headed towards recession, there was no threat to the goal of price stability, and the Fed saw its task as cutting interest rates and providing generous liquidity to the banking system in the attempt to avoid recession. Concern about the future weakness of the economy intensified following the attack on the World Trade Centre and the Pentagon on 11 September.

It is clear from the actions and comments of the FOMC that it believes that monetary policy does have powerful real effects, at least in the short to medium term. This was despite the fact that the interest rate cuts were well anticipated by the financial markets. Differences of opinion regarding likely cuts largely centred on whether the cut would be one-quarter or one-half of one per cent or on whether the cut would be this or next month. The markets were never genuinely taken by surprise. This confirms that monetary policy is thought by practitioners to have powerful real effects whether policy is anticipated or not. This does not, of course, refute the proposition that money is neutral in the long run, but market practitioners act as if:

- the long-run is quite distant and

- short-run gains in employment and output are well worth having.

We return in these circumstances to simple Keynesian truths:

- if unemployment is rising and people fear for their jobs, they will reduce their spending

- if consumers reduce their spending, profits will fall and firms will reduce their output

- as profits fall, firms will cut investment

- as output and investment fall, firms will lay off workers.

The role of monetary policy in these circumstances is to encourage people to spend and firms to invest by lowering the cost of doing so. These points were made throughout 2001 in FOMC statements.

The decade of the 1990s had started with interest rates relatively high. At the beginning of July 1990, the target Fed funds rate stood at 8.25 per cent. The early 1990s, however, saw a downturn in all developed economies and the Fed set out on a long series of interest cuts, which saw the target rate fall sharply. In 1991, the Fed was extraordinarily active, making 10 cuts in the intended Fed funds rate, bringing it down from 7 per cent to 4 per cent. That is, the FOMC not only cut the interest rate at each of its 8 regular meetings, but also made further reductions in two special telephone linkups. Three more cuts followed in 1992, bringing the rate to 3 per cent by September, but this was as far as the Fed was prepared to go and the rate was then left unchanged for seventeen months until February 1994, by which time the US economy had started on a long period of rapid growth. The Fed, worried now about developing inflationary pressure, then pushed the rate up sharply. It made six increases in the target rate in 1994, two of fifty basis points and one (November) by the unusually large amount of 75 basis points. A further 50-basis-point increase in February 1995 meant that the rate had doubled from 3 per cent to 6 per cent in just twelve months. Perhaps this had been too far and too fast. In the following twelve months, three 25-point cuts had restored the target to 5.25 per cent.

Then came a period of extraordinary calm. Almost nothing happened from January 1996 until September 1998. In a period of two and three-quarter years, there was only a small increase in March 1997 as the economy kept growing but without generating serious concerns of inflation. Towards the end of 1998, a crisis developed in Asian financial markets and spread to

Russia and Latin America. An influential New York hedge fund, Long-Term Capital Management, was caught up in the financial market turmoil and a rescue had to be organized. There were short-lived fears that the world was headed for a serious financial crash. The Fed responded by cutting the intended Federal funds rate in its meetings in September, October, and November to leave it at 4.75 per cent by the end of 1998.

When the crash did not occur, the Fed turned its attention back to the US growth rate and the Chairman of the Board of Governors, Alan Greenspan, became worried by what he saw as excessive speculation leading to the overvaluation of equities, especially in the technology sector. The Fed cautioned calm and tried to bring this about through Greenspan's public statements and by steadily raising rates. Three increases in the intended rate in the second half of 1999, followed by three further rises in the first half of 2000, brought it up from 4.75 per cent to 6.5 per cent in a year. All of these changes are shown in Table 14.1.

At its meeting of 19 December 2000, the FOMC noted the slowing down of the US economy but left the intended Fed funds rate at 6.5 per cent. However, they had been sufficiently worried to signal the possibility of an emergency meeting before the regular meeting due at the end of January 2001. They took advantage of this and reduced the target rate by 50 points on January 3 and by a further 50 points at the regular meeting on January 31. Two interesting questions occur here:

1. To what extent was the FOMC looking ahead at its December 2000 meeting?

2. Were the two fifty-point cuts in January at all influenced by the fact that the Chairman's report to Congress was rapidly approaching?

We cannot know the answer to either of these questions but the minutes of the December 2000 meeting reported that the FOMC had, *inter alia*, been told that:

• economic activity, which had expanded at an appreciably lower pace since midyear, might have slowed further in recent months

• consumer spending and business purchases of equipment and software had decelerated markedly after having registered extraordinary gains in the first half of the year

• housing construction, though still relatively firm, was noticeably below its robust pace of earlier in the year

- inventory overhangs had emerged in a number of goods-producing industries with manufacturing production declining as a consequence

- initial claims for unemployment insurance continued to trend upward, and the civilian unemployment rate edged up to 4 percent in November, its average thus far this year

- the weakening of factory output in November was reflected in a further decline in the rate of capacity utilization in manufacturing to a point somewhat below its long-term average and

- consumer spending appeared to be decelerating noticeably further in the fourth quarter in an environment of diminished consumer confidence, smaller job gains, and lower stock prices.

Certainly not all the news was bad. The economy had grown very rapidly in the first half of 2000 and some slowdown was to be expected and possibly welcomed given the tight labour markets. However, inflationary pressures seemed to be declining quite rapidly. The Committee were told that one measure of inflation had 'remained at a relatively subdued level'. Another, it is true, 'appeared to be increasing very gradually' but this was attributed to the indirect effects of higher energy costs following earlier oil price increases.

Rather oddly, in making its statement regarding the assessment of risks, the Committee moved from 'risks weighted towards rising inflation' inflation in November to 'risks weighted toward economic weakness' in December, not taking advantage of the intermediate balanced risks assessment. Despite this, no change was made to the target Fed funds rate. Overall, the case for doing nothing on December 19 but then dropping the intended Fed funds rate by 50 points 15 days later does not suggest that the FOMC was looking very far forward on December 19.

As Table 14.1 shows, once the Fed settled into its rate-cutting mood, things started happening quickly. The intended Fed funds rate was cut at each scheduled FOMC meeting between January 31 and August 21, as well as at another unscheduled telephone meeting on April 18. The first four of these cuts were of 50 basis points with the result that the target rate plummeted by 3 per cent in fewer than eight months. Although in the early part of the year, the financial markets remained confident that the Fed would through its sharp cuts in interest rates keep the US economy out of recession, the need to cut rates so quickly as the economy headed down again raised doubts about the ability of central banks to forecast sufficiently well ahead.

In his explanation of Fed policy to Congress on 18 July 2001, Alan Greenspan raised an interesting point about the length of time lags. He defended the rapid series of cuts in the intended Federal flows rate by argu-

Table 14.1: Intended Federal Funds Rate
January 1991 to December 2001

Year	Date	New intended Fed funds rate (%)	Change (basis points)
1991	January 9	6.75	- 25
	February 1	6.25	- 50
	March 8	6.00	- 25
	April 30	5.75	- 25
	August 6	5.50	- 25
	September 13	5.25	- 25
	October 31	5.00	- 25
	November 6	4.75	- 25
	December 6	4.50	- 25
	December 20	4.00	- 50
1992	April 9	3.75	- 25
	July 2	3.25	- 50
	September 4	3.00	- 25
1994	February 4	3.25	+ 25
	March 22	3.50	+ 25
	April 18	3.75	+ 25
	May 17	4.25	+ 50
	August 16	4.75	+ 50
	November 15	5.50	+ 75
1995	February 1	6.00	+ 50
	July 6	5.75	- 25
	December 19	5.50	- 25
1996	January 31	5.25	- 25
1997	Mar 25	5.50	+ 25
1998	September 29	5.25	- 25
	October 15	5.00	- 25
	November 17	4.75	- 25
1999	January 30	5.00	+ 25
	August 24	5.25	+ 25
	November 16	5.50	+ 25
2000	February 2	5.75	+ 25
	March 21	6.00	+ 25
	May 16	6.50	+ 50
2001	January 3	6.00	- 50
	January 31	5.50	- 50
	March 20	5.00	- 50
	April 18	4.50	- 50
	May 15	4.00	- 50
	June 27	3.75	- 25
	August 21	3.50	- 25
	September 17	3.00	- 50
2001	October 2	2.50	- 50
	November 6	2.00	- 50
	December 11	1.75	- 25

ing that the depth of the downturn had been increased by the 'especially prompt and synchronous adjustment of production by business utilizing the faster flow of information coming from the adoption of new technologies'. This was expanded later in his statement in the following way:

> Because the extent of the slowdown was not anticipated by businesses, some backup in inventories occurred, especially in the United States. Innovations, such as more advanced supply-chain management and flexible manufacturing technologies, have enabled firms to adjust production levels more rapidly to changes in sales. But these improvements apparently have not solved the thornier problem of correctly anticipating demand.[18]

If all this is so, forecasts of turning points and depths of recessions, already difficult, will become more so. Monetary policy will have little choice other than to respond to events as they occur. Yet, we were told that in making the decision to cut rates by only 25 points in July (rather than the 50 points of the previous five reductions), the FOMC 'recognized that the effects of policy actions are felt with a lag'. If lags in the economy generally are changing and becoming shorter but time lags in monetary policy remain as long as ever, the practice of monetary policy will become ever more precarious.

The direction of US monetary policy in 2001 may well have been changed by the events of September 11. Although on August 21, the FOMC had continued to see the risks 'weighted mainly toward conditions that may generate economic weakness in the foreseeable future', there may well not have been a further cut in the target interest rate at the next scheduled meeting on October 2. However, the attack on the World Trade Centre and the Pentagon changed that as it led to immediate fears of a further loss in consumer confidence and serious problems for industries associated with air travel. The prospect that the downturn would be deeper than previously thought led the FOMC to have an emergency meeting on September 17, at which rates were cut by 50 points and further 50-point cuts followed on October 2 and November 6. A 25-point cut on December 11 reduced the target rate to 1.75 per cent, 4.75 per cent below the rate of 12 months earlier.

Of course, the sharp cuts in interest rate in the aftermath of September 11 were also, probably principally, intended to provide support for financial markets. The New York Stock Exchange remained closed for a week after the attack on the World Trade Centre and there were considerable fears regarding the way the markets would respond when it reopened. We thus had here another example of a Greenspan put option (see Section 12.3).

Although there were some relatively long periods of calm in the 1990s, there were, as Table 14.1 shows, other periods when the interest rate has been rushed down or up in a great hurry, notably, in 1990-91 (down) and in 1994-5 (up). The question we need to ask is whether this suggests that monetary policy is safe in the hands of the Fed since it shows the Fed as being decisive in the face of rapidly economic conditions. Alternatively, does it indicate that, for all the sophisticated policy models and the placing of monetary policy in the hands of experts, central banks are still largely flying by the seats of their pants?

14.6 Summary

The US central bank, the Federal Reserve System is not a single bank but a set of twelve regional reserve banks coordinated by a board in Washington D C. This structure can be explained by a look at the story of the development of the US banking system. This was dominated by two fears — of centralization with power concentrated in New York or Washington D C and of domination by the 'moneyed interests' of the financial sector. The result was a highly decentralized banking system with very large numbers of small banks. Two attempts in the late 18th and 19th centuries failed because of the fears of centralization. Consequently, the Federal Reserve System was not set up until 1913. The bank was required to be politically independent and independent of the financial sector. Initially, much of the power rested with the regional reserve banks. However, continued multi-bank panics and the lack of coordination evident at the time of the Great Depression in the 1930s led to a number of changes being made. This replaced the old Federal Reserve Board with the Board of Governors of the Federal Reserve and placed monetary policy in the hands of the Federal Open Market Committee (FOMC), which consisted of the seven members of the Board of Governors and five representatives of the regional reserve banks. One of the regional bank representatives is always from the Federal Reserve Bank of New York because it carries out open market operations on behalf of the FOMC. Power now rests with the centre, with the regional banks largely acting as local agencies of the Board of Governors. However, the presence of regional representatives on the FOMC means that it still pays more attention to economic conditions in the different parts of the country than is the case with many other central banks.

The Federal Reserve (the Fed) was required to act against both inflation and deflation and to act to encourage high employment and economic growth. However, over the past 25 years, price stability has become dominant in the bank's set of goals. The Fed has neither a target rate of inflation nor a target rate of growth of the money supply, but pays attention to a wide range of real and monetary indicators. It is required by law to calculate monetary growth ranges for M2 and M3 consistent with its price stability objective but does not believe that these are a reliable guide to policy.

The Fed carries out its policy through open market operations that seek to keep the Federal funds rate of interest — the interest rate that depository institutions pay when they borrow reserves overnight to meet reserve requirements. The reserve requirements are set to help the Fed control liquidity within the system but the ratios are seldom changed and are not used as a way of attempting to control the money supply. The Fed made half-hearted attempts to influence reserves in the 1970s and early 1980s (firstly through establishing a target range for the Fed funds rate, allowing for variations in the interest rate; and secondly by targeting non-borrowed and then borrowed reserves). However, these did not succeed in making the money supply exogenous. There is no doubt that the money supply is now endogenous.

Borrowed reserves are borrowings through the discount window, through which the Fed lends to banks as lender of last resort. The discount rate is usually kept below the Fed funds rate, but banks are discouraged from borrowing in this way except in emergencies.

The Fed is certainly politically independent but has in place a number of features that make it relatively accountable to the political system. However, the extent to which it can be said to independent of the financial sector is open to doubt. The recent performance of the Fed also raises questions regarding the extent to which it succeeds in looking ahead and adjusting interest rates sufficiently early to control problems that are developing in the economy.

Key concepts in this chapter

bank charters

state-chartered banks

federal-chartered banks

multi-bank panics

elastic currency

Federal Open Market Committee (FOMC)

monitoring ranges

lagged reserve accounting

contemporaneous reserve accounting

discount window

federal funds rate

reserve ratios

matched transactions

frown costs (non-pecuniary costs)

open market operations

central bank independence

transparency

accountability

Questions and exercises

1. List all of the possible functions of a central bank and consider which ones can be adequately performed without a central bank being in existence. What particular problems were caused by the absence of a central bank in the USA between 1836 and 1913.

2. Consider the extent to which the current structure of the Federal Reserve System is a product of

    (a) geography;
    (b) history;
    (c) planning.

3. How centralized is the US central bank system now? Do the regional Reserve Banks have more or less power than the national central banks within the European System of Central Banks?

4. Discuss whether the change in the balance of the objectives of the Federal Reserve over the years is a product of:
    (a) our greater knowledge of economics;
    (b) shifts in the balance of economic power within the country;
    (c) fashion (doing what other monetary authorities do).

5. If the Fed wishes to discourage banks from borrowing at the discount window except in emergencies, why does it keep the discount rate below the Federal funds rate?

6. Why does the Fed feel the need to maintain a system of reserve ratios when the Bank of England does not (apart from the small prudential ratio)?

7. Why do you think the Fed currently has a reserve ratio for sight deposits but not for demand deposits?

8. Does the FOMC engage in:

(a) inflation targeting;
(b) money supply targeting;
(c) nominal demand targeting?

Explain your answer in each case. If you think it does none of the above three, what does it do?

9. How useful are the phrases from which the FOMC chooses for describing its view of likely future developments in the US economy? What is the purpose of making statements of this kind?

10. A distinction is usually made between the 'transparency' of a central bank and its accountability. What is the difference? Consider the proposition that, while the monetary policy of the Fed is transparent, the FOMC is not genuinely accountable. Is it possible for a central bank to be accountable without being transparent?

Further reading

For a brief but good history of the Federal Reserve System, see *The New Palgrave Dictionary of Money and Finance*, (1992). A brief account of the whole US banking and financial system can be found in Howells and Bain (2002). A great deal of useful material is available on the web from the sites of the Federal Reserve System (www.federalreserve.gov) and the Federal Reserve Bank of New York (www.ny.frb.org). Wray (1990) and Moore (1988) provide detailed evidence to explain precisely why the money supply in the United States is endogenous.

Appendix 1:
The *IS/LM* model

Although it is not without its critics, the IS/LM model has been the dominant framework for the analysis of monetary impulses in the macroeconomy, almost since the day it was developed and published by Hicks (1937). This being the case, we make frequent reference throughout this book to the way in which particular issues might be represented in that model, or how the model may need to be modified in order to represent a particular state of affairs. For students not familiar with the model, therefore, this appendix provides firstly a formal algebraic and geometric derivation of the model, followed by a list of those issues raised in this book which might have some effect upon the *LM* curve, with some indication of what that effect might be.

Before we begin, however, some words of caution about interest rates are essential. 'The rate of interest' in the IS/LM model has to fulfil two roles: it has to represent the cost of funds for real investment projects (its *IS* role) and represent the opportunity cost of money (its *LM* role). The usual convention is to take i to be the long bond rate. This would be an appropriate rate at which to discount the returns from investment projects and is at least one of many returns available on non-money assets. (If one adopts Keynes's assumption of only two assets, it becomes the only rate available for non-money holders). If i is the long bond rate and it is meant to represent the opportunity cost of money, then we have to make the further assumption that money does not itself pay interest, i.e. money's own rate, i_m, $= 0$, otherwise we should need a change in the $i\text{-}i_m$ differential to represent a change in the opportunity cost. However, putting such a differential on the vertical axis would violate our first requirement that the interest term also represents the cost of investment funds. We can, as we shall see, introduce the idea of interest-bearing money but money's own rate has to be thought of as one of the many 'services' that money yields. Thus changes in i_m cause the money demand curve to shift.

Derivation

The *IS/LM* model is a comparative static representation of simultaneous equilibrium in the goods market ('real' sector) and the money market. The need for such a representation stems from the role of the rate of interest, which, on the one hand, serves to balance the demand for money with its supply, while at the same time determining the level of real investment spending to which savings must adjust — giving rise to a level of income that determines (in part) the demand for active money balances. It is this simultaneous oscillation between money market and goods market events, which the *IS/LM* model so conveniently captures, that accounts for its long popularity, other shortcomings notwithstanding.

Equilibrium in the goods market, shown by the *IS* curve, is defined as a situation in which planned injections are equal to planned withdrawals or:

$$J = W \qquad \text{...A1}$$

In a closed economy, this amounts to:

$$I + G = S + T \qquad \text{...A2}$$

where *I* and *G* stand for investment and government spending respectively and *S* and *T* indicate saving and taxation. If *I* is assumed to be negatively related to the rate of interest, while government spending is assumed to be exogenously determined as a policy decision, then:

$$J = Z - ii + \bar{G} \qquad \text{...A3}$$

If saving and taxation are both assumed to be proportional to income, *Y*, then:

$$W = sY + tY = (s + t)Y \qquad \text{...A4}$$

For equilibrium, therefore:

$$Z - ii + \bar{G} = (s + t)Y \qquad \text{...A5}$$

and:

$$Y = \frac{\bar{G} + Z - ii}{(s + t)} \qquad \text{...A6}$$

is the equation for the *IS* curve, giving the equilibrium value of income for any value of *i*. Notice that the curve has a negative slope given by $-(s + t)/i$. Thus any increase in the interest sensitivity of investment, *i*, causes the curve to be flatter, while increases in the savings propensity, s, or tax rate, t, have the same effect. Notice, too, that a new series of Y values for i is generated (the IS curve will shift) for any change in Z or G and the extent of the shift is given by $1/(s + t)$, the 'full multiplier' effect.

Figure A1: Derivation of the IS curve

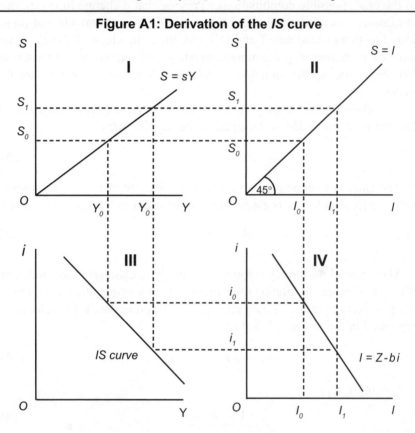

The same result can be achieved with a four quadrant diagram of the kind drawn in Figure A.1. To simplify the labelling of the diagram, we assume that a fixed amount of government spending is included in quadrant IV. The 'investment' schedule is really an 'investment plus government spending' schedule corresponding to equation A.3. Similarly, the 'savings' schedule in quadrant I is a 'savings plus taxation' schedule corresponding to equation A.4). At a rate of interest, i_0, injections in quadrant IV (including the interest sensitive component of investment) require a matching level of withdrawals indicated by S_0. These are forthcoming, in quadrant I, at a level of income Y_0. A fall in interest rates to i_1 induces some increase in injections — how much depends on the interest elasticity of investment, shown by the slope in quadrant IV. In equilibrium, these greater injections require a greater level of withdrawals, S_1. These are forthcoming only at Y_1. Plotting the two combinations, i_0/Y_0 and i_1/Y_1, in quadrant III enables us to draw the *IS* curve, from which we can read off all the other possible combinations. Proving that a change in tax, saving and interest coefficients changes the slope of the withdrawals and injections functions (quadrants I and IV) and, thus, the slope of the *IS* curve, and that a change in government spending and autonomous investment shift the injections function and the *IS* curve, is left as an exercise for the reader.)

Equilibrium in the money market, shown by the *LM* curve, requires the demand for money, *Md*, to be equal to the supply, *Ms*:

$$Md = Ms \qquad \qquad \text{...A6}$$

The latter is assumed to be fixed exogenously by the monetary authorities. At its simplest, it is assumed to be invariant to interest rates. Thus,

$$Ms = \bar{Ms} \qquad \qquad \text{...A7}$$

The demand for money responds positively to changes in income, negatively to changes in interest rates on non-money assets, the term i above, and positively to money's own rate, i_m. The responsiveness in each case is expressed in the terms a, b and c:

$$Md = aY - bi + ci_m \qquad \qquad \text{...A8}$$

Solving for *Y*:

$$Y = \frac{\bar{Ms} + bi - ci_m}{a} \qquad \qquad \text{...A9}$$

This is the equation for the *LM* curve enabling us to plot equilibrium values for Y and i in the money market. Notice that its slope with respect to i, the rate on non-money assets, is a/b. Since this is positive, the *LM* curve slopes upward with respect to i. The larger the income elasticity, a, the steeper the slope while the greater the coefficient, b, on the (non-money) interest rate the flatter the curve. A change in the exogenous money supply, $\bar{Ms}$, or in money's own rate, i_m, yields a new set of Y values for each value of i (ie the *LM* curve shifts) and a change in the coefficient c, changes the extent of the shift resulting from any change in money's own rate.

Figure A2: Derivation of the *LM* curve

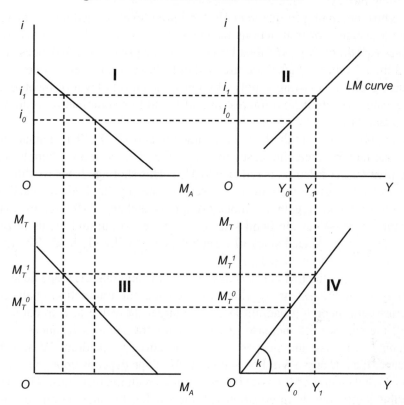

These relationships can be seen diagrammatically in Figure A2. The exogenous money supply is shown in quadrant II and is shown either by the distance O to M_A or O to M_T. The line joining the two axes at 45° indicates the money stock may be held either for transactions purposes, M_T, or asset purposes, M_A. Thus, at M_T the whole of the money supply is held for transactions purposes, while at M_A it is held entirely for asset purposes. Intermediate positions show the trade-off between money held for each purpose. Changes in the money stock are shown by parallel shifts (in or out) of the line in quadrant II.

Quadrants I and IV show the demand for money, broken down into the demand for asset balances and the demand for transactions balances respectively. It is assumed that prices are given and therefore, that in quadrant IV, the demand for transactions balances is a positive function of the level of real income. In quadrant I, the asset demand varies inversely with the rate of interest, which is assumed to represent the opportunity cost of holding money.

Thus, beginning in quadrant IV, the initial level of income, Y_0, generates a demand for transactions balances, M_T^0, leaving M_A^0 for asset purposes (quadrant IV). M_A^0 thus becomes the supply of asset balances, and quadrant I tells us that these are willingly held at an interest rate of i_0. Thus, given the existing supply of money, the current level of income, Y_0 generates an equilibrium interest rate of i_0 and this combination is shown in quadrant II.

Suppose now that the level of income increases to Y_1. The demand for transactions balances increases to M_T^1. With a fixed money supply, the supply of asset balances is reduced to M_A^1. This shortage leads wealthholders to try to restore their desired asset balances by (individually) selling bonds. In the aggregate, the money supply is unchanged (though its ownership changes) but the bond sales cause prices to fall and yields to rise until, at i_0, the reduced stock of asset balances is willingly held. The new equilibrium position is at Y_1, i_1.

Notice that the LM curve is upward sloping and that the slope depends firstly upon the extent to which the demand for transactions balances varies with income (quadrant IV). The larger the value of a in equation A9, the sharper the increase in demand for transactions balances when income increases; the steeper the demand curve in quadrant IV and the steeper the *LM* curve will be. Secondly, the slope depends upon the extent to which the demand for asset balances varies with interest rates. The larger the coefficient, b, in equation A9, the smaller the interest rate change required to accommodate a change in the supply of asset balances; the flatter is the demand curve in quadrant I and the *LM* curve in quadrant II.

Note, next, that a change in the quantity of money, shown by a shift of the curve in quadrant III, leads to a new set of equilibrium interest rates for each level of income (the *LM* curve shifts). The *LM* curve shifts downward following an increase in money stock and upward following a reduction. Lastly, note that a change in money's own rate of return, i_m, causes a shift of the asset demand curve in quadrant I. An increase in i_m, *ceteris paribus* causes an increase in the demand for money as an asset, the demand curve shifts out and a new, higher, level of (non-money) interest rates is generated. In these circumstances the *LM* curve shifts upward. A reduction in i_m results in a downward shift of the *LM* curve.

We turn now to some of the issues discussed elsewhere in this book and their representation in the *IS/LM* framework.

A taxonomy of LM impacts

The elasticity of the demand for money (mainly Chapter 5)

The coefficient, b, on i is larger (for high interest elasticity) and smaller (for low elasticity). In figure A.2 the demand curve is steep when the elasticity is low making for a steep LM curve. Notice that in the extreme case where $b = 0$, equation A9 reduces to:

$$Y = \frac{\overline{M}s - ci_m}{a} \qquad \qquad ...A10$$

and the LM curve is vertical. Conversely, when $b = ¥$, the LM curve is horizontal.

Financial innovation and the demand for money (Sections 6.2 and 11.3)

The effect depends upon the nature of the innovation.

i) Where the innovations result in the creation of additional money substitutes, the effect is to increase the elasticity of the demand for money with respect to non-money interest rates. The coefficient on i is larger, and the Md and LM curves are flatter.

ii) Where the innovations lead to a rise in interest rates paid on bank deposits, or to an increase in the proportion of such deposits which pay interest, then there is a rise in money's own rate, i_m. *Ceteris paibus* the demand for money increases. In figure A2 the demand curve in quadrant I lies further from the origin and so the non-money rate is higher. The LM curve shifts upward.

iii) Where the innovations are part of increased competition on the lending side, a reduction in the spread between lending rates and money's own rate $(i_L - i_m)$ also leads to an increase in the demand for money with the formal consequences described in the last paragraph. This arises because people are more inclined to finance a deficit by borrowing than by running down existing holdings of liquid assets. Notice that the same effect follows from a reduction in the non-pecuniary costs of borrowing (lower collateral, higher lending multiples, fewer administrative requirements etc). In our derivation of the LM curve, we make no reference to the demand for money being affected by lending rates. Neither does anyone else. But empirical studies of the demand for money do recognize a connection.

Wealth effects (mainly Chapter 6)

In the basic goods and money market equations above, both savings and the demand for money are given as functions of current income (Y). However, it has long been recognized that the economy's stock of wealth plays a role in both markets. Although it is possible simply to re-write these equations substituting wealth (or permanent income - the income expected to be generated in the future by the existing stock of wealth) for current income, the conventional *IS/LM* approach is to treat wealth as an additional element in the equations. Thus, a change in the stock of wealth causes the *IS* and *LM* curves to shift.

An increase in wealth, *ceteris paribus*, causes an increase in demand for assets of all types including consumer durables. Thus, consumption increases at each level of income and savings fall. To maintain equilibrium, investment must also fall and this only occurs at a higher rate of interest. Thus, each level of income is associated in equilibrium with a higher rate of interest than before and the *IS* curve shifts out to the right. It should also be noted that an increase in wealth produces an increase in the demand for investment (particularly in the demand for housing) at each rate of interest. If we consider this separately from the consumption effect, we see that to maintain equilibrium following the increase in wealth, savings must increase and this requires a higher current income level. Again, the *IS* curve shifts to the right.

This contrasts with the negative effect on the *LM* curve. This arises because an increase in wealth produces also an increase in the demand for money. But since the supply of money is assumed to be exogenously determined, it does not change. Thus, to maintain equilibrium the demand for money cannot change and there must be an offsetting change in the other variables influencing the demand for money — either the interest rate must rise, causing a fall in the asset or speculative demand for money; or current income must fall causing a fall in the transactions demand for money. Whichever way one looks at it, the *LM* curve moves up to the left. This is shown in Figures 7.5 and 7.6.

How much the *IS* and *LM* curves shift depends on the strength of the wealth effect in the consumption, investment and demand for money functions.

Instability of the demand for money (Chapter 5)

The *LM* curves we have drawn to this point have assumed that the demand for money is a stable function of income and interest rate and can be fully explained by them. Thus, a change in Y or i causes a predictable movement along the LM curve, while a change in i_m causes the LM curve to shift by a predictable amount, with the size of the shift depending on the size of the constant c. However, if the demand for money is influenced by variables not included in the equation it shifts around in an unpredictable way. As we see in Chapter 5, a crucial part of Keynes's argument was that the demand for money was influenced not just by the current interest rate (i) but also by the expected future interest rate and that this would also be influenced by a change in i. It follows that a fall in the current interest rate causes a movement down the existing LM curve but may also a produce a shift in the whole curve, to the extent that an expectation of a future interest rate change is generated. It may also be the case that expectations of future interest rate changes arise from other sources - changes in foreign interest rates, political disturbances, forecast rates of inflation etc.. Then the LM curve may shift with no change in any of the variables listed in equation A8.

What is crucial to the outcome in this example is whether we can successfully model expectations and incorporate them into our equation. If we can, we shall simply have another variable to which the demand for money is stably related. If we cannot, the demand for money function is unstable and the LM curve moves around in an unpredictable way. Other potential sources of instability in the demand for money function are discussed in Chapter 6.

Elasticity of money supply (Chapter 3)

We derived the LM curve under the normal assumption that $Ms = \overline{Ms}$. More realistically, one might expect Ms to respond positively to changes in (non-money) interest rates, even when reserve requirements and the quantity of monetary base are fixed exogenously. This arises because banks' clients switch from cash to deposits and from non-interest bearing to interest bearing deposits as interest rates rise. The switch from cash makes more of the monetary base available to banks while the switch between deposits usually amounts to a switch towards time deposits against which banks need to hold smaller reserves. This is a way of saying that the bank deposit multiplier is positively related to interest rates. In these circumstances, we could specify $Ms = M + gi$, where M is determined by the size of base, reserve requirements and the value of the multiplier when $i = 0$. In Figure 3.1, Ms is drawn with a slight positive slope. The reader should confirm that shifting the demand curve up a positively sloped Ms curve generates a lower value of i for each shift of the demand curve and the LM curve is flatter. In these circumstances equation A9 should be modified to:

$$Y = \frac{M + gi + bi - ci_m}{a} \qquad \qquad \text{...A11}$$

g is the slope of the Ms curve. An increase in g increases the slope and makes the LM curve flatter.

Endogeneity of money supply (Chapters 3 and 4)

In allowing Ms a positive slope we have continued the assumption of exogeneity. The curve shifts only when the monetary authorities choose to change the quantity of money through changes in the monetary base, reserve requirements or whatever. As we have seen, however, the authorities target the level of interest rates. In this situation the quantity of money is determined by the demand for loans and the willingness to hold the resulting deposits at that level of interest rates. The demand (for loans and deposits) at the going level of interest rates is assumed to be determined by the price level and output. In these circumstances, the money supply is determined by other variables within the economy, that is to say, endogenously. It has become a common practice to represent an endogenously determined money supply by a horizontal Ms curve. The reader can easily check that if Ms is drawn horizontally, and the demand curve shifts as a result of income changes, then the LM curve must also be horizontal. This is a convenient practice but is best thought of as a 'stylized fact'. A horizontal Ms curve implies that $g = \infty$ in equation A11, i.e. that the multiplier is infinitely elastic with respect to the interest rate on non-money assets. No one has ever suggested this to be the case. Supporters of the endogenous money case point to the authorities being willing to supply whatever quantity of monetary base is required, given the demand for loans and money at the pre-set level of interest rates. It is M in equation A11 that adjusts without limit. The strictly correct diagrammatic representation of this is an Ms curve which is free to shift without limit. If the MS curve shifts at exactly the same rate as the Md curve, then the LM curve could still be horizontal, but only in these circumstances. (Perfectionists might also care to note that an Ms curve drawn horizontally is drawn horizontally with respect to the wrong rate of interest. The endogeneity case is that the money supply is perfectly elastic at the discount rate set by the central bank. As we pointed out at the start of this appendix, the rate of interest in Figures A1 and A2 must be the long bond rate. This is not the same thing at all.)

Financial innovation and the money supply (Chapter 11)

As with the demand for money, the effect depends upon the nature of the innovation. It also depends upon the monetary regime in question and whether the money supply is exogenously or endogenously determined. Since this is sometimes a matter of controversy and/or judgement, the perception of the effects of innovation is also a matter of controversy.

i) Where the money supply is exogenously determined, the key variables are the size of the monetary base, the size of the multiplier and the elasticity of the multiplier with respect to interest rates. If the base is defined unambiguously to include only liabilities of the central bank, the base is held wholly and exclusively by banks and banks are subject to a mandatory reserve requirement, then the scope for innovation to affect the money stock through the three channels we have mentioned is very limited (though in such a case innovations to facilitate disintermediation may develop rapidly, taking business offshore, for example). In the UK, most of *M0* is notes and coin and notes and coin are held outside the banking system. Thus any innovation which enables the non-bank public to economise on cash increases the quantity of base available to banks. The *Ms* (and *LM*) curves shift to the right. Such innovations may also make the switch between cash and deposits easier, increasing the interest-sensitivity of the multiplier. In equation A11, the value of *g* increases, the *Ms* curve becomes more elastic and the *LM* curve becomes flatter.

ii) Where the money supply is endogenously determined, the authorities' control is limited to setting interest rates and accepting the resulting quantities. What is at issue here is the effect of innovation upon the interest elasticity of demand for bank lending and upon the demand for money. The picture can be very complex since it is often the behaviour of relative interest rates that is crucial. The major innovation of interest bearing bank sight deposits in the UK in the 1980s is a good example since it simultaneously lowered the cost of bank lending as a source of finance relative to drawing on existing deposits and made it more difficult for the authorities to raise the relative cost of bank borrowing by raising the official discount rate since all (relevant) rates tended to move together. one can show none of this in the stylized world of horizontal *LM* curves. The best one can say is that if an innovation makes borrowing more attractive the *Ms* curve shifts (the authorities providing the base to make this possible); if the innovation makes the demand for bank loans less responsive to interest rates then the *Ms* curve shifts more rapidly over time (the money supply growing more quickly and the authorities having to validate the growth by expanding the base).

IS/LM and the Open Economy (Chapter 10)

The *IS/LM* model must be adjusted in a number of ways to enable it to be used to deal with open economy issues. Most notably, we need a third curve, the *BP* line, which expresses balance in the balance of payments. For the balance of payments to be in balance, any surplus/deficit in the current account must be offset by an equivalent deficit/surplus in the capital account. Thus:

$$B = Bc + Bk \qquad\qquad ...\text{A}12$$

where B is the overall balance of payments, Bc is the balance on current account and Bk represents net capital inflow.

In a simple version, the current account is represented by the balance of trade (exports – imports). Exports are taken to be a function of world income and the international competitiveness of home exports and this, in turn, depends on home prices relative to those abroad, expressed through the exchange rate, in a common currency. Since the *IS/LM* model assumes both constant home prices and a fixed exchange rate, and since both world income and foreign prices are outside of the control of the home government, exports may be written as an exogenous variable. Imports, on the other hand, are a function of domestic income and the international competitiveness of home goods. The net result is that domestic income is the only endogenous variable affecting the current account balance and we may write:

$$B_c = \overline{X} - IM(Y) \qquad\qquad ...\text{A}13$$

It follows that as income increases, *ceteris paribus*, imports increase and the balance on current account worsens. The extent to which it worsens as income increases depends upon the country's marginal propensity to import (*IM*). This changes over time (in the UK's case it has steadily increased) but can be assumed to be constant in the short run.

Net capital inflow (the capital account balance) depends on home interest rates relative to those in the rest of the world and the expected change in exchange rates. In a fixed exchange rate model, the second term drops out and net capital inflow is seen to depend on home interest rates in comparison with the exogenous world interest rates. Consequently, we have:

$$B_k = f(i - i^*) \qquad\qquad ...\text{A}14$$

where *i* represents domestic interest rates and *i** interest rates in the rest of the world. As *i* increases, *ceteris paribus*, capital inflow increases. The extent to which this happens depends on the degree of international capital mobility. The more mobile capital is among countries, the greater is the change in net capital inflow following a change in relative interest rates.

By putting together information from (A13) and (A14) we can come to a conclusion about the general shape of the *BP* curve. Remember, that as income increases, ceteris paribus, the balance on current account worsens. Thus, for the overall balance of payments to remain in balance, the balance on capital account must be improving. But this only occurs if the domestic interest rate is rising relative to world interest rates. It is clear then that the *BP* curve must have a positive slope in the general case. It is also clear that, other things being equal:

(a) it is more steeply sloped, the higher is the marginal propensity to import;

(b) it is less steeply sloped, the more mobile is international capital.

In practice, for developed countries at least, the degree of international capital mobility is the dominating factor and it is common to draw as a special case a perfectly elastic *BP* curve, which assumes perfect mobility of capital. This implies that domestic interest rates cannot vary from world rates (any slight movement of domestic rates above/below world rates causes immediate inflows/outflows of capital, which drive domestic rates back to the world rate). The general case is shown as BP_0 in Figure A.3 while BP_1 represents the case of perfect capital mobility.

Figure A3: Open economy *IS/LM*

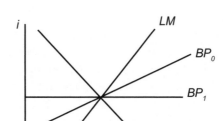

As indicated in Figure A3, it is normal to draw the *BP* curve for developed countries as having a less steep slope than the *LM* curve, implying that net capital inflow is significantly more interest elastic than the demand for money. A *BP* curve for a less developed economy might, on the other hand, be drawn more steeply sloped than the *LM* curve. Readers should consider what this implies.

The final step with the *BP* curve is to consider what happens when the exchange rate changes. A depreciation of the exchange rate (a fall in the value of the domestic currency), *ceteris paribus*, increases a country's exports and reduces its imports resulting in an improvement in the current account at every level of income. It follows that to maintain overall balance in the balance of payments, there must be a matching capital outflow and this only occurs if the domestic interest rate is lower at every level of domestic income. In other words, the *BP* curve shifts down. Equally, an exchange rate appreciation will push the *BP* curve up.

Appendix II:
The Term Structure of Interest Rates

The relationship between interest rates on assets differentiated solely by their term to maturity is known as the 'term structure of interest rates' and a graphical representation is known as a 'yield curve'. We look at this relationship here for two reasons. The first is that in Section 4.2 we noted that changes in short-term interest rates might not be fully reflected in changes in medium and long-rates because other factors played a part. We look in a moment at these factors. Secondly, in Section 12.4 we noted that the shape of the yield curve (and changes in its shape) have often played a role in policy-making. We explain the argument behind this use of the curve.

Figure A4: The yield curve

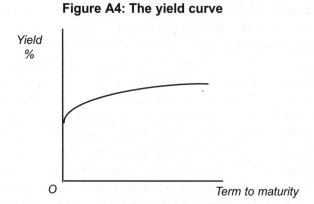

Figure A4 shows what is often referred to as a 'typical' or 'normal' yield curve. Notice that it is upward-sloping and thus shows yields increasing with the term to maturity. The idea that this is a 'normal' shape must be based upon an argument that there is something so systematically unattractive about long dated assets (bonds, for example), that people have to be paid an inducement (a premium) to hold them. It is tempting to jump to the conclusion that the premium must be due to the comparative illiquidity of long-dated bonds: if investors are to commit their funds for a long period there must be an additional reward. But this confuses 'term to maturity' with 'holding period'. An investor can buy short- or long-dated bonds today and sell them tomorrow. There is a large and active market for bonds of all maturities and she can hold a bond of any maturity for any period that she likes, up to the date of its redemption. The characteristic that is strictly speaking responsible for the positive term-premium is that long bonds show a greater price sensitivity to changes in interest rates than do short-dated bonds. If we define 'duration' as the weighted average length of time that it takes for an investor to receive the total cashflows from a bond, then it is pretty clear that duration increases with the term to maturity. Note also that, for a given term to maturity, duration is also inversely related to the size of the coupon since the effect of a high coupon is to bring forward the bulk of cashflows and thus to reduce the weighted average length of time that it takes to receive them. Now assume that a bond's market price equals the present value of the future cashflows. The present value is arrived at by discounting and the effect of discounting depends upon both the size of the discount rate and the length of time that we have to wait for the payment. Consequently, long-deferred payments are more seriously affected by a change in discount rate than payments which accrue in the near-term. All of this can be demonstrated by the arithmetic of bond pricing and some further arithmetic can show that duration measures the elasticity of bond prices with respect to changes in interest rates (Howells and Bain, 2002, ch.16; Blake, 2000, ch.5)

Even this characteristic, however, is not sufficient on its own to explain a systematic upward bias to the yield curve. We need the further assumption that investors do not like this characteristic or, more strictly, that more investors dislike this characteristic of long-dated bonds than prefer the positive characteristic of long-dated bonds, namely that they provide an absolutely guaranteed income if held to maturity. We need the assumption that, on balance, the bond market is dominated by capital-risk averse, as opposed to income-risk averse investors. If this is true, the majority of investors in long-dated bonds need some additional compensation for the risk of price fluctuations. Other things being equal, the steepness of the curve indicates the strength of this aversion capital-risk aversion and thus it follows that changes in the degree of capital risk aversion will cause changes in the slope and thus in the relation between short and long rates.

Furthermore, the slope of the curve is likely to be influenced by expectations of future short-term rates. Imagine an investor who is prepared to invest in bonds for more than the shortest possible period, then he or she has the choice of making a single investment for the whole period or a series of shorter-term investments. In the simplest case we might take the investor who wishes to invest for two years and can thus buy now a two-year bond (which we shall call 'long') or a one-year bond ('short'), reinvesting the proceeds in another one-year bond in one year's time. Now let us assume that the current structure of interest rates (whatever it is) is an equilibrium structure. Investors are happy, in other words, with this structure (this is a reasonable assumption, since, if they were not, they could buy and sell bonds of different maturities causing yields to change until they were happy). Being happy with this structure means that investors (like ours) must be indifferent between holding a two-year bond and a succession of two one-year bonds. Formally speaking, the following must hold:

$$(1+i_2)^2 = (1+i_1) \times (1 + E^2 i_1) \qquad \text{...A15}$$

where i_2 is the *current* two-year interest rate (the rate available now on a two-year) bond, i_1 is the *current* one-year rate and E^2i^1 is the one-year rate *expected* in the second year. Now suppose that $i_1 = 6$ per cent while $i_2 = 7$ per cent. It is a fairly simple task to calculate what investors must be expecting about the one year rate in one year's time, by rearranging A15.

$$E^2 i_1 = \frac{(1+i_2)^2}{(1+i_1)} - 1 \qquad \text{...A16}$$

Using our figures we have:

$$^2i_1 = \frac{(1.07)^2}{(1.06)} - 1 = \frac{1.1449}{1.06} - 1 = 1.0801 - 1 = .0801 \text{ or } 8.01\% \qquad \text{...A17}$$

Thus, if the current one year rate is 6 per cent while the current two year rate is 7 per cent, it must be the case that investors expect to be able to reinvest in one year's time at slightly more than 8 per cent. Clearly, if current one year rates are 6 per cent and two year rates are 7 per cent, the yield curve is upward sloping. In these circumstances, it seems that investors must expect future short-term rates to be higher, and not just higher than current short term rates but higher even than current long rates (8.01>7). In short, an upward sloping yield curve implies higher short rates in future while a downward sloping yield curve implies lower short rates in future.

If there were no other influences on the yield curve (no capital risk aversion, for example) then expectations that current short rates were not going to change would produce a horizontal yield curve. But these influences are not mutually exclusive. If capital-risk aversion is generally present then all yield curve will have an upward bias added to whatever slope would result from interest rate expectations. If these were neutral, for example, then the yield curve would not be horizontal but would have an upward slope as a result of the risk premium; if investors expected interest rates to fall, then the yield curve might be downward sloping, but less steeply than it would have been if expectations were the only influence. If expectation about the future course of interest rates are normally distributed around a mean of 'no change', then capital risk aversion means that the curve will slope upwards more frequently than it will slope downwards. Hence the idea of the upward slope as 'normal'.

Now we can see why (in Section 4.2) we suggested that the communication of changes in central banks' official interest rates, at the very short end of the maturity spectrum, to medium and long-term rates is complex. We can see that a rise (for example) in official rates could be modified at medium and long parts of the spectrum by changes in capital risk aversion. More likely the effect will be modified by expectations.

Thus, if financial markets believe that an increase in the official rate is the first of a series of rises (because they can see inflationary pressures developing), longer-term rates will follow short-term rates up. However, an increase in the official rate might persuade the markets that inflation will fall in future, allowing official rates to come down again. In this case, a rise in the official rate would produce expectations of lower future interest rates and long rates might even fall, while short rates go up. This is more likely to occur when short rates are moved to what appear to be historically 'extreme' levels in pursuit of policy objectives. Hence, downward sloping ('inverted') yield curves do sometimes appear when short rates are raised to counter inflationary pressure. As we note in 4.2, much depends here on demand conditions in the other major economies, especially that of the USA, and the expected policies of other central banks, notably the Federal Reserve Board (the Fed).

The expectations theory of the term structure has been subjected to intensive empirical testing over the years (see Malkiel, 1992 for a survey). Generally, speaking, the tests have not been encouraging though it is not clear, strictly speaking, whether this is because interest differentials are not driven by expectations or whether they are driven by expectations but the expectations are incorrect. The testing continues, however, partly because the dataset is almost limitless (different definitions of short/long, different time periods etc); partly because changes in econometric techniques allow new tests to be carried out; and partly because it just is very hard to believe that agents make forecasts of interest rates which are frequently incorrect or that they are irrational and do not do the sort of calculations we have done above. There is another reason, however, for the reluctance to abandon the expectations theory and this is that there is a big policy prize at the end of this particular rainbow.

This can be most easily understood if we introduce what is frequently called the Fisher hypothesis which states that the nominal (risk-free, short-term) rate of interest is composed of a real rate of interest which is stable and an inflation premium which varies with inflation so as to maintain the stability of the real rate. In symbols:

$$i = r + \pi \qquad\qquad ...\text{A18}$$

where i is the nominal rate, r is the real rate and π is the rate of inflation. Now, just suppose that the current term structure did enable us to make reliable forecasts of future short-term rates. We could take our earlier example which suggested that short-term rates would rise from 6 to 8 per cent in the near future. Then if we knew, from past observation, that the real rate was usually about 3 per cent, then our yield curve would enable us to forecast future inflation rates as well as future short-term interest rates. This would be immensely useful for central banks and other policy makers.

Unfortunately, as we have said, tests of the term structure's forecasting ability have not been very encouraging. Furthermore, the evidence suggests that real interest rates are not so stable as would be required for the simple kind of calculation that we have just done. At the moment, it does not seem possible to make accurate forecasts about either the level of future interest rates or the level of future inflation rates.

However, the fact that the term structure cannot be used to forecast a particular value, does not mean that it has no value to policy makers. Provided we think that expectations play some part in determining the shape of the curve and that an inflation premium plays some part in the nominal interest rate, then, with some degree of caution, we might be prepared to regard changes in the shape of the yield curve as indicating something about changes in inflationary pressures. A sudden steepening of the yield curve, for example, might be read as indicating that markets expect the rate of inflation to rise in future (even if it cannot tell us the actual rate). Similarly, a flattening of the curve might suggest a future reduction in inflationary pressure and serve as an indication to a central bank that it can reduce the official interest rate, especially if there is other supporting evidence of a moderation of inflation. In this limited role, the yield curve, and more especially changes in the shape of the yield curve has come to be one of the many information variables which central banks have come to use in setting interest rates. We look at attempts to extract information from the bond and other markets in Section 12.4.

Endnotes

Chapter 1

1. This includes the idea that, in past societies, money has taken the form of colourful objects such as 'cattle, tobacco, leather and hides, furs, olive oil, beer or spirits, slaves or wives, copper, iron, gold, silver, rings, diamonds, wampum beads or shells, huge rocks and landmarks, and cigarette butts'. This list is taken from Samuelson (9e, 1973).

2. It is possible for a firm to be bankrupted because their resources are insufficiently liquid but this implies an inability to borrow and, thus, a judgement by financial intermediaries about the true value of the firm's illiquid resources.

3. Essentially notes and coins (see Chapter 1).

4. In making this argument, Wray quotes extensively from Polanyi (1971).

5. In modern economies, seigniorage takes many forms. For example, in international economics, the willingness of countries and central banks to hold and use US dollars after World War II converted US dollars into a world currency and the US government obtained benefits (or seigniorage) as the issuer of the currency. It gave the USA the ability to run Balance of Payments deficits and thus to expand the economy to a greater extent than would otherwise have been possible and to spend freely abroad.

6. This led to Gresham's Law stated by Sir Thomas Gresham in 1558 as 'bad money always drives out good'.

Chapter 3

1. In many systems the expression 'non-bank private sector' is used to denote the general (non-government) public whose holdings of deposits are part of the money stock. In the UK, M4 includes building society as well as bank deposits and so the relevant deposit holders have to be identified as the 'non-bank, non-building society, private sector'. Fortunately, this is usually shortened to 'M4 private sector' or simply 'M4PS'.

2. The suggestion that deposits and loans (and changes in them) must match may seem strange. It does involve a small simplification in that it abstracts from shareholders' funds on the liabilities side. But this apart, the statement is correct since all bank assets are loans in some shape or form. Securities/investments are loans (mainly to government) backed by securities. Since notes and coin are issued by government, holdings of these are also in effect loans to the

public sector as are deposits at the central bank — since the central bank is also part of the public sector. If necessary, changes in shareholders funds can be incorporated in the following derivations by the addition of a term, ΔNDL for changes in 'non-deposit liabilities'.

Chapter 4

1. 'This, alas, is not a caricature...Indeed this is how the determination of the money supply is introduced in macromodels in most of the current leading textbooks.' (Goodhart, 2002, p.16). The textbooks include Mankiw, (4e, 2000, ch.18) and Burda and Wyplosz (1997, ch.9) amongst others.

2. They need also to be able to make transfers of funds to other banks as payments take place between clients of different banking firms.

3. Or, indeed, a tightening of monetary policy itself. Assume that this leads to a rise in price, increase in collateral requirements, and reduction in supply of credit from non-bank sources. The inevitable consequence will be a jump in overdraft utilisation and the liquidity problems described here unless the Central Bank relieves the shortage.

4. This illustration also draws attention to an asymmetry in the loan/deposit creation process. Central Banks can initiate a monetary expansion, through open market operations and expansion of the base; they cannot (at tolerable cost) initiate a reduction by reversing the process (see Moore, 1986, 1988a).

5. Supporters of the view that central bank behaviour matters little include Minsky (1982, 1986), Rousseas (1986), Pollin (1991) and Dow (1993, 1994). Niggle (1991) points out that the degree of (and the possibilities for) reserve-economising innovation will depend upon institutional features of the regime.

6. In its explanation of the 'new monetary policy framework' the UK Treasury makes no reference to 'reserves' or 'monetary base' though it does explain at length the Monetary Policy Committee's responsibility (and procedures) for setting interest rates. It also points out that the responsibility for the management of government debt was transferred from the Bank to the Treasury's Debt Management Office in 1998, thus denying the Bank access to the open market operations that would be essential for the targeting of reserves. (Treasury, 2002, ch.3).

7. Consider the flow of funds approach again. In this framework changes in the quantity of money are 'explained' by changes in the components of aggregate bank lending. As Cuthbertson pointed out '..the reader may be wondering what has happened to the demand for money in this analysis. There is an implicit demand for money in the model but only in *equilibrium*.' (1985a, p.173. Emphasis in original).

8. In the 'Post-Keynesian' tradition it is sometimes argued that the demand for money is completely irrelevant: agents will hold whatever quantity of deposits are generated by loans. Where money creation is concerned, loan demand is

everything. (See Kaldor (1982), and Moore (1997)). For an alternative view see Howells (1995 and 1997).

9. At the end of 1995, OFI and ICC shares combined accounted for only 40 per cent of the outstanding stock. The remaining 60per cent was held by the personal sector.

10. For the results of causality tests see Moore (1988a, 1989); Palley (1994); Howells and Hussein (1998); Caporale and Howells (2001).

11. After initially arguing that targeting the (exogenous) money stock was misguided because of infinitely variable velocity, by the early 1980s Kaldor was adopting the position here, namely that changes in money were an *effect* not a cause. (See Kaldor, 1982).

12. A situation recognised by Sprenkle and Miller as long ago as 1980 and much referred to since in demand for money studies, without apparent recognition of its significance.

Chapter 5

1. For a brief but clear survey of pre-Quantity Theory views and of the development of the Quantity Theory, see Visser (1974). More detail is provided in Harris, 1985 and Humphrey, 1974. For a discussion of the contributions of Alfred Marshall and earlier writers to the Quantity Theory tradition, see Eshag, 1963.

2. Harris, 1985, examines the pre-Keynesian Quantity Theory tradition in some detail and stresses the complexity of the body of thought surrounding it. He refers to the expression of the Quantity Theory in terms of a change in the quantity of money producing a proportional change in the absolute price level as the Crude Quantity Theory.

3. See Bain and Howells (1991)

4. Patinkin, 1965, argued that the Cambridge approach was quite different from the Quantity Theory because the Quantity Theory made no assumption as to why money was held. It operated through changes in the money stock influencing the goods market via a real balance effect. In this view, the Quantity Theory should be represented by a hyperbolic market equilibrium curve rather than a demand for money curve. For a full account of the derivation of the real balance effect, the problems associated with it, and its significance see Harris, 1985.

5. In other words, people were assumed to hold regressive expectations

6. Short but helpful explanations of the finance motive can be found in Chick, 1983, and Rousseas, 1986. Keynes's original article can be found in JMK, 1973, vol XIV pp 201-23.

7. For details of theoretical extensions and criticisms of the basic model see, in particular, Akerlof and Milbourne (1978, 1980). Gowland, 1991, provides a good account of both the model and its defects.

8. Sprenkle (1969, 1972) claimed the theory to be useless in regard to large firms with multiple branches and accounts. See also Cuthbertson, 1985a, and Cuthbertson and Barlow, 1991.

9. For this criticism, see Fisher, 1989, and Karni, 1974. Gowland (1991) illustrates the point with some approximate calculations.

10. A number of other writers have produced risk aversion models based upon the same broad premises as Tobin. For a discussion of these and later models see Cuthbertson and Barlow, 1991.

11. The original (1956) version of the equation had the demand for nominal balances as a function of a similar set of variables plus the general price level (P). To produce the 1970 version, Friedman assumed the function homogeneous of degree one in both prices and permanent income, enabling him to divide throughout by P and Yp.

12. Much to Patinkin's displeasure.

Chapter 6

1. The *Foundations of Monetary Economics* (Laidler, 1999), a recent three-volume collection, contains 17 essays on the demand for money and nothing on the supply of money!

2. Flow variables are measured per period of time (e.g. GDP per annum); stock variables are measured at a particular time (the supply of money at 31 December 2001).

3. The date of the 'Big Bang' in the equities and bonds markets, in which many changes were made in institutional arrangements.

4. Mayer (1978) includes 'reliance on small macroeconometric models' as one of his 12 propositions associated with monetarism.

5. Other US studies which indicated instability in the demand for money function at this time include Pierce (1975), Enzler *et al* (1976) and Meyer (1976).

6. Note, however, that where the income elasticity of demand for money is used to gather up exogenous changes not reflected elsewhere in the demand for money function, we cannot draw conclusions about the rate at which the supply of money should increase in relation to increases in real income. Thus, Friedman's high (1959) estimate of the income elasticity of M2 in the USA is now generally accepted to have reflected influences such as the growth of banking. This high income elasticity (1.8) led Friedman to call money a luxury good.

Chapter 7

1. Or, of course, if the government controlled the printing presses, through the printing of money.

2. The increase in wealth, to the extent that it causes people to feel better off, might lead them to choose a higher degree of liquidity — increasing hoarding rather than expenditure. Then, the wealth elasticity of demand for money might be higher than for illiquid financial or real assets.

3. The strongest Keynesian argument against the Ricardian equivalence position can be found in Dow and Earl, 1982, p.128, where it is rejected as 'absolute nonsense'.

Chapter 8

1. It could equally well be called the non-decelerating-inflation rate of unemployment since any level of unemployment above the natural rate will also only be temporary and will be the result of inflation decelerating below workers' expected inflation rate.

2. In most formulations of adaptive expectations, much heavier weights are applied to recent experience but people give some weight to experience from many previous years. This causes workers' inflationary expectations to approach the new rate of inflation relatively quickly but it might be many years before the expectations are actually correct

3. Although all rejections of hypotheses about expectations-determined events, are hard to interpret since they may be rejections of the theory of expectations formation rather than of the hypothesis itself.

4. Compare this list with the points mentioned in Box 13.4

5. That is a central banker who is more concerned about fluctuations in inflation (as compared to fluctuations in output) than is true of the society in general

Chapter 9

1. This omits other possibilities e.g. that, in periods of high unemployment, it may be possible to reduce unemployment without inflationary consequences.

2. A prior question is the standard of measurement to be used e.g. in the case of inflation, which price index provides the best guide to the success or failure of policy: the retail price index, the underlying rate of inflation, the wholesale price index, the GDP deflator, a deflator of value added in manufacturing industry, the rate of increase of private final demand .... This is in turn complicated by the regular changes in statistical series introduced by the authorities.

3. In dynamic optimal control models, the objective function includes the instruments as well as the policy objectives, on the realistic assumption that there are costs involved in changing the values of instruments.

4. A vast literature exists on the relationship between democracy and social welfare, stemming from Arrow's impossibility theorem that demonstrates the impossibility of forming a social preference through the aggregation of individual preferences, without breaking at least one of a number of rules that Arrow takes to be requirements of a democratic system (Arrow, 1951).

5. The discussion here assumes that the purpose of the setting of targets by government is the maximization of welfare through stabilization policy. However, there may be other reasons for the setting of targets, for example the setting of money supply growth targets to provide information to the private sector about government policy intentions and hence to influence inflationary expectations.

6. This implies that national economies are single entities and that their long-term interests can be identified. This, in turn, stems from a willingness of macro-economists to ignore questions of income distribution and regional balance. For example, it may well be that people in the North of England would prefer a slower rate of growth for the UK as a whole, if it meant a more equal distribution of income between North and South.

7. An early statement of this argument can be found in Friedman, 1948.

8. For a survey of this work see Blanchard (1990).

9. For good discussions of the relevance of rational expectations to stabilization policy see Visser (1991) and Cuthbertson and Taylor (1987a).

10. For further discussion of Poole's model and criticisms of it see Benjamin Friedman in Friedman and Hahn (1990) and Gowland (1991).

11. The argument regarding the suboptimality of intermediate targets can also be found in Chick (1977) and in B Friedman (1975).

12. DCE = the increase in the money supply — the change in the overseas component of the money supply.

Chapter 10

1. For a development of this argument in relation to the EMS see Giavazzi and Pagano, 1988; and Giavazzi and Giovannini, 1989.

2. The phrase used in the agreement governing the Bretton Woods adjustable peg fixed exchange rate system, which operated from 1945-72.

3. In the event, the 15 per cent remained in force until the establishment of monetary union in January 1999.

4. Padoa Schioppa, 1988, p 373.

5. Rogoff, 1985a; Fratianni and von Hagen, 1990.

6. Mélitz, 1988.

7. Purchasing power parity requires that the exchange rate between two currencies is determined by the price levels of a comparable bundle of goods in the two countries (absolute PPP), or that expected future spot exchange rates reflect the expected future inflation rates in the two countries (relative PPP).

8. Nash non-cooperative games are classed as either Nash-Cournot (actions by other countries taken as given) or Nash-Stackelberg (one country acts as leader and anticipates how the other country will respond to its actions).

9. Williamson and Miller, 1987; McKinnon, 1988.

10. see, for example, Krugman (1991)

11. Kindleberger, 1988, p.137.

12. Portes, 1990, p.226.

13. Walters, 1990, p.54.

14. Horne and Masson, 1988, p.273.

15. Currie, 1990, p.144.

Chapter 11

1. Lord Kaldor was one of several economists on the Radcliffe Committee and argued this particular case against monetary targets. As we shall see later, his rejection of monetary targeting strengthened over the years but the basis for rejection changed fundamentally.

2. Sterling, along with other major European currencies, became convertible for foreign holders of it in 1958. Full sterling convertibility for UK residents dates from 1979. Other European currencies moved towards full convertibility during the 1980s and early 1990s.

3. The Bank of England itself had been nationalised in 1946.

4. Domestic credit expansion is the sum of the domestic credit counterparts of the money supply. In Equation 3.18, for example, DCE is found by ignoring $\pm$ ext. The logic was that under a fixed exchange rate regime, there is little that government can do about the impact of external flows, but it could at least be asked to control the domestic sources of money.

5. This process was more eloquently christened 'the regulatory dialectic' by Kane (1984). More examples of regulation-induced innovation are given in section 4.3.

6. e.g. in Zawadzki (1981), Gowland (1984), Hall (1983). See also Bank 1971b).

7. Details of interest rate movements and volume and types of debt sold are in Hall (1983) pp.28-30.

8. See Hall (1983) ch..4.

9. Gowland (1982) p.109.

10. Goodhart (2002) p.17.

11. We return to the issue of relative interest rates and monetary policy in our dis cussion of liability management later in this chapter.

12. See Goodhart (1984).

13. See Lewis and Davis (1987) section 9.7.

14. See also Howells and Bain (2002) ch.12.

15. Bank of England, *Statistical Abstract*, 1997, vol. I, tables 19.3, 19.4).

16. '...monetary targeting is simply a limiting case of inflation targeting in which the policymaker assigns a weight of unity to money and of zero to all other variables'. M King (1997) p.440.

Chapter 13

1. A strict application of optimum currency area theory might, for example, lead to the conclusion that south-east and central England should share a common currency with northern France but that the north of England and Scotland should have a separate currency.

2. H M Treasury (1997) *UK membership of the single currency: an assessment of the five economic tests*, available on the HM Treasury website: www.hm-treasury.gov.uk

3. The assessment is due to be completed by June 2003, see H M Treasury (November, 2001), *Preliminary and technical work to prepare for the assessment of the five tests for UK membership of the single currency*, available on the Treasury website, www.hm-treasury.gov.uk

4. Although we generally use the term European Union (EU) in this book, direct reference to the *Treaty on European Union* must use the term European Community (EC) because, according to the Treaty, the Economic Community is the economic and monetary pillar of the three-pillared European Union, the other two of which relate to common foreign and security policies.

5. Formally, the exchange rate strategy of the euro area rests with the European Council, not with the ECB. However, since the value of the euro has some impact on the future rate of inflation, the ECB must take it into account in making interest rate decisions.

6. This appears to give a target range for inflation of 1-2 per cent, hence Svensson's proposal of 1.5 per cent as the point inflation target.

7. See Box 4.1 in Chapter 4 for an explanation of repurchase agreements.

8. Interest rate decisions are announced fortnightly, except in August when there is normally only on meeting of the Council

9. 'Structural operations' are also possible. These are intended to adjust the structural liquidity of the Eurosystem in relation to the banking system. For an outline of these, see European Central Bank (2001).

10. This rate was known as the Lombard rate in the Bundesbank's system.

11. ECB, *Monthly Report*, December 2001, p. 5.

Chapter 14

1. In each case the bank was granted a 20-year charter, which was not renewed

2. Quoted in Davies (1994).

3. Even by the end of the year 2000, despite large falls in numbers over many years, there remained 8,315commercial banks in the USA.

4. State governments have the power to charter banks under the US constitution. The National Banking Act of 1863 empowered a federal agency to issue bank charters also.

5. No two members were to come from the same Federal Reserve region.

6. Multi-bank panics occurred in 1914, 1930 and 1933, with the panic of 1933 leading to widespread restrictions on the convertibility of deposits into currency.

7. See section 11.3 for the part played by Regulation Q in the development of the eurocurrency system.

8. Federal Reserve Bank of New York, *About the Fed*, available on www.ny.frb.org

9. Quoted in Handa (2000), p. 253.

10. Testimony of Chairman Alan Greenspan. Federal Reserve Board's semiannual monetary policy report to the CongressBefore the Committee on Financial Services, U.S. House of Representatives July 18, 2001.

11. Indeed, the Fed is legally required to do this.

12. The MCA required that in 1980 only 3 per cent of the first $25 million of a bank's demand deposits and another banking act in 1982 established a zero per

cent reserve requirement for the first $2 million of a bank's deposits. Both the $2 million and the $25 million figures to which the reduced percentages apply are adjusted annually to reflect the growth in total demand deposits in the USA. These concessions were intended to reduce the burden of maintaining reserves for small banks.

13. As we explain in Section 4.3, the use of average deposits eliminates day-to-day fluctuations and leaves interest rates less volatile at the end of the maintenance period. That is, it is intended to smooth out interest rate fluctuations.

14. For an explanation of how repos (known in the USA as RPs) work, see Box 4.1.

15. Matched sale-purchase transactions (MSPs) involve a contract for immediate sale of Treasury bills to, and a linked matching contract for subsequent purchase from, each participating dealer.

16. Although there are only 8 FOMC meetings a year, decisions can be altered by special telephone link-ups — see below in relation to September 11, 2001.

17. Wray (1990) p.249.

18. Testimony of Chairman Alan Greenspan, *Federal Reserve Board's semiannual monetary policy report to the Congress* before the Committee on Financial Services, U.S. House of Representatives, July 18, 2001

References

Acocella N (1998) *Economic Policy*, Cambridge: Cambridge U P

Adam C S (1991) 'Financial innovation and the demand for M3 in the UK 1975-86', *Oxford Bulletin of Economics and Statistics*, 53, 401-24

Akerlof G A and Milbourne R D (1978) 'New calculations of Income and Interest Elasticities in Tobin's Model of the Transactions Demand for Money', *Review of Economics and Statistics*, 60

Akerlof G A and Milbourne R D (1980) 'The short-run demand for money', *Economic Journal*, 90, 885-900

Akhtar M A (1983) 'Financial innovations and their implications for monetary policy: an international perspective', BIS Economic Papers 9

Alesina A and Summers L (1993) 'Central bank independence and macroeconomic performance: some comparative evidence', *Journal of Money, Credit and Banking*, 25, 151-62

Anderson N and Sleath J (1999) 'New estimates of the UK real and nominal yield curves', *Bank of England Quarterly Bulletin*, 39 (4), 384-92

Arestis P, Biefang-Frisancho I, Hagemann, H, Howells P and Trautwein M (1995) 'Financial Innovation and the Long-run Demand for Money in the UK and in Germany: A Comparative Application of Cointegration Modelling', *Weltwirtschaftsliches Archiv*, 131 (2), 302-325

Arrow K (1951) *Social Choice and Individual Values*, Cowles Foundation Monograph 12. New York: J Wiley

Artis M J and Lewis M K (1974) 'The demand for money: stable or unstable', *The Banker*, 124, 239-47

Artis M J and Lewis M K (1976) 'The demand for money in the UK, 1963-73', *Manchester School*, 44, 147-81

Artis M J and Lewis M K (1990) 'Money supply and demand' in Bandyopadhyay T and Ghatak S (eds)

Artis M J and Lewis M K (1991) *Money in Britain: Monetary Policy, Innovation and Europe*, Oxford: Philip Allan

Artis M J, Mizen P and Kontolemis Z (1998) 'In flation Targeting: what can the ECB learn from the recent experience of the Bank of England', *Economic Journal*, 108 (451), 1810-25

Association for Payment Clearing Systems, *Yearbook of Statistics*, 2000, (London: APACS)

Atkinson P and Chouraqui J-C (1987) 'The formulation of monetary policy: a reassessment in the light of recent experience', *Monetary Policy and Financial Systems* No. 1, OECD Working Paper No 32

Baba Y, Hendry D F and Starr R M (1992) 'The demand for M1 in the USA, 1960-88', *Review of Economic Studies*, 59, 25-61

Bain K (1998) 'Some problems with the use of "credibility" and "reputation" to support the independence of central banks', in Arestis P and Sawyer M (eds), *The Political Economy of Central Banking*, Cheltenham: Edward Elgar

Bain K and Howells P G A (1991) 'The income and transactions velocities of money', *Review of Social Economy*, XLIX (3), 383-95

Bain K and Howells P (1996) 'Central Banks, Governments and Markets: an examination of central bank independence and power', *Economies et Sociétés,* Cahiers de l'ISMEA, Serie Monnaie et Production, Feb/March

Ball L N (1994) 'Credible disinflation with staggered price setting', *American Economic Review*, 84, 282-9

Ball L (1997) 'Disinflation and the NAIRU', in Romer C D and D H (eds), *Reducing Inflation: Motivation and Strategy*, Chicago: University of Chicago Press

Ball L (1999), 'Efficient rules for monetary policy', *International Finance*, 2, 63-83

Bandyopadhyay T and S Ghatak (eds) (1990) *Current Issues in Monetary Economics*, Hemel Hempstead: Harvester Wheatsheaf

Bank of England (annual) *Statistical Abstract* parts 1 and 2

Bank of England Quarterly Bulletin (1971a) 'Key issues in monetary and credit policy — an address by the Governor', June

Bank of England Quarterly Bulletin (1971b) 'Competition and Credit Control', June

Bank of England (1983) 'Competition, innovation and regulation in British banking' *Bank of England Quarterly Bulletin*, 363-76

Bank of England Quarterly Bulletin (1997a) 'The Operation of Monetary Policy', February, 5-20

Bank of England Quarterly Bulletin (1997b) 'The Bank of England's Operations in the Sterling Money Markets', May

Bank of England Quarterly Bulletin (1999a) 'The Transmission Mechanism of Monetary Policy', May

Bank of England (1999b) 'Monetary Policy in the United Kingdom', Bank of England Fact Sheet (available at www.bankofengland.co.uk)

Barnett W A, Offenbacher E K and Spindt P A (1984) 'The new Divisia monetary aggregates', *Journal of Political Economy*, 92 (6), 1049-85

Barro R J (1974) 'Are government bonds net wealth', *Journal of Political Economy*, 82, 1095-1117

Barro R J (1977) 'Unanticipated money growth and unemployment in the United States', *American Economic Review*, 67, 101-15

Barro R J (1978) 'Unanticipated money, output and the price level in the United States', *Journal of Political Economy*, 86, 549-80

Barro R J and Gordon D B (1983) 'Rules, Discretion and Reputation in a Model of Monetary Policy', *Journal of Monetary Economics*, 12, 101-21

Barro R and Grossman H (1976) *Money, Employment and Inflation*, Cambridge: Cambridge University Press

Baumol W J (1952) 'The transactions demand for cash: an inventory theoretic approach', *Quarterly Journal of Economics,* 66, 545-56

Bean C R (1984) 'Targeting nominal income: an appraisal', *Economic Journal*, 93, 806-19

Bean C R and Jenkinson N (2001) 'The formulation of monetary policy at the Bank of England' *Bank of England Quarterly Bulletin*, winter 2001, 434-41

Belongia M T (1996) 'Measurement matters: some recent results in monetary economics re-examined', *Journal of Political Economy*, 104 (5), 1065-83

Benassy J-P (1975), 'Neo-Keynesian disequilibrium theory in a monetary economy', *Review of Economic Studies*, 42, 503-24

Bernard H and Gerlach S (1996) 'Does the term structure predict recessions? The international evidence', BIS Working Paper no. 37, Geneva: Bank for International Settlements

Bernanke B S (1996) 'What does the Bundesbank target?', NBER Working Paper, no.5764

Bertocchi G and M Spagat (1993) 'Learning, experimentation and monetary policy', *Journal of Monetary Economics,* 32 (1), Aug, 169-83

Blackburn K (1992) 'Credibility and time-consistency in monetary policy', in K Dowd and M K Lewis (eds)

Blanchard O J and Fischer S (1989) *Lectures in Macroeconomics*, Cambridge, Mass: MIT Press

Blanchard O J (1990) 'Why does money affect output? A survey', in Friedman B M and Hahn F H (eds), *Handbook of Monetary Economics* vol II, Amsterdam: North-Holland, 779-835

Blinder A (1987) 'Credit Rationing and Effective Supply Failures', *Economic Journal*, 97, 327-52

Blinder A S (1997) 'What central bankers could learn from academia – and vice versa,' *Journal of Economic Perspectives*, 11 (2), 3-19

Bomberger W A and Makinen G E (1980) 'Money demand in open economies: alternative specifications', *Southern Economic Journal*, 47 (1), 30-39

Bordo M and Jonung L (1981) 'The long-run behaviour of the income velocity of money in five advanced countries, 1879-1975: An Institutional Approach', *Economic Inquiry*, 19, 96-116

Bordo M and Jonung L (1987) *The Long-Run Behaviour of the Velocity of Circulation: The International Evidence*, New York: Cambridge U P

Bordo M and Jonung L (1990) 'The long-run behaviour of velocity: the institutionalist approach revisited', *Journal of Policy Modelling*, 12, 165-97

Borio C E V (1997) 'Monetary policy operating procedures in industrial countries', Bank for International Settlements, Working Paper no. 40

Bowen A (1995) ' Inflation targetry in the United Kingdom' in Haldane A G (ed), *Targeting Inflation*, London: Bank of England

Brainard W C (1967) 'Uncertainty and the effectiveness of policy', *American Economic Review*, May, 411-25

Brainard W C and Tobin J (1968) 'Econometric models: their problems and usefulness: pitfalls in financial model building', *American Economic Review*, 58, 411-25

Bronfenbrenner M and T Mayer (1960) 'Liquidity functions in the American economy', *Econometrica*, October, 28, 810-34

Brooke M, Cooper N and Scholtes C (2000) 'Inferring market interest rate expectations from money market rates', *Bank of England Quarterly Bulletin*, 40 (4), 392-402

Browning P (1986) *The Treasury and Economic Policy, 1964-85*, Harlow: Longman

Brunner K (1968) 'The role of money and monetary policy', *Federal Reserve Bank of St Louis Review*, 50, 8-24

Brunner K and Meltzer A H (1972) 'Money, debt and economic activity', *Journal of Political Economy,* 80, 951-75

Brunner K and Meltzer A H (1989) *Monetary Economics*, Oxford: Basil Blackwell

Budd A (1998) 'The role and operations of the Bank of England Monetary Policy Committee' *Economic Journal*, 108, 1783-94

Burda M and Wyplosz C (2e, 1997) *Macroeconomics: A European Text*, Oxford: Oxford, U P

Burns A F and Mitchell W C (1946), *Measuring Business Cycles,* New York: NBER

Campillo M and Miron J (1997) 'Why does inflation differ across countries?', in Romer C D and D H (eds), *Reducing Inflation: Motivation and Strategy*, Chicago: University of Chicago Press, 335-57

Canzoneri M and Gray J A (1985) 'Monetary policy games and the consequences of noncooperative behaviour", *International Economic Review* 26

Caporale G M and Howells P G A (2001) 'Money, Credit and Spending: Drawing Causal Inferences', *Scottish Journal of Political Economy*, 48 (5), 447-57

Cecchetti S G, Genberg H, Lipsky J and Wadhwani S (2000) *Asset Prices and Central Bank Policy*, Geneva Reports on the World Economy 2, International Center for Monetary and Banking Studies,Geneva; London: Centre for Economic Policy Research

Chick V (2nd ed 1977) *The Theory of Monetary Policy*, Oxford: Blackwell

Chick V (1983) *Macroeconomics after Keynes*, Oxford: Philip Allan

Chick V (1986) 'The evolution of the banking system and the theory of saving, investment and interest', *Économies et sociétés*, Cahiers de l'ISMEA, Série 'Monnaie et Production, 3, 111-26

Chick V (1993) 'The evolution of the banking system and the theory of monetary policy', in S F Frowen (ed) *Monetary Theory and Monetary Policy*: New Tracks for the 1990s, London: Macmillan

Chick V and Dow S C(1996) 'Regulation and differences in financial institutions', *Journal of Economic Issues*, 30 (2), 517-23

Chow G C (1966) 'On the long-run and short-run demand for money', *Journal of Political Economy*, April, 74, 111-31

Chrystal K (ed.) (1990) *Monetarism,* 2 Vols, Aldershot: Edward Elgar

Chrystal K A and MacDonald R (1994) 'Exchange rates and financial innovation: the sterling dollar rate 1972-90', *Federal Reserve Bank of St Louis Review*, 76 (2), 73-109

Clare A (2001) 'The information in UK company warnings', *Bank of England Quarterly Bulletin*, 41(1), 104-109

Clarida R, Gali J and Gertler M (1998) 'Monetary policy rules in practice: some international evidence', *European Economic Review*, 42, 1033-1067

Clayton G, J C Gilbert and R Sedgewick (eds) *Monetary Theory and Policy in the 1970s*, Oxford: Oxford UP

Clews R, Panigirtzoglou N and Proudman J (2000) 'Recent developments in extracting information from options markets, *Bank of England Quarterly Bulletin*, 40 (1), 50-59

Clower R W (1967) 'A reconsideration of the microfoundations of monetary theory', *Western Economic Journal*, 6 (December), 1-8

Cook T and Hahn T (1989) 'Effects of changes in the Federal Funds rate target on market rates in the 1970s', *Journal of Monetary Economics*, 24, 331-51

Cooper N, Hillman R and Lynch D (2001) 'Interpreting movements in high-yield corporate bond market spreads', *Bank of England Quarterly Bulletin*, 41 (1), 110-120

Cooper R N (1969) 'Macroeconomic policy adjustments in interdependent economies', *Quarterly Journal of Economics*, 83 (1), 1-24

Cooper R N (1985) 'Economic interdependence and coordination of economic policies', in Jones R W and Kenen P B (eds) *Handbook of International Economics* II, Amsterdam: North Holland

Copeland L S (2000) *Exchange Rates and International Finance*, Harlow: Pearson Education

Cornford A and Kregel J (1996) 'Globalisation, capital flows and international regulation', Jerome Levy Institute, Working Paper no. 161

Cottrell A (1986) 'The endogeneity of money and money-income causality', *Scottish Journal of Political Economy,* 33 (1), 2-27

Cramer J S (1981) 'The volume of transactions and of payments in the UK, 1968-77', *Oxford Economic Papers*, 33 (2), 234-55

Cramer J S (1986) 'The volume of transactions and the circulation of money in the United States 1950-79', *Journal of Business and Economic Statistics*, 2 (4), 225-32

Crawford M (1993) *One Money for Europe? The Economics and Politics of Maastricht*, Basingstoke: Macmillan

Cukierman A (1992) *Central Bank Strategy, Credibility, and Independence: Theory and Evidence*, Cambridge Mass.: MIT Press

Currie D (1990) 'International policy coordination', in Llewellyn D T and Milner C (eds) *Current Issues in International Monetary Economics*, Basingstoke: MacMillan

Cuthbertson K (1985a) *The Supply and Demand for Money*, Oxford: Blackwell

Cuthbertson K (1985b) 'Sterling bank lending to UK industrial and commercial companies', *Oxford Bulletin of Economics and Statistics*, 42 (2), 91-118

Cuthbertson K (1993) 'Monetary control: theory, empirics and practicalities', in P Arestis (ed), *Money and Banking: Essays for the Twenty-First Century,* (London: Macmillan) 192-219

Cuthbertson K and Barlow D (1991) 'Money demand analysis: an outline', in Taylor M P (ed) (1991) *Money and Financial Markets*, Oxford: Blackwell

Cuthbertson K and Foster N (1982) 'Bank lending to industrial and commercial companies in three models of the UK economy', *National Institute of Economic Review*, 102, 63-77

Cuthbertson K and Slow J (1990) 'Bank advances and liquid assets of UK industrial and commercial companies', University of Newcastle, Deparment of Economics, mimeo

Cuthbertson K and Taylor M P (1987a) 'Monetary anticipations and the demand for money: some evidence for the UK', *Weltwirtschaftlichesarchiv*, 123(3), 503-19

Cuthbertson K and M P Taylor (1987b), 'The demand for money: a dynamic rational expectations model', *Economic Journal*, 97, 65-76

Cuthbertson K and Taylor M P (1989) 'Anticipated and unanticipated variables in the demand for M1 in the UK', *The Manchester School*, 57, 319-39

Dale S (1993) 'Effects of changes in official UK rate upon money market rates since 1987', *Manchester School, Proceedings of the Money, Macroeconomics and Finance Research Group*, 76-94.

Dale S and Haldane A G (1993) 'Interest rate control in a model of monetary policy', Bank of England, Working Papers Series no.17

Darby M R (1972) 'On economic policy with rational expectations', *Journal of Monetary Economics*, 3 (2), 118-26

Davidson P (1988) 'Endogenous money, the production process and inflation analysis', *Economie Appliquée*, XLI (1), 151-69

Davidson P (1996) 'Reality and economic theory', *Journal of Post Keynesian Economics*, 18 (4), 479-508

Davies G (1994) *A History of Money. From Ancient Times to the Present Day*, Cardiff: University of Wales Press

Davis E P (1992) 'Credit Quality Spreads, Bond Market Efficiency and Financial Efficiency', *Manchester School*, 55 (supplement), 21-46

Davis E P and Henry S G B (1993) 'The Use of Financial Spreads as Indicators of Real Activity', in P Arestis (ed) *Money and Banking: Issues for the Twenty First Century,* London: Macmillan, 261-286

Dennis R (2001) 'Inflation expectations and the stability properties of nominal GDP targeting', *Economic Journal,* Jan, 103-113

Deutsche Bundesbank (ed) *The Monetary Transmission Process: Recent Developments and Lessons for Europe*, New York: Palgrave

Diamond D W (1984) 'Financial intermediation and delegated monitoring', *Review of Economic Studies*, 51, 393-414

Dornbusch R (1976) 'Expectations and exchange rate dynamics', *Journal of Political Economy*, 84, 1161-76

Dotsey M (1998) 'The predictive content of the interest rate term spread for future economic growth', *Federal Reserve Bank of Richmond*

Quarterly Review, 84 (3), 30-51

Dow J C R and Saville I D (1988) *A Critique of Monetary Policy*, Oxford: Oxford U P

Dow S C and Chick V (1988) 'A Post Keynesian perspective on the relation between banking and regional development', in P Arestis (ed) *Post Keynesian Monetary Economics: New Approaches to Financial Modelling*, Aldershot: Edward Elgar,

Dow S C (1993) *Money and the Economic Process*, Aldershot: Elgar

Dow S C (1994) 'Horizontalism: a critique', *Cambridge Journal of Economics*, 20 (4) 497-508

Dow S C (1996) 'Regulation and differences in financial institutions', *Journal of Economic Issues*, 30 (2), 517-23 (with V Chick)

Dow S C and Earl P E (1982) *Money Matters: a Keynesian Approach to Monetary Economics,* Oxford: Martin Robertson

Dowd K (1990) 'The value of time and the transactions demand for money', *Journal of Money, Credit and Banking,* 22 (February), 51-64

Dowd K and Lewis M K (eds) (1992) *Current Issues in Financial and Monetary Economics*, Basingstoke: Macmillan

Downward P (forthcoming), 'Econometrics', in King J (ed) *The Encyclopedia of Post Keynesian Economics*, Cheltenham: Edward Elgar

Driffil J (1988) 'The stability and sustainability of the European Monetary System with perfect capital markets', in Giavazzi F, Micossi S and Miller M (eds) (1988) *The European Monetary System*, Cambridge: Cambridge U P

Eijffinger S and de Haan J (1996) *The Political Economy of Central Bank Independence*, Princeton University, Special Papers in Economics, 19, May

Enzler J, Johnson L and Paulus J (1976), 'Some problems of money demand', *Brookings Papers on Economic Activity*, 1, 261-80

Eshag E (1963), 'The internal value of money: review of Marshall's work', reprinted in Chrystal K (ed) (1990)

European Central Bank (2001) *The Monetary Policy of the ECB*, Frankfurt: ECB

Faig M (1989) 'Seasonal fluctuations and the demand for money', *Quarterly Journal of Economics*, 104 (November), 847-61

Fazzari S and Minsky H P (1984) 'Domestic monetary policy: if not monetarism, what?', *Journal of Economic Issues*, 18 (1), 101-16

Feige E L (1967) 'Expectations and adjustments in the monetary sector', *American Economic Review*, 57, 462-73

Financial Times, 'George damps prospects of interest rate rises', 20th February 2002

Fisher D (1989) *Money Demand and Monetary Policy*, London: Harvester Wheatsheaf

Fisher I (1907) *The Rate of Interest*, New York: Macmillan

Fisher I (1911), *The Purchasing Power of Money*, New York: Macmillan. Reprinted (1963) New York: Augustus M Kelley

Fisher P and Whitley J (2000) 'Macroeconomic models at the Bank of England' in S Holly and M Weale (eds) *Econometric Modelling*, Cambridge: NIESR

Fleming J M (1962) 'Domestic financial policies under fixed and floating exchange rates', IMF Staff Papers, 9, 369-77

Forder J (1998) 'Central bank independence – conceptual clarifications and interim assessment', *Oxford Economic Papers*, 50, 307-34

Forder J (1999) 'Central bank independence: reassessing the measurements', *Journal of Economic Issues*, 33 (1), 23-40

Foster J (1992) 'The determination of sterling M3, 1963-88: an evolutionary macroeconomic approach', *Economic Journal*, 102

Frankel J A (1979) 'On the mark: a theory of floating exchange rates based on real interest rate differentials', *American Economic Review*, 69, 610-22

Frankel J A with M Chinn (1995) 'The stabilising properties of a nominal GNP rule', *Journal of Money, Credit and Banking*, 27 (2), 318-334

Fratianni M and von Hagen J (1990) 'German dominance in the EMS: the empirical evidence', *Open Economies Review*, 1

Friedman B M (1975) 'Targets, instruments and indicators of monetary policy', *Journal of Monetary Economics,* 1, 443-73

Friedman B M and Hahn F H (eds) (1990) *A Handbook of Monetary Economics*, 2 vols., Amsterdam: North-Holland

Friedman M (1948) 'A monetary and fiscal framework for economic stability', reprinted in *Essays in Positive Economics*, Chicago: University of Chicago Press (1953)

Friedman M (1956) 'The quantity theory of money: a restatement', in Friedman M (ed) *Studies in the Quantity Theory of Money*, Chicago: University of Chicago Press

Friedman M (1957) A Theory of the Consumption Function, Princeton: Princeton U P (for NBER)

Friedman M (1959) 'The demand for money: some theoretical and empirical results', *Journal of Political Economy*, 67

Friedman M (1960) *A Program for Monetary Stability*, New York: Fordham U P

Friedman M (1963) *Inflation: Causes and Consequences*, Bombay: Asia Publishing House

Friedman M (1968) 'The role of monetary policy', *American Economic Review,* 58, 1-17

Friedman M (1986) 'The resource cost of irredeemable paper money', *Journal of Political Economy*, 94, 642-7

Friedman M (1988) 'Money and the stockmarket', *Journal of Political Economy*, 96

Friedman M (1970), 'A theoretical framework of monetary analysis', *Journal of Political Economy*, 78, 193-238

Friedman M and Schwartz A (1963) *A Monetary History of the United States*, 1867-1960, Princeton: Princeton U P

Friedman M and Schwartz A (1982) *Monetary Trends in the United States and the United Kingdom: Their Relation to Income, Prices and Interest Rates, 1867-1975*, Chicago: University of Chicago Press

Galbraith J K (1954), *The Great Crash*, London: Hamish Hamilton

Galbraith J K (1975) *Money: Whence it came, where it went*, Harmondsworth: Penguin Books

Gerlach S and Schnabel G (2000) 'The Taylor Rule and interest rates in the EMU area: a note', *Economic Letters*, 67 (2), 165-71

Giavazzi F and Giovannini A (1989) *Limiting Exchange-Rate Flexibility. The EMS Experience*, Cambridge Mass: MIT Press

Giavazzi F and Pagano M (1988) 'The advantage of tying one's hand: EMS discipline and central bank credibility', *European Economic Review*, 32, Jun, 1055-82

Goldfeld S M (1973) 'The demand for money revisited', *Brookings Papers on Economic Activity*, 3, 577-638

Goldfeld S M (1976) 'The case of the missing money', *Brookings Papers on Economic Activity*, 3, 683-739

Goldfeld S M (1992) 'Demand for money: empirical studies', in Newman P, Milgate M and Eatwell J (eds)

Goldfeld S M and Sichel D (1990) 'The demand for money', in Friedman B M and Hahn F H (eds)

Goodhart C A E (1984) *Monetary Theory and Practice*, London: Macmillan

Goodhart C A E (1986) 'Financial innovation and monetary control', *Oxford Review of Economic Policy*, 2 (4)

Goodhart C A E (1989a) *Money, Information and Uncertainty* 2nd edn, London: Macmillan

Goodhart C A E (1989b) 'The conduct of monetary policy', *Economic Journal*, 99 (396), June, 293-346

Goodhart C A E (1994) 'What should central banks do? What should be their macroeconomic objectives and operations', *Economic Journal*, 104, November, 1424-36

Goodhart C A E (2002), 'The endogeneity of money', in Arestis P, Desai M and Dow S (eds) *Money, Macroeconomics and Keynes Essays in Honour of Victoria Chick* Vol 1 London: Routledge

Goodhart C A E and Crockett A D (1970) 'The importance of money', *Bank of England Quarterly Bulletin*, 10, 159-98

Gordon R J (1982) 'Price inertia and policy ineffectiveness in the United States 1890-1980', *Journal of Political Economy,* December, 90(6), 1087-117

Gowland D H (1978) *Monetary Policy and Credit Control*, London: Croom Helm

Gowland D H (2e, 1984) *Controlling the Money Supply*, London: Croom Helm

Gowland D (1990), *Understanding Macroeconomics*, Aldershot: Edward Elgar

Gowland D H (2e, 1991) *Money, Inflation and Unemployment* 2nd edn, Hemel Hempstead: Harvester Wheatsheaf

Grandmont J (1977) 'Temporary general equilibrium theory', *Econometrica*, 43, 535-72

de Grauwe P (4e, 2000) *The Economics of Monetary Integration*, 4th edn, Oxford: Oxford UP

Greenaway D (ed) (1989) *Current Issues in Macroeconomics*, Basingstoke: Macmillan

Greider W (1987) *Secrets of the Temple: How the Federal Reserve runs the Country*, New York: Simon and Schuster

Grice J and Bennett A (1984) 'Wealth and the demand for £M3 in the United Kingdom 1963-78', *Manchester School*, 52 (September), 239-70

Gurley J G and Shaw E S (1960) *Money in a Theory of Finance*, Washington: Brookings Institution

Hacche G (1974) 'The demand for money in the UK: experience since 1971', *Bank of England Quarterly Bulletin*, 14, 284-305

Hafer R W (1985) 'Monetary stabilization policy: evidence from money demand forecasts', *Federal Reserve Bank of St Louis Review*, 67 (5)

Hafer R W and Hein S E (1979) 'Evidence on the temporal stability of the demand for money relationship in the United States', *Federal Reserve Bank of St Louis Review*, 61 (12)

Haldane A G (1995a) 'Inflation targets', *Bank of England Quarterly Bulletin*, 35 (3), 250-9

Haldane A G (ed) (1995b), *Targeting Inflation*, London: Bank of England

Haldane A G (1999) 'Monetary policy and the yield curve', *Bank of England Quarterly Bulletin*, 39 (2) , 171-76

Hall M J B (1983) *Monetary Policy since 1971*, London: Macmillan

Hall R E (1986) 'Optimal monetary institutions and policy' in Campbell C and Dougan W (eds) *Alternative Monetary Regimes*, Baltimore: Johns Hopkins Press

Hall S G, Henry S G B, and Wilcox J B (1989), 'The long run determinants of UK monetary aggregates', Bank of England Discussion Paper, 41

Hall S G, Henry S G B, and Wilcox J B (1990) 'The long-run determination of UK monetary aggregates, in Henry S G B and Patterson K D (eds), *Economic Modelling at the Bank of England*, London: Chapman and Hall

Hamada K (1976) 'A strategic analysis of monetary independence', *Journal of Political Economy*, 84, 677-700

Hamada K (1985) *The Political Economy of International Monetary Interdependence*, Cambridge Mass.: MIT Press

Handa J (2000) *Monetary Economics*, London: Routledge

Harris L (1985) *Monetary Theory*, New York: McGraw-Hill

Heffernan S A (1993) 'Competition in British retail banking', *Journal of Financial Services Research,* 7, 309-32

Heffernan S A (1997) 'Modelling British interest rate adjustment: an error correction approach', *Economica*, May, 291-31

Heller H R (1965) 'The demand for money: the evidence from the short-run data', *Quarterly Journal of Economics*, May, 78, 291-303

Hendry D F (1985) 'Monetary economic myth and econometric reality, *Oxford Review of Economic Policy*, 1, 72-84

Hendry D F, Pagan A R and Sargan J D (1984) 'Dynamic specification' in Griliches Z and Intriligator M D (eds), *Handbook of Econometrics*, Vol 2, Amsterdam: North Holland

Hicks J R (1937) 'Mr Keynes and the "Classics": a suggested interpretation', *Econometrica*, 5, 147-59

Hicks J R (1967) *Critical Essays in Monetary Theory*, Oxford: Clarendon Press

Hicks J R (1979) *Causality in Economics*, Oxford: Blackwell

Horne J and Masson P R (1988) 'Scope and limits of international economic cooperation and policy coordination', IMF Staff Papers, 35(2), 259-96

Howells P G A (1995) 'The demand for endogenous money', *Journal of Post Keynesian Economics,* 18 (1), 89-106

Howells P G A (1997), 'The Demand for Endogenous Money: A Rejoinder', *Journal of Post Keynesian Economics*, 19 (3), 429-35

Howells P G A (2001) 'The endogeneity of money' in P Arestis and M C Sawyer (eds) *Money, Finance and Capitalist Development*, Cheltenham: Edward Elgar

Howells P G A and Bain K (2002) *The Economics of Money, Banking and Finance,* London:Pearson Education

Howells P G A and Biefang-Frisancho Mariscal I (1992) 'An explanation for the recent behaviour of income and transactions velocities in the United Kingdom', *Journal of Post Keynesian Economics*, 14 (3), 85-105

Howells P G A and Hussein K A, 'The endogeneity of money: evidence from the G7', *Scottish Journal of Political Economy*, 45 (3), 329-40

Howells P G A and Hussein (1999), 'The demand for bank loans and the "State of Trade"', *Journal of Post Keynesian Economics*, 21 (3), 441-54

Hughes-Hallett A (1989) 'Macroeconomic interdependence and the coordination of economic policy', in Greenaway D (ed)

Humphrey T M (1974) 'The quantity theory of money: its historical evolution and role in policy debates', *Federal Reserve Bank of Richmond Economic Review*, 60, May/June. Reprinted in Chrystal K (ed.) (1990)

Issing, Otmar (1993) *Central Bank Independence and Monetary Stability*, Occasional Paper 89, London: Institute of Economic Affairs

Judd J P and Scadding J L (1982) 'The search for a stable money demand function: a survey of the post-1973 literature', *Journal of Economic Literature*, XX, 993-1023

Kaldor N (1982) *The Scourge of Monetarism*, Oxford: Oxford U P

Kaldor N (1985) 'How monetarism failed', *Challenge*, 28 (2), 4-13

Kane E J (1984) 'Technological and regulatory forces in the development of financial services competition', *Journal of Finance*, July, 759-73

Karni E (1974) 'The Value of Time and the Demand for Money', *Journal of Money, Credit and Banking*, 6, 45-64

Kavanagh N J and Walters A A (1966) 'The Demand for Money in the United Kingdom, 1877-1961', *Bulletin of the Oxford University Institute of Economics and Statistics*, 28, 93-116

Keynes J M (1923) *A Tract on Monetary Reform*, London: Macmillan, Vol. IV of Moggridge D and Johnson E (eds) (1973) *Collected Works of John Maynard Keynes*, London: Macmillan

Keynes J M (1930) *A Treatise on Money*, London: Macmillan, Vols. V and VI of Moggridge D and Johnson E (eds) (1973) *Collected Works of John Maynard Keynes*, London: Macmillan

Keynes J M (1936) *The General Theory of Employment, Interest and Money*, London: Macmillan, Vol VII of Moggridge D and Johnson E (eds) (1973) *Collected Works of John Maynard Keynes,* London: Macmillan

Keynes JM (1939) 'Professor Tinbergen's Method', *Economic Journal,* 44, 558-568

Keynes J M (1973) *The General Theory and After: Part II, Defence and Development,* Vol. XIV of Collected Works of John Maynard Keynes Moggridge D and Johnson E (eds) (1973) *Collected Works of John Maynard Keynes,* London: Macmillan

Khusro A M (1952) 'An investigation of liquidity preference', *Yorkshire Bulletin of Economic and Social Research,* 4, 1-20

Kindleberger C P (1996), *Manias, Panics and Crashes. A History of Financial Crashes* 3rd edn, New York: John Wiley and Sons

King M (1994) 'The transmission mechanism of monetary policy', *Bank of England Quarterly Bulletin,* August, 261-267

King M (1995) 'Credibility and monetary policy: theory and evidence', *Scottish Journal of Political Economy,* 42 (1), 1-19

King M (1997) 'The inflation target five years on', *Bank of England Quarterly Bulletin,* 37 (4), 431-42.

Klein B (1974) 'Competitive interest payments on bank deposits and the long-run demand for money', *American Economic Review,* 64, 931-49

Klovland J T (1983) 'The demand for money in secular perspective: the case of Norway 1867-1980', *European Economic Review,* 22

Kohn D L (2000) *Report to the non-executive directors of the Court of the Bank of England on monetary policy process and the work of monetary analysis,* Bank of England

Krugman P (1991) 'Target zones and exchange rate dynamics', *Quarterly Journal of Economics,* 106, 669-82

Kydland F and E Prescott (1977) ' "Rules rather than discretion": the inconsistency of optimal plans', *Journal of Political Economy,* 85 (3), 473-92

Laidler D E W (1966) `Some evidence on the demand for money', *Journal of Political Economy*, February, 74, 55-68

Laidler D E W (1971) 'The influence of money on economic activity: a survey of some current problems' in Clayton G, Gilbert J C and Sedgewick R (eds)

Laidler D E W (1980) 'The demand for money in the United States — yet again' in Brunner K and Meltzer A H (eds), *On the State of Macroeconomics,* Carnegie-Rochester Conference Series on Public Policy, vol 12, Amsterdam: North Holland

Laidler D E W (1982) *Monetarist Perspectives*, Oxford: Phillip Allan

Laidler D E W (1984) 'The buffer stock notion in monetary economics', *Economic Journal Conference Papers Supplement*, 94, 17-34

Laidler D E W (1990) *Taking Money Seriously,* Hemel Hempstead: Philip Allan

Laidler D E W (4e,1993) *The Demand for Money*, New York: HarperCollins

Laidler D E W (ed) (1999) *The Foundations of Monetary Economics*, 3 vols., Cheltenham: Edward Elgar

Laidler D E W (2002) 'The transmission mechanism with endogenous money', in Arestis P, Desai M and Dow S (eds) *Money, Macroeconomics and Keynes. Essays in Honour of Victoria Chick* Vol 1 London: Routledge

Laidler D E W and Parkin J M (1970) 'The demand for money in the United Kingdom 1955-67: preliminary estimates', *Manchester School,* 38, 187-208

Lastrapes W D and Selgin G (1994) 'Buffer-Stock Money: Interpreting Short-run Dynamics using Long-Run Restrictions', *Journal of Money, Credit and Banking*, 26, 34-54

Latané H A (1954) 'Cash balances and the interest rates: a pragmatic approach', *Review of Economics and Statistics*, 36, 456-60

Lavoie M (1985) 'Credit and Money: The Dynamic Circuit, Overdraft Economics and Post Keynesian Economics' in M Jarsulic (ed) *Money and Macro Policy*, Boston: Kluwer-Nijhoff

Lee T H (1967) 'Alternative interest rates and the demand for money: the empirical evidence', *American Economic Review*, 57 (5), 1168-81

Leland H and Pyle D (1977) 'Information asymmetries, financial structures and financial intermediaries', *Journal of Finance,* 32, 371-87

Lewis M K (1988) 'Off balance sheet activities and financial innovation in banking', *Banca Nationale del Lavoro*, 387-410

Lewis M K and Davis K T (1987) *Domestic and International Banking*, Hemel Hempstead: Philip Allan

Lewis M K and Mizen P D (2000) *Monetary Economics*, Oxford: Oxford U P

Lindsey D E and P A Spindt (1986), 'An evaluation of monetary indices', Federal Reserve Board, Division of Research and Statistics, Special Studies Paper No 195, March

Lipsey R G (1960) 'The relationship between unemployment and the rate of change of money wage rates in the U.K., 1861-1957: a further analysis', *Economica*, 27, 1-31

Lohman S (1996), 'Quis custodiet ipsis custodes?', in Siebert H (ed) (1996) *Monetary Policy in an Integrated World Economy*: Symposium 1995, Kiel: J C B Mohr

Lucas R E (1972) 'Expectations and the neutrality of money', *Journal of Economic Theory*, 4 (1), 102-24

Lucas R E (1973) 'Some international evidence on output-inflation trade-offs', *American Economic Review*, 63, 326-34

MacKinnon J G and Milbourne R D (1988) 'Are price equations really money demand equations on their heads?', *Journal of Monetary Economics*, 3, 295-305

Malinvaud E (1977) *The Theory of Unemployment Reconsidered*, Oxford: Basil Blackwell

Malz A (1995) 'Using options prices to estimate re-alignment probabilities in the European Monetary System' Federal Reserve Bank of New York Staff Reports, no.5.

Malz A (1997) 'Estimating the probability distribution of future exchange rates from options prices', *Journal of Derivatives*, winter, 18-36

Mankiw N G (4e 2000) *Macroeconomics,* New York: Worth Publishers.

Mankiw N G (2001) 'The inexorable and mysterious trade-off between inflation and unemployment', *Economic Journal*,111 (471), C45-C61

Mankiw N G and Summers L H (1986) 'Money demand and the effects of fiscal policies', *Journal of Money, Credit and Banking,* Nov, 18, 415-29

Mayer T (1978) *The Structure of Monetarism*, New York: W W Norton

McCallum B T (1989) *Monetary Economics: Theory and Policy*, New York: Macmillan

McCallum B T (1997), 'Issues in the design of monetary policy rules', NBER working paper, 6016

McCallum, B T (1999) 'Issues in the design of monetary policy rules', in Taylor J B and Woodford M (eds) *Handbook of Macroeconomics*, Amsterdam: North Holland.

McCallum B T and Goodfriend M (1992) 'Demand for Money: Theoretical Studies' in Newman P, Milgate M and Eatwell J (eds)

McKinnon R I (1982) 'Currency substitution and instability in the world dollar standard', *American Economic Review*, 72 (3), 320-33

McKinnon R I (1984a) 'Why floating exchange rates fail', Discussion Paper, Banca d'Italia, no 72

McKinnon R I (1984b) *An International Standard for Monetary Stabilization*, Washington D C: Institute for International Economics

McKinnon R I (1988) 'Monetary and exchange rate policies for international financial stability: a proposal', *Journal of Economic Perspectives*, 2 (1), 83-103

Meade J E (1978) 'The meaning of internal balance', *Economic Journal*, 88, 423-35

Mélitz J (1988) 'Monetary discipline and cooperation in the European

Monetary System: a synthesis', in Giavazzi F, Micossi S and Miller M (eds), *The European Monetary System*, Cambridge: Cambridge U P

Meltzer A H (1963) 'The demand for money: the evidence from the time series', *Journal of Political Economy*, June, 219-46

Merton R C (1974) 'On the pricing of corporate debt: the risk structure of interest rates', *Journal of Finance*, 29, 449-70.

Meyer L H (1976) 'Alternative definition of the money stock and the demand for money', *Federal Reserve Bank of New York Monthly Review*

Milbourne R D (1987) 'Re-examining the buffer stock model of money', *Economic Journal*, 97, supplement, 130-42

Miles D K and Wilcox J (1991) 'The Money Transmission Mechanism' in Green C and Llewellyn D T (eds), *Surveys in Monetary Economics* Vol I, Oxford: Blackwell

Milesi-Ferretti G (1995) 'The disadvantage of tying their hands: on the political economy of policy commitments', *Economic Journal*, 105 (433), 1381-1402

Miller M and Orr D (1966) 'A model of the demand for money by firms', *Quarterly Journal of Economics*, 80, 413-35

Miller M and Orr D (1968) 'The demand for money by firms: extension of analytic results', *Journal of Finance*, 23, 735-59

Miller M, Weller P and Zhang L (2002) 'Moral hazard and the US stock market: Analysing the "Greenspan put"', *Economic Journal*, 112, C171-C186

Minsky H P (1978) 'The financial instability hypothesis: a restatement', Thames Papers in Political Economy, Thames Polytechnic

Minsky H P (1982) *Can it happen again? Essays on Instability and Finance*, Armonk N Y: M E Sharpe

Minsky H P (1986) *Stabilizing an Unstable Economy*, New Haven CT: Yale U P

Minsky H P (1991) 'The financial instability hypothesis: a clarification', in M Feldstein (ed), *The Risk of Economic Crisis*, Chicago: University of Chicago Press

Mishkin F S (1982) 'Does anticipated policy matter? an econometric investigation', *Journal of Political Economy*, 90, 22-51

Moore B J (1986) 'How credit drives the money supply: The significance of institutional developments', *Journal of Economic Issues*, XX (2), 113-452

Moore B J (1988a), *Horizontalists and Verticalists*, Cambridge: Cambridge U P

Moore B J (1988b), 'The endogenous money supply', *Journal of Post Keynesian Economics,* 10 (3), 372-85

Moore B J (1989) 'A simple model of bank intermediation', *Journal of Post Keynesian Economics*, 12 (1)

Moore B J (1997) 'Reconciliation of the supply and demand for endogenous money', *Journal of Post Keynesian Economics*, 19 (3), 423-35

Moore B J and Threadgold A R (1980), 'Bank Lending and the Money Supply', Bank of England Discussion Paper No. 10

Moore B J and Threadgold A R (1985), 'Corporate Bank Borrowing in the UK, 1965-81', *Economica*, 52, 65-78

Mosley L (1997) 'International Financial Markets and Government Economic Policy: The importance of financial market operations', unpublished paper given at the 1997 Annual Meeting of the American Political Science Association, Duke University, N.C.

Mullineux A (1996) *Financial Innovation, Banking and Monetary Aggregates*, Cheltenham:Edward Elgar

Mundell R A (1962) 'The appropriate use of monetary and fiscal policy for internal and external stability', International Monetary Fund Staff Papers, IX

Mundell R A (1963) 'Capital mobility and stabilization policy under fixed and flexible exchange rates', *Canadian Journal of Economics and Political Science*, 29 (4), 475-85

Muscatelli V A, Tirelli P and Trecroci C (2000) 'Does institutional change really matter? Inflation targets, central bank reform and interest rate policy in the OECD countries', CES-Ifo Working Paper no. 278, Munich: CES-Ifo

Myrdal G (1939) *Monetary Equilibrium*, London: William Hodge and Co

Newman P, M Milgate and J Eatwell (eds) (1992) *The New Palgrave Dictionary of Money and Finance*, London: Macmillan

Niggle C J (1990) 'The evolution of money, financial institutions and monetary economics', *Journal of Economic Issues*, 24, June, 443-50

Niggle C J (1991) 'The endogenous money supply theory: an institutionalist appraisal' *Journal of Economic Issues,* 25 (1) 137-151

Padoa Schioppa T (1988) 'The European Monetary System: A long-term view', in Giavazzi F, Micossi S and Miller M (eds) *The European Monetary System*, Cambridge: Cambridge U P

Palley T I (1991) 'The endogenous money supply: consensus and disagreement', *Journal of Post Keynesian Economics*, 13 (3), 397-403

Palley T I (1994) 'Competing views of the money supply process: theory and evidence', *Metroeconomica*, 45 (1), 67-88

Patinkin D (2e 1965) *Money, Interest and Prices*, New York: Harper and Row

Pesek B and Saving T (1967) *Money, Wealth and Economic Theory*, New York: Collier Macmillan

Phelps E S (1967) 'Phillips curves, expectations of inflation and optimal employment over time', *Economica*, 34, 254-281

Phillips A W (1958) 'The relation between unemployment and the rate of change of money wage rates in the United Kingdom, 1861-1957', *Economica*, 25, 283-99

Pierce J L (1975) 'Interest rates and their prospect in the recovery', Brookings Papers on Economic Activity, I

Pigou A C (1949) *The Veil of Money,* London: Macmillan

Pilbeam K (2e, 1998) *International Finance*, Basingstoke: Macmillan

Polanyi K (1971) 'Aristotle discovers the economy', in Polanyi K, Arensberg C M and Pearson H W (eds), *Trade and Market in the Early Empires,* Chicago: Regnery and Company

Pollin R (1991) 'Two theories of money supply endogeneity: some empirical evidence', *Journal of Post Keynesian Economics*, 13(3), 366-396

Poole W (1970) 'Optimal choice of monetary instruments', *Quarterly Journal of Economics*, 84, 197-216

Poole W (1991) 'Interest rates and the conduct of monetary policy: a comment', *Carnegie-Rochester Series on Public Policy*, 34, 31-40

Portes R (1990) 'Macroeconomic Policy Coordination and the European Monetary System', in P Ferri (ed) *Prospects for the European Monetary System,* London: Macmillan, 222-35

Radcliffe Committee (1959) *Report of the Committee on the Working of the Monetary System*, Cmnd 827, London: HMSO

Rogoff K (1985a) 'Can exchange rate predictability be achieved without monetary convergence? evidence from the EMS', *European Economic Review*, 28

Rogoff K (1985b) 'Can international monetary policy coordination be counter-productive?', *Journal of International Economics* 18, 199-217

Rogoff K (1985c) 'The optimal degree of commitment to an intermediate monetary target', *Quarterly Journal of Economics*, 100(4), 1169-89

Rousseas S (1986) *Post Keynesian Monetary Economics*, London: Macmillan

Sargent T J and Wallace N (1975) 'Rational expectations, the optimal monetary instrument and the optimal money supply rule', *Journal of Political Economy,* April, 83, 241-54

Sargent T J and Wallace N (1982) 'The real bills doctrine versus the quantity theory: a reconsideration', *Journal of Political Economy,* 90, 1212-36

Samuelson P (9e, 1973) *Economics*, New York: McGraw-Hill

Shackle G L S (1971), Discussion Paper in G Clayton, J C Gilbert and R Sedgewick (eds)

Shiller R (2000) *Irrational Exuberance*, Princeton: Princeton U P.

Siklos P L (1993) 'Income velocity and institutional change: some new time series evidence. 1870-1986', *Journal of Money, Credit and Banking*, 25 (3), 377-92

Simons H (1948) *Economic Policy for a Free Society*, Chicago: University of Chicago Press

Sims C A (1972) 'Money, income and causality', *American Economic Review*, 62, 540-52

Smith A (1776) *The Wealth of Nations*, London

Sprenkle C M (1969) 'The uselessness of transactions demand models', *Journal of Finance*, 4, 835-47

Sprenkle C M (1972) 'On the observed transactions demand for money', *The Manchester School*, 40, 261-7

Sprenkle C and Miller M H (1980) 'The precautionary demand for broad and narrow money', *Economica*, 47, 407-21

Stiglitz J E and Weiss A (1981) 'Credit rationing in markets with imperfect information', *America Economic Review*, 71, 393-410.

Stock J H and Watson M W, (1989) 'New Indices of Coincident and Leading Economic Indicators' in S Fischer and O Blanchard (eds) *NBER Macroeconomic Annual* (Cambridge: MIT Press).

Stone C T and Thornton D L (1987) 'Solving the 1980s Velocity Puzzle: A Progress Report', *Federal Reserve Bank of St Louis Review*, Aug/Sept, 5-23

Struthers J and Speight H (1986) *Money: Institutions Theory and Policy*, Harlow: Longman

Svensson L (1997) 'Inflation forecast targeting: implementing and monitoring inflation targets', *European Economic Review*, 41, 1111-1146

Svennson L E O (1999) 'Inflation targeting as a monetary policy rule', *Journal of Monetary Economics*, 43, 655-79

Svensson L E O (2000), 'The first year of the eurosystem: inflation targeting or not?' *American Economic Review, Papers and Proceedings*, 95-99

Svensson, L E O (2001) 'Price stability as a target for monetary policy: defining and maintaining price stability', in Deutsche Bundesbank (ed) *The Monetary Transmission Process: Recent Developments and Lessons for Europe*, New York: Palgrave

Taylor J (1979), 'Staggered price setting in a macro model', *American Economic Review*, 83, 108-13

Taylor J B (1993) 'Discretion versus Policy Rules in Practice', Carnegie-Rochester Series on Public Policy, 39, 195-214

Taylor J B (1999a), 'A historical analysis of monetary policy rules' in Taylor J B (ed)

Taylor J B (1999b) (ed) *Monetary Policy Rules*, Chicago: Chicago U P.

Taylor J B (1999c) 'The robustness and efficiency of monetary policy rules as guidelines for interest rate setting by the European Central Bank', *Journal of Monetary Economics*, 43 (3), 655-679

Taylor M P (1987) 'Financial innovation, inflation and the stability of the demand for broad money in the United Kingdom', *Bulletin of Economic Research,* 39(2), 225-33

Taylor M P (ed) (1991) *Money and Financial Markets*, Oxford: Blackwell

Temin P (1976) *Did Monetary Forces Cause the Great Depression?*, New York: Norton

Theil H (1964) *Optimal Decision Rules for Government and Industry*, Amsterdam: North Holland

Tinbergen J (1952) *On the Theory of Economic Policy*, Amsterdam: North Holland

Tinbergen J (1956), *Economic Policy: Principles and Design*, Amsterdam: North Holland

Tobin J (1947) 'Money, wage rates and employment', in Harris S (ed), *The New Economics*, New York: Knopf

Tobin J (1956) 'The interest-elasticity of transactions demand for cash', *Review of Economics and Statistics*, 38(3), 241-7

Tobin J (1958) 'Liquidity preference as behaviour towards risk', *Review of Economic Studies*, 25(1), 65-86

Tobin J (1969) 'A general equilibrium approach to monetary theory', *Journal of Money, Credit and Banking*, 1(1), 15-29

Tödter K-H and H-E Reimers (1994), 'P-Star as a link between money and prices in Germany', *Weltwirtschaftlishes Archiv*, 130, 273-89

Treasury H M (1997) *UK membership of the single currency: an assessment of the five economic tests*, available on the HM Treasury website: www.hm-treasury.gov.uk

Treasury H M (November, 2001) *Preliminary and technical work to prepare for the assessment of the five tests for uk membership of the single currency*, available on the Treasury website, www.hm-treasury.gov.uk

Treasury H M (2002) *Reforming Britain's Economic and Financial Policy*, London: Palgrave

Visser H (1974), *The Quantity of Money*, London: Martin Robertson

Visser H (1991) *Modern Monetary Theory*, Aldershot: Edward Elgar

Walsh C E (1995) 'Optimal contracts for central bankers', *American Economic Review*, 85, 150-67

Walters A (1990) *Sterling in Danger. The Economic Consequences of Pegged Exchange Rates*, London: Fontana/Collins in association with the Institute of Economic Affairs

Waud R N (1973) 'Proximate targets and monetary policy', *Economic Journal*, 83, 1-20

Weintraub S (1978) *Keynes, Keynesians and Monetarists*, Philadelphia: University of Philadelphia Press

West K (1986) 'Targeting nominal income: a note', *Economic Journal*, 96, 1077-83

Wicksell K (1898) *Interest and Prices*, London: Macmillan

Williamson J and Miller M (1987) *Targets and Indicators: A Blueprint for the International Coordination of Economic Policy*, Washington DC: Institute for International Economics

Wood G E, Mills T C and Capie F H (1993) *Central Bank Independence: What Is It and What Will It Do For Us?*, London: Institute of Economic Affairs

Wray L R (1990) *Money and Credit in Capitalist Economies. The Endogenous Money Approach*, Aldershot: Edward Elgar

Wren-Lewis S (1984) 'Omitted variables in equations relating prices to money', *Applied Economics*, 16, 483-96

Yates A (1995) 'On the design of inflation targets', in Haldane A G (ed), *Targeting Inflation*, London: Bank of England

Zawadzki K K F (1981) *Competition and Credit Control*, Oxford: Basil Blackwell

Index

Acocella N 224
Adam C 138, 155
Akhtar M 154
Alesina L 233
Anderson N 365
Arestis P 155
Artis M 148, 158, 159, 168, 261–3
asset prices 362–4
asymmetric information 11, 80, 203, 221
aymmetric shocks 386
Atkinson P 148

Baba Y 149
Bain K 130, 165, 230, 233
Ball L 223, 267, 270
Banks
 balance sheets 51–6
Bank of England 40, 45, 46, 89, 99, 172, 178,
  237, 270, 271, 315, 317, 319–20, 325, 327,
  344, 354, 376, 401, 412, 413, 423, 425,
  429, 432, 443
 independence of 344
 and interest rates 75–6, 78, 82
bank lending
 demand for 66, 69, 81, 89–90
 and money supply 53–69, 81, 89–92
Banking Acts 1979 and 1987 325
Banking School 23
Barber A 322
Barnett W 135
Barro R 190, 220, 224, 227
Barro-Gordon model 228–30
barter 16–20, 34, 126
base rate 77
basis point 77
Basel Committee 334
Basel-Nyborg Agreement (1987) 286
Baumol W 113, 116, 152, 160
Bean C 267, 347, 363
Belongia M 135
Benassy J-P 220
Bennett A 137
Bernanke B S 270
Bernard H 368
Bertocchi G 251

Biefang-Frisancho Mariscal 166
'bill leak' 331–32
Blackburn K 230
Blanchard O 258
Blinder A 203, 238
Board of Governors of the Federal Reserve
  System 423, 431, 440
Bomberger W 165
Bordo M 154
Borio C E V 69, 74, 83
Brainard W 251
Bretton Woods 156, 157, 197, 279, 283, 285,
  286, 297, 303, 305, 314, 316
Bronfenbrenner M 143
Brooke M 366
Browning P 323
Brunner K 16, 121, 193
buffer stock money 158–61
building societies 336–7
Bundesbank 82, 90, 234, 235, 236, 270, 345,
  382, 394, 397
Burns A 363

Callaghan J 324
Campillo M 236
Canzoneri M 298
capital asset pricing model 360
Cecchetti S 362
central banks 57, 87, 356
 accountability 237, 370, 393–4, 395, 397,
  412, 413, 417, 431–2
 credibility 209, 224–8, 342, 358, 370
 independence 231–8, 248, 265–6
 policy rules 268–72
 transparency 237, 370–1, 394, 432
certificates of deposit (CDs) 87, 354
Chick V 51, 118, 152, 191
Chinn M 267
Chouraqui J-C 148
Chow G 138
Chrystal A 135
Clare A 369, 372
Clarida R 269
Clews R 367
Clower R 20

commodity money   3–4, 16, 21, 23
Competition and Credit Control   69, 79,
      317–327, 336
consumption   174–5
contemporaneous reserve accounting   426,
      429
convergence of economies   378, 380, 382, 383,
      390
Cook T   79
Cooper N   366n   368
Cooper R   297, 298
Cornford A   353, 360
'corset', see supplementary special
      deposits
Cottrell A   161
Cramer J   165
Crawford M   234
credit   6–8, 10–13, 15, 21–23, 32, 33, 35, 46,
      100, 420, 422, 425
   availability of   173, 202
   counterparts   65
   demand for   11–12, 15
   rationing   203
currency   4–5, 98, 420, 424, 425
Currency School   22–23
currency substitution   157, 158
Currie D   305
Cuthbertson K   89, 146, 159, 161

Dale S   78, 79
Darby M   159
Davidson P   64, 167, 307
Davies G   6, 26
Davis E P   368
Debt Managemnt Office (DMO)   345
Dennis R   267
Diamond D W   69
discount window   423, 426, 427, 430, 441
Divisia indexes   39, 40, 44–5
Dornbusch R   290, 293
Dotsey M   368
Dow J C R   357
Dow S C   51, 118
Dowd K   126
Downward P   167
Driffil J   230
Duisenberg, Wim   404
'Duke of York' tactics   321

Earl P   118
elastic currency   425
equation of exchange   97, 128, 313
eurocurrency   329–30

European Central Bank (ECB)   90, 173, 237,
      262, 266, 305, 345, 361, 370, 376,
      388–414, 425, 432
European Exchange Rate Mechanism (ERM)
      81, 342–3, 359, 367
European Monetary System (EMS)   282, 283,
      284, 285, 286, 287, 305, 341
European System of Central Banks (ESCB)
      345, 388–92,   394, 401
exchange   2–9, 13, 16–22, 24, 95, 102, 103
exchange rate   1, 157, 197–202, 275–96, 322,
      330, 340–1, 359–61
exchange rate bands   282–3
exchange rate overshooting   290–3
Executive Board of the ECB   388, 391, 392,
      395, 404
expectations   14, 157, 177, 433
   adaptive   138, 146, 211–12, 217
   inflationary   177–8, 278
   rational (forward-looking)   138, 142, 146,
      161, 216–17, 226–9, 253, 254

Faig M   138
Federal funds rate (of interest)   425, 426, 427,
      428, 429, 430, 433, 435, 436, 437, 438, 441
Federal Open Market Committee (FOMC)   417,
      423, 425, 427, 428–30, 431, 433–7, 439, 440
Federal Reserve Act (1913)   419
Federal Reserve banks   419–20, 424, 431
Federal Reserve Board   419, 421
Federal Reserve System (the Fed)   88, 235,
      237, 305, 361, 406, 417–40
Feige E   138
First Bank of the United States   418
Fischer S   258
Fisher D   48
Fisher I   29, 35, 97, 98, 101, 102, 103, 104,
      107, 127, 165, 367
'Fisher hypothesis'   366
Fisher P   363
five economic tests (for UK member
   ship of euro area)   382–8, 412
fixed rate tenders   399
Fleming J   197
flow of funds   64–70, 73, 81, 90, 320
foreign exchange markets   176, 424, 428
Foster N   89, 163
Frankel J   267, 293
Friedman B   258
Friedman M   9, 35, 37, 38, 95, 103, 121–5,
      126, 127, 128, 129, 131, 138, 142, 144,
      147, 154, 156, 208, 211, 212, 215, 237,
      251, 252, 422

frown costs 427

Galbraith J K 3, 22, 422
Gali J 269
Gerlach S 270, 368
Gertler M 269
Glass-Steagal Act (1933) 421–2
Goldfeld S 138, 146, 148, 154
Goodfriend M 126, 130
Goodhart C 5, 16, 20, 25, 51, 74, 82, 83, 85,
    87, 158, 159, 190, 224, 258, 323, 340, 357,
    361, 430
Gordon D 224, 227
Governing Council of the ECB 388, 391, 392,
    394, 399, 400, 401, 403, 408, 409, 412
government debt 65, 320–22, 345
Gowland D 112, 113, 130, 259, 323, 334, 340
Grandmont J 220
Gray J 298
Greenspan Alan 417, 425, 436, 438
Greenspan put option 439
Greider W 431
Grice J 137
Grossman H 220
Gurley J 190

Hacche G 148
Hafer R 153
Hahn T 79
Haldane A G 79, 263, 371
Hall R E 266
Hall S 138
Hamada K 299, 301
Handa J 48, 130, 143, 169
Harmonised Index of Consumer Prices (HICP)
    396, 397, 403, 405, 406, 412
Heffernan S 79
Hein S 153
Hendry D F 150, 158
Henry S G B 138, 368
Hicks J R 51, 92
Hillman R 368
Horne J 304
Howells P 89, 130, 165, 166
Hughes Hallett A 299
Hussein K A 89

indicators 248
income
    current 28, 31, 104, 107, 114, 123, 125, 132,
        138, 146, 151, 174, 192
    expected 118, 120, 121, 122, 126, 161, 174,
        175

nominal 31, 39, 74, 85, 89, 90, 105, 118,
    121, 127, 143, 147, 171, 173, 184, 185,
    192, 194, 197, 198, 203, 207, 208, 229,
    256, 259, 260, 266, 268, 275, 314, 318,
    324, 397
permanent 122, 123, 124, 125, 132, 137,
    138, 147
real 28, 38, 74, 95, 97, 101, 115, 124, 126,
    127, 139, 143, 149, 158, 168, 182, 191,
    203, 207, 212, 252, 289, 291, 397
transitory 125
inflation 1, 12, 14, 15, 23, 27, 32, 38, 39, 59,
    69, 85, 93, 101, 122, 123, 124, 126, 128,
    171, 178, 179, 191, 195, 196, 198, 201,
    207, 209–40, 243, 244–54, 259, 260–71,
    278, 279, 281–8, 293–300, 302, 303, 308,
    323, 324, 345, 382, 389–90, 396–98,
    400–14, 419, 425, 433–37, 439, 441
    Report 344, 347, 367, 370
    target 344, 361, 396, 397, 401, 412, 413,
        414
    targeting 259–66
innovation 87–8, 328–30, 367–8
insider-outsider (model of labour market) 221–2
interest rates
    and monetary growth 69, 81
    and definitions of money 36, 37, 39, 40, 45,
        46
    and the demand for money 1, 10–15, 21, 23,
        95, 99, 103, 105–114, 116, 118–21, 123,
        126, 127, 128
    and monetary authorities 34, 38
    normal rate of 106–9, 110, 111, 112, 113, 163
    relative 78–80, 328–9, 342, 367–8
    setting of 74–7, 81, 346–7, 354–5
interest rate control 172, 173, 195, 255,
    319–20, 326, 429, 430
International Monetary Fund (IMF) 316, 318
IS/LM 103, 180, 184, 185, 187, 188, 191, 192,
    197, 198, 199, 200, 201, 204, 256, 257,
    258, 313
Issing O 234
investment 175–6

Jackson Andrew 418
Jonung L 154
Judd J 154, 166

Kaldor N 85, 86
Keynes J M 15, 44, 95, 96, 103–4, 106,
    109–13, 118, 127, 128m 130, 143, 148,
    163, 164, 165, 167, 168, 183–5, 186, 187,
    204, 207, 208, 209, 307, 314, 320

Khusro A 137
Kindleberger C 304, 422
King M 89, 371
Klein B 155
Klovland J 154
Kontolemis Z 261–3
Kregel J 353, 360
Kydland F 226, 227, 254

labour market flexibility 378, 379, 384, 386
lagged reserve accounting 87, 429
Laidler D 130, 138, 140, 146, 158, 159, 161,
    195–6, 255
Lastrapes W 161
Lavoie M 85
Lee T 155
Leland H and Pyle D 69
lender of last resort 76, 85, 86, 320–22, 357
Lewis M K 130, 148, 158, 159, 168, 170, 332,
    333, 430
liability management 87, 328, 334–40
LIBOR 366
Lindsey D 135
Lipsey R G 211
liquidity 9, 31, 37, 39, 41, 112, 113, 122, 134,
    148, 420, 422, 424, 434
liquidity trap 109, 113, 146, 163, 164, 339
Lohman S 238
long-run v short-run 14–15, 99, 102, 103, 110,
    124, 128, 161, 215, 239
Louvre Accord 303, 304, 305
Lucas R 214
Lynch D 368

Maastricht convergence conditions 381, 385,
    395, 401
Maastricht Treaty 236, 381, 392, 393, 401
MacDonald R 135
MacKinnon J G 159
main refinancing rate of the ECB (refi) 173,
    399–400, 401, 404, 405, 406, 407
Makinen G 165
Malinvaud E 220
Malz A 367
Mankiw N 138, 222–3
marginal lending facility 400
Masson P 304
matched transactions 427, 428
Mayer T 121, 143, 144, 193
McCallum B 126, 130, 267, 268
McKinnon R 157, 302
Meade J 248
Medium Term Financial Strategy (MTFS) 251,
    253, 324, 337

Meltzer A 16, 138, 146, 193
Merton R C 367
Milbourne R 117, 159
Miles D 203
Milesi Ferretti G 230
Miller M 117, 139, 302, 362, 363
minimum lending rate (MLR) 322
minimum reserve ratios 400
Minsky H 164
Miron J 236
Mishkin F 224
Mitchell W 364
Mizen P 130, 170, 261–3, 430
monetary base 49, 57–8, 62–4, 67, 74
monetary base control 83–5
monetary conditions index 268
Monetary Control Act (MCA), 1980 426
monetary growth reference values 398, 404, 409
monetary policy
    before 1985 312–327
    and credibility 342, 358
    coordination 296–305
    in the euro area 375–414
    in the USA 417–43
    importance of 1, 14–15, 40
    objectives of 82, 358
    strength or weakness of 115, 121, 128,
        184–202
    transmission mechanism of 13–14, 27, 118,
        127, 171–203, 270, 276–85, 422
Monetary Policy Committee (of Bank of
    England) 14, 262, 290, 344, 346–7, 371,
    412, 413, 43
monetary target 397, 409
money
    as bank deposits 52
    as means of payment 20, 21, 30, 31, 32, 36,
        41
    as medium of exchange 3, 4, 7, 34, 35, 36,
        46, 102
    as store of value 34, 35, 102
    as unit of account 4, 8, 20, 34, 35
    broad 33, 37, 40, 41, 44, 49, 134, 137, 138,
        147, 149, 155, 156
    DCE 40, 42, 316, 324
    economists' definitions of 33–39, 95, 100
    endogenous 11, 13. 33, 89–92, 96, 101,
        104, 162–3, 172, 312, 317, 422, 428, 430
    exogenous 11, 12, 13, 17, 23, 28, 39, 57–63,
        90, 92, 97, 101, 103, 120, 121, 124, 127,
        128, 158, 172, 215–16, 422, 44157–63,
        90, 92
    gains from use of 16
    inside 36, 39, 189

money – *continued*
  meaning of word   2–7
  M0   42, 46, 49–50, 55
  M1   41, 42, 49–43, 161, 326
  M2   41, 42, 425, 426, 441
  M3   41, 42, 44, 49–53, 68, 324, 326, 389,
      398, 406, 409, 425, 426, 441
  M3c   42
  M3H   43
  M4   40, 43, 44, 45, 46, 49–50, 55, 68
  M4c   43, 44
  M5   40, 43, 44, 45
  narrow   35, 36, 37, 40, 41, 49, 134, 137, 147,
      149, 152, 153, 154, 158, 159
  NIBM1   41, 42, 44
  neutrality of   3, 17–18, 24, 31, 38, 97, 104,
      128, 218, 422, 434
  official measures of   39–46
  outside   36, 39
  PSL1   40, 41, 43
  PSL2   40, 41, 43, 44, 327
money balances
  active   105, 116
  idle   106–9, 113, 121
money demand   5, 8, 10–14, 17, 31, 38, 46
  Cambridge approach to   96, 101–3, 124,
      128
  interest elasticity of   107, 109, 110, 116, 121,
      128, 181, 192
  inventory theoretic model of   113–17
  portfolio models of   101, 103, 117–21,
      186–7
  shopping time models of   126–7
  stability of   12, 13, 38, 39, 46, 95, 106,
      108–11, 117–8, 121, 124–5, 127–9, 158,
      162–4, 185, 207–8, 215, 318
  theories of   95–129
money markets,   354–7
money supply
  base-multiplier model of   57–8, 62–4, 67, 74,
      83, 90, 313, 315
  direct controls of   11, 315–17, 323
  endogenous   11, 13, 89–92, 312, 317
  exogenous   11, 12, 13, 23, 28, 39, 57, 63,
      90, 92
  growth rate of   1, 36, 75, 81, 324, 339
  flow of funds model of   64–70, 73
monitoring ranges   425
Moore B J   85, 87, 89
motives for holding money
  finance   109
  precautionary   96, 104, 105, 116–7, 128
  speculative   96, 104, 106–9, 111, 113, 117,
      118, 127, 128, 163

transactions   96, 104, 105, 113, 115, 116,
      117, 126, 422
Mullineux A   134
multi-bank panics   419, 421, 440
multiplier
  bank deposit   55–64
  and exogenous money   57, 63–4
Mundell R   197, 247
Mundell-Fleming model   197–202, 276–285
Muscatelli V   270
Myrdal G   85

nationally-chartered banks   419
New Classical model   208–9, 216–220
new Keynesian models (of the labour market)
      220–3
New York Federal Reserve bank   421, 422,
      423, 427, 428, 429
Niggle C J   51, 152
nominal income targeting   266–8
Off-balance sheet operations   332
open market operations   172, 182, 199, 421,
      424, 426, 427, 428, 430, 440, 441
optimum currency area theory   377
Orr D   117
overdrafts   86
overfunding   327

Palley T   88
Panigirtzoglou N   367
Parkin M   138
Pesek B   190
Phelps E   208, 211
Phillips A W   208
Phillips curve   208–16, 226, 228, 239, 244,
      246, 267, 268, 287
  expectations-augmented (Friedman/Phelps)
      208, 211–16, 218, 223, 232
Pigou A C   17
Plaza Agreement   303, 305
policy goals   244–5
policy instruments   245–6
policy irrelevance (ineffectiveness)   216, 217–8
political business cycle   232
Pollin R   88
Poole W   49, 256, 258
Portes R   304
pre-commitment (in monetary policy)   225
Prescott E   226, 227, 254
Proudman J   367
public sector borrowing requirement (PSBR)
      65–6, 315, 321, 323, 324, 327
Purchasing Power Parity (PPP)   289, 290, 292,
      294

Quantity Theory of Money 27, 29, 96–101, 102, 103, 124, 128, 181, 207, 212, 239, 314

Radcliffe Report 202, 314, 316, 318, 320
Reimers H-E 252
'regulation Q' 328, 340, 423
repurchase agreements ('repos') 76–8, 173, 345, 347–8, 354, 357, 366, 399
reputation (in monetary policy) 224, 279
reserves
    bank 52–62, 66, 74–6, 83, 87–8
    ratio to deposits 52–62, 70, 320, 325
Revised Quantity Theory 123, 126
Ricardian equivalence 190
Rogoff K 231, 237, 300
Rousseas S 130
RPIX 262, 348, 397
rules versus discretion 82

sacrifice ratio 215, 239
Samuelson P 17
Sargent T 252
Saville I D 357
Saving T 190
Scadding J 154, 166
Schnabel G 270
Scholtes C 366
Schwartz A 144, 152, 158, 422
Second Bank of the United States 418
Securitization 333
seigniorage 21–2, 231
Selgin G 161
Shaw E 190
Shiller R 362
Siklos P 154
Simons H 422
Sims A C 88
Sleath J 365
Slow 89
Smith Adam 1, 2
Spagat M 251
special deposits 319
Speight H 35, 48
Sprenkle C 139
Spindt P 135
Stability and Growth Pact 384–5, 394, 411
state-chartered banks 418, 419
sterilization 159, 199–200, 275, 279, 281, 286, 295, 296, 307
Stiglitz J E 69
Stock J H 368
Struthers J 35, 48
Summers L 138, 233

supplementary special deposits 323, 328
Svensson L 264, 265, 267, 270, 397, 411
symmetric shocks 378
synchronized business cycles 378, 410

Taylor J B 82, 221, 268, 269
Taylor M 148, 155, 159, 161, 170
Taylor rules 268–72
Temin P 422
Theil H 246, 251, 358
Threadgold A 89
time consistency in monetary policy 224–8
time lags (in monetary policy) 161, 178–9, 195, 250
Tinbergen J 246, 358
Tinbergen's Rule 247
Tobin J 96, 103, 113, 116–18, 127, 143, 144, 146, 152, 160, 306
Tobin tax 276, 305–7
Tödter K-H 252
Treasury H M 90, 323, 358
    Select Committee 344
treasury bills 76, 78,

uncovered interest rate parity (UIRP) 289, 290, 295, 297
unemployment
    non-accelerating-inflation rate of (NAIRU) 213–14, 217
    natural rate of 212–13, 223–4, 239, 245

variable rate tenders 400
velocity of money 12, 13, 22, 29, 144, 147, 150, 151, 152, 154, 158, 163, 164, 313, 327, 328, 337
    income velocity 15, 29, 30, 31, 33, 107, 124, 149, 152, 153, 156, 166, 182, 207
    transactions velocity 97, 99, 128, 166
Visser H 20, 21, 25, 166

wage flexibility 378, 379, 384
Wallace N 252
Walsh C 238
Watson M W 368
Waud R 259
wealth 2–3, 5, 7–9, 13, 18, 23, 24, 37, 41, 97, 100, 101, 102, 121, 222, 123, 125, 126, 132, 133, 137, 138, 142, 144, 147, 154
    effects in monetary policy 187–92
    human or non-human 9, 122, 123, 125, 126, 137, 138
Weintraub S 85
Weiss A 69

Weller P   362, 363
West K   267
Whitley J   363
Wicksell K   252, 259
Wilcox J   138, 203
Williamson J   302
World Trade Organisation   359

Wray L   17, 19, 26, 86, 130, 162
Wren-Lewis S   158

Yates A   263
Yield curve   364–6, 371

Zhang L   362, 363